Language Arts

PATTERNS OF PRACTICE

SEVENTH EDITION

Gail E. Tompkins
California State University, Fresno, Emerita

Merrill
is an imprint of

PEARSON

Upper Saddle River, New Jersey
Columbus, Ohio

Library of Congress Cataloging-in-Publication Data

Tompkins, Gail E.
   Language arts : patterns of practice / Gail E. Tompkins. — 7th ed.
      p. cm.
   Includes bibliographical references and index.
   ISBN 0-13-159789-2 (alk. paper)
1.   Language arts (Elementary)   I. Title.
   LB1576.T655 2009
   372.6—dc22   2007017265

Vice President and Executive Publisher: Jeffery W. Johnston
Senior Editor: Linda Ashe Bishop
Senior Development Editor: Hope Madden
Senior Project Manager: Mary M. Irvin
Senior Editorial Assistant: Laura Weaver
Design Coordinator: Diane C. Lorenzo
Cover Designer: Candace Rowley
Cover Images: Cher Cartwright and Linda Bronson
Operations Specialist: Laura Messerly
Director of Marketing: Quinn Perkson
Marketing Manager: Darcy Betts Prybella
Marketing Coordinator: Brian Mounts

This book was set in Optima by S4Carlisle Publishing Services. It was printed and bound by Edwards Brothers. The cover was printed by Phoenix Color Corp.

Photo Credits: "Meeting the Needs" feature photos by Ingram/Jupiter Images, David Mager/Pearson Learning Photo Studio, and Anne Vega. All photos in the color insert by Gail E. Tompkins

Pearson Education Ltd.   Pearson Education Australia Pty. Limited
Pearson Education Singapore Pte. Ltd.   Pearson Education North Asia Ltd.
Pearson Education Canada, Ltd.   Pearson Educación de Mexico, S.A. de C.V.
Pearson Education—Japan   Pearson Education Malaysia Pte. Ltd.

Merrill
is an imprint of

PEARSON

10 9 8 7 6 5 4 3 2 1
ISBN 13: 978-0-13-159789-1
ISBN 10:   0-13-159789-2

For Judy,
my Cape Cod "sister,"
and the Chase family
with love and gratitude
for adopting me

PREFACE

*H*elping children and adolescents learn to communicate using all six language competencies—reading, writing, listening, speaking, viewing, and visually representing–can seem like an overwhelming task for a new or even an experienced teacher. Making this goal possible for *all* children in our culturally diverse, technologically changing society can be even more daunting. However, this thoroughly revised and streamlined seventh edition of *Language Arts: Patterns of Practice* models for you the integration of the six language arts into the literacy curriculum and presents the most effective and practical methods for working with the diverse abilities and literacy experiences of children in today's K–8 classrooms.

The text begins with the background information you need to understand your students, their classroom environment, and the research and theories behind solid language arts teaching. It goes on to clarify the specific instructional approaches best suited to an integrated study of language arts, modeling instruction and pinpointing the topics, strategies, and skills you will need to cover. Within this presentation, the text describes four patterns of practice—*literature circles, literature focus units, reading and writing workshop,* and *thematic units*—each developed to illustrate how to integrate the teaching of language competencies depending on instructional goals. The use of each of these patterns of practice is clarified within every chapter topic. Seamlessly, the text illustrates the way the language arts and instructional methodologies fit together, like the carefully constructed pieces of a quilt, crafted and organized to form one complete picture.

Language Arts: Patterns of Practice has long been a highly valued resource to preservice teachers. Built on a solid research base, this exceptionally applied and teacher-friendly text brings teaching methods to life through the use of authentic student artifacts, classroom vignettes, and video footage of master teachers in their language arts classrooms. The seventh edition of the text, streamlined to provide a succinct model of language arts instruction, retains the rich classroom orientation, accessible writing style, and numerous features that have been the text's hallmark, adding a sharpened focus on English learners, deepened classroom application of the four patterns of practice, and integrated treatment of the almost limitless resources of MyEducationLab. These new ideas and revisions have been crafted to help you prepare for, plan for, and implement successful language arts instruction.

Preparing for the Language Arts Classroom

- **New!** *Patterns of Practice* features pinpoint the ways to use the four patterns of practice—literature focus units, literature circles, reading and writing workshop, and thematic units—with each chapter's topic.

- Colorful inserts in Chapter 2 identify the patterns of practice—the four instructional approaches most appropriate for integrating the six language arts. These pages provide detailed classroom examples of teachers in action, identifying procedures and processes for using each instructional approach. These colorful classroom glimpses illustrate how motivating and engaging each approach can be for students learning language arts.

- Chapter-opening vignettes describe how individual teachers use the different instructional approaches to develop language arts competencies. These features set the tone for each chapter, clearly illustrating chapter concepts as they are played out in successful language arts classrooms.

- Authentic samples of student work pepper every chapter, modeling the kind of interaction and response you can expect in your own classroom.

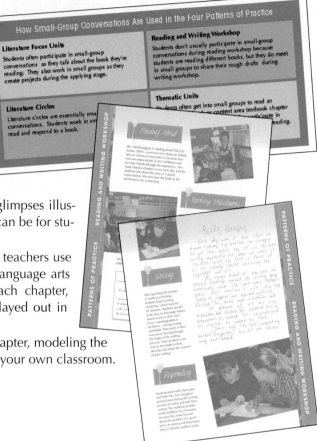

Planning for the Language Arts Classroom

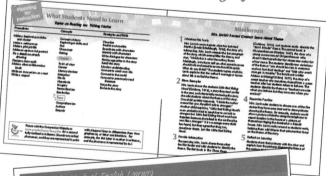

- **New!** *Planning for Instruction* features throughout the text help you prepare for teaching with three elements. First, a list of concepts, strategies, and topics help you plan meaningful minilessons. Second, a detailed minilesson example models effective instructional practice. Finally, connection to MyEducationLab deepens the text's authentic classroom exploration by leading you to video clips that illustrate other minilessons from the list of topics in live language arts classrooms.

- **New!** *Meeting the Needs of English Learners* features help prepare you for the needs of today's students with concrete advice for planning instruction to address the needs of culturally and linguistically diverse learners.

Tools for the Language Arts Classroom

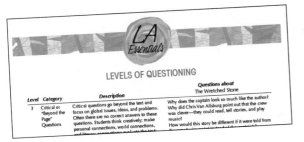

LA Essentials provide guidelines, lists, tools, and resources ready to take right into the classroom. These practical, informative teaching tips are foundational tools all teachers can refer to again and again as they teach.

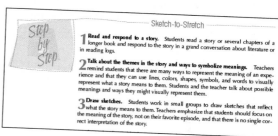

Step by Step features provide detailed instructions for preparing and carrying out specific instructional strategies. These tools become a clear and precise map for teachers to use in their classrooms.

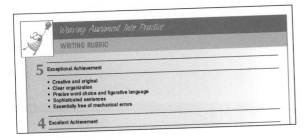

Weaving Assessment Into Practice features present authentic artifacts and guidelines for assessing the development of language arts strategies and skills.

Booklists provide thematically organized lists of trade books that you can incorporate into your teaching.

MyEducationLab This online website, available with this text, contains classroom clips, strategies, artifacts, lesson-planning guidance and software, standards information, and research articles—countless resources for a prospective teacher. Deepen your understanding of language arts teaching by visiting this valuable website.

Language Arts: Patterns of Practice provides consistent models of language arts instruction and is infused with a rich array of strategies and ideas, adaptable to suit your personal instructional style and your students' individual needs.

MyEducationLab

Your Class. Your Career. Everyone's Future.

"Teacher educators who are developing pedagogies for the analysis of teaching and learning contend that analyzing teaching artifacts has three advantages: it enables new teachers time for reflection while still using the real materials of practice; it provides new teachers with experience thinking about and approaching the complexity of the classroom; and in some cases, it can help new teachers and teacher educators develop a shared understanding and common language about teaching. . . ."[1]

As Linda Darling-Hammond and her colleagues point out, grounding teacher education in real classrooms—among real teachers and students and among actual examples of students' and teachers' work—is an important, and perhaps even an essential, part of training teachers for the complexities of teaching today's students in today's classrooms. For a number of years, we have heard the same message from many of you as we sat in your offices learning about the goals of your courses and the challenges you face in teaching the next generation of educators. Working with a number of our authors and with many of you, we have created a website that provides you and your students with the context of real classrooms and artifacts that research on teacher education tells us is so important. Through authentic in-class video footage, interactive simulations, rich case studies, examples of authentic teacher and student work, and more, **MyEducationLab** offers you and your students a uniquely valuable teacher education tool.

MyEducationLab is easy to use! Wherever the MyEducationLab logo appears in the margins or elsewhere in the text, you and your students can follow the simple link instructions to access the MyEducationLab resource that corresponds with the chapter content. These include:

Video: Authentic classroom videos show how real teachers handle actual classroom situations.

Homework & Exercises: These assignable activities give students opportunities to understand content more deeply and to practice applying content.

1. Darling-Hammond, l., & Bransford, J., Eds. (2005). *Preparing Teachers for a Changing World.* San Francisco: John Wiley & Sons.

Case Studies: A diverse set of robust cases drawn from some of our best-selling books further expose students to the realities of teaching and offer valuable perspectives on common issues and challenges in education.

Simulations: Created by the IRIS Center at Vanderbilt University, these interactive simulations give hands-on practice at adapting instruction for a full spectrum of learners.

Student & Teacher Artifacts: Authentic student and teacher classroom artifacts are tied to course topics and offer practice in working with the actual types of materials encountered every day by teachers.

Readings: Specially selected, topically relevant articles from ASCD's renowned *Educational Leadership* journal expand and enrich students' perspectives on key issues and topics.

Other Resources:

Lesson & Portfolio Builders: With this effective and easy-to-use tool, you can create, update, and share standards-based lesson plans and portfolios.

News Articles: Looking for current issues in education? Our collection offers quick access to hundreds of relevant articles from the New York Times Educational News Feed.

MyEducationLab is easy to assign, which is essential to providing the greatest benefit to your student. Visit www.myeducationlab.com for a demonstration of this exciting new online teaching resource.

ACKNOWLEDGMENTS

I'm privileged to work with very talented teachers. I want to express my heartfelt thanks to the teachers highlighted in the Patterns of Practice features: Judith Kenney, Laurie Goodman, Laura McCleneghan, and Susan McCloskey—and the teachers profiled in the chapter opener vignettes—Manuel Hernandez, Kathleen Kakutani, Arnold Keogh, Patty LaRue, Mike Martinez, Kristi McNeal, Ro Meinke, and Jennifer Miller-McColm. I also want to acknowledge the teachers who have influenced my teaching over the years: Eileen Boland, Kimberly Clark, Stephanie Collom, Florence Crimi, Pat Daniel, Roberta Dillon, Whitney Donnelly, Sandy Harris, Terry Kasner, Carol Ochs, Judy Reeves, Jenny Reno, and Susan Zumwalt. Thanks for welcoming me into your classrooms. I learned as I watched you and worked side by side with you and your students. The students whose writing samples and photographs appear in the book deserve special recognition. You've breathed life into the pages of this book.

I am grateful to everyone on Jeff Johnston's remarkable team at Merrill who enthusiastically embrace each new edition of *Language Arts*. I want to thank Linda Bishop, my acquisitions editor, for nurturing our vision for the seventh edition and ensuring that it became a reality. My development editor, Hope Madden, is my taskmaster, nudging me toward impossible deadlines. All taskmasters should have your spirit! My project manger, Mary Irvin, is a marvel! You've moved this book through production with your usual thoroughness and efficiency. Melissa Gruzs, my copyeditor and proofreader, has become an indispensable member of the production team. I appreciate your dogged attention to detail, and since we've been working together, you've taught me to be a more careful writer. Thanks, too, to quiltmaker Cher Cartwright and illustrator Linda Bronson, whose dynamic work is featured on the cover and inside this edition of *Language Arts*. Your talent enriches my words.

Finally, I want to acknowledge my colleagues who served as reviewers for this edition: Diane Bottomley, Ball State University; Helen Hoffner, Holy Family University; Cindy J. Hopper, University of North Carolina – Charlotte; Lonnie R. McDonald, Henderson State University; Debra Price, Sam Houston State University; and Janet Young, Brigham Young University. I also want to thank Patricia DeMay, University of West Alabama; Deanna Gilmore, Washington State University—Tri-Cities; and Rebecca Kaminski, Clemson University, who painstakingly reviewed the ancillaries for instructors to verify their accuracy and usefulness. I remain grateful to reviewers of previous editions, as well: Helen Abadiano, Central Connecticut State University; Doreen Bardsley, Arizona State University; Bobbie W. Berry, Clarion University of Pennsylvania; Scott Busley, Grand Canyon University; Irene Cota, California State University, Northridge; Betty Goerss, Indiana University East; Gail Gerlach, Indiana University of Pennsylvania; Catherine Kurkjian, Central Connecticut State University; Lonnie R. McDonald, Henderson State University; Marjorie S. Wynn, University of South Florida, Lakeland; and Janet R. Young, Brigham Young University. I appreciate your thoughtful analyses and insights. This text is more effective because of your efforts.

ABOUT THE AUTHOR AND ILLUSTRATORS

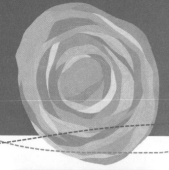

Gail Tompkins   I'm a teacher, first and foremost. I began my career as a first-grade teacher in Virginia in the 1970s. I remember one first grader who cried as the first day of school was ending. When I tried to comfort him, he sobbed accusingly, "I came to first grade to learn to read and write and you forgot to teach me." I've never forgotten that child's comment and what it taught me: Teachers must understand their students and meet their expectations.

My first few years of teaching left me with more questions than answers, and I wanted to become a more effective teacher, so I started taking graduate courses. In time I earned a master's degree and then a doctorate in reading/language arts, both from Virginia Tech. Through my graduate studies, I learned a lot of answers, but more important, I learned to keep asking questions.

Then I began teaching at the university level. First I taught at Miami University in Ohio, then at the University of Oklahoma, and finally at California State University, Fresno. I've taught preservice teachers and practicing teachers working on master's degrees, and I've directed doctoral dissertations. I've received awards for my teaching, including the Provost's Award for Excellence in Teaching at California State University, Fresno, and I was inducted into the California Reading Association's Reading Hall of Fame. Throughout the years, my students have taught me as much as I taught them. I'm grateful to all of them for what I've learned.

I've been writing college textbooks for more than 20 years, and I think of the books I write as teaching, too. I'll be teaching you as you read this text.

When I'm not teaching, I like to make quilts, and piecing together a quilt is a lot like planning effective language arts instruction. Instead of cloth, teachers use the patterns of practice and other instructional procedures to design instruction for the diverse students in today's classrooms. That's why I like to use quilts on the cover of *Language Arts*. ◆

Cher Cartwright   After a lifetime of relying on words to communicate—first as a teacher and then as a lawyer—I discovered the language of visual art, which allows more articulate and subtle expression than can be achieved with mere words. Originally drawn to quilting by my appreciation of traditional quilts, I use the quilt form as a springboard for creative expression. I am proud to be an award-winning textile artist, and I rely exclusively on my own hand-dyed fabric, creating purely imaginative visuals that are abstract, bold, and dramatic. My quilts are primarily explorations of form and color and the emotions evoked by these elements, but I also hope to elicit a physical response in the viewer. My work has been exhibited internationally, with pieces juried into the prestigious Quilt National exhibitions in 2003 and 2007. I live with my husband and two dogs in White Rock, British Columbia. You can see more of my work at my website: **www.chercartwright.com** ◆

Linda Bronson   I grew up on the hustling bustling Jersey Shore, spending summers at the beach covering my brother up to his neck in sand and decorating him to look like a starfish. At home I played dress up and ran around the backyard pretending to be Wonder Woman, and my mom taught me how to draw.

It wasn't until attending art college at the Rhode Island School of Design that I truly blossomed. Suddenly, I was expected to spend all of my time making art! What a treat! I took so many interesting classes—everything from photography and graphic design to stained glass and ceramics. I learned that artists could make careers out of doing what they love!

Nowadays, you can find my painting in picture books, magazines, advertisements, posters, and greeting cards. I think I have the world's best job! You can see more of my work at **www.lindabronson.com/** ◀

CONTENTS

Chapter 1   *Learning and the Language Arts*   2

HOW CHILDREN LEARN   6
   The Process of Learning   6
   Learning Strategies   7
   Social Contexts of Learning   8
   Implications for Learning Language Arts   9

LANGUAGE LEARNING AND CULTURE   9
   The Four Language Systems   9
   Academic Language   13
   Culturally and Linguistically Diverse Students   13
   Critical Literacy   16
   Implications for Learning Language Arts   18

HOW STUDENTS LEARN LANGUAGE ARTS   18
   Creating a Community of Learners   20
   Motivation for Learning   23
   The Six Language Arts   24
   Language Arts Strategies and Skills   26
   The Goal of Language Arts Instruction   30

REVIEW   31
PROFESSIONAL REFERENCES   32
CHILDREN'S BOOK REFERENCES   33

Chapter 2   *Teaching and Assessing Language Arts*   34

PATTERNS OF PRACTICE   40
   Literature Focus Units   41
   Literature Circles   43
   Reading and Writing Workshop   44
   Thematic Units   47

THE TEACHER'S ROLE   48
   What About Teaching?   49
   Differentiating Instruction   49

ASSESSING STUDENTS' LEARNING   52
   Monitoring Students' Progress   52

Implementing Portfolios in the Classroom   56
Assigning Grades   60

REVIEW   65

PROFESSIONAL REFERENCES   65

CHILDREN'S BOOK REFERENCES   66

Chapter
3

The Reading and Writing Processes   *68*

THE READING PROCESS   72
Aesthetic and Efferent Reading   72
Stage 1: Prereading   73
Stage 2: Reading   74
Stage 3: Responding   78
Stage 4: Exploring   79
Stage 5: Applying   80
Teaching the Reading Process   80

THE WRITING PROCESS   84
Stage 1: Prewriting   84
Stage 2: Drafting   86
Stage 3: Revising   87
Stage 4: Editing   91
Stage 5: Publishing   93
Teaching the Writing Process   96
The Qualities of Effective Writing   97
Connections Between Reading and Writing   102

REVIEW   104

PROFESSIONAL REFERENCES   105

CHILDREN'S BOOK REFERENCES   106

Chapter
4

Emerging Into Literacy   *108*

FOSTERING YOUNG CHILDREN'S INTEREST IN LITERACY   113
Concepts About Written Language   113
Concepts About the Alphabet   115

YOUNG CHILDREN EMERGE INTO READING   126
Shared Reading   126
Language Experience Approach   130

YOUNG CHILDREN EMERGE INTO WRITING   131
Introducing Young Children to Writing   132
Interactive Writing   134
Minilessons   137

REVIEW   138

PROFESSIONAL BOOKS   140

CHILDREN'S BOOK REFERENCES   141

Chapter 5

Looking Closely at Words 142

HISTORY OF THE ENGLISH LANGUAGE 146
Old English (A.D. 450–1100) 146
Middle English 1100–1500) 147
Modern English (1500–present) 148
Learning About Word Histories 148

WORDS AND THEIR MEANINGS 150
Root Words and Affixes 150
Synonyms and Antonyms 154
Homonyms 156
Multiple Meanings 158
Figurative Language 158
Borrowed Words 161

TEACHING STUDENTS ABOUT WORDS 162
Direct and Indirect Instruction 164
Choosing Words to Teach 165
Word Walls 166
Word-Study Activities 167
Minilessons 169
Assessing Students' Vocabulary Knowledge 173

REVIEW 174

PROFESSIONAL REFERENCES 174

CHILDREN'S BOOK REFERENCES 175

Chapter 6

Personal Writing 176

WRITING IN JOURNALS 180
Personal Journals 182
Dialogue Journals 184
Reading Logs 185
Double-Entry Journals 188
Language Arts Notebooks 188
Learning Logs 190
Simulated Journals 191
Teaching Students to Write in Journals 194
Assessing Students' Journal Entries 196

LETTER WRITING 196
Friendly Letters 198
Business Letters 201
Simulated Letters 201
Teaching Students to Write Letters 202
Assessing Students' Letters 203

REVIEW   206

PROFESSIONAL REFERENCES   207

CHILDREN'S BOOK REFERENCES   207

Chapter

7

Listening to Learn   208

AESTHETIC LISTENING   213
Interactive Read-Alouds   214
Responding to Stories   219
Listening and Viewing   220
Teaching Aesthetic Listening   220
Assessing Students' Aesthetic Listening   222

EFFERENT LISTENING   222
Reading Aloud Informational Books   225
Teaching Efferent Listening   227
Assessing Students' Efferent Listening   230

CRITICAL LISTENING   231
Persuasion and Propaganda   231
Teaching Critical Listening   235
Assessing Students' Critical Listening   237

REVIEW   238

PROFESSIONAL REFERENCES   239

CHILDREN'S BOOK REFERENCES   239

Chapter

8

Sustaining Talk in the Classroom   240

CONVERSATIONS   244
Small-Group Conversations   244
Grand Conversations   246
Instructional Conversations   249

TALK AS A LEARNING TOOL   250
Asking Questions   250
K-W-L Charts   253
Minilessons   254
Oral Reports   255
Interviews   258
Debates   261

THE POWER OF DRAMA   262
Improvisation   263
Process Drama   263
Playing With Puppets   265
Theatrical Productions   265

REVIEW 268

PROFESSIONAL REFERENCES   268

CHILDREN'S BOOK REFERENCES   269

Chapter
9

Reading and Writing Stories   270

CHILDREN'S CONCEPT OF STORY   275
    Elements of Story Structure   277
    Genres   287
    Literary Devices   288
    Teaching Students About Stories   290

READING STORIES   291
    Guided Reading   291
    Readers Theatre   291
    Independent Reading   294
    Responding to Stories   297
    Retelling Stories   298

WRITING STORIES   303
    Writing Retellings of Stories   303
    Writing Innovations   305
    Writing Sequels   306
    Writing Genre Stories   306
    Writing Original Stories   307
    Assessing Students' Stories   308

REVIEW   309

PROFESSIONAL REFERENCES   309

CHILDREN'S BOOK REFERENCES   310

Chapter
10

Reading and Writing Information   312

LEARNING ABOUT INFORMATIONAL BOOKS   317
    Types of Informational Books   317
    Expository Text Structures   320
    Teaching Students About Informational Books   322

RESEARCHING AND WRITING REPORTS   326
    Visual Reports   326
    "All About ..." Books   330
    Collaborative Reports   333
    Individual Reports   334
    Multigenre Projects   337
    Teaching Students to Write Reports   338
    Assessing Students' Reports   341

LIFE STORIES   341
    Reading Biographies   342
    Teaching Students to Write Autobiographies   343
    Teaching Students to Write Biographies   344
    Assessing Students' Life Stories   347

REVIEW   349

PROFESSIONAL REFERENCES   349

CHILDREN'S BOOK REFERENCES   350

Chapter 11

Reading and Writing Poetry   352

PLAYING WITH WORDS   357
  Laughing With Language   357
  Creating Word Pictures   359
  Experimenting With Rhyme   359
  Poetic Devices   360

READING POEMS   363
  Types of Poems   363
  Reading and Responding to Poems   364
  Assessing Students' Experiences With Poems   371

WRITING POEMS   371
  Formula Poems   372
  Free-Form Poems   377
  Syllable- and Word-Count Poems   380
  Rhymed Verse Forms   381
  Model Poems   382
  Teaching Students to Write Poems   383
  Assessing the Poems Students Write   387

REVIEW   388

PROFESSIONAL REFERENCES   388

CHILDREN'S BOOK REFERENCES   389

Chapter 12

Learning to Spell Conventionally   392

STUDENTS' SPELLING DEVELOPMENT   397
  What Is Invented Spelling?   397
  Stages of Spelling Development   398
  Analyzing Students' Spelling Development   401

TEACHING SPELLING   406
  Components of the Spelling Program   408
  Minilessons   418
  Weekly Spelling Tests   418
  Assessing Students' Progress in Spelling   423

REVIEW   424

PROFESSIONAL REFERENCES   425

Chapter 13

Language Tools: Grammar and Handwriting 426

GRAMMAR 431
Grammar Concepts 431
Teaching Grammar 436

HANDWRITING 447
Handwriting Forms 447
Children's Handwriting Development 449
Teaching Handwriting 452
Keyboarding: An Alternative to Handwriting 458

REVIEW 460

PROFESSIONAL REFERENCES 460

CHILDREN'S BOOK REFERENCES 461

Chapter 14

Putting It All Together 462

LITERATURE FOCUS UNITS 467
How to Develop a Literature Focus Unit 467
A Primary-Grade Literature Focus Unit on *The Mitten* 473
An Upper-Grade Literature Focus Unit on *The Giver* 473

LITERATURE CIRCLES 475
How to Organize for Literature Circles 475

READING AND WRITING WORKSHOP 479
Establishing a Workshop Environment 481
How to Set up a Reading Workshop 481
How to Set up a Writing Workshop 484

THEMATIC UNITS 489
How to Develop a Thematic Unit 490
Using Content-Area Textbooks 494
A Middle-Grade Thematic Unit on Flight 495

REVIEW 497

PROFESSIONAL REFERENCES 497

CHILDREN'S BOOK REFERENCES 498

Name Index 499

Subject Index 504

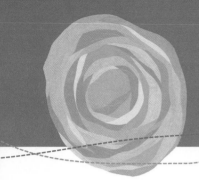

SPECIAL FEATURES

LA Essentials

Roles Students Play in Literature Circles   45
Guidelines for Authentic Assessment   53
Key Features of the Reading Process   73
Key Features of the Writing
   Process   85
The Most Useful Phonics
   Generalizations   125
Root Words   151
Affixes   153
Types of Journals   181
Response Patterns   187
Forms for Friendly and Business
   Letters   199
Guidelines for Using Videos in the Classroom   221
Guidelines for Reading Aloud Informational Books   227
Levels of Questioning   252
Ways to Respond to Stories   299
Genres for Multigenre Projects   339
Guidelines for Reading Poems   366
Guidelines for Writing Poems   385
Characteristics of the Stages of Spelling Development   399
Components of a Comprehensive Spelling Program   409
Individualized Spelling Tests   422
Components of Grammar Instruction   432
Guidelines for Teaching Grammar   438
Sequence of Handwriting Development   453
Guidelines for Successful Keyboarding   459
Steps in Developing a Literature Focus Unit   468
Steps in Organizing Literature Circles   477
Steps in Setting up a Reading Workshop   482
Steps in Setting up a Writing Workshop   486
Steps in Setting up a Thematic Unit   491

Planning for Instruction

What Students Need to Know About the Reading and
   Writing Processes   98
What Emergent Readers and Writers Need to Learn   138
What Students Need to Learn About Vocabulary   172
What Students Need to Learn About Personal Writing   204
What Students Need to Learn About Listening   232

What Students Need to Learn About Talk   256
What Students Need to Learn About Stories   292
What Students Need to Learn About Informational Books
   324
What Students Need to Learn About Poetry   372
What Students Need to Learn About Spelling   420
What Children Need to Learn About Language Tools   454

Step by Step

Minilessons   43
Writing Groups   88
Shared Reading   127
Language Experience Approach   131
Interactive Writing   136
Word Walls   166
Writing Letters   202
Interactive Read-Alouds   216
Anticipation Guides   225
Creating Commercials and Advertisements   236
Grand Conversations   247
Instructional Conversations   250
K-W-L Charts   258
Oral Reports   259
Hot Seat   261
Debates   262
Process Drama   264
Sketch-to-Stretch   286
Guided Reading   294
Readers Theatre   295
Retelling Stories   301
Cubing   329
Collaborative Reports   333
Individual Reports   336
Choral Reading   368
Gallery Walks   386
Making Words   412

Meeting the Needs of English Learners

How Can Teachers Support English Learners' Language
   Development?   16
How Do Teachers Adapt Instruction for English Learners?   51

How Do Teachers Adapt the Writing Process for English Learners?   94

How Can Teachers Develop Students' Vocabularies?   162

How Can Teachers Use Journals With English Learners?   197

Why Is Listening Crucial for English Learners?   223

How Do English Learners Use Talk as a Learning Tool?   251

How Do Teachers Scaffold English Learners' Knowledge of Stories?   276

How Do English Learners Use Writing as a Learning Tool?   327

Shouldn't English Learners Be Doing Something More Important Than Reading and Writing Poetry?   374

How Do Teachers Teach Spelling to English Learners?   407

What's the Best Way to Teach Grammar to English Learners?   440

chapter one

Learning and the Language Arts

The first graders in Mrs. McNeal's classroom are rereading their collaborative retelling of Maurice Sendak's *Where the Wild Things Are* (2003). It's written on three large charts, one for the beginning, one for the middle, and one for the end. Here is their retelling:

Beginning *Max wore his wolf suit and made mischief. His mother called him, "Wild Thing!" He was sent to bed without any supper!*

Middle *Max went to his room and a forest grew. Max got into his private boat and sailed to where the wild things are.*

End *Max wanted to go home to where somebody loved him best of all. When he got home his supper was waiting for him and it was still hot!*

Mrs. McNeal used interactive writing to write the retelling so that all of the words would be spelled correctly, and the children could easily reread it. The "middle" chart is shown on page 4. The boxes around some letters and words represent the correction tape that Mrs. McNeal used to correct spelling errors and poorly formed letters.

***H**ow do teachers incorporate the six language arts in their teaching?*

Listening, talking, reading, writing, viewing, and visually representing are the six language arts; two of the language arts are oral, two are written, and two are visual. Effective teachers integrate instruction and incorporate opportunities for children to use all six every day in their language arts programs. As you read this vignette about first graders participating in writing workshop, notice that Mrs. McNeal provides opportunities for her students to use all six language arts.

Japmeet holds the pointer and leads the class in rereading the "beginning" chart, moving the pointer from word to word as the children read aloud. Next, Henry leads the rereading of the "middle" chart, and Noelle does the "end" chart. As they finish reading, the children clap their hands because they're proud of their retelling of a favorite story.

Mrs. McNeal's students are learning about stories; they know that stories have beginnings, middles, and ends. They can pick out the three parts in stories that Mrs. McNeal reads aloud, and they try to include all three parts in the stories they write.

The first graders participate in an hourlong writing workshop each day. It begins with a 15-minute word work lesson that focuses on reading and writing high-frequency words. The first graders sit on the floor in front of the word wall, a bulletin-board display with 20 sheets of construction paper on which the letters are printed in alphabetical order and word cards with high-frequency words are posted according to beginning letter. Currently, 52 words are posted on the word wall, and several new words are added each week. The word wall is shown on page 4.

The lesson begins with a review of the words. First, Hanna holds the pointer and leads the children in reading the words. Next, Mrs. McNeal passes out small dry-erase boards, pens, and erasers, and they play a word game: The teacher gives phonological, semantic, and syntactic clues about a word on the word wall, and the first graders identify the word. Mrs. McNeal says, "I'm thinking of a word with three letters. It begins with /y/ and it fits in this sentence: _____ are my friend. What is the word?" The children identify *you* and write it on their dry-erase boards. They hold up their boards so Mrs. McNeal can check their work. Then the children erase their boards and the game continues.

Next, Mrs. McNeal teaches a 15-minute minilesson on a writing concept, such as adding details, writing titles, or using punctuation marks correctly. Today, she reviews beginning, middle, and end. She asks Sachit to read his draft aloud. He reads:

I love school. I have lots of friends. One is Yaman.

Children's Retelling of the "Middle" of the Story

Max w[ent] to [his] room and a forest gr[ew]. Max [go]t into his pri[vate] bo[at] and [sailed] to where the wi[ld] things are.

Mrs. McNeal's Word Wall

Aa	Bb	Cc	Dd	Ee
at any	by	can	do	eat
and are		can't	don't	
all				

Ff	Gg	Hh	Ii/Jj/Kk	Ll
fun	got	house had	I	like
friend	get	her have	jump	look
	going	him how		

Mm/Nn	Oo	Pp/Qq	Rr	Ss
me	other one	quiet	run	sister
make	of	play		some
new	or	people		said

Tt	Uu	Vv	Ww	Xx/Yy/Zz
they there	used	very	went with	You
time	us		want	
then			was	

He is a good friend to me. We play with Alex. We play basketball. We are good friends. I can't get a ball in the hoop.

The children pick out the beginning and middle sections of the story but notice that Sachit's story needs an ending. After several children suggest possible endings, Sachit decides to use Yaman's suggestion and finishes his story this way: *But I still play basketball anyway.*

A 25-minute writing period follows. On most days, children write stories independently, but sometimes they work together to write collaborative compositions, as they did to retell *Where the Wild Things Are.* Today, some children are beginning new stories. They sit knee-to-knee with a classmate and plan their stories by telling them aloud. Some children work on stories they began the previous day, and others meet with Mrs. McNeal to share their writings. They read their stories to Mrs. McNeal and talk about them, checking that they make sense and have a beginning, a middle, and an end. If the story is ready to be published, Mrs. McNeal types it on the computer, leaving space at the top for an illustration and correcting spelling and other mechanical errors so that the children can read it.

Noelle's Story

The Birthday Party

Once it was my grandpa's birthday. We had a party. We played lots of games. My dad played and my sister played and my cousin played. All of us had fun.

For the last 5 minutes of the workshop, children share their newly published compositions. Noelle reads aloud her story, "The Birthday Party," which is shown here. The children tell her that they like her story because it reminds them of the times they spend with their grandparents. Mrs. McNeal ceremoniously hangs Noelle's story in a special section of the bulletin board for everyone to reread.

*T*oday, **teachers face new challenges** and opportunities. The students who come to your classroom may speak a different language at school than they speak at home, and they're growing up in varied family structures: Many live in two-parent families, but others live with single parents or grandparents, in blended families, or with two moms or dads. Far too many children are growing up in poverty, some with parents in prison and siblings in gangs. Still others are homeless. Sadly, some have lost sight of the American dream, believing that a college education is out of reach. Clearly, the way you teach language arts must address not only your beliefs about how children learn but also the language and culture of the students you teach.

In this chapter, you'll read about theories of language and learning and how they apply to language arts instruction. As you continue reading this chapter, think about these questions:

- ♦ How do children learn?
- ♭ How do language and culture influence learning?
- ♦ What are the language arts?
- ⚑ How do children learn language arts?

HOW CHILDREN LEARN

Swiss psychologist Jean Piaget (1886–1980) radically changed our understanding of how children learn with his constructivist framework (Piaget & Inhelder, 2000). He described learning as the modification of children's cognitive structures as they interact with and adapt to their environment. He believed that children construct their own knowledge from their experiences. Related to Piaget's theory is information-processing theory (Flavell, Miller, & Miller, 2001), which focuses on how learners use cognitive processes and think about what and how they're learning.

The Process of Learning

Children's knowledge is not just a collection of isolated bits of information; it is organized in the brain, and this organization becomes increasingly integrated as their knowledge grows (Tracey & Morrow, 2006). The organization of knowledge is the cognitive structure, and knowledge is arranged in category systems called *schemata*. (A single category is a *schema*.) Within the schemata are three components: categories of knowledge, features or rules for determining what constitutes a category and what's included in each category, and a network of interrelationships among the categories.

These schemata can be likened to a conceptual filing system in which children and adults organize and store the information derived from their past experiences. Taking this analogy further, information is filed in the brain in "file folders." As children learn, they add file folders to their filing system, and as they study a topic, its file folder becomes thicker.

As children learn, they enlarge existing schemata or construct new ones. Two cognitive processes—*assimilation* and *accommodation*—are responsible (Piaget & Inhelder, 2000). Assimilation takes place when information is integrated into existing schemata, and accommodation occurs when schemata are modified or new schemata are created. Through assimilation, children add new information to their picture of the world; through accommodation, they change that picture to reflect new information.

Learning occurs through the process of equilibration. When children encounter something they don't understand, disequilibrium, or cognitive conflict, results. This disequilibrium typically produces confusion and agitation, feelings that impel children to seek equilibrium, a comfortable balance with the environment. In other words, when confronted with new or discrepant information, children are intrinsically motivated to try to make sense of it. If their schemata can assimilate or accommodate the new information, then the disequilibrium caused by the new experience will motivate them to learn. Equilibrium is then regained at a higher developmental level. These are the steps in the process:

1. Equilibrium is disrupted by the introduction of new or discrepant information.
2. Disequilibrium occurs, and the dual processes of assimilation and accommodation function.
3. Equilibrium is attained at a higher developmental level.

The process of equilibration happens again and again during the course of a day. In fact, it is occurring right now as you are reading this chapter. Learning doesn't always occur when we are presented with new information, however: If the new information is too difficult and we cannot relate it to what we already know, we don't learn. The new information must be puzzling, challenging, or, in Piaget's words, "moderately novel."

Learning Strategies

We all have skills that we use automatically as well as self-regulated strategies for things that we do well—driving defensively, playing volleyball, training a new pet, or maintaining classroom discipline. We unconsciously apply skills we have learned and choose among strategies. The strategies we use in these activities are problem-solving mechanisms that involve complex thinking processes. When we are learning how to drive a car, for example, we learn both skills and strategies. Some of the first skills we learn are how to make left turns and parallel park. With practice, these skills become automatic. One of the first strategies we learn is how to pass another car. At first, we have only a small repertoire of strategies, and we don't always use them effectively; that's one reason why we get a learner's permit that requires a more experienced driver to ride along with us. With practice and guidance, we become more successful drivers, able to anticipate driving problems and take defensive actions.

Children develop a number of learning strategies or methods for learning. Rehearsal—repeating information over and over—is a learning strategy children use to remember something. Here are other learning strategies:

Predicting: Anticipating what will happen
Organizing: Grouping information into categories
Elaborating: Expanding on the information presented
Monitoring: Regulating or keeping track of progress

Information-processing theory suggests that as children grow older, their use of learning strategies improves (Flavell, Miller, & Miller, 2001). As they acquire more effective methods for learning and remembering information, children also become more aware of their own cognitive processes and better able to regulate them. They can reflect on their literacy processes and talk about themselves as readers and writers. For example, third grader Mario reports that "it's mostly after I read a book that I write" (Muhammad, 1993, p. 99), and fifth grader Hobbes reports that "the pictures in my head help me when I write stuff down 'cause then I can get ideas from my pictures" (Cleary, 1993, p. 142).

Children become more realistic about the limitations of their memories and more knowledgeable about which learning strategies are most effective in particular situations. They also become increasingly aware of what they know and don't know. The term *metacognition* refers to this knowledge that children acquire about their own cognitive processes and to children's regulation of their cognitive processes to maximize learning (Tracey & Morrow, 2006).

Teachers play an important role in developing children's metacognitive abilities. During large-group activities, teachers introduce and model learning strategies. In small-group lessons, they provide guided practice, talk with children about learning strategies, and ask them to reflect on their own use of these cognitive processes. Teachers also guide children about when to use particular strategies and which strategies are more effective with various activities.

Social Contexts of Learning

Children's cognitive development is enhanced through social interaction. Russian psychologist Lev Vygotsky (1896–1934) asserted that children learn through socially meaningful interactions and that language is both social and an important facilitator of learning (Vygotsky, 1986, 2006). Children's experiences are organized and shaped by society, but rather than merely absorbing these experiences, children negotiate and transform them as a dynamic part of culture. They learn to talk through social interactions and to read and write through interactions with literate children and adults (Dyson, 1997, 2003). Community is important for both readers and writers: Children talk about books they are reading with classmates, and they turn to classmates for feedback about their writing (Zebroski, 1994).

Through interactions with adults and collaboration with classmates, children learn things they could not learn on their own (Tracey & Morrow, 2006). Adults guide and support children as they move from their current level of knowledge toward a more advanced level. Vygotsky (2006) described these two levels as the actual developmental level, the level at which children can perform a task independently, and the level of proximal development, the level at which children can perform a task with assistance. Children can typically do more difficult things in collaboration than they can on their own, which is why teachers are important models for their students and why children often work with partners and in small groups.

A child's "zone of proximal development" is the range of tasks that the child can perform with guidance from others but cannot yet perform independently. Vygotsky believed that children learn best when what they are attempting to learn is within this zone. He felt that children learn little by performing tasks they can already do independently—tasks at their actual developmental level—or by attempting tasks that are too difficult, or beyond their zone of proximal development.

Vygotsky and Jerome Bruner (2004) used the term *scaffold* as a metaphor to describe adults' contributions to children's learning. Scaffolds are support mechanisms that teachers, parents, and others provide to help children successfully perform a task within their zone of proximal development. Teachers serve as scaffolds when they model or demonstrate a procedure, guide children through a task, ask questions, break complex tasks into smaller steps, and supply pieces of information. As children gain knowledge and experience about how to perform a task, teachers gradually withdraw their support so that children make the transition from social interaction to internalized, independent functioning.

Implications for Learning Language Arts

How children learn has important implications for how they learn language arts. Contributions from the constructivist and sociolinguistic theories include these ideas:

- Children are active participants in learning.
- Children learn by relating the new information to prior knowledge.
- Children organize their knowledge in schemata.
- Children use skills automatically and strategies consciously as they learn.
- Children learn through social interactions with classmates and the teacher.
- Teachers provide scaffolds for children.

Think about these implications and how they will affect your teaching.

LANGUAGE LEARNING AND CULTURE

Language is a complex system for creating meaning through socially shared conventions (Halliday, 1978). Before children enter kindergarten, they learn the language of their community. They understand what community members say to them, and they share their ideas with others through that language. In an amazingly short period of 3 or 4 years, children master the exceedingly complex system of their native language, which allows them to understand sentences they have never heard before and to create sentences they have never said before. Young children are not taught how to talk; this knowledge about language develops tacitly, or unconsciously.

The Four Language Systems

Language is organized using four systems, sometimes called *cueing systems*, which together make oral and written communication possible. Here are the language systems:

The phonological, or sound, system of language

The syntactic, or structural, system of language

The semantic, or meaning, system of language

The pragmatic, or social and cultural use, system of language

The four language systems and their terminology are summarized in Figure 1–1.

Children have an implicit understanding of these systems, and they integrate information simultaneously from them in order to communicate. No one system is more important than any other one, even though the phonological system (sometimes called the *visual system*) plays a prominent role in early literacy.

The Phonological System. There are approximately 44 speech sounds in English. Children learn to pronounce these sounds as they learn to talk, and they associate the sounds with letters as they learn to read and write. Sounds are called *phonemes*, and they are represented in print with diagonal lines to differentiate them from *graphemes*, or letter combinations. For example, the first letter in *mother* is written *m,* and the phoneme is represented by /m/; the /ō/ phoneme in *soap* represented by the grapheme *oa.*

FIGURE 1–1

Overview of the Four Language Systems

System	Terms	Applications
Phonological System *The sound system of English with approximately 44 sounds*	• Phoneme (the smallest unit of sound) • Grapheme (the written representation of a phoneme using one or more letters) • Phonological awareness (knowledge about the sound structure of words, at the phoneme, onset-rime, and syllable levels) • Phonemic awareness (the ability to manipulate the sounds in words orally) • Phonics (instruction about phoneme-grapheme correspondences and spelling rules)	• Pronouncing words • Detecting regional and other dialects • Decoding words when reading • Using invented spelling • Reading and writing alliterations and onomatopoeia
Syntactic System *The structural system of English that governs how words are combined into sentences*	• Syntax (the structure or grammar of a sentence) • Morpheme (the smallest meaningful unit of language) • Free morpheme (a morpheme that can stand alone as a word) • Bound morpheme (a morpheme that must be attached to a free morpheme)	• Adding inflectional endings to words • Combining words to form compound words • Adding prefixes and suffixes to root words • Using capitalization and punctuation to indicate beginnings and ends of sentences • Identifying the parts of speech • Writing simple, compound, and complex sentences • Combining sentences
Semantic System *The meaning system of English that focuses on vocabulary*	• Semantics (meaning) • Synonyms (words with similar meanings) • Antonyms (opposites) • Homonyms (words that sound alike)	• Learning the meanings of words • Discovering that some words have multiple meanings • Studying synonyms, antonyms, and homonyms • Using a dictionary and a thesaurus • Reading and writing comparisons (metaphors and similes) and idioms
Pragmatic System *The system of English that varies language according to social and cultural uses*	• Function (the purpose for which a person uses language) • Standard English (the form of English used in textbooks and by television newscasters) • Nonstandard English (other forms of English)	• Varying language to fit specific purposes • Reading and writing dialogue in dialects • Comparing standard and nonstandard forms of English

The phonological system is important in both oral and written language. Regional and cultural differences exist in the way people pronounce phonemes. For example, Jimmy Carter's speech is characteristic of the southeastern United States, and John F. Kennedy's was typical of New England. Similarly, the English spoken in Australia is different from American English. English learners must learn to pronounce English sounds, and sounds that are different from those in their native language are particularly difficult for children to learn. For example, Spanish does not have /th/, and children who have immigrated to the United States from Mexico and other Spanish-speaking countries have difficulty pronouncing this sound; they often substitute /d/ for /th/ because the sounds are articulated in similar ways (Nathenson-Mejia, 1989). Younger children usually learn to pronounce the difficult sounds more easily than do older children and adults.

Children use their knowledge of the phonological system as they learn to read and write. In a purely phonetic language, there would be a one-to-one correspondence between letters and sounds, and teaching students to sound out words would be a simple process. But English is not a purely phonetic language, because there are 26 letters and 44 sounds and many ways to combine the letters—especially the vowels—to spell some of the sounds. Consider the different ways of spelling long *e* in these words: *sea, green, Pete, me,* and *people.* And sometimes the patterns used to spell long *e* don't work, as in *head* and *great.* Phonics, which describes the phoneme-grapheme correspondences and related spelling rules, is an important part of beginning reading instruction, because students use phonics information to decode words. However, because readers do much more than decode words when they read, phonics instruction cannot be the entire reading program.

Young children also use their understanding of the phonological system to create invented spellings. First graders, for example, might spell *home* as *hm* or *hom,* and second graders might spell *school* as *skule,* based on their knowledge of phoneme-grapheme relationships and the spelling patterns. As children become better readers and writers, their spellings become increasingly sophisticated and finally conventional. Also, English learners' spellings typically reflect their pronunciations of words.

The Syntactic System. The syntactic system is the structural organization of English. This system is the grammar that regulates how words are combined into sentences. The word *grammar* here means the rules governing how words are combined in sentences, not the grammar of English textbooks or the conventional etiquette of language. Children use the syntactic system as they combine words to form sentences. Word order is important in English, and English speakers must arrange words into a sequence that makes sense. Young Spanish-speaking English learners, for example, learn to say, "This is my red sweater," not "This is my sweater red," which is the literal translation from Spanish.

Children use their knowledge of the syntactic system as they read. They anticipate that the words they are reading have been strung together into sentences. When they come to an unfamiliar word, they recognize its role in the sentence even if they don't know the terms for parts of speech. For example, in the sentence "The horses galloped through the gate and out into the field," children may not be able to decode the word *through,* but they can easily substitute a reasonable word or phrase, such as *out of* or *past.* Many of the capitalization and punctuation rules that children learn reflect the syntactic system. Similarly, when they learn about simple, compound, and complex sentences, they are learning about the syntactic system.

Another component of syntax is word forms. Words such as *dog* and *play* are morphemes, the smallest meaningful units in language. Word parts that change the meaning of a word are also morphemes. When the plural marker *-s* is added to *dog* to make *dogs,* for instance, or the past-tense marker *-ed* is added to *play* to make *played,* these words now contain two morphemes because the inflectional endings change the meaning of the words. The words *dog* and *play* are free morphemes because they convey meaning while standing alone. The endings *s* and *ed* are bound morphemes because they must be attached to a free morpheme to convey meaning. As they learn to talk, children quickly learn to combine words and word parts, such as adding *-s* to *cookie* to create a plural and adding *-er* to *high* to indicate a comparison. They also learn to combine two or more free morphemes to form compound words; *birthday,* for example, is a compound word created by combining two free morphemes.

Children also learn to add affixes to words. Affixes added at the beginning of a word are prefixes, and affixes added at the end are suffixes. Both kinds of affixes are bound morphemes. For example, the prefix *un-* in *unhappy* is a bound morpheme, whereas *happy* is a free morpheme because it can stand alone as a word.

The Semantic System. The third language system is the semantic, or meaning, system. Vocabulary is the key component of this system. Researchers estimate that children have a vocabulary of 5,000 words by the time they enter school, and they continue to acquire 3,000 words each year (Stahl & Nagy, 2005). Considering how many words children learn each year, it is unreasonable to assume that they learn words only through formal instruction. Children probably learn 7 to 10 words a day, many of which are learned informally through reading and through social studies, science, and other curricular areas.

At the same time children are learning new words, they are also learning that many words have more than one meaning. Meaning is usually based on the context, or the surrounding words. The common word *run,* for instance, has more than 30 meanings. Read these sentences to see how the meaning of *run* is tied to the context in which it is used:

> Will the mayor run for reelection?
> The bus runs between Dallas and Houston.
> The advertisement will run for three days.
> Did you run in the 50-yard dash?
> The plane made a bombing run.
> Will you run to the store and get a loaf of bread for me?
> The dogs are out in the run.

Children often don't have the full range of meanings of many words; rather, they learn meanings through a process of refinement.

Children learn other sophisticated concepts about words as well. They learn about shades of meaning—for example, the differences among these *sad* words: *unhappy, crushed, desolate, miserable, disappointed, cheerless, down,* and *grief stricken.* They also learn about synonyms and antonyms, wordplay, and figurative language, including idioms.

The Pragmatic System. The fourth language system is pragmatics, which deals with the social and cultural aspects of language use. People use language for many purposes, and how they talk or write varies according to purpose and audience. Language use varies among social classes, cultural and ethnic groups, and geographic regions; these varieties are known as *dialects*. School is one cultural community, and the language of school is Standard English. This register, or style, is formal—the one used in textbooks, newspapers, and magazines and by television newscasters. Other forms, including those spoken in inner cities, in Appalachia, and by Mexican Americans in the Southwest, are generally classified as nonstandard English. These nonstandard forms of English are alternatives in which the phonology, syntax, and semantics differ from those of Standard English, but they are neither inferior nor substandard. They reflect the communities of the speakers, and the speakers communicate as effectively as those who use Standard English in their communities. The goal is for students to add Standard English to their repertoire of language registers, not to replace their home dialect with Standard English.

Academic Language

The type of English used for instruction is called *academic language*. It's different than the social or conversational language we speak at home and with friends in two ways. First, academic language is more cognitively demanding and decontextualized than social language in which speakers carry on face-to-face conversations about everyday topics (Wong-Fillmore & Snow, 2002). Teachers use academic language when they teach language arts, math, and other content areas and when they give directions for completing assignments. It's also the language used in content-area textbooks and standardized achievement tests.

Second, academic language has semantic, syntactic, and pragmatic features that distinguish it from social language. The ideas expressed are more complex; the meaning is less obvious and takes more effort to understand. The vocabulary is more technical and precise; many words are unfamiliar or are used in new ways. The sentence structure is different: Academic language uses longer, more complex sentences that may be difficult to understand. Academic language has a different style, too: Speakers and writers present detailed, well-organized information about complex and abstract topics, usually without becoming personally involved in the topic. The contrasts between social and academic language are summarized in Figure 1–2.

Even when students are proficient users of social language, they are likely to have difficulty understanding and using academic language in the classroom without instruction (Wong-Fillmore & Snow, 2002). Through instruction and frequent opportunities to use talk and other language arts in meaningful ways, children learn the knowledge, vocabulary, and language patterns associated with academic English. Although learning academic language is essential for all children, the challenge is greater for English learners.

Culturally and Linguistically Diverse Students

The United States is a culturally pluralistic society, and our ethnic, racial, and socioeconomic diversity is reflected in classrooms. Today nearly a third of us classify ourselves as non-European Americans (Wright, 2004). The percentage of culturally

FIGURE 1–2

Contrasts Between Social and Academic Language

	Social Language	Academic Language
Topics	Topics are familiar, everyday, and concrete; they are often examined superficially with few details being presented.	Topics are unfamiliar, complex, and abstract. More details are provided, and they are examined in more depth.
Vocabulary	Everyday, familiar words are used.	Technical terms, jargon, and many multisyllabic words are used.
Sentence Structure	Sentences are shorter and dependent on the context.	Sentence structure is longer and more complicated.
Viewpoints	One opinion or viewpoint is shared, and it is often subjective or biased.	Multiple viewpoints are considered and analyzed, usually objectively.

diverse students is even higher: In California, more than 50% of school-age children belong to ethnic minority groups, and in New York state, 40% do. It has been estimated that given current birthrates and immigration patterns, within a few years, Hispanic American and Asian American populations will have grown by more than 20%, and the African American population will have grown by 12%. These changing demographic realities are having a significant impact on schools, as more and more students come from linguistically and culturally diverse backgrounds.

Because the United States is a nation of immigrants, dealing with cultural diversity is not a new responsibility for public schools; however, the magnitude of diversity is much greater now. In the past, the United States was viewed as a melting pot in which language and cultural differences would be assimilated or combined to form a new, truly American culture. What actually happened, though, was that the European American culture remained dominant. The concept of cultural pluralism has replaced the idea of assimilation. Cultural pluralism respects people's right to retain their cultural identity within American society, recognizing that each culture contributes to and enriches the total society.

Children of diverse cultures come to school with a broad range of language and literacy experiences, although their experiences may be different than those of mainstream or European American children (Samway & McKeon, 1999). They have learned to communicate in at least one language, and, if they don't speak English, they want to learn English in order to make friends, learn, and communicate just like their classmates. Brock and Raphael (2005) emphasize that teachers should take children's diverse backgrounds into account as they plan instruction, making sure to provide a variety of opportunities for children to participate in classroom activities.

English Learners. Learning a second language is a constructive process, and children learn English in a predictable way through interactions with other children and with adults. Jim Cummins (1996) theorized that English learners must develop two types of English proficiency. First, children learn social or everyday language, which Cummins called Basic Interpersonal Conversational Skills (BICS). Social language is characterized as context-embedded because context cues that make the language easier to understand are available to speakers and listeners. This type of language is easy to learn, according to Cummins, because it is cognitively undemanding and can usually be acquired in only 2 to 3 years.

Cummins's second type of language is called Cognitive Academic Language Proficiency (CALP). CALP is academic language, the type of language that students need to understand and use for school success, and it's much harder for learners to understand because it's context reduced and more cognitively demanding. Context-reduced language is more abstract and less familiar, and it's cognitively demanding because technical terms, complex sentence structures, and less familiar topics are involved. English learners require 5 to 7 years or more to become proficient in this type of English, and too many English learners never reach proficiency.

How quickly English learners learn academic English depends on many factors, including their native language proficiency, school experiences, motivation, and personality. The family's literacy level, their socioeconomic status, and their cultural isolation are other considerations. In addition, when families flee from social unrest or war in their native countries, children often take longer to learn English because of the trauma they experienced.

Michael Newman/PhotoEdit Inc.

The Four Language Systems
These Spanish-speaking first graders use the four language systems as they learn to speak, read, and write in English. They have already developed the language systems in their native language, and now they add linguistic information about English. Their teacher helps them understand how English is similar to their native language and how it is different. The errors that these English learners make, such as pronouncing *j* like *h* and placing modifiers after the noun instead of before it (e.g., the *baby little* instead of the *little baby*), often reflect the language systems of their native language.

Meeting the Needs of English Learners

How Can Teachers Support English Learners' Language Development?

- Create a stress-free environment in the classroom.
- Show genuine interest in children, their language, and their culture.
- Build students' background knowledge using artifacts, videos, photos, maps, and picture books.
- Use language that is neither too hard nor too easy for students.
- Embed language in context-rich activities.
- Highlight important words on word walls and encourage students to use these words orally and in writing.
- Have students dramatize vocabulary words they are learning, stories they have read, historical events they are studying, and other topics to enhance their learning.
- Demonstrate how to do projects, and show samples so students understand what they are expected to do.
- Read aloud to students every day.
- Avoid forcing students to speak.
- Expand the two- and three-word sentences that students produce.
- Have students work together with partners and in cooperative groups.
- Have students share ideas with a partner as a rehearsal before sharing with the whole class.
- Provide many opportunities for students to listen to and speak English and to read and write English in low-risk situations.
- Don't lower your expectations for any group of students.

So that children can grow in their knowledge of and use of academic language, Courtney Cazden (2001) challenges teachers to make changes in classroom language use to incorporate more academic language. Finding ways to help all children develop academic language has become more urgent because of the enactment of the No Child Left Behind Act of 2001.

Critical Literacy

It's easy for teachers to focus on teaching children how to read and write without considering how language works in our society, but language is more than just a means of communication; it shapes our perceptions of society, justice, and acceptance. Standard English is the language of school, but today, many children speak a different language or a nonstandard form of English at home. These language differences and the way that teachers and classmates respond to them affect how children think about themselves and their expectations for success at school. Some children are more eager to share their ideas than others, and research suggests that teachers call on boys more often than girls. Also, classmates encourage some children to participate more than others. These language behaviors silence some children and marginalize others.

Language is not neutral. The reasons why people use language are another consideration. Both children and adults use language for a variety of purposes—to entertain, inform, control, and persuade, for example. Language used for these purposes can affect our beliefs, opinions, and behavior. Martin Luther King Jr.'s "I Have a Dream" speech, for example, had a great impact on American society, calling people to action in the Civil Rights movement. Essays, novels, and other written materials also affect us in powerful ways. Think about the impact of *Anne Frank: The Diary of a Young Girl* (Frank, 1995): The madness of the Holocaust appalled us.

Critical literacy focuses on the empowering role of both oral and written language. This theory emphasizes the use of all six language arts to communicate, solve problems, and persuade others to a course of action. It emphasizes the interactions of students in the classroom and in their neighborhoods, and the relationship between language and students in the context of the classroom, the neighborhood, and society.

Critical literacy grew out of the critical pedagogy theory that suggests that teachers and students ask fundamental questions about knowledge, justice, and equity (Wink, 2005). Language becomes a means for social action. Teachers do more than just teach students to use the six language arts; both teachers and students become agents of social change. The increasing social and cultural diversity in our society adds urgency to resolving inequities and injustices.

Language arts instruction doesn't take place in a vacuum; the content that teachers teach and the ways they teach it occur in a social, cultural, political, and historical context (Freire & Macedo, 1987). Consider the issue of grammar instruction, for example. Some people argue that grammar shouldn't be taught because it is too abstract and won't help children become better readers or writers; however, others believe that not teaching grammar is one way the majority culture denies access to nonstandard English speakers. Both proponents and detractors of grammar instruction want what is best for students, but their views are diametrically opposed. Think about these issues related to teaching and learning:

Does school perpetuate the dominant culture and exclude others?
Do all students have equal access to learning opportunities?
How are students who speak nonstandard English treated?
Is school more like family life in some cultures than in others?
Do teachers interact differently with boys and girls?
Are some students silenced in classrooms?
Do teachers have different expectations for minority students?
Are English learners marginalized?
Does the literature that students read reflect diverse voices?

Language arts is not simply a body of knowledge, but rather is a way of organizing knowledge within a cultural and political context. Giroux (1997) challenges teachers not to accept the status quo, but to be professionals and to take control of their own teaching and consider the impact of what they do in the classroom.

Luke and Freebody's (1997) model of reading includes critical literacy as the highest level. I have adapted their model to incorporate both reading and writing:

Level 1. Code Breakers: Students learn phonics, word-identification strategies, and high-frequency words to read and write fluently.

Level 2. Text Participants: Students comprehend what they are reading, learn about text structures and genres, and develop coherent ideas in the texts they write.

Level 3. Text Users: Students read and write multigenre texts and compare the effect of genre and purpose on texts.

Level 4. Text Critics: Students examine the issues raised in books they read and write.

Teachers take students to the fourth level, text critics, when they read and discuss books such as *Rosa* (Giovanni, 2005), the story of the Rosa Parks's refusal to give up her seat on a city bus; *The Breadwinner* (Ellis, 2000), the story of a girl in Taliban-controlled Afghanistan who must pretend to be a boy to support her family; *The Watsons Go to Birmingham—1963* (Curtis, 2000), the story of an African American family caught in the Birmingham church bombing; and *Homeless Bird* (Whelan, 2000), the story of an Indian girl who has no future when she is widowed. These stories describe injustices that primary-, middle-, and upper-grade students can understand and discuss (Foss, 2002; Lewison, Flint, & Van Sluys, 2002). In fact, teachers report that their students are often more engaged in reading stories about social issues than other books and that students' interaction patterns change after reading them (Wolk, 2004).

Implications for Learning Language Arts

What you've read about language and culture has important implications for how students learn language arts in school:

- Students use the four language systems simultaneously as they communicate.
- Students need to understand and use academic language.
- Students from each cultural group bring their unique backgrounds of experience to the process of learning.
- Students' cultural and linguistic diversity provides an opportunity to enhance and enrich the learning of all students.
- Students use language arts to reflect on cultural, social, and political injustices and work to change the world.

Think about these implications and how they will affect how you teach language arts.

HOW STUDENTS LEARN LANGUAGE ARTS

Language arts instruction is changing to reflect our greater oral, written, and visual communication needs. The Steering Committee of the Elementary Section of the National Council of Teachers of English (NCTE, 1996) identified seven characteristics of competent language users, which are presented in Figure 1–3. Students exemplify these characteristics of competent language users as they do the following activities:

- Compare the video and book versions for the same story
- Interview community resource people who have special knowledge, interests, or talents in connection with literature focus units and social studies and science thematic units
- Examine propaganda techniques used in print advertisements and television commercials
- Use the Internet to gather information as part of social studies and science thematic units
- Assume the role of a character while reading a story, and write simulated journal entries as that character
- Use the writing process to write stories, and share the stories with classmates
- Analyze an author's writing style during an author unit

These activities exhibit the three characteristics—meaningful, functional, and genuine—of all worthwhile experiences with language. First, they use language in meaningful rather than contrived situations. Second, they are functional, or real-life,

---

FIGURE 1–3

Characteristics of Competent Language Users

Personal Expression

Students use language to express themselves, to make connections between their own experiences and their social world, to choose books they want to read and topics they want to write about, and to create a personal voice.

Aesthetic Appreciation

Students use language aesthetically to read literature, talk with others, and enrich their lives.

Collaborative Exploration

Students use language as a learning tool as they learn in collaboration with classmates.

Strategic Language Use

Students use strategies as they create and share meaning through language.

Creative Communication

Students use text forms and genres creatively as they share ideas through oral and written language.

Reflective Interpretation

Students use language to organize and evaluate learning experiences, question personal and social values, and think critically.

Thoughtful Application

Students use language to solve problems, persuade others, and take action.

activities. And third, they are genuine rather than artificial activities, because they communicate ideas.

Creating a Community of Learners

Language arts classrooms are social settings. Together, students and their teacher create the classroom community, and the type of community they create strongly influences students' learning. Effective teachers establish a community of learners in which students are motivated to learn and are actively involved in language arts activities. Teachers and students work collaboratively and purposefully. Perhaps the most striking quality of classroom communities is the partnership that the teacher and students create. Students are a "family" in which all the members respect one another and support each other's learning. They value culturally and linguistically diverse classmates and recognize that everyone makes important contributions to the classroom (Wells & Chang-Wells, 1992).

Students and the teacher work together for the good of the community. Consider the differences between renting and owning a home. In a classroom community, students and the teacher are joint owners of the classroom. Students assume responsibility for their own learning and behavior, work collaboratively with classmates, complete assignments, and care for the classroom. In contrast, in traditional classrooms, the classroom belongs to the teacher, and students are simply renters for the school year. This doesn't mean that in a classroom community, teachers abdicate their responsibility to students. On the contrary, teachers retain their roles as organizer, facilitator, participant, instructor, model, manager, diagnostician, evaluator, coordinator, and communicator. These roles are often shared with students, but the ultimate responsibility remains with the teacher.

Researchers have identified many characteristics of effective classroom communities. Ten of these characteristics, which are described in Figure 1–4, show how the learning theories presented earlier in this chapter are translated into practice.

Teachers begin the process of establishing a community of learners when they make deliberate decisions about the kind of classroom culture they want to create (Whatley & Canalis, 2002). School is "real" life for students, and they learn best when they see a purpose for learning to read and write. The social contexts that teachers create are key. Teachers must think about their roles and what they believe about how children learn. They must decide to have a democratic classroom where students' abilities in reading and writing develop through meaningful literacy activities.

Teachers are more successful when they take the first 2 weeks of the school year to establish the classroom environment (Sumara & Walker, 1991). Teachers can't assume that students will be familiar with the procedures and routines used in language arts or that they will instinctively be cooperative, responsible, and respectful of classmates. Teachers explicitly explain classroom routines, such as how to get supplies out and put them away and how to work with classmates in a cooperative group, and they set the expectation that students will adhere to the routines. Next, they demonstrate literacy procedures, including how to choose a book from the classroom library, how to provide feedback in a writing group, and how to participate in a grand conversation or discussion about a book. Third, teachers model ways of interacting with students, responding to literature, respecting classmates, and assisting classmates with reading and writing projects.

FIGURE 1–4

Characteristics of Effective Classroom Communities

Responsibility

Students are responsible for their learning, their behavior, and the contributions they make in the classroom. They see themselves as valued and contributing members of the classroom community. Students become more self-reliant when they make choices about the language arts activities in which they are involved.

Opportunities

Students have opportunities to participate in language arts activities that are meaningful, functional, and genuine. They read real books and write books for real audiences—their classmates, their parents and grandparents, and other members of their community.

Engagement

Students are motivated to learn and to be actively involved in language arts activities. In a student-centered classroom, the activities are interesting, and students sometimes choose which books to read, how they will respond to a book, topics for writing, and the writing form they will use.

Demonstration

Students learn procedures, concepts, skills, and strategies through demonstrations— with modeling and scaffolding—that teachers provide.

Risk Taking

Students are encouraged to explore topics, make guesses, and take risks. Rather than viewing learning as the process of getting the answer right, teachers promote students' experimentation with new skills and strategies.

Instruction

Teachers are expert language users, and they provide instruction through minilessons on procedures, skills, strategies, and other concepts related to language arts. These minilessons are planned and taught to small groups, the whole class, or individual students so that students can apply what they are learning in meaningful literacy projects.

Response

Students have opportunities to respond after reading and viewing and to share their interpretations of stories. Through writing in reading logs and participating in discussions called *grand conversations,* students share personal connections to the story, make predictions, ask questions, and deepen their comprehension. When they write, students share their rough drafts in writing groups to get feedback on how well they are communicating, and they celebrate their published books by sharing them with classmates and other "real" audiences.

Choice

Students often make choices about the language arts activities in which they are involved. They choose what books they will read and what projects they will create after reading. Students make choices within the parameters set by the teacher.

Continues

FIGURE 1–4

Continued

When they are given the opportunity to make choices, students are often more highly motivated to do the activity, and they value their learning experience more because it's more meaningful to them.

Time

Students need large chunks of time to pursue language arts activities. It doesn't work well for teachers to break the classroom schedule into many small time blocks for phonics, reading, spelling, handwriting, grammar, and writing. Students need 2 or 3 hours of uninterrupted time each day for language arts instruction. It is important to minimize disruptions during the time set aside, and administrators should schedule computer, music, art, and other pull-out programs so that they don't interfere. This is especially important in the primary grades.

Assessment

Teachers and students work together to establish guidelines for assessment, and students monitor their own work and participate in the evaluation. Rather than imposing assessment on students, teachers share with their students the responsibility for monitoring and evaluating their progress.

Adapted from Cambourne & Turbill, 1987.

Teachers are the classroom managers or administrators. They set expectations and clearly explain to students what is expected of them and what is valued in the classroom. The classroom rules are specific and consistent, and teachers also set limits. For example, students might be allowed to talk quietly with classmates when they are working, but they are not allowed to shout across the classroom or talk when the teacher is talking or when classmates are making a presentation to the class. Teachers also model classroom rules themselves as they interact with students. According to Sumara and Walker, the process of socialization at the beginning of the school year is planned, deliberate, and crucial for establishing an environment that's conducive to learning.

Not everything can be accomplished quickly, however, so teachers continue to reinforce classroom routines and language arts procedures. One way is to have student leaders model the desired routines and behaviors and encourage classmates to follow the lead. Teachers also continue to teach additional literacy procedures as children are involved in new activities. The classroom community evolves during the school year, but the foundation is laid during the first 2 weeks.

Teachers develop a predictable classroom environment with familiar routines and a consistent schedule. Students feel comfortable, safe, and more willing to take risks in a predictable environment. This is especially true for students from varied cultures, English learners, and less capable readers and writers.

Motivation for Learning

Motivation is intrinsic and internal—a driving force within us. Children in the primary grades are usually eager to learn. They are enthusiastic participants in classroom activities and confident that they will be successful in school. Their teachers play a crucial role in engaging them, monitoring their progress, and providing encouragement. They plan instructional activities that are interesting, incorporate authentic materials, and often involve children in cooperative groups. Pressley, Dolezal, Raphael, Mohan, Roehrig, and Bogner (2003) studied nine second-grade teachers, examined the most engaging teachers' instructional practices, and identified these motivating teacher behaviors:

- Teachers create a community of learners.
- Teachers create a positive classroom environment with books, charts, and posters used as teaching tools, colorful bulletin board displays, and a display of student work.
- Teachers set clear expectations for behavior and learning, and children know what is expected of them.
- Teachers encourage cooperation rather than competition.
- Teachers provide positive feedback and compliment children for good behavior and learning.
- Teachers encourage children to take risks and to be persistent.
- Teachers plan instruction thoroughly with little "down time" between activities.
- Teachers provide authentic, hands-on activities.
- Teachers model and scaffold learning.
- Teachers teach strategies and skills through direct instruction and modeling.
- Teachers monitor children's behavior and learning.
- Teachers stimulate children's creativity, curiosity, and critical thinking.
- Teachers emphasize depth over breadth as they teach.
- Teachers make home–school connections.
- Teachers model interest and enthusiasm for learning.
- Teachers emphasize the value of education.
- Teachers genuinely enjoy being with children and communicate that they care for them.

Edmunds and Bauserman (2006) found similar results when they interviewed students in prekindergarten through fifth grade.

Often students' motivation for language arts diminishes as they reach the upper grades. Penny Oldfather (1995) conducted a 4-year study to examine the factors influencing students' motivation and found that when students had opportunities for authentic self-expression as part of language arts activities, they were more highly motivated. The students she interviewed reported that they were more highly motivated when they had ownership of the learning activities. Specific activities that they mentioned included opportunities to choose their own topics for writing and books for reading, to express their own ideas and opinions and talk about books they're reading, to share their writings with classmates, and to pursue "authentic" activities—not worksheets—using the language arts.

Some students are not strongly motivated for language arts, and they adopt strategies for avoiding failure rather than strategies for success. These strategies are defensive tactics (Paris, Wasik, & Turner, 1991). Unmotivated students often give up or remain passive, uninvolved in reading and other language arts activities. Some students feign interest or pretend to be involved even though they are not. Others don't think language arts is important, and they choose to focus on other curricular areas—math or physical education, for instance. Some students complain about feeling ill or that classmates are bothering them. They place the blame on anything other than themselves.

Other students avoid language arts entirely. They just don't do it. Another group of students read books that are too easy for them or write short pieces so that they don't have to exert much effort. Students use these strategies because they lead to short-term success. The long-term result, however, is devastating because these students fail to learn to read and write.

The Six Language Arts

Traditionally, language arts educators have defined the language arts as the study of the four modes of language: listening, talking, reading, and writing, but more recently, the National Council of Teachers of English and the International Reading Association (*Standards,* 1996) proposed two additional language arts—viewing and visually representing. These new language arts reflect the growing importance of visual literacy (Whitin, 1996).

Listening. Beginning at birth, a child's contact with language is through listening. Listening instruction is often neglected at school because teachers believe that children already know how to listen and that instructional time should be devoted to reading and writing. This book presents an alternative view of listening and listening instruction and focuses on these key concepts:

- Listening is a process of which hearing is only one part.
- Students listen differently according to their purpose.
- Students listen aesthetically to stories, efferently to learn information as part of thematic units, and critically to persuasive appeals.
- Students use listening strategies and monitor their comprehension in order to listen more effectively.

Talking. As with listening, teachers often neglect instruction in talk because they believe students already know how to talk. Research has emphasized the importance of talk in the learning process (Dwyer, 1991). For example, students use talk to respond to literature, provide feedback about classmates' writing in writing groups, and present oral reports as part of social studies and science units. You'll learn more about these key concepts about talk as you continue reading:

- Talk is an essential part of learning.
- Students use talk for both aesthetic and efferent purposes.
- Students participate in grand conversations as they respond to literature.
- Students give presentations, including oral reports and debates.
- Drama provides a valuable method of learning and a powerful way of communicating.

Reading. Reading is a process, and students use strategies and skills to decode words and comprehend what they are reading. Students vary the way they read according to their purpose: They read for pleasure differently than they do to locate and remember information (Rosenblatt, 2005). Here are the key concepts about reading:

- Reading is a strategic process.
- The goal of reading is comprehension, or meaning making.
- Students read differently for different purposes.
- Students participate in five types of reading: independent reading, shared reading, guided reading, buddy reading, and reading aloud to children.

Writing. Like reading, writing is a strategic process (Dean, 2006). Students use the writing process to write stories, reports, poems, and other genres (Graves, 1994). They also do informal writing, such as writing in reading logs and making graphic organizers. As you continue reading, you'll learn about these key concepts about writing:

- Writing is a process in which students cycle recursively through the stages of prewriting, drafting, revising, editing, and publishing.
- Students experiment with many written language genres.
- Informal writing is used to develop writing fluency and as a learning tool.
- Spelling and handwriting are tools for writers.

Viewing. Visual media include film and videos, print advertisements and commercials, photographs and book illustrations, the Internet, and DVDs. Because visual media, including the Internet, are commonplace in American life today, students need to learn how to comprehend them and to integrate visual knowledge with other literacy knowledge (Williams, 2007). Heide and Stilborne (1999) explain that the Internet has "a wide range of resources available for electronic field trips involving pictures, text, sound, and sometimes interactivity" (p. 19). Here are the key concepts about viewing:

- Viewing is an important component of literacy.
- Students view visual media for a variety of purposes.
- Viewing is much like reading, and students use comprehension strategies in both reading and viewing.
- Students use the Internet as a learning tool.
- Students learn about propaganda techniques in order to critically analyze commercials and advertisements.

Visually Representing. Students create meaning through multiple sign systems such as video productions, Inspiration® and other computer programs, dramatizations, story quilts, and illustrations on charts, posters, and books they are writing (Moline, 1995). According to Harste, "seeing something familiar in a new way is often a process of gaining new insights" (1993, p. 4). Projects involving visual texts are often completed as part of literature focus units, literature circles, and thematic units. This book presents these key concepts about visually representing:

- Students consider audience, purpose, and form as they create visual texts.
- Visual texts, like writing, can be created to share information learned during literature focus units and thematic units.

Relationships Among the Language Arts. Discussing the language arts one by one suggests a division among them, as though they could be used separately. In reality, they are used simultaneously and reciprocally, just as Mrs. McNeal's students in the vignette at the beginning of the chapter used all six language arts during writing workshop. Almost any language arts activity involves more than one of the language arts. In a seminal study, researcher Walter Loban (1976) documented the language growth and development of a group of 338 students from kindergarten through 12th grade (ages 5–18). Two purposes of his longitudinal study were to examine differences between students who used language effectively and those who did not, and to identify predictable stages of language development. Three of Loban's conclusions are especially noteworthy. First, he reported positive correlations among listening, talking, reading, and writing. Second, he found that students with less effective oral language abilities tended to have less effective written language abilities. And third, he found a strong relationship between students' oral language ability and their overall academic ability. Loban's study demonstrates clear relationships among the language arts and emphasizes the need to teach listening and talking as well as reading and writing.

Language Arts Strategies and Skills

Students learn both strategies and skills through language arts instruction. Strategies are problem-solving methods or behaviors, and students develop and use both general learning strategies and specific strategies related to language arts. Although there isn't a definitive list of language arts strategies, researchers have identified a number of strategies that capable readers and writers use (Fletcher & Portalupi, 1998). I focus on these strategies in this text:

Activating background knowledge	Organizing
Blending	Playing with language
Brainstorming	Predicting
Connecting	Proofreading
Evaluating	Questioning
Identifying big ideas	Revising
Identifying root words	Segmenting
Inferencing	Setting purposes
Monitoring	Summarizing
Noticing nonverbal cues	Visualizing

These strategies are described in Figure 1–5. Some strategies, such as blending, are used specifically in phonemic awareness, phonics, and spelling, and many others are applied in all six language arts. Consider revising, for example. Probably the best-known application is in writing: Students revise as they add, substitute, delete, and move information in their rough drafts. Revising visual representations works the same way. But students also revise meaning while they talk on the basis of feedback from the audience, and as they listen to a speaker, view a DVD, or read a book.

Skills, in contrast, are information-processing techniques that students use automatically and unconsciously as they construct meaning. Many skills focus at the word level, but some require students to attend to larger chunks of text. For example, readers use skills such as decoding unfamiliar words, noting details, and sequencing events, and writers employ skills such as forming contractions, using punctuation marks, and capitalizing people's names. Skills and strategies are not the same thing. The important difference between skills and strategies is how they are used: Skills are used unconsciously, and strategies are used deliberately (Paris et al., 1991).

FIGURE 1–5

Strategies That Capable Readers and Writers Use

Strategy	Description
Activating background knowledge	Students think about what they already know about a topic.
Blending	Students combine sounds to pronounce a word.
Brainstorming	Students think of many ideas related to a topic.
Connecting	Students relate a topic to themselves, the world around them, and literature.
Evaluating	Students reflect on, make judgments about, and value an experience.
Identifying big ideas	Students determine the most important ideas.
Identifying root words	Students pick out the root in a longer word.
Inferencing	Students draw conclusions from clues presented in the text.
Monitoring	Students keep track of their understanding or success with an activity.
Noticing nonverbal cues	Students interpret gestures, symbols, and nonalphabetic features.
Organizing	Students put ideas in a coherent and logical arrangement.
Playing with language	Students notice figurative and novel uses of language and use language creatively themselves.
Predicting	Students anticipate events.
Proofreading	Students identify mechanical errors in their writing.
Questioning	Students ask questions to clarify or expand meaning.
Revising	Students make changes or a new version.
Segmenting	Students break a word into sounds.
Setting purposes	Students identify a goal for themselves.
Summarizing	Students pick out the big ideas to remember.
Visualizing	Students draw pictures in their minds.

Students learn to use five types of skills. Although many of the skills are oriented to reading and writing, some are used for listening, talking, viewing, and visually representing. Here are the five types of skills:

◆ *Comprehension Skills.* These include separating facts and opinions, comparing and contrasting, and recognizing literary genres and structures. Students apply comprehension skills as they create meaning using all six language arts.

◆ *Print Skills.* These include sounding out words, noticing word families, using root words and affixes to decode and spell words, and using abbreviations. Students use print skills as they decode words when reading and as they spell words when writing.

◆ *Study Skills.* These include skimming and scanning, taking notes, making clusters, and previewing a book before reading. Students use study skills during thematic units, while reading informational books, and while collecting information to use in writing reports.

◆ *Language Skills.* These include identifying and inferring meanings of words, noticing idioms, dividing words into syllables, and choosing synonyms. Students are continuously interacting with words as they use the language arts, and they use language skills to analyze words when they are listening and reading and to choose more precise language when they are talking and writing.

◆ *Reference Skills.* These include alphabetizing a list of words, using a dictionary, and reading and making graphs and other diagrams. Students learn to use reference skills to read newspaper articles, locate information in encyclopedias and other informational books, and consult library resources.

Examples of each of the five types of skills are presented in Figure 1–6. Students use these skills for various language arts activities. For example, they use some of the skills when giving an oral report and others when writing in learning logs or making a graphic organizer to compare several versions of a folktale.

Teachers often wonder which skills they should teach and when to teach them. School districts often prepare frameworks and curriculum guides that include the skills to be taught at each grade level, and skills are usually listed in basal reading programs. These resources provide guidelines, but teachers should decide which skills to teach and when to teach them based on students' level of development.

Teachers use a combination of direct and indirect instruction to provide information that students need to know about skills and strategies. Direct instruction is planned. Teachers often teach minilessons, brief 15- to 30-minute lessons, in which they explicitly explain a particular strategy or skill, model its use, and provide examples and opportunities for practice. Indirect instruction involves taking advantage of teachable moments to reexplain a strategy or skill to a student or clarify a misconception. Both types of instruction are necessary in order to meet students' needs.

Teachers plan strategy and skill instruction that grows out of language arts activities using a whole-part-whole sequence: The language arts activity is the first *whole*, the minilesson is the *part*, and having students apply what they are learning in other language arts activities is the second *whole*. This instructional sequence is recommended to ensure that the instruction is meaningful and that students learn to use the strategies and skills independently (Mazzoni & Gambrell, 2003).

The goal of instruction is for students to be able to use the strategies and skills that they've learned independently. Dorn and Soffos (2001) have identified four

FIGURE 1–6

Language Arts Skills

Category	Skills	
Print	Sound out words using phonics Notice word families Decode by analogy Use classroom resources Apply spelling rules	Recognize high-frequency words Divide words into syllables Capitalize proper nouns and adjectives Use abbreviations
Comprehension	Chunk words into phrases Sequence Categorize Classify Separate facts and opinions Note details Identify cause and effect Compare and contrast	Use context clues Notice organizational patterns of poetry, plays, business and friendly letters, stories, essays, and reports Recognize literary genres (traditional stories, fantasies, science fiction, realistic fiction, historical fiction, biography, autobiography, and poetry)
Language	Notice compound words Use contractions Use possessives Notice propaganda Use similes and metaphors Notice idioms and slang Choose synonyms Recognize antonyms Differentiate among homonyms Use root words and affixes Appreciate rhyme and other poetic devices	Use punctuation marks (period, question mark, exclamation point, quotation marks, comma, colon, semicolon, and hyphen) Use simple, compound, and complex sentences Combine sentences Recognize parts of sentences Avoid sentence fragments Recognize parts of speech (nouns, pronouns, verbs, adjectives, adverbs, conjunctions, prepositions, and interjections)
Reference	Sort in alphabetical order Use a glossary or dictionary Locate etymologies in the dictionary Use the pronunciation guide in the dictionary Locate synonyms in a thesaurus Locate information in an encyclopedia, atlas, or almanac	Use a table of contents Use an index Use a card catalog Read and make graphs, tables, and diagrams Read and make time lines Read newspapers and magazines Use bibliographic forms
Study	Skim Scan Preview Follow directions	Make outlines and clusters Take notes Paraphrase

behaviors that teachers use as part of both direct and indirect instruction to develop self-regulated learners:

Modeling: Teachers demonstrate how to use strategies and skills.

Coaching: Teachers direct students' attention and encourage their active engagement in activities.

Scaffolding: Teachers adjust the support they provide according to students' needs.

Fading: Teachers relinquish control as students become more capable of using a strategy or performing an activity.

It's not enough to simply explain strategies and skills or remind students to use them. If teachers want their students to be able to use strategies and skills independently, they must actively engage students, encourage and scaffold them while they are learning, and then gradually withdraw their support.

The Goal of Language Arts Instruction

The goal of language arts instruction is for students to develop communicative competence, the ability to use language appropriately in both social and academic contexts (Hymes, 1972). Communicative competence is context specific: This means that students may participate effectively in classroom conversations but not know how to give a more formal oral presentation. Similarly, students may know how to read informational books but not how to write a report to share information. At each grade level, teachers expand students' abilities to use the six language arts in new contexts. Through language arts instruction, students acquire the characteristics of competent language users. They become more strategic and more creative in their use of language, better able to use language as a tool for learning, and more reflective in their interpretations.

In recent years, state and federal mandates have increasingly dictated which instructional approaches and materials teachers use in teaching language arts and developing students' communicative competence. Those that are grounded in scientific evidence are endorsed (Lyon & Chhabra, 2004). The most far-reaching initiative is George W. Bush's No Child Left Behind (NCLB) Act of 2001, which was designed to close the achievement gap between white, affluent students and other students. This initiative, based on the report of the National Reading Panel (2000), has mandated an increased emphasis on teaching basic skills and holds schools accountable for students' performance. Schools are now required to administer standardized tests each year to students in grades 3–8 to monitor their progress. Guidelines for preparing students for "high-stakes" testing are presented in Figure 1–7.

The NCLB Act affects every school in the United States. All schools set annual achievement goals, and those that meet their goals are labeled "schools of choice." If schools don't make adequate yearly progress for 2 consecutive years, they are required to implement special programs to improve test scores, and parents may transfer their children to higher-achieving schools.

The NCLB initiative's emphasis on basic skills has narrowed the goal of language arts instruction in many schools to having students meet grade-level standards on standardized achievement tests; to achieve that goal, teachers are increasingly being required to use scripted basal reading programs under the mistaken assumption that they were recommended by the National Reading Panel (Shanahan, 2003).

Because of the NCLB Act, state-designated lists of grade-level standards, and other mandated programs, teachers feel a loss of professional autonomy in determining what and how to teach. There is increased pressure from parents, administrators, and politicians for teachers to "teach to the test" rather than to develop students' communicative competence by engaging their students in meaningful, functional, and genuine language arts activities. Some teachers have embraced the new instructional programs, and others have quietly resisted them and continued to use student-centered approaches as often as they could. Still others are actively resisting the imposition of these programs because they reject the conformity and loss of teacher control inherent in new state and federal mandates (Garan, 2004; Novinger & Compton-Lilly, 2005).

FIGURE 1–7

How to Prepare Students for High-Stakes Testing

Test-Taking Strategies

Teach test-taking strategies by modeling how to read, think about, and answer test items.

Practice Tests

Design practice tests with the same types of items used on the tests that students will take.

Easy-to-Read Materials

Use easy-to-read reading materials for practice tests so students can focus on practicing test-taking strategies.

Variety of Passages

Include a combination of unrelated narrative and expository passages on practice tests.

Regular Schedule

Have students take practice tests on a regular schedule.

Untimed and Timed Tests

Begin with untimed tests and move to timed tests as students gain experience with test-taking strategies.

Testing Conditions

Simulate testing conditions in the classroom, or take students to where the test will be administered for the practice sessions.

Graphs of Test Results

Graph students' results on practice tests so they can see their progress.

Teachers, administrators, and parents can point to both positive and negative outcomes of these state and federal mandates (Valencia & Villarreal, 2003). Some teachers feel more confident about their teaching ability now because they are being told how to teach language arts, and in many schools, students' test scores are rising. At the same time, however, other teachers are discouraged and frustrated because they are not allowed to use the instructional approaches that have been effective for them in the past. Some of their students continue to fail because they cannot do work at their grade level, and they also are concerned about the amount of time diverted from instruction for testing. In some schools, testing takes more than one month of the school year. In addition, some parents have expressed concern that their children have developed test anxiety and are preoccupied with the "high-stakes" tests they must pass each spring.

Review

Language arts instruction should be based on theories and research about how children learn. Language and culture also have an impact on how students learn language arts. The goal of language arts instruction is for students to develop communicative competence in the six language arts—listening, talking, reading, writing, viewing, and visually representing. Here are the key concepts presented in this chapter:

- Constructivist, information-processing, and sociolinguistic theories of learning inform our understanding of how students learn language arts.
- Students learn through active involvement in listening, talking, reading, writing, viewing, and visually representing activities.

- Teachers should provide instruction within students' zone of proximal development.
- Teachers scaffold or support students' learning.
- Students use all four language systems—phonological, syntactic, semantic, and pragmatic—in listening, talking, reading and writing.
- Students learn cognitively demanding and decontextualized academic language at school.
- Teachers create a community of learners in their classrooms.
- Students learn and use language arts strategies, including predicting, visualizing, revising meaning, summarizing, and monitoring.
- Students learn and use language arts skills, including choosing synonyms, skimming, capitalizing words, and using a dictionary.
- Students need opportunities to participate in language arts activities that are meaningful, functional, and genuine.

Professional References

Brock, C. H., & Raphael, T. E. (2005). *Windows to language, literacy, and culture.* Newark, DE: International Reading Association.

Bruner, J. S. (2004). *Toward a theory of instruction.* Cambridge, MA: Harvard University Press.

Cambourne, B., & Turbill, J. (1987). *Coping with chaos.* Rozelle, NSW, Australia: Primary English Teaching Association.

Cazden, C. B. (2001). *Classroom discourse: The language of teaching and learning* (2nd ed.). Portsmouth, NH: Heinemann.

Cleary, L. M. (1993). Hobbes: "I press rewind through the pictures in my head." In S. Hudson-Ross, L. M. Cleary, & M. Casey (Eds.), *Children's voices: Children talk about literacy* (pp. 136–143). Portsmouth, NH: Heinemann.

Cummins, J. (1989). *Empowering minority students.* Sacramento: California Association for Bilingual Education.

Dean, D. (2006). *Strategic writing.* Urbana, IL: National Council of Teachers of English.

Dorn, L. J., & Soffos, C. (2001). *Shaping literate minds: Developing self-regulated learners.* York, ME: Stenhouse.

Dwyer, J. (Ed.). (1991). *A sea of talk.* Portsmouth, NH: Heinemann.

Dyson, A. H. (1997). *Writing superheroes.* New York: Teachers College Press.

Dyson, A. H. (2003). *The brothers and sisters learn to write.* New York: Teachers College Press.

Edmunds, K. M., & Bauserman, K. L. (2006). What teachers can learn about reading motivation through conversations with children. *The Reading Teacher, 59,* 414–424.

Faltis, C. J. (2006). *Teaching English language learners in elementary school communities* (4th ed.) Upper Saddle River, NJ: Merrill/Prentice Hall.

Flavell, J. H., Miller, P. H., & Miller, S. A. (2001). *Cognitive development* (4th ed.). Upper Saddle River, NJ: Prentice Hall.

Fletcher, R., & Portalupi, J. (1998). *Craft lessons: Teaching writing K–8.* Portland, ME: Stenhouse.

Foss, A. (2002). Peeling the onion: Teaching critical literacy with students of privilege. *Language Arts, 79,* 393–403.

Freire, P., & Macedo, D. (1987). *Literacy: Reading the word and the world.* South Hadley, MA: Bergin & Garvey.

Garan, E. (2004). *In defense of our children: When politics, profit, and education collide.* Portsmouth, NH: Heinemann.

Giroux, H. (1997). *Pedagogy and the politics of hope, theory, culture, and schooling.* Boulder, CO: Westview Press.

Graves. D. H. (1994). *A fresh look at writing.* Portsmouth, NH: Heinemann.

Halliday, M. A. K. (1978). *Language as social semiotic: The social interpretation of language and meaning.* Baltimore: University Park Press.

Harste, J. (1993, April). Inquiry-based instruction. *Primary Voices K–6, 1,* 2–5.

Heide, A., & Stilborne, L. (1999). *The teacher's complete and easy guide to the Internet.* New York: Teachers College Press.

Hymes, D. (1972). On communicative competence. In J. B. Pride & J. Holmes (Eds.), *Sociolinguistics* (pp. 269–285). Harmondsworth, Middlesex, UK: Penguin.

Lewison, M., Flint, A. S., & Van Sluys, K. (2002). Taking on critical literacy: The journey of newcomers and novices. *Language Arts, 79,* 382–392.

Loban, W. (1976). *Language development: Kindergarten through grade twelve* (Research Report No. 18). Urbana, IL: National Council of Teachers of English.

Luke, A., & Freebody, P. (1997). Shaping the social practices of reading. In S. Muspratt, A. Luke, & P. Freebody (Eds.),

Constructing critical literacies (pp. 185–225). Cresskill, NJ: Hampton.

Lyon, G. R., & Chhabra, V. (2004). The science of reading research. *Educational Leadership, 61*(6), 12–17.

Mazzoni, S. A., & Gambrell, L. B. (2003). Principles of best practice. In L. M. Morrow, L. B. Gambrell, & M. Pressley (Eds.), *Best practices in literacy instruction* (2nd ed., pp. 9–22). New York: Guilford Press.

Moline, S. (1995). *I see what you mean: Children at work with visual information.* York, ME: Stenhouse.

Muhammad, R. J. (1993). Mario: "It's mostly after I read a book that I write." In S. Hudson-Ross, L. M. Cleary, & M. Casey (Eds.), *Children's voices: Children talk about literacy* (pp. 92–99). Portsmouth, NH: Heinemann.

Nathenson-Mejia, S. (1989). Writing in a second language: Negotiating meaning through invented spelling. *Language Arts, 66,* 516–526.

National Reading Panel. (2000). *Teaching children to read: An evidence-based assessment of the scientific research literature on reading and its implications for reading instruction, reports of the subgroups.* Washington, DC: National Institute of Child Health and Human Development.

NCTE Elementary Section Steering Committee. (1996). Exploring language arts standards within a cycle of learning. *Language Arts, 73,* 10–13.

Novinger, S., & Compton-Lilly, C. (2005). Telling our stories: Speaking truth to power. *Language Arts, 82,* 195–203.

Oldfather, P. (1995). Commentary: What's needed to maintain and extend motivation for literacy in the middle grades? *Journal of Reading, 38,* 420–422.

Paris, S. G., Wasik, B. A., & Turner, J. C. (1991). The development of strategic readers. In R. Barr, M. L. Kamil, P. B. Mosenthal, & P. D. Pearson (Eds.), *Handbook of reading research* (Vol. 2, pp. 609–640). New York: Longman.

Piaget, J., & Inhelder, B. (2000). *The psychology of the child.* New York: Basic Books.

Pressley, M., Dolezal, S. E., Raphael, L. M., Mohan, L., Roehrig, A. D., & Bogner, K. (2003). *Motivating primary-grade students.* New York: Guilford Press.

Rosenblatt, L. M. (2005). *Making meaning with texts: Selected essays.* Portsmouth, NH: Heinemann.

Samway, K. D., & McKeon, D. (1999). *Myths and realities: Best practices for language minority students.* Portsmouth, NH: Heinemann.

Shanahan, T. (2003). Research-based reading instruction: Myths about the National Reading Panel report. *The Reading Teacher, 56,* 646–655.

Stahl, S. A., & Nagy, W. E. (2005). *Teaching word meanings.* Mahwah; NJ: Erlbaum.

Standards for the English Language Arts. (1996). Urbana, IL: National Council of Teachers of English and the International Reading Association.

Sumara, D., & Walker, L. (1991). The teacher's role in whole language. *Language Arts, 68,* 276–285.

Tracey, D. H., & Morrow, L. M. (2006). *Lenses on reading.* New York: Guilford Press.

Valencia, R. R., & Villarreal, B. J. (2003). Improving students' reading performance via standards-based school reform: A critique. *The Reading Teacher, 56,* 612–621.

Vygotsky, L. S. (1986). *Thought and language.* Cambridge, MA: MIT Press.

Vygotsky, L. S. (2006). *Mind in society.* Cambridge, MA: Harvard University Press.

Wells, G., & Chang-Wells, G. L. (1992). *Constructing knowledge together: Classrooms as centers of inquiry and literacy.* Portsmouth, NH: Heinemann.

Whatley, A., & Canalis, J. (2002). Creating learning communities through literacy. *Language Arts, 79,* 478–487.

Whitin, P. E. (1996). *Sketching stories, stretching minds.* Portsmouth, NH: Heinemann.

Williams, T. L. (2007). "Reading" the painting: Exploring visual literacy in the primary grades. *The Reading Teacher, 60,* 636–642.

Wink, J. (2005). *Critical pedagogy: Notes from the real world* (3rd ed.). New York: Longman.

Wolk, S. (2004). Using picture books to teach for democracy. *Language Arts, 82,* 26–35.

Wong-Fillmore, L., & Snow, C. E. (2002). What teachers need to know about language. In C. T. Adger, C. E. Snow, & D. Christian (Eds.), *What teachers need to know about language* (pp. 7–54). Washington, DC: Center for Applied Linguistics.

Wright, J. W. (Ed.). (2004). *The New York Times 2005 almanac.* New York: Penguin.

Zebroski, J. T. (1994). *Thinking through theory: Vygotskian perspectives on the teaching of writing.* Portsmouth, NH: Boynton/Cook.

Children's Book References

Curtis, C. P. (2000). *The Watsons go to Birmingham—1963.* New York: Delacorte.

Ellis, D. (2000). *The breadwinner.* Toronto: Groundwood Books.

Frank, A. (1995). *Anne Frank: The diary of a young girl* (new ed.). New York: Doubleday.

Giovanni, N. (2005). *Rosa.* New York: Henry Holt.

Sendak, M. (2003). *Where the wild things are.* New York: HarperCollins.

Whelan, G. (2000). *Homeless bird.* New York: Scholastic.

chapter two

Teaching and Assessing Language Arts

Mrs. Miller-McColm sits down on her teacher's stool and picks up Natalie Babbitt's *Tuck Everlasting* (2002), the highly acclaimed story of a family who drinks from a magical spring and becomes immortal. "Yesterday, we stopped halfway through Chapter 6," she says to her sixth graders. "Who remembers what was happening?" A sea of hands go up, and Mrs. Miller-McColm calls on Junior. "Winnie wanted to run away from home, but she got kidnapped by the Tucks. I don't know why though," he says. Next, Isabel says, "I think she goes with the Tucks because she wants to. I think she wants an adventure so she'll stay with them forever."

The students continue talking about the story for several minutes, and then Mrs. Miller-McColm begins reading aloud. After she reads the middle of page 34, she stops and asks, "Why does Mae Tuck say, 'We're not bad people, truly we're not. We had to bring you away—you'll see why in a minute—and we'll take you back just as soon as we can. Tomorrow. I promise'?" The students break into small groups to talk for several minutes about whether the Tucks are "bad" people for kidnapping Winnie and to speculate about why they abducted her. Their desks are arranged in five groups, and the classmates in each group talk eagerly. After several minutes, Mrs. Miller-McColm brings the class back together to continue the discussion. "We don't think the Tucks are bad people," Noemi offers, "because bad people aren't nice, and

How do teachers organize for instruction?

Teachers organize for instruction using four patterns of practice—literature focus units, literature circles, reading and writing workshop, and thematic units. Teachers vary the patterns they choose and sometimes add other programs, including basal readers. No matter which patterns teachers use, they combine direct instruction, small-group activities, and independent activities into their plans. As you read this vignette, notice how Mrs. Miller-McColm incorporates all four patterns of practice in her language arts program.

Mae Tuck is. They must have a good reason for what they did." Donavon says, "They may be nice people but we don't think Winnie will get free 'tomorrow.'" Iliana agrees, "Winnie won't get free until the book ends, and there are a lot of pages still to read." After the students share their ideas, the teacher reads to the end of this chapter and continues reading the next one, where the Tucks explain to Winnie about their "changelessness" and why they abducted her. She finishes reading the last page of Chapter 7, puts the book down, and looks at the students. They look back at her, dazed; no one says a word.

To help the sixth graders sort out their ideas and feelings, Mrs. Miller-McColm asks them to quickwrite in their reading logs. The students take about 5 minutes to write, and then they're ready to talk. Some read their reading log entries aloud, and others share their ideas. Mrs. Miller-McColm asks, "Do you believe the Tucks? Are they telling the truth?" About half of the students agree that the Tucks are telling the truth; others aren't so sure. Next, she asks them to write in their reading logs again, this time about whether they believe the Tucks' story.

Mrs. Miller-McColm uses the novels she reads aloud to teach about story structure. Her focus is on plot development as she reads *Tuck Everlasting.* She has talked about how authors develop stories, and the students understand that in the beginning, authors introduce the problem; in the middle, the problem gets worse; and in the end, it is resolved. Yesterday, they learned the problem in this story—Winnie Foster is abducted by the Tucks. The teacher has also taught them about conflict situations, and at this point in the story, they think the conflict is between characters—between Winnie and the Tucks. Later, they'll see that the conflict is within Winnie herself as she decides whether to drink from the spring and live with the Tucks forever.

Mrs. Miller-McColm spends the first hour of the language arts period teaching a literature focus unit using a book from her district's list of "core" literature selections. She reads the book aloud because about half of her sixth graders couldn't read it on their own. She has already read *Holes* (Sachar, 1998) and

A Wrinkle in Time (L'Engle, 2007); by the end of the school year, she will have read 11 or 12 novels.

Mrs. Miller-McColm's daily schedule is shown in the box below. Her students participate in a variety of language arts activities using the four patterns of practice during the morning and connect language arts to social studies and science through thematic units in the afternoon.

Mrs. Miller-McColm's Daily Schedule

8:30–8:45 *Opening*

8:45–9:45 *Literature Focus Unit*
Mrs. Miller-McColm reads aloud a featured book, involves students in response activities, and teaches story structure, vocabulary, and other strategies and skills.

9:45–10:30 *Book Groups*
Students divide into groups according to reading level and participate in literature circles. They choose books to read, read them independently, and meet with Mrs. Miller-McColm to discuss them. They also apply what they are learning about story structure during the literature focus unit to the books they are reading now and create graphic displays that they post on a special bulletin board.

10:30–10:45 *Recess*

10:45–11:15 *Word Work*
Mrs. Miller-McColm teaches minilessons on word-identification and spelling strategies and skills, including idioms, synonyms, syllabication, root words, and affixes. Students also study spelling words and take weekly spelling tests.

11:15–12:15 *Writing Workshop*
Students use the writing process to write stories and other genres. They meet in writing groups to revise their writing and editing conferences to correct spelling, capitalization, punctuation, and sentence structure errors. They share their published writing from the author's chair. Mrs. Miller-McColm also teaches minilessons on writing procedures, concepts, strategies, and skills.

12:15–1:00 *Lunch and Recess*

1:00–2:00 *Math*

2:00–3:15 *Social Studies/Science*
Mrs. Miller-McColm alternates teaching monthlong social studies and science thematic units. Students apply what they are learning in language arts as they participate in content-area study and develop projects to share their learning.

3:15–3:25 *Clean-up and Dismissal*

Next, Mrs. Miller-McColm's students participate in book groups, another name for literature circles. They read at fourth- through eighth-grade levels, and she divides them into seven book groups according to reading level. The students choose novels to read after their teacher introduces several choices for each group. Currently, they are reading these books:

Stone Fox (Gardiner, 2003) (level 4)

Sarah, Plain and Tall (MacLachlan, 2004) (level 4)

Shiloh (Naylor, 2000) (level 5)

Ralph the Mouse (Cleary, 1993) (level 5)

Maniac Magee (Spinelli, 2002) (level 6)

The BFG (Dahl, 1998) (level 6)

Harry Potter and the Goblet of Fire (Rowling, 2002) (level 8)

The students meet with their groups to set reading schedules. They read during this period and at home and meet with Mrs. Miller-McColm two or three times each week to talk about their books. Groups create displays about the books they're reading on a bulletin board on one side of the classroom. For this round of book groups, the focus is on plot development: Each group makes a sign with the title and author of the book and then creates a graphic display emphasizing the conflict situations in their novel.

Mrs. Miller-McColm meets with the group reading *Sarah, Plain and Tall,* a story about a mail-order bride in the early 1900s. She begins by asking the students to summarize the story so far, and Gabrielle says, "A woman named Sarah is coming to stay at a farm. She might marry the dad and be a mom for the children, Anna and Caleb." "Has she arrived yet?" Mrs. Miller-McColm asks, and April responds, "She just arrived. She came on a train and everyone is very nervous." Then students make connections between the story and their own lives, the world around them, and other literature, and Mrs. Miller-McColm helps them analyze the plot and identify the conflict situation; it's between Sarah and the other characters. The students decide to draw open-mind portraits of the characters to post in their section of the bulletin board. For their portraits, they will draw pictures of the characters and attach three sheets of paper behind the pictures where they will draw and write about the conflict each character feels at the beginning of the story, in the middle, and at the end.

Next, she meets with the group reading *Shiloh*. These students have just finished reading this novel about a boy who sticks out his neck to save an abused dog. They're eager to talk about the book and make connections to personal experiences and to other dog stories they've read. Mrs. Miller-McColm asks them to think more deeply about the story and rereads the last paragraph of the story aloud:

> I look at the dark closing in, sky getting more and more purple, and I'm thinking how nothing is as simple as you guess—not right or wrong, not Judd Travers, not even me or this dog I got here. But the good part is I saved Shiloh and opened my eyes some. Now that ain't bad for eleven. (p. 144)

She asks what Marty, the main character in the story, means when he says, "nothing is as simple as you guess . . . " Omar begins, "At first Marty thought he was all good and Judd Travers was all bad, but then Marty did something dishonest to get Shiloh. He didn't like doing bad things but he did them for a good reason so I think that's ok." The students continue talking about being responsible for your own actions, both good and bad. After the discussion ends, the teacher checks the group's section of the bulletin board, and the students make plans to finish it before the end of the week.

The teacher also takes them over to the classroom library and introduces them to *Shiloh Season* (Naylor, 1996) and *Saving Shiloh* (Naylor, 2006), the other books in the Shiloh trilogy, and the students eagerly decide to read these two books next.

After the recess break, Mrs. Miller-McColm teaches a word work lesson on suffixes, beginning with the word *changelessness* from *Tuck Everlasting*. She points out the two suffixes, *-less,* meaning "without," and *-ness,* meaning "state of being." The students talk about the word's meaning and how the suffixes affect the root word. Then she shares a list of other words ending in *-less,* including *weightless, effortless,* and *careless.* They talk about the meaning of each word and how it changes when it takes on the suffix *-ness,* such as *weightlessness.* Then students use the last 10 minutes of the period to practice their spelling words.

Next, Mrs. Miller-McColm begins writing workshop with a minilesson on writing narrative leads. She displays a chart of four techniques that writers use to hook their audience and explains each one:

Action: The main character does something interesting.

Dialogue: The main character says something interesting.

A thought or a question: The main character shares something that he or she is thinking or asks a question.

A sound: The author begins with an interesting sound related to the story.

She reads aloud the first sentences from *The Sign of the Beaver* (Speare, 2005), *The Breadwinner* (Ellis, 2000), and other novels, and the students identify the hook used in each one. Tomorrow, they will work together as a class to write sample leads using each technique, and the next day, they'll write leads with partners.

After the minilesson, students write independently for 40 minutes. For the past month, they've been writing on self-selected topics; many are writing stories, but some are writing poetry and informational books. Mrs. Miller-McColm has already announced that students should finish the pieces they are working on by Friday because beginning next week, they'll be using writing workshop time to write reports as part of their unit on ancient Egypt.

Some students are working independently, and others are meeting in small groups to revise their writing, conferencing with the teacher, or working with partners to proofread their writing. The four computers are all occupied, too, as students word process their compositions and print out final copies. They place their final copies in a box on Mrs. Miller-McColm's desk and she binds their compositions—handwritten or word processed—into books for them.

During the last 5 minutes of writing workshop, students take turns sitting in the author's chair to read their completed writings aloud. Students sit on the floor and listen attentively as their classmate reads. Ricky, who wants to be a race car driver, reads a book he has researched and written about the Winston Cup Series. He has also included this year's schedule of races and a map of the United States showing where the tracks are. After he finishes reading, students clap and ask questions. Junior asks, "What does NASCAR stand for?" and Ricky explains that it is an acronym for the National Association for Stock Car Automobile Racing. Omar asks for more clarification about how the races are run, and Briana asks how winners of each race gain points. The students get so interested that they don't want to end the discussion, even though it is lunchtime!

In the afternoon, Mrs. Miller-McColm teaches thematic units on social studies and science topics. Currently the topic is ancient Egypt. The students are reading from a text set of books and Internet articles, making notes of important information about ancient Egypt in their learning logs. Mrs. Miller-McColm taught a series of mini-lessons on notetaking at the beginning of the unit, and students are applying what they learned as they read and take notes. For 30 minutes, students finish reading text set materials and taking notes.

Next, Mrs. Miller-McColm brings the class together to talk about the reports they will write. She begins by asking them to highlight the achievements of the ancient Egyptian civilization and they brainstorm a list, including:

the remarkable pyramids
gods and goddesses
how the Egyptians farmed near the Nile River
the mummification process
the hieroglyphic system of writing
Egyptian women's make-up and jewelry

Then she explains that students will choose one achievement that particularly interests them, research it, and share what they learn in a report. They'll also make an artifact to go with the report. If their topic is hieroglyphics, for example, they might make a scroll. The students are excited; they quickly choose topics and suggest artifacts they can make. Mrs. Miller-McColm distributes the rubric that students will use to self-assess their projects and that she'll use to grade them and they read it together. Then she passes around several reports from last year, which the students examine and compare to the rubric to better understand what their teacher wants them to do.

---

*T*eachers use four patterns of practice to involve students in meaningful, functional, and genuine language-learning activities: literature focus units, literature circles, reading and writing workshop, and thematic units. Teachers incorporate a combination of these approaches in their instructional programs, just as Mrs. Miller-McColm did in the vignette. It's not enough to teach language arts using a basal reader or other textbook.

Assessment goes hand in hand with teaching. It should be authentic—based on students using the language arts in genuine and worthwhile ways. Teachers begin by determining students' background knowledge before instruction, and they continue as they monitor students' progress during instruction. Teachers and students collaborate to document students' learning; there are innovative ways to involve students in assessing their own learning and determining grades.

As you read this chapter, you'll learn how to organize for instruction and to assess students' learning. Think about these questions as you continue reading:

- ◆ What are literature focus units?
- ◘ What are literature circles?
- ◆ What is reading and writing workshop?
- ◢ What are thematic units?
- ◆ How do teachers assess students' learning?

PATTERNS OF PRACTICE

Just as there are many quilt patterns, there are many ways to organize language arts instruction. This text focuses on these four patterns or instructional approaches for teaching language arts: literature focus units, literature circles, reading and writing workshop, and thematic units. All four patterns embody the characteristics of learning described in Chapter 1 and provide opportunities for students to use oral and written language in meaningful, functional, and genuine ways. Teachers organize their instructional programs in different ways, but students need to have opportunities to participate in all four approaches during each school year. Figure 2–1 provides an overview of the four patterns of practice.

FIGURE 2–1

Overview of the Four Patterns of Practice

Features	Literature Focus Units	Literature Circles
Description	Teachers and students read and respond to one text together as a class or in small groups. Teachers choose texts that are high-quality literature selections. After reading, students explore the text and apply their learning by creating projects.	Teachers choose five or six books and collect multiple copies of each one. Students choose the book they want to read and form groups or "book clubs" to read and respond to the book. They develop a reading and discussion schedule, and the teacher participates in some of the discussions.
Strengths	• Teachers develop units using the reading process. • Teachers select picture books or chapter books for units. • Teachers scaffold reading instruction as they read with the whole class. • Teachers teach minilessons on reading strategies and skills. • Students explore vocabulary and literary language. • Students develop projects to apply their reading.	• Books are available at a variety of reading levels. • Students are more strongly motivated because they choose the books they read. • Students have opportunities to work with their classmates. • Students participate in authentic literacy experiences. • Activities are student directed, and students work at their own pace. • Teachers may participate in discussions to help students clarify misunderstandings and think more deeply about the book.
Limitations	• Students all read the same book whether or not they like it and whether or not it's their reading level. • Many of the activities are teacher directed.	• Teachers often feel a loss of control because students are reading different books. • Students must learn to be task oriented and to use time wisely in order to be successful. • Sometimes students choose books that are too difficult or too easy for them.

Teachers usually organize their daily schedule to include two or more of the instructional approaches, as Mrs. Miller-McColm did in the vignette at the beginning of the chapter. When teachers don't have that much time available, they alternate teacher-led literature focus units with student-selected literature circles or reading and writing workshop. Both teacher-led and student-selected instructional patterns provide valuable language-learning opportunities, and no one approach provides all the opportunities that students need. The logical solution is to use a combination of patterns.

Literature Focus Units

Teachers organize literature focus units around a featured selection. Books chosen for literature focus units represent the finest in children's literature; they're books that

---

FIGURE 2–1

Continued

Features	Reading and Writing Workshop	Thematic Units
Description	Students choose books and read and respond to them independently during reading workshop and write books on self-selected topics during writing workshop. Teachers monitor students' work through conferences. Students share the books they read and the books they write with classmates during a sharing period.	Students study social studies or science topics. They use the six language arts as they participate in activities and demonstrate learning. Although content-area textbooks may be used, they are only one resource. Students also identify topics they want to study, so thematic units are authentic learning opportunities.
Strengths	• Students read books appropriate for their reading levels. • Students are more strongly motivated because they choose the books they read. • Students work through the steps of the writing process during writing workshop. • Teachers teach minilessons on reading strategies and skills. • Activities are student directed, and students work at their own pace. • Teachers have opportunities to work individually with students during conferences.	• Students read text sets of stories, informational books, and poetry related to the unit. • Students write in learning logs. • Teachers and students make clusters and other charts to organize information. • Teachers scaffold instruction as students work independently, in small groups, and together as a class. • Students use talk to clarify meanings and give presentations. • Students use computers and technology tools to enhance learning. • Students create projects.
Limitations	• Teachers often feel a loss of control because students are reading different books and working at different stages of the writing process. • Students must learn to be task oriented and to use time wisely in order to be successful.	• Teachers must design thematic units and locate needed resources and other materials. • Thematic units are more time-consuming than textbook-driven social studies and science units.

Booklist

BOOKS FOR LITERATURE FOCUS UNITS

Kindergarten
Brett, J. (1989). *The mitten*. New York: Putnam.

Henkes, K. (1991). *Chrysanthemum*. New York: Greenwillow.

Simont, M. (2001). *The stray dog*. New York: HarperCollins.

Grade 1
Choi, Y. (2001). *The name jar*. New York: Knopf.

Dorros, A. (1991). *Abuela*. New York: Dutton.

Rathmann, P. (1995). *Officer Buckle and Gloria*. New York: Putnam.

Grade 2
Bunting, E. (1999). *Smoky night*. San Diego: Harcourt Brace.

Look, L. (2004). *Ruby Lu, brave and true*. New York: Atheneum.

Meddaugh, S. (1995). *Hog-eye*. Boston: Houghton Mifflin.

Grade 3
Cohen, B. (1998). *Molly's pilgrim*. New York: Lothrop, Lee & Shepard.

MacLachlan, P. (2004). *Sarah, plain and tall*. New York: HarperCollins.

White, E. B. (2006). *Charlotte's web*. New York: HarperCollins.

Grade 4
Naylor, P. R. (2000). *Shiloh*. New York: Aladdin Books.

Ryan, P. M. (2000). *Esperanza rising*. New York: Scholastic.

Gardiner, J. R. (2003). *Stone Fox*. New York: HarperTrophy.

Grade 5
Curtis, C. P. (2000). *The Watsons go to Birmingham—1963*. New York: Delacorte.

DiCamillo, K. (2003). *The tale of Despereaux*. New York: Candlewick Press.

Lowry, L. (2005). *Number the stars*. New York: Yearling.

Grade 6
Babbitt, N. (2002). *Tuck everlasting*. New York: Farrar, Straus & Giroux.

Hale, S. (2005). *Princess Academy*. New York: Bloomsbury.

Paulsen, G. (2006). *Hatchet*. New York: Aladdin Books.

Grade 7
Avi. (2003). *Nothing but the truth: A documentary novel*. New York: Orchard Books.

Sachar, L. (1998). *Holes*. New York: Farrar, Straus, & Giroux.

Whelan, G. (2000). *Homeless bird*. New York: Scholastic.

Grade 8
Cushman, K. (1994). *Catherine, called Birdy*. New York: HarperCollins.

Hesse, K. (2001). *Witness*. New York: Scholastic.

Lowry, L. (2006). *The giver*. New York: Delacorte.

every student should read. Several books for each grade level are suggested in the Booklist on page 42. The books must be appropriate for students' interest level, but sometimes they aren't written at their reading level. When they're too difficult for students to read themselves, teachers read them aloud.

Students read the featured selection as a class, and they develop their understanding of the story with the teacher's guidance. In the vignette, for example, Mrs. Miller-McColm was teaching a literature focus unit on *Tuck Everlasting* (Babbitt, 2002). Here are the four components of literature focus units:

◆ *Reading.* Students read books together as a class or in small groups. They may read independently or together with a partner, or they may read along as the teacher reads the book aloud or guides their reading.

◆ *Responding.* Students respond to the selection to record their initial impressions of it and to develop their comprehension. They write in reading logs and participate in discussions called *grand conversations*.

◆ *Teaching Minilessons.* Teachers teach minilessons on language arts procedures, concepts, strategies, and skills and connect the minilessons to books students are reading or compositions they are writing (Atwell, 1998). The steps in teaching a minilesson are shown in the Step by Step box below.

◆ *Creating Projects.* Students create projects to apply their learning (Luongo-Orlando, 2001). Projects may involve any of the language arts, but children usually choose the projects they create based on their interests and the opportunities the selection presents to them.

Literature Circles

Students meet in small-group literature circles to read and respond to self-selected books (Daniels, 2002; Day, Spiegel, McLellan, & Brown, 2002). What matters most is that students are reading and discussing something that interests them and is manageable in a supportive community of learners. As students participate in literature

---

Minilessons

Step by Step

1 Introduce the topic.   Teachers introduce the strategy or skill by naming it and making a connection between the topic and the activities going on in the classroom.

2 Share examples.   Teachers show how to use the topic with examples from students' writing or from children's books.

3 Provide information.   Teachers provide information, explaining and demonstrating the strategy or skill.

4 Supervise practice.   Students practice using the strategy or skill with teacher supervision.

5 Assess learning.   Teachers monitor students' progress and evaluate their use of newly learned strategies or skills.

circles, they learn to view themselves as readers. They have opportunities to read high-quality books that they might not have chosen on their own and read widely (Evans, 2001). They also learn responsibility for completing assignments and to self-assess their learning and work habits (Hill, Johnson, & Noe, 1995; Samway & Whang, 1996). Here are the components of literature circles:

◆ *Reading.* Teachers collect five or six copies of each of six books and give a book talk to introduce each book. Students sign up for the book they want to read and form literature circles to read the book. After working together as a group to create a reading and responding schedule, students read the first part of the book to be ready to participate in the discussion.

◆ *Responding.* Students meet to discuss the book and to reflect on their reading. To facilitate their responding, they often assume roles ranging from discussion director to illustrator and word wizard, and they prepare for their roles before they meet to discuss the book. A list of roles is presented in the LA Essentials box on page 45.

◆ *Creating Projects.* After finishing a book, students prepare projects to present when they share the book with classmates. Students choose the type of project they create. Projects range from murals and dramatizations to poems and choral readings of excerpts.

◆ *Sharing.* Students meet as a class, and each group shares its book. Sometimes students prepare a book talk to share the book; at other times, they create projects to tell about the book. They provide enough information to create interest in the book, but they never tell the ending because they want to encourage classmates to read the book through the sharing activity.

Mrs. Miller-McColm's students in the vignette at the beginning of the chapter participated in literature circles that they called book clubs. These sixth graders participated in activities representing all four components of literature circles.

Reading and Writing Workshop

Two types of workshops are reading workshop and writing workshop. Reading workshop fosters real reading of self-selected stories, poems, and informational books, and writing workshop fosters real writing for genuine purposes and authentic audiences (Atwell, 1998; Cohle & Towle, 2001). Teachers often use the two workshops concurrently, but if their schedule doesn't allow them to do so, they may alternate them. Schedules for reading and writing workshop at the second-, fifth-, and eighth-grade levels are presented in Figure 2–2.

Some teachers fear that their students' standardized achievement test scores will decline if they implement a workshop approach in their classrooms, even though many have reported either an increase in test scores or no change at all. Kathleen Swift (1993) presented the results of a yearlong study comparing two groups of her students, one group reading basal reader stories, and the other participating in reading workshop. The workshop group showed significantly greater improvement, and Swift also reported that students participating in reading workshop showed more positive attitudes toward reading.

Reading Workshop. Students read self-selected books independently during reading workshop and respond to books by writing in reading logs (Atwell, 1998). There are many benefits to reading workshop: Students become more fluent readers and deepen their appreciation of books and reading, they develop lifelong reading habits,

ROLES STUDENTS PLAY IN LITERATURE CIRCLES

Discussion Director
The discussion director guides the group's discussion and keeps the group on task. To get the discussion started or to redirect the discussion, the discussion director may ask:

- What did the reading make you think of?
- What questions do you have about the reading?
- What do you predict will happen next?

Passage Master
The passage master focuses on the literary merits of the book. This student chooses several memorable passages to share with the group and tells why he or she chose each one.

Word Wizard
The word wizard is responsible for vocabulary. This student identifies four to six important, unfamiliar words from the reading and looks them up in the dictionary. The word wizard selects the most appropriate meaning and other interesting information about the word to share.

Connector
The connector makes meaningful personal, world, or literary connections. These connections might include events at school or in the community, current events or historical events, or something from the connector's own life. Or the connector can make comparisons with other books.

Summarizer
The summarizer prepares a brief summary of the reading to convey the main ideas to share with the group. This student often begins the discussion by reading the summary aloud to the group.

Illustrator
The illustrator draws a picture or diagram related to the reading. It might involve a character, an event, or a prediction. The student shares the illustration with the group, and the group talks about it before the illustrator explains it.

Investigator
The investigator locates some information about the book, the author, or a related topic to share with the group. This student may search the Internet, check an encyclopedia, or interview a person with special expertise.

FIGURE 2–2

Schedules for Reading and Writing Workshop

Second-Grade Schedule

15 minutes	Reading aloud to students
15 minutes	Teaching a minilesson (on a reading or writing topic)
30 minutes	Reading and responding
15 minutes	Sharing
	—Later—
30 minutes	Writing
15 minutes	Sharing

This 2-hour schedule is broken into two parts. The first 75 minutes, scheduled in the morning, focuses on reading, and the last 45 minutes, scheduled after lunch, is devoted to writing.

Fifth-Grade Schedule

40 minutes	Reading and responding
20 minutes	Teaching a minilesson (on a reading or writing topic)
40 minutes	Writing
20 minutes	Sharing

This schedule is also planned for 2 hours. The minilesson separates the two independent work sessions, and during the sharing session, students share books they have read, response projects they have created, and compositions they have published.

Eighth-Grade Schedule

40 minutes	Reading and responding or writing
15 minutes	Teaching a minilesson (on Mondays–Thursdays)
	Sharing (on Fridays)

The eighth-grade schedule is for 55 minutes. Because of time limitations, students alternate reading and writing workshop, minilessons are scheduled for 4 days each week, and sharing is held on Fridays.

they're introduced to different genres, and they choose favorite authors. Most important, students come to think of themselves as readers (Daniels, 2002). Here are the components of reading workshop:

◆ *Reading and Responding.* Students spend 30 to 60 minutes independently reading books and other reading materials. They also keep reading logs for writing responses to their reading and participate in conferences with the teacher to enrich their understanding of favorite books.

◆ *Sharing.* For the last 15 minutes of reading workshop, the class gathers together to share books they've read and enjoyed.

◆ *Teaching Minilessons.* The teacher spends approximately 15 minutes teaching minilessons on reading workshop procedures, literary concepts, and reading strategies and skills.

Writing Workshop. Writing workshop is a way of implementing the writing process (Atwell, 1998; Calkins, 1994; Fletcher & Portalupi, 2001). Students usually write on topics they choose themselves, and they assume ownership of their learning. The classroom becomes a community of writers who write and share their writing, and students come to see themselves as writers (Samway, 2006). They practice writing skills and strategies and learn to choose words carefully to articulate their ideas. Perhaps most important, they see firsthand the power of writing to entertain, inform, and persuade.

Students' writing grows out of their personal experiences, books they have read or listened to read aloud, and content-area study (Gillet & Beverly, 2001; Graves, 1994; Heffernan, 2004). They write personal narratives about experiences and events in their lives, create sequels to favorite books, and retell stories from different viewpoints. Young children often use the pattern or refrain from a familiar book, such as *Brown Bear, Brown Bear, What Do You See?* (Martin, 2007) and *The Important Book* (Brown, 1990), to structure their stories. Students experiment with other genres, such as poetry and scripts, after reading examples of the genre and learning about them. They also use writing workshop to write letters, book reviews, reports, and other projects as part of thematic units. In the vignette at the beginning of the chapter, Mrs. Miller-McColm's sixth graders were writing reports on ancient Egypt during writing workshop.

Writing workshop is a 60- to 90-minute period scheduled each day. During this time, the teacher and the students are involved in these activities:

◆ *Writing.* Students spend 30 to 45 minutes working independently on writing projects. They move at their own pace through all five stages of the writing process—prewriting, drafting, revising, editing, and publishing. Many times, students compile their final copies to make books during writing workshop, but sometimes they attach their writing to artwork, make posters, write letters that are mailed, or perform scripts as skits or puppet shows.

◆ *Sharing.* Students gather together to share their new publications with the class and to make related announcements. For example, a student who has just finished writing a puppet-show script and making puppets may ask for volunteers to help perform the puppet show, which could be presented several days later during sharing time. Younger children often sit in a circle or gather together on a rug for sharing time. The student who is sharing sits in a special chair, labeled the "author's chair," to read his or her composition. After the reading, classmates clap and offer compliments. They may also make other comments and suggestions, but the focus is on celebrating completed writing projects, not on revising the composition to make it better.

◆ *Teaching Minilessons.* During this 15- to 30-minute period, teachers present minilessons on writing workshop procedures, literary concepts, and writing skills and strategies (Fletcher & Portalupi, 1998; Portalupi & Fletcher, 2001). They also talk about authors of children's trade books and the writing strategies and skills these authors use.

Teachers often add a fourth component to writing workshop in which they read stories aloud to share examples of good writing with students. This activity helps students to feel a part of the community of writers.

Thematic Units

Thematic units integrate language arts with social studies, science, and other curricular areas (Lindquist & Selwyn, 2000). Students use all the language arts as they investigate, solve problems, and learn during a unit (Rief, 1999). They also use language arts to demonstrate their new learning at the end of the unit. These language arts activities occur during thematic units:

◆ *Reading.* Students read informational books and magazines, stories, and poems related to the unit as well as content-area textbooks. They also research topics on the Internet.

◆ *Keeping Learning Logs.* Students keep learning logs in which they write entries about new concepts they are learning, record new and interesting words, make charts and diagrams, and reflect on their learning.

◆ *Making Visual Representations.* Students create clusters, maps, time lines, Venn diagrams, data charts, and other diagrams and displays. They use these visual representations as tools to organize information and represent relationships about the topic they are studying (Moline, 1995).

◆ *Creating Projects.* Students create projects to apply their learning and demonstrate their new knowledge. These projects range from alphabet books and oral reports to posters and dramatizations.

In the vignette, Mrs. Miller-McColm's students were involved in a thematic unit on ancient Egypt, and they participated in all four language arts activities during the unit.

THE TEACHER'S ROLE

The teacher's role is complex and multidimensional. No longer are teachers simply providers of knowledge, nor do they assign an endless series of worksheets and busywork. Instead, teachers understand that students' literacy develops most effectively through meaningful social contexts. These teachers plan for instruction

Bob Daemmrich / The Image Works

A Teacher at Work
This third-grade teacher organizes instruction into literature focus units, literature circles, reading/writing workshop, and thematic units. Now the students are involved in writing workshop. One group meets with the teacher while others write independently or confer with classmates. This teacher is an instructor and a participant; she teaches the students and learns along with them. She manages the classroom effectively; the classroom is arranged to facilitate learning. The third graders understand the routines and their teacher's expectations.

using the four patterns of practice to meet the needs of their students. Their goal is to help children develop communicative competence and to excite them about literacy.

Teachers direct the life of the classroom. They are instructors, coaches, facilitators, and managers. Figure 2–3 lists some of the roles teachers assume.

What About Teaching?

You could say that everything a teacher does during the four patterns of practice is teaching, and in a sense it is. Although teaching is defined as providing information, teachers do two kinds of teaching. One kind is direct instruction, where teachers teach minilessons in which they explicitly present information, provide opportunities for supervised practice, and then have students apply what they have learned through reading and writing activities. Direct instruction has been associated with skill-and-drill activities, but it doesn't have to be. This kind of teaching is necessary to provide information and opportunities for students to apply what they are learning with guidance from the teacher.

The second kind is indirect instruction. Teachers use indirect instruction for brief, on-the-spot lessons as they respond to students' questions or when students demonstrate the need to know something. These interactions take place during whole-class activities, during conferences with students, and while working with small groups.

Differentiating Instruction

Teachers know that students vary—their interests and motivation, their background knowledge and prior experiences, and their culture and language proficiency as well as their language arts capabilities—so it's important to allow for these differences as they plan for instruction. According to Carol Ann Tomlinson (2001), differentiated instruction "means 'shaking up' what goes on in the classroom so that students have multiple options for taking information, making sense of ideas, and expressing what they learn" (p. 1). Differentiating instruction is especially important for students who haven't been successful and who can't handle grade-level reading and writing assignments and for very capable students who aren't challenged by grade-level assignments.

Teachers differentiate instruction as they implement the patterns of practice in their classrooms. Here are five ways to differentiate instruction:

◆ *Offer Choices.* Teachers offer choices when students select books to read in literature circles and in reading workshop, and students often choose their writing topics and genres during writing workshop. Students also make choices about the projects they create during literature focus units and thematic units.

◆ *Use Small Groups.* Teachers group students flexibly for literature circles, guided reading, writing groups, and other instructional activities. Students also work in small groups to develop projects and to write reports and other compositions.

◆ *Set Up Centers.* Teachers set up centers with instructional materials for students to practice concepts they're studying and to extend their learning.

◆ *Integrate All Six Language Arts.* Teachers provide opportunities for students to develop expertise in all six language arts, not just reading and writing. Because many students are better able to understand and express themselves through the oral

FIGURE 2–3

Teacher Roles During Language Arts Instruction

Role	Description
Organizer	Creates a language-rich environment. Sets time schedules. Uses the four patterns of practice. Uses the language arts as tools for learning across the curriculum.
Facilitator	Develops a community of learners. Stimulates students' interest in language and literacy. Allows students to choose books to read and topics for projects. Provides opportunities for students to use language in meaningful, functional, and genuine ways. Involves parents in classroom and out-of-classroom literacy activities.
Participant	Reads and writes with students. Learns along with students. Asks questions and seeks answers to questions.
Instructor	Provides information about books, authors, and illustrators. Explains language arts procedures. Teaches minilessons on concepts, skills, and strategies. Activates and builds background knowledge before reading, writing, and viewing. Groups students flexibly for instruction.
Model	Demonstrates procedures, strategies, and skills. Reads aloud to students every day.
Manager	Sets expectations and responsibilities. Monitors students' progress. Keeps records. Arranges the classroom to facilitate learning. Provides technology hardware and software to support language arts activities.
Diagnostician	Conferences with students. Observes students participating in language arts activities. Assesses students' strengths and weaknesses. Plans instruction based on students' needs.
Evaluator	Assesses students' progress in language arts. Helps students self-assess their learning. Assigns grades. Examines the effectiveness of the language arts program.
Coordinator	Works with librarians, aides, and parent volunteers. Works with other teachers on grade-level projects, pen pal programs, and cross-age reading programs.
Communicator	Expects students to do their best. Encourages students to become lifelong readers and writers. Communicates the language arts program to parents and administrators. Shares language arts goals and activities with parents and the community.

and visual language arts than through the written language arts, using all six language arts scaffolds their learning. Other students who are capable readers and writers may have less expertise in the other language arts and need to develop those abilities, too.

◆ *Incorporate Projects.* Teachers have students create projects as the final step in literature focus units and thematic units so that they have opportunities to explore topics that interest them and demonstrate their learning in authentic ways.

When teachers consider the needs of their students and incorporate these five ways to differentiate instruction into their plans, students are more likely to be successful.

Meeting the Needs of English Learners

How Do Teachers Adapt Instruction for English Learners?

Classroom Environment

Create a community of learners so that students feel valued and are comfortable taking risks and admitting when they are confused or need assistance.

Grouping Patterns

Vary grouping patterns so that English learners have regular opportunities to work in small groups, individually, and with the whole class. When students work in small groups, they collaborate and learn from their classmates.

Minilessons

Teach minilessons regularly, and reteach the minilessons to small groups of English learners who need additional practice.

Visuals

Integrate visuals, including realia, photographs, charts, maps, and diagrams, into the language arts program.

Background Knowledge

Take time to build students' background knowledge, and introduce important vocabulary words before teaching difficult concepts.

Oral Language

Provide opportunities for students to talk with classmates, and use talk to support their written language development.

Centers

Incorporate centers so English learners have an opportunity to work collaboratively on activities and projects and learn from their classmates.

Monitor Students

Monitor students' progress closely and provide assistance when needed so they can be successful.

ASSESSING STUDENTS' LEARNING

Assessing students' learning in language arts is a difficult task. Although it may seem fairly easy to develop and administer a criterion-referenced test, tests measure language skills rather than students' ability to use language in authentic ways. Nor do tests measure listening, talking, and viewing very well. A test on punctuation marks, for example, doesn't demonstrate students' ability to use punctuation marks correctly in their own writing. Instead, such a test typically evaluates whether students can add punctuation marks to a set of sentences created by someone else or proofread to spot punctuation errors in someone else's writing. A far better alternative approach is to examine how students use punctuation marks in their own writing.

Traditional assessment reflects outdated views of how students learn to read and write and offers an incomplete picture of students' language abilities. Tests focus on only a few aspects of what readers do as they read, what listeners do as they listen, and what writers do as they write. Traditional assessment fails to use authentic language tasks or to assist teachers in finding ways to help students succeed.

Assessment should resemble real language use (Valencia, Hiebert, & Afflerbach, 1994). A better approach is authentic assessment, in which teachers examine both the processes that students use as they listen, talk, read, write, view, and visually represent and the artifacts or products they create, such as projects and reading logs. Students, too, participate in reflecting on and assessing their own learning. Authentic assessment has five purposes:

- To document milestones in students' language and literacy development
- To identify students' strengths in order to plan for instruction
- To document students' language arts activities and projects
- To determine grades
- To help teachers learn more about how students become strategic readers and writers

Assessment is more than testing; it is an integral part of teaching and learning (Tierney, 2005). The purpose of classroom assessment is to inform and influence instruction. Through authentic assessment, teachers learn about their students, about themselves as teachers, and about the impact of the instructional program. Similarly, when students reflect on their learning and use self-assessment, they learn about themselves as learners and also about their learning. The LA Essentials box on page 53 presents guidelines for authentic assessment and describes how teachers use authentic assessment tools in their classrooms.

Monitoring Students' Progress

Teachers monitor students' progress as they are involved in language arts activities during literature focus units, literature circles, reading and writing workshop, and thematic units, and they use the results of their monitoring to inform their teaching. Four ways to monitor students' progress are classroom observations, anecdotal notes, conferences, and checklists.

Classroom Observations. Language arts teachers engage in "kid watching," a term that Yetta Goodman coined and defined as "direct and informal observation

LITERATURE FOCUS UNIT

Reading

The fifth graders in Mrs. Kenney's class are reading Roald Dahl's delicious fantasy, *Charlie and the Chocolate Factory* (2004). It's the story of Charlie Bucket, an honest and kind boy, who finds the fifth winning Golden Ticket, entitling him to a visit inside Willy Wonka's famous chocolate factory. Charlie and the four other children who also found winning tickets have a wild time visiting the factory, and, in the end, Mr. Wonka gives Charlie the best present of all—his factory!

Mrs. Kenney varies the ways students read each chapter. She reads the first chapter aloud, using whole-class shared reading, and students follow along in their copies of the book. For the other chapters, students alternate reading independently, reading with a buddy, reading in small groups, and reading together as a class.

Create your own Wonka goodie.

Responding

Mrs. Kenney's students respond to the story in two ways. They participate in small-group and whole-class discussions called grand conversations.

In these lively discussions, they share their ideas about the story, ask questions to clarify misunderstandings, and make connections to their own lives. Mrs. Kenney participates in the whole-class grand conversations and often asks students to think about Charlie and compare him to the other four children who visit Willy Wonka's chocolate factory.

The fifth graders also write in double-entry reading logs. At the beginning of the literature focus unit, students staple together booklets of paper for their journals and divide each page into two columns. After reading each chapter, they choose a quote and write it in the left column and then write a response in the right column.

Quote	Response
Ch. 19 Pg. 94 "The place was like a witch's kitchen!"	I chose this quote because did you know — it's a simile!

QUOTE	MY THOUGHTS
Ch 11 Pg 50 "You've got a Golden Ticket! You found the last Golden Ticket! Hey, what do you know?"	I feel excited and happy because Charlie never had anything much in his life. Maybe now his life will take a turn for the better.

Teaching Minilessons

Mrs. Kenney and her students choose important words from each chapter as they read *Charlie and the Chocolate Factory*. The words are organized by parts of speech on the word wall because Mrs. Kenney is teaching a series of minilessons about the parts of speech. The noun list includes *hooligan*, *precipice*, and *verdict*; the verb list includes *beckoned*, *revolt*, *stammer*, and *criticize*. The adjective list includes *despicable*, *scraggy*, and *repulsive*; *ravenously*, *violently*, and *frantically* are on the adverb list.

Mrs. Kenney also uses the words from the word wall as she teaches minilessons on root words and affixes to small groups of students. Students take turns choosing a word from the word wall and breaking apart the word's prefix, root, and suffix as Mrs. Kenney writes the information on the dry-erase board. Then students record the information on small, individual dry-erase boards.

In this literature focus unit, Mrs. Kenney is focusing on character. During a series of minilessons, students investigate how Roald Dahl developed Charlie's character and compare him with Willy Wonka and the other four children with winning Golden Tickets.

After studying about the characters, students create open-mind portraits of one of the characters. One student's open-mind portrait of Willy Wonka is shown here. The portrait goes on top and the page showing his thoughts goes underneath.

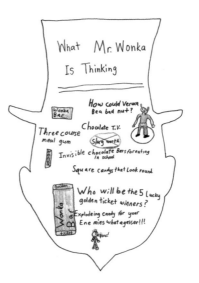

Creating Projects

Students create a variety of projects to extend the book and apply their learning. These two boys created a model of Willy Wonka's chocolate factory. Other students researched how chocolate is made and created a poster to display what they learned, wrote poems about each of the characters in *Charlie and the Chocolate Factory*, or read another of Roald Dahl's stories.

As the concluding activity, Mrs. Kenney and her students view *Willy Wonka and the Chocolate Factory*, the film version of the story starring Gene Wilder. Afterwards, students work in small groups to create Venn diagrams comparing the book and the film versions. One student's Venn diagram is shown here. After discussing the differences, most students agree that they preferred the book.

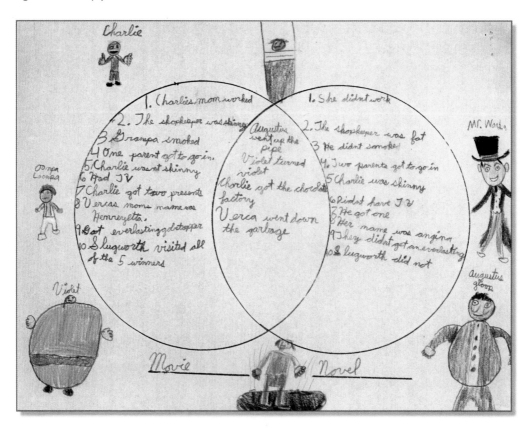

LITERATURE CIRCLES

Reading

Mrs. Goodman's eighth graders participate in literature circles. Mrs. Goodman introduces eight books written at varying levels of difficulty, and students sign up for the book they want to read. The students are currently reading these books:

- *The Outsiders,* by S. E. Hinton (2006)
- *The Face on the Milk Carton,* by Caroline Cooney (1990)
- *Holes,* by Louis Sachar (1998)
- *I Am the Cheese,* by Robert Cormier (1977)
- *To Kill a Mockingbird,* by Harper Lee (2002)
- *What Jamie Saw,* by Carolyn Coman (1997)

Students have set a reading schedule and they spend time reading during class and at home.

Students in each literature circle assume roles to deepen their understanding of the story and ensure the smooth functioning of their group. They rotate these roles each day so that everyone has the opportunity to experience all roles.

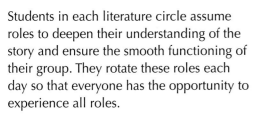

ROLES IN A LITERATURE CIRCLE		
1	Discussion Leader	This student keeps classmates focused on the big ideas in the story.
2	Harmonizer	This student helps everyone stay on task and show respect to classmates.
3	Wordsmith	This student identifies important words in the story and checks the meaning of words in a dictionary.
4	Connector	This student connects events in the story with real-life experiences.
5	Illustrator	This student draws pictures to help classmates visualize events in the story.

Responding

Students frequently meet in their literature circles to discuss the story they are reading, and students fulfill their roles. They talk about what's happening in the story, ask questions to clarify confusion, make connections to their own lives, and predict what will happen next. As students talk, Mrs. Goodman circulates around the classroom, joining each group for a few minutes.

Students also write in reading logs. Sometimes they write summaries and make predictions, and at other times they write reflections and ask questions. After writing, students often divide into groups of two or three to read their entries to classmates.

Reading Log

I am liking To Kill a Mockingbird a lot. But it's very different from other books I've read. Instead of describing the scenery and how the people look, it tells the history of everything. The book tells you what has happened. That makes it harder to picture what is happening but easier to make up what you want. I don't think I've ever read a description of Scout anywhere in the book. I didn't quite understand the beginning of the book because it was introducing everything really fast. But now, I'm beginning to understand what is going on.

Reading Log

My questions are:

- Why don't Scout and Jim call their father Dad but use his real name (Atticus)?

- Why doesn't Scout play with other girls?

- What does everyone look like?

- Why doesn't anyone search for the truth about the Radleys?

Creating Projects

Students create projects after they finish reading and discussing a story. They write poems and sequels, research a topic on the Internet, develop PowerPoint presentations, create artifacts related to the story, and design story quilts.

After students identify a project they want to develop, they meet with Mrs. Goodman and she approves their choice and helps them get started.

"When Jamie saw Van Throw Nin"

This picture is a square from a story quilt about *What Jamie Saw*, a story about child abuse. Students in the literature circle draw pictures to represent events from the book and put them together to make the quilt, which presents a strong message about the effects of child abuse.

Sharing

Sharing is the concluding activity. Students in each literature circle share the book they have read and their project with Mrs. Goodman and the class. Sometimes students work together to give a group presentation to the class, and sometimes students develop individual presentations. The students demonstrate their understanding of the story through their presentation, and they hope to interest their classmates in choosing the book and reading the story.

Mrs. Goodman explains how students will be graded before the literature circle begins and posts the criteria in the classroom. For this literature circle, students are graded on four items; each item is worth 25 points. At the end of the literature circle, Mrs. Goodman prepares a grading sheet with the criteria, grades students' work, and assigns the grades.

GRADING SHEET

Name _Justin_

Book _The Face on the Milk Carton_

1. Reading Log	20
2. Roles in the Literature Circle	25
3. Working Together in a Group	25
4. Project at the End	22
	(92)

READING AND WRITING WORKSHOP

Reading & Responding

Mrs. McClenaghan's fifth and sixth graders participate in reading workshop for an hour each morning. The students read books they have selected from the classroom library, including *A Wrinkle in Time* (L'Engle, 2007), *The Sign of the Beaver* (Speare, 2005), *Harry Potter and the Sorcerer's Stone* (Rowling, 1997), *Missing May* (Rylant, 1992), and *Tuck Everlasting* (Babbitt, 2002).

Students also respond to the books they're reading, and their response activities vary according to what Mrs. McClenaghan is teaching. This week's focus is on a reading strategy—forming interpretations. The students identify a big idea in the chapter they are reading and provide evidence from the text to support the idea on T-charts they have made.

Conferencing

As her students read and respond, Mrs. McClenaghan moves around the classroom, stopping to conference with students. She asks students to read a short excerpt and tell about their reading experience and the reading strategies they are using. They talk about the story so Mrs. McClenaghan can monitor their comprehension and clarify any misunderstandings. She carries a clipboard with her and writes notes about each student, including what book the student is reading and the progress he or she is making.

Reading Aloud

Mrs. McClenaghan is reading aloud *The Cay* (Taylor, 2003), a survival story about an elderly African American man and a Caucasian boy who are shipwrecked in the Caribbean and become friends through the experience. She reads aloud a chapter or two each day, and the students talk about the story in a grand conversation. She also uses the book in the minilessons she is teaching.

Teaching Minilessons

These fifth and sixth graders have been examining the strategies that good readers use, such as asking questions, making connections, and visualizing, in a series of minilessons. Today, Mrs. McClenaghan focuses on making inferences. She explains that good readers read between the lines to figure out the author's message. She rereads a passage from *The Cay* and asks the students to identify the big idea in the passage. Then she makes a T-chart on a dry-erase board and records their answers. In the first column, she writes the big idea, and in the second, a quote from the text to support the big idea. Then she reads another passage several pages later in the text, and they rephrase the big idea to clarify it and finish the chart.

BIG Idea	Text Evidence
It's about friendship.	p. 76 I said to Timothy, "I want to be your friend." He said softly, "Young bahss, you 'ave always been my friend."
It doesn't matter what color you are, you can still be friends.	p. 79 "I don't like some white people my own self, but 'twould be outrageous if I didn't like any o' dem."

Really Hungry

One day, when it was close to dinner time, my big brother was so hungry he got there before any of us. He was waiting impatiently and when we were at the table with our food in front of us he already started devouring the vegetables and rice.

My mother looked at him, and he stopped stuffing himself. He waited very impatiently while she said grace. Mother's grace isn't short but it isn't very long either. He fidgeted and squirmed untill she finished. "You should make it shorter," he said.

He gobbled all of his rice, vegetables and chicken. We watched him in amazement. He asked for seconds and he started to swallow his food.

"Don't eat like that," snapped my mother. "Disgusting!" She bit her chicken wing and chewed.

Writing

After spending 60 minutes in reading workshop, students begin writing workshop, which lasts for 45 minutes. Students usually write two- to four-page stories about events in their own lives—autobiographical incidents— during writing workshop. They work at their own pace, moving through the stages of the writing process. Most students write four or five drafts as they develop and refine the content of their writing.

Responding

Students meet with classmates and with Mrs. McClenaghan several times during the writing process to revise and edit their writing. The students provide useful feedback to classmates because they have learned about the qualities of a good piece of writing and they know how to identify problem spots.

Teaching Minilessons

In this writing minilesson, Mrs. McClenaghan shares an essay written by a student from another class. She asks the students to rate it using their district's 6-point writing rubric. They raise their hands and show with their fingers the score they would give the paper. Most students rate it a 4, and Mrs. McClenaghan agrees. They talk about the strong points in the paper and the areas where improvement is needed.

Then Mrs. McClenaghan reviews the asking-questions and magnifying-a-sentence revision strategies and the symbols students use to represent the two strategies. Next, students reread the essay and attach small self-stick notes to the paper with the symbols written on them to indicate revision points. Students also underline the specific sentence to which each note refers.

Sharing

During the last 5 minutes of writing workshop, one student sits in the author's chair and shares a newly published composition. The classmates clap and offer compliments after the student finishes reading. They are an appreciative audience because Mrs. McClenaghan and her students have developed a supportive classroom community.

THEMATIC UNITS

Reading

Ms. McCloskey works with 40 kindergarten through third-grade students in their multiage classroom. The children are engaged in a thematic unit on insects, integrating all areas of the curriculum. They participate in a variety of reading activities. They listen to Ms. McCloskey read books aloud and read along with her as she shares big books. During centers time, they reread familiar books with buddies and read independently. They also read other books at their own reading levels during guided reading.

Learning Logs

Each day, children write entries for their learning logs at the writing center. They meet with Ms. Russell, a student teacher working in the classroom, to write about insects. Many of the students are English learners, so Ms. Russell helps them to expand their sentences and include science words in their entries. She also reviews spelling, capitalization, punctuation, and grammar skills with individual children. Then children file their papers in their learning log folders, which are kept at the writing center. At the end of the thematic unit, children compile their learning logs and decorate the covers.

This entry, titled "Wings," was written by a kindergartner who is still learning about capital letters and punctuation marks. He added the second part, "because it has wings," in response to Ms. Russell's question, "How can a ladybug fly?"

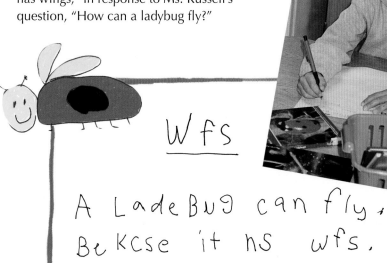

Wfs

A LadeBug can fly,
BeKCSe it hs wfs.

Visual Representations

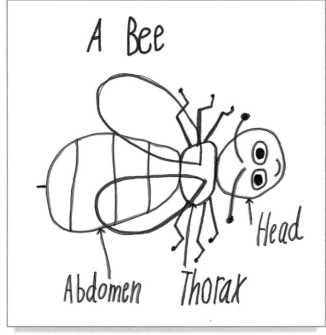

A Bee

Head

Abdomen   Thorax

SPIDERS   INSECTS

2 body parts
  1. head
  2. abdomen

3 body parts
  1. head
  2. thorax
  3. Abdomen

8 Legs

6 legs

No wings

Wings

Spin webs

No webs

The children make diagrams, charts, and drawings to record information they are learning about insects. They learn to draw insects accurately with three body parts and six legs. They use diagrams to organize information they are learning as Ms. McCloskey reads a book or presents a demonstration. They also use attribute charts to record descriptive words as they observe insects in the "Look and Learn" science center.

Creating Projects

The children are creating a multigenre display on insects. Each child writes a story, poem, or report for the display, which will cover an entire wall of the classroom. The children use the writing process to develop their compositions, and all children, even the kindergartners, type their final copies on the computer with Ms. McCloskey's assistance.

What body Parts?
thorax
head
abdomen
wings
stinger
antennae
legs
eyes

Where do they live?
colony
hive

Bees

What type of bees?
queen bee
drone bee
worker bees

What do they eat?
pollen
nectar

The Bees

Bees have three body parts: a thorax, an abdomen, and a head. On their body they have some little and big wings, a stinger, two antennae, six legs, and two large black eyes.

The bees live in a hive. Sometimes bees live in a group of bees, and it is called a colony. A lot of bees live in a colony and a lot of bees live in a hive.

There are three kinds of bees. There is a queen bee, a drone bee, and worker bees. The queen lays eggs on the hive and the worker bees take car of the baby bees. One of the worker bees gets pollen from the flowers. Whe the worker bees get pollen, they danc because they can't talk.

Bees eat pollen and nectar to ma honey. When bees make honey they have to go get pollen and nectar. W need bees because bees could ma honey for us. If bees is not in this stat there will be no honey for us.

Dragonfly

Dragonfly fly, fly, fly.
Dragonfly fly around the pond.
Dragonfly fly by the flower.
Dragonfly fly by me.
Dragonfly fly, fly, fly.

GUIDELINES FOR AUTHENTIC ASSESSMENT

- **Choose Appropriate Assessment Tools**

  Teachers identify their purpose for assessment and choose an appropriate assessment tool. To judge spelling development, for example, teachers examine students' spelling in books they write and their use of proofreading, as well as their performance on spelling tests.

- **Use a Variety of Assessment Tools**

  Teachers regularly use a variety of authentic assessment tools, including anecdotal notes, that reflect current theories about how children learn.

- **Integrate Instruction and Assessment**

  Teachers use the results of assessment to inform their teaching. They observe and conference with students as they teach and supervise students during language arts activities.

- **Keep a Positive Focus**

  Teachers focus on what students can do, not what they can't do. They focus on how to facilitate students' development as readers, writers, and users of language.

- **Examine Both Processes and Products**

  Teachers examine both the language processes students use and the products they create. They notice the strategies students use for language activities as well as assess the quality of students' work.

- **Consider Multiple Contexts**

  Teachers assess students' language arts development in a variety of contexts, including literature focus units, thematic units, and reading and writing workshop. Multiple contexts are important because students often do better in one context than in another.

- **Focus on Individual Students**

  In addition to whole-class assessments, teachers make time to observe, conference with, and do other assessment procedures with individual students in order to develop clear understandings of each student's development.

- **Teach Students to Self-Assess Their Learning**

  Self-assessment is an integral part of assessment. Students reflect on their progress in reading, writing, and the other language arts.

Weaving Assessment Into Practice

NOTES ABOUT MATTHEW

March 5	Matthew selected Ben Franklin as historical figure for American Revolution project.
March 11	Matthew fascinated with information he has found about B. F. Brought several sources from home. Is completing B. F.'s lifeline with many details.
March 18	Simulated journal. Four entries in four days! Interesting how he picked up language style of the period in his journal. Volunteers to share daily. I think he enjoys the oral sharing more than the writing.
March 24	Nine simulated journal entries, all illustrated. High level of enthusiasm.
March 28	Conferenced about cluster for B. F. biography. Well-developed with five rays, many details. Matthew will work on "contributions" ray. He recognized it as the least developed one.
April 2	Three chapters of biography drafted. Talked about "working titles" for chapters and choosing more interesting titles after writing that reflect the content of the chapters.
April 7	Drafting conference. Matthew has completed all five chapters. He and Dustin are competitive, both writing on B. F. They are reading each other's chapters and checking the accuracy of information.
April 11	Writing group. Matthew confused Declaration of Independence with the Constitution. Chapters longer and more complete since drafting conference. Compared with autobiography project, writing is more sophisticated. Longer, too. Reading is influencing writing style—e.g., "Luckily for Ben." He is still somewhat defensive about accepting suggestions except from me. He will make 3 revisions—agreed in writing group.
April 14	Revisions: (1) eliminated "he" (substitute), (2) resequenced Chapter 3 (move), and (3) added sentences in Chapter 5 (add)
April 23	Editing conference—no major problems. Discussed use of commas within sentences, capitalizing proper nouns. Matthew and Dustin more task-oriented on this project; I see more motivation and commitment.
April 29	Final copy of biography completed and shared with class.

of students" (1978, p. 37). To be effective kid watchers, teachers must understand how children develop language and must understand the role of errors in language learning. Teachers use kid watching spontaneously when they interact with students and are attentive to their behavior and comments. Other observation times should be planned when the teacher focuses on particular students and makes anecdotal notes about their involvement in literacy events and other language arts activities. The focus is on what students do as they use oral and written language, not on whether they are behaving properly or working quietly. Of course, little learning can occur in disruptive situations, but during these observations, the focus is on language, not behavior.

Anecdotal Notes. Teachers write brief notes as they observe students; the most useful notes describe specific events, report rather than evaluate, and relate the events to other information about the students (Rhodes & Nathenson-Mejia, 1992). Teachers make notes about students' performance in listening, talking, reading, writing, viewing, and visually representing activities; about the questions students ask; and about the strategies and skills they use fluently or indicate confusion about. These records document students' growth and pinpoint instructional needs (Boyd-Batstone, 2004). A yearlong collection of records provides a comprehensive picture of a student's learning in language arts. An excerpt from a fifth-grade teacher's anecdotal notes about one student's progress during a unit on the American Revolution appears in the Weaving Assessment Into Practice feature on page 54.

Several organizational schemes for anecdotal notes are possible, and teachers should use the format that is most comfortable for them. Some teachers make a card file with dividers for each child and write anecdotes on notecards. They feel comfortable jotting notes on these small cards or even carrying around a set of cards in a pocket. Other teachers divide a spiral-bound notebook into sections for each student and write anecdotes in the notebook, which they keep on their desk. A third technique is to write anecdotes on small sheets of paper and clip the sheets in students' assessment folders.

Conferences. Teachers talk with students to monitor their progress in language arts activities as well as to set goals and help students solve problems (Gill, 2000). Seven types of conferences are described in Figure 2–4. Often these conferences are brief and impromptu, held at students' desks as the teacher moves around the classroom; at other times, the conferences are planned, and students meet with the teacher at a designated conference table.

The teacher's role is to be listener and guide. Teachers can learn a great deal about students and their learning if they listen as students talk about their reading, writing, or other activities. When students explain a problem they are having, the teacher is often able to decide on a way to work through it. Graves (1994) suggests that teachers balance the amount of their talk with the student's talk during the conference and, at the end, reflect on what the student has taught them, what responsibilities the student can take, and whether the student understands what to do next.

Checklists. Teachers use checklists as they observe students; as they track students' progress during literature focus units, literature circles, reading and writing workshop, and thematic units; and as they document students' use of language arts skills, strategies, procedures, and concepts. For example, when students participate in writing conferences in which they read their compositions to small groups of classmates and ask for suggestions for improving their writing, teachers can note whether students participate fully in the group, share their writing with classmates, gracefully accept suggestions about improving their writing, and make substantive changes in their writing based on some of their classmates' suggestions. Students can even help develop the checklists so that they understand what types of behavior are expected of them.

A "Weekly Reading-Writing Workshop Activity Sheet" appears in the Weaving Assessment Into Practice feature on page 57. Third graders complete this checklist each week to monitor their work during reading and writing workshop. Notice that

FIGURE 2–4

Types of Conferences

On-the-Spot Conferences

The teacher visits with students at their desks to monitor some aspect of the students' work or to check on progress. These conferences are brief; the teacher may spend less than a minute at each student's desk.

Prereading or Prewriting Conferences

The teacher and the student make plans for reading or writing at the conference. At a prereading conference, they may talk about information related to the book, difficult concepts or vocabulary words related to the reading, or the reading log the student will keep. At a prewriting conference, they may discuss possible writing topics or how to narrow a broad topic.

Revising Conferences

A small group of students meet with the teacher to get specific suggestions about revising their compositions. These conferences offer student writers an audience to provide feedback on how well they have communicated.

Book Discussion Conferences

Students and the teacher meet to discuss the book they have read. They may share reading log entries, discuss plot or characters, compare the story to others they have read, or make plans to extend their reading.

Editing Conferences

The teacher reviews students' proofread compositions and helps them correct spelling, punctuation, capitalization, and other mechanical errors.

Minilesson Conferences

The teacher meets with students to explain a procedure, strategy, or skill (e.g., writing a table of contents, using the visualization strategy when reading, or capitalizing proper nouns).

Assessment Conferences

The teacher meets with students after they have completed an assignment or project to talk about their growth as readers or writers. Students reflect on their competences and set goals.

students are directed to write a letter to the teacher on the back of the sheet, reflecting on their work during that week.

Implementing Portfolios in the Classroom

Portfolios are systematic and meaningful collections of artifacts documenting students' language arts learning and development over a period of time (Porter & Cleland, 1995). These collections are dynamic, and they reflect students' day-to-day learning activities in language arts and across the curriculum. Students' work samples provide windows on the strategies they employ as language users—readers, writers, listeners, viewers, and talkers.

Portfolio programs complement language arts instruction in many ways. The most important benefit is that students become more involved in the assessment of their work and more reflective about the quality of their reading, writing, and other language use. There are other benefits as well:

- Students feel ownership of their work.
- Students become more responsible about their work.
- Students set goals and are motivated to work toward accomplishing them.
- Students reflect on their accomplishments.
- Students make connections between learning and assessing.
- Students' self-esteem is enhanced.
- Students recognize the connection between process and product.

In addition, portfolios eliminate the need to grade all student work. Portfolios are useful for student and parent conferences, and they complement the information provided in report cards.

Weaving Assessment Into Practice

WEEKLY READING-WRITING WORKSHOP ACTIVITY SHEET

Name _____   Week _____

Read independently	M T W Th F	Made a cluster	M T W Th F
Wrote in a reading log	M T W Th F	Wrote a rough draft	M T W Th F
Listened to the teacher read aloud	M T W Th F	Went to a writing group	M T W Th F
Read with a classmate	M T W Th F	Made revisions	M T W Th F
Read at the listening center	M T W Th F	Proofread my own writing	M T W Th F
Had a reading conference	M T W Th F	Had a writing conference	M T W Th F
Shared a book with classmates	M T W Th F	Shared my writing with classmates	M T W Th F
Other		Other	

Interesting words read this week   Spelling words needed this week

_____   _____
Titles of books read   Titles of writings

_____
Write a letter on the back, thinking about the week and your reading and writing.

Collecting Work in Portfolios. Portfolios are folders, large envelopes, or boxes that hold students' work. Teachers often have students label and decorate folders and then store them in plastic crates or cardboard boxes. Students date and label items as they place them in their portfolios, and they attach notes to the items to explain the context for the activity and why they selected a particular item for inclusion in the portfolio. Students' portfolios should be stored in a place where they are readily accessible to students. Students review their portfolios periodically and add new pieces to them.

Students usually choose the items to place in their portfolios within the guidelines the teacher provides. Some students submit the original piece of work; others want to keep the original, so they place a copy in the portfolio instead. In addition to the writing and art samples that can go directly into portfolios, students also record oral language and drama samples on audio- and videotapes to place in their portfolios. Large-size art and writing projects can be photographed, and the photographs placed in the portfolio. The following types of student work might be placed in a portfolio:

autobiographies	oral readings (on videotape)
biographies	oral reports (on videotape)
books	poems
choral readings (on videotape)	projects
clusters	readers theatre performances
copies of letters, along with replies	(on videotape)
received	reading log entries
drawings, diagrams, and charts	reports
learning log entries	simulated-journal entries
lists of books read	stories
multigenre projects	

This variety of work samples takes into account all six language arts. Also, samples from workshops, literature focus units, literature circles, and thematic units should be included.

Not all work that is placed in a student's portfolio needs to be graded for quality. Teachers, of course, will be familiar with most pieces, but it is not necessary to correct them with a red pen. Many times, students' work is simply graded as "done" or "not done." When a piece of work is to be graded, students should choose it from the items being placed in their portfolios.

Many teachers collect students' work in folders, and they assume that portfolios are basically the same as work folders; however, the two types of collections differ in several important ways. Perhaps the most important difference is that portfolios are student oriented, whereas work folders are usually teachers' collections. Students choose which samples will be placed in portfolios, and teachers often place all completed assignments in work folders (Clemmons, Lasse, Cooper, Areglado, & Dill, 1993). Next, portfolios focus on students' strengths, not their weaknesses. Because students choose items for portfolios, they choose samples that they believe best represent their language development. Another difference is that portfolios involve reflection (D'Aoust, 1992). Through reflection, students become aware of their

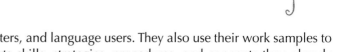

strengths as readers, writers, and language users. They also use their work samples to identify the language arts skills, strategies, procedures, and concepts they already know and the ones they need to focus on.

Involving Students in Self-Assessment. Portfolios are a useful vehicle for engaging students in self-reflection and goal setting (Courtney & Abodeeb, 2005). Students can learn to reflect on and assess their own reading and writing activities and their development as readers and writers. Teachers begin by asking students to think about their language arts abilities in terms of contrast. For example, in reading, students identify the books they have read that they liked most and least and ask themselves what these choices suggest about themselves as readers. They also identify what they do well in reading and what they need to improve about their reading. By making these comparisons, students begin to reflect on their language arts development.

Teachers use minilessons and conferences to talk with students about the characteristics of good listeners, good writers, good storytellers, and good viewers. In particular, they discuss these characteristics:

- What good listeners do as they listen
- How to view a film or videotape
- What fluent reading is
- How to prepare to give an oral report
- Which language arts strategies and skills students use
- How students choose books for reading workshop
- How students demonstrate comprehension
- What makes a good project to extend reading
- How students decide what to write in journals
- How students adapt their writing to their audience
- How students visually represent important concepts
- How to use writing rubrics
- How to participate in a grand conversation

As students learn about what it means to be effective language users, they acquire both the tools they need to reflect on and evaluate their own language development and vocabulary to use in their reflections, such as *goal, strategy,* and *rubric.*

Students write notes on the items they choose to put into their portfolios. In these self-assessments, students explain the reasons for their selections and identify strengths and accomplishments in their work. In some classrooms, students write their reflections and comments on index cards; in other classrooms, students design special comment sheets that they attach to the items in their portfolios. A first grader wrote this reflection to explain why she chose to make a poster about author Eric Carle and his books and to include it in her portfolio: "I have a favorite author. Mr. Eric Carle. I read five of his books!" A fifth grader chose to put the reading log he wrote while reading *Shiloh* (Naylor, 2000) in his portfolio. He wrote this reflection: "I put my journal on the computer. It looks good! I used the SPELCHEK. I put in lots of details like I was him. I should of put some illustrations in the book."

Showcasing Students' Portfolios. At the end of the school year, many teachers organize "Portfolio Share Days" to celebrate students' accomplishments and to provide an opportunity for students to share their portfolios with classmates and the wider community (Porter & Cleland, 1995). Often family members, local businesspeople and politicians, school administrators, college students, and others are invited to attend. Students and community members form small groups, and the students share their portfolios, pointing out their accomplishments and strengths. This activity is especially useful in involving community members in the school and showing them the types of language arts activities students are doing as well as how students are becoming effective readers, writers, and language users.

These sharing days also help students accept responsibility for their own learning—especially those students who have not been as motivated as their classmates. When less motivated students listen to their classmates talk about their work and how they have grown as readers, writers, and language users, they often decide to work harder the next year.

Assigning Grades

Assigning grades is one of the most difficult responsibilities placed on teachers. "Grading is a fact of life," according to Donald Graves (1983, p. 93), but he adds that teachers should use grades to encourage students, not to hinder their achievement. The authentic assessment procedures described in this chapter encourage students because they document how students are using all the language arts in authentic ways. The difficult part is reviewing and translating this documentation into grades.

Assignment Checklists. One way for students to keep track of assignments during literature focus units and thematic units is to use assignment checklists. Teachers create the assignment checklist as they plan the unit. Students receive a copy of the checklist at the beginning of the unit and keep it in their unit folder. As students complete the assignments, they check them off, so it is easy for the teacher to review students' progress periodically. At the end of the unit, the teacher collects the unit folders and grades the work.

A checklist for a second-grade thematic unit on hermit crabs is presented in the Weaving Assessment Into Practice feature at the top of page 61. Eight assignments on the checklist include both science and language arts activities. Students put a check in the boxes in the "Student's Check" column when they complete each assignment, and the teacher adds the grade in the right-hand column.

Teachers of middle- and upper-grade students often assign points to each activity in the unit checklist so that the total point value for the unit is 100 points; activities that involve more time and effort earn more points. The checklist shown in the Weaving Assessment Into Practice feature at the bottom of page 61 is for a fifth-grade literature focus unit on *Number the Stars* (Lowry, 2005); the point value for each activity is listed in parentheses. Students make checkmarks on the lines on the left side of the grading sheet, and the teacher marks the numerical grades on the right side.

Rubrics. Teachers and students develop rubrics, or scoring guides, to assess students' growth as writers or to evaluate other language arts activities (Skillings & Ferrell,

Weaving Assessment Into Practice

CHECKLIST FOR THEMATIC UNIT ON HERMIT CRABS

Name _____

Begin _____
End _____

	Student's Check	Teacher's Grades

1. Keep an observation log on the hermit crab on your table for 10 days. ☐ _____
2. Make a chart of a hermit crab and label the parts. ☐ _____
3. Make a map of the hermit crab's habitat. ☐ _____
4. Read three books about hermit crabs and do quickwrites about them. ☐ _____

   _____ Hermit Crabs

   _____ A House for Hermit Crab

   _____ Is This a House for Hermit Crab?

5. Do two science experiments and write lab reports. ☐ _____

   _____ Wet-Dry Experiment

   _____ Light-Dark Experiment

6. Write about hermit crabs. Do one. ☐ _____

   _____ All About Hermit Crabs book

   _____ A poem about hermit crabs

   _____ A story about hermit crabs

7. Do a project about hermit crabs. Share it. ☐ _____
8. Keep everything neatly in your hermit crab tolder. ☐ _____

Weaving Assessment Into Practice

NUMBER THE STARS GRADING SHEET

Name _____   Date _____

_____ 1. Read Number the Stars. _____

_____ 2. Write 5 entries in a reading log or simulated journal. (25) _____

_____ 3. Talk about your reading in 5 grand conversations. (25) _____

_____ 4. Make a Venn diagram to compare characters. Summarize what you learned
from the diagram in an essay. (10) _____

_____ 5. Make a cluster about one word on the word wall. (5) _____

_____ 6. Make a square with a favorite quote for the story quilt. (10) _____

_____ 7. Do a project. (25) _____

Total (100) _____

Weaving Assessment Into Practice

WRITING RUBRIC

5 Exceptional Achievement

- Creative and original
- Clear organization
- Precise word choice and figurative language
- Sophisticated sentences
- Essentially free of mechanical errors

4 Excellent Achievement

- Some creativity, but more predictable than an exceptional paper
- Definite organization
- Good word choice, but little figurative language
- Varied sentences
- Only a few mechanical errors

3 Adequate Achievement

- Predictable paper
- Some organization
- Adequate word choice
- Little variety of sentences and some run-on sentences
- Some mechanical errors

2 Limited Achievement

- Brief and superficial
- Little organization
- Imprecise language
- Incomplete and run-on sentences
- Many mechanical errors

1 Minimal Achievement

- No ideas communicated
- Lacks organization
- Inadequate word choice
- Sentence fragments
- Overwhelming mechanical errors

Weaving Assessment Into Practice

RUBRIC FOR ASSESSING REPORTS ON ANCIENT EGYPT

4 Excellent Report

_____ Three or more chapters with titles
_____ Main idea clearly developed in each chapter
_____ Three or more illustrations
_____ Effective use of Egypt-related words in text and illustrations
_____ Very interesting to read
_____ Very few mechanical errors
_____ Table of contents

3 Good Report

_____ Three chapters with titles
_____ Main idea somewhat developed in each chapter
_____ Three illustrations
_____ Some Egypt-related words used
_____ Interesting to read
_____ A few mechanical errors
_____ Table of contents

2 Average Report

_____ Three chapters
_____ Main idea identified in each chapter
_____ One or two illustrations
_____ A few Egypt-related words used
_____ Some mechanical errors
_____ Sort of interesting to read
_____ Table of contents

1 Poor Report

_____ One or two chapters
_____ Information in each chapter rambles
_____ No illustrations
_____ Very few Egypt-related words used
_____ Many mechanical errors
_____ Hard to read and understand
_____ No table of contents

2000). Rubrics make the analysis of writing simpler and the assessment process more reliable and consistent. Rubrics may have 3, 4, 5, or 6 levels, with descriptors at each level related to ideas, organization, language, and mechanics. Some rubrics are general and appropriate for almost any writing project, whereas others are designed for a specific writing assignment.

The Weaving Assessment Into Practice feature on page 62 shows a general, 5-level writing rubric that teachers and students can use to assess almost any type of formal writing assignment. In contrast, the rubric shown in the Weaving Assessment Into Practice feature on page 63 is designed to assess a particular writing assignment—a class of sixth graders designed this 4-level rubric to assess their reports on ancient Egypt. In contrast to the general rubric, the report rubric lists specific components that students were to include in their reports.

Both teachers and students can assess writing with rubrics. They read the composition and highlight words or check statements in the rubric that best describe the composition. It is important to note that rarely are all the highlighted words or checked statements at the same level; the score is determined by examining the highlighted words or checked statements and determining which level best represents the overall quality of the composition.

To assess students' learning systematically, teachers should use at least three evaluation approaches. Approaching an evaluation from at least three viewpoints is called *triangulation*. In addition to tests, teachers can use kid watching, anecdotal records, conferences, portfolios, assignment checklists, and rubrics. Using a variety of techniques enables teachers to be much more accurate in charting and assessing students' language growth.

What About Tests? With the current emphasis on accountability, it's important to understand the differences between authentic assessment and tests. Consider the often-confused terms *assessment* and *evaluation*. Assessment is diagnostic and ongoing. Teachers use assessment tools to plan instruction and monitor student progress. In contrast, evaluation is used to judge students' learning (Cobb, 2003). It often involves testing, using teacher-made tests, unit tests that accompany textbooks, or end-of-year standardized achievement tests. Teachers use evaluation after instruction to assign grades and at the end of the year to determine if students have met grade-level standards and should progress to the next grade level.

Authentic assessment tools and tests provide different kinds of information. Authentic assessment gives a more complete picture of what students know about language arts and the strategies and skills they can use, whereas tests judge student performance against a grade-level standard (Wilson, Martens, & Arya, 2005). A student who scores 95% on a unit test is judged to have learned more than one who scores 70%, but it usually isn't clear exactly what the student knows or which strategies and skills he or she has learned to use.

Most teachers are required to administer end-of-year standardized achievement tests to show students' growth and demonstrate accountability. Even with this emphasis on tests, it's important that teachers continue to use authentic assessment to inform their instruction and monitor student learning.

Review

This chapter focused on how teachers teach language arts. Teachers plan language arts instruction using four patterns of practice: literature focus units, literature circles, reading and writing workshop, and thematic units. Key points presented in this chapter include the following:

- Classrooms should be authentic learning environments that encourage students to use all six language arts.
- Literature focus units include four components: reading books, responding, teaching minilessons, and creating projects.
- In literature circles, students read and discuss self-selected books in small groups.
- Reading workshop components are reading and responding, sharing, and teaching minilessons.
- Writing workshop components are writing, sharing, and teaching minilessons.
- Thematic units are interdisciplinary units that integrate language arts with social studies, science, and other curriculuar areas.
- Teachers play many roles during language arts instruction: organizer, facilitator, participant, instructor, model, manager, diagnostician, evaluator, coordinator, and communicator.
- Teachers differentiate instruction to meet the needs of all students.
- Assessment is an integral part of instruction.
- Teachers use authentic assessment procedures, including observations, anecdotal notes, conferences, checklists, portfolios, and rubrics, to monitor and assess students' learning.

Professional References

Atwell, N. (1998). *In the middle: New understandings about writing, reading, and learning* (2nd ed.). Portsmouth, NH: Heinemann.

Boyd-Batstone, P. (2004). Focused anecdotal records assessment: A tool for standards-based, authentic assessment. *The Reading Teacher, 58,* 230–239.

Calkins, L. M. (1994). *The art of teaching writing* (2nd ed.). Portsmouth, NH: Heinemann.

Cambourne, B. (2001). What do I do with the rest of the class? The nature of teaching-learning activities. *Language Arts, 79,* 124–135.

Clemmons, J., Lasse, L., Cooper, D., Areglado, N., & Dill, M. (1993). *Portfolios in the classroom: A teacher's sourcebook.* New York: Scholastic.

Cobb, C. (2003). Effective instruction begins with purposeful assessments. *The Reading Teacher, 57,* 386–388.

Cohle, D. M., & Towle, W. (2001). *Connecting reading and writing in the intermediate grades: A workshop approach.* Newark, DE: International Reading Association.

Courtney, A. M., & Abodeeb, T. L. (2005). Diagnostic-reflective portfolios. In S. J. Barrentine & S. M. Stokes (Eds.), *Reading assessment: Principles and practices for elementary teachers* (2nd ed., pp. 215–222). Newark, DE: International Reading Association.

Daniels, H. (2002). *Literature circles: Voice and choice in book clubs and reading groups* (2nd ed.). Portland, ME: Stenhouse.

D'Aoust, C. (1992). Portfolios: Process for students and teachers. In K. B. Yancy (Ed.), *Portfolios in the writing classroom* (pp. 39–48). Urbana, IL: National Council of Teachers of English.

Day, J., Spiegel, D. L., McLellan, J., & Brown, V. (2002). *Moving forward with literature circles.* New York: Scholastic.

Evans, K. S. (2001). *Literature discussion groups in the intermediate grades.* Newark, DE: International Reading Association.

Fletcher, R., & Portalupi, J. (1998). *Craft lessons: Teaching writing K–8.* Portland, ME: Stenhouse.

Fletcher, R., & Portalupi, J. (2001). *Writing workshop: The essential guide.* Portsmouth, NH: Heinemann.

Gill, R. S. (2000). Reading with Amy: Teaching and learning through reading conferences. *The Reading Teacher, 53,* 500–509.

Gillet, J. W., & Beverly, L. (2001). *Directing the writing workshop: An elementary teacher's handbook.* New York: Guilford Press.

Goodman, Y. M. (1978). Kid watching: An alternative to testing. *National Elementary Principals Journal, 57,* 41–45.

Graves, D. H. (1983). *Writing: Teachers and children at work.* Portsmouth, NH: Heinemann.

Graves, D. H. (1994). *A fresh look at writing.* Portsmouth, NH: Heinemann.

Heffernan, L. (2004). *Critical literacy and writer's workshop: Bringing purpose and passion to student writing.* Newark, DE: International Reading Association.

Hill, B. C., Johnson, N. J., & Noe, K. L. S. (Eds.). (1995). *Literature circles and response.* Norwood, MA: Christopher-Gordon.

Lindquist, T., & Selwyn, D. (2000). *Social studies at the center: Integrating kids, content, and literacy.* Portsmouth, NH: Heinemann.

Luongo-Orlando, K. (2001). *A project approach to language learning: Linking literary genres and themes in elementary classrooms.* Markham, ON: Pembroke.

Moline, S. (1995). *I see what you mean: Children at work with visual information.* York, ME: Stenhouse.

Portalupi, J., & Fletcher, R. (2001). *Nonfiction craft lessons: Teaching information writing K–8.* Portland, ME: Stenhouse.

Porter, C., & Cleland, J. (1995). *The portfolio as a learning strategy.* Portsmouth, NH: Heinemann.

Rhodes, L. K., & Nathenson-Mejia, S. (1992). Anecdotal records: A powerful tool for ongoing literacy assessment. *The Reading Teacher, 45,* 502–511.

Rief, L. (1999). *Vision and voice: Extending the literacy spectrum.* Portsmouth, NH: Heinemann.

Samway, K. D. (2006). *When English learners write: Connecting research to practice, K–8.* Portsmouth, NH: Heinemann.

Samway, K. D., & Whang, G. (1996). *Literacy study circles in a multicultural classroom.* York, ME: Stenhouse.

Skillings, M. J., & Ferrell, R. (2000). Student-generated rubrics: Bringing students into the assessment process. *The Reading Teacher, 53,* 452–455.

Swift, K. (1993). Try reading workshop in your classroom. *The Reading Teacher, 46,* 366–371.

Tierney, R. J. (2005). Literacy assessment reform: Shifting beliefs, principled possibilities, and emerging practices. In S. J. Barrentine & S. M. Stokes (Eds.), *Reading assessment: Principles and practices for elementary teachers* (2nd ed., pp. 23–40). Newark, DE: International Reading Association.

Tomlinson, C. A. (2001). *How to differentiate instruction in mixed-ability classrooms* (2nd ed.). Alexandria, VA: Association for Supervision and Curriculum Development.

Valencia, S. W., Hiebert, E. H., & Afflerbach, P. P. (1994). *Authentic reading assessment: Practices and possibilities.* Newark, DE: International Reading Association.

Wilson, P., Martens, P., & Arya, P. (2005). Accountability for reading and readers: What the numbers don't tell. *The Reading Teacher, 58,* 622–631.

Children's Book References

Babbitt, N. (2002). *Tuck everlasting.* New York: Farrar, Straus & Giroux.

Brown, M. W. (1990). *The important book.* New York: HarperCollins.

Cleary, B. (1993). *Ralph the mouse.* New York: Morrow.

Coman, C. (1997). *What Jamie saw.* New York: Puffin Books.

Cooney, C. (1990). *The face on the milk carton.* New York: Bantam.

Cormier, R. (1977). *I am the cheese.* New York: Knopf.

Dahl, R. (1998). *The BFG.* New York: Puffin Books.

Dahl, R. (2004). *Charlie and the chocolate factory.* New York: Knopf.

Ellis, D. (2000). *The breadwinner.* Toronto: Groundwood Books.

Gardiner, J. R. (2003). *Stone Fox.* New York: HarperTrophy.

Hinton, S. E. (2006). *The outsiders.* New York: Penguin.

Lee, H. (2002). *To kill a mockingbird.* New York: HarperCollins.

L'Engle, M. (2007). *A wrinkle in time.* New York: Square Fish.

Lowry, L. (2005). *Number the stars.* New York: Yearling.

MacLachlan, P. (2004). *Sarah, plain and tall.* New York: HarperCollins.

Martin, B., Jr. (2007). *Brown bear, brown bear, what do you see?* New York: Holt.

McMillan, B. (1995). *Summer ice: Life along the Antarctic peninsula.* Boston: Houghton Mifflin.

Naylor, P. R. (1996). *Shiloh season.* New York: Atheneum.

Naylor, P. R. (2000). *Shiloh.* New York: Aladdin Books.

Naylor, P. R. (2006). *Saving Shiloh.* New York: Atheneum.

Rowling, J. K. (1998). *Harry Potter and the sorcerer's stone.* New York: Levine.

Rowling, J. K. (2002). *Harry Potter and the goblet of fire.* New York: Scholastic.

Rylant, C. (1992). *Missing May.* New York: Orchard Books.

Sachar, L. (1998). *Holes.* New York: Farrar, Straus & Giroux.

Speare, E. G. (2005). *The sign of the beaver.* New York: Yearling.

Spinelli, J. (2002). *Maniac Magee.* New York: Scholastic.

Taylor, T. (2003). *The cay.* New York: Laurel Leaf.

The Reading and Writing Processes

During the first week of school, Ms. Kakutani reads aloud *Granny Torrelli Makes Soup* (Creech, 2003) to her fourth graders. It's a story about friendship, which is her theme for the first month of school. In the story, Granny Torrelli helps her granddaughter Rosie smooth out her relationship with best friend Bailey. Ms. Kakutani makes connections between what Rosie learns about being a friend and how she wants the students to behave toward their classmates. It's the teacher's first step in creating a community of learners in the classroom.

After they finish the book, Ms. Kakutani and her students prepare spaghetti and meatballs and invite parents, grandparents, and siblings to join them for a lunch. The students write invitations, and parents volunteer to supply many of the ingredients and help prepare the food in the classroom. Others bring salad, bread, fruit, and dessert to complete the meal. It's a festive occasion where children introduce their families to Ms. Kakutani and show them around their classroom.

For the next 2 weeks, Ms. Kakutani and her students read *Amber Brown Goes Fourth* (Danziger, 1995), the third in a series of chapter-book stories about a spunky girl with a two-color name. This book, also with a friendship theme, is written at the third-grade reading level; it's appropriate for this class because most students read a year below grade level. The teacher has a class set of this Amber Brown book that she

*H*ow do teachers use the reading process to organize literature focus units?

Good teaching isn't accidental! Teachers organize literature focus units to ensure that students comprehend what they're reading. Some activities introduce the book and activate background knowledge, some guide students as they interpret the story, and others provide opportunities to teach students about literature and for students to apply what they're learning. As you read this vignette, notice how Ms. Kakutani incorporates the prereading, reading, responding, exploring, and applying stages of the reading process in the unit.

distributes to students and a text set with multiple copies of the other books in the series that she places in the classroom library for students to read independently.

Ms. Kakutani reads this story with her students using shared reading because she wants to ensure that everyone can read the story, and she wants to introduce the comprehension strategies that she will emphasize this year. The students follow along in their copies as she reads the book aloud, chapter by chapter. The class spends 9 days reading the 14 chapters in the book; on some days, they read one chapter, and on other days, they read two. As they read, Ms. Kakutani pauses off and on to think aloud about the comprehension strategies she is using—monitoring, visualizing, connecting, summarizing, and evaluating.

After they finish reading, the students participate in a grand conversation with Ms. Kakutani. Participating in a free-flowing discussion about the story is new to many students. The teacher explains the activity, models it, and teaches them how to ask questions, offer opinions, and make connections to their own lives and to *Granny Torrelli Makes Soup*. They talk about the events in the story, the importance of having friends, and their own nervousness about beginning fourth grade.

When the grand conversation slows down, Ms. Kakutani often returns to the book and rereads a sentence to redirect the conversation. After reading Chapters 6 and 7, for example, she rereads the bottom part of page 47 and asks, "What does Brandi mean when she says, 'I am NOT Justin'?" At first the students are unsure, but as they talk about how Brandi might feel, they recognize that one child cannot replace another one. Then the teacher asks, "Do you think Brandi and Amber will become best friends?" The students make predictions that guide their reading for the second half of the story.

After reading and discussing Chapter 14, Ms. Kakutani rereads Amber's comment, "I guess there will always be changes in my life" (p. 100), and asks students what they think it means. They reflect on the changes in Amber's life—her friend Justin moving away, her parents getting divorced, her father moving to Paris, her mother dating Max, and

Amber starting fourth grade. Then Ms. Kakutani asks students if they expect to have changes in their lives, and the conversation continues as they talk about the changes in their lives—parents who are soldiers in Iraq, new babies born into their families, mothers going to work, families moving to a new community, grandparents dying, older siblings being sent to prison, and, of course, starting fourth grade.

After they talk about the story, the students write entries in their reading logs. Ms. Kakutani provides questions to guide their responses. She makes her questions open-ended to encourage students to continue to think more deeply about the story and make connections to their own lives. Here are Ms. Kakutani's questions:

Chapters 1 and 2	*What have you learned about Amber?*
	How do you think her life is going to change?
Chapter 3	*What's hard about starting fourth grade?*
Chapters 4 and 5	*How is Amber's fourth grade different from third grade?*
	How is fourth grade different for you?
Chapters 6 and 7	*Do you think Amber and Brandi will become best friends?*
	Do you agree with Amber that everyone should have a best friend?
Chapter 8	*What funny things have you done with your mom or dad?*
Chapter 9	*Do you think it was fair for the girls to get detention for laughing?*
Chapters 10 and 11	*Why do you think Brandi and Amber are getting to be better friends?*
	Would you want to be the Burp Queen or Burp King of fourth grade?
Chapters 12 and 13	*What should Amber do to be a good friend?*
	Do you think Amber is ever going to like Max?
Chapter 14	*Do you think Max was trying to bribe Amber with the mermaid?*
	What changes have you had in your life?

The students make small journals by stapling together sheets of lined paper and adding construction paper covers. They illustrate the covers to reflect the book they are reading. They begin each entry on a new page and add the chapter number, a title, and the date at the top of the page. Bella writes this entry after reading Chapters 6 and 7, in response to the question, "Do you think Amber and Brandi will become best friends?":

> *I feel sorry for Amber Brown. She has too many changes in her life. She needs a new best friend. Her old best friend moved away and she is lonely. I am thinking Brandi will be her best friend because she needs one, too. I hope there are no more changes for her!*

Jordan writes this entry after reading Chapter 14 and adds this title—"The Change in My Life":

I'm having a change right now and it scares me. My Dad is in Iraq. He is a sergeant. I pray to God to watch over him. He says he's safe but I think he could get killed. I'm proud of him because he is brave. I pray he comes back safe.

Ms. Kakutani also emphasizes the important vocabulary in the story. She posts a word wall—a large chart divided into alphabetized sections—and after reading each chapter or two, students choose the most important words to add to the word wall. They take turns writing the words on the chart, and they refer to the word wall whenever they need help spelling or thinking of a word. The class word wall is shown in the box below. She also points out the wordplay in the story. The students get interested in reading jokes after reading the ones in Chapter 1 and Chapter 6, and Ms. Kakutani locates several joke books in the classroom library to share with them.

Amber Brown Goes Fourth **Word Wall**			
AB Amber Brown best friend Brandi Colwin Burp Queen bossy	**CD** divorce colorful change do-over detention	**EF** empty feeling feet-feat fourth-forth fiend	**GH** Hannah Burton Her Dweebness humongous
IJ Justin Daniels immature	**KL** London knapsack laughing	**M** Max Mrs. Holt musical mermaid	**NOP** Paris name dropper nervous
QRS sole-soul scared snap fingers spaghetti-slurping contest	**TU** trophy	**VW** vacancies	**XYZ**

Ms. Kakutani also shares information about author Paula Danziger and does a book talk to introduce the other Amber Brown books. Then students spend the last week in the unit reading other Amber Brown stories individually, with partners, and in small groups. Even after the unit ends, many students will trade books and continue reading about Amber Brown's adventures during independent reading time.

---

*R*eading and writing involve similar processes. The reading process is a series of stages during which readers read, explore, and reflect on the text they're reading. The writing process is similar, involving a variety of activities as students gather and organize their ideas, write rough drafts, revise and edit the drafts, and, finally, publish their writings. The goal of both processes is making meaning. Readers create meaning through negotiation with the texts they're reading, and, similarly, writers create meaning through negotiation with the texts they're writing. Readers use their life and literature experiences and their knowledge of written language as they read, and writers bring similar knowledge and experiences to writing. It's quite common for two people to read a text and come away with different interpretations and for two writers to write different accounts of the same event. Meaning doesn't exist on the pages of the book that a reader is reading or in the words of the composition that a writer is writing; instead, meaning is created through the transaction between readers and what they are reading or between writers and what they are writing.

In this chapter, you will read about the reading and writing processes and see how teachers use these processes in organizing language arts instruction. As you read, think about these questions:

- ◆ What are the stages in the reading process?
- ▣ How do children comprehend what they're reading?
- ◆ What are the stages in the writing process?
- ▣ How do teachers use these two processes in teaching language arts?

THE READING PROCESS

Reading is a process in which readers negotiate meaning in order to comprehend, or create an interpretation. During reading, the meaning does not go from the page to the readers. Instead, it involves a complex negotiation between the text and readers that is shaped by many factors: readers' knowledge about the topic; readers' purpose for reading; the language community readers belong to and how closely that language matches the language used in the text; readers' culturally based expectations about reading; and readers' expectations about reading based on their previous experiences.

Aesthetic and Efferent Reading

Readers read for different purposes, and the way they approach the reading process varies according to their purpose. Often they read for enjoyment, but at other times, they read for information. When reading to be entertained, readers assume an *aesthetic* stance and focus on the lived-through experience of reading. They concentrate on the thoughts, images, feelings, and associations evoked during reading. Readers also respond to these thoughts, images, feelings, and associations. For example, as students read *Princess Academy* (Hale, 2005), they may imagine themselves in Miri's village on the isolated Mt. Eskel. When reading to carry away information, readers assume an *efferent* stance: They concentrate on the public, common referents of the words and symbols in the text. For example, as children read *Sea Horse: The Shyest Fish in the Sea* (Butterworth, 2006), their focus is on the information in the text and illustrations, not on the experience of reading.

Almost every reading experience calls for a balance between aesthetic and efferent reading (Rosenblatt, 2005); readers do not simply read stories and poems aesthetically and informational books efferently. As they read, readers move back and forth between the aesthetic and efferent stances. Literature, however, should be read primarily from the aesthetic stance.

Readers move through the five stages of the reading process: prereading, reading, responding, exploring, and applying. The key features of each stage are summarized in the LA Essentials box on the next page.

KEY FEATURES OF THE READING PROCESS

- **Stage 1: Prereading**

  Activate or build background knowledge.
  Set purposes for reading.
  Preview the text.

- **Stage 2: Reading**

  Read independently, with a buddy, using shared reading, or through guided reading, or listen to the text read aloud.
  Read the entire text from beginning to end or read one or more sections to learn specific information.
  Apply strategies and skills.
  Read the illustrations, charts, and diagrams.

- **Stage 3: Responding**

  Respond in reading logs.
  Discuss the text with classmates and the teacher.

- **Stage 4: Exploring**

  Reread and think more deeply about the text.
  Examine the author's craft.
  Learn vocabulary words.
  Participate in minilessons.

- **Stage 5: Applying**

  Create a project.
  Connect with related books.
  Value the reading experience.

Stage 1: Prereading

The reading process begins before readers open a book to read. The first stage is prereading. As readers prepare to read, they do the following:

- Activate background knowledge
- Set purposes
- Plan for reading

Activating Background Knowledge. Readers activate their background knowledge or schemata about the book before beginning to read; the topic of the book, the title, the author, the genre, the cover illustration, a comment someone makes about the book, or something else may trigger this activation. When students are reading independently—during reading workshop, for example—they choose the books they will read and activate their background knowledge themselves. At other times, such as during literature focus units, teachers help students activate and build their background knowledge. They share information on a topic related to the book or introduce a book box with a collection of objects connected to the book. Or, they show a video or film, tell about the author, read the first paragraph aloud, or ask students to make a prediction about the book. For example, before reading *The Giver* (Lowry, 2006), teachers build a concept of what a "perfect" society might be like by having students brainstorm a list of problems in today's society and think of possible remedies.

Setting Purposes. Readers are more successful when they have a purpose for reading the selection (Blanton, Wood, & Moorman, 1990). During literature focus units, purpose setting is usually directed by the teacher, but in reading workshop, students set their own purposes because everyone is reading different books. For teacher-directed purpose setting, teachers explain how students are expected to read and what they will do after reading. The goal of teacher-directed purpose setting is to help students learn how to set personally relevant purposes when they are reading independently.

When readers have a purpose for reading, comprehension of the selection they are reading is enhanced in several ways (Blanton et al., 1990). First, the purpose guides the reading process that students use. Having a purpose provides motivation and direction for reading as well as a mechanism that students use to monitor their reading. As they monitor their reading, students ask themselves whether they are fulfilling their purpose. Second, purpose setting activates a plan for teachers to use in teaching reading. They help students draw on background knowledge as they set purposes, consider strategies they might use as they read, and think about the structure of the text they are reading. Third, when students have a purpose in mind, they are better able to identify important information to remember as they read.

Planning for Reading. Students often preview the reading selection, especially articles and nonfiction books, as they prepare to read. They examine illustrations, read the table of contents, and determine the reading difficulty of the selection. For longer books, they also decide how much to read each day. Previewing serves an important function as students connect their background knowledge, identify their purpose for reading, and take their first look at the selection.

Stage 2: Reading

Students do the actual reading in the second stage. Sometimes they read independently, but at other times, they listen to the teacher read aloud or read with classmates and the teacher. There are five types of reading that take place in classrooms:

- Shared reading
- Guided reading
- Independent reading
- Buddy reading
- Reading aloud to students

FIGURE 3–1

The Five Types of Reading

Type	Advantages	Disadvantages
Shared Reading Teachers read aloud while students follow along using individual copies of a book, a class chart, or a big book.	• Students have access to books they could not read independently. • Teachers model fluent reading. • Teachers model reading strategies. • A community of readers is developed.	• Multiple copies, a class chart, or a big book version of the text is needed. • Text may not be appropriate for all students. • Some students may not be interested in the text.
Guided Reading Teachers support students as they read texts at their reading levels. Students are grouped homogeneously.	• Teachers provide direction and scaffolding. • Students practice reading strategies. • Students read independently. • Students practice the prediction cycle.	• Multiple copies of the text are needed. • Teachers control the reading experience. • Some students may not be interested in the text.
Independent Reading Students read a text independently and often choose the text themselves.	• Students develop responsibility and ownership. • Students self-select texts. • Readers have a more authentic experience.	• Students may need assistance to read the text. • Teachers have little involvement or control.
Buddy Reading Two students read or reread a text together.	• Students are encouraged to collaborate. • Students reread familiar texts. • Students develop reading fluency. • Students talk about texts to deepen comprehension.	• Teachers' involvement and control are limited. • One student may depend on the other to do the reading.
Reading Aloud to Students Teachers or other fluent readers read aloud to students.	• Students have access to books they could not read independently. • Teachers model fluent reading. • Teachers model reading strategies. • A community of readers is developed. • Only one copy of the text is required.	• Students have no opportunity to read. • Text may not be appropriate for some students. • Some students may not be interested in the text.

The type of reading that teachers choose depends on the difficulty level of the text, students' reading levels, and the teacher's purpose. The advantages and disadvantages of each type of reading are outlined in Figure 3–1.

Shared Reading. Students follow along as the teacher reads the selection aloud. Kindergarten and first-grade teachers often use big books—enlarged versions of the selection—for shared reading (Holdaway, 1979). Children sit so that they can see the book, and they listen to the teacher read aloud and read along as the teacher reads refrains and other familiar words. The teacher or a child points to each line of text as it is read to draw children's attention to the words, to show the direction of print on a page, and to highlight important concepts about letters, words, and sentences.

Teachers in other grades also use shared reading when students have individual copies of the reading selection but it's too difficult for them to read independently (Fisher & Medvic, 2000). The teacher reads aloud as students follow along in their copies. Sometimes teachers read the first chapter or two of a chapter book together with the class, using shared reading, and then students use other types of reading as they read the rest of the book. Only those students for whom the book is too difficult continue to use shared reading and read along with the teacher.

Guided Reading. Teachers read with small groups of students who read at the same level or who use similar reading strategies and skills. They scaffold students' reading to enable them to develop and use reading strategies and skills in guided reading (Fountas & Pinnell, 1996, 2001). Selections used for guided reading should be written at students' instructional reading levels, that is, slightly beyond their ability to read the text independently. Teachers usually read the first page or two with students, and then the students read the rest of the selection silently. Teachers often group and regroup students for guided reading so that the book selected is appropriate for all students in a group.

Independent Reading. Students read silently by themselves and at their own pace (Taylor, 1993). Independent reading is the most authentic type of reading. This is what most people do when they read, and it's the way students develop a love of reading and come to think of themselves as readers. It's essential that the reading selection is either at an appropriate level of difficulty or very familiar so that students can read it independently. Otherwise, teachers use one of the other types of reading to support students and make it possible for them to participate in the reading experience.

Buddy Reading. Students read or reread a selection with a classmate in buddy reading. Sometimes students read with buddies because it's an enjoyable social

Anthony Magnacca/Merrill

Buddy Reading

These two good friends like to read chapter books together during DEAR time (Drop Everything And Read, a 20-minute daily independent reading time). They choose the books that interest them and are at their reading level from the classroom library and take turns doing the reading. Their teacher has taught them several strategies for cooperative reading, so they are able to help each other with unfamiliar words, stop reading when necessary to ask clarifying questions, and often make personal, world, and literary connections to the story. Buddy reading is a good alternative to independent reading for students who are very social or students who don't like to read.

activity, and sometimes they read together to help each other. Often students can read selections together that neither one could read individually. By working together, they are often able to figure out unfamiliar words and talk out comprehension problems. Teachers show students how to support each other as they read together. Unless students know how to work collaboratively, buddy reading often deteriorates into the better reader reading aloud to the other student, but that isn't the intention of this type of reading. Students need to take turns reading aloud to each other or read in unison. They often stop and help each other identify an unfamiliar word or take a minute or two at the end of each page to talk about what they have read. It's a valuable way of providing the practice that beginning readers need to become fluent readers.

Reading Aloud to Students. At every grade level, teachers read aloud to children for a variety of purposes each day. Teachers read aloud books that are appropriate for students' interest level but too difficult for them to read by themselves. When they read aloud, teachers do two things: They model what good readers do and how good readers use reading strategies, and they actively involve students in the reading experience by asking them to make predictions and use other comprehension strategies.

Reading aloud to students is not the same as round-robin reading, in which children take turns reading paragraphs aloud as the rest of the class listens. Round-robin reading has been used for reading chapter books aloud, but it is more commonly used for reading chapters in content-area textbooks, even though there are more effective ways to teach content-area information and read textbooks. Round-robin reading is no longer recommended, for several reasons (Opitz & Rasinski, 1998). First, students should read fluently if they are going to read aloud to the class. When less capable readers read, their reading is often difficult to listen to and embarrassing to them personally. Less capable readers need reading practice, but performing in front of the entire class is not the most productive way for them to practice. They can read with

How the Types of Reading Fit Into the Four Patterns of Practice

Literature Focus Units

Teachers usually read featured selections aloud or use shared reading because the books are often difficult for students to read on their own, even though the content is grade-level appropriate. Students should read independently, when they can.

Literature Circles

Students usually read books independently, but students read more difficult books with buddies. Teachers also use guided reading procedures when they're introducing literature circles to primary-grade students.

Reading and Writing Workshop

Reading workshop is designed to provide opportunities for students to read self-selected books independently, and teachers also read books aloud to the class and use them to teach minilessons about reading strategies and the author's craft.

Thematic Units

Teachers read many informational books aloud to students during thematic units, and students use shared reading, buddy reading, and independent reading to read other books and content-area textbooks.

buddies and in small groups during guided reading. Second, if the selection is easy enough for students to read aloud, they should read independently instead. During round-robin reading, many students follow along only just before it is their turn to read, so they don't do much reading. Third, round-robin reading is often tedious and boring, so students lose interest in reading.

Stage 3: Responding

Readers respond to their reading and continue to negotiate meaning to deepen their comprehension. They make tentative and exploratory comments by writing in reading logs and participating in grand conversations immediately after reading.

Writing in Reading Logs. Students write and draw thoughts and feelings about what they have read in reading logs. Rosenblatt (2005) explains that as readers write about what they have read, they unravel their thinking and at the same time elaborate on and clarify their responses. Students often choose their own topics for reading log entries, but many teachers hang a list of open-ended prompts in the classroom to guide students' responses. Possible prompts include the following:

> I really don't understand . . .
> I like/dislike (character) because . . .
> This book reminds me of . . .
> (Character) reminds me of myself because . . .
> I think (character) is feeling . . .
> I wonder why . . .
> (Event) makes me think about the time I . . .
> If I were (character), I'd . . .
> I noticed that (the author) is . . .
> I predict that . . .

These open-ended prompts allow students to make connections to their own lives, the world, and other literature. At other times, teachers ask specific questions to direct students' attention to some aspect of a book, as Ms. Kakutani did in the vignette at the beginning of the chapter.

Participating in Grand Conversations. Students talk about the text with classmates in discussions called *grand conversations*. Peterson and Eeds (1990) explain that in this type of discussion, students share their personal responses and tell what they liked about the selection. After sharing personal reactions, they shift the focus to "puzzle over what the author has written and . . . share what it is they find revealed" (p. 61). Often students make connections between the selection and their own lives, the world around them, or other literature they have read. If they are reading a chapter book, they also make predictions about what will happen in the next chapter. Teachers often participate in grand conversations, but they act as interested participants, not as leaders.

Grand conversations can be held with the whole class or with small groups. Young children usually meet as a class, but older students often prefer to talk with classmates in small groups. When students get together as a class, there is a feeling of community, and the teacher can be part of the group. When students meet in small groups, students have more opportunities to participate in the discussion and share their responses, but fewer viewpoints are expressed in each group and teachers must move around, spending only a few minutes with each group. Some teachers compromise and have students begin their discussions in small groups and then come together as a class and have the groups share what they discussed.

Stage 4: Exploring

Teachers lead students back into the text to explore it more analytically in this stage. They are involved in these activities:

- Rereading the selection
- Examining the author's craft
- Focusing on new vocabulary words
- Participating in minilessons

Rereading the Selection. Students often reread picture books, articles, and other brief selections several times. If the teacher used shared reading to read the selection, then students might reread it once or twice with a buddy or read it with their parents, and after these experiences, read it independently. Each time they reread, students benefit in specific ways (Yaden, 1988): They enrich their comprehension and make deeper connections between the selection and their own lives or between the selection and other literature they have read.

Examining the Author's Craft. Teachers plan exploring activities to focus students' attention on the genre, the structure of the text, and the literary language that authors use (Eeds & Peterson, 1995). Students sequence events in the story using storyboards (pages of a picture book cut apart and glued on tagboard cards) and make story maps to visually represent the plot and other story elements (Bromley, 1996). To focus on literary language, students often reread favorite excerpts in a read-around and write memorable quotes on story quilts that they create. Teachers also share information about the author and introduce other books by that author. Sometimes teachers have students compare several books written by a particular author.

Focusing on Words. Students add "important" words related to the book to word walls posted in the classroom, and then they refer to the word walls for a variety of activities during the exploring stage. Researchers emphasize the importance of immersing students in words, teaching strategies for learning words, and personalizing word learning (Blachowicz & Fisher, 2006). Students make word clusters and posters to highlight particular words. They also make word chains, sort words, create a semantic feature analysis to analyze related words, and play word games.

Teaching Minilessons. Teachers present minilessons on reading procedures, concepts, strategies, and skills during the exploring stage. They introduce the topic and make connections between the topic and examples in the featured selection so that students can connect the information with their own reading process. A list of topics for minilessons about the reading process is presented on page 98.

Stage 5: Applying

Readers continue to deepen their interpretations and value the reading experience in this last stage of the reading process. Students build on their reading experiences, the responses they made immediately after reading, and the exploring activities as they create projects. These projects can involve reading, writing, talk and drama, viewing, visually representing, or research, and can take many forms, including murals, readers theatre scripts, oral presentations, and individual books and reports, as well as reading other books. A list of projects is presented in Figure 3–2. Providing a variety of project options takes into account Howard Gardner's (2000) theory of multiple intelligences, that students have preferred ways of learning and showing knowledge. Usually students choose which projects they will do rather than working as a class on the same project. Sometimes, however, the class works together on a project.

Teaching the Reading Process

Teachers apply the five-stage reading process in the reading lessons they teach, whether they organize instruction into literature focus units, literature circles, reading workshop, or thematic units. Successful language arts instruction doesn't just happen; teachers bring students together as a community of learners and teach them the procedures for various language arts activities. Each pattern of practice requires that teachers carefully structure activities, provide appropriate books and other materials, present instruction, create time and space for students to work, and plan for assessment.

What's Important in Reading? Everyone—parents, teachers, and politicians—has an opinion about what's important in reading instruction. Often the debate centers on phonics: Some people believe that phonics is the most important factor

---

How the Reading Process Fits Into the Four Patterns of Practice

Literature Focus Units

Students use the reading process as they read a featured book. Teachers build background knowledge before reading, and afterward students respond, explore, and apply what they've learned.

Literature Circles

Students use the reading process as they read self-selected books in literature circles. More emphasis is placed on reading and responding, but students also participate in other activities, too.

Reading and Writing Workshop

Although the focus in reading workshop is on reading, students activate background knowledge before reading and are involved in other stages afterward, but to a lesser degree.

Thematic Units

Students often read stories and informational books as part of thematic units, and teachers incorporate activities representing all five stages in the reading process.

FIGURE 3–2

Projects for the Applying Stage of the Reading Process

Visually Representing Projects

Create a collage to represent the theme of a book.
Make a story can or box. Decorate a coffee can or cardboard box using scenes from a book. Fill the can with objects and quotes related to the book.
Construct a shoe box or other miniature scene of an episode for a favorite book.
Make a set of storyboards with one card for each episode or chapter. Include an illustration and a paragraph describing the section of the book.
Make a map or relief map of a book's setting or something related to the book.
Prepare bookmarks for a book and distribute them to classmates.
Use or prepare illustrations of the events in the story for clothesline props to use in retelling the story.
Create a quilt about a book.
Draw a graphic organizer of the big ideas in an informational book.

Writing Projects

Write a review of a favorite book for a class review file.
Write a postcard or letter about a book to a classmate, friend, or pen pal.
Write another episode or a sequel for a book.
Write and mail a letter to a favorite author.
Write a simulated letter from one book character to another.
Copy five quotable quotes from a book and list them on a poster.
Make a scrapbook about the book.
Create a found poem, or write a poem related to the book.
Keep a simulated journal from the perspective of one character in the book.
Rewrite the story from another point of view.
Prepare a multigenre project.

Reading Projects

Read another book by the same author.
Read and compare two versions of a story.
Read a biography about the author or illustrator of the book.

Viewing Projects

View a film version of the book.
Analyze the illustrator's craft.

Talk and Drama Projects

Present a book talk about the book to the class.
Create a song about a book, or choose a tune for a poem and sing the song for the class.
Dress as a character from the book and answer questions from classmates about the character.
Videotape a commercial for a book.

Research Projects

Research the author or illustrator of the book on the Internet and compile information in a chart or summary.
Research a topic related to the book. Present the information in an oral or written report.

because students need to be able to decode the words they're reading, but others consider phonics to be less important than comprehension because the purpose of reading is to make meaning from text. The view taken in this text is that there are four important factors in developing capable readers:

- Word identification
- Fluency
- Vocabulary
- Comprehension

Teachers address all of these factors through direct instruction, by reading aloud to students every day, and by providing daily opportunities for students to read books at their own reading level.

◆ *Word identification* Capable readers have a large bank of words that they recognize instantly and automatically because they can't stop and analyze every word as they read. Students learn to read phonetically regular words, such as *baking* and *first,* and high-frequency words, such as *there* and *said.* In addition, they learn word-identification strategies to figure out unfamiliar words they encounter while reading. They use phonic analysis to read *raid, strap,* and other phonetically regular words, syllabic analysis to read *jungle, election,* and other multisyllabic words, and morphemic analysis to read *omnivorous, millennium,* and other words with Latin and Greek word parts. Through a combination of instruction and reading practice, students' knowledge of words continues to grow.

Phonics, the set of phoneme-grapheme relationships, is an important part of word-identification instruction in the primary grades, but it's only one part of word identification because English is not an entirely phonetic language. During the primary grades, children also learn to recognize at least 300 high-frequency words, such as *what* and *come,* that can't be sounded out. Older students learn more sophisticated word-identification strategies about dividing words into syllables and recognizing root words and affixes.

◆ *Fluency* Capable readers have learned to read fluently—quickly and with expression. Three components of fluency are reading speed, word recognition, and prosody (Rasinski, 2004). Students need to read at least 100 words per minute to be considered fluent readers, and most children reach this speed by third grade. Speed is important because it's hard for students to remember what they're reading when they read slowly. Word recognition is related to speed because readers who automatically recognize most of the words they're reading read more quickly than those who don't. Prosody, the ability to read sentences with appropriate phrasing and intonation, is important because when readers read expressively, the text is easier to understand (Dowhower, 1991).

Developing fluency is important because readers don't have unlimited cognitive resources, and both word identification and comprehension require a great deal of mental energy. During the primary grades, the focus is on word identification, and students learn to recognize hundreds of words, but in fourth grade—after most students have become fluent readers—the focus changes to comprehension. Students who are fluent readers have the cognitive resources available for comprehension, but students who are still word-by-word readers are focusing on word identification.

◆ *Vocabulary* Capable readers have larger vocabularies than less capable readers do (National Reading Panel, 2000). They learn words at the amazing rate of

7 to 10 per day. Learning a word is developmental: Children move from recognizing that they've seen or heard the word before to learning one meaning, and then to knowing several ways to use the word (Allen, 1999). Vocabulary knowledge is important in reading because it's easier to decode words that you've heard before, and it's easier to comprehend what you're reading when you're already familiar with some words related to the topic.

Reading is the most effective way that students expand their vocabularies. Capable readers do more reading than less capable students, so they learn more words. Not only do they do more reading, but the books capable students read contain more age-appropriate vocabulary than the easier books that lower-performing students read (Stahl, 1999).

◆ *Comprehension* Readers use their past experiences and the text to construct comprehension, a meaning that's useful for a specific purpose (Irwin, 1991). Comprehension is a complex process that involves both reader and text factors (Sweet & Snow, 2003). While they're reading, readers are actively involved in thinking about what they already know about a topic. They set a purpose for reading, read strategically, and

FIGURE 3–3

How the Reading Process Nurtures Capable Readers

Stages	Word Identification	Fluency	Vocabulary	Comprehension
Stage 1 Prereading	Teachers introduce new words and teach word-identification strategies.		Teachers introduce key vocabulary words as they build background knowledge.	Students activate their background knowledge, and teachers build knowledge when necessary. Also, students set purposes for reading.
Stage 2 Reading	Students use phonics and other word-identification strategies as they read.	Students read texts at their reading levels independently.	Teachers read aloud books that students can't read independently.	Students use comprehension strategies as they read.
Stage 3 Responding				Students deepen their comprehension as they write in reading logs and talk about books.
Stage 4 Exploring	Teachers teach phonics, high-frequency words, and word-identification strategies.	Students reread familiar texts.	Students post words on word walls and participate in vocabulary activities.	Teachers teach students about comprehension strategies, genres, and the structure of texts.
Stage 5 Applying		Students create choral reading projects.	Students independently read texts at their reading levels.	Students extend their comprehension as they create projects.

make inferences using clues in the text. Readers also use their knowledge about texts. They think about the genre and the topic of the text, and they use their knowledge of text structure to guide their reading.

Capable readers are strategic: They use predicting, visualizing, connecting, questioning, summarizing, and other strategies to think about and understand what they're reading (Pressley, 2002). They also learn to monitor whether they're comprehending and learn how to take action to solve problems and clarify confusions when they occur. Teaching comprehension involves introducing strategies through mini-lessons, demonstrating how capable readers use them, and involving students in supervised practice activities.

Through these activities, teachers scaffold students and then gradually release responsibility for comprehending to students (Pearson & Gallagher, 1983). Teachers withdraw support slowly once students show that they can use strategies independently while they're reading. Of course, even when students are using strategies independently, they may need increased scaffolding when they're reading more difficult text, texts about unfamiliar topics, or different genres (Pardo, 2004).

Students develop into capable readers as they use the reading process. Activities are included in each stage to develop these four factors. Figure 3–3 shows how word identification, fluency, vocabulary, and comprehension are developed through the reading process.

THE WRITING PROCESS

The focus in the writing process is on what students think and do as they write; it is writer centered (Gillet & Beverly, 2001). The five stages are prewriting, drafting, revising, editing, and publishing, and the key features of each stage are shown in the box on page 85. The labeling and numbering of the stages does not mean, however, that the writing process is a linear series of neatly packaged categories. Research has shown that the process involves recurring cycles, and labeling is only an aid to identifying and discussing writing activities (Barnes, Morgan, & Weinhold, 1997; Graves, 1994; Perl, 1994). In the classroom, the stages merge and recur as students write.

Stage 1: Prewriting

Prewriting is the getting-ready-to-write stage. Writers begin the writing process before they have their topic completely thought out. They begin tentatively—talking, reading, writing—to discover what they know and decide what direction they want to take (Flower & Hayes, 1994). Prewriting has probably been the most neglected stage in the writing process; however, it is as crucial to writers as a warm-up is to athletes. Murray (1982) believes that at least 70% of writing time should be spent in prewriting. During the prewriting stage, students

- choose a topic;
- consider purpose, form, and audience;
- generate and organize ideas for writing.

KEY FEATURES OF THE WRITING PROCESS

- **Stage 1: Prewriting**
  Students engage in rehearsal activities.
  Students identify the audience and the purpose of the writing activity.
  Students choose an appropriate genre or form based on audience and purpose.

- **Stage 2: Drafting**
  Students write a rough draft.
  Students mark their writing as a rough draft.
  Students emphasize content rather than mechanics.

- **Stage 3: Revising**
  Students reread their own writing.
  Students share their writing in writing groups.
  Students participate constructively in discussions about classmates' writing.
  Students make changes in their compositions to reflect the reactions and comments of both teacher and classmates.
  Students make substantive rather than minor changes.

- **Stage 4: Editing**
  Students proofread their own compositions.
  Students help proofread classmates' compositions.
  Students increasingly identify and correct their own mechanical errors.
  Students meet with the teacher for a final editing.

- **Stage 5: Publishing**
  Students make the final copy of their writing, often using word processing.
  Students publish their writing in an appropriate form.
  Students sit in the author's chair to share their writing.

Choosing a Topic. Students often choose their own topics so that they write about things they're interested in and knowledgeable about. It's the first step in helping students become responsible for their own writing. At other times, however, teachers assign topics for writing assignments. They may ask students to write in response to a book they've read in a literature focus unit, for example, as Ms. Kakutani did in the vignette at the beginning of the chapter, or to do a writing project as part of a thematic unit. Whenever possible, teachers keep the topics general so that students can narrow them in a way that interests them.

Considering Purpose. As students prepare to write, they think about their purpose for writing. Are they writing to entertain? to inform? to persuade? Understanding the purpose of a piece of writing is important because it influences other decisions students make about audience and form. When students have no purpose in mind other than to complete the assignment, their writing is usually lackluster—without a strong voice or controlling idea.

Considering Audience. Students' writing is influenced by their sense of audience. Britton, Burgess, Martin, McLeod, and Rosen (1975) define sense of audience as "the manner in which the writer expresses a relationship with the reader in respect to the writer's understanding" (pp. 65–66). Students may write primarily for themselves or for others. Possible audiences include classmates, younger children, parents, children's authors, and pen pals. Other audiences are more distant and less well known, such as when students write letters to businesses to request information. Students adapt their writing to fit their audience, just as they vary their speech to meet the needs of the people who are listening to them.

Considering Form. One of the most important considerations is the form the writing will take: a story? a letter? a poem? a report? Five genres that students learn to use are informational writing, journals and letters, persuasive writing, poetry, and stories. Figure 3–4 reviews these genres and lists some writing activities exemplifying each one. Through reading and writing, students develop a strong sense of these genres and how they are structured. Langer (1985) found that by third grade, children responded in distinctly different ways to story- and report-writing assignments; they organized the writing differently and included varied kinds of information and elaboration. Because children are clarifying the distinctions between various genres, it is important that teachers use the correct terminology and not label all children's writing "stories."

Gathering and Organizing Ideas. Students engage in activities to gather and organize ideas for writing. Graves (1994) calls what writers do to prepare for writing "rehearsal" activities. When students read books, take field trips, view videos and DVDs, and dramatize stories, for example, they are participating in rehearsal activities because they are building and activating background knowledge. Young children use drawing to gather and organize ideas for writing, and older students prepare for writing by making graphic organizers.

Stage 2: Drafting

Students get their ideas down on paper during the drafting stage (Gillet & Beverly, 2001). They write on every other line to leave space for revisions. Teachers often make a small *x* on every other line of students' papers as a reminder to skip lines as students draft their compositions. Students label their drafts by writing "Rough Draft" in ink at the top of the paper or by stamping them with a ROUGH DRAFT stamp; this label indicates to the writer, other students, parents, and administrators that the composition is a draft in which the emphasis is on content, not mechanics. It also explains why the teacher has not graded the paper or marked mechanical errors.

Drafting is messy. Students write quickly, trying to capture the ideas they're thinking. It's not uncommon for them to leave out a word here and there and make careless spelling errors. They cross out sentences that aren't working, use carets to

FIGURE 3–4

Writing Genres

Genre	Purpose	Activities
Informational Writing	Students collect and synthesize information for informational writing. This writing is objective, and reports are the most common type of informational writing. Students use informational writing to give directions, sequence steps, compare one thing to another, explain causes and effects, or describe problems and solutions.	Alphabet books Autobiographies Biographies Directions Interviews Reports
Journals and Letters	Students write to themselves and to specific, known audiences in journals and letters. Their writing is personal and often less formal than for other genres. They share news, explore new ideas, and record notes. Letters and envelopes require special formatting, and children learn these formats during the primary grades.	Business letters E-mail messages Friendly letters Learning logs Postcards Reading logs
Persuasive Writing	Persuasion is winning someone to your viewpoint or cause. The three ways people are persuaded are by appeals to logic, moral character, and emotion. Students present their position clearly and then support it with examples and evidence.	Advertisements Book and movie reviews Persuasive letters Persuasive posters
Poetry Writing	Students create word pictures and play with rhyme and other stylistic devices as they create poems. As students experiment with poetry, they learn that poetic language is vivid and powerful but concise, and they learn that poems can be arranged in different ways on a page.	Diamante poems Five-senses poems Found poems Free verse Haiku "I am" poems
Story Writing	Students retell familiar stories, develop sequels for stories they have read, write stories called *personal narratives* about events in their own lives, and create original stories. They organize their stories into three parts: beginning, middle, and end.	Original short stories Personal narratives Retellings of stories Sequels to stories Scripts of stories

insert new ideas, and draw arrows to rearrange text. As students write rough drafts, it is important not to emphasize correct spelling and neatness. In fact, pointing out mechanical errors during the drafting stage sends students a message that mechanical correctness is more important than content (Sommers, 1994). Later, during editing, students can clean up mechanical errors and put their composition into a neat, final form.

Stage 3: Revising

Revising is the time when writers clarify and refine the ideas in their compositions (Angelillo, 2005). Novice writers often break the writing process cycle as soon as they complete a rough draft, believing that once they have jotted down their ideas, the writing task is complete. Experienced writers, however, know that they must turn to others for reactions and revise on the basis of these comments (Sommers, 1994).

Revision is not just polishing; it is meeting the needs of readers by adding, substituting, deleting, and rearranging material. The word *revision* means "seeing again," and in this stage, writers see their compositions again with the help of their classmates and teacher. Here are activities in the revising stage:

- Rereading the rough draft
- Sharing the rough draft in a writing group
- Revising on the basis of feedback
- Conferencing with the teacher

Rereading the Rough Draft. After finishing the rough draft, writers need to distance themselves from it for a day or two, then reread it from a fresh perspective, as a reader might. As they reread, students make changes—adding, substituting, deleting, and moving—and place question marks by sections that need work. It is these trouble spots that students ask for help with in their writing groups.

Writing Groups

1 The writer reads. Students take turns reading their compositions aloud. Classmates listen politely, thinking about compliments they will make after the writer finishes reading. Only the writer looks at the composition, because when others look at it, they quickly notice and comment on mechanical errors, even though the emphasis during revising is on content. Listening to the writing read aloud keeps the focus on content.

2 Listeners offer compliments. Writing-group members say what they liked about the writing. These positive comments should be specific, rather than the often heard "I liked it" or "It was good."

3 The writer asks questions. Writers ask for assistance with trouble spots they identified earlier when rereading their writing, or they ask questions that reflect more general concerns about how well they are communicating.

4 Listeners offer suggestions. Members of the writing group ask questions about things that were unclear to them and make revision suggestions. Because it's difficult for students to appreciate suggestions, it's important to teach them what kinds of suggestions are acceptable and how to word their comments in helpful ways.

5 The process is repeated. Students repeat the first four steps as they share their rough drafts.

6 Writers plan for revision. At the end of the writing-group session, students make a commitment to revise their writing. When students verbalize their planned revisions, they are more likely to complete the revision stage. After the group disbands, students make the revisions.

Sharing in Writing Groups. Students meet in writing groups to share their compositions with classmates. Because writing must meet the needs of readers, feedback is crucial. Writing groups provide a scaffold in which teachers and classmates talk about plans and strategies for writing and revising (Calkins, 1994). The Step by Step feature on page 88 describes the procedure for writing groups.

Teaching students how to work in writing groups takes patience and practice. Teachers explain the purpose of writing groups and the steps in the procedure, and next, they model the steps using a rough draft they have written. Then small groups of students model the steps while their classmates watch, and teachers point out how to provide useful feedback to writers. Teachers often have students develop a list of meaningful comments and post it in the classroom for students to refer to during this stage. Figure 3–5 shows a sixth-grade class list of compliments, questions, and suggestions that students can offer to classmates. Teachers also coach students

---

FIGURE 3–5

Sixth Graders' List of Writing-Group Comments

Compliments	Questions	Suggestions
I liked the part where _____ .	Did my introduction grab your attention?	Could you add more about _____ ?
Your lead grabbed my attention because _____ .	What do you want to know more about?	I think the part about _____ is long, and you could delete some of that.
My favorite sentence is _____ .	Did you understand my organization?	Which part is your conclusion?
I like the way you described _____ .	What do you think the best part of my paper is?	I think you should substitute a better word for _____ , such as _____ .
I noticed this metaphor: _____ .	Are there some words that I need to change?	Your organization isn't clear because _____ .
I could hear your "voice" when you wrote _____ .	Did you like my title?	I think you might try moving the part about _____ to _____ .
I like your conclusion because _____ .	Does my dialogue sound "real" to you?	I think you used _____ too many times. Can you combine some sentences?
I liked your organization because _____ .	Is there something that isn't clear to you?	
Your sequence is _____ .	Is there something that I need to delete?	
Your writing is powerful because it made me feel _____ .	Is there something I should move from one part of my writing to another part?	

on how to accept their classmates' compliments and suggestions for revision without getting upset.

Writing groups can form spontaneously when several students are ready to share their compositions, or they can be formal groupings with identified leaders. In some classrooms, writing groups form when four or five students finish their rough drafts. The students gather around a conference table or in a corner of the classroom. They take turns reading their rough drafts aloud, and classmates in the group listen and respond, offering compliments and suggestions for revision. Sometimes the teacher joins the writing group, but if the teacher is involved in something else, students work independently. In other classrooms, the writing groups are established. Students get together to share their writing when everyone in the group is ready. Sometimes the teacher participates in these groups, providing feedback along with the students. At other times, the writing groups can function independently. Four or five students are assigned to each group, and a list of groups and their members is posted in the classroom. Students take turns serving as group leader.

Making Revisions. Students make four types of changes—additions, substitutions, deletions, and moves—as they revise (Faigley & Witte, 1981). They add words, substitute sentences, delete paragraphs, and move phrases. Students often use a blue pen to cross out, draw arrows, and write in the space left between the double-spaced lines of their rough drafts so that revisions will show clearly. This way teachers can examine the types of revisions students make. Revisions are an important gauge of students' growth as writers.

Conferencing With the Teacher. Sometimes the teacher participates in the writing groups and provides revision suggestions along with the students, and at other times, the teacher conferences individually with students about their rough drafts. The teacher's role during conferences is to help students make choices and define directions for revision. Barry Lane (1993, 1999) offers these suggestions for talking with students about their papers:

- Have students come to a conference prepared to begin talking about their concerns. Students should talk first in a conference.
- Ask questions rather than give answers. Ask students what is working well for them, what problems they are having, and what questions they have.
- React to students' writing as a reader, not as a teacher. Offer compliments first; give suggestions later.
- Keep the conference short, and recognize that not all problem areas or concerns can be discussed.
- Limit the number of revision suggestions, and make all suggestions specific.
- Have students meet in writing groups before conferencing. Then students can share the feedback they received from classmates.
- To conclude the conference, ask students to identify the revisions they plan to make.
- Take notes during conferences and summarize students' revision plans. These notes are a record of the conference, and the revision plans can be used in assessing students' revisions.

It is time-consuming to meet with every student, but it's worth the time (Calkins, Hartman, & White, 2005). In a 5-minute conference, teachers listen to students talk about their writing processes, guide students as they make revision plans, and offer feedback during the writing process, when it is most usable.

Stage 4: Editing

Editing is putting the piece of writing into its final form. Until this stage, the focus has been primarily on the content of students' writing. Now the focus changes to mechanics. Students polish their writing by correcting misspellings and other mechanical errors. The goal here is to make the writing "optimally readable" (Smith, 1982). Writers who write for readers understand that if their compositions aren't readable, they have written in vain because their ideas will never be read.

Mechanics are the commonly accepted conventions of written Standard English; they include capitalization, punctuation, spelling, sentence structure, usage, and formatting considerations specific to poems, scripts, letters, and other writing forms. The use of these commonly accepted conventions is a courtesy to those who will read the composition.

Mechanical skills are best taught during the editing stage. When editing a composition that will be shared with a genuine audience, students are more interested in using mechanical skills correctly so that they can communicate effectively. In a study of two third-grade classes, Calkins (1980) found that the students in the class who learned punctuation marks as a part of editing could define or explain more marks than the students in the other class, who were taught punctuation skills in a traditional manner, with instruction and practice exercises on each punctuation mark. In other words, the results of this research, as well as other studies (Graves, 1994; Routman, 1996; Weaver, 1996), suggest that students learn mechanical skills better as part of the writing process than through practice exercises.

Students move through these activities during editing:

- Getting distance from the composition
- Proofreading to locate errors
- Correcting errors

Getting Distance. Students are more efficient editors if they set the composition aside for a few days before beginning to edit. After working so closely with a piece of writing during drafting and revising, they're too familiar with it to be able to locate many mechanical errors. With the distance gained by waiting a few days, children are better able to approach editing with a fresh perspective and gather the enthusiasm necessary to finish the writing process by making the paper optimally readable.

Proofreading. Students proofread their compositions to locate and mark possible errors. Proofreading is a unique type of reading in which students read slowly, word by word, hunting for errors rather than reading quickly for meaning. Concentrating on mechanics is difficult because our natural inclination is to read for meaning. Even experienced proofreaders often find themselves reading for meaning and overlooking errors that don't inhibit meaning. It's important, therefore, to take time to explain proofreading and demonstrate how it differs from regular reading.

To demonstrate proofreading, the teacher copies a piece of student writing on the chalkboard or displays it on an overhead projector. The teacher reads it several times, each time hunting for a particular type of error. During each reading, the teacher reads the composition slowly, softly pronouncing each word and touching the word with a pencil or pen to focus attention on it. The teacher circles possible errors as they are located.

Errors are marked or corrected with special proofreaders' marks. Students enjoy using these marks, the same ones that adult authors and editors use. Proofreaders' marks that children can learn to use in editing their writing are presented in Figure 3–6. Editing checklists help students focus on particular types of errors. Teachers develop checklists with two to six items appropriate for the grade level. A first-grade checklist, for example, might contain only two items—one about capital letters at the beginning of sentences and another about periods at the end of sentences. In contrast, a middle-grade checklist might have items such as using commas in a series, indenting paragraphs, capitalizing proper nouns, and spelling homonyms correctly. Teachers can revise the checklist during the school year to focus attention on skills that have recently been taught.

A third-grade editing checklist is presented in Figure 3–7. First, children proof-read their own compositions, searching for errors in each category on the checklist; after proofreading, they check off each item. Then, after completing the checklist, children sign their names and trade checklists and compositions with a classmate. Now they become editors and complete each other's checklists. Having both writer and editor sign the checklist helps them take the activity seriously.

FIGURE 3–6

Proofreaders' Marks

Delete	ℰ	There were cots to sleep on and food to eat on at the shelter.
Insert	∧	Mrs. Kim's cat is the color of carrots.
Indent paragraph	¶	¶Riots are bad. People can get hurt and buildings can get burned down but good things can happen too. People can learn to be friends.
Capitalize	≡	Daniel and his mom didn't like mrs. Kim or her cat.
Change to lowercase	/	People were Rioting because they were angry.
Add period	⊙	I think Daniel's mom and Mrs. Kim will become friends ⊙
Add comma	⁀	People hurt other people, they steal things, and they burn down buildings in a riot.
Add apostrophe	⋁	Daniel's cat was named Jasmine.

FIGURE 3–7

A Third-Grade Editing Checklist

Editing Checklist

Author   Editor

1. I have circled the words that might be misspelled.

2. I have checked that all sentences begin with a capital letter.

3. I have checked that all sentences end with a punctuation mark.

4. I have checked that all proper nouns begin with a capital letter.

Signatures

Author: _____   Editor: _____

Correcting Errors. After students proofread their compositions, they correct the errors they've found individually or with an editor's assistance. Some errors are easy to correct, some require use of a dictionary, and others involve instruction from the teacher. It's unrealistic to expect students to locate and correct every mechanical error in their compositions. Not even published books are error free! Once in a while, students change a correct spelling and make it incorrect, but they correct far more errors than they create.

Editing can end after students and their editors correct as many mechanical errors as possible, or after students conference with the teacher for a final editing. When mechanical correctness is crucial, this conference is important. Teachers proofread the composition with the student, and they make the remaining corrections together, or the teacher makes checkmarks in the margin to note errors for the student to correct independently.

Stage 5: Publishing

During this stage, students bring their compositions to life by publishing them or sharing them orally with an appropriate audience. When they share their writing with classmates, other students, parents, and community members, students come to think of themselves as authors. In this stage, students

- make final copies of their writing;

- read from the author's chair;
- share their writing.

Making Final Copies. One of the most popular ways for students to publish their writing is by making books. Simple booklets can be made by folding a sheet of paper into quarters, like a greeting card. Students write the title on the front and use the three remaining sides for their compositions. They can also construct booklets by stapling sheets of writing paper together and adding construction paper covers. These stapled booklets can be cut into various shapes, too. Students can make more sophisticated books by covering cardboard covers with contact paper, wallpaper, or cloth; pages are sewn or stapled together, and the first

Meeting the Needs of English Learners

How Do Teachers Adapt the Writing Process for English Learners?

Stage 1: Prewriting

- Use drawing as a rehearsal activity.
- Have students "talk out" their compositions with a classmate before beginning to write.
- Brainstorm ideas and vocabulary words with students.

Stage 2: Drafting

- Have students dictate their rough drafts.
- Reassure students that spelling and other mechanical skills aren't important in this stage.

Stage 3: Revising

- Have students share their rough drafts with a trusted classmate before meeting in a writing group.
- Expect students to make only one or two revisions at first.

Stage 4: Editing

- Focus on one type of grammar/usage error at a time.
- Have students mark possible errors; then correct errors with them.
- Have students identify and correct errors on the first page of their compositions; then correct the remaining errors with students.

Stage 5: Publishing

- Provide opportunities for students to share their writing with classmates.
- Don't correct any remaining errors on the final copy.

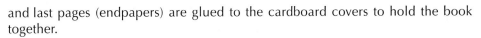

and last pages (endpapers) are glued to the cardboard covers to hold the book together.

The Author's Chair. Teachers designate a special chair in their classroom as "the author's chair" (Graves & Hansen, 1983). This chair might be a rocking chair, a lawn chair with a padded seat, a wooden stool, or a director's chair, and it should be labeled "Author's Chair." Students sit in the chair to read aloud books they have written, and this is the only time anyone sits there.

When students share their writing, one student sits in the author's chair, and a group of classmates sit on the floor or in chairs in front of the author's chair (Karelitz, 1993). The student sitting in the author's chair reads the writing aloud and shows the accompanying illustrations. After the reading, classmates who want to comment raise their hands, and the author chooses several classmates to ask questions and give compliments. Then the author chooses another student to share and takes a seat in the audience.

Most students really enjoy reading their writing aloud to their classmates, and they learn about the importance of audience as they watch for their classmates' reactions. And classmates benefit from the experience as well: They get ideas for their own writing as they listen to how other students use sentence patterns and vocabulary that they might not be familiar with. The process of sharing their writing brings closure to the writing process and energizes students for their next writing project.

Sharing Writing. In addition to reading their writing to classmates, students share their writing in other ways, too. They may share it with larger audiences through hardcover books placed in the class or school library, plays performed for classmates, or letters sent to authors, businesses, and other correspondents. Here are other ways to share writing:

- Submit the piece to writing contests
- Display the writing as a mobile
- Contribute to a class anthology
- Submit it to a literary magazine
- Read it at a school assembly
- Share at a read-aloud party
- Share with parents and siblings
- Send it to a pen pal
- Post it on an e-zine
- Design a poster about the writing
- Read it to children in other classes

Through this sharing, students communicate with audiences who respond to their writing in meaningful ways.

Sharing writing is a social activity that helps students develop sensitivity to audiences and confidence in themselves as authors. Dyson (1985) advises that teachers consider the social interpretations of sharing—students' behavior, teacher's behavior, and interaction between students and teacher—within the classroom context. Individual students interpret sharing differently. More than just providing the opportunity for students to share writing, teachers need to teach students how to respond to their classmates. Teachers themselves serve as a model for responding to students' writing without dominating the sharing.

Teaching the Writing Process

Students learn to use the writing process as they write compositions in literature focus units and thematic units and as they participate in writing workshop. Learning to use the writing process is more important than any particular writing projects students might be involved in, because the writing process is a tool.

One way to introduce the writing process is to write a collaborative or group composition. The teacher models the writing process and provides an opportunity for students to practice the process approach to writing in a supportive environment. As students and teacher write a composition together, they move through the five stages of the writing process, just as writers do when they work independently. The teacher demonstrates the strategies writers use and clarifies misconceptions during the group composition, and students offer ideas for writing as well as suggestions for tackling common writing problems.

The teacher begins by introducing the idea of writing a group composition and reviewing the project. Students dictate a rough draft, which the teacher records on the chalkboard or on chart paper. The teacher notes any misunderstandings students have about the writing assignment or process and, when necessary, reviews concepts and offers suggestions. Then the teacher and students read the composition and identify ways to revise it. Some parts of the composition will need reworking, and other parts may be deleted or moved. More specific words will be substituted for less specific ones, and redundant words and sentences will be deleted. Students may also want to add new parts to the composition. After making the necessary content changes, students proofread the composition, checking for mechanical errors, for paragraph breaks, and for sentences to combine. They correct errors and make changes. Then the teacher or a student copies the completed composition on chart paper or on a sheet of notebook paper. Copies can be made and given to each student. Collaborative compositions are an essential part of many writing experiences,

How the Writing Process Fits Into the Four Patterns of Practice

Literature Focus Units

Students use the writing process as they create projects during the applying stage of the reading process.

Literature Circles

The writing process is not usually associated with literature circles because the focus is on reading, not writing.

Reading and Writing Workshop

Students regularly move through the stages of the writing process as they write stories, informational books, and other compositions.

Thematic Units

Students often create writing projects as part of thematic units, and they use the writing process to develop and refine their projects.

especially when students are learning to use the writing process because they serve as a dry run during which students' questions and misconceptions can be clarified.

Teachers also use minilessons to teach students how to gather and organize ideas for writing, how to participate in writing groups, how to proofread, and how to share their writing. Teachers teach these procedures, concepts, and strategies and skills during minilessons. Minilessons can be taught as part of class collaborations, during literature focus units and thematic units, and in writing workshop. Topics for minilessons on the writing process are listed on page 98, and a minilesson on one of the topics, revising, is presented on page 99. Many teachers use the editing stage as a time to informally assess students' spelling, capitalization, punctuation, and other mechanical skills and to give minilessons on a skill that students are having trouble with.

The Qualities of Effective Writing

Vicki Spandel (2005, 2008) and her colleagues at the Northwest Regional Educational Laboratory examined student writing to identify the traits or qualities of effective writing. Through their research, they identified these six traits: ideas, organization, voice, word choice, sentence fluency, and conventions. When students learn about these traits, they grow in their understanding of what effective writing looks like and develop a vocabulary to talk about writing. In a multiyear study, Culham (2003) found that teaching students about the six traits improves the quality of their writing.

◆ **Trait 1: Ideas** Ideas are the "heart of the message" (Culham, 2003, p. 11). When ideas are well developed, the writing is clear and focused. Effective details elaborate the big ideas and create images in readers' minds. As students examine this trait, they develop these abilities:

- Choosing original and interesting ideas
- Narrowing and focusing ideas
- Choosing details to develop an idea
- Using the senses to add imagery

Esperanza Rising (Ryan, 2000), the story of a girl and her mother who flee from Mexico and find work in California as migrant workers, demonstrates how effective authors develop ideas. The book's title emphasizes the theme: The main character's name is Esperanza, the Spanish word for *hope*, and she rises above her difficult circumstances. At the beginning of the book, Pam Muñoz Ryan paints a vivid picture of Esperanza's comfortable life on her family's ranch in Mexico, and later in the story, she creates a powerful contrast as she describes Esperanza's harsh existence in a migrant labor camp. As the story ends, Esperanza remains hopeful, telling her good friend Isabel never to be afraid of starting over.

◆ **Trait 2: Organization** Organization is the internal structure of a composition; its function is to enhance the central idea. Spandel (2001) explains that organization is putting "information together in an order than informs, persuades, or entertains" (p. 39). The logical pattern of the ideas varies according to genre; stories, for example, are organized differently than nonfiction or poetry. As students learn about organization, they develop these abilities:

- Using structural patterns in their writing
- Crafting leads to grab the readers' attention

What Students Need to Learn About the Reading and Writing Processes

Topics

Procedures	Concepts	Strategies and Skills
The Reading Process	**The reading process**	
Do shared reading		Predict
Do buddy reading	Aesthetic reading	Visualize
Do guided reading	Efferent reading	Make connections
Do independent reading	Comprehension	Make inferences
Respond in reading logs		Summarize
Participate in grand conversations		Monitor
Create projects		
The Writing Process	**The writing process**	
Choose a topic		Gather ideas
Cluster	Functions of writing	Organize ideas
Quickwrite	Writing forms	Draft
Participate in writing groups	Audience	*Revise*
Write "All About the Author" pages	Proofreaders' marks	
Share published writing	Author's chair	Proofread

I invite you to explore some of these topics by visiting MyEducationLab. To examine how a sixth-grade teacher involves students in a prewriting activity and how fourth graders participate in editing, go to the topic "Writing" and click on the videos "Prewriting" and "Editing." If you'd like to see how third graders create charts about the writing process, go to the topic "Visually Representing" and click on the video "Charts: The Writing Process."

Minilesson

Ms. Yarborough Introduces Revising to Third Graders

1 **Introduce the topic**

Ms. Yarborough names the five stages of the writing process as she points to the writing process charts hanging in the classroom. She explains that the focus today is on revising and points to that chart. She reminds children that the purpose of revising is to make their writing better and explains that writers add, delete, substitute, and move words and sentences as they revise.

2 **Share examples**

Ms. Yarborough shares this paragraph on the chalkboard and explains that she wrote it because they are studying about amphibians:

> *Amphibians live in water and on land. They live in water when they are babies. They live on land when they grow up. Frogs are some amphibians.*

She reads the paragraph aloud and asks the class to help her make it better by adding, deleting, substituting, and moving words and sentences.

3 **Provide information**

Children work with Ms. Yarborough to revise the paragraph. They add words and sentences and reorder sentences in the paragraph. As children make suggestions, Ms. Yarborough writes the changes on the chalkboard. Here is the revised paragraph:

> *Amphibians live part of their lives in water and part on land. Frogs, toads and salamanders are amphibians. They hatch from eggs in water, grow up, and live on land when they are adults. This process of changing is called metamorphosis.*

4 **Supervise practice**

Ms. Yarborough divides children into small groups and gives each group another paragraph about amphibians to revise. Children work together to make revisions, using blue pens and making marks as Ms. Yarborough demonstrated. Ms. Yarborough circulates as they work, and then children share their rough drafts and revised paragraphs with the class.

5 **Reflect on learning**

Ms. Yarborough asks children to compare the rough drafts and revised paragraphs and decide which are better. Then children brainstorm a list of reasons why revision is important. Their list includes: "The writing is more interesting," "It's more fun to read," and "The words are more scientific."

- Using transition words to link ideas together
- Writing satisfying endings

Louis Sachar's award-winning novel *Holes* (1998) is a well-organized story about a hapless boy named Stanley Yelnats who is wrongly convicted of theft and sent to Camp Green Lake, a juvenile detention facility where he spends every day digging holes. The beginning, middle, and end of the story are easy to pick out: The beginning is before Stanley arrives at Camp Green Lake, the middle is while he's there, and the end is when he escapes and redeems himself. What makes this book unique is the second plot about a curse that has followed the Yelnats family for generations. As the book ends, Stanley fulfills his destiny by digging up the truth and unraveling the family curse.

◆ *Trait 3: Voice* Voice is the writer's style; it's what breathes life into writing. Culham (2003) calls it "the soul of the piece" (p. 12). The writer's voice can be humorous or compelling, reflective or persuasive. What matters most is that the author connects with readers. Students develop their own voices in these ways:

- Retelling familiar stories from the viewpoints of different characters
- Assuming a persona and writing from that person's viewpoint
- Using strong verbs
- Avoiding redundancy and vague wording

Catherine, Called Birdy (Cushman, 1994), the fictional diary of a rebellious teenager in medieval England, has a compelling voice that keeps you reading from the first page to the last. In this witty first-person account of daily life, Birdy recounts how she avoids marrying any of the rich suitors that her father brings to meet her. Her journal entries have an authentic ring because they're infused with period details and sprinkled with exclamations, such as "corpus bones" and "God's thumbs," that sound plausible.

◆ *Trait 4: Word choice* Carefully chosen words have the power to clarify meaning or to create a mood. It's important for writers to choose words that fit both their purpose and the audience to whom their writing is directed. Students increase their word knowledge through literature focus units and lots of reading. As students experiment with word choice, develop these abilities:

- Using precise nouns, vivid verbs, and colorful modifiers
- Consulting a thesaurus to consider options
- Avoiding tired words and phrases
- Using wordplay

Readers appreciate the importance of careful word choice in Pamela Duncan Edwards's collection of alliterative stories, including *Clara Caterpillar* (2001), *Some Smug Slug* (1996), and *The Worrywarts* (2003). These tongue-twister books are fun to read aloud.

◆ *Trait 5: Sentence fluency* Sentence fluency is "the rhythm and flow of carefully structured language that makes it both easy and pleasurable to read aloud" (Spandel, 2001, p. 101). Effective sentences vary in structure and length, and students are now encouraged to include some sentence fragments to add rhythm and energy to their writing (Culham, 2003). Teachers teach students about sentence structure so that they develop these abilities:

- Varying sentence structure and length
- Including some sentence fragments

- Beginning sentences in different ways
- Combining or expanding sentences

In *Old Black Fly* (Aylesworth, 1992), a pesky fly goes on an alphabetical rampage until he is finally stopped by a fly swatter. The rhythm and flow of the snappy couplets make this a popular read-aloud book, and after reading, students are eager to try their hand at creating an imitative poem featuring an old grinning grasshopper or an old slippery seal.

◆ *Trait 6: Conventions* Conventions guide readers through the writing. Mechanics, paragraphing, and design elements are three types. Writers check that they've used Standard English mechanics—spelling, punctuation, capitalization, and grammar—as a courtesy to readers. They verify that their division of the text into paragraphs enhances the organization of the ideas. They also create a design for their compositions and arrange the text on the page to enhance readability. Students learn to apply these conventions during the editing and publishing stages of the writing process:

- Proofreading to identify mechanical errors
- Using a dictionary to correct spelling errors
- Checking paragraphing
- Adding design elements to the final copy

The importance of punctuation is highlighted in *Punctuation Takes a Vacation* (Pulver, 2003). After reading the book, teachers can remove the punctuation in excerpts from a familiar book so students can see what happens when "punctuation takes a vacation." The page layout is important in many picture books. In Jan Brett's *The Umbrella* (2004), a story set in the rain forest, and in many of her other books, illustrations on the edge of the left-hand pages show what happened on the previous page, and illustrations on the edge of the right-hand pages show what will happen next.

Teaching the Six Traits. A good way to introduce the six traits is by having students examine what makes a favorite book effective. For example, in Janet Stevens and Susan Stevens Crummel's *Jackalope* (2003), the story of a jackrabbit who wishes to be feared so his fairy godrabbit gives him horns, there's a lot to like. A class of fourth graders identified these qualities:

- The story is told by an armadillo. (Ideas, Organization)
- Armadillo sounds like he's a cowboy. (Voice)
- The story mentions fairy tales and nursery rhymes. (Ideas)
- The beginning, middle, and end are easy to pick out. (Organization)
- Some of the sentences rhyme. (Sentence fluency)
- What the armadillo says is typed in colored boxes. (Conventions)
- The funny vegetable wordplays are italicized so you are sure to notice them. (Word choice, Conventions)
- Jack is a good character because he saved the fairy godrabbit. (Ideas)
- The theme is clear: You should be happy being yourself. (Ideas)
- We didn't find any spelling or punctuation or capitalization mistakes. (Conventions)

Later, the students reread their comments and classified them according to the traits they illustrate, and like many of the best books available for children today, *Jackalope* exemplifies all of them!

Teachers introduce the six traits one by one through a series of minilessons. They explain the characteristics of the trait using stories and other books as models. Once students have some knowledge of the trait, they examine how other students applied the trait in sample compositions, and then they revise other sample compositions to incorporate the trait. Next, they apply what they've learned in their own writing.

Linking the Six Traits to the Writing Process. The writing process is a cyclical series of activities that students use as they draft and refine their writing, but it doesn't specify how to make writing better. That's where the six traits come in: Students apply what they've learned about the traits to improve the quality of their writing, particularly during the revising and editing stages (Culham, 2003).

As students reread their rough drafts, they can check that their writing exemplifies each of the traits. Teachers can develop rubrics that focus on one or more traits that students can use to self-assess their writing. Students also ask classmates in a revising group for feedback about how they might improve their sentence fluency, organization, or another trait. The six traits provide another reason for students to carefully proofread their rough drafts. They learn that they correct mechanical errors and check paragraphing to improve the readability of their compositions. Students also think about the design for their published compositions. They decide how to arrange the text on the page in order to make their writing more understandable, and with word processing, students can make their writing look very professional.

Connections Between Reading and Writing

Reading and writing are both meaning-making processes, and readers and writers are involved in remarkably similar activities. Tierney (1983) explains that reading and writing involve concurrent, complex transactions between readers and writers. Writers participate in several types of reading activities; for example, they read other authors' works to obtain ideas and to learn about the structure of stories and other texts, but they also read and reread their own work to discover, monitor, and clarify. The quality of these reading experiences seems closely tied to success in writing. Readers are writers, too: They participate in many of the same activities that writers use—generating ideas, organizing, monitoring, problem solving, and revising.

The reading and writing processes have comparable stages (Butler & Turbill, 1984). Figure 3–8 shows the stages of reading and writing and the similar activities at each stage. For example, notice the similarities between the activities listed for the third stage of reading and writing—responding and revising, respectively. Fitzgerald (1989) analyzed these activities and concluded that they draw on similar processes of author-reader-text interactions. Similar analyses can be made for activities in the other stages as well.

Readers and writers use similar strategies for constructing meaning as they interact with print. As readers, we use a variety of problem-solving strategies to make decisions about an author's meaning and to construct meaning for ourselves. As writers, we also use problem-solving strategies to decide what our readers need as we construct meaning for them and for ourselves. Tierney and Pearson (1983) compare reading to writing by describing reading as a composing process because readers compose and refine meaning through reading, much as writers do.

FIGURE 3–8

A Comparison of the Reading and Writing Processes

	What Readers Do	**What Writers Do**
Stage 1	*Prereading*	*Prewriting*
	Readers use knowledge about • the topic • reading • literature • language systems	Writers use knowledge about • the topic • writing • literature • language systems
	Readers' expectations are cued by • previous reading/writing experiences • genre • purpose for reading • audience for reading	Writers' expectations are cued by • previous reading/writing experiences • genre • purpose for writing • audience for writing
	Readers preview the text and make predictions.	Writers gather and organize ideas.
Stage 2	*Reading*	*Drafting*
	Readers • use word-identification strategies • use comprehension strategies • monitor reading • create meaning	Writers • use spelling strategies • use writing strategies • monitor writing • create meaning
Stage 3	*Responding*	*Revising*
	Readers • respond to the text • clarify misunderstandings • develop interpretations	Writers • respond to the text • clarify misunderstandings • develop interpretations
Stage 4	*Exploring*	*Editing*
	Readers examine the text by • considering the impact of words and literary language • exploring structural elements • comparing the text to others	Writers examine the text by • correcting mechanical errors • reviewing paragraph and sentence structure
Stage 5	*Applying*	*Publishing*
	Readers • develop projects to extend knowledge • share projects with classmates • reflect on the reading process • value the piece of literature • feel success • want to read again	Writers • produce the finished copy of their compositions • share their compositions with genuine audiences • reflect on the writing process • value the composition • feel success • want to write again

Adapted from Butler & Turbill, 1984.

Teachers can help students appreciate the similarities between reading and writing and understand the importance of connecting the two language arts when they follow these guidelines:

- Involve students in daily reading and writing activities.
- Introduce the reading and writing processes in kindergarten.
- Talk with students about the similarities between the reading and writing processes.
- Teach students about the reading and writing strategies.
- Emphasize both the processes and the products of reading and writing.
- Emphasize the purposes for which students use reading and writing.
- Teach reading and writing using genuine literacy experiences.

Tierney explains: "What we need are reading teachers who act as if their students were developing writers and writing teachers who act as if their students were readers" (1983, p. 151). Reading contributes to students' writing development, and writing contributes to students' reading development (Schulze, 2006; Shanahan, 1988).

Review

Reading and writing are similar processes of constructing meaning. Teachers organize reading and writing instruction using the five stages of the reading and writing processes. Students learn to use the reading and writing processes through literature focus units, literature circles, reading and writing workshop, and thematic units. Here are the key concepts presented in this chapter:

- Students use aesthetic reading when they read for enjoyment and efferent reading when they read for information.
- Four factors in developing capable readers are word identification, fluency, vocabulary, and comprehension.
- The five stages of the reading process are prereading, reading, responding, exploring, and applying.
- Five ways to read a selection are shared reading, guided reading, independent reading, buddy reading, and listening as it is read aloud.
- Students use the reading process during literature focus units, literature circles, reading workshop, and thematic units.
- The five stages of the writing process are prewriting, drafting, revising, editing, and publishing.
- Purpose, form, and audience influence students' compositions.
- Students use the writing process as they write during literature focus units, writing workshop, and thematic units.
- Teachers present minilessons on procedures, concepts, and strategies and skills in the reading and writing processes.
- The goal of both reading and writing is to construct meaning, and the two processes have comparable activities at each stage.

Professional References

Allen, J. (1999). *Words, words, words*. Portsmouth, NH: Heinemann.

Angelillo, J. (2005). *Making revision matter*. New York: Scholastic.

Barnes, D., Morgan, K., & Weinhold, K. (Eds.). (1997). *Writing process revisited: Sharing our stories*. Urbana, IL: National Council of Teachers of English.

Blachowicz, C., & Fisher, P. (2006). *Teaching vocabulary in all classrooms* (3rd ed.). Upper Saddle River, NJ: Merrill/Prentice Hall.

Blanton, W. E., Wood, K. D., & Moorman, G. B. (1990). The role of purpose in reading instruction. *The Reading Teacher, 43*, 486–493.

Britton, J., Burgess, T., Martin, N., McLeod, A., & Rosen, H. (1975). *The development of writing abilities, 11–18*. London: Schools Council Publications.

Bromley, K. D. (1996). *Webbing with literature: Creating story maps with children's books* (2nd ed.). Boston: Allyn & Bacon.

Butler, A., & Turbill, J. (1984). *Towards a reading-writing classroom*. Portsmouth, NH: Heinemann.

Calkins, L. M. (1980). When children want to punctuate: Basic skills belong in context. *Language Arts, 57*, 567–573.

Calkins, L. M. (1994). *The art of teaching writing* (2nd ed.). Portsmouth, NH: Heinemann.

Calkins, L., Hartman, A., & White, Z. (2005). *One to one: The art of conferring with young writers*. Portsmouth, NH: Heinemann.

Culham, R. (2003). *6 + 1 traits of writing: The complete guide, grades 3 and up*. New York: Scholastic.

Dowhower, S. L. (1991). Speaking of prosody. Fluency's unattended bedfellow. *Theory Into Practice, 30*, 165–173.

Dyson, A. H. (1985). Second graders sharing writing: The multiple social realities of a literacy event. *Written Communication, 2*, 189–215.

Dyson, A. H. (1986). The imaginary worlds of childhood: A multimedia presentation. *Language Arts, 63*, 799–808.

Eeds, M., & Peterson, R. L. (1995). What teachers need to know about the literary craft. In N. L. Roser & M. G. Martinez (Eds.), *Book talk and beyond: Children and teachers respond to literature* (pp. 10–23). Newark, DE: International Reading Association.

Faigley, L., & Witte, S. (1981). Analyzing revision. *College Composition and Communication, 32*, 400–410.

Fisher, B., & Medvic, E. F. (2000). *Perspectives on shared reading: Planning and practice*. Portsmouth, NH: Heinemann.

Fitzgerald, J. (1989). Enhancing two related thought processes: Revision in writing and critical thinking. *The Reading Teacher, 43*, 42–48.

Flower, L., & Hayes, J. R. (1994). The cognition of discovery: Defining a rhetorical problem. In S. Perl (Ed.), *Landmark essays on writing process* (pp. 63–74). Davis, CA: Heragoras Press.

Fountas, I. C., & Pinnell, G. S. (1996). *Guided reading: Good first teaching for all children*. Portsmouth, NH: Heinemann.

Fountas, I. C, & Pinnell, G. S. (2001). *Guiding readers and writers, grades 3–6*. Portsmouth, NH: Heinemann.

Gardner, H. (2000). *Intelligence reframed: Multiple intelligences for the 21st century*. New York: Basic Books.

Gillet, J. W., & Beverly, L. (2001). *Directing the writing workshop: An elementary teacher's handbook*. New York: Guilford Press.

Graves, D. H. (1994). *A fresh look at writing*. Portsmouth, NH: Heinemann.

Graves, D. H., & Hansen, J. (1983). The author's chair. *Language Arts, 60*, 176–183.

Holdaway, D. (1979). *The foundations of literacy*. Portsmouth, NH: Heinemann.

Irwin, J. W. (1993). *Teaching reading comprehension processes* (2nd ed.). Boston: Allyn & Bacon.

Karelitz, E. B. (1993). *The author's chair and beyond: Language and literacy in a primary classroom*. Portsmouth, NH: Heinemann.

Lane, B. (1993). *After the end: Teaching and learning creative revision*. Portsmouth, NH: Heinemann.

Lane, B. (1999). *The reviser's toolbox*. Shoreham, VT: Discover Writing Press.

Langer, J. A. (1985). Children's sense of genre. *Written Communication, 2*, 157–187.

Murray, D. H. (1982). *Learning by teaching*. Montclair, NJ: Boynton/Cook.

National Reading Panel. (2000). *Teaching children to read: An evidence-based assessment of the scientific research literature on reading and its implications for reading instruction, reports of the subgroups*. Washington, DC: National Institute of Child Health and Human Development.

Opitz, M. F., & Rasinski, T. V. (1998). *Good-bye round robin: Twenty-five effective oral reading strategies*. Portsmouth, NH: Heinemann.

Pardo, L. W. (2004). What every teacher needs to know about comprehension. *The Reading Teacher, 58*, 272–280.

Pearson, P. D., & Gallagher, M. (1983). The instruction of reading comprehension. *Contemporary Educational Psychology, 8*, 317–344.

Perl, S. (1994). Understanding composing. In S. Perl (Ed.), *Landmark essays on writing process* (pp. 99–106). Davis, CA: Heragoras Press.

Peterson, R., & Eeds, M. (1990). *Grand conversations: Literature groups in action*. New York: Scholastic.

Pressley, M. (2002). Comprehension strategies instruction: A turn-of-the-century status report. In C. C. Block & M. Pressley (Eds.), *Comprehension instruction: Research-based practices* (pp. 11–27). New York: Guilford Press.

Rasinski, T. V. (2004). Creating fluent readers. *Educational Leadership, 61*(6), 46–51.

Rosenblatt, L. M. (2005). *Making meaning with texts: Selected essays*. Portsmouth, NH: Heinemann.

Routman, R. (1996). *Literacy at the crossroads: Crucial talk about reading, writing, and other teaching dilemmas*. Portsmouth, NH: Heinemann.

Schulze, A. C. (2006). *Helping children become readers through writing*. Newark DE: International Reading Association.

Shanahan, T. (1988). The reading-writing relationship: Seven instructional principles. *The Reading Teacher, 41*, 636–647.

Smith, F. (1982). *Writing and the writer*. New York: Holt, Rinehart and Winston.

Sommers, N. (1994). Revision strategies of student writers and experienced adult writers. In S. Perl (Ed.), *Landmark essays on writing process* (pp. 75–84). Davis, CA: Heragoras Press.

Spandel, V. (2001). *Books, lessons, ideas for teaching the six traits: Writing in the elementary and middle grades*. Wilmington, MA: Great Source Education Group.

Spandel, V. (2005). *Creating writers: Through 6-trait writing assessment and instruction* (4th ed.). Boston: Allyn & Bacon.

Spandel, V. (2008). *Creating young writers: Using the six traits to enrich writing process in primary classrooms* (2nd ed.). Boston: Allyn & Bacon.

Stahl, S. A. (1999). *Vocabulary development*. Cambridge, MA: Brookline Books.

Sweet, A. P., & Snow, C. E. (2003). Reading for comprehension. In A. P. Sweet & C. E. Snow (Eds.), *Rethinking reading comprehension* (pp. 1–11). New York: Guilford Press.

Taylor, D. (1993). *From the child's point of view*. Portsmouth, NH: Heinemann.

Tierney, R. J. (1983). Writer-reader transactions: Defining the dimensions of negotiation. In P. L. Stock (Ed.), *Forum: Essays on theory and practice in the teaching of writing* (pp. 147–151). Upper Montclair, NJ: Boynton/Cook.

Tierney, R. J., & Pearson, P. D. (1983). Toward a composing model of reading. *Language Arts, 60*, 568–580.

Weaver, C. (1996). *Teaching grammar in context*. Portsmouth, NH: Heinemann.

Yaden, D. B., Jr. (1988). Understanding stories through repeated read-alouds: How many does it take? *The Reading Teacher, 41*, 556–560.

Children's Book References

Aylesworth, J. (1992). *Old black fly*. New York: Henry Holt.

Brett, J. (2004). *The umbrella*. New York: Putnam.

Butterworth, C. (2006). *Sea horse: The shyest fish in the sea*. Cambridge, MA: Candlewick Press.

Creech, S. (2003). *Granny Torrelli makes soup*. New York: HarperCollins.

Curtis, C. P. (1999). *Bud, not Buddy*. New York: Delacorte.

Cushman, K. (1994). *Catherine, called Birdy*. New York: HarperCollins.

Danziger, P. (1995). *Amber Brown goes fourth*. New York: Putnam.

Edwards, P. D. (1996). *Some smug slug*. New York: HarperCollins.

Edwards, P. D. (2001). *Clara caterpillar*. New York: HarperCollins.

Edwards, P. D. (2003). *The worrywarts*. New York: HarperCollins.

Fowler, A. (1990). *It's a good thing there are insects*. Chicago: Childrens Press.

Hale, S. (2005). *Princess academy*. New York: Bloomsbury.

Howe, D., & Howe, J. (2006). *Bunnicula: A rabbit-tale of mystery*. New York: Aladdin Books.

Lowry, L. (2006). *The giver*. New York: Delacorte.

Pulver, R. (2003). *Punctuation takes a vacation*. New York: Holiday House.

Ryan, P. M. (2000). *Esperanza rising*. New York: Scholastic.

Sachar, L. (1998). *Holes*. New York: Farrar, Straus & Giroux.

Stevens, J., & Crummel, S. S. (2003). *Jackalope*. San Diego: Harcourt Brace.

chapter four

Emerging Into Literacy

In Mrs. Kirkpatrick's kindergarten–first grade multiage classroom, the children participate in weeklong literature focus units. She uses the featured book for shared reading and center activities that children work on while she teaches guided reading groups using leveled books at children's reading levels. This week's featured book is *If You Give a Mouse a Cookie* (Numeroff, 1985), a circular story about a mouse who, after receiving a cookie, wants a glass of milk, a straw, a napkin, other items, and finally another cookie. Mrs. Kirkpatrick has copies of both the regular-size and the big book versions of the story as well as copies of four other books by the same author that incorporate the same circular pattern, *If You Give a Moose a Muffin* (Numeroff, 1991), *If You Give a Pig a Pancake* (Numeroff, 1998), *If You Take a Mouse to the Movies* (Numeroff, 2000), and *If You Take a Mouse to School* (2002).

Mrs. Kirkpatrick teaches language arts for 2 1/2 hours each morning. Children sample cookies and talk about their favorite cookies on Monday before Mrs. Kirkpatrick begins to read the featured book using shared reading. Children read and reread the big book version of the story several times, and each time they are able to read more of the words themselves. The predictable pattern of the text and picture clues make it easier for the children to be successful. Later in the week, the children read the regular-size versions of the book individually or with buddies. Mrs. Kirkpatrick moves through the

*H*ow do teachers support children's emergence into reading and writing?

In kindergarten and first grade, children acquire phonemic awareness and phonics knowledge, learn to recognize and print the letters of the alphabet, and develop concepts about print. Literature focus units facilitate children's emergence into literacy because the book provides the foundation for a combination of direct instruction and authentic reading and writing activities. As you read this vignette, notice how Mrs. Kirkpatrick provides instruction and opportunities to nurture her students' emergence into literacy.

reading process as children respond to the story in a grand conversation, compare it to other circular stories that Laura Numeroff has written, and draw pictures and write in reading logs.

The children also participate in exploring-stage activities. Mrs. Kirkpatrick draws their attention to specific words in the story, and together they write vocabulary words on a word wall. She also teaches high-frequency words, which are posted on another word wall in the classroom. One of the high-frequency words this week is *you*; the children locate the word again and again in the story and reread all the high-frequency words that have been posted on the word wall in the classroom. Mrs. Kirkpatrick teaches minilessons on phonics concepts, using sample words from the featured book to make the connection that phonics knowledge is useful for reading and writing. She also teaches minilessons about irregular plurals after children ask whether *mouses* or *mice* is the correct plural form. They also practice reading skills at centers.

Children work on two culminating projects. They write pages for a class book following Laura Numeroff's pattern and using their own names. For example: *If you give Graciela a bag of popcorn, she will want a glass of juice.* They also make a cookie quilt to hang on the wall of the classroom. Each child makes a square for the paper quilt by designing a cookie in the center of the square and writing or dictating a sentence that is written underneath. The box on page 110 presents a stage-by-stage outline showing how Mrs. Kirkpatrick teaches the book *If You Give a Mouse a Cookie.*

Later in the morning, Mrs. Kirkpatrick meets with children in small groups for guided reading while their classmates work in centers. Two sixth graders come to the classroom to help supervise centers so Mrs. Kirkpatrick can concentrate on the reading groups. The activities at most of the centers are related to the featured book. For example, at one center, children retell the story by sequencing objects or cards with pictures of objects related to the story. A list of the centers in Mrs. Kirkpatrick's classroom is shown on page 111. Three of the centers are required, and they are marked with an asterisk in

Outline for a Literature Focus Unit on *If You Give a Mouse a Cookie*

1. **Prereading**
   - The teacher brings in several types of cookies for children to sample. Children talk about their favorite cookies, and they create a graph to chart their favorite cookies.
   - The teacher introduces the book using a big book version of the story.
   - The teacher shares a book box of objects or pictures of objects mentioned in the story (cookie, glass of milk, straw, napkin, mirror, scissors, broom, etc.), and children talk about how some of the items might be used in the story.
   - Children and the teacher begin the word wall with *cookie* and *mouse.*

2. **Reading**
   - The teacher reads the big book version of *If You Give a Mouse a Cookie* using shared reading.
   - The teacher rereads the book, and children join in when they can or they repeat each sentence after the teacher reads it.

3. **Responding**
   - The children and the teacher participate in a grand conversation about the book.
   - Children dramatize the story using objects in the book box.
   - Children draw pictures in reading logs and add words and sentences (using invented spelling) to record their reactions to the book.

4. **Exploring**
   - Children and teacher add interesting and important words to the word wall.
   - Children read regular-size versions of the book with partners and reread the book independently.
   - The teacher teaches minilessons on the /m/ sound or other phonemic awareness or phonics concepts.
   - The teacher explains the concept of a circular story, and children sequence picture cards of the events in the story to make a circle diagram.
   - The teacher presents a minilesson about the author, Laura Numeroff, and reads other books by the author.
   - Children make word posters of words on the word wall.
   - The teacher teaches a minilesson on irregular plurals (e.g., *mouse–mice, child–children*).
   - The teacher sets up centers for children to sort objects related to the phonemic awareness/phonics lesson, listen to *If You Give a Moose a Muffin* (Numeroff, 1991) and other books by the author, write books about cookies, and use cards to sequence story events.

5. **Applying**
   - Children write their own versions of the story or original circle stories.
   - Children create a cookie quilt.

The Centers in Mrs. Kirkpatrick's Classroom

Comprehension Center
Children wear a mouse hand puppet as they sequence objects and retell *If You Give a Mouse a Cookie.* Copies of the book are available at the center to use to check the order of events in the story.

Phonics Center*
Children sort a collection of objects into baskets labeled with letters. *Mm* is this week's featured letter and sound, and Mrs. Kirkpatrick has set out these *Mm* objects: toy mouse, milk carton, marble, toy monkey, macaroni, play money, mitten, and toy man. In addition, she sets out books with other phonics activities that are appropriate for children in each of the guided reading groups.

Listening Center
Children listen to books written by Laura Numeroff and write and draw pictures in their reading logs.

Writing Center*
Children make books about cookies, write a retelling of the story, or write a new version of the story. A poster with cookie labels and names of cookies and a word wall with words related to the story are posted nearby.

Quilt Center
Children make cookie blocks for the class paper quilt. A variety of art materials are available at the center for children to use.

High-Frequency Word Center
Children mark *you,* the high-frequency word of the week, and other familiar high-frequency words on charts posted at the center using Wikki-Stix (pipe cleaners covered in wax) shaped into circles. They also use magnetic letters, plastic linking letters, or foam letters to practice spelling the words.

Reading Center*
Children select and read leveled books independently. Leveled books arranged in plastic tubs are available at the center for children to choose from.

---

*Required centers

the figure. The others are free choice, and children must complete at least two of them during the week. They work at their own pace and move freely from center to center, carrying their work folders with them. Stapled inside the folders is a weekly list of centers, and the sixth-grade aides place a stamp beside the name of the center when children complete work there.

---

*I*s there a magic age when children become readers and writers? Researchers used to think that at the age of 6, most children were ready to learn to read and write, but now we know that children begin the process of becoming literate gradually during the preschool years. Very young children notice signs, logos, and other environmental print. Who hasn't observed children making scribbles on paper as they try to "write"? As children are read to, they learn how to hold a book and turn pages, and they observe how the text is read. Most children come to kindergarten and first grade with sophisticated knowledge about written language and experiences with reading and writing.

The current approach to language arts instruction in kindergarten through second grade reflects the process known as *emergent literacy*. New Zealand educator Marie Clay (1967) is credited with coining the term. Now, researchers look at literacy learning from the child's point of view, and the age range has been extended to include children as young as 12 or 14 months of age who listen to stories being read aloud, notice labels and signs in their environment, and experiment with pencils. The concept of literacy has broadened, too, to incorporate the cultural and social aspects of language learning, and children's experiences with and understanding of written language—both reading and writing—are included as part of emergent literacy.

Teale and Sulzby (1989) paint a portrait of young children as literacy learners with these characteristics:

- Learning the functions of literacy through observing and participating in real-life settings in which reading and writing are used
- Developing reading and writing abilities concurrently and interrelatedly through experiences in reading and writing
- Constructing their understanding of reading and writing through active involvement with literacy materials

They describe young children as active learners who construct their own knowledge about reading and writing with the assistance of parents and other literate people. These caregivers help by demonstrating literacy as they read and write, by supplying materials, and by structuring opportunities for children to be involved in reading and writing. The environment is positive, with children experiencing reading and writing in many facets of their everyday lives and observing others who are engaged in literacy activities.

The No Child Left Behind Act of 2001 has brought unprecedented attention to how young children learn to read and write. Teachers and administrators, parents, researchers, and policy makers are all focused on ensuring that every child reads at grade level by the end of third grade. Although all of the interested groups have the same goal, they are divided on the most effective ways to teach language arts in the primary grades. Many state and national policy makers contend that "scientific" evidence specifies that a skills-based, direct instruction approach is the most effective way, but many teachers and researchers believe in a balanced approach of blending direct instruction with reading and writing (Barone & Morrow, 2003; Burns, Griffin, & Snow, 1999; International Reading Association/National Association for the Education of Young Children, 1998; Moats, 1999; National Reading Panel, 2000; Stanovich, 2000). The approach taken in this book is that children are more successful when teachers use research-based practices to provide direct instruction within the context of meaningful literacy activities.

As you continue reading about young children's literacy development, think about these questions:

- How do teachers foster young children's interest in literacy?
- How do young children develop as readers and writers?
- What teaching strategies do teachers use in teaching reading and writing?

FOSTERING YOUNG CHILDREN'S INTEREST IN LITERACY

Children's introduction to written language begins before they come to school (Vuke-lich & Christie, 2004). Parents and other caregivers read to young children, and the children observe adults reading. They learn to read signs and other environmental print in their community. Children experiment with writing and have parents write for them. They also observe adults writing. When young children come to kindergarten, their knowledge about written language expands quickly as they participate in meaningful experiences with reading and writing.

Students also grow in their ability to stand back and reflect on language. The ability to talk about concepts of language is called *metalinguistics* (Yaden & Templeton, 1986), and children's ability to think metalinguistically develops through experiences with reading and writing.

Concepts About Written Language

Through experiences at home and at school, young children learn that print carries meaning and that reading and writing are used for a variety of purposes (Bennett-Armistead, Duke, & Moses, 2005). They read menus in restaurants to know what foods are being served, write and receive letters to communicate with friends and relatives, and read (and listen to) stories for enjoyment. Children also learn as they observe parents and teachers using written language for all of these purposes.

Children's understanding about the purposes of reading and writing reflects how written language is used in their community. Although reading and writing are part of daily life for almost every family, families use written language for different purposes in different communities (Heath, 1983). It is important to realize that children have a wide range of literacy experiences in both middle- and working-class families, even though those experiences might be different (Taylor & Dorsey-Gaines, 1987). In some communities, written language is used mainly as a tool for practical purposes, such as paying bills, and in some communities, reading and writing are also used for leisure-time activities. In other communities, written language serves even wider functions, such as debating social and political issues.

Teachers demonstrate the purposes of written language and provide opportunities for children to experiment with reading and writing in these ways:

- Posting signs in the classroom
- Making a list of classroom rules
- Using literacy materials in dramatic play centers
- Writing notes to students in the class
- Exchanging messages with classmates
- Reading and writing stories
- Making posters about favorite books
- Labeling classroom items
- Drawing and writing in journals
- Writing morning messages
- Recording questions and information on charts
- Writing notes to parents

- Reading and writing letters to pen pals
- Reading and writing charts and maps

Concept of a Word. Children's understanding of the concept of a "word" is an important part of becoming literate. Young children have only vague notions of language terms, such as *word, letter, sound,* and *sentence,* that teachers use in talking about reading and writing (Invernizzi, 2003). Preschoolers equate words with the objects the words represent. As they are introduced to reading and writing experiences, children begin to differentiate between objects and words, and finally they come to appreciate that words have meanings of their own.

Several researchers have investigated children's understanding of a word as a unit of language. Papandropoulou and Sinclair (1974) identified four stages of word consciousness. At the first level, young children don't differentiate between words and things. At the next level, children describe words as labels for things. They consider words that stand for objects as words, but don't classify articles and prepositions as words because words such as *the* and *with* cannot be represented with objects. At the third level, children understand that words carry meaning and that stories are built from words. At the fourth level, more fluent readers and writers describe words as autonomous elements having meanings of their own with definite semantic and syntactic relationships. Children might say, "You make words with letters." Also, at this level, children understand that words have different appearances—they can be spoken, listened to, read, and written.

Environmental Print. Young children's "reading" experiences often begin with environmental print. Many children begin reading by recognizing logos on fast-food restaurants, department stores, grocery stores, and commonly used household items within familiar contexts (Harste, Woodward, & Burke, 1984). They recognize the golden arches of McDonald's and say "McDonald's," but when they are shown the word *McDonald's* written on a sheet of paper without the familiar sign and restaurant setting, they cannot yet read the word. Researchers have found that young emergent readers depend on context to read familiar words and memorized texts (Sulzby, 1985). Slowly, children develop relationships linking form and meaning as they learn concepts about written language and gain more experience reading and writing.

When children begin writing, they use scribbles or single letters to represent complex ideas (Clay, 1991). As they learn about letter names and phoneme-grapheme correspondences, they use one, two, or three letters to stand for a word. At first they run their writing together, but they slowly learn to segment words and leave spaces between words. They sometimes add dots or lines as markers between words, or they draw circles around words. They also move from capitalizing words randomly to using a capital letter at the beginning of a sentence and to mark proper nouns. Similarly, children move from using periods at the end of each line of writing to marking the ends of sentences with periods. Then they learn about other end-of-sentence markers and, finally, about punctuation marks that are embedded in sentences.

Literacy Play Centers. Young children learn about the functions of reading and writing as they use written language in their play. As they construct block buildings, children write signs and tape them on the buildings; as they play doctor, they write prescriptions on slips of paper; and as they play teacher, they read stories aloud to friends who are pretending to be students or to doll and stuffed-animal "students." Young children use these activities to reenact familiar, everyday activities and to

Anne Vega/Merrill

Literacy Play Centers
These kindergartners use reading and writing as they play in the housekeeping center. They read recipes and food-package labels as they cook, for example, and write telephone messages when they answer the telephone. They also leave messages for classmates who will visit this center. After "baking" clay cookies, these children wrote this message using invented spelling: GD KE R U (good cookies for you). Through these activities, young children learn to value reading and writing because of the important role literacy can play in their lives.

pretend to be someone or something else. Through these literacy-enriched play activities, children use reading and writing for a variety of functions.

Kindergarten teachers adapt play centers and add literacy materials to enhance their value for literacy learning. Housekeeping centers are probably the most common play centers in kindergarten classrooms, but teachers can transform them into grocery stores, post offices, or medical centers by changing the props (Bennett-Armistead, Duke, & Moses, 2005). Materials for reading and writing can be included in each of these centers. Food packages, price stickers, and money are props in grocery store centers; letters, stamps, and mailboxes in post office centers; and appointment books, prescription pads, and folders for patient records in medical centers. A variety of literacy play centers can be set up in classrooms to coordinate with thematic units. Ideas for literacy play centers are offered in Figure 4–1; each center includes authentic literacy materials that children can experiment with and use to learn more about the functions of written language.

Concepts About the Alphabet

Young children also develop concepts about the alphabet and how letters are used to represent phonemes. Children use this phonics knowledge to decode unfamiliar words as they read and to create spellings for words as they write. Too often it is assumed that phonics instruction is the most important component of the reading

---

FIGURE 4–1

Literacy Play Centers With Reading and Writing Materials

Post Office Center

mailboxes	wrapping paper	package seals
envelopes	tape	address labels
stamps (stickers)	packages	cash register
pens	scale	money

Hairdresser Center

hair rollers	towel	curling iron (cordless)
brush and comb	posters of hairstyles	ribbons, barrettes, clips
mirror	wig and wig stand	appointment book
empty shampoo bottle	hair dryer (cordless)	open/closed sign

Restaurant Center

tablecloth	napkins	aprons/vests for waitstaff
dishes	menus	hat and apron for chef
glasses	tray	
silverware	order pad and pencil	

Medical Center

appointment books	stethoscope	folders (for patient
white shirt/jacket	thermometer	records)
medical bag	tweezers	prescription bottles
hypodermic syringe	bandages	and labels
(play)	prescription pad	walkie-talkie

Grocery Store Center

grocery cart	price stickers	marking pen
food packages	cash register	cents-off coupons
plastic fruit and	money	advertisements
artificial foods	grocery bags	

---

program for young children, but phonics is only one of the four language systems. Emergent readers and writers use all four language systems—phonological, semantic, syntactic, and pragmatic—as well as their knowledge about written language concepts as they read and write.

The Alphabetic Principle. The one-to-one correspondence between the phonemes (or sounds) and graphemes (or letters), such that each letter consistently represents one sound, is known as the *alphabetic principle*. In phonetic languages, there is a one-to-one correspondence; however, English is not a purely phonetic language. The 26 letters represent approximately 44 phonemes, and three letters—*c, q,* and *x*—are superfluous because they do not represent unique phonemes. The letter *c*, for example, can represent either /k/ as in *cat* or /s/ as in *city*, and it can be joined with *h* for the digraph /ch/. To further complicate matters, there are more than 500 spellings to represent the 44 phonemes. Consonants are more consistent and predictable than vowels. Long *e*, for instance, is spelled more than 10 ways in common words.

Words are spelled phonetically approximately half the time (Hanna, Hanna, Hodges, & Rudorf, 1966). The nonphonetic spellings of many words reflect morphological information. The word *sign*, for instance, is a shortened form of *signature*, and the spelling shows this relationship. Spelling the word phonetically (i.e., *sine*) might seem simpler, but the phonetic spelling lacks semantic information (Venezky, 1999).

Letter Names. The most basic information children learn about the alphabet is to identify letter names and form the letters in handwriting. They notice letters in environmental print, and they often learn to sing the ABC song. Five-year-olds can usually recognize some letters, especially those in their own names, in names of family members and pets, and in common words in their homes and communities. They can also write some of these familiar letters.

Young children associate letters with meaningful contexts—names, signs, T-shirts, and cereal boxes. Research suggests that children do not learn alphabet letter names in any particular order or by isolating letters from meaningful written language. McGee and Richgels (2003, 2007) concluded that learning letters of the alphabet requires many, many experiences with meaningful written language. They recommend that teachers take three steps to encourage children's alphabet learning:

◆ *Capitalize on children's interests.* Teachers provide letter activities that children enjoy and talk about letters when children are interested in talking about them. Teachers know what features to comment on because they observe children during reading and writing activities to find out which letters or letter features children are exploring. Children's questions also provide insights into what they are curious about.

◆ *Talk about the role of letters in reading and writing.* Teachers talk about how letters represent sounds and how letters combine to spell words, and they point out capital and lowercase letters. Teachers often talk about the role of letters as they write with children.

◆ *Teach routines and provide opportunities for alphabet learning.* Teachers use children's names and environmental print in literacy activities, do interactive writing, encourage children to use invented spellings, share alphabet books, and play letter games to teach the letters of the alphabet.

Teachers begin teaching letters of the alphabet using two sources of words—children's own names and environmental print. They also teach children to sing the ABC song so that they will have a strategy to use to identify a particular letter: Children sing the song and point to each letter on an alphabet chart until they reach the unfamiliar letter. This is an important strategy because it gives them a real sense of independence in identifying letters. Teachers also provide routines, activities, and games for talking about and manipulating letters. During these familiar, predictable activities, teachers and children say letter names, manipulate magnetic letters, and write letters on dry-erase boards. At first the teacher structures and guides the activities, but with experience, the children internalize the routine and do it independently, often at a literacy center. Figure 4–2 presents 10 routines to teach the letters of the alphabet.

It's crucial that instruction to teach children to identify and print the letters of the alphabet be embedded in meaningful and authentic reading and writing experiences (McGee & Richgels, 2003). Instruction is meaningful when children can tie what they are learning to their own world and authentic when children can apply what they are learning to reading and writing stories and other books. Children recognize and write

FIGURE 4–2

Routines to Teach the Letters of the Alphabet

Environmental Print
Teachers collect food labels, toy traffic signs, and other environmental print for children to use in identifying letters. Children sort labels and other materials to find examples of a letter being studied.

Alphabet Books
Teachers read aloud alphabet books to build vocabulary and teach the names of words that represent each letter. Then children reread the books and consult them to think of words when making books about a letter.

Magnetic Letters
Children pick all examples of one letter from a collection of magnetic letters or match upper- and lowercase letterforms of magnetic letters. They also arrange the letters in alphabetical order and use the letters to spell their names and other familiar words.

Letter Stamps
Students use letter stamps and ink pads to stamp letters on paper or in booklets. They also use letter-shaped sponges to paint letters and letter-shaped cookie cutters to make cookies and to cut out clay letters.

Key Words
Teachers use alphabet charts with a picture of a familiar object for each letter. It is crucial that children be familiar with the objects or they won't remember the key words. Teachers recite the alphabet with children, pointing to each letter and saying, "A—apple, B—bear, C—cat," and so on.

Letter Containers
Teachers collect coffee cans or shoe boxes, one for each letter of the alphabet. They write upper- and lowercase letters on the outsides of the containers and place several familiar objects or pictures of objects that represent the letter in each one. Teachers use these containers to introduce the letters, and children use them at a center for sorting and matching activities.

Letter Frames
Teachers make circle-shaped letter frames from tagboard, collect large plastic bracelets, or shape pipe cleaners or Wikki-Stix (pipe cleaners covered in wax) into circles for students to use to highlight particular letters on charts or in big books.

Letter Books and Posters
Children make letter books with pictures of objects beginning with a particular letter on each page. They add letter stamps, stickers, or pictures cut from magazines. For posters, the teacher draws a large letterform on a chart and children add pictures, stickers, and letter stamps.

Letter Sorts
Teachers collect objects and pictures representing two or more letters. Then children sort the objects and place them in containers marked with the specific letters.

Dry-Erase Boards
Children practice writing upper- and lowercase forms of a letter and familiar words on dry-erase boards.

the letters found in environmental print and in their classmates' names, find familiar letters and words on classroom signs and in books, write letters and words as they respond to literature, and make books.

Being able to name the letters of the alphabet is a good predictor of beginning reading achievement, even though knowing the names of the letters doesn't directly affect a child's ability to read (Adams, 1990). A more likely explanation for this relationship between letter knowledge and reading is that children who have been actively involved in reading and writing activities before entering first grade know the names of the letters, and they are more likely to begin reading quickly. Simply teaching children to name the letters without the accompanying reading and writing experiences does not have this effect.

Phonemic Awareness. *Phonemic awareness* is children's basic understanding that speech is composed of a series of individual sounds, and it provides the foundation for phonics (Yopp, 1992). When children can choose a duck as the animal that begins with /d/ from a collection of toy animals, identify *duck* and *luck* as rhyming words, or blend the sounds /d/ /ŭ/ /k/ to pronounce *duck*, they're phonemically aware. (Note that the emphasis is on the sounds of spoken words, not reading letters or pronouncing letter names.) Developing phonemic awareness enables children to use sound-symbol correspondences to read and spell words. It isn't sounding out words for reading or using spelling patterns to write words; rather, it's the ability to manipulate sounds orally.

Understanding that words are composed of smaller units—phonemes—is a significant achievement for young children because phonemes are abstract language units. Phonemes carry no meaning, and children think of words according to their meanings, not their linguistic characteristics (Griffith & Olson, 1992). When children think about ducks, for example, they think of animals covered with feathers that swim in ponds and make noises we describe as "quacks"; they don't think of *duck* as a word with three phonemes or four graphemes or as a word beginning with /d/ and rhyming with *luck*. Phonemic awareness requires that children treat speech as an object. They shift their attention away from the meaning of words to the linguistic features of speech. This focus on phonemes is even more complicated because phonemes are not discrete units in speech. Often they are slurred together; think about the blended initial sound in *tree* and the ending sound in *eating*.

Children develop phonemic awareness in two ways. They learn playfully as they sing songs, chant rhymes, and listen to parents and teachers read wordplay books to them. Yopp (1995) recommends that teachers read books with wordplay aloud and encourage children to talk about the books' language. Teachers ask questions and make comments, such as "Did you notice how _____ and _____ rhyme?" and "This book is fun because of all the words beginning with the _____ sound." Once children are very familiar with the book, they can create new verses or make other variations. Books such as *Cock-a-doodle-moo!* (Most, 1996), *The Hungry Thing* (Slepian & Seidler, 2001), and *The Stuffed Animals Get Ready for Bed* (Inches, 2006) stimulate children to experiment with sounds, create nonsense words, and become enthusiastic about reading. When teachers read books with alliterative or assonant patterns, such as *Busy Buzzing Bumblebees and Other Tongue Twisters* (Schwartz, 1992), children attend to the smaller units of language.

Teachers also teach lessons to help children understand that their speech is composed of sounds (Ball & Blachman, 1991). The goal of phonemic awareness activities is to break down and manipulate spoken words. Children who have developed phonemic awareness can manipulate spoken language in these five ways:

- Match words by sounds
- Isolate a sound in a word
- Blend individual sounds to form a word
- Substitute sounds in a word
- Segment a word into its constituent sounds (Yopp, 1992)

Teachers teach minilessons focusing on each of these tasks using familiar songs with improvised lyrics, riddles and guessing games, and wordplay books. These activities should be playful and gamelike. Five types of activities are described in Figure 4–3.

Children experiment with oral language in phonemic awareness activities. Teachers have avoided asking children to read and write letters and words during these activities because the focus is on speech. More recently, however, teachers are finding that once children develop a rudimentary level of phonemic awareness, the activities are more effective when teachers begin with an oral language activity and then move into decoding and spelling words.

The relationship between phonemic awareness and learning to read is extremely important, and researchers have concluded that at least some level of phonemic awareness is a prerequisite for learning to read (Gillon, 2004). In fact, phonemic awareness seems to be both a prerequisite for and a consequence of learning to read (Perfitti, Beck, Bell, & Hughes, 1987). As they become phonemically aware, children recognize that speech can be segmented into smaller units, and this knowledge is very useful when children learn about sound-symbol correspondences and spelling patterns. Moreover, phonemic awareness has been shown to be the most powerful predictor of later reading achievement (Lomax & McGee, 1987). Klesius, Griffith, and Zielonka (1991) found that children who began first grade with strong phonemic awareness did well regardless of the kind of reading instruction they received.

Phonics. *Phonics* is the set of relationships between phonology (the sounds in speech) and orthography (the spelling patterns of written language). Sounds are spelled in different ways, for several reasons. One reason is that sounds, especially vowels, vary according to their location in a word (e.g., *go–got*). Adjacent letters often influence how letters are pronounced (e.g., *bed–bead*), as do vowel markers such as the final *e* (e.g., *bit–bite*) (Shefelbine, 1995).

Phonics is a very controversial topic. Some parents and politicians, as well as even a few teachers, believe that most of the educational ills in the United States could be solved if children were taught to read using phonics. A few people still argue that phonics is a complete reading program, but that view ignores what we know about the interrelatedness of the four language systems. Reading is a complex process, and the phonological system works in conjunction with the semantic, syntactic, and pragmatic systems, not in isolation.

The controversy now centers on how to teach phonics. Marilyn Adams (1990), in her landmark review of the research on phonics instruction, recommends that phonics be taught within a balanced approach that integrates instruction in reading skills and strategies with meaningful opportunities for reading and writing. She emphasizes that phonics instruction should focus on the most useful information for identifying words; it also should be systematic and intensive, and it should be completed by the third grade.

FIGURE 4–3

Types of Phonemic Awareness Activities

Sound-Matching Activities

Teachers create matching games using familiar objects and pictures. From a collection, including a football, a car, a fish, and a toothbrush, children choose the two that begin with the same sound. Or, children choose one of several items beginning with a particular sound. Children also identify rhyming words. They name a word that rhymes with a given word and identify rhyming words from familiar songs and books.

Sound-Isolation Activities

Children identify the sounds at the beginning, middle, or end of the word, or teachers can set out a tray of objects and ask children to choose the one that doesn't belong because it doesn't begin with the sound. From a tray with a toy pig, a puppet, a teddy bear, and a pen, for example, the teddy bear doesn't belong. Yopp (1992) created new verses to the tune of "Old MacDonald Had a Farm":

> What's the sound that starts these words:
> Chicken, chin, and cheek?
> (wait for response)
> /ch/ is the sound that starts these words:
> Chicken, chin, and cheek.
> With a /ch/, /ch/ here, and a /ch/, /ch/ there,
> Here a /ch/, there a /ch/, everywhere a /ch/, /ch/.
> /ch/ is the sound that starts these words:
> Chicken, chin, and cheek. (p. 700)

Teachers change the question at the beginning of the verse to focus on medial and final sounds.

Sound-Blending Activities

Children play the "What am I thinking of?" guessing game. The teacher identifies several characteristics of an object and then pronounces its name, articulating each of the sounds separately (Yopp, 1992). Then children blend the sounds together and identify the word using both the phonological and the semantic information that the teacher provided. For example:

> I am thinking of an animal that lives in a pond when it's young, but that lives on land when it's an adult. It's a /f/ /r/ /ŏ/ /g/. What is it?

The children blend the sounds together to pronounce the word *frog*.

Sound-Addition or -Substitution Activities

Students create nonsense words as they add or substitute sounds in words in songs they sing or in books that are read aloud to them. Teachers read wordplay books, such as Hutchins's *Don't Forget the Bacon!* (1976), in which a boy leaves for the store with a mental list of four items to buy. As he walks, he repeats his list, substituting sounds and creating new words each time. "A cake for tea" changes to "a cape for me" and then to "a rake for leaves." Children suggest other substitutions, such as "a pail for maple sugar trees." They also substitute sounds in refrains of songs (Yopp, 1992). For example, children can change the "Ee-igh, ee-igh, oh!" refrain in "Old MacDonald Had a Farm" to "Bee-bigh, bee-bigh, boh!" to focus on the initial /b/ sound. Teachers choose one sound, such as /sh/, and have children substitute this sound for the beginning sound in their names and in familiar words. For example, *José* becomes *Shosé* and *clock* becomes *shock*.

Segmentation Activities

Children slowly pronounce a word, identifying all its sounds. Yopp (1992) suggests singing a song to the tune of "Twinkle, Twinkle, Little Star" in which children segment entire words. Here is one example:

> Listen, listen, to my word.
> Then tell me all the sounds you heard: *coat*
> /k/ is one sound, /o/ is two
> /t/ is last in *coat*; it's true. (p. 702)

After several repetitions of the verse segmenting other words, the song ends this way:

> Thanks for listening to my words
> And telling all the sounds you heard! (p. 702)

Teachers teach sound-symbol correspondences, how to blend sounds to decode words and segment sounds for spelling, and the most useful phonics generalizations, or "rules." Phonics concepts build on phonemic awareness. The most important concepts that primary-grade students learn—consonants, vowels, rimes and rhymes, phonics generalizations—are explained in the next sections.

◆ *Consonants* Letters are classified as either consonants or vowels. The consonants are *b, c, d, f, g, h, j, k, l, m, n, p, q, r, s, t, v, w, x, y,* and *z.* Most consonants represent a single sound consistently, but there are some exceptions. *C,* for example, does not represent a sound of its own: When it is followed by *a, o,* or *u,* it is pronounced /k/ (e.g., *castle, coffee, cut*), and when it is followed by *e, i,* or *y,* it is pronounced /s/ (e.g., *cell, city, cycle*). *G* represents two sounds, as the word *garbage* illustrates. It is usually pronounced /g/ (e.g., *glass, go, green, guppy*), but when *g* is followed by *e* or *i,* it is pronounced /j/, as in *giant. Gy* is not a common English spelling, but when *g* is followed by *y* (e.g., *energy, gypsy, gymnasium*), it is usually pronounced /j/. *X* is also pronounced differently according to its location in a word. When *x* is at the beginning of a word, it is often pronounced /z/, as in *xylophone,* but sometimes the letter name is used, as in *x-ray.* At the end of a word, *x* is pronounced /ks/, as in *box.*

The letters *w* and *y* are particularly interesting. At the beginning of a word or syllable, they are consonants (e.g., *wind, yard*), but when they are in the middle or at the end of a word or syllable, they are vowels (e.g., *saw, flown, day, by*).

Two kinds of combination consonants are blends and digraphs. *Consonant blends* are two or three consonants that appear next to each other in words and whose individual sounds are blended together, as in *grass, belt,* and *spring. Consonant digraphs* are letter combinations that represent single sounds. The four most common are *ch* as in *chair* and *each, sh* as in *shell* and *wish, th* as in *father* and *both,* and *wh* as in *whale.* Another consonant digraph is *ph,* as in *graph* and *photo.*

◆ *Vowels* The remaining five letters—*a, e, i, o,* and *u*—represent vowels, and *w* and *y* are also vowels when used in the middle and at the end of syllables and words. Vowels represent several sounds. The most common are short and long vowels. The short vowel sounds are /ă/ as in *cat,* /ĕ/ as in *bed,* /ĭ/ as in *win,* /ŏ/ as in *hot,* and /ŭ/ as in *cup.* The long vowel sounds are the same as the letter names, and they are illustrated in the words *make, feet, bike, coal,* and *suit.* Long vowels are usually spelled with two vowels, except when *e* or *y* is used at the end of a word or syllable (e.g., *belong, try*).

When *y* is a vowel at the end of a word, it is pronounced as long *e* or long *i,* depending on the length of the word. In one-syllable words, such as *by* and *try,* the *y* is pronounced as long *i,* but in most longer words, such as *baby* and *happy,* the *y* is pronounced as long *e.*

Vowel sounds are more complicated than consonant sounds, and many vowel combinations represent long vowels and other vowel sounds. Consider these combinations:

ai as in *nail*	*oa* as in *soap*
au as in *laugh* and *caught*	*oi* as in *oil*
aw as in *saw*	*oo* as in *cook* and *moon*
ea as in *peach* and *bread*	*ou* as in *house* and *through*
ew as in *sew* and *few*	*ow* as in *now* and *snow*
ia as in *dial*	*oy* as in *toy*
ie as in *cookie*	

Most vowel combinations are vowel digraphs or diphthongs. When two vowels represent a single sound, the combination is a vowel digraph (e.g., *nail, snow*), and when two vowels represent a glide from one sound to another, the combination is a diphthong. Two vowel combinations that are consistently diphthongs are *oi* and *oy*, but other combinations, such as *ou* in *house* (but not in *through*) and *ow* in *now* (but not in *snow*) are diphthongs when they represent a glided sound. In *through*, the *ou* represents the o͞o sound as in *moon*, and in *snow*, the *ow* represents the ō sound.

When *r* follows one or more vowels in a word, it influences the pronunciation of the vowel sound, as in *car, air, are, ear, bear, first, for, more, murder*, and *pure*. These sounds are called *r*-controlled vowels. Because they are difficult to sound out, students learn many of these words as sight words.

The vowels in the unaccented syllables of multisyllabic words are often softened and pronounced "uh," as in the first syllable of *about* and *machine* and the final syllable of *pencil, tunnel, zebra*, and *selection*. This vowel sound is called a *schwa* and is represented in dictionaries with ə, which looks like an inverted *e*.

Rimes and Rhymes. One-syllable words and syllables in longer words can be divided into two parts, the onset and the rime. The onset is the consonant sound, if any, that precedes the vowel and the rime is the vowel and any consonant sounds that follow it. For example, in *show, sh* is the onset and *ow* is the rime, and in *ball, b* is the onset and *all* is the rime. For *at* and *up*, there is no onset; the entire word is the rime. Research has shown that children make more errors decoding and spelling final consonants than initial consonants and that they make more errors on vowels than on consonants (Treiman, 1985). These problem areas correspond to rimes, and educators now speculate that teaching onsets and rimes could provide a key to developing children's phonemic awareness.

Children can focus their attention on a rime, such as *ay*, and create rhyming words, including *bay, day, lay, may, play, say*, and *way*. These words can be read and spelled by analogy because the vowel sounds are consistent in rimes. Wylie and Durrell (1970) identified 37 rimes that can be used to produce nearly 500 words that primary-grade students read and write. These rimes and some common words using them are presented in Figure 4–4.

Phonics Generalizations. Because English does not have a one-to-one correspondence between sounds and letters, both linguists and educators have created rules or generalizations to clarify English spelling patterns. One rule is that *q* is followed by *u* and pronounced /kw/ (e.g., *queen* and *earthquake*). There are very few exceptions to this rule. Another generalization that has few exceptions relates to *r*-controlled vowels: *r* influences the preceding vowel so that its sound is neither long nor short (e.g., *car, market, birth*, and *four*). There are exceptions, however; for instance, *fire*.

Many generalizations aren't very useful because there are more exceptions to the rule than words that conform (Clymer, 1996). A good example is the "when two vowels go walking" rule: When there are two vowels side by side, the long vowel sound of the first one is pronounced and the second is silent. Examples of words conforming to this rule are *meat, soap*, and *each*. There are more exceptions, however, including *food, said, head, chief, bread, look, soup, does, too, again*, and *believe*.

Only a few phonics generalizations have a high degree of utility for readers. The generalizations that work most of the time are the ones that students should learn because they are the most useful (Adams, 1990). Eight high-utility generalizations are listed in the LA Essentials box on the next page. Even though these rules are fairly reliable, very few of them approach 100% utility. The *r*-controlled vowel rule is useful in 78% of words in which the letter *r* follows the vowel (Adams, 1990). Other commonly taught, useful rules have even lower percentages of utility. The CVC pattern rule—which says that when a one-syllable word has only one vowel and the vowel comes between two consonants, it is usually short, as in *bat, land*, and *cup*—is estimated to work 62% of the time. Exceptions include *told, fall, fork*, and *birth*. The CVCe pattern rule—which says that when there are two vowels in a one-syllable word and one vowel is an *e* at the end of the word, the first vowel is long and the final *e* is silent—is estimated to work in 63% of CVCe words. Examples of conforming words are *came, hole*, and *pipe*, and two very common exceptions are *have* and *love*.

Children learn phonics as a natural part of reading and writing activities, but teachers also teach phonics directly and systematically. They explain many phonics concepts as they engage children in authentic literacy activities using children's names, titles of books, and environmental print in the classroom. During these teachable moments, teachers answer children's questions about words, model how to use phonics knowledge to decode and spell words, and have children share the strategies they use for reading and writing (Mills, O'Keefe, & Stephens, 1992). For example, as part of a literature focus unit on *The Very Hungry Caterpillar* (Carle, 2001), teachers might point out that *very* begins with *v* but that not many words start with *v*. Children might mention other *v* words, such as *valentine*. Teachers also demonstrate how to apply phonics information as they read big books with the class and do interactive writing. As they read and spell words, teachers break words apart into sounds and apply phonics rules and generalizations.

FIGURE 4–4

37 Common Rimes

Rime	Examples	Rime	Examples
-ack	black, pack, quack, stack	-ide	bride, hide, ride, side
-ail	mail, nail, sail, tail	-ight	bright, fight, light, might
-ain	brain, chain, plain, rain	-ill	fill, hill, kill, will
-ake	cake, shake, take, wake	-in	chin, grin, pin, win
-ale	male, sale, tale, whale	-ine	fine, line, mine, nine
-ame	came, flame, game, name	-ing	king, sing, thing, wing
-an	can, man, pan, than	-ink	pink, sink, think, wink
-ank	bank, drank, sank, thank	-ip	drip, hip, lip, ship
-ap	cap, clap, map, slap	-ir	fir, sir, stir
-ash	cash, dash, flash, trash	-ock	block, clock, knock, sock
-at	bat, cat, rat, that	-oke	choke, joke, poke, woke
-ate	gate, hate, late, plate	-op	chop, drop, hop, shop
-aw	claw, draw, jaw, saw	-or	for, or
-ay	day, play, say, way	-ore	chore, more, shore, store
-eat	beat, heat, meat, wheat	-uck	duck, luck, suck, truck
-ell	bell, sell, shell, well	-ug	bug, drug, hug, rug
-est	best, chest, nest, west	-ump	bump, dump, hump, lump
-ice	ice, mice, nice, rice	-unk	bunk, dunk, junk, sunk
-ick	brick, pick, sick, thick		

THE MOST USEFUL PHONICS GENERALIZATIONS

Pattern	Description	Examples	
Two sounds of *c*	The letter *c* can be pronounced as /k/ or /s/. When *c* is followed by *a, o,* or *u*, it's pronounced /k/—the hard *c* sound. When *c* is followed by *e, i,* or *y*, it's pronounced /s/—the soft *c* sound.	cat cough cut	cent city cycle
Two sounds of *g*	The sound associated with the letter *g* depends on the letter following it. When *g* is followed by *a, o,* or *u*, it's pronounced /g/—the hard *g* sound. When *g* is followed by *e, i,* or *y*, it's usually pronounced /j/—the soft *g* sound. Exceptions include *get* and *give*.	gate go guess	gentle giant gypsy
CVC pattern	When a one-syllable word has only one vowel and the vowel comes between two consonants, it's usually short. One exception is *told*.	bat cup land	
Final *e* or CVCe pattern	When there are two vowels in a one-syllable word and one of them is an *e* at the end of the word, the first vowel is long and the final *e* is silent. Two exceptions are *have* and *love*.	home safe dune	
CV pattern	When a vowel follows a consonant in a one-syllable word, the vowel is long. Exceptions include *the, to,* and *do*.	go be	
r-controlled vowels	Vowels that are followed by the letter *r* are overpowered and are neither short nor long. One exception is *fire*.	car for birthday	
-igh	When *gh* follows *i*, the *i* is long and the *gh* is silent. Two exceptions are *neighbor* and *eight*.	high night	
kn- and *wr-*	In words beginning with *kn-* and *wr-*, the first letter isn't pronounced.	knee write	

Adapted from Clymer, 1996.

Teachers also present minilessons on specific high-utility phonics concepts, skills, and generalizations as part of a systematic program. According to Shefelbine, the program should be "systematic and thorough enough to enable most students to become independent and fluent readers; yet still efficient and streamlined" (1995, p. 2). Phonics instruction is always tied to reading and writing because without meaningful reading and writing activities, children see little reason to learn phonics (Cunningham, 2005; Freppon & Dahl, 1991).

YOUNG CHILDREN EMERGE INTO READING

Children move through three stages as they learn to read: emergent reading, beginning reading, and fluent reading (Juel, 1991). In emergent reading, children gain an understanding of the communicative purpose of print. They notice environmental print, dictate stories for the teacher to record, and reread predictable books after they have memorized the pattern. From this foundation, children move into the beginning reading stage. In this stage, children learn phoneme-grapheme correspondences and begin to decode words. In the third stage, fluent reading, children have learned how to read. They recognize most words automatically and can decode unfamiliar words quickly. Children should reach this fluent stage by third grade. Once they are fluent readers, children are able to concentrate more of their cognitive energy on comprehension. This accomplishment is significant because beginning in fourth grade, children read more informational books and content-area textbooks as reading becomes a learning tool.

Primary-grade teachers organize language arts instruction into the same four patterns of practice that teachers of middle- and upper-grade students use, but they make special adaptations to accommodate young children's developing literacy abilities. Two instructional adaptations that primary-grade teachers use are shared reading and the Language Experience Approach. Through these approaches, kindergartners, first graders, and second graders read big books aloud with classmates, independently read books appropriate for their reading levels, and create texts by dictating their own words for teachers to record.

Shared Reading

Teachers and children read books together in shared reading. Usually the teacher reads aloud as children follow along in regular-size or enlarged, big book picture books. Teachers use this approach to share the enjoyment of high-quality literature when students cannot read the books independently (Fisher & Medvic, 2000; Holdaway, 1979). As they read, teachers also demonstrate how print works, provide opportunities for children to use the prediction strategy, and increase children's confidence in their ability to read. Shared reading is often used with emergent readers; however, teachers also use shared reading with older students who cannot read independently. The steps in shared reading are listed in the Step by Step feature on the next page.

Predictable Books. The stories and other books teachers use for shared reading with young children often have repeated words and sentences, rhyme, or other patterns. Books that use these patterns are known as *predictable books*. They are a valuable instructional tool because the repeated words and sentences, patterns, and sequence enable children to predict the next sentence or episode in the story

Shared Reading

1 Introduce the book. Teachers introduce the book by activating children's prior knowledge about the topic or by presenting new information on a topic related to the book, and then by showing the cover of the book and reading the title and the author's name. Then children make predictions about what will happen in the book.

2 Read the book. The teacher reads the book aloud while children follow along in individual copies or on a big book positioned on a chart rack beside the teacher. The teacher models fluent reading and uses a dramatic style to keep the children's attention. Teachers encourage children to chime in on words they know and on refrains. Periodically, teachers ask children to make predictions to redirect their attention to the text.

3 Respond to the book. Children respond to the book by drawing and writing in reading logs and by sharing their responses in grand conversations.

4 Reread the book. Children take turns turning pages and using the pointer to track the text as they reread the book. Teachers invite children to join in reading familiar and predictable words. Also, they take advantage of teachable moments to explain graphophonic cues and reading strategies.

5 Continue the process. Teachers continue to reread the book with children one or two more times over a period of several days, again having them turn pages and take turns using the pointer to track the text while reading. They encourage children who can read the text to read along with them.

6 Have children read independently. After children become familiar with the text, teachers distribute individual copies of the book for them to read independently.

or other book (Tompkins & Webeler, 1983). Here are four characteristics of predictable books:

◆ *Repetition.* Phrases and sentences are repeated to create a predictable pattern in many books for young children. Examples include *I Went Walking* (Williams, 1990), *Barnyard Banter* (Fleming, 1994), and *Polar Bear, Polar Bear, What Do You Hear?* (Martin, 1992). Sometimes each episode or section ends with the same words or a refrain, and in other books, the same statement or question is repeated. For example, in *The Little Red Hen* (Pinkney, 2006), the animals repeat "Not I" when the Little Red Hen asks them to help her plant the seeds, harvest the wheat, and bake the bread. After their refusals to help, the hen each time says, "Then I will."

◆ *Cumulative Sequence.* Phrases or sentences are repeated and expanded in each episode in these books. In the traditional story *The Gingerbread Boy* (Galdone, 1983), for instance, Gingerbread Boy repeats and expands his boast as he meets each character on his run away from Little Old Man and Little Old Woman. Other examples include *Jack's Garden* (Cole, 1995) and *Jump, Frog, Jump!* (Kalan, 2002).

◆ *Rhyme and Rhythm.* Rhyme and rhythm are important devices in some books. Many of the popular Dr. Seuss books, such as *Hop on Pop* (2003), are good examples. The sentences have a strong beat, and rhyme is used at the end of each line or in another poetic scheme. Also, some books have an internal rhyme—within lines rather than at the ends of lines. Other books in this category include familiar songs, such as *Shoo Fly!* (Trapani, 2000), and booklong verses, such as *Pattern Fish* (Harris, 2000).

◆ *Sequential Patterns.* Some books use a familiar sequence—such as months of the year, days of the week, numbers 1 to 10, or letters of the alphabet—to structure the text. For example, *The Very Hungry Caterpillar* (Carle, 2001) combines number and day-of-the-week sequences as the caterpillar eats through an amazing array of foods, and *Shiver Me Letters: A Pirate ABC* (Sobel, 2006) incorporates an alphabet sequence. A list of predictable books illustrating each of these patterns is presented in the Booklist below.

Big Books. Teachers use enlarged picture books called *big books* in shared reading, most commonly with primary-grade students (Ditzel, 2000). In this technique, developed in New Zealand, teachers place the enlarged picture book on an easel or chart rack where all children can see it; the teacher reads the big book with small groups of children or with the whole class (Holdaway, 1979). Trachtenburg and Ferruggia (1989) used big books with their class of transitional first graders and found that making and reading big books dramatically improved children's reading scores on standardized achievement tests. The teachers reported that children's self-concepts as readers were decidedly improved as well.

Booklist

YOUNG CHILDREN'S BOOKS WITH PREDICTABLE PATTERNS

Repetitive Sentences ---

Florian, D. (2000). *A pig is big.* New York: Greenwillow.
Guarino, D. (1997). *Is your mama a llama?* New York: Scholastic.
Hoberman, M. A. (2001). *"It's simple," said Simon.* New York: Knopf.

Martin, B., Jr. (1992). *Brown bear, brown bear, what do you see?* New York: Holt.
Westcott, N. B. (2003). *The lady with the alligator purse.* Boston: Little, Brown.

Cumulative Sequence ---

Brett, J. (2004). *The umbrella.* New York: Putnam.
Egielski, R. (1997). *The gingerbread boy.* New York: HarperCollins.
Pinkney, J. (2006). *The little red hen.* New York: Dial Books.

Taback, S. (1997). *There was an old lady who swallowed a fly.* New York: Viking.
West, C. (1996). *"I don't care!" said the bear.* Cambridge, MA: Candlewick Press.

Rhyme and Rhythm ---

Harris, P. (2006). *The night pirates.* New York: Scholastic.
Lies, B. (2006). *Bats at the beach.* Boston: Houghton Mifflin.

Martin, B., Jr., & Archambault, J. (1989). *Chicka chicka boom boom.* New York: Aladdin Books.
Raffi. (1999). *Down by the bay.* New York: Crown.

Sequential Patterns ---

Carle, E. (1984). *The very busy spider.* New York: Philomel.
Kraus, R. (1995). *Come out and play, little mouse.* New York: HarperCollins.
Numeroff, L. J. (2002). *If you take a mouse to school.* New York: HarperCollins.

Wadsworth, O. A. (2002). *Over in the meadow.* New York: North-South Books.
Wood, A. (2004). *The napping house.* San Diego: Harcourt Brace.

Many popular picture books, including *Silly Sally* (Wood, 1999), *How Much Is a Million?* (Schwartz, 1994), *There was an Old Lady Who Swallowed a Fly* (Taback, 1997), *Click, Clack, Moo: Cows That Type* (Cronin, 2000), and *Eating the Alphabet: Fruits and Vegetables From A to Z* (Ehlert, 2006), are available in big book editions from Scholastic. Teachers and children can also make big books themselves by printing the text of a book on large sheets of posterboard and adding illustrations.

Cross-Age Reading Buddies. Another way to use shared reading in kindergarten and first grade is with cross-age reading buddies. Upper-grade students are paired with emergent readers, and the students become reading buddies. Older students read books with younger children, using shared reading techniques so that the younger children do more and more of the reading as they become familiar with the book. Research supports the effectiveness of cross-age tutoring, and teachers report that children's reading fluency increases and their attitudes toward school and learning become more positive (Caserta-Henry, 1996).

Teachers arranging a buddy reading program decide when the students will get together, how long each session will last, and what the reading schedule will be. Primary-grade teachers explain the program to their students and talk about activities the buddies will be doing together. Upper-grade teachers teach a series of minilessons about how to work with young children, how to read aloud and encourage children to make predictions, how to use shared reading, how to select books to appeal to younger children, and how to help them respond to books. Then older students choose books to read aloud and practice reading them until they can read the books fluently.

At the first meeting, students pair off, get acquainted, and read together. They also talk about the books they have read and perhaps write in special reading logs. Buddies also may want to go to the library and choose the books they will read at the next session.

There are significant social benefits to cross-age tutoring programs. Children get acquainted with other children that they might otherwise not meet, and they learn how to work with older or younger children. As they talk about books they have read, they share personal experiences. They also talk about reading strategies, how to choose books, and their favorite authors or illustration styles. Sometimes reading buddies write notes back and forth, or they plan holiday celebrations together to strengthen the social connections between the children.

Traveling Bags of Books. Another way to encourage shared reading is to involve parents by using traveling bags of books. Teachers collect text sets of three, four, or five books on various topics for children to take home and read with their parents (Reutzel & Fawson, 1990). For example, teachers might collect copies of *The Gingerbread Boy* (Galdone, 1975), *Gingerbread Baby* (Brett, 1999), *Red Fox Dances* (Baron, 1996), and *Rosie's Walk* (Hutchins, 2005) for a traveling bag of fox stories. Then children and their parents read one or more of the books and draw or write a response to the books they have read in the reading log that accompanies the books in the traveling bag. One family's response after reading *The Gingerbread Boy* is shown in Figure 4–5. In this entry, the kindergartner drew a picture of Gingerbread Boy, an older sibling wrote the sentence the kindergartner dictated to accompany the picture, and the children's mother also wrote a comment. Children keep the bag at home for several days and then return it to school so that another child can borrow it. Teachers can also

---

FIGURE 4–5

A Family's Reading Log Entry Written After Reading *The Gingerbread Boy*

SHAYLA

A gingerbréd boy
is runing away.

SHAYLA LOVES THIS BOOK! WE ALL DO! LAST NIGHT

WE MADE YUMMY GINGERBREAD COOKIES. THIS

WAS A FUN BOOK BAG. *Alice Garcia*

---

add small toys, stuffed animals, audiotapes of one of the books, or other related objects to the bags.

Teachers often introduce traveling bags at a special parents' meeting or an open house get-together and explain how parents use shared reading to read with their children. It is important for parents to understand that their children may not be familiar with the books and that they aren't expected to be able to read them independently. Teachers also talk about the responses that children and parents write in the reading log and show sample entries from the previous year.

Language Experience Approach

The Language Experience Approach (LEA) is based on children's language and experiences (Ashton-Warner, 1965; Stauffer, 1970). Children dictate words and sentences about their experiences, and the teacher takes down the dictation for them; the text they develop becomes the reading material. Because the language comes from the children themselves, and because the content is based on their experiences, they are usually able to read the text easily. Reading and writing are connected because children are actively involved in reading what they have written. The steps are shown in the Step by Step feature on page 131.

The Language Experience Approach is an effective way to help children emerge into reading. Even students who have not been successful with other types of reading activities can read what they have dictated. There is a drawback, however: Teachers

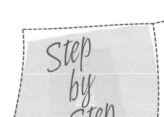

-------- Language Experience Approach --------

1 Provide an experience.   A meaningful experience is identified to serve as the stimulus for the writing. For group writing, it can be a book read aloud, a field trip, or some other experience—such as having a pet or playing in the snow—that all children are familiar with. For individual writing, the stimulus can be any experience that is memorable for the particular child.

2 Talk about the experience.   Children and the teacher discuss the experience prior to writing. The purpose of the talk is to review the experience and generate words so that children's dictation will be more interesting and complete. Teachers often begin with an open-ended question, such as, "What are you going to write about?" As children talk about their experiences, they generate and organize ideas and brainstorm more specific vocabulary.

3 Record the dictation.   Teachers write down the child's dictation. Texts for individual children are written on sheets of writing paper or in small booklets, and group texts are written on chart paper. Teachers print neatly and spell words correctly, but they preserve children's language as much as possible. For individual texts, teachers continue to take the child's dictation and write until he or she hesitates. Then the teacher rereads what has been written and encourages the child to continue. For group texts, children take turns dictating sentences, and after writing each sentence, the teacher rereads it.

4 Read the text.   After the text has been dictated, the teacher reads it aloud, pointing to each word. This reading reminds children of the content of the text and demonstrates how to read it aloud with appropriate intonation. Then children join in the reading. After reading group texts together, individual children can take turns rereading. Group texts can also be copied so that each child has a copy to read independently.

provide a "perfect" model when they take children's dictation—they write neatly and spell all words correctly. After Language Experience activities, some young children aren't eager to do their own writing, because they prefer their teacher's "perfect" writing to their own childlike writing. To avoid this problem, teachers have young children do their own writing concurrently with the Language Experience activities so that they learn that sometimes they do their own writing, and at other times, the teacher takes their dictation.

YOUNG CHILDREN EMERGE INTO WRITING

Many young children become writers before entering kindergarten; others are introduced to writing during their first year of school (Schulze, 2006). Young children's writing development follows a pattern similar to their reading development: emergent writing, beginning writing, and fluent writing. In the first stage, emergent writing, children make scribbles to represent writing. At first, the scribbles appear randomly on a page, but with experience, children line up the letters or scribbles from left to right and from top to bottom. Children also begin to "read," or tell what their writing says. The next stage is beginning writing, and it signals children's growing awareness of the alphabetic principle. Children use invented spelling to represent words, and as they learn more about phoneme-grapheme correspondences, their writing approximates conventional spelling. They move from writing single words to writing sentences and experiment with capital letters and punctuation marks. The third stage is fluent writing, when children write in paragraphs and vary their writing according to genre. They use mainly correct spelling and other conventions of written language, including capital letters and punctuation marks.

Opportunities for writing begin on the first day of kindergarten and continue daily throughout the primary grades, regardless of whether children have already learned to read or write letters and words. Children often begin using a combination of art and scribbles or letterlike forms to express themselves (Ditzel, 2000). Their writing moves toward conventional forms as they apply concepts that they are learning about written language.

Four samples of young children's writing are shown in Figure 4–6. The first sample is a kindergartner's letter to the Great Pumpkin; the writing is at the emergent stage. The child wrote using scribbles, much like cursive, and followed the left-to-right, top-to-bottom orientation. The Great Pumpkin's comment, "I love you all," can be deciphered. The second sample is characteristic of the beginning stage. A kindergartner wrote this list of favorite foods as part of a literature focus unit on *The Very Hungry Caterpillar* (Carle, 2001). The list reads, "orange, strawberry, apple, pizza, birthday cake." The third sample is another example of beginning-stage writing, which was taken from a first grader's reading log. The child used invented spelling to list the animal characters that appear in *The Mitten* (Brett, 1989). The fifth animal from the top is a badger. The fourth sample is a page from a first grader's dinosaur book. The text reads, "No one ever saw a real dinosaur," and this child used a capital letter to begin the sentence and a period to mark the end. This sample shows the transition from beginning to fluent writing.

Introducing Young Children to Writing

Young children's writing grows out of talking and drawing (Schickedanz & Casbergue, 2004). As they begin to write, their writing is literally their talk written down, and children can usually express in writing the ideas they talk about. At the same time, children's letterlike marks develop from their drawing. With experience, children learn to differentiate between their drawing and their writing. Kindergarten teachers often explain to children that they should use crayons when they draw and pencils when they write. Teachers also differentiate where on a page children will write and draw: The drawing might go at the top of a page and the writing at the bottom, or children can use paper with space for drawing at the top and lines for writing at the bottom.

Teachers help children emerge into writing beginning on the first day of kindergarten when they give children pencils and encourage them to write. You might call

FIGURE 4–6
Four Samples of Young Children's Writing

young children's writing "kid writing" and contrast it with teachers' writing, or "adult writing." When young children understand that their writing is allowed to look different from adults' writing, they are more willing to experiment with writing. Teachers show children how to hold a pencil and do kid writing with scribbles; random, letter-like marks; or letters. During kindergarten and first grade, children's writing gradually comes more closely to approximate adult writing because teachers are modeling adult writing for children, teaching minilessons about written language, and involving them in writing activities.

Kid writing takes many different forms. Their scribbles may resemble letterlike forms, or sometimes children imitate adults' cursive writing. At first, the letters they string together don't have phoneme-grapheme correspondences, but with more experience, children invent spellings that represent more sound features of words and apply some spelling rules. A child's progressive writings of "Abbie is my dog. I love her very much" over a period of 18 months are presented in Figure 4–7. This child moves from using scribbles, to using single letters to represent words (top two entries), to spelling phonetically and misapplying a few spelling rules in the third and fourth entries. Note that in the fourth example, the child is experimenting with using periods to mark spaces between words. In the fifth example, the child's writing is more conventional, and more than half of the words are spelled correctly. The message is written as two sentences, which are marked at the beginning with capital letters and at the end with periods.

Kid writing gives young children permission to experiment with written language. Too often, children assume that they should write and spell like adults do, and they cannot. Without this ability, children do not want to write, or they ask teachers to spell every word or copy text out of books or from charts. Kid writing offers several strategies for writing and allows children to invent spellings that reflect their knowledge of written language.

Interactive Writing

Teachers use interactive writing to model conventional writing (Button, Johnson, & Furgerson, 1996; Tompkins & Collom, 2004). Children and the teacher collaborate on constructing the text to be written and then write it together. Teachers reinforce concepts about written language as they focus children's attention on individual words and on sounds within words. This procedure grew out of the Language Experience Approach, and conventional writing is used so that everyone can read the completed text.

Topics for interactive writing can come from stories students have read, classroom news, and information learned during thematic units. Children take turns holding the marking pen and doing the writing themselves. They usually sit in a circle on the carpet and take turns writing the text they construct on chart paper that is displayed on an easel. While one child is writing at the easel, the others are writing on small dry-erase boards in their laps.

Teachers begin by collecting the necessary materials. For whole-class or small-group activities, they collect chart paper, colored marking pens, white correction tape, an alphabet chart, magnetic letters, and a pointer. They also collect small

---

FIGURE 4–7

The Development of One Child's Kid Writing

Scribble Writing

One-Letter Labeling

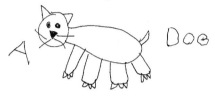

Invented Spelling Without Spacing

AZMIDDDiLRETS

More Sophisticated Invented Spelling With Spacing

ABe.isMi. doG.I.(uv hn. Vre ms.

More Conventional Writing in Sentences

Abie is my dog. I love hur vrey mus.

---

dry-erase boards, pens, and erasers for children to use. The steps in interactive writing are shown in the Step by Step feature on page 136.

When children begin interactive writing in kindergarten, they write letters to represent the beginning sounds in words and write familiar words such as *the, a,* and *is*. The first letters that children write are often the letters in their own names. As children learn more about sound-symbol correspondences and spelling patterns, they do more of the writing. Once children are writing words fluently, they can continue to do interactive writing as they work in small groups. Each child in the group uses a particular color pen, and children take turns writing letters, letter clusters, and words.

---- Interactive Writing ----

1 Collect materials. Teachers collect chart paper, colored marking pens, white correction tape, an alphabet chart, magnetic letters or letter cards, and a pointer. They also collect small dry-erase boards, pens, and erasers for individual children's writing.

2 Set a purpose. Teachers present a stimulus activity or set a purpose for the interactive writing activity. Often they read or reread a trade book, but children also write daily news, compose a letter, or brainstorm information they are learning in a thematic unit.

3 Pass out writing supplies. Teachers distribute individual dry-erase boards, pens, and erasers for children to use to write the text individually as it is written on chart paper. They periodically ask children to hold their boards up so they can see what each child is writing.

4 Choose a sentence to write. Teachers negotiate the text—often a sentence or two—with children. They repeat the sentence several times and segment it into words. The teacher also helps them remember the sentence as it is being written.

5 Write the first sentence word by word. Before writing the first word, teachers slowly pronounce the word, "stretching" it out. Then children take turns writing the letters in the first word. The teacher chooses children to write a sound or the entire word, depending on each child's knowledge of phonics and spelling. Teachers often have children use one color pen for the letters they write, and they use another color and write the parts of words that children can't spell. In that way, teachers can keep track of how much writing children are able to do. Teachers keep a poster with the upper- and lowercase letters of the alphabet to refer to when a child is unsure about a letterform, and they use white correction tape (sometimes called "boo-boo" tape) when a child writes a letter incorrectly or writes the wrong letter. After each word is written, one child serves as the "spacer" and uses his or her hand to mark the space between words and sentences. Teachers have children reread the sentence from the beginning each time a new word is completed. When appropriate, teachers call children's attention to capital letters, punctuation marks, and other conventions of print. They repeat this procedure to write additional sentences to complete the text.

6 Display the interactive writing. Teachers post the finished chart in the classroom and have children reread the text using shared or independent reading. They may also add artwork to "finish" the chart.

They also learn to use the white correction tape to correct poorly formed letters and misspelled words.

Figure 4–8 presents an interactive writing chart about brushing teeth, which was written over several days by a kindergarten class after a visit to a dentist. Notice that the children knew most beginning and ending sounds and the sight words *you* and *the*. Underlining has been added to show the letters the teacher wrote, and the boxes around letters indicate the use of correction tape.

Minilessons

Teachers teach minilessons about written language concepts and other reading and writing topics to children in kindergarten and the primary grades. Children learn about how reading and writing are used to convey messages and how children behave as readers and writers. A list of minilesson topics is presented on page 138, and a minilesson showing how to teach children to make predictions on page 139. These minilessons can be taught during literature focus units, in reading and writing workshop, and through other activities.

FIGURE 4–8

A Kindergarten Class's Interactive Writing Chart

Brushing Teeth

Brush your teeth after you eat food.

Brush your teeth in the morning and at night.

If You don't you will get cavities.

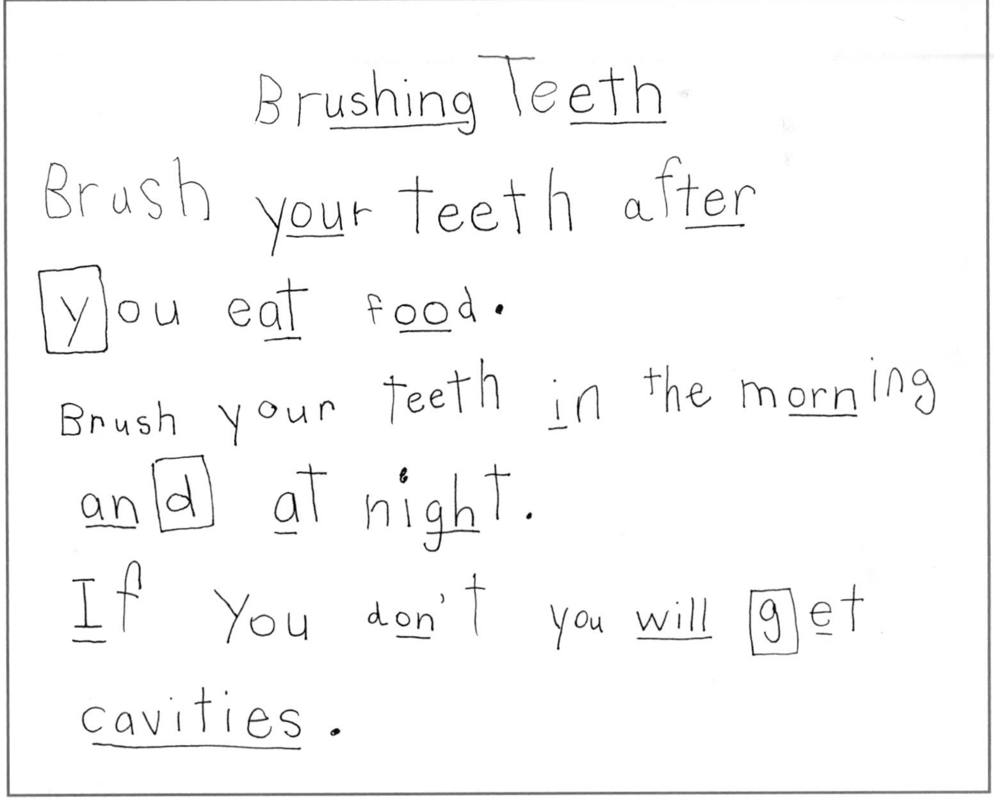

What Emergent Readers and Writers Need to Learn

Topics

Procedures	Concepts	Strategies and Skills
Hold a book correctly Turn pages correctly Separate words into 　onsets and rimes Match printed words 　with words read aloud **Do shared reading**	Direction of print A word A sentence Uppercase letters Lowercase letters Alphabetic principle Rhyming words The author's chair Kid writing	Identify letter names Match upper- and lowercase 　letterforms Identify phoneme-grapheme 　correspondences "Stretch" words **Make predictions**
Dictate Language 　Experience stories **Do interactive writing**		Use capital letters Use punctuation marks Use invented spelling

To learn more about how teachers work with young children, please visit MyEducationLab. You can watch a first-grade teacher teach a guided reading lesson by going to the topic "Reading" and clicking on the video "Shared Reading." If you'd like to see an interactive writing lesson, go to the topic "Writing" and click on the video "Interactive Writing." And to see a first-grade teacher lead a daily news activity, click on the video "Daily News" in the topic "Viewing."

Review

Emergent literacy is based on research about how children learn to read and write. Young children learn concepts about written language as they experiment with reading and writing, and teachers demonstrate reading and writing through shared reading, interactive writing, and other teaching strategies. Children emerge into writing as they learn to use graphic symbols to represent their thoughts, and they refine their kid writing as they learn about phoneme-grapheme correspondences. Here are the key concepts presented in this chapter:

- Emergent literacy has replaced the traditional readiness approach.
- As children learn about words, they move from recognizing environmental print to reading decontextualized words in books.
- Children use phonics as well as information from the other three language systems as they learn to read.

Minilesson

Mr. Voss's Kindergartners Learn to Predict

1 Introduce the topic

Mr. Voss explains to his kindergarten class that before he begins to read a book, he thinks about it. He looks at the illustration on the book cover, reads the title, and makes a prediction or guess about the story.

2 Share examples

Mr. Voss shows the cover of *The Wolf's Chicken Stew* (Kasza, 1996) and thinks aloud about it. He says, "This book is about a wolf who is going to cook some delicious chicken stew. Yes, that makes sense because I know that wolves like to eat chickens. I think the wolf on the cover is looking for chickens to cook in the stew." Then Mr. Voss asks the kindergartners to agree or disagree. Most agree, but one child suggests that the wolf is looking for a supermarket to buy the chickens.

3 Provide information

Mr. Voss reads the book aloud, stopping several times to confirm or revise predictions. Children confirm the prediction once the hen and her chicks are introduced, but by the end, no one is surprised when the wolf befriends the chickens. After reading, they talk about how their predictions changed as they read the story.

4 Supervise practice

During story time for 5 days, the kindergartners make predictions before reading aloud. If the prediction seems far-fetched, Mr. Voss asks the child to relate it to the book or make a new prediction. Children confirm or revise predictions as they listen and discuss their predictions after reading.

5 Reflect on learning

Mr. Voss's students make a chart about predicting. The kindergartners dictate these sentences for the chart:

> *You have to turn on your brain to think before you read. You can make a prediction. Then you want to find out if you are right.*

- Both reading and writing development have three stages: emergent, beginning, and fluent.
- Teachers use shared reading to read books with young children.
- Other ways to use shared reading are cross-age reading buddies and traveling bags of books.
- Teachers use children's own language to create reading materials in the Language Experience Approach.
- Children are introduced to writing as they watch their parents and teachers write and as they experiment with writing.
- Children use "kid writing" to experiment with written language concepts and invented spelling.
- Teachers use interactive writing to teach concepts about print, phonics, spelling, high-frequency words, and written language conventions.

Professional References

Adams, M. J. (1990). *Beginning to read: Thinking and learning about print.* Cambridge, MA: MIT Press.

Ashton-Warner, S. (1965). *Teacher.* New York: Simon & Schuster.

Ball, E., & Blachman, B. (1991). Does phoneme segmentation training in kindergarten make a difference in early word recognition and developmental spelling? *Reading Research Quarterly, 26,* 49–86.

Barone, D. M., & Morrow, L. M. (2003). *Literacy and young children: Research-based practices.* New York: Guilford Press.

Bennett-Armistead, V. S., Duke, N. K., & Moses, A. M. (2005). *Literacy and the youngest learner: Best practices for educators of children from birth to 5.* New York: Scholastic.

Burns, S., Griffin, P., & Snow, C. E. (1999). *Starting out right: A guide to promoting children's reading success.* Washington, DC: National Academy Press.

Button, K., Johnson, M. J., & Furgerson, P. (1996). Interactive writing in a primary classroom. *The Reading Teacher, 49,* 446–454.

Caserta-Henry, C. (1996). Reading buddies: A first-grade intervention program. *The Reading Teacher, 49,* 500–503.

Clay, M. M. (1967). The reading behaviour of five year old children: A research report. *New Zealand Journal of Educational Studies, 2*(1), 11–31.

Clay, M. M. (1991). *Becoming literate: The construction of inner control.* Portsmouth, NH: Heinemann.

Clymer, T. (1996). The utility of phonic generalizations in the primary grades. *The Reading Teacher, 50,* 182–187.

Cunningham, P. A. (2005). *Phonics they use: Words for reading and writing* (4th ed.). Boston: Allyn & Bacon.

Ditzel, R. J. (2000). *Great beginnings: Creating a literacy-rich kindergarten.* Portsmouth, ME: Stenhouse.

Fisher, B., & Medvic, E. F. (2000). *Perspectives on shared reading: Planning and practice.* Portsmouth, NH: Heinemann.

Freppon, P. A., & Dahl, K. L. (1991). Learning about phonics in a whole language classroom. *Language Arts, 68,* 190–197.

Gillon, G. T. (2004). *Phonological awareness: From research to practice.* New York: Guilford Press.

Griffith, F., & Olson, M. (1992). Phonemic awareness helps beginning readers break the code. *The Reading Teacher, 45,* 516–523.

Hanna, P. R., Hanna, J. S., Hodges, R. E., & Rudorf, E. H. (1966). *Phoneme-grapheme correspondences as cues to spelling improvement.* Washington, DC: US Government Printing Office.

Harste, J. C., Woodward, V. A., & Burke, C. L. (1984). *Language stories and literacy lessons.* Portsmouth, NH: Heinemann.

Heath, S. B. (1983). *Ways with words: Language, life, and work in communities and classrooms.* Cambridge: Cambridge University Press.

Holdaway, D. (1979). *The foundations of literacy.* Portsmouth, NH: Heinemann.

International Reading Association and the National Association for the Education of Young Children. (1998). Learning to read and write: Developmentally appropriate practices for young children. A joint position statement of the International Reading Association and the National Association for the Education of Young Children. *Young Children, 53,* 524–546.

Invernizzi, M. (2003). Concepts, sounds, and the ABCs: A diet for a very young reader. In D. M. Barone & L. M. Morrow (Eds.), *Literacy and young children: Research-based practices* (pp. 140–156). New York: Guilford Press.

Juel, C. (1991). Beginning reading. In R. Barr, M. L. Kamil, P. Mosenthal, & P. D. Pearson (Eds.), *Handbook of reading research* (Vol. 2, pp. 759–788). New York: Longman.

Klesius, J. P., Griffith, P. L., & Zielonka, P. (1991). A whole language and traditional instruction comparison: Overall effectiveness and development of the alphabetic principle. *Reading Research and Instruction, 30,* 47–61.

Lomax, R. G., & McGee, L. M. (1987). Young children's concepts about print and meaning: Toward a model of word reading acquisition. *Reading Research Quarterly, 22,* 237–256.

McGee, L. M., & Richgels, D. J. (2003). *Designing early literacy programs.* New York: Guilford Press.

McGee, L. M., & Richgels, D. J. (2007). *Literacy's beginnings: Supporting young readers and writers* (5th ed.). Boston: Allyn & Bacon.

Mills, H., O'Keefe, T., & Stephens, D. (1992). *Looking closely: Exploring the role of phonics in one whole language classroom.* Urbana, IL: National Council of Teachers of English.

Moats, L. (1999). *Teaching reading* is *rocket science.* Washington, DC: American Federation of Teachers.

National Reading Panel. (2000). *Report of the National Reading Panel.* Washington, DC: National Institute of Child Health and Human Development Clearinghouse.

Papandropoulou, I., & Sinclair, H. (1974). What is a word? Experimental study of children's ideas on grammar. *Human Development, 17,* 241–258.

Perfitti, C., Beck, I., Bell, L., & Hughes, C. (1987). Phonemic knowledge and learning to read are reciprocal: A longitudinal study of first grade children. *Merrill-Palmer Quarterly, 33,* 283–319.

Reutzel, D. R., & Fawson, P. C. (1990). Traveling tales: Connecting parents and children in writing. *The Reading Teacher, 44,* 222–227.

Schickedanz, J. A., & Casbergue, R. M. (2004). *Writing in preschool: Learning to orchestrate meaning and marks.* Newark, DE: International Reading Association.

Schulze, A. C. (2006). *Helping children become readers through writing: A guide to writing workshop in kindergarten.* Newark, DE: International Reading Association.

Shefelbine, J. (1995). *Learning and using phonics in beginning reading* (Literacy research paper, vol. 10). New York: Scholastic.

Stanovich, K. E. (2000). *Progress in understanding reading: Scientific foundations and new frontiers.* New York: Guilford Press.

Stauffer, R. G. (1970). *The language experience approach to the teaching of reading.* New York: Harper & Row.

Sulzby, E. (1985). Kindergartners as readers and writers. In M. Farr (Ed.), *Advances in writing research, vol. 1: Children's early writing development* (pp. 127–199). Norwood, NJ: Ablex.

Taylor, D., & Dorsey-Gaines, C. (1987). *Growing up literate: Learning from inner-city families.* Portsmouth, NH: Heinemann.

Teale, W. H., & Sulzby, E. (1989). Emerging literacy: New perspectives. In D. S. Strickland & L. M. Morrow (Eds.), *Emerging literacy: Young children learn to read and write* (pp. 1–15). Newark, DE: International Reading Association.

Tompkins, G. E., & Collom, S. (Eds.). (2004). *Sharing the pen: Interactive writing with young children.* Upper Saddle River, NJ: Merrill/Prentice Hall.

Tompkins, G. E., & Webeler, M. B. (1983). What will happen next? Using predictable books with young children. *The Reading Teacher, 36,* 498–502.

Trachtenburg, R., & Ferruggia, A. (1989). Big books from little voices: Reaching high risk beginning readers. *The Reading Teacher, 42,* 284–289.

Treiman, R. (1985). Phonemic analysis, spelling, and reading. In T. H. Carr (Ed.), *The development of reading skills* (pp. 5–18). San Francisco: Jossey-Bass.

Venezky, R. L. (1999). *The American way of spelling: The structure and origins of American English orthography.* New York: Guilford Press.

Vukelich, C., & Christie, J. (2004). *Building a foundation for preschool literacy.* Newark, DE: International Reading Association.

Wylie, R. E., & Durrell, D. D. (1970). Teaching vowels through phonograms. *Elementary English, 47,* 787–791.

Yaden, D. B., Jr., & Templeton, S. (Eds.). (1986). *Metalinguistic awareness and beginning literacy: Conceptualizing what it means to read and write.* Portsmouth, NH: Heinemann.

Yopp, H. K. (1992). Developing phonemic awareness in young children. *The Reading Teacher, 45,* 696–703.

Yopp, H. K. (1995). Read-aloud books for developing phonemic awareness: An annotated bibliography. *The Reading Teacher, 48,* 538–542.

Children's Book References

Baron, A. (1996). *Red fox dances.* Cambridge, MA: Candlewick Press.

Brett, J. (1989). *The mitten.* New York: Putnam.

Brett, J. (1999). *Gingerbread baby.* New York: Putnam.

Carle, E. (2001). *The very hungry caterpillar.* New York: Philomel.

Cole, H. (1995). *Jack's garden.* New York: Greenwillow.

Cronin, D. (2000). *Click, clack, moo: Cows that type.* New York: Simon & Schuster.

Ehlert, L. (2006). *Eating the alphabet: Fruits and vegetables from A to Z.* San Diego: Harcourt.

Fleming, D. (1994). *Barnyard banter.* New York: Henry Holt.

Galdone, P. (1975). *The gingerbread boy.* New York: Seabury.

Harris, T. (2000). *Pattern fish.* Brookfield, CT: Millbrook Press.

Hutchins, P. (1976). *Don't forget the bacon!* New York: Mulberry Books.

Hutchins, P. (2005). *Rosie's walk.* New York: Aladdin Books.

Inches, A. (2006). *The stuffed animals get ready for bed.* San Diego: Harcourt Brace.

Kalan, R. (2002). *Jump, frog, jump!* New York: HarperFestival.

Kasza, K. (1996). *The wolf's chicken stew.* New York: Putnam.

Martin, B., Jr. (1992). *Polar bear, polar bear, what do you hear?* New York: Holt, Rinehart and Winston.

Most, B. (1996). *Cock-a-doodle-moo!* San Diego: Harcourt Brace.

Numeroff, L. J. (1985). *If you give a mouse a cookie.* New York: HarperCollins.

Numeroff, L. J. (1991). *If you give a moose a muffin.* New York: HarperCollins.

Numeroff, L. J. (1998). *If you give a pig a pancake.* New York: HarperCollins.

Numeroff, L. J. (2000). *If you take a mouse to the movies.* New York: HarperCollins.

Numeroff, L. (2002). *If you take a mouse to school.* New York: HarperCollins.

Pinkney, J. (2006). *The little red hen.* New York: Dial Books.

Schwartz, A. (1992). *Busy buzzing bumblebees and other tongue twisters.* New York: HarperCollins.

Schwartz, D. M. (1994). *How much is a million?* New York: Morrow.

Seuss, Dr. (2003). *Hop on pop.* New York: Scholastic.

Slepian, J., & Seidler, A. (2001). *The hungry thing.* New York: Scholastic.

Sobel, J. (2006). *Shiver me letters: A pirate ABC.* San Diego: Harcourt Brace.

Taback, S. (1997). *There was an old lady who swallowed a fly.* New York: Viking.

Trapani, I. (2000). *Shoo fly!* Watertown, MA: Charlesbridge.

Williams, S. (1990). *I went walking.* San Diego: Harcourt Brace.

Wood, A. (1999). *Silly Sally.* San Diego: Red Wagon Books.

chapter five

Looking Closely at Words

During a unit on the Middle Ages, Ms. Boland's eighth graders develop a word wall. They identify words to put on the word wall as they read books about the Middle Ages, including *Catherine, Called Birdy* (Cushman, 1994), *Castle Diary: The Journal of Tobias Burgess, Page* (Platt, 1999), *Ms. Frizzle's Adventures: Medieval Castle* (Cole, 2002), and *Castle* (Macaulay, 1977). Students choose 10 important words and draw word clusters on index cards, and they also write the words in their learning logs so that they can refer more easily to them during the thematic unit. The word wall is shown on page 144.

Ms. Boland uses the words on the word wall for a series of vocabulary mini-lessons. To review the meaning of the words, she uses a semantic feature analysis chart with the categories "castle," "knights," "peasants," "crusades," and "cathedral" and 20 words for students to categorize. For *villein,* the "peasants" category would be checked, and for *fortress,* the "castle" category would be checked, for example. For other words, such as *Black Death,* more than one category would be checked. She demonstrates how to fill in the chart using the first two words as examples, and then students work in small groups to complete the chart.

In the second minilesson, Ms. Boland focuses on etymology, or word history, and students learn that words about the Middle Ages come from English, French,

What is the best way to teach vocabulary?

Students are expected to learn many technical terms in thematic units, but in too many classrooms, having students look up the definition of words and write sentences using the words substitutes for teaching vocabulary. Researchers tell us that students learn many words incidentally through multiple exposures and others through word-study activities that go beyond looking up definitions. As you read this vignette, notice how Ms. Boland involves students in a variety of meaningful word-study activities.

Latin, and Greek. Ms. Boland shares some guidelines for determining the language source, such as that compound words are usually English, words in which *ch* is pronounced /sh/ are French, words that end in -*tion* are Latin, and words in which *ch* is pronounced /k/ are Greek. Then students sort these words according to language:

> English: *freeman, drawbridge, landlord, knight, forenoon, heathen, scabbard,* and *king*
>
> French: *chivalry, heraldry, garderobe, lute, troubadour,* and *tournament*
>
> Latin: *apprentice, illumination, humor, joust, entertainment, cathedral, solar, Renaissance,* and *medieval*
>
> Greek: *alchemy, monk,* and *monastery*

In the next minilesson, students examine root words and affixes to determine the meaning of *Renaissance* (rebirth), *monk* and *monastery* (alone), *manuscript* (handwritten), *medieval* (Middle Ages), *Crusades* (cross), *solar* (sun), *unicorn* (one horn). They also compare related English and Latin words—for example, *church* and *cathedral, Middle Ages* and *medieval, kingly* and *royal, sun* and *solar,* and *Black Death* and *plague*—to discover that the more common words in each pair are English and the more sophisticated ones are Latin.

In the fourth minilesson, Ms. Boland compares the English word *hand* with the Latin word *manus* ("hand") and words made from these two root words. To begin, students brainstorm a list of words with the root word *hand: handwriting, handle, handy, handmade, handshake, handsome, handicraft, right- (or left-) handed,* and *handbag.* Then Ms. Boland introduces the Latin root word *manus,* which is used in *manuscript* and a "handful" of other words, including *manufacture, manual,* and *manicure.* Students make root-word clusters for the two words in their learning logs.

In the last minilesson, Ms. Boland reviews synonyms and how to use a thesaurus. Together the students examine synonyms for *knight* and choose these five appropriate ones: *warrior, defender, protector, gallant,* and *cavalier.* Next, Ms. Boland divides students into small

Word Wall on the Middle Ages				
A archery alchemy acre archer apprentice armorer	**B** breaking fast battering ram bailey Black Death barter battlements baron bloodletting	**C** cathedral chain mail castle coat of arms constable clergy Crusades chivalry	**D** dizzard dub drawbridge	**E** estate entertainmentl ear
F fairs fortress feudal system fanfare forenoon fresco flying buttresses freeman	**G** gatehouse guilds garderobe great hall	**H** heraldry harvest heathen humors heraldic arms herbs huntsman	**I** illumination **J** Jerusalem jousts	**K** keep kings knight knighthood
L lance landlord lord lute leprosy	**M** manor minstrel mercenary moat medieval Magna Carta merchants monastery Middle Ages monk missionaries	**N** **O** Notre Dame nave nobles	**P** pagan pillory peasant plague parchment pilgrims pennant poacher pike portcullis	
Q quartering quill pens **R** reeve royal Renaissance	**S** scabbard siege serf steward suit of armor squire shield solar	**T** tournament turrets trencher troubadours transepts twelvemonth	**U** **X** unicorn **V** **Y** vernacular yeoman villein **W** **Z** watchtower	

groups, and each group investigates the synonyms for another word-wall word and chooses the five most appropriate ones.

After reading about the Middle Ages, students divide into research teams to learn more about a particular aspect of life at that time. One group researches the building of a castle, and other groups investigate medical practices; the Crusades; monks and life in a monastery; knighthood; the feudal social system; food, drink, and celebrations; the life of a serf; and the life of the nobles. The students in each group research a topic and develop a display with artifacts and a PowerPoint presentation to document what they have learned. A page from a PowerPoint presentation on the

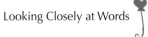

Crusades is shown here; this excerpt shows how students incorporated the word-history information they learned about the word *Crusades*.

A Page From a PowerPoint Presentation

CRUSADES

- A Crusade is a holy war that is started by a religious leader.
- Crusade comes from the Latin word "crux" or cross.
- So a Crusade was the War of the Cross.

At the end of the thematic unit, students transform their classroom into a museum. They dress in costumes and set up their displays at stations in the classroom. Parents and other students at the school visit the displays, and students share what they have learned about the Middle Ages.

Students' word knowledge plays a critical role in their academic success. Reading comprehension, for instance, depends on vocabulary knowledge; when many of the words are unfamiliar, students are unlikely to grasp the text's meaning. It's not surprising that high-achieving students know many more words than low-achieving students; in fact, researchers report that the vocabularies of high-achieving third graders are equal to the lowest-achieving high school seniors (Beck, McKeown, & Kucan, 2002).

Differences in students' word knowledge are apparent in kindergarten and first grade, and these differences appear to relate to the families' socioeconomic status (SES). Researchers have noticed that children from high SES homes know twice as many words as those from low SES homes (Beck et al., 2002). How does a family's SES contribute to these differences? High SES children's vocabulary is enhanced in these ways:

◆ *Background Knowledge.* High SES children participate in a broader array of vocabulary-enriching experiences with their families.

◆ *Book Experiences.* High SES children are more likely to be read to every day, regularly visit the library and check out books, and have their own collection of books.

◆ *Parents' Vocabulary Level.* High SES parents use more sophisticated vocabulary when they talk with their children.

One way to demonstrate these differences is by comparing kindergartners' knowledge of color words. Some 5- and 6-year-olds know 25 color words or more, including *silver, magenta, turquoise, navy,* and *tan,* whereas others can't name the eight basic colors.

It's difficult for children with less vocabulary knowledge to catch up with their classmates because high achievers learn more words and they learn them more quickly than lower achievers. High SES children's vocabularies grow at an astonishing rate of 3,000 to 4,000 words a year, whereas low SES children learn words at a much slower rate. By the time children graduate from high school, high-achieving students' vocabularies reach 50,000 words or more.

As you read this chapter, think about how students develop their knowledge of words. Ask yourself these questions:

- ◆ How has the history of the English language affected vocabulary?
- ◧ What important vocabulary concepts do students learn?
- ◆ How do teachers develop students' vocabularies?
- ◪ How do teachers focus on words during the four patterns of practice?

HISTORY OF THE ENGLISH LANGUAGE

Understanding the history of English and how words entered the language contributes greatly to understanding words and their meanings. English is a historical language, which accounts for word meanings and some spelling inconsistencies (Tompkins & Yaden, 1986). English has a variety of words for a single concept, and the etymology of the words explains many apparent duplications. Consider these words related to water: *aquatic, hydrant, aquamarine, waterfall, hydroelectric, watercress, watery, aquarium, waterproof, hydraulic, aqualung,* and *hydrogen.* These words come from three root words, each meaning "water": *water* is English, of course, whereas *aqua* is Latin and *hydro* is Greek. The root word used depends on the people who created the word, the purpose of the word, and when the word entered English.

The development of the English language is divided into three periods: Old English, Middle English, and Modern English (Stevenson, 1999). The beginning and end of each period are marked by a significant event, such as an invasion or an invention.

Old English (A.D. 450–1100)

The recorded history of English begins in A.D. 449, when Germanic tribes, including the Angles and Saxons, invaded Britain. The invaders pushed the original inhabitants, the Celts, to the northern and western corners of the island. This annexation is romanticized in the King Arthur legends. Arthur is believed to have been a Celtic military leader who fought bravely against the Germanic invaders.

The English language began as an intermingling of the dialects spoken by the Germanic tribes in Britain. Many people assume that English is based on Latin, but it has Germanic roots and was brought to Britain by these invaders. Although 85% of Old English words are no longer used, many everyday words remain (e.g., *child, foot, hand, house, man, mother, old,* and *sun*). In contrast to Modern English, Old English had a highly developed inflectional system for indicating number, gender, and verb tense. The Anglo-Saxons added affixes to existing words, including *be-, for-, -ly, -dom,* and *-hood.* They also invented vividly descriptive compound words; the Old English word for "music," for example, was *ear-sport.* The folk epic *Beowulf,* the great literary work of the period, illustrates the poetic use of words; for instance, the sea is described as a "whale-path" and a "swan's road."

Foreign words also made their way into the predominantly Germanic word stock. The borrowed words came from two main sources: Romans and Vikings. Contact between the Roman soldiers and traders and the Germanic tribes on the continent, before they had invaded England, contributed some words, including *cheese, mile, street,* and *wine.* The missionaries who reintroduced Christianity to Britain in 597 also brought with them a number of religious words (e.g., *angel, candle, hymn*). In 787, the Vikings began a series of raids against English villages, and for several centuries, they occupied much of England. The Vikings' contributions to the English language were significant. They provided the pronouns *they, their, them;* introduced the /g/ and /k/ sounds (e.g., *get, kid*); contributed most of our *sk-* words (e.g., *skin, sky*) and some of our *sc-* words (e.g., *scalp, score*); and enriched our vocabulary with more than 500 everyday words, including *husband* and *window.*

The structure, spelling, and pronunciation of Old English were significantly different from those of Modern English, so much so that we would not be able to read an Old English text or understand someone speaking Old English. Some consonant combinations were pronounced that are not heard today, including the /k/ in words such as *knee.* The letter *f* represented both /f/ and /v/, resulting in the Modern English spelling pattern of *wolf* and *wolves.* The pronunciation of the vowel sounds was very different, too; for example, the Old English *stan* (*a* as in *father*) became our word *stone.*

Middle English (1100–1500)

The Norman Conquest in 1066 changed the course of the English language and ushered in the Middle English period. William, Duke of Normandy defeated King Harold at the Battle of Hastings and claimed the English throne. For more than 200 years, French was the official language in England, spoken by the nobility, even though the lower classes continued to speak English, but before the end of the 14th century, English was restored as the official language. Chaucer's *Canterbury Tales,* written in the late 1300s, provides evidence that English was replacing French. Political, social, and economic changes contributed to this reversal.

The Middle English period was one of tremendous change. Many Old English words were lost as 10,000 French words were added to the language, reflecting the Norman impact on English life, including military words (e.g., *soldier, victory*), political words (e.g., *government, princess*), medical words (e.g., *physician, surgeon*), and words related to the arts (e.g., *comedy, music, poet*) (Baugh & Cable, 2002). Many of the new loan words duplicated Old English words. Typically, one word was eventually lost; often, it was the Old English word that disappeared. If both words remained, they developed slightly different meanings. For example, *hearty* (Old English) and *cordial* (French) were originally synonyms, both meaning "from the heart," but in time they differentiated, and they now have different but related meanings.

During this period, there was a significant reduction in the use of inflections, or word endings. Many irregular verbs were lost, and others developed regular past and past-participle forms (e.g., *climb, talk*), although Modern English still retains some irregular verbs (e.g., *sing, fly, be, have*) that contribute to our usage problems. By 1000, *-s* had become the accepted plural marker, although the Old English plural form *-en* was used in some words. This artifact remains in a few plurals, such as *children*.

Modern English (1500–Present)

William Caxton's introduction of the printing press in England marks the beginning of the Modern English period. It was a powerful force in standardizing English spelling, and from this point the lag between pronunciation and spelling began to widen. The tremendous increase in travel to many parts of the world during the 1600s and 1700s resulted in a wide borrowing of words from more than 50 languages. Borrowings include *alcohol* (Arabic), *chocolate* (Spanish), *cookie* (Dutch), *czar* (Russian), *hallelujah* (Hebrew), *hurricane* (Spanish), *kindergarten* (German), *smorgasbord* (Swedish), *tycoon* (Chinese), and *violin* (Italian).

Many Latin and Greek words were added to English during the Renaissance to increase the language's prestige; for example, *congratulate, democracy,* and *education* came from Latin, and *catastrophe, encyclopedia,* and *thermometer* from Greek. Many modern Latin and Greek borrowings are scientific words (e.g., *aspirin, vaccinate*), and some of the more recently borrowed forms (e.g., *criterion, focus*) have retained their native plural forms, adding confusion about how to spell these forms in English. Also, some recent loan words from French have retained their native spellings and pronunciations, such as *hors d'oeuvre* and *cul-de-sac*.

In addition to the vocabulary expansion during this period, there have been extensive sound changes. The short vowels have remained relatively stable, but there was a striking change in the pronunciation of long vowels. This change, known as the Great Vowel Shift, was gradual, occurring during the 1500s. Because spelling had become fixed before the shift, the vowel letter symbols no longer corresponded to the sounds. For example, the word *name* had two syllables and rhymed with *comma* during the Middle English period, but during the Great Vowel Shift, the pronunciation of *name* shifted to rhyme with *game* (Hook, 1975).

The Modern English period brought changes in syntax, particularly the disappearance of double negatives and double comparatives and superlatives. Eliminations came about slowly; for instance, Shakespeare still wrote, "the most unkindest cut of all." Also, the practice of using *-er* or *-est* to form comparatives and superlatives in shorter words and *more* or *most* with longer words was not standardized until after Shakespeare's time.

Learning About Word Histories

The best source of information about word histories is an unabridged dictionary, which provides etymological information about words: the language the word was borrowed from, the spelling of the word in that language or the transliteration of the word into the Latin alphabet, and the original meaning of the word. Etymologies are enclosed in square brackets and appear at the end of a dictionary entry. They are written in a shortened form to save space, using abbreviations for language names, such as *Ar* for *Arabic* and *L* for *Latin*. Let's look at etymologies for three words derived from very different sources: *king, kimono,* and *thermometer.* Each etymology is elaborated, beginning with *king:*

> **king** [bef. 900; ME, OE *cyng*]

> *Elaboration:* The word *king* is an Old English word originally spelled *cyng.* It was used in English before the year 900. In the Middle English period, the spelling changed to its current form.

Next, let's consider *kimono:*

> **kimono** [1885–1890; < Japn clothing, garb, equiv. to *ki* wear + *mono* thing]

> *Elaboration:* Our word *kimono* comes from Japanese, and it entered English between 1885 and 1890. *Kimono* means "clothing" or "garb," and it is equivalent to the Japanese words *ki,* meaning "wear," and *mono,* meaning "thing."

Finally, we examine *thermometer:*

> **thermometer** [1615–1625; thermo < Gr *thermos,* hot + meter < *metron,* measure]

> *Elaboration:* The first recorded use of the word *thermometer* in English was between 1615 and 1625. Our word was created from two Greek words meaning "hot" and "measure."

A list of recommended books about the history of English is shown in the box below. The books include fascinating stories about how words grew and changed because of historical events and linguistic accidents.

Booklist

BOOKS ABOUT THE HISTORY OF ENGLISH

American Heritage editors. (2004). *Word histories and mysteries: From abracadabra to Zeus.* Boston: Houghton Mifflin. (U)

American Heritage editors. (2006). *More word histories and mysteries: From aardvark to zombie.* Boston: Houghton Mifflin. (U)

Brook, D. (1998). *The journey of English.* New York: Clarion Books. (M)

Claiborne, R. (2001). *Loose cannons, red herrings, and other lost metaphors.* New York: Norton. (U)

Clements, A. (1996). *Frindle.* New York: Simon & Schuster. (M)

Collins, H. (1987). *101 American English idioms.* New York: McGraw-Hill. (M–U)

Collins, H. (1990). *101 American English proverbs.* New York: McGraw-Hill. (M–U)

Funk, C. E. (2002). *Heavens to Betsy! And other curious sayings.* New York: Collins. (U)

Funk, C. E. (2002). *Horsefeathers and other curious words.* New York: Collins. (U)

Funk, C. E. (2002). *Thereby hangs a tale: Stories of curious word origins.* New York: Collins. (U)

Merriam-Webster editors. (1995). *Merriam-Webster new book of word histories.* Springfield, MA: Merriam-Webster. (U)

Metcalf, A. (1997). *America in so many words: Words that have shaped America.* Boston: Houghton Mifflin. (U)

Metcalf, A. (1999). *The world in so many words: A country-by-country tour of words that have shaped our language.* Boston: Houghton Mifflin. (U)

Morris, E. (2004). *From altoids to zima: The surprising stories behind 125 famous brand names.* Palmer, AK: Fireside Books. (U)

Terban, M. (1983). *In a pickle and other funny idioms.* Boston: Houghton Mifflin. (M)

Terban, M. (1988). *Guppies in tuxedos: Funny eponyms.* New York: Clarion Books. (M)

Terban, M. (2006). *Scholastic dictionary of idioms.* New York: Scholastic. (M–U)

Towle, W. (1993). *The real McCoy: The life of an African-American inventor.* New York: Scholastic. (M)

P = primary grades (K–2); M = middle grades (3–5); U = upper grades (6–8)

WORDS AND THEIR MEANINGS

Children begin kindergarten with approximately 5,000 words in their vocabularies, and their vocabularies grow at a rate of about 3,000 words a year (Graves, 2006). Through literature focus units, literature circles, reading and writing workshop, and thematic units, children experiment with words and concepts, and their knowledge of words and meanings grows. Young children assume that every word has only one meaning, and words that sound alike, such as *son* and *sun*, are confusing to them. Through continuing experiences with language, children become more sophisticated about words and their literal and figurative meanings. Children learn about words and word parts, words that mean the same thing as and the opposite of other words, words that sound alike, words with multiple meanings, the figurative language of idioms, and how words have been borrowed from languages around the world. They also learn about how words are created and have fun playing with words.

Root Words and Affixes

A root word is a morpheme, the basic part of a word to which affixes are added. Many words are developed from a single root word; for example, the Latin word *portare* ("to carry") is the source of at least nine Modern English words: *deport, export, import, port, portable, porter, report, support,* and *transportation.* Latin is one source of English root words, and Greek and Old English are two other sources.

Some root words are whole words, and others are parts of words. Some root words have become free morphemes and can be used as separate words, but others cannot. For instance, the word *act* comes from the Latin word *actus,* meaning "doing." English uses part of the word and treats it as a root word that can be used independently or in combination with affixes, as in *actor, activate, react,* and *enact.* In the words *alias, alien, inalienable,* and *alienate,* the root word *ali* comes from the Latin word *alius,* meaning "other"; it is not used as an independent root word in English. A list of English, Latin, and Greek root words appears in the LA Essentials box on the next page. Students can compile lists of words developed from these root words, and they can draw root word clusters to illustrate the relationship of the root word to the words developed from it. Figure 5–1 shows a root word cluster for the Greek root *graph,* meaning "write," made by a seventh-grade class. Recognizing basic elements from word to word helps students cut down on the amount of memorizing necessary to learn meanings and spellings.

Affixes are bound morphemes that are added to words and root words. Affixes can be prefixes or suffixes: Prefixes are added to the beginnings of words, such as *re-* in *reread,* and suffixes are added to the ends of words, such as *-ing* in *singing* and *-er* in *player.* Like root words, affixes come from English, Latin, and Greek. They often change a word's meaning, such as adding *un-* to *happy* to form *unhappy.* Sometimes they change the part of speech: For example, when *-tion* is added to *attract* to form *attraction,* the verb *attract* becomes a noun.

When an affix is "peeled off," or removed from a word, the remaining word is usually a real word. For example, when the prefix *pre-* is removed from *preview,* the word *view* can stand alone; and when the suffix *-able* is removed from *lovable,* the word *love* can stand alone (when the final *e* is added, anyway). Some words include letter sequences that might be affixes, but because the remaining word cannot stand

LA Essentials

ROOT WORDS

Root	Language	Meaning	Sample Words
ann/enn	Latin	year	anniversary, annual, centennial, millennium, perennial
arch	Greek	ruler	anarchy, archbishop, architecture, hierarchy, monarchy,
astro	Greek	star	aster, asterisk, astrology, astronaut, astronomy, disaster
auto	Greek	self	autobiography, automatic, automobile, autopsy
bio	Greek	life	biography, biohazard, biology, biodegradable, bionic
capit/capt	Latin	head	capital, capitalize, capitol, captain, decapitate, per capita
cent	Latin	hundred	bicentennial, cent, centigrade, centipede, century, percent
circ	Latin	around	circle, circular, circus, circuit, circumference, circumstance
corp	Latin	body	corporal, corporation, corps, corpuscle
cosmo	Greek	universe	cosmic, cosmopolitan, microcosm
cred	Latin	believe	credit, creditable, creed, discredit, incredulity
cycl	Greek	wheel	bicycle, cycle, cyclist, cyclone, recycle, tricycle
dict	Latin	speak	contradict, dictate, dictator, prediction, verdict
graph	Greek	write	autobiography, biographer, cryptograph, graphic, paragraph
gram	Greek	letter	cardiogram, diagram, grammar, monogram, telegram
jus/jud/jur	Latin	law	injury, injustice, judge, juror, jury, justice, justify, prejudice
lum/lus/luc	Latin	light	illuminate, lucid, luminous, luster
man	Latin	hand	maneuver, manicure, manipulate, manual, manufacture
mar/mer	Latin	sea	aquamarine, Margaret, marine, marshy, mermaid, submarine
meter	Greek	measure	centimeter, diameter, speedometer, thermometer
mini	Latin	small	miniature, minimize, minor, minimum, minuscule, minute
mort	Latin	death	immortal, mortality, mortuary, postmortem
nym	Greek	name	anonymous, antonym, homonym, pseudonym, synonym
ped	Latin	foot	biped, pedal, pedestrian, pedicure
phono	Greek	sound	earphone, microphone, phonics, saxophone, symphony
photo	Greek	light	photograph, photographer, photosensitive, photosynthesis
pod/pus	Greek	foot	octopus, podiatry, podium, tripod
port	Latin	carry	exporter, import, port, portable, reporter, support, transportation
quer/ques/quis	Latin	seek	inquisitive, query, quest, question
scope	Latin	see	horoscope, kaleidoscope, microscope, periscope, telescope
scrib/scrip	Latin	write	describe, inscription, postscript, prescribe, scribble, script
sphere	Greek	ball	atmosphere, atmospheric, hemisphere, sphere, stratosphere
struct	Latin	build	construction, destruction, indestructible, instruct, reconstruct
tele	Greek	far	telecast, telegram, telephone, telescope, telethon, television
terr	Latin	land	subterranean, terrace, terrain, terrarium, terrier, territory
vers/vert	Latin	turn	advertise, anniversary, controversial, divert, reversible, versus
vict/vinc	Latin	conquer	convict, convince, evict, invincible, victim, victory
vis/vid	Latin	see	improvise, invisible, revise, television, video, visitor
viv/vit	Latin	live	revive, survive, vital, vitamin, vivacious, vivid, viviparous
volv	Latin	roll	convolutions, evolution, involve, revolutionary, revolver, volume

FIGURE 5–1

A Cluster for the Root Word *Graph*

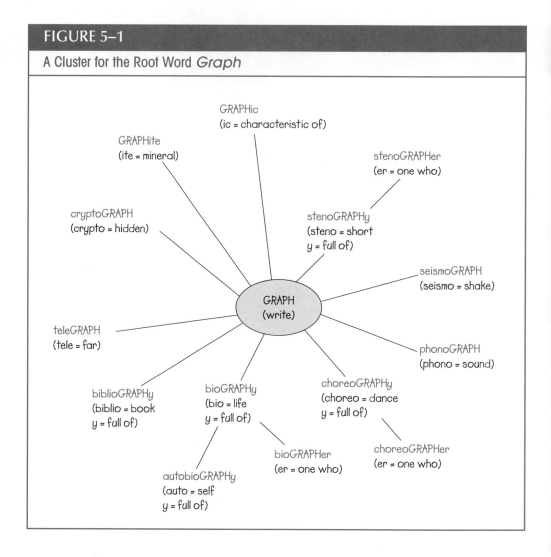

GRAPHic
(ic = characteristic of)

GRAPHite
(ite = mineral)

stenoGRAPHer
(er = one who)

cryptoGRAPH
(crypto = hidden)

stenoGRAPHy
(steno = short
y = full of)

seismoGRAPH
(seismo = shake)

GRAPH
(write)

teleGRAPH
(tele = far)

phonoGRAPH
(phono = sound)

biblioGRAPHy
(biblio = book
y = full of)

bioGRAPHy
(bio = life
y = full of)

choreoGRAPHy
(choreo = dance
y = full of)

bioGRAPHer
(er = one who)

choreoGRAPHer
(er = one who)

autobioGRAPHy
(auto = self
y = full of)

alone, they are not affixes. For example, the *in-* at the beginning of *include* isn't a prefix because *clude* isn't a word, and the *-ic* at the end of *magic* isn't a suffix because *mag* can't stand alone as a word, but the *-ic* at the end of *atomic* is a suffix because *atom* is a word. Sometimes, however, the root word can't stand alone. One example is *legible:* The *-ible* is a suffix and *leg-* is the root word even though it can't stand alone.

Some affixes have more than one form. For example, the prefixes *il- im-* and *ir-* are forms of the prefix *in-*, with the meanings of "in," "into," and "on"; these prefixes are used with verbs and nouns. The prefixes *il-, im-, ir-,* and *ig-* are also forms of the prefix *in-*, with the meaning "not"; these prefixes are used with adjectives. Both *in-* prefixes are borrowed from Latin. The prefix *a-* and its alternate form *an-* are borrowed from Greek and also mean "not"; the alternate form is used when the word it is being added to begins with a vowel. Similarly, some suffixes have alternate forms; for example, the suffix *-ible* is an alternate form of *-able*. The alternate form is used in words, such as *legible,* whose root words can't stand alone. There are exceptions, however, such as *collectible.*

A list of prefixes and suffixes is presented in the LA Essentials box on page 153. White, Sowell, and Yanagihara (1989) identified the affixes most commonly used in

AFFIXES

Language	Prefixes	Suffixes
English	**over-* (too much): overflow *self-* (by oneself): self-employed **un-* (not): unhappy **un-* (reversal): untie *under-* (beneath): underground	*-ed* (past tense): played *-ful* (full of): hopeful *-ing* (participle): eating, building *-ish* (like): reddish *-less* (without): hopeless *-ling* (young): duckling **-ly* (in the manner of): slowly **-ness* (state or quality): kindness *-s/-es* (plural): cats, boxes **-y* (full of): sleepy
Greek	*a-/an-* (not): atheist, anaerobic *amphi-* (both): amphibian *anti-* (against): antiseptic *di-* (two): dioxide *hemi-* (half): hemisphere *hyper-* (over): hyperactive *hypo-* (under): hypodermic *micro-* (small): microfilm *mono-* (one): monarch *omni-* (all): omnivorous *poly-* (many): polygon *sym-/syn-/sys-* (together): synonym	*-ism* (doctrine of): communism *-ist* (one who): artist *-logy* (the study of): zoology
Latin	*bi-* (two, twice): bifocal, biannual *de-* (away): detract **dis-* (not): disapprove **dis-* (reversal): disinfect *ex-* (out): export **il-/im-/in-/ir-* (not): illegible, impolite, inexpensive, irrational **in-* (in, into): indoor *inter-* (between): intermission *milli-* (thousandth): millisecond **mis-* (wrong): mistake *multi-* (many): multimillionaire *post-* (after): postwar *pre-* (before): precede *quad-/quart-* (four): quadruple, quarter *re-* (again): repay **re-/retro-* (back): replace, retroactive **sub-* (under): submarine *trans-* (across): transport *tri-* (three): triangle	*-able/-ible* (worthy of, can be): lovable, audible **-al/-ial* (action, process): arrival, denial *-ance/-ence* (state or quality): annoyance, absence *-ant* (one who): servant *-ary/-ory* (person, place): secretary, laboratory *-cule* (very small): molecule *-ee* (one who is): trustee **-er/-or/-ar* (one who): teacher, actor, liar *-ic* (characterized by): angelic *-ify* (to make): simplify *-ment* (state or quality): enjoyment *-ous* (full of): nervous **-sion/-tion* (state or quality): tension, attraction *-ure* (state or quality): failure

*= most common affixes

English words; these are marked with an asterisk in the LA Essentials feature. White and his colleagues recommend that the commonly used affixes be taught to middle- and upper-grade students because of their usefulness. Some of the most commonly used prefixes can be confusing because they have more than one meaning. The prefix *in-,* for instance, can mean either "not" or "again," and *un-* can mean "not" or it can reverse the meaning of the word (e.g., *tie–untie*).

Synonyms and Antonyms

Synonyms are words that have the same or nearly the same meaning. English has many synonyms because so many words have been borrowed from other languages. Synonyms provide options, allowing us to express ourselves precisely. Think of all the synonyms for the word *cold: cool, chilly, frigid, icy, frosty,* and *freezing,* for example. Each word has a different shade of meaning: *Cool* means moderately cold; *chilly* is uncomfortably cold; *frigid* is intensely cold; *icy* means very cold; *frosty* means covered with frost; and *freezing* is so cold that water changes into ice. Our language would be limited if we had only the word *cold.*

Many synonyms entered English during the Norman occupation of Britain. Compare these pairs of synonyms: *end–finish, clothing–garments, forgive–pardon, buy–purchase, deadly–mortal.* The first word in each pair comes from Old English; the second was borrowed from the Normans. The Old English words are more basic words, and the French loan words are more sophisticated. Perhaps that's why both words in each pair have survived—they express slightly different ideas. Other pairs of synonyms come from different languages. For example, in the pair *comfortable* and *cozy, comfortable* is a Latin loan word, whereas *cozy* is English, probably of Scandinavian origin.

Students can check a dictionary or thesaurus to locate synonyms for words. A fifth-grade class examined the word *wretched* after reading Chris Van Allsburg's picture-book fantasy *The Wretched Stone* (1991), the story of a strange, glowing stone picked up on a sea voyage that captivates a ship's crew and has a terrible transforming effect on them. They guessed from context clues that the word meant something "bad" or "evil," but they didn't know the exact meaning. One student checked a dictionary and found three meanings for the word—"unfortunate," "causing misery," and "of poor quality." He reported back to his classmates, and they immediately recognized that the second meaning—"causing misery"—was the most appropriate. Then they checked the word in a thesaurus and found seven synonyms. The students divided into seven groups and each group studied one of the synonyms, checking its meaning in a dictionary and thinking about how the word was used in the story. Then the groups reported back that *terrible, miserable,* and *dreadful* were the three most appropriate synonyms. Finally, the students collaborated to make a class chart for *wretched,* which is shown in Figure 5–2. The word being studied is written at the top of the chart, the word is used in a sentence in the middle section, and the synonyms are listed in a T chart in the bottom section to indicate their appropriateness in this context.

Antonyms are words that express opposite meanings. Antonyms for *loud* include *soft, subdued, quiet, silent, inaudible, sedate, somber, dull,* and *colorless.* These words express shades of meaning, just as synonyms do, and some opposites are more appropriate for one meaning of *loud* than for another. When *loud* means *gaudy,* for instance, appropriate opposites might be *somber, dull,* and *colorless.*

FIGURE 5–2

Students' T-Chart of Synonyms for *Wretched*

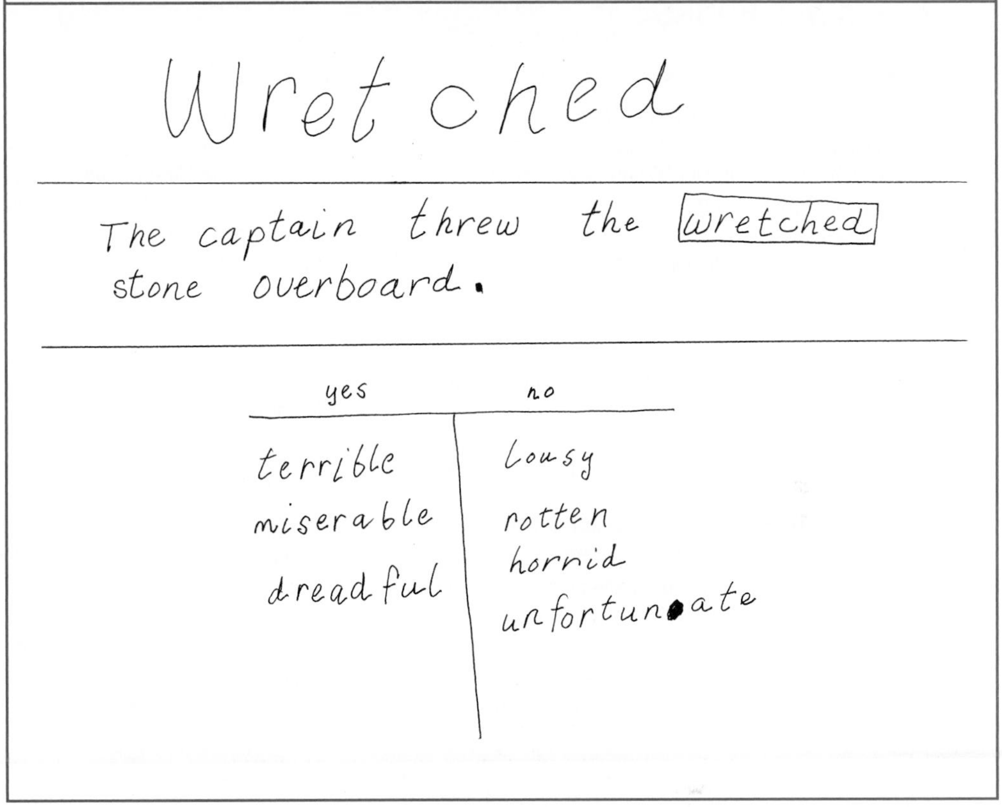

Wretched

The captain threw the [wretched] stone overboard.

yes	no
terrible	lousy
miserable	rotten
dreadful	horrid
	unfortunate

Two important reference books for examining the meanings of words are dictionaries and thesauri. Both list synonyms and antonyms, but dictionaries also explain the shades of meaning of related words. Series of dictionaries published by American Heritage, Merriam-Webster, and other publishing companies are available for children. Most series include a first dictionary for primary-grade (K–2) students, a children's dictionary for middle-grade (3–5) students, and a student's dictionary for upper-grade (6–8) students. The *Merriam-Webster Children's Dictionary* (2006), with more then 32,000 entries and 3,000 illustrations, is an excellent reference. This dictionary takes into account children's interests and was designed with visually exciting illustrations and diagrams that expand word definitions. In addition, synonym boxes suggest word choices, and word-history boxes present interesting information about how words entered English and have changed in meaning over the centuries.

An easy-to-use thesaurus is *A First Thesaurus* (Wittels & Greisman, 2001), which contains more than 2,000 entry words. Synonyms are printed in black type for each entry word, and the antonyms follow in red type. Another good thesaurus is the *Scholastic Children's Thesaurus* (Bollard, 2006). More than 2,500 synonyms are grouped under 500 entries in the thesaurus. Under the entry *common,* for example, the synonyms *ordinary, typical, familiar, everyday,* and *widespread* are listed along with a brief definition and sample sentence for each. These and other reference books are annotated in the Booklist on page 156.

Booklist

REFERENCE BOOKS

Dictionaries

The American Heritage children's dictionary. (2006). Boston: Houghton Mifflin. (M) This appealing hardcover dictionary contains 14,000 entries and more than 600 color photos and illustrations. Word history, language detective, synonym, and vocabulary-builder boxes provide additional interesting information. A phonics guide and thesaurus are also included. It's available on CD-ROM, too.

The American Heritage first dictionary. (2006). Boston: Houghton Mifflin. (P) More than 2,000 entries and 650 color photographs and graphics are presented in this attractive reference book. A clearly stated definition and an easy-to-read sentence are provided for each entry.

The American Heritage picture dictionary. (2006). Boston: Houghton Mifflin. (P) The 900 common words in this book designed for kindergartners and first graders are listed alphabetically and illustrated with lively color drawings.

The American Heritage student dictionary. (2006). Boston: Houghton Mifflin. (U) This comprehensive dictionary for middle school students has 65,000 detailed entries with sentence examples and etymologies and more than 2,000 photographs. Synonym lists, word-history boxes, and word-building features are highlighted in the text. Charts on the periodic table, geological eras, and weights and measures add to the book's usefulness.

Levey, J. S. (2006). *Scholastic first dictionary.* New York: Scholastic. (P) More than 1,500 entries are in this visually appealing dictionary for beginning readers. Each entry word is highlighted, defined, and used in a sentence.

Merriam-Webster children's dictionary. (2006). New York: Dorling Kindersley. (M–U) This stunning volume pairs the 32,000 entries from *Merriam-Webster's Elementary Dictionary* with the striking design and color illustrations that DK is famous for. This visually appealing book includes more than 3,000 photos and charts.

Scholastic children's dictionary. (2002). New York: Scholastic. (M) More than 30,000 entries are presented with color illustrations and bright page decorations. Attractively designed boxes with information about synonyms, affixes, and word histories are featured throughout the book.

Thesauri

Bollard, J. K. (2006). *Scholastic children's thesaurus.* New York: Scholastic. (M) This attractive reference book for middle-grade students contains 500 entries and 2,500 synonyms grouped under the entries. All synonyms are defined and used in sample sentences. Antonyms are not listed.

Hellweg, P. (2006). *The American Heritage children's thesaurus.* Boston: Houghton Mifflin. (M–U) This well-designed and attractive reference book contains more than 4,000 entries and 36,000 synonyms. For each entry, synonyms are listed with the best matches first, and each is used in a sentence to clarify its meaning. Antonym and word-group boxes provide additional information and extend the book's usefulness.

Hellweg, P. (2006). *The American Heritage student thesaurus.* Boston: Houghton Mifflin. (U) This comprehensive, dictionary-style thesaurus with 6,000 entries and more than 70,000 synonyms is designed for middle school and high school students. Clear sample sentences are provided for each synonym. In addition, word-group features list related vocabulary for words with no true synonyms.

Wittels, H., & Greisman, J. (2001). *A first thesaurus.* Racine, WI: Golden Books. (P–M) More than 2,000 entries are listed, with the main words printed in bold type in this easy-to-read reference. Synonyms are printed in regular type and antonyms in red.

Homonyms

Homonyms, words that have sound and spelling similarities, are divided into three categories: homophones, homographs, and homographic homophones. *Homophones* are words that sound alike but are spelled differently. Most homophones developed from entirely different root words, and it is only by accident that they have come to sound alike; for example, the homophones *right* and *write* entered English before the year 900 and were pronounced differently. *Right* was spelled *riht* in Old English; during the Middle

English period, the spelling was changed by French scribes to the current spelling. The verb *write* was spelled *writan* in Old English and *writen* in Middle English. *Write* is an irregular verb, suggesting its Old English heritage, and the silent *w* was pronounced hundreds of years ago. In contrast, a few words were derived from the same root words, such as *flea–flee, flower–flour, stationary–stationery,* and *metal–medal–mettle,* and the similar spellings have been retained to demonstrate the semantic relationships.

Homographs are words that are spelled the same but pronounced differently. Examples of homographs are *bow, close, lead, minute, record, read,* and *wind. Bow* is a homograph that has three unrelated meanings. The verb form, meaning "to bend in respect," was spelled *bugan* in Old English; the noun form, meaning "a gathering of ribbon" or "a weapon for propelling an arrow," is of Old English origin and was spelled *boga.* The other noun form of *bow,* meaning "forward end of a ship," did not enter English until the 1600s from German.

Homographic homophones are words that are both spelled and pronounced alike, such as *bark, bat, bill, box, fair, fly, hide, jet, mine, pen, ring, row, spell, toast,* and *yard.* Some are related words; others are linguistic accidents. The different meanings of *toast,* for example, came from the same Latin source word, *torrere,* meaning "to parch or bake." The derivation of the noun *toast* as heated and browned slices of bread is obvious. However, the relationship between the source word and *toast* as a verb, "drinking to someone's honor or health," is not immediately apparent; the connection is that toasted, spiced bread flavored the drinks used in making toasts. In contrast, *bat* is a linguistic accident: *Bat* as a cudgel comes from the Old English word *batt;* the verb *to bat* is derived from the Old French word *batre;* and the nocturnal *bat* derives its name from an unknown Viking word and was spelled *bakke* in Middle English. Not only do the three forms of *bat* have unrelated etymologies, but they were borrowed from three languages!

There are many books of homonyms for children, including Gwynne's *The King Who Rained* (1988b), *A Chocolate Moose for Dinner* (1988a), and *A Little Pigeon Toad* (1998). Children enjoy reading these books and making their own word books. Figure 5–3 shows a page from a second grader's homophone book.

FIGURE 5–3

A Page From a Second Grader's Homophone Book

Multiple Meanings

Many words have more than one meaning. The word *bank,* for example, may refer to a piled-up mass of snow or clouds, the slope of land beside a lake or river, the slope of a road on a turn, the lateral tilting of an airplane in a turn, to cover a fire with ashes for slow burning, a business establishment that receives and lends money, a container in which money is saved, a supply for use in emergencies (e.g., blood bank), a place for storage (e.g., computer's memory bank), to count on, similar things arranged in a row (e.g., a bank of elevators), or to arrange things in a row. You may be surprised that there are at least 12 meanings for the common word *bank.* Why does this happen? The meanings of *bank* just listed come from three sources. The first five meanings come from a Viking word, and they are related because they all deal with something slanted or making a slanted motion. The next five meanings come from the Italian word *banca,* a money changer's table. All these meanings deal with financial banking except for the 10th meaning, "to count on," which requires a bit more thought. We use the saying "to bank on" figuratively to mean "to depend on," but it began more literally from the actual counting of money on a table. The last two meanings come from the Old French word *banc,* meaning "bench." Words acquired multiple meanings as society became more complex and finer shades of meaning were necessary; for example, the meanings of *bank* as an emergency supply and a storage place are fairly new. As with many words with multiple meanings, it is a linguistic accident that three original words from three languages, with unrelated meanings, came to be spelled the same way.

Students can create posters with word clusters to show multiple meanings of words (Bromley, 1996). Figure 5–4 shows a cluster with 10 meanings for the word *hot* sketched on a poster made by three seventh graders. The students drew rays and wrote the meanings, listed examples, and drew illustrations.

Words assume additional meanings when an affix is added or when they are combined with another word, or compounded. Consider the word *fire* and the variety of words and phrases that incorporate *fire: fire hydrant, firebomb, fireproof, fireplace, firearm, fire drill, under fire, set the world on fire, fire away,* and *open fire.* Students can compile a list of words or make a booklet illustrating the words. Other common words with many variations include *short, key, water, book, rain, shoe, head, make, walk, cat,* and *side.*

Figurative Language

Many words have both literal and figurative meanings; literal meanings are the explicit, dictionary meanings, and figurative meanings are metaphorical or use figures of speech. For example, to describe winter as the coldest season of the year is literal, but to say that winter has icy breath is figurative. Two types of figurative language are idioms and metaphors.

Idioms are groups of words, such as "spill the beans," that have a special meaning. Idioms can be confusing to students because they must be interpreted figuratively rather than literally. "Spill the beans" dates back to ancient Greece when many Greek men belonged to secret clubs, and the members took a vote to decide whether to admit new members. They wanted the vote to remain secret, so they voted by each placing a white or brown bean in a special jar; a white bean indicated a yes vote, and a brown bean was a no vote. The club leader would then examine

FIGURE 5–4

Seventh Graders' Poster of 10 Meanings for *Hot*

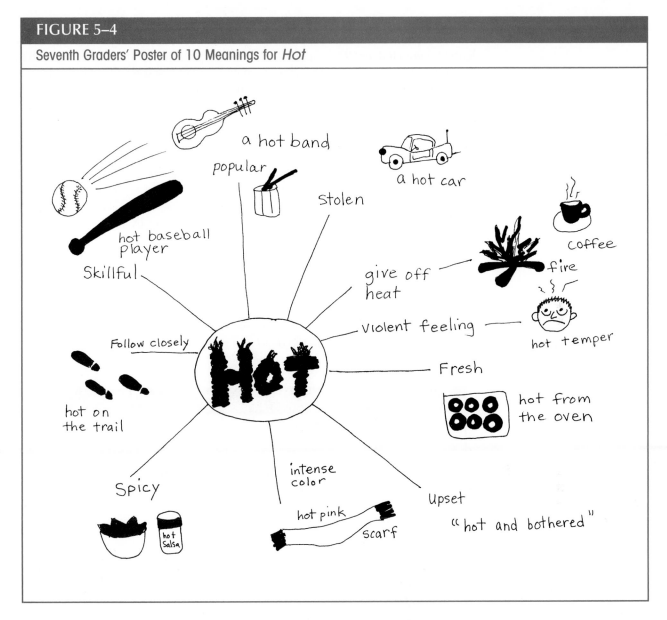

the beans, and if they were all white, the person was admitted to the club. The vote was kept secret to avoid hurting the person's feelings in case the members voted not to admit him to the club. Sometimes during the voting, one member would accidentally (or not so accidentally) knock the jar over, spilling the beans, and the vote would no longer be a secret. The Greeks turned this real happening into a saying that we still use today. Another idiom with a different history but a similar meaning is "let the cat out of the bag."

There are hundreds of idioms in English, and we use them every day to create word pictures that make language more colorful. Some examples are "out in left field," "a skeleton in the closet," "stick your neck out," "a chip off the old block," and "don't cry over spilt milk." Some of these idioms are new, and others are hundreds or thousands of years old; some are American in origin, and others come from around the world.

Three excellent books of idioms for students are the *Scholastic Dictionary of Idioms, Phrases, Sayings, and Expressions* (Terban, 2006), *Punching the Clock: Funny Action Idioms* (Terban, 1990), and *In a Pickle and Other Funny Idioms* (Terban, 1983). Because idioms are figurative sayings, many children—especially those who are English learners—have difficulty using them. It is crucial that children move beyond the literal meanings, thus learning flexibility in using language. One way for children to learn flexibility is to create idiom posters showing the literal and figurative meanings of the sayings. A fourth grader's drawing of the literal meaning of "hold your horses" is shown in Figure 5–5.

Metaphors and similes compare something to something else. A *simile* is a comparison signaled by the use of *like* or *as:* "The crowd was as rowdy as a bunch of marauding monkeys" and "In the moonlight, the dead tree looked like a skeleton" are two examples. In contrast, a *metaphor* compares two things by implying that one is something else, without using *like* or *as.* "The children were frisky puppies playing in the yard" is an example. Metaphors are a stronger comparison, as these examples show:

Simile: *The two old men crossed the street as slowly as snails.*
Metaphor: *The two old men were snails crossing the street.*

Simile: *In the moonlight, the dead tree looked like a skeleton.*
Metaphor: *In the moonlight, the dead tree was a skeleton.*

FIGURE 5–5

A Fourth Grader's Idiom Poster

Differentiating between the terms *simile* and *metaphor* is less important than understanding the meaning of comparisons in books students are reading and having students use comparisons to make their writing more vivid.

Students begin by learning traditional comparisons, such as "happy as a clam" and "high as a kite," and then they learn to notice and invent fresh, unexpected comparisons. To introduce traditional comparisons to primary-grade students, teachers use Audrey Wood's *Quick as a Cricket* (1994). Middle- and upper-grade students locate comparisons in books they are reading and invent their own as they write poems, stories, and other types of writing.

Borrowed Words

The most common way of expanding vocabulary is to borrow words from other languages. Perhaps as many as 75% of our words have been borrowed from other languages and incorporated into English. Word borrowing has occurred during every period of language development, beginning when the Angles and Saxons borrowed more than 400 words from the Romans. During the eighth and ninth centuries, the Vikings contributed approximately 900 words. The Norman conquerors introduced thousands of French words into English, reflecting every aspect of life; for example, *adventure, fork, juggler,* and *quilt.* Later, during the Renaissance, when scholars translated Greek and Latin classics into English, they borrowed many words from Latin and Greek to enrich the language, including *chaos, encyclopedia, pneumonia,* and *skeleton.* More recently, words from at least 50 languages have been added to English through exploration, colonization, and trade. These are some of the loan words from other languages (Tompkins & Yaden, 1986, p. 31):

Aboriginal Australian: *kangaroo, kiwi*
African (many languages): *banjo, cola, gumbo, safari, zombie*
Arabic: *alcohol, apricot, assassin, magazine*
Chinese: *chop suey, kowtow, tea, wok*
Dutch: *caboose, easel, pickle, waffle*
French: *ballet, beige, chauffeur*
German: *kindergarten, poodle, pretzel, waltz*
Greek: *atom, cyclone, hydrogen*
Hebrew: *cherub, kosher, rabbi*
Hindi: *dungaree, juggernaut, jungle, shampoo*
Italian: *broccoli, carnival, macaroni, opera, pizza*
Japanese: *honcho, judo, kimono, origami*
Persian: *bazaar, divan, khaki, shawl*
Portuguese: *cobra, coconut, molasses*
Russian: *czar, sputnik, steppe, troika, vodka*
Scandinavian: *egg, fjord, husband, ski, sky*
Spanish: *alligator, guitar, mosquito, potato*
Turkish: *caviar, horde, khan, kiosk, yogurt*

Native Americans have also contributed a number of words to English. The early American colonists encountered many unfamiliar animals, plants, foods, and aspects of Native American life in North America; they borrowed the Native

American terms for these objects or events and tried to spell them phonetically. Native American loan words include *chipmunk, hickory, moccasin, moose, muskrat, opossum, papoose, powwow, raccoon, skunk, toboggan, tomahawk,* and *tepee.*

TEACHING STUDENTS ABOUT WORDS

Learning a word isn't as simple as you might think. It's not that you either know a word or you don't; instead, there's a continuum of word knowledge, moving from never having seen or heard the word before to knowing it well and being able to use it effectively in a variety of contexts (Allen, 1999). Beck and her colleagues (2002) suggest that there's a continuum of word knowledge that moves from not knowing a word to knowing it well:

No Knowledge. Students are not familiar with the word.

Incidental Knowledge. Students have seen or heard the word, but they don't know its meaning.

Partial Knowledge. Students know one definition for the word or can use it in one context.

Full Knowledge. Students have a deep understanding of the word's multiple meanings and are able to use it effectively in multiple contexts.

It takes time for students to move from having little or no knowledge of a word to full knowledge. During a week's study of a word, for example, students may move from the no knowledge or incidental knowledge level to partial knowledge, but it's

Meeting the Needs of English Learners

How Can Teachers Develop Students' Vocabularies?

Many English learners have small vocabularies, and their limited understanding of words impedes their school success. As you continue reading, you'll learn about three ways to help English learners enrich their vocabularies. However, it's wrong to assume that all English learners have limited vocabularies because when students have rich vocabularies in their first language, they learn English words fairly easily because translating words from one language to another is much easier than learning new words.

Provide Meaningful Contexts for Learning

Graves and Fitzgerald (2006) advise teachers to provide a variety of rich, meaningful language experiences for English learners so that they can acquire new vocabulary just like native English speakers do. One way to accomplish this is by reading aloud stories, informational books, and books of poetry. Another way is through independent reading of interesting, age-appropriate books at students' reading levels (Akhavan, 2006). A third way is through thematic units where students expand their background knowledge as they develop concepts and related words (Peregoy & Boyle, 2005).

Teach Useful Words

English learners need explicit instruction to rapidly expand their vocabularies and to develop both conversational English and academic English (Graves, 2006). Teachers must be selective in choosing words to teach because they can't possibly teach all unfamiliar words related to a book students are reading or to a thematic unit. Akhavan (2006) recommends using the word's usefulness as a guide in determining which words to teach. Whenever possible, teachers group the words they've chosen to teach thematically and focus on related words and the concepts underlying the words. Words are posted on the wall so students can read and think about them.

Teaching a word involves more than looking it up in a dictionary and explaining its meanings. Teachers also focus on how to pronounce the word, use it in sentences, and spell it. English learners learn best when they're actively engaged in learning words using all six language arts (Peregoy & Boyle, 2005). They can use improvisation, for example, to dramatize how they would use a word in informal conversation, or they can create a diagram to explain its relationship to related words.

Foster Word-Learning Strategies

Word-learning strategies are especially important for English learners because they have so many words to learn (Graves & Fitzgerald, 2006). Students learn to use these strategies so that they can independently unlock the meaning of unfamiliar words:

- *Context Clues.* Students use context to infer the meaning of an unfamiliar word.
- *Morphology.* Students apply knowledge of root words and affixes to deduce the meaning of a word.
- *Multiple Meanings.* Students consider alternative meanings of a word.
- *Dictionaries.* Students use the dictionary to check the meaning of an unfamiliar word.
- *Cognates.* Students recognize that an English word is similar to a word in their native language. (Carlo, August, McGlaughlin, Snow, Dressler, Lippman, Lively, & White, 2004). Cognates are especially useful for English learners who are native Spanish speakers because so many English words have Spanish cognates.

What's Not Recommended

Too often, vocabulary instruction is equated with giving students lists of words to look up in the dictionary, but this isn't a worthwhile instructional practice. Instead, Beck, McKeown, and Kucan (2002) emphasize that teaching vocabulary to English learners involves teaching concepts about words so students can make sense of the new information and expand their background knowledge.

unlikely they'll reach the full knowledge level. In fact, it may take several years of using a word to develop a rich, decontextualized understanding of its meaning and related words.

To reach the full knowledge level, students develop "ownership" of the word, meaning that they know or can do these things:

- Pronounce the word correctly
- Understand the word's multiple meanings
- Use the word appropriately in sentences
- Identify related noun, verb, and adjective forms
- Recognize other words that come from the same root word
- Name synonyms and antonyms

With this knowledge, students will be able to understand the word when they are listening and reading and use it to express ideas in talk and writing.

Direct and Indirect Instruction

Even though students learn hundreds or thousands of words incidentally through reading and content-area study each year, teaching vocabulary directly is an essential part of language arts instruction for all students and especially for struggling students and English learners (Graves, 2006). Blachowicz and Fisher (2006) have reviewed the research on effective vocabulary instruction and identified these guidelines for teaching vocabulary:

- Teachers immerse students in vocabulary by creating a word-rich environment in the classroom. When teachers post words on word walls, students are more likely to learn them incidentally and through direct instruction.
- Teachers prepare students to become independent word learners. When teachers involve students in choosing some of the words they will study and teach word-learning tools, such as how to use root words to analyze words and how to use a dictionary, students are more likely to take control of their own learning.
- Teachers model word-learning strategies while teaching vocabulary. When teachers demonstrate ways, such as making clusters and sorting words, to become actively involved in learning word meanings and students participate in these activities, they are more likely to personalize the words and remember their meanings.
- Teachers assess both the depth and the breadth of vocabulary knowledge. When teachers choose assessment techniques based on their instructional goals, they can evaluate both how well students understand the words they've studied and the range of words they learned.

Vocabulary instruction fits into all four patterns of practice, as shown in the box on the next page. Teachers apply Blachowicz and Fisher's guidelines as they teach vocabulary. During thematic units, for example, teachers, like Ms. Boland in the vignette at the beginning of the chapter, highlight important words on word walls and teach minilessons using these words.

How Vocabulary Fits Into the Four Patterns of Practice

Literature Focus Units

Students post important words on the word wall and participate in a variety of vocabulary activities, including word maps and word sorts, during the exploring stage of the reading process.

Literature Circles

Students identify important words in books they're reading, check the meanings of these words in a dictionary, and talk about them as they participate in literature circle discussions.

Reading and Writing Workshop

Students learn hundreds, if not thousands, of new words incidentally as they use word-learning strategies while reading books independently and listening to the teacher read books aloud.

Thematic Units

Students post words on a word wall during thematic units and participate in a variety of vocabulary activities, including tea party, word chains, and semantic feature analysis.

Choosing Words to Teach

Teachers often feel overwhelmed when they think about all of the unfamiliar words in a book students are reading or in a thematic unit they're teaching. Of course, it's not possible to teach every unfamiliar word. Teachers need to choose the words that are most useful—those that are most important to understand the book or the big ideas in the unit. In addition, the words chosen for instruction should be common enough that students can use them in other contexts.

Words have different levels of usefulness. Some words, such as *comfortable* and *lonely,* are words that we use frequently, whereas words such as *brawny, frolic,* and *tolerate* are less common but still useful. Other words, such as *bailey* and *nebula,* are specialized and used infrequently. Beck, McKeown, and Kucan (2002) classified words into three tiers:

Tier 1 Words: Basic, everyday words that don't usually have to be taught in school.
Tier 2 Words: Useful words that students need to learn in school.
Tier 3 Words: Less common, specialized words that not all students need to learn before high school.

The Tier 2 words are those that teachers should post on word walls and use for instruction. They're part of academic language—the words that students need to learn to be successful in school.

Instead of teaching 50 or more unfamiliar words from a book or a thematic unit, teachers identify the Tier 2 words to focus on. There are some questions to consider when choosing words:

- Is the word important to understand the book or the big idea?
- Do students already understand the concept?
- Can students explain the unfamiliar word using words they already know?
- Can students use the word in other contexts?

After considering these questions, teachers can choose 5 to 10 words or more, depending on the grade level, for direct instruction.

Word Walls

The most important way to focus students' attention on words is to write important words on word-wall charts and post them in the classroom. Before beginning instruction, teachers hang up blank word walls made from large sheets of butcher paper that have been divided into alphabetized sections. Students and the teacher write on the word wall interesting, confusing, and important words from books they are reading and concepts they are learning during thematic units. Usually students choose the words to write on the word wall during the exploring stage of the reading process, and they may even do the writing themselves. Teachers add any key words students have not chosen. Words are added to the word wall as they come up—in books students are reading during literature focus units or during thematic units—usually not in advance; also, separate charts are used for each unit. The procedure for creating a word wall is described in the Step by Step feature below.

---------- Word Walls ----------

1 Prepare the word wall.   Teachers hang a long sheet of butcher paper on a blank wall in the classroom, divide it into 12 to 16 boxes, and label with letters of the alphabet.

2 Introduce the word wall.   Teachers introduce the word wall and write several key words on it during preparing activities before reading.

3 Add words to the word wall.   After reading a picture book or after reading each chapter of a chapter book, students suggest "important" words for the word wall. Students and the teacher write the words on the word wall, making sure to write large enough so that most students can see the words. If a word is misspelled, it should be corrected because students will be reading and using the word in various activities. Sometimes the teacher adds a small picture or writes a synonym for a difficult word, puts a box around the root word, or writes the plural form or other related words nearby.

4 Use the word wall for exploring activities.   Students use the words for a variety of activities, and teachers expect them to spell the words correctly. During literature focus units, students refer to the word wall when they are making words, writing in reading logs, doing word sorts, or working on projects. During thematic units, students use the word wall in similar ways.

5 Write the words on word cards.   Teachers transfer the words from the word wall to word cards at the end of the unit. They can write the words on index cards, sentence strips, or small sheets of decorated paper that correspond to the topic of the unit. They punch holes in one corner of the cards and use metal rings or yarn to make a booklet. They place the word booklets in the writing center for students to refer to as needed.

Teachers choose the most important words from books to teach. Important words include words that are essential to understanding the text, words that may confuse students, and words students will use as they read other books. As teachers choose words for word walls and other vocabulary activities, they consider the book being read as well as the instructional context. Even though all these words and perhaps more will be added to the word wall, not all will be directly taught to students. As they plan, teachers create lists of words that they anticipate will be written on word walls during the unit. They try to identify which words will be recognizable sight words for their students and which words represent new concepts, new words, and new meanings for them. From this list, teachers choose the key words—the ones that are critical to understanding the book or the theme—and these are the words they plan to highlight or include in minilessons. They also choose any words that must be introduced before reading. According to Vygotsky's notion of a "zone of proximal development," teachers need to be alert to individual students and what words they are learning so that they can provide instruction when students are most interested in learning more about a word.

Identifying some words on the word wall as key words doesn't mean that the other words are unimportant. Students have many opportunities to use all the word wall words as they write and talk about what they are reading and studying. For example, students often use the word wall to locate a specific word they want to use to make a point during a discussion or to check the spelling of a word they are writing in a reading log or in a report. Teachers also use the words listed on the word wall for word-study activities.

Word-Study Activities

Word-study activities provide opportunities for students to explore the meanings of words listed on word walls, other words related to books they are reading, and words they are learning during social studies or science units. Through these activities, they explore the word meanings and make associations among words. None of these activities ask students to simply write words and their definitions or to use the words in sentences or a contrived story. Here are eight types of activities:

◆ *Word Posters.* Students choose a word from the word wall and write it on a small poster. Then they draw and color a picture to illustrate the word. They may also want to use the word in a sentence.

◆ *Word Maps.* Students create diagrams called *word maps* to highlight a word they're studying and its meanings. They incorporate different kinds of information about the word, including its etymology, word forms, related words, and ways to use the word in a sentence. The information that's included depends on students' knowledge of words and the word itself. Figure 5–6 shows two word maps; a fourth grader created the *alien* word map when she was learning that *alien* can mean "a person who isn't a citizen," and a fifth grader created the *repel* word map to focus on the four meanings of that word.

◆ *Dramatizing Words.* Students choose a word from the word wall and dramatize it for classmates to guess. Teachers might also want to choose a word from the word wall for a "word of the day."

◆ *Word Sorts.* Students sort a collection of words taken from the word wall into two or more categories (Bear, Invernizzi, Templeton, & Johnston, 2008). Usually students choose which categories they will use for the sort, but sometimes the teacher chooses. For example, words from a story might be sorted by character, or words from a theme on machines might be sorted according to whether they are machines or according to type of machine. The words can be written on cards, and then students sort a pack of word cards into piles. Or, students can cut apart a list of words, sort the words into categories, and then paste each group on a sheet of paper. Figure 5–7 shows a word sort done by a small group of fifth graders during a theme on the colonies. Students chose the three categories—New England colonies, middle colonies, and Southern colonies—and sorted word cards for each category. Then they glued the word cards onto a large sheet of paper.

◆ *Books About Words.* A variety of books for children are collections of words or explain words related to particular concepts. *Zin! Zin! Zin! A Violin* (Moss, 2005), for instance, explains words for groups of musicians (e.g., *solo, duo, trio, quartet*), and Ruth Heller introduces *batch, school, fleet, bevy,* and *flock* in *A Cache of Jewels and Other Collective Nouns* (1987). Marvin Terban, the author of more than a dozen books about words, explains *hocus-pocus, razzmatazz, hodgepodge, knickknack,* and 103 other words in *Superdupers! Really Funny Real Words* (1989). These and other recommended books about words are listed in the box on page 171.

◆ *Tea Party.* Teachers prepare a set of cards with text (sentences or paragraphs) from a story or informational book students are reading. At least one "important" word from the word wall is included in each excerpt, and the word is highlighted. Students have a "tea party" and read the cards to classmates. They also talk about the highlighted word and its meaning. Sometimes teachers write the definition of the word or a synonym on the back of the card.

◆ *Word Chains.* Students choose a word from the word wall and then identify three or four words to sequence before or after the word to make a chain. For example, the word *tadpole* can be chained this way: *egg, tadpole, frog;* and the word *aggravate* can be chained like this: *irritate, bother, aggravate, annoy.* Students can draw and write their chains on a sheet of paper, or they can make a construction paper chain and write the words on each link.

FIGURE 5–6

Two Students' Word Maps

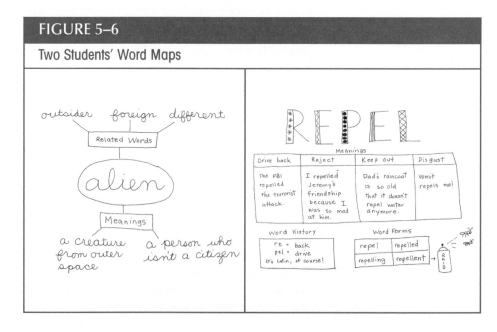

FIGURE 5–7

A Word Sort on the American Colonies

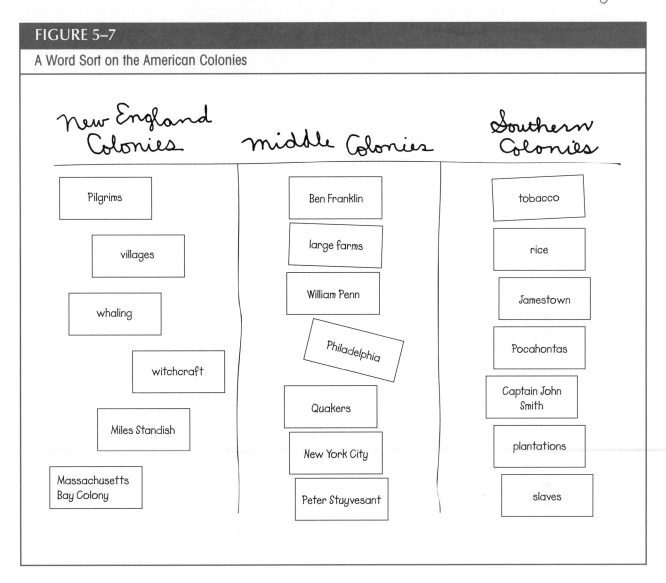

◆ *Semantic Feature Analysis.* Students select a group of related words, such as names of different kinds of birds, and then make a grid or chart to classify them according to distinguishing characteristics. A semantic feature analysis that Ms. Boland's class created during their thematic unit on medieval life is presented in Figure 5–8. This activity reinforces students' organization of knowledge and related words into schemata (Pittelman, Heimlich, Berglund, & French, 1991).

Minilessons

Traditionally, vocabulary instruction involved assigning students to look up the definitions of a list of words in a dictionary and use the words in sentences, but this approach often failed to produce in-depth understanding. Instead, teachers should teach minilessons about specific words as well as word-learning strategies

FIGURE 5–8

A Semantic Feature Analysis on Medieval Life

	castle	knights	peasants	Crusades	cathedral
apprentice	◯	✓	◯	◯	◯
bailey	✓	◯	◯	◯	◯
Black Death	◯	✓	✓	◯	◯
chivalry	◯	✓	◯	◯	◯
clergy	◯	◯	◯	?	✓
dub	◯	✓	◯	◯	◯
flying buttress	◯	◯	◯	◯	✓
fortress	✓	◯	◯	◯	◯
garderobe	✓	◯	◯	◯	◯
jousts	◯	✓	◯	◯	◯
keep	✓	◯	◯	◯	◯
mercenary	◯	?	◯	✓	◯
moat	✓	◯	◯	◯	◯
pilgrims	◯	?	◯	✓	◯
portcullis	✓	◯	◯	◯	◯
serf	◯	◯	✓	◯	◯
siege	✓	◯	◯	◯	◯
tournament	◯	✓	◯	◯	◯
villein	◯	◯	✓	◯	◯

Code: ✓ = yes

◯ = no

? = don't know

Scott Cunningham/Merrill

Minilessons

This teacher is reviewing how to take notes using key vocabulary words. She taught the minilesson to the whole class, and then students were to continue to take notes as they read the next chapter. These four students were unsure how to proceed, so the teacher reviewed the steps in taking notes and next will work with students as they read, make a cluster, and take notes on the next chapter together. Teachers provide direct instruction through minilessons and are then available to give additional assistance to students who need more support.

Booklist

BOOKS ABOUT WORDS AND WORDPLAY

Agee, J. (2002). *Palindromania!* New York: Farrar, Straus & Giroux. (See other wordplay books by the same author.) (M–U)

Cleary, B. P. (2005). *How much can a bare bear bear? What are homonyms and homophones?* Brookfield, CT: Millbrook Press. (M)

Clements, A. (1996). *Frindle.* New York: Simon & Schuster. (M–U)

DeGross, M. (1998). *Donavan's word jar.* New York: HarperCollins. (M)

Evans, D. (2004). *MVP*.* Blodgett, OR: Hand Print Press. (U)

Falwell, C. (1998). *Word wizard.* New York: Clarion Books. (M)

Fine, E. H. (2004). *Cryptomania: Teleporting into Greek and Latin with cryptokids.* Berkeley, CA: Triangle Press. (M–U)

Frasier, D. (2000). *Miss Alaineus: A vocabulary disaster.* San Diego: Harcourt Brace. (M)

Heller, R. (1998). *A cache of jewels and other collective nouns.* New York: Putnam. (M–U)

Mammano, J. (2001). *Rhinos who play soccer.* San Francisco: Chronicle Books. (See other books in the series.) (P–M)

Moss, L. (2005). *Zin! Zin! Zin! A violin.* New York: Aladdin Books. (P–M)

Most, B. (1992). *There's an ant in Anthony.* New York: HarperCollins. (P–M)

Pallotta, J. (2006). *The construction alphabet book.* Watertown, MA: Charlesbridge. (See other alphabet books by the same author.) (M)

Terban, M. (1988). *Guppies in tuxedos: Funny eponyms.* New York: Clarion Books. (M–U)

Terban, M. (1993). *It figures! Fun figures of speech.* New York: Clarion Books. (M)

Terban, M. (2006). *Building your vocabulary and making it great!* New York: Scholastic. (U)

Terban, M. (2006). *The Scholastic dictionary of idioms.* New York: Scholastic. (M–U)

What Students Need to Learn About Vocabulary

Topics

Procedures	*Concepts*	*Strategies and Skills*
Choose words for word walls	*Word Histories*	Use phonics to pronounce a word
Extrapolate the etymology	Root words	Use structural analysis to identify a word
"Peel off" affixes	*Prefixes*	Use context clues to identify a word
Make a word poster	*Suffixes*	Consider shades of meaning in
Make a word map	Synonyms	selecting a word
Do a word sort	Antonyms	Use a thesaurus to choose a better word
Make a word chain	Homophones	Use a dictionary to identify a word
Do a semantic feature analysis	Homographs	Consider multiple meanings of
Locate a word in a dictionary	Homographic homophones	words
Locate a word in a thesaurus	Idioms	
	Literal meanings	
	Figurative meanings	

 I invite you to learn more about teaching vocabulary by visiting MyEducationLab. To see how sixth graders examine root words and affixes, go to the topic "Language Tools" and click on the video "Apply Affixes."

(Baumann & Kame'enui, 2004). To teach specific words, they provide in-depth information about words, provide multiple opportunities to learn a word, and get students to actively investigate words in order to deepen their level of knowledge. To teach word-learning strategies, teachers explain and demonstrate strategies for unlocking word meanings, such as peeling off affixes or using the root word to determine the word's meaning. A list of topics for minilessons and a sample minilesson showing how a sixth-grade teacher explains to her students how related words develop from English, Latin, and Greek root words presented are here and on page 173.

Minilesson

Mrs. Monroe Teaches Her Sixth Graders About Word Histories

1 Introduce the topic

Mrs. Monroe asks her sixth-grade students to brainstorm a list of words about teeth, and students suggest words, including *teeth, toothbrush, floss, dentist, cavities, cleaning, tooth fairy, dental, orthodontist, braces,* and *dentures.* She points out that it seems unusual that words such as *toothbrush, dentist,* and *orthodontist* all relate to teeth, but look so different.

2 Share examples

Mrs. Monroe explains that many words dealing with teeth come from three root words—*tooth* (English), *dent* (Latin), and *dont* (Greek). They sort the words from the brainstormed list into four columns:

tooth	*dent*	*dont*	*other*
teeth	dentist	orthodontist	floss
toothbrush	dental		cavities
tooth fairy	dentures		braces

She points out that Latin and Greek words are likely to be medical or scientific.

3 Provide information

Mrs. Monroe explains that there are other trios of related words:

star (E), *stell* (L), and *astr* (Gr)
sound (E), *sono* (L), and *phon* (Gr)
people (E), *pop* (L), and *demo* (Gr)
foot (E), *ped* (L), and *pod* (Gr)
water (E), *aqua* (L), and *hydro* (Gr)

The students brainstorm some examples of the trios and ask why words come from different root words. The teacher explains that many words in English come from different languages because people wanted to be able to express various ideas, and that at different historical times, the English liked to invent new words from other languages, especially Latin and Greek.

4 Supervise practice

Mrs. Monroe divides the class into five groups and gives each group a set of word cards representing a different trio of words. The students read the word cards, check the meanings of any unfamiliar words, sort the words, glue the sorted words on a poster, and add other related words.

5 Reflect on learning

Students share their posters with the class and marvel at the complexity of English.

Assessing Students' Vocabulary Knowledge

Teachers assess students' word knowledge in a variety of ways. They listen while students talk during the unit, examine students' writing and projects, and ask students to talk or write about what they have learned. Here are some specific strategies to determine whether students have learned and are applying new words:

- Check reading logs, learning logs, or simulated journals for newly taught words.
- Listen for new vocabulary words when students give an oral report.

- Ask students to draw a word map or other diagram highlighting a word.
- Check students' reports, biographies, poems, stories, or other writings for unit-related words.
- Check students' projects for these words.
- Ask students to write a letter to you, telling what they have learned in the unit.

It's probably not very useful to give tests on the vocabulary words because a correct answer on a test does not indicate whether students have ownership of a word or whether they are applying it in meaningful and genuine ways.

Review

Learning about words is an important part of language arts. Few words have only one meaning, and students gradually learn about multiple meanings as well as about root words and affixes; homonyms, synonyms, and antonyms; and figurative meanings of words, such as idioms and metaphors. The best measure of students' learning of words is their ability to use the words in meaningful ways. Here are the key points in this chapter:

- English is a historical language, and its diverse origins account for word meanings and some spelling inconsistencies.
- The fact that children's vocabularies grow at a rate of about 3,000 to 4,000 words a year suggests that they learn many words incidentally.
- Students use their knowledge of root words and affixes to unlock the meaning of unfamiliar words.
- Many words have more than one meaning, and students learn additional word meanings through the four patterns of practice.
- Idioms and metaphors can be confusing because they must be interpreted figuratively rather than literally.
- Reading and writing are the most important ways students learn vocabulary, but direct instruction is also important.
- Students need to use a word many times in order to learn it well.
- Words are not all equally difficult or easy to learn; the degree of difficulty depends on what students already know about a word.
- Students use reference books, including dictionaries and thesauri, to expand their knowledge of words.
- Word-study activities include word walls, word posters, word clusters, word sorts, word chains, and semantic feature analysis.

Professional References

Akhavan, N. (2006). *Help! My kids don't all speak English: How to set up a language workshop in your linguistically diverse classroom.* Portsmouth, NH: Heinemann.

Allen, J. (1999). *Words, words, words.* Portsmouth, NH: Heinemann.

Baugh, A. C., & Cable, T. (2002). *The history of the English language.* Oxford, UK: Routledge Books.

Baumann, J. F., & Kame'enui, E. J. (Eds.). (2004). *Vocabulary instruction: Research to practice.* New York: Guilford Press.

Bear, D. R., Invernizzi, M., Templeton, S., & Johnston, F. (2008). *Words their way: Word study for phonics, vocabulary, and spelling instruction* (4th ed.). Upper Saddle River, NJ: Merrill/Prentice Hall.

Beck, I. L., McKeown, M. G., & Kucan, L. (2002). *Bringing words to life: Robust vocabulary instruction.* New York: Guilford Press.

Blachowicz, C., & Fisher, P. (2006). *Teaching vocabulary in all classrooms* (3rd ed.). Upper Saddle River, NJ: Merrill/Prentice Hall.

Bromley, K. D. (1996). *Webbing with literature: Creating story maps with children's books* (2nd ed.). Boston: Allyn & Bacon.

Carlo, M. S., August, D., McGlaughlin, B., Snow, C. E., Dressler, C., Lippman, D. N., Lively, T. J., & White, C. E. (2004). Closing the gap: Addressing the vocabulary needs of English-language learners in bilingual and mainstream classes. *Reading Research Quarterly, 39,* 188–215.

Graves, M. F. (2006). *The vocabulary book: Learning and instruction.* New York: Teachers College Press.

Graves, M. F., & Fitzgerald, J. (2006). Effective vocabulary instruction for English language learners. In C. C. Block & J. N. Mangieri (Eds.), *The vocabulary-enriched classroom: Practices for improving the reading performance of all students in grades 3 and up* (pp. 118–137). New York: Scholastic.

Hook, J. N. (1975). *History of the English language.* New York: Ronald Press.

Nagy, W. E. (1988). *Teaching vocabulary to improve reading comprehension.* Urbana, IL: ERIC Clearinghouse on Reading and Communication Skills and the National Council of Teachers of English and the International Reading Association.

Nagy, W. E., & Herman, P. (1985). Incidental vs. instructional approaches to increasing reading vocabulary. *Educational Perspectives, 23,* 16–21.

Peregoy, S. F., & Boyle, O. F. (2005). *Reading, writing, and learning in ESL: A resource book for K–12 teachers* (4th ed.). Boston: Allyn & Bacon.

Pittelman, S. D., Heimlich, J. E., Berglund, R. L., & French, M. P. (1991). *Semantic feature analysis: Classroom applications.* Newark, DE: International Reading Association.

Stevenson, V. (1999). *The world of words.* New York: Sterling.

Tompkins, G. E. (2008). *Teaching writing: Balancing process and product* (5th ed.). Upper Saddle River, NJ: Merrill/Prentice Hall.

Tompkins, G. E., & Yaden, D. B., Jr. (1986). *Answering students' questions about words.* Urbana, IL: National Council of Teachers of English.

White, T. G., Sowell, J., & Yanagihara, A. (1989). Teaching elementary students to use word-part clues. *The Reading Teacher, 42,* 302–308.

Children's Book References

Bollard, J. K. (2006). *Scholastic children's thesaurus.* New York: Scholastic.

Cole, J. (2002). *Ms. Frizzle's adventures: Medieval castle.* New York: Scholastic.

Cushman, K. (1994). *Catherine, called Birdy.* New York: HarperCollins.

Gwynne, F. (1988a). *A chocolate moose for dinner.* New York: Aladdin Books.

Gwynne, F. (1988b). *The king who rained.* New York: Aladdin Books.

Gwynne, F. (1998). *A little pigeon toad.* New York: Aladdin Books.

Heller, R. (1987). *A cache of jewels and other collective nouns.* New York: Grosset & Dunlap.

Macaulay, D. (1977). *Castle.* Boston: Houghton Mifflin.

Merriam-Webster children's dictionary. (2006). New York: Dorling Kindersley.

Moss, L. (2005). *Zin! Zin! Zin! A violin.* New York: Aladdin Books.

Platt, R. (1999). *Castle diary: The journal of Tobias Burgess, page.* Cambridge, MA: Candlewick Press.

Terban, M. (1983). *In a pickle and other funny idioms.* New York: Clarion Books.

Terban, M. (1989). *Superdupers! Really funny real words.* New York: Clarion Books.

Terban, M. (1990). *Punching the clock: Funny action idioms.* New York: Clarion Books.

Terban, M. (1996). *Scholastic dictionary of idioms, phrases, sayings, and expressions.* New York: Scholastic.

Van Allsburg, C. (1991). *The wretched stone.* Boston: Houghton Mifflin.

Wittels, H., & Greisman, J. (2001). *A first thesaurus.* Racine, WI: Golden Books.

Wood, A. (1994). *Quick as a cricket.* New York: Scholastic.

chapter six

Personal Writing

Ms. Meinke teaches seventh-grade language arts, and her students often participate in literature circles. One group of six students is reading *The Great Gilly Hopkins* (Paterson, 1987), the story of Gilly, an angry, mistrustful, disrespectful foster child who eventually finds love and acceptance. To begin their 3-week period of literature circles, the students sign up to read one of the six books that Ms. Meinke has introduced. The students divide into groups, after which each group selects a group leader and sets its schedule for reading and discussing the book. Students also construct reading logs by stapling paper into booklets and adding construction paper covers.

Ms. Meinke meets with *The Great Gilly Hopkins* group to talk about the book. She explains that the story is about a girl named Gilly Hopkins who is a foster child. They talk about foster care and how children become foster children. Several students mention that they know someone who is a foster child. She also passes out a list of topics for reading log entries, and students place the sheet in their reading logs. A copy of the topics sheet is shown on page 178.

Ms. Meinke varies the types of entries that she asks students to write in reading logs. She does this for two reasons. First of all, she believes that each chapter is different and that the content of the chapter should determine the type of response. Also, she has found that students tire of writing regular reading log entries because of their repetitiveness and predictability.

The students read in class and at home, and every two days, they meet to discuss their reading. Often Ms. Meinke sits in on at least part of their discussions.

During the discussions, students ask questions and clarify misunderstandings, share their favorite excerpts, and make predictions about what will happen next. Sometimes, too, they share their reading log entries or talk about how they will write their entries.

Timothy wrote this simulated-journal entry after reading Chapter 2:

Dear Diary,

I can't live here, it's a dump. I have to live with Miss Trotter and that colored (or black) man Mr. Randolph. I will have to get out of this dump and fast. Today was the first day Mr. Randolph came and I can't escort him every day to dinner. I don't belong here, even Mrs. Nevin's house was better than here.

I cannot believe Miss Ellis took me to this awful place. I got to find a way to call Courtney Hopkins. She'll take me outta this place. Everyone's trying to be nice to me but I'll show them who's the boss, and I bet there is something wrong with W. E.

After reading Chapter 6, about how mean Gilly is to her teacher, Miss Harris, Steven wrote this simulated letter to Gilly:

Hey Gilly,

That was the best note you have ever written. That was cool because you actually made Miss Harris curse. I bet you none of the kids at this school could ever make a teacher do that. I wish I could write cards like that and make teachers curse. You are also very brave because you wrote that to a teacher. No kid is crazy enough to do something like that. That is how crazy I think you are.

Your classmate,

Steven

Johanna wrote this response about whether it is ever right to lie and steal after reading Chapter 7:

I think she shouldn't be forgiven. I know she has

Reading Log Assignments for *The Great Gilly Hopkins*

Chapter 1 "Welcome to Thompson Park"
What is a foster child? How do foster children feel and behave? Why?

Chapter 2 "The Man Who Comes to Supper"
Write a diary entry from Gilly's viewpoint.

Chapter 3 "More Unpleasant Surprises"
Write a double entry with a quote from the chapter and your response.

Chapter 4 "Sarsaparilla to Sorcery"
Write a diary entry from Gilly's viewpoint.

Chapter 5 "William Ernest and Other Mean Flowers"
Do a character study on Maime Trotter. Identify and list three characteristics. Then locate and copy two quotes as evidence for each characteristic.

Chapter 6 "Harassing Miss Harris"
Write a letter to Gilly telling her what you think of what she did to Miss Harris.

Chapter 7 "Dust and Desperation"
Gilly does two things that are considered immoral: she lies and she steals. She has had a rough life, so maybe doing these things is excusable. Perhaps, however, lying and stealing are wrong under any circumstances. Take a position and support it with evidence from the book.

Chapter 8 "The One Way Ticket"
Draw a scene from the chapter and write a brief description of the scene.

Chapter 9 "Pow"
There is a definite change in Gilly's behavior and feelings in this chapter. Describe how she changes and then describe the causes of these changes using examples from the book.

Chapter 10 "The Visitor"
Draw a picture of Gilly and her family at Thanksgiving dinner. Then, in a paragraph, describe Gilly's foster family and how they make each other feel needed. Or, draw Nonnie, Gilly's grandmother. Then, in a paragraph, tell what she looks like, what kind of person she seems to be, how she behaves, and how she gets along with her daughter, Courtney.

Chapter 11 "Never and Other Canceled Promises"
So where should Gilly go? List three reasons why she should stay with Trotter and list three reasons why she should go with her grandmother Nonnie. Then write a short paragraph telling where you would like her to go and why.

Chapters 12 and 13 "The Going" and "Jackson, Virginia"
Select eight to ten images, details, interesting phrases, or parts of sentences from the book and arrange the "found" parts into a poem.

Chapters 14 and 15 "She'll Be Riding Six White Horses" and "Homecoming"
In this final response, write about your feelings. What did you like? dislike? Why?

---

had a horrible life, but it's never right. It is one thing to steal and it's another to steal from a blind man. That is just mean. I kind of feel bad for her because of everything she's been through. She lies, cheats, and steals. I am not sure which side to take because in one way she should be forgiven but on another side she shouldn't be because she's done too many bad things. Especially stealing from Mr. Randolph.

Sarah wrote about how Gilly has changed after reading Chapter 9:

> *Gilly changes because she sees that Trotter really cares for her. Trotter got in an argument about what Gilly did. Miss Ellis wanted to take Gilly back but Trotter wouldn't let her. Gilly becomes more liking toward Trotter. Gilly even starts liking W. E. Gilly doesn't think he is dumb any more. Another example is "Look, W. E.," she bent over close to his ear and whispered hoarsely into it, "I'm going to teach you how to fight. No charge or anything. Then when some big punk comes up to you and tries to start something, you can just let them have it," said Gilly.*

After reading Chapters 12 and 13, Timothy wrote this found poem:

> *He tore a piece of him and gave it to you.*
> *Don't make it harder for us, baby.*
> *This was supposed to be a party, not a funeral.*
> *Sometimes it's best not to go visiting.*
> *You make me proud.*
> *Why would anybody leave peace for war?*
> *Stop hovering over me.*
> *Inside her head, she was screaming.*

Steven reflects on the book in his last entry:

> *I thought that at the end Gilly was going to go with her mom. I also thought Gilly's mom was going to be nice and sweet. I thought this was very good because it had an unexpected ending. I didn't think that Gilly's mom would be so rude and mean. Now I wish that Gilly would go back with Trotter because Courtney is mean. Those are my reasons why she should be with Trotter.*

Ms. Meinke is especially interested in the students' responses in this last entry. She finds that many students, like Steven, want Gilly to stay with Trotter, but she is pleased when they realize that Nonnie, who never even knew of Gilly's existence, is family and is delighted to provide a home for her only granddaughter.

Ms. Meinke collects the students' reading logs twice—once halfway through the literature circle and again at the end—to grade them. She has found that students appreciate the opportunity to pace themselves as they read and write the entries. She awards points for each journal entry, and these points are part of students' grades for the literature circle.

----

*A*ll kinds of people—artists, scientists, dancers, politicians, writers, and assassins—do personal writing. They write letters and keep journals. People record the everyday events of their lives and the issues that concern them. The personal writing of some public figures has survived for hundreds of years and provides a fascinating glimpse of their authors and the times in which they lived. For example, the Renaissance genius Leonardo da Vinci recorded his daily activities, dreams, and plans for his painting and engineering projects in more than 40 notebooks. American explorers Meriwether Lewis and William Clark kept a journal of their travels across the North American continent, more for geographical than personal use. Dutch artist Vincent Van Gogh wrote more than 1,000 letters during his lifetime, many to his brother Theo; these letters, which often contained striking drawings, document the artist's tragic life. Anne Frank, who wrote while in hiding from the Nazis during World War II, is probably the best-known child diarist.

Children write journals and letters for many of the same reasons that public figures write—to record events in their lives and to share information with others. And, there are other reasons for using personal writing. Young children use personal writing to develop writing fluency. As they write, they practice writing conventions, handwriting skills, and spelling high-frequency words. Students use personal writing as a tool to enhance their learning in language arts and across the curriculum. They write in learning logs, for instance, as part of thematic units, and as they write, they learn to take notes, summarize, and reflect on learning.

As you continue reading about journals and letters and how to incorporate personal writing in your language arts program, think about these questions:

- ◈   What types of journals do students use?
- ▣   How do students use journals as tools for learning in language arts and across the curriculum?
- ◈   What types of letters do students write?
- ▰   How do teachers incorporate letter writing in their instructional programs?

WRITING IN JOURNALS

Students use journals for a variety of purposes. Seven types of journals are described in the LA Essentials box on page 181. In most types of journals, the focus is on the writer; the writing is personal and private. Students' writing is spontaneous and loosely organized, and it often contains mechanical errors because they're focusing on thinking, not on spelling, capitalization, and punctuation. James Britton and his colleagues (1975) compare this type of writing to a written conversation, which may be with oneself or with trusted readers who are interested in the writer. Here are some of the purposes for journal writing:

- Record experiences
- Stimulate interest in a topic
- Explore thinking
- Personalize learning
- Develop interpretations
- Wonder, predict, and hypothesize
- Engage the imagination
- Ask questions
- Activate prior knowledge
- Assume the role of another person
- Share experiences with trusted readers

TYPES OF JOURNALS

Personal Journals
Students write in personal journals about events in their own lives and about other topics of special interest. These journals are the most private type. Teachers respond as interested readers, often asking questions and offering comments about their own lives.

Dialogue Journals
Dialogue journals are similar to personal journals except they're written to be shared with the teacher or a classmate. Whoever receives the journal reads the entry and responds to it. The entries are like written conversations.

Reading Logs
Students respond in reading logs to stories, poems, and informational books they're reading. They write and draw entries after reading, record key vocabulary words, make charts and other diagrams, and record memorable quotes.

Double-Entry Journals
Students divide each page of their journals into two columns and write different types of information in each column. Sometimes they write quotes from a story in one column and add reactions to the quotes in the other, or they write predictions in one column and what actually happened in the story in the other.

Language Arts Notebooks
Students take notes, write rules and examples, draw diagrams, and write lists of other useful information about language arts topics in these notebooks. Students use these notebooks during minilessons and refer to the information during literature focus units, literature circles, and reading and writing workshop.

Learning Logs
Students write in learning logs as part of thematic units. They write quickwrites, draw diagrams, take notes, and write vocabulary words.

Simulated Journals
Students assume the role of a book character or a historical personality and write journal entries from that person's viewpoint. They include details from the story or historical period in their entries.

Journal writing gives students valuable writing practice. Kindergartners use a combination of drawing and writing in their journal entries (McGee & Richgels, 2007). They write scribbles, random letters and numbers, simple captions, or extended texts using invented spelling. Their invented spellings often seem bizarre by adult standards, but they are reasonable in terms of children's knowledge of phoneme-grapheme correspondences and spelling patterns. In first and second grades, children gain fluency and confidence that they can write through journal writing. Older children experiment with writing conventions that must be considered in more public writing. If they decide to make an entry "public," they can later revise and edit their writing.

Personal Journals

Personal journals are usually the first type of journal writing that young children do. Kindergartners begin writing in journals early in the school year, and their writing becomes more conventional as they learn concepts about print, letters of the alphabet, and phonics skills. Hannon (1999) recommends beginning with personal or dialogue journals. Two kindergartners' journal entries are presented in Figure 6–1. In the left entry, a 5-year-old draws a detailed picture of a football game (note that the player in the middle-right position has the ball) and adds five letters for the text so that his entry will have some writing. In the entry on the right, another child writes, "I spent the night at my dad's house."

FIGURE 6–1

Two Kindergartners' Journal Entries

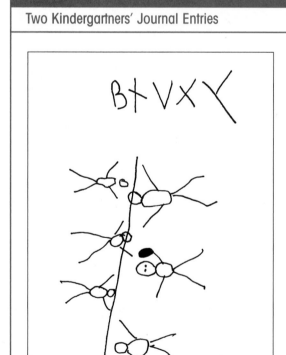

FIGURE 6–2

Fourth and Fifth Graders' List of Writing Topics

Things to Write About in Personal Journals

my favorite place in town	if I had three wishes
boyfriends/girlfriends	my teacher
things that make me happy or sad	TV shows I watch
music	my favorite holiday
an imaginary planet	if I were stranded on an island
cars	what I want to be when I grow up
magazines I like to read	private thoughts
what if snow were hot	how to be a superhero
cartoons	dinosaurs
places I've been	my mom/my dad
favorite movies	my friends
if I were a movie/rock star	my next vacation
poems	if I were an animal or something else
pets	books I've read
football	favorite things to do
astronauts	my hobbies
the president	if I were a skydiver
jokes	when I get a car
motorcycles	if I had a lot of money
things that happen in my school	if I were rich
current events	wrestling and other sports
things I do on weekends	favorite colors

or ANYTHING else I want to write about

Students often keep personal journals in which they recount events in their lives and write about topics of their choosing. They choose to write about a variety of topics and explore their feelings in these entries. It's normal for students to misspell a few words in their entries; when they write in personal journals, the emphasis is on what they say, not how correctly they write. It's helpful to develop a list of possible journal-writing topics on a chart in the classroom or make copies for students to clip inside their journal notebooks. Students choose their own topics for personal journals. Although they can write about almost anything, some students will complain that they don't know what to write about, so a list of topics gives them a crutch. Figure 6–2 shows a list of possible journal-writing topics developed by a class of fourth and fifth graders. They continue to add topics to their list so that it may include more than 100 topics by the end of the school year. Referring students to the list or asking them to brainstorm a list of topics encourages them to become more independent writers.

Privacy becomes an important issue as students grow older. Most young children are willing to share what they have written, but by third or fourth grade, they grow less willing to read their journal entries aloud to the class, although they are usually willing to share the entries with a trusted teacher. Teachers must be scrupulous about respecting students' privacy and not insist that they share their writing when they are unwilling to do so. It is important to talk with students about respecting classmates' privacy and not reading each other's journals. Also, many teachers keep personal journals on an out-of-the-way shelf when they are not in use.

When students share personal information with teachers through their journals, a second issue arises: Sometimes teachers learn details about students' problems and family life that they don't know how to deal with. Entries about child abuse, suicide, or drug use may be a student's way of asking for help. Although teachers are not counselors, they have a legal obligation to protect their students and to report possible problems to appropriate school personnel. Occasionally a student invents a personal problem as an attention-getting tactic; however, asking about the journal entry or having a school counselor do so will help to ensure that the student's safety is fully considered.

Dialogue Journals

Students converse in writing with the teacher or with a classmate through dialogue journals. These journals are interactive and conversational in tone. Most important, dialogue journals are an authentic writing activity and provide the opportunity for real communication between students or between a student and the teacher. Students write informally about something of interest, a concern, a book they are reading, or what they are learning in a thematic unit. They choose their own topics and usually control the direction the writing takes.

When teachers or classmates respond to students' entries, they answer as they would in an oral conversation. They react to their comments, ask questions, and offer suggestions. Teachers acknowledge students' ideas and encourage them to continue to write about their interests. They also provide new information about topics, so that students will want to read their responses. Teachers try to avoid unspecific comments, such as "good idea" or "very interesting." Their responses don't need to be lengthy; a sentence or two is often enough. Even so, it's time-consuming to respond to 25, 30, or more journal entries every day. To solve this problem, many teachers read and respond to students' journal entries on a rotating basis; they might respond to one group one week and another group the next week.

In this fifth grader's dialogue journal, Daniel shares the events and problems in his life with his teacher, and she responds sympathetically. Daniel writes:

> Over spring break I went down to my grandma's house and played basketball in their backyard and while we were there we went to see some of my uncles who are all Indians. Out of my whole family down there they are all Indians except Grandpa Russell.

And Daniel's teacher responds:

> What a fun spring break! That is so interesting to have Indians in your family. I think I might have some Indian ancestors too. Do you still plan to go to Padre Island for the summer?

The next day Daniel writes:

> My family and I plan to go to Padre Island in June and I imagine we will stay there for quite a while. I think the funnest part will probably be swimming or camping or something like that. When we get there my mom says we will probably stay in a nice motel.

Daniel's teacher responds:

> That really sounds like a fun vacation. I think swimming is the most fun, too. Who will go with you?

Daniel continues to talk about his family, now focusing on the problems he and his family are facing:

> *Well, my mom and dad are divorced so that is why I am going to court to testify on Tuesday but my mom, me, and my sister and brother are all going and that kind of makes me sad because a couple of years ago when my mom and dad were together we used to go a lot of places like camping and hiking but now after what happened we hardly go anywhere.*

His teacher responds:

> *I am so sorry your family is having problems. It sounds as if your mom and dad are having problems with each other, but they both love you and want to be with you. Be sure to keep talking to them about how you feel.*

Daniel replies:

> *I wish my mom and dad did not have problems because I would have a lot more fun and get to go and do a lot more things together, but since my mom and dad are divorced I have to take turns spending time with both of them.*

This journal is not a series of teacher questions and student answers; instead, the student and teacher are having a conversation, and the interchange is built on mutual trust and respect.

Dialogue journals are especially effective in promoting the writing development of children who are English learners. Researchers have found that these students are more successful writers when they choose their own topics for writing and when their teachers contribute to the dialogue with requests for a reply, statements, and other comments (Reyes, 1991). Not surprisingly, researchers found that students wrote more when teachers requested a reply than when teachers made comments that did not require a response. Also, when a student was particularly interested in a topic, it was less important what the teacher did, and when the teacher and the student were both interested in a topic, the topic seemed to take over as they shared and built on each other's writing. Reyes also found that English learners were much more successful in writing dialogue journal entries than in writing in response to books they had read.

Students use dialogue journals to write to classmates or the teacher about books they are reading (Nash, 1995). In these journal entries, students write about the books they are reading, compare the books to others by the same author or books by other authors they have read, and offer opinions about the book and whether a classmate or the teacher might enjoy reading it. They also write about their book-selection strategies and their reading behavior. This approach is especially effective in reading workshop classrooms when students are reading different books. They're often paired and write back and forth to their reading buddies. This activity provides the socialization that independent reading does not. Depending on whether students are reading relatively short picture books or longer chapter books, they can write dialogue journal entries every other day or once a week, and then classmates write back.

Reading Logs

Students write in reading logs about the stories and other books they are reading or listening to the teacher read aloud during literature focus units, literature circles, and reading workshop. Rather than simply summarize their reading, students delve into important ideas and relate their reading to their own lives or to other literature they have read. They may also list interesting or unfamiliar words, jot down memorable quotes, and take notes about characters, plot, or other story elements; but the primary purpose is for them to think about the book and develop their own interpretations, as Ms. Meinke's students did in the vignette at the beginning of the chapter.

Even kindergartners write in reading logs. They use a combination of drawing and writing, as the two samples in Figure 6–3 show. A kindergartner wrote the entry on the left after listening to his teacher read *The Three Billy Goats Gruff* (Finch, 2001). As he shared his entry with classmates, he read the text this way: "You are a mean, bad troll." Another child wrote the entry on the right after listening to her teacher read *The Jolly Postman, or Other People's Letters* (Ahlberg & Ahlberg, 2006). This child drew a picture of the three bears receiving a letter from Goldilocks. She labeled the mom, dad, and baby bear in the picture and wrote, "I [am] sorry I ate your porridge."

Hancock (2007) examined students' responses and noticed patterns in their reading log entries; she identified nine categories, which are listed in the LA Essentials box on page 187. The first four are immersion responses in which students make inferences about characters, offer predictions, ask questions, or discuss confusions. The next three categories focus on students' involvement with the story. The last two are literary connections, in which students make connections and evaluate the book they're reading.

These categories can extend the possibilities of response by introducing teachers and students to a wide variety of response options. Teachers can assess the kinds of responses students are currently making by reading their reading logs, categorizing

FIGURE 6–3

Two Kindergartners' Reading Log Entries

RESPONSE PATTERNS

Immersion Responses

Understanding	Students write about their understanding of characters and plot. Their responses include personal interpretation as well as summarizing.
Character Introspection	Students share their insights into the feelings and motives of a character. They often begin their comments with "I think."
Predicting	Students speculate about what will happen later in the story and confirm predictions they made previously.
Questioning	Students ask "I wonder why" questions and write about confusions.

Involvement Responses

Character Identification	Students show personal identification with a character, sometimes writing "If I were _____, I would . . . " They express empathy, share related experiences from their own lives, and sometimes give advice to the character.
Character Assessment	Students judge a character's actions and often use evaluative terms such as *nice* or *dumb*.
Story Involvement	Students reveal their involvement as they express satisfaction with how the story is developing. They may comment on their desire to continue reading or use terms such as *disgusting, weird,* or *awesome* to react to sensory aspects of the story.

Literary Connections

Connections	Students make text-to-self, text-to-world, text-to-text, and text-to media (television shows and movies) connections.
Literary Evaluation	Students evaluate part or all of the book. They may offer "I liked/I didn't like" opinions and praise or condemn an author's style.

Adapted from Hancock, 2007.

the entries, and tallying the categories. Often students use only a few types of responses, not the wide range that's available. In this event, teachers can teach minilessons and model types of responses that students aren't using, and they can ask questions when they read journals to prompt students to think in new ways about the story they're reading.

Seventh graders' reading log entries about *The Giver* (Lowry, 2006) are shown in Figure 6–4. In these entries, students react to the book, make predictions, deepen their understanding of the story, ask questions, assume the role of the main character, and value the story. Each entry is categorized according to Hancock's patterns of response. As you read the students' excerpts, you might notice other patterns, too.

Double-Entry Journals

Students divide each entry into two columns when they write double-entry journals (Berthoff, 1981). In the left column, they usually write quotes from the story or other book they're reading, and in the right column, they relate each quote to their own life, the world around them, and other literature they've read. Through this type of journal, students become more engaged in what they are reading, note sentences that have personal connections, and become more sensitive to the author's language.

Students in a fifth-grade class wrote double-entry journals as they read C. S. Lewis's classic *The Lion, the Witch and the Wardrobe* (2005). After they read each chapter, students reviewed the chapter and selected one or two brief quotes. They wrote these excerpts in the left column of their journals, and they wrote reactions beside each quote in the right column. Excerpts from a fifth grader's journal are presented in Figure 6–5. This student's responses indicate that she is engaged in the story and is connecting the story to her own life.

Double-entry journals can be used in several other ways. Instead of recording quotes from the book, students can write "Reading Notes" in the left column and then add "Reactions" in the right column. In the left column, they write about the events they read about in the chapter. Then in the right column, they make personal connections to the events.

As an alternative, students can use the heading "Reading Notes" for one column and "Discussion Notes" for the other column. They write reading notes as they read or immediately after reading. Later, after discussing the story, or chapter of a longer book, students add discussion notes. As with other types of double-entry journals, it is in the second column that students make more interpretive comments.

Young children can use the double-entry format for a prediction journal (Macon, Bewell, & Vogt, 1991), labeling the left column "Predictions" and the right column "What Happened." In the left column, they write or draw a picture of what they predict will happen in the story or chapter before reading it. Then, after reading, they draw or write what actually happened in the right column.

Language Arts Notebooks

Language arts notebooks are a specialized type of journal in which students record a variety of information about language arts topics. Often students use these notebooks to take notes about procedures, concepts, strategies, and skills during minilessons. Procedure entries include the steps in giving a book talk, participating in a grand conversation, and proofreading a paper. Concept entries include information on authors and genres, contractions, homophones, parts of speech, plot diagrams, affixes, poetic formulas, and types of sentences. Strategy entries include explanations of visualization or connecting to personal experience, and student reflections about how they use the strategy during language arts activities. Skill entries include charts about forming plurals, using quotations in writing dialogue, alphabetizing a list of words, and skimming a content-area textbook.

FIGURE 6–4

Entries From Seventh Graders' Reading Logs About *The Giver*

Student	Excerpt	Response Pattern
Tiffany	I think the book *The Giver* is very scary because when you do something wrong you get released from the community. I think it would be terrible to be pushed out of your community and leave your family. Your family would be ashamed and embarrassed. It is like you are dead.	Story involvement
Scott	I don't think I could handle being a friend of Jonas's. In other words NO I would not like to be a friend of his. There would be too much pain involved and most of the time I wouldn't see Jonas.	Character identification
Rob	The part that hooked me was when the book said Jonas took his pills and did not have feelings about Fiona.	Understanding
Jared	As I'm reading I'm wondering if they get married at twelve because they get jobs at twelve.	Questioning
Elizabeth	Something that surprised me so far in the story was when Lily said she wanted to be a birthmother. Lily's mom became mad and said three years, three births, and then you're a laborer. Being a birthmother is not a good job at least after the three years. I hope that doesn't happen to Lily but I don't know what other job she should have.	Character assessment
Graciela	So far I think that the story is really sad. The story is sad because everyone has sameness except Jonas and the Giver. Jonas and the Giver are the only ones who can see color because of the memories. The story is also sad because no one has feelings.	Story involvement
Rob	Why didn't Jonas use the fire in his favorite memory to stay warmer on his long journey through the rain and snow, and the terrible coldness? Also, why didn't the author explain more about the things that are between the lines so the reader could really grasp them?	Literary evaluation
Marcos	Well, I can't really make a prediction of what is going to happen because I already read the book. If I hadn't read ahead my prediction would be that Jonas would get drowned in the river because he couldn't handle the pain.	Understanding
Rob	I think Jonas will confront his father. He won't ever forget what he saw his father do and it is wrong. Just wrong, wrong, wrong. If my father ever did that to an innocent little baby I would never forgive him. It's like abortion. I would confront him and tell him that I know. I will always know and so will God.	Predicting
Elizabeth	I don't exactly understand what happens at the end. It sounds like they froze to death. I think they died but I wish they found freedom and happiness. It is very sad.	Questioning
Mark	The ending is cool. Jonas and Gabe come back to the community but now it is changed. There are colors and the people have feelings. They believe in God and it is Christmas.	Story involvement
Graciela	At first I thought it would be good to have a perfect community. There would be no gangs and no crime and no sickness. But there is a lesson in this story. Now I think you can't have a perfect community. Even though we have bad things in our community we have love and other emotions and we can make choices.	Connections

FIGURE 6–5

Excerpts From a Fifth Grader's Double-Entry Journal About *The Lion, the Witch and the Wardrobe*

In the Text	My Response
Chapter 1 I tell you this is the sort of house where no one is going to mind what we do.	I remember the time that I went to Beaumont, Texas to stay with my aunt. My aunt's house was very large. She had a piano and she let us play it. She told us that we could do whatever we wanted to.
Chapter 5 "How do you know?" he asked, "that your sister's story is not true?"	It reminds me of when I was little and I had an imaginary place. I would go there in my mind. I made up all kinds of make-believe stories about myself in this imaginary place. One time I told my big brother about my imaginary place. He laughed at me and told me I was silly. But it didn't bother me because nobody can stop me from thinking what I want.
Chapter 15 Still they could see the shape of the great lion lying dead in his bonds.	When Aslan died I thought about when my Uncle Carl died.
They're nibbling at the cords.	This reminds me of the story where the lion lets the mouse go and the mouse helps the lion.

By recording this information in a notebook, students create a permanent reference book to use during language arts activities. Older students often divide their language arts notebooks into several sections, and they add information to sections on authors, words, spelling, parts of speech, sentences, strategies, poetry, stories, and study skills.

Learning Logs

Students write entries in learning logs to record and think about what they are learning in math, science, social studies, or other content areas. As they write in these journals, students reflect on their learning, discover gaps in their knowledge, and explore relationships between what they are learning and their past experiences. For example, in math class, they record explanations and examples of concepts presented in class and react to the mathematical concepts they are learning and any problems they may be having. Figure 6–6 presents an entry from a sixth grader's learning log in which she describes how to change improper fractions. Notice that after she describes the steps in sequence, she includes a review of the six steps. In addition, some upper-grade teachers allow students the last 5 minutes of math class to summarize the day's lesson and react to it in their learning logs.

Students can make daily entries in science logs to track the growth of plants or animals. For instance, a second-grade class observed caterpillars as they changed from caterpillars to chrysalides to butterflies over a period of 4 to 6 weeks. They each kept a log with daily entries, in which they noted the changes they observed using words describing shape, color, size, and other properties. Two pages from a second grader's log documenting the caterpillars' growth and change are presented in Figure 6–7.

FIGURE 6–6

A Sixth Grader's Math Learning Log Entry

Changing to Improper Fractions

To Change a mixed number such as $5\frac{2}{3}$, you must must multiply the denominator, which is the bottom number, times the whole number which is 5. So now we have: $3 \times 5 = 15$. Next you add the numerator to the problem like this! $15 + 2 = 17$. Put the same denominator, the bottom number, and it should look like this! $\frac{17}{3}$. To check your answer, find out how many times 3, the bottom number, goes into the top number, 17. It goes in 5 times. There are two left over, so the answer is $5\frac{2}{3}$. It is correct.

6 Steps!

1. $5\frac{2}{3}$
2. $3 \times 5 = 15$
3. $15 + 2 = 17$
4. $\frac{17}{3}$
5. $3\overline{)17} = 5\frac{2}{3}$
6. $5\frac{2}{3}$ – correct

Simulated Journals

Some children's books, such as *Catherine, Called Birdy* (Cushman, 1994), the story of a disenchanted English noble woman of the 13th century, are written as journals; authors research the time period, assume the role of a character, and write from the character's point of view. These books might be considered simulated journals. They are rich with historical details and incorporate both the words and phrasing of the period. At the end of these books, authors often include information about how they researched the period and explanations about the liberties they took with the character, setting, or events that are recorded. Scholastic Books publishes historical journals appropriate for fourth through eighth graders. The books include *I Walk in Dread: The Diary of Deliverance Trembley, Witness to the Salem Witch Trials* (Fraustino, 2004), which recounts events during the Salem witch hunts of 1692; *The Journal of Jesse Smoke: A Cherokee*

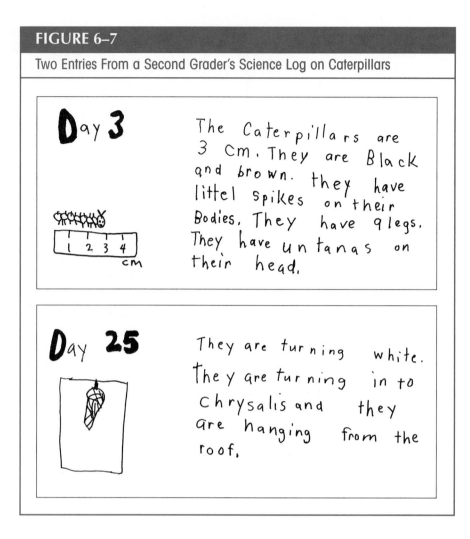

FIGURE 6–7

Two Entries From a Second Grader's Science Log on Caterpillars

Day **3**

The Caterpillars are 3 cm. They are Black and brown. they have littel spikes on their Bodies. They have 9 legs. They have untanas on their head.

1 2 3 4
cm

Day **25**

They are turning white. They are turning in to Chrysalis and they are hanging from the roof.

Boy (Bruchac, 2001), which records the Cherokee removal on the Trail of Tears in 1838; and *Catherine: The Great Journey* (Gregory, 2005), which chronicles the 14th year in the life of the German princess who became empress of Russia. Each book provides a glimpse into history from a young girl's or boy's perspective and is handsomely bound to look like an old journal. The paper is heavy and rough cut around the edges, and a ribbon page marker is bound into the book.

Students also write simulated journals, assuming the role of another person and writing from that person's viewpoint. For example, they can assume the role of a historical figure when they read biographies or as part of thematic units. As they read stories, they can assume the role of a character in the story. In this way, students gain insight into other people's lives and into historical events. A look at a series of diary entries written by a fifth grader who has assumed the role of Betsy Ross shows how she carefully chose the dates for each entry and wove in factual information:

May 15, 1773

Dear Diary,

This morning at 5:00 I had to wake up my husband John to get up for work but he wouldn't wake up. I immediately called the doc. He came over as fast as he

could. He asked me to leave the room so I did. An hour later he came out and told me he had passed away. I am so sad. I don't know what to do.

June 16, 1776

Dear Diary,

Today General Washington visited me about making a flag. I was so surprised. Me making a flag! I have made flags for the navy, but this is too much. But I said yes. He showed me a pattern of the flag he wanted. He also wanted six-pointed stars but I talked him into having five-pointed stars.

July 8, 1776

Dear Diary,

Today in front of Carpenter Hall the Declaration of Independence was read by Tom Jefferson. Well, I will tell you the whole story. I heard some yelling and shouting about liberty and everyone was gathering around Carpenter Hall. So I went to my next door neighbors to ask what was happening but Mistress Peters didn't know either so we both went down to Carpenter Hall. We saw firecrackers and heard a bell and the Declaration of Independence was being read aloud. When I heard this I knew a new country was born.

June 14, 1777

Dear Diary,

Today was a happy but scary day. Today the flag I made was adopted by Congress. I thought for sure that if England found out that a new flag was taking the

Anthony Magnacca/Merrill

Using Learning Logs

A third grader takes notes in her learning log as her classmates perform a science experiment. Her focus is on capturing ideas and using scientific words. Students often brainstorm a list of words, draw and label diagrams, record the steps in completing a task, and answer questions in their learning logs. Because the writing is informal, it's messier than other types of writing, but it must be legible. Writing is an important tool for learning because as they write, students clarify ideas and practice vocabulary.

old one's place something bad would happen. But I'm happy because I am the maker of the first American flag and I'm only 25 years old!

Students can use simulated journals in two ways: as a tool for learning or as a project. When students use simulated journals as a tool for learning, they write the entries as they are reading a book in order to get to know the character better or during a thematic unit as they are learning about the historical period. In these entries, students are exploring concepts and making connections between what they are learning and what they already know. These journal entries are less polished than when students write a simulated journal as a project. Students might choose to write a simulated journal as a culminating project for a literature focus unit or a thematic unit. For a project, students plan out their journals carefully, choose important dates, and use the writing process to draft, revise, edit, and publish their journals.

Teaching Students to Write in Journals

Journals are typically written in notebooks or booklets. Spiral-bound notebooks are useful for long-term personal and dialogue journals and for language arts notebooks, whereas small booklets of paper stapled together are more often used for reading logs, learning logs, and simulated journals that are used for one literature focus unit, literature circle, or thematic unit. Most teachers prefer to keep the journals in the classroom so that they will be available for students to write in each day, but students could write at home, too.

Students usually write at a particular time each day. Many teachers have students make personal or dialogue journal entries while they take attendance or immediately after recess. Language arts notebooks are often used during minilessons to record information about topics being studied. Teachers may assign the same types of journals throughout the school year, or they may alternate them, starting and stopping with particular literature focus units and thematic units.

How Journals Fit Into the Four Patterns of Practice

Literature Focus Units

Students usually write in reading logs, but sometimes they keep simulated journals where they write from one character's viewpoint as they read each chapter. They also write in language arts notebooks about information presented during minilessons.

Literature Circles

Students create reading logs for each book they read and discuss in a literature circle. They write notes while they're reading and take notes as classmates share information during the small-group discussions.

Reading and Writing Workshop

During reading workshop, students keep reading logs where they list books they've read and write responses, and during writing workshop, they can write lists of writing topics and first drafts in personal journals.

Thematic Units

Students write in learning logs. They can also keep double-entry journals where they write information in one column and their responses in the other, or they write simulated journals from the viewpoint of a historical personality or scientist.

Booklist

BOOKS IN WHICH CHARACTERS AND HISTORICAL PERSONALITIES KEEP JOURNALS

Cronin, D. (2005). *Diary of a spider.* New York: HarperCollins. (P)

Cruise, R. (1998). *The top-secret journal of Fiona Claire Jardin.* San Diego: Harcourt Brace. (M)

Cunningham, L. S. (2005). *The midnight diary of Zoya Blume.* New York: HarperCollins. (M–U).

Danticat, E. (2005). *Anacaona: Golden flower.* New York: Scholastic. (M–U)

Garland, S. (1998). *A line in the sand: The Alamo diary of Lucinda Lawrence.* New York: Scholastic. (M–U)

George, J. C. (2001). *My side of the mountain.* New York: Puffin Books. (M–U)

Hesse, K. (2000). *Stowaway.* New York: McElderry. (M–U)

Hite, S. (2003). *Journal of Rufus Rowe, witness to the battle of Fredericksburg.* New York: Scholastic. (M–U)

Lewis, C. C. (1998). *Dilly's big sister diary.* New York: Millbrook Press. (P)

Ma, Y. (2005). *The diary of Ma Yan: The struggles and hopes of a Chinese schoolgirl.* New York: HarperCollins. (M–U)

McKissack, P. C. (2000). *Nzingha: Warrior queen of Matamba.* New York: Scholastic. (M–U)

Morpurgo, M. (2006). *The amazing story of Adolphus Tips.* New York: Scholastic. (M–U)

Moss, M. (2002). *Galen: My life in imperial Rome.* San Diego: Harcourt Brace. (M–U)

Myers, W. D. (1999). *The journal of Scott Pendleton Collins: A World War II soldier.* New York: Scholastic. (M–U)

Parker, S. (1999). *It's a frog's life.* Pleasantville, NY: Reader's Digest. (P)

Perez, A. I. (2002). *My diary from here to there/Mi diario de aquí hasta allá.* San Francisco: Children's Book Press. (P)

Philbrick, R. (2001). *The journal of Douglas Allen Deeds: The Donner party expedition.* New York: Scholastic. (M–U)

Platt, R. (2005). *Egyptian diary: The journal of Nakht.* New York: Candlewick Press. (M)

Veciana-Suarez, A. (2002). *Flight to freedom.* New York: Scholastic. (U)

Watts, L. (2002). *Stonecutter.* San Diego: Harcourt Brace. (U)

P = primary grades (K–2); M = middle grades (3–5); U = upper grades (6–8)

Teachers introduce students to journal writing using minilessons in which they explain the purpose of the journal-writing activity and the procedures for gathering ideas, writing the entry, and sharing it with classmates. Teachers often model the procedure by writing a sample entry on chart paper as students observe. This sample demonstrates that the writing is to be informal, with ideas emphasized over correctness. Then students make their own first entries, and several read their entries aloud. Through this sharing, students who are still unclear about the activity have additional models on which to base their own writing. Similar minilessons are used to introduce each type of journal. Even though most types of journals are similar, the purpose of the journal, the information included in the entries, and the writer's viewpoint vary according to type.

Students write in journals on a regular schedule, usually daily. After they know how to write the appropriate type of entry, they can write independently, and some students usually read their journal entries aloud afterward. If the sharing becomes too time-consuming, they can share in small groups or with partners. Then, after everyone has had a chance to share, several students can be selected to share with the entire class.

The Reading-Writing Connection. Journal writing can also be introduced with examples from literature. Characters in children's literature, such as Amelia in *Amelia's Notebook* (Moss, 2006) and Birdy in *Catherine, Called Birdy* (Cushman, 1994), keep journals in which they record events in their lives and their thoughts and dreams. A list of books in which characters and historical personalities keep journals is presented in the Booklist on page 195. In these books, the characters demonstrate the process of journal writing and illustrate both the pleasures and the difficulties of keeping a journal.

Minilessons. Teachers teach minilessons on procedures, concepts, strategies, and skills about writing in journals. A list of minilesson topics is presented in the box on pages 204. It is especially important to teach a minilesson when students are learning a new type of journal or when they are having difficulty with a particular procedure or strategy, such as changing point of view for simulated journals or writing in two columns in double-entry journals.

Assessing Students' Journal Entries

Students can write in journals independently with little or no sharing with the teacher, or they can make daily entries that the teacher monitors or reads regularly. Typically, students are accustomed to having teachers read all or most of their writing, but the quantity of writing students produce in journals is often too great for teachers to keep up with. Some teachers rarely check students' journals; others read selected entries and monitor the remaining ones; still others try to read all entries. These three management approaches can be termed *private journals, monitored journals*, and *shared journals*. When students write private journals, they write primarily for themselves, and sharing with classmates or the teacher is voluntary; the teacher does not read the journals unless invited to. When students write monitored journals, they write primarily for themselves, but the teacher monitors the writing to ensure that entries are being made regularly. The teacher simply checks that entries have been made and does not read the entries unless they are marked "Read me." Students write shared journals primarily for the teacher; the teacher regularly reads all entries, except those marked "private," and offers encouragement and suggestions.

Many teachers have concerns about how to grade journal entries. Because the writing is usually not revised and edited, teachers should not grade the quality of the entries. One option is to give points for each entry made, especially in personal journals. However, some teachers grade the content in learning logs and simulated journals because they can check to see whether the entries include particular pieces of information. For example, if students are writing simulated journals about the Crusades, they may be asked to include five pieces of historically accurate information in their entries. (It is helpful to ask students to identify the five pieces of information by underlining and numbering them.) Rough-draft journal entries should not be graded for mechanical correctness. Students need to complete the writing process and revise and edit their entries if they are to be graded for mechanical correctness.

LETTER WRITING

Letters are a way of talking to people who live too far away to visit. Audience and purpose are important considerations, but form is also important in letter writing. Although letters may be personal, they involve a genuine audience of one or more persons. Through letter writing, students have the opportunity not only to sharpen their writing skills, but also to increase their awareness of audience. Because letters are written to communicate with a specific and important audience, students

Writing can be difficult for English learners, and journals are the best way to introduce writing. It's essential that English learners have daily opportunities to practice writing because they need to develop writing fluency, the ability to get words down on paper. Through sustained writing, their handwriting skills improve, and their ability to spell high-frequency English words increases. In addition, there's less pressure because when students write in journals, the emphasis is on ideas rather than on correctness and neatness.

Students usually write about events in their own lives before writing about books they're reading and the content they're learning in thematic units. Peregoy and Boyle (2005) recommend that English learners write in buddy journals, which are a lot like dialogue journals: Students write back and forth to other English learners, and in these entries that are like written conversations, they write about topics that interest them, sharing ideas and asking questions. And as they're developing writing fluency, students are also learning that the purpose of writing is communicating ideas.

Many English learners write brief entries, often using and reusing familiar words and sentence patterns, and their entries are typically sprinkled with grammatical errors and misspelled words. Too often, teachers conclude that their English learners just can't write, but they can help these students write better journal entries. The first step involves examining students' entries to determine whether the problems center on undeveloped ideas, limited vocabulary, nonstandard grammar, or spelling errors. Often teachers notice problems in all four areas, but they prioritize the problem areas and then work to resolve them.

Ideas and Vocabulary

Ideas and vocabulary usually go hand in hand. Teachers model how to brainstorm ideas and related words before beginning to write, and they also demonstrate how to write entries with interesting, well-developed ideas. Teachers can also help individual students talk out their ideas and brainstorm a bank of words before they begin writing.

Grammar

To focus on correcting nonstandard grammar errors, teachers teach minilessons on particular grammar concepts and then have students locate examples of the concept in their journal entries and make any needed corrections.

Spelling

Even though students usually misspell some words in their journals entries, they should be expected to spell most high-frequency words correctly. Teachers explain how useful high-frequency words are to writers, and they demonstrate how to locate high-frequency words on the classroom word wall or on individual word walls that students keep in their journals. English learners can also return to a previously written journal entry and check for misspelled words using the word wall as a resource.

take more care to think through what they want to say, to write legibly, and to use spelling, capitalization, and punctuation conventions correctly.

Children's letters are typically classified as friendly or business letters. Formats for friendly and business letters are shown in the LA Essentials box on page 199. The choice of format depends on the purpose of the letter. Friendly letters might be informal, chatty letters to pen pals or thank-you notes to a television newscaster who has visited the classroom. When students write to the National Park Service requesting information about the Grand Canyon or another park or send letters to the president expressing an opinion about current events, they use the more formal, business-letter style. Before students write both types of letters, they need to learn how to format them.

Friendly Letters

After teachers have introduced the format for friendly letters, students need to choose a "real" someone to write to. Writing authentic letters that will be delivered is much more valuable than writing practice letters to be graded by the teacher. Students write friendly letters to classmates, friends who live out of town, relatives, and pen pals. They may want to keep a list of addresses of people to write friendly letters to on a special page in their journals or in address booklets. In these casual letters, they share news about events in their lives and ask questions to learn more about the person they are writing to and to encourage that person to write back. Receiving mail is the real reward of letter writing!

Robinson, Crawford, and Hall (1991) examined the effects of personal letter writing on young children's writing development. In the study, a group of 20 kindergartners wrote back and forth to the researchers over a 2-year period. In their early letters, the children told about themselves, promised to be friends with their correspondent, and asked the correspondent questions. Over the 2-year period, they matured as letter writers and continued to be eager correspondents. Their letters became more sophisticated, and they developed letter-writing strategies that took their readers into account. The researchers concluded that authentic, purposeful, and sustained letter-writing experiences are extremely valuable for children.

Pen Pal Letters. Teachers can arrange for their students to exchange letters with students in another class by contacting a teacher in a nearby school or local educational associations, or by answering advertisements online or in educational magazines. Another possible arrangement is to have your class become pen pals with college students in a language arts methods class. Over a semester, the children and the preservice teachers can write back and forth four, five, or six times, and perhaps even meet at the end of the semester. The children have the opportunity to be pen pals with college students, and the preservice teachers have the opportunity to get to know a student and examine his or her writing development.

Courtesy Letters. Invitations and thank-you notes are two other types of friendly letters that students write. They may write to parents to invite them to an after-school program, to the class across the hall to invite them to visit a classroom exhibit, or to a person in the community to invite him or her to be interviewed as part of a thematic unit. Students also write letters to thank people who have been helpful.

FORMS FOR FRIENDLY AND BUSINESS LETTERS

Friendly Letter

Street
City, State ZIP
Date   ←— Return address

Greeting —→   Dear _____,

Body {

Your friend,   ←— Complimentary closing

Signature

Business Letter

Street
City, State ZIP
Date   ←— Return address

Inside —→   Person's Name
address   Company Name
             Street
             City, State ZIP

Greeting —→ Dear _____,

Body {

Sincerely,   ←— Complimentary closing

Signature

E-mail Messages. The Internet has created a completely new way for students to send messages electronically to correspondents anywhere in the world. It's a fast and simple way to send and reply to mail, and messages can be saved and stored on the computer, too. Students can use e-mail message forms. They type the correspondent's e-mail address in the top window, specify a topic in the subject window, and then write their message in the large window. They begin by greeting their correspondent, and then they write their message. Students should keep their messages short—no longer than one or two screens—so that they can easily be read on the computer screen. They end their messages with a closing, much as in other types of letters. McKeon (1999) studied the e-mail messages that a class of third graders wrote about the books they were reading and concluded that e-mail is a constructive way to enhance students' learning as well as an effective strategy for teachers to personalize their interaction with students.

Letters to Authors and Illustrators. Students write letters to favorite authors and illustrators to share their ideas and feelings about the books they have read. They ask questions about how a particular character was developed or why the illustrator used a certain art medium. Students also describe the books they have written. Here's a letter that a fourth grader wrote to Eve Bunting at the end of an author study, after the class had read and responded to eight of her books.

> *Dear Eve Bunting,*
>
> *I have read some of your books. All of them had friendship in them. My favorite book is Smoky Night. I think the theme is get along and respect each other. My family needs to learn to respect each other and to get along because I fight with my brother and he fights with my sister.*
>
> *How many picture books have you written? I have read eight of them. Have you ever met Chris Van Allsburg because we did an author study on him also. Why do you write your books?*
>
> *Sincerely,*
>
> *Jeffrey*

Most authors and illustrators reply to children's letters when possible, and Eve Bunting answered this fourth grader's letters. However, they receive thousands of letters from children every year and cannot be pen pals with students. Beverly Cleary's award-winning book *Dear Mr. Henshaw* (1983) offers a worthwhile lesson about what students (and their teachers) can realistically expect from authors and illustrators. Here are some guidelines for writing to authors and illustrators:

- Follow the correct letter format with return address, greeting, body, closing, and signature.
- Use the process approach to write, revise, and edit the letter.
- Recopy the letter so that it will be neat and easy to read.
- Write the return address on both envelope and letter.
- Include a stamped, self-addressed envelope for a reply.
- Be polite in the letter.

Students should write genuine letters to share their thoughts and feelings about the author's writing or the illustrator's artwork, and they should write only to authors and illustrators whose work they are familiar with. In their letters, students should avoid asking personal questions, such as how much money the author or illustrator earns. They should not ask for free books, because authors and illustrators usually don't have copies of their books to give away. Students send their letters to the author or illustrator in care of the publisher (the publisher's name appears on the book's title page, and the address usually appears on the copyright page, the page following the title page). If students cannot find the complete mailing address, they can check online.

Business Letters

Students write business letters to seek information, to complain and compliment, and to transact business. They use this more formal letter style and format (as shown in the LA Essentials box on page 199) to communicate with businesses, local newspapers, and government agencies. Students may write to businesses to order products, to ask questions, and to complain about or compliment specific products; they write letters to the editors of local newspapers and magazines to comment on articles and to express their opinions. It is important that students support their comments and opinions with facts if they hope to have their letters published. Students can also write to local, state, and national government officials to express concerns, make suggestions, or seek information.

Simulated Letters

Students can write simulated letters, in which they assume the identity of a historical or literary figure (Roop, 1995). Simulated letters are similar to simulated journals except that they are formatted as letters. Students can write letters as though they were Davy Crockett or another of the men defending the Alamo, or Thomas Edison, describing his invention of the lightbulb. They can write from one book character to another; for example, after reading *Sarah, Plain and Tall* (MacLachlan, 2004), students can assume the persona of Sarah and write a letter to her brother William, as a third grader did in this letter:

> *Dear William,*
>
> *I'm having fun here. There was a very big storm here. It was so big it looked like the sea. Sometimes I am very lonesome for home but sometimes it is very fun here in Ohio. We swam in the cow pond and I taught Caleb how to swim. They were afraid I would leave. Maggie and Matthew brought some chickens.*
>
> *Love,*
>
> *Sarah*

Even though these letters are never mailed, they are written to a specific audience. Classmates assume the role of the person to whom the letter is addressed and respond to the letter from that point of view. Also, these letters show clearly how well students comprehend the story, and teachers can use them to monitor students' learning.

Teaching Students to Write Letters

Students use the process approach to write letters so that they can make their letters interesting, complete, and readable. The steps are shown in the Step by Step feature below.

The Reading-Writing Connection. A variety of books that include letters have been published for children. Some of these are stories with letters that children can take out of envelopes and read. *With Love, Little Red Hen* (Ada, 2001) is a collection of letters that tells a story, and Ann Turner's *Nettie's Trip South* (1987) is a book-length letter about the inhumanity of slavery in the antebellum South. Other books are epistolary novels in which the story is told through a collection of letters, such as *Dear Whiskers* (Nagda, 2000), the story of a fourth grader who befriends her second-grade pen pal, a Saudi Arabian girl who has recently come to the United States. The Booklist on the next page lists books that teachers can share as part of letter-writing activities.

Minilessons. Teachers present minilessons about letters, including how they are formatted and how to craft letters to encourage correspondents to respond. A list of minilesson topics and a sample minilesson on writing letters to favorite authors are presented in the box on pages 204 and 205. These lessons are sometimes presented as part of language arts, but at other times teachers teach minilessons on letter writing as part of social studies or science lessons because students often write letters as part of thematic units. For example, students write business letters to request information during a science unit on ecology or write simulated letters as part of a history-based thematic unit.

-------------- Writing Letters --------------

1 **Gather and organize information for the letter.** Students participate in prewriting activities, such as brainstorming or clustering, to decide what information to include in their letters. If they are writing friendly letters, particularly to pen pals, they also identify several questions to ask.

2 **Review the friendly- or business-letter form.** Before writing the rough drafts of their letters, students review the friendly- or business-letter form.

3 **Draft the letter.** Students write a rough draft, incorporating the information developed during prewriting and following either the friendly- or the business-letter style.

4 **Revise and edit the letter.** Students meet in a writing group to share their rough drafts and get feedback to use in revising their letters. They also edit their letters with a partner, proofreading to identify errors and correcting as many as possible.

5 **Make the final copy of the letter.** Students recopy their letters and address envelopes. Teachers often review how to address an envelope during this step, too.

6 **Mail the letter.** The crucial last step is to mail the letters and wait for a reply.

BOOKLIST

BOOKS THAT INCLUDE LETTERS

Ada, A. F. (1998). *Yours truly, Goldilocks.* New York: Atheneum. (P)

Ada, A. F. (2001). *With love, Little Red Hen.* New York: Atheneum. (P)

Avi. (2003). *Nothing but the truth.* New York: Orchard Books. (U)

Ayres, K. (1998). *North by night: A story of the Underground Railroad.* New York: Delacorte. (M–U)

Bonners, S. (2000). *Edwina victorious.* New York: Farrar, Straus & Giroux. (M)

Cherry, L. (1994). *The armadillo from Amarillo.* New York: Gulliver Green. (M)

Danziger, P., & Martin, A. M. (1998). *P. S. Longer letter later.* New York: Scholastic. (M)

Danziger, P., & Martin, A. M. (2000). *Snail mail no more.* New York: Scholastic. (M)

Klise, K. (1999). *Letters from camp.* New York: Avon. (U)

Klise, K. (2006). *Regarding the bathrooms: A privy to the past.* San Diego: Harcourt. (U)

Lyons, M. E. (1992). *Letters from a slave girl: The story of Harriet Jacobs.* New York: Scribner. (U)

Nagda, A. W. (2000). *Dear Whiskers.* New York: Holiday House. (M)

Nolen, J. (2002). *Plantzilla.* San Diego: Harcourt Brace. (P–M)

Olson, M. W. (2000). *Nice try, tooth fairy.* New York: Simon & Schuster. (P)

Pak, S. (1999). *Dear Juno.* New York: Viking. (P)

Pinkney, A. D. (1994). *Dear Benjamin Banneker.* San Diego: Gulliver/Harcourt Brace. (M)

Stewart, S. (1997). *The gardener.* New York: Farrar, Straus & Giroux. (P)

Teague, M. (2002). *Dear Mrs. LaRue: Letters from obedience school.* New York: Scholastic. (P)

Teague, M. (2004). *Detective LaRue: Letters from the investigation.* New York: Scholastic. (P)

Woodruff, E. (1994). *Dear Levi: Letters from the Overland Trail.* New York: Knopf. (M–U)

Assessing Students' Letters

Traditionally, students wrote letters and turned them in for the teacher to grade. The letters were returned to the students after they were graded, but they were never mailed. Teachers now recognize the importance of having an audience for student writing, and research suggests that students write better when they know that their writing will be read by someone other than the teacher. Although it's often necessary to assess student writing, it would be inappropriate for the teacher to put a grade on the letter if it's going to be mailed to someone. Teachers can instead develop a checklist or rubric for evaluating students' letters without marking on them.

A third-grade teacher developed the checklist in the Weaving Assessment Into Practice feature on page 206; the checklist identifies specific behaviors and measurable products. The teacher shares the checklist with students before they begin to write so that they know what is expected of them and how they will be graded. At an evaluation conference before the letters are mailed, the teacher reviews the checklist with each student. The letters are mailed without evaluative comments or grades written on them, but the completed checklist goes into students' writing folders. A grading scale can be developed from the checklist; for example, points can be awarded for each checkmark in the Yes column so that five checkmarks can equal a grade of A, four checkmarks a B, and so on.

What Students Need to Learn About Personal Writing

Topics

Procedures	Concepts	Strategies and Skills
Journals		
Write a journal entry	Personal journals	Choose a topic
Share entries	Dialogue journals	Generate
Respond in dialogue journals	Language arts notebooks	Organize
Write in language arts notebooks	*Reading logs*	Predict
Write reading log entries		Incorporate key vocabulary
Write double-entry journals	Double-entry journals	Assume another viewpoint
Use learning logs	Learning logs	
Write simulated journals	Simulated journals	
Letters		
Write pen pal letters	Friendly-letter format	Use letter formats correctly
Write courtesy letters	Business-letter format	Ask questions to elicit information
Write e-mail messages		Respond to correspondent's questions
Write letters to authors and illustrators		
Write business letters		
Write simulated letters		

To learn more about personal writing, please visit MyEducationLab. You can watch fourth graders responding in reading logs to the books their teacher is reading aloud by going to the topic "Writing" and clicking on the video "Reading Logs."

Minilesson

Mr. Rinaldi's Eighth Graders Write Simulated Letters

1 Introduce the topic

Mr. Rinaldi's eighth graders are studying the American Civil War, and each student has assumed the persona of someone who lived in that period. Many students have become Union or Confederate soldiers and given themselves names and identities. Today, Mr. Rinaldi asks his students to think about the war as their persona would. He explains that they will write simulated letters to Abraham Lincoln or Jefferson Davis, arguing an issue as their persona might. He explains that a simulated letter is a letter that is written as if the writer were someone else.

2 Share examples

Mr. Rinaldi assumed the persona of a Confederate bugle boy when his students assumed personas, and he reads a letter he has written to Abraham Lincoln as that bugle boy, begging Lincoln to end the war. He gives three reasons why the war should end: the South has the right to choose its own destiny; the South is being destroyed by the war; and too many boys are dying. He ends his emotional letter this way: *I 'spect I'ma gonna die, too, Mr. President. What ya' gonna do when there be no more of us to shoot? No more Johnny Rebs to die. When the South has all died away, will you be a-smilin' then?* The students are stunned by the power of their teacher's simulated letter.

3 Provide information

Mr. Rinaldi explains that he did three things in his simulated letter to make it powerful: He wrote in persona—the way a scared, uneducated boy might write—he included vocabulary words about the war, and he argued his point of view persuasively. Together they brainstorm a list of arguments or persuasive appeals—for better food and clothing for soldiers and to end the war or to continue the war. He passes out a prewriting form that students use to plan their simulated letters.

4 Supervise practice

The students write their letters using the writing process. The planning sheet serves as prewriting, and students draft, revise, and edit their letters as Mr. Rinaldi conferences with students, encouraging them to develop the voice of their personas. Afterward, students share their letters with the class.

5 Reflect on learning

After the lesson, Mr. Rinaldi talks with his students about their simulated letters. He asks them to reflect on what they have learned, and the students emphasize that what they learned was about the inhumanity of war, even though they thought they were learning about letters.

Weaving Assessment Into Practice

A CHECKLIST FOR ASSESSING STUDENTS' PEN PAL LETTERS

Pen Pal Letter Checklist

Name _____

	Yes	No
1. Did you complete the cluster?	☐	☐
2. Did you include questions in your letter?	☐	☐
3. Did you put your letter in the friendly letter form?	☐	☐

_____ return address
_____ greeting
_____ 3 or more paragraphs
_____ closing
_____ salutation and name

	Yes	No
4. Did you write a rough draft of your letter?	☐	☐
5. Did you revise your letter with suggestions from people in your writing group?	☐	☐
6. Did you proofread your letter and correct as many errors as possible?	☐	☐

Review

Two types of personal writing are journals and letters. Journals are an important learning tool that students at all grade levels can use effectively. Students use journal writing to share events in their lives and to record what they are learning in literature focus units, literature circles, and thematic units. Students write three kinds of letters: friendly letters, business letters, and simulated letters. Here are the key concepts presented in this chapter:

- Students write in seven kinds of journals: personal journals, dialogue journals, reading logs, double-entry journals, language arts notebooks, learning logs, and simulated journals.
- Dialogue journals are especially useful for English learners.
- Reading logs, double-entry journals, and simulated journals are often used during literature focus units and literature circles.
- Learning logs and simulated journals are used for thematic units.
- Even young children can draw and write in personal journals and reading logs.
- Teachers teach minilessons about how to write in journals.
- Students often share entries with classmates, although personal journal entries are usually private.
- The friendly and business letters that children write should be mailed to authentic audiences.

- Students write simulated letters in connection with literature focus units, literature circles, and thematic units.
- The focus in personal writing is on developing writing fluency and using writing for authentic purposes.

Professional References

Berthoff, A. E. (1981). *The making of meaning.* Montclair, NJ: Boynton/Cook.

Bode, B. A. (1989). Dialogue journal writing. *The Reading Teacher, 42,* 568–571.

Britton, J., Burgess, T., Martin, N., McLeod, A., & Rosen, H. (1975). *The development of writing abilities, 11–18.* London: Schools Council Publications.

Hancock, M. R. (2007). *Language arts: Extending the possibilities.* Upper Saddle River, NJ: Merrill/Prentice Hall.

Hannon, J. (1999). Talking back: Kindergarten dialogue journals. *The Reading Teacher, 53,* 200–203.

Macon, J. M., Bewell, D., & Vogt, M. E. (1991). *Responses to literature, grades K–8.* Newark, DE: International Reading Association.

McGee, L. M., & Richgels, D. J. (2007). *Literacy's beginnings: Supporting young readers and writers* (5th ed.). Boston: Allyn & Bacon.

McKeon, C. A. (1999). The nature of children's e-mail in one classroom. *The Reading Teacher, 52,* 698–706.

Nash, M. F. (1995). "Leading from behind": Dialogue response journals. In N. L. Roser & M. G. Martinez (Eds.), *Book talk and beyond: Children and teachers respond to literature* (pp. 217–225). Newark, DE: International Reading Association.

Peregoy, S. F., & Boyle, W. F. (2005). *Reading, writing, and learning in ESL: A resource book for K–12 teachers* (4th ed.). Boston: Allyn & Bacon.

Reyes, M. de la Luz. (1991). A process approach to literacy using dialogue journals and literature logs with second language learners. *Research in the Teaching of English, 25,* 291–313.

Robinson, A., Crawford, L., & Hall, N. (1991). *Someday you will no (sic) all about me: Young children's explorations in the world of letters.* Portsmouth, NH: Heinemann.

Roop, P. (1995). Keep the reading lights burning. In M. Sorensen & B. Lehman (Eds.), *Teaching with children's books: Paths to literature-based instruction* (pp. 197–202). Urbana, IL: National Council of Teachers of English.

Children's Book References

Ada, A. F. (2001). *With love, Little Red Hen.* New York: Atheneum.

Ahlberg, J., & Ahlberg, A. (2006). *The jolly postman, or other people's letters.* New York: LB Kids.

Bruchac, J. (2001). *The journal of Jesse Smoke: A Cherokee boy.* New York: Scholastic.

Bunting, E. (1999). *Smoky night.* San Diego: Harcourt Brace.

Cleary, B. (1983). *Dear Mr. Henshaw.* New York: Morrow.

Cushman, K. (1994). *Catherine, called Birdy.* New York: Harper-Collins.

Finch, M. (2001). *The three billy goats Gruff.* Cambridge, MA: Barefoot Books.

Fraustino, L. R. (2004). *I walk in dread: The diary of Deliverance Trembley, Witness to the Salem witch trials.* New York: Scholastic.

Gregory, K. (2005). *Catherine: The great journey.* New York: Scholastic.

Lewis, C. S. (2005). *The lion, the witch and the wardrobe.* New York: HarperCollins.

Lowry, L. (2006). *The giver.* New York: Delacorte.

MacLachlan, P. (2004). *Sarah, plain and tall.* New York: HarperCollins.

Moss, M. (2006). *Amelia's notebook.* New York: Simon & Schuster.

Nagda, A. W. (2000). *Dear Whiskers.* New York: Holiday House.

Paterson, K. (1987). *The great Gilly Hopkins.* New York: Harper & Row.

Turner, A. (1987). *Nettie's trip south.* New York: Macmillan.

chapter seven

Listening to Learn

The second graders in Mr. Hernandez's classroom are involved in a monthlong study of folktales, and this week they're comparing several versions of "The Little Red Hen." On Monday, Mr. Hernandez read aloud Paul Galdone's *Little Red Hen* (2006), and the children reread it with buddies the next day. Next, he read aloud Jerry Pinkney's *The Little Red Hen* (2006), and they compared it to Galdone's version. On Wednesday and Thursday, the children read "The Little Red Hen" in their reading textbooks and compared this version with the others.

Parent volunteers came into the classroom on Wednesday to make bread with the students. The second graders learned how to read a recipe and use measuring cups and other cooking tools as they made the bread. They baked the bread in the school kitchen, and what they enjoyed was eating freshly baked bread—still warm from the oven—dripping with butter and jam.

The next day, Mr. Hernandez read aloud *Bread, Bread, Bread* (Morris, 1993), an informational book about the breads that people eat around the world, and parents brought in different kinds of bread for the children to sample, including tortillas, rye bread, corn bread, bagels, Jewish matzoh, blueberry muffins, Indian chapatty, and Italian breadsticks. As they sampled them, the children took turns talking about the kinds of bread their families eat.

Today, Mr. Hernandez is reading aloud *Cook-a-Doodle-Doo!* (Stevens & Crummel, 1999), the story of the Little Red Hen's great-grandson, Big Brown Rooster, who manages to bake a strawberry shortcake with the help of three friends—Turtle, Iguana, and Pig. He sets out a story box of objects related to the story: a chef's hat,

Should teachers encourage discussion during a read-aloud or postpone it until afterward?

Some teachers ask children to listen quietly while they read aloud and then talk about it afterward. Other teachers, however, invite children to become actively involved as they read aloud. These teachers stop reading periodically to pose questions to stimulate discussion, ask them to make predictions, and encourage children to offer spontaneous comments while they are listening. As you read this vignette, notice how Mr. Hernandez uses discussion to support his second graders' comprehension.

a flour sifter, an egg beater, a plastic strawberry, an oven mitt, a shortcake pan, a timer, a pastry blender, and measuring cups and spoons. The students identify the objects, and Mr. Hernandez prepares a word card for each one so that they can practice matching objects and word cards at a center. Almost immediately, Mikey guesses, "I know what the story is about! Little Red Hen is going to cook something, but it isn't bread. Um . . . Maybe it is strawberry jam to put on the bread."

"That's a good prediction, Mikey, but let me get one more clue for this story box," Mr. Hernandez says, as he reaches over to a nearby rack of puppets. He selects a rooster puppet and adds it to the box. He looks at the students expectantly, and Mallory asks, "Is that a hen?" "No, it isn't," Mr. Hernandez replies. Again he waits until Cristina offers, "I think it's a rooster." "You're right! A rooster is a male chicken, and a hen is a female chicken," he explains. Then Mikey revises his prediction, "Now I know! It's a story about a rooster who cooks something with strawberries."

Mr. Hernandez shows the cover of *Cook-a-Doodle-Doo!* and reads the title. At first the children laugh at the title, and then several of them repeat it aloud. "What does the title make you think of?" Mr. Hernandez asks. Jesus jumps up and imitates a rooster as he calls, "Cock-a-doodle-doo! Cock-a-doodle-doo!" The children compare the sound a rooster makes to the book's title and conclude that the rooster in this book is going to do some cooking.

The teacher draws the students' attention back to the book and asks, "What do you think the rooster is going to cook?" Lacey and Connor both answer "strawberry pancakes," and everyone agrees. Mr. Hernandez asks if anyone has ever tasted strawberry shortcake, but no one has. He explains what it is and tells the class it's his favorite dessert. Then he looks back at the cover illustration and says, "I keep looking at this picture, and I think it looks just like strawberry shortcake."

"Let's start reading," Mr. Hernandez says, and he reads the first two pages of the story that introduce the Little Red Hen's great-grandson, Big Brown Rooster, who is the main character. The children point out the similarity between Little Red Hen's and Big Brown Rooster's names: They are each three words long, they each have a size word, a color word, and an animal name, and words are in the same order in each name.

Mr. Hernandez continues reading, and they learn that the Rooster does plan to make strawberry shortcake—their teacher's favorite dessert. "What's shortcake?" Larry asks. "Is it the opposite of long cake?" Everyone laughs, including Mr. Hernandez. He explains that shortcake is flatter than cake, more like a biscuit. Mikey asks, "Is it like a brownie? Brownies are flatter than chocolate cake." "That's a good comparison," Mr. Hernandez says. Sammy offers: "A tortilla is flatter than a piece of bread." "Good! That's another good comparison," the teacher responds. "All this talk about food is making me hungry."

"Look at this," Mr. Hernandez says, and he points to the cookbook that Big Brown Rooster is holding in the illustration. "That's Little Red Hen's cookbook—*The Joy of Cooking Alone*," he laughs. "My wife's favorite cookbook is called *The Joy of Cooking*," he explains. "I wonder why the illustrator added the word *alone* to the title of her cookbook?" "That's because no one would help her make bread," Mallory explains.

The teacher continues reading the story. He turns the page and shows the illustration, a picture of Big Brown Rooster talking to a dog, a cat, and a goose, and the children, remembering the events from "Little Red Hen," spontaneously call out to Rooster, "No, don't ask them. They won't help you!" Big Brown Rooster does ask the three animals to help him, and as the children predicted, they refuse. As Mr. Hernandez reads the "Not I" refrain, everyone joins in. Sondra comments on the similarities to the "Little Red Hen" story: "There's a dog, a cat, and a goose like in the other story, and they won't listen to the Big Brown Rooster either." Then the children predict that Big Brown Rooster, like Little Red Hen, will have to cook alone.

On the next several pages, they learn that three other animals—Turtle, who can read recipes, Iguana, who can get "stuff," and Pig, who is a tasting expert—offer to help. The children get excited. "I think this story is going to be different. It's better," Cristina comments. Mr. Hernandez wonders aloud if these three animals will be good helpers, and the children agree that they will be.

The rooster calls the four of them a "team" on the next page, and Mr. Hernandez asks, "What is a team?" The second graders mention basketball teams, so the teacher rephrases his question: "What makes a group of basketball players a team? What do they do when they are a team?" Students respond that players work together to make a score and win a game. "So, what kind of team are the rooster, the turtle, the iguana, and the pig?" Connor explains, "They are a cooking team. I predict they will work together to cook strawberry shortcake." Then Raymond adds, "And Mr. Hernandez is the captain of the team!"

Mr. Hernandez continues reading, as Turtle reads the recipe and Iguana collects the ingredients for strawberry shortcake. In the story, Iguana doesn't know the difference between a *flower* and *flour* and because the children seem confused, too, the teacher explains the homophones. Iguana doesn't know about cooking tools and procedures either. He wants to use a ruler instead of a measuring cup to measure flour and he looks for teaspoons in a teapot, for example. Because the children recently used measuring cups and spoons when they baked bread, they are more knowledgeable than Iguana, and Sammy says, "That iguana is silly. He's not very smart either." On the next page,

Iguana misunderstands "stick of butter." He breaks a stick from a tree branch, and Lacey calls out, "No, Iguana, that's the wrong kind of stick."

As each ingredient is added, Pig offers to taste the batter, but Big Brown Rooster replies "not yet." Mr. Hernandez pauses after he reads this and reflects, "Pig is eager to taste the shortcake batter. I wonder how long he'll wait patiently for his turn to taste." "Maybe Big Brown Rooster should give him something else to do," Sondra offers. "I'd tell him to go in the living room and watch a video because that's what my mama tells my brother," says Connor. Mr. Hernandez continues reading, and in the story, Pig is getting more desperate to taste the batter. Jesus calls out, "Oh no! Now Pig really, really wants to taste it. Something bad is going to happen." Everyone agrees.

The teacher continues reading. The characters finish mixing the ingredients and put the batter in the oven to bake. "Wow! I'm surprised that Pig is being so good," Mallory offers. "I thought he would gobble up all the shortcake from the mixing bowl." The others agree. "So, now you think the shortcake is going to turn out right?" Mr. Hernandez asks. Most of the children think that it will, but Jesus and Mikey predict trouble ahead.

Mr. Hernandez continues reading. The characters cut the strawberries in half and make whipped cream while the shortcake is in the oven. As he reads, some of the children spontaneously pretend to cut strawberries or pretend to use the egg beater to whip the cream. They dramatize cooking activities again as the teacher reads. The next several pages tell how Rooster takes the shortcake out of

A Second Grader's Chart

We are a Team!

Rooster	Iguana	Turtle	Pig
I need a Team.	I can get stuf!	I can read the recipe!	I am the taster! I like to eat.

the oven, lets it cool, and slices it in half, and assembles the layers of cake, whipped cream, and strawberries. Mikey notices that Pig smells the shortcake when it comes out of the oven and really wants to taste it. "I still think that Pig is bad news," he says.

Finally, the strawberry shortcake is ready to eat, and Rooster says, "If Great-Granny could see me now!" Mr. Hernandez asks what the sentence means. Connor answers, "Rooster wants her to know he is a good cook, too!" Lacey suggests, "Rooster is really proud of himself." Raymond says, "I think Rooster wants Little Red Hen to know that he has a team to help him cook."

Mr. Hernandez turns the page and the students gasp. The illustration shows the strawberry shortcake falling off the plate as Iguana carries it to the table. "Oh no, it's ruined!" Mallory says. "They can't eat it because it's on the floor." "Pig can! Yes, Pig can. Now it really is his turn," Mikey says gleefully. Jesus cheers. "Well, I guess pigs can eat food on the floor," Mallory allows.

"What about the other animals?" Mr. Hernandez asks. "Won't they get to eat strawberry shortcake?" At first the children guess that they won't, and then Jacob offers, "Well, they could go to the store and buy more food and make another strawberry shortcake." Most of the children agree that Jacob has a good idea, but Larry disagrees, "No way. 'Snip, snap, snout. This story's told out,' said Pig." Everyone laughs as Larry suggests an alternative ending using the final words from the "Gingerbread Man" story they read several weeks before.

Mr. Hernandez reads the last few pages in the book, and the children learn that the animals do make another delicious strawberry shortcake for everyone to eat. They're satisfied with how the story turned out. "I'm really glad everyone got to eat some strawberry shortcake," Cristina says. "It's a really good story," Sammy reflects, "because it's funny and serious, too." "What's funny in the story?" the teacher asks. The children say that Iguana is the funniest character, and the funniest part is when the shortcake falls on the floor and Pig gobbles it up. Then Mr. Hernandez asks, "What's serious in the story?" The students recognize the authors' message and identify it as the serious part of the book. They say that the book's message is that a job is easier to do when you work together as a team. "I'm glad Rooster had a team," said Sondra. "What about us?" Mr. Hernandez asks, "Do we have a team?" Mikey says, "I think that our class is a team." Mr. Hernandez responds, "What do you think makes us a team?" "We help each other learn and do our work," Larry answers. The other children agree.

Finally, Mr. Hernandez shows the last page with Little Red Hen's recipe for strawberry shortcake, and he surprises everyone by announcing that he brought the ingredients and that they'll make strawberry shortcake after lunch.

The second graders regularly make charts in their reading logs to help them remember an important idea about each story they read or listen to read aloud. After reading *Cook-a-Doodle-Doo!*, they make charts about how the characters in the story were a team. One child's chart about the team is shown in the box on page 211. Mr. Hernandez helps them brainstorm a list of words to use on their charts and writes the words on the chalkboard so that the children can spell them correctly. The words they brainstorm include *team, Big Brown Rooster, Turtle, Iguana, Pig, Little Red Hen, strawberry shortcake, helper, recipe,* and *taster.*

*W*hy do people listen? Children often say that they listen to learn or to avoid punishment, but according to Wolvin and Coakley (1996), people listen differently according to their purpose. They've identified these purposes:

◆ *Discriminative Listening.* People use discriminative listening to distinguish sounds. Young children use discriminative listening as they develop phonemic awareness, the ability to blend and segment the sounds in spoken words. Children also "listen" to nonverbal messages. They learn the meanings of more sophisticated forms of body language and recognize how teachers emphasize that something they are teaching is important, such as by writing it on the chalkboard, speaking more loudly, or repeating information.

▨ *Aesthetic Listening.* People listen aesthetically when they're listening for enjoyment to stories read aloud, as Mr. Hernandez's students did in the vignette at the beginning of the chapter. The focus is on the lived-through experience of the literature and the connections children make to their own lives, the world around them, and other literature. Viewing film, DVD, and videotape versions of stories are other examples of aesthetic listening.

▨ *Efferent Listening.* People listen efferently to understand a message and remember important information. This is the type of listening required in many instructional activities, including minilessons. Children use efferent listening as they listen to teachers present information or read informational books aloud. They determine the speaker's purpose, identify the main ideas, and organize the information in order to remember it.

▨ *Critical Listening.* People listen critically to evaluate a message. Critical listening is an extension of efferent listening. Children listen to understand a message, but they also filter the message to detect propaganda devices, persuasive language, and emotional appeals. It's used when people listen to debates, commercials, political speeches, and other arguments.

The four types of listening are reviewed in Figure 7–1.

As you continue reading, you will learn about these four kinds of listening. Keep these points in mind as you read:

- ◆ How do children listen aesthetically?
- ▨ How do children listen efferently?
- ◆ How do children listen critically?
- ▨ How is each type of listening taught and assessed?

AESTHETIC LISTENING

Louise Rosenblatt (2005) coined the term *aesthetic reading* to describe the stance readers take when they are concerned with the experience they are living through and with their relationship to the literature they are reading. The focus is on their experience during reading, not on the information they will carry away from the experience. Similarly, the term *aesthetic listening* can be used to describe the type of listening children and adults do as they listen to teachers read aloud stories, poets recite poems, actors perform a play, and singers sing songs, and as they view films and videotape versions of stories. Children also use aesthetic listening as they listen

FIGURE 7–1

Overview of the Four Types of Listening

Types	Characteristics	Examples
Discriminative	Distinguish among sounds	Participate in phonemic awareness activities Notice rhyming words in poems and songs Recognize alliteration and onomatopoeia Experiment with tongue twisters
Aesthetic	Listen for pleasure or enjoyment	Listen to stories and poems read aloud View video versions of stories Listen to stories at a listening center Watch students perform a play or readers theatre reading Participate in grand conversations Participate in tea party activities
Efferent	Listen to understand messages	Listen to informational books read aloud or at a listening center Use anticipation guides Listen to oral reports Use clusters and graphic organizers View informational videos Listen to book talks Participate in instructional conversations Participate in writing groups Do note taking/note making Listen during minilessons Listen to students share projects
Critical	Evaluate messages	Listen to debates and political speeches View commercials and other advertisements Evaluate themes and arguments in books read aloud

to stories at the listening center. The focus of this type of listening is on the lived-through experience and the connections the listeners are making to the literature they are listening to. More traditional names for aesthetic listening are appreciative listening and listening for pleasure.

Interactive Read-Alouds

Reading aloud to children is a cherished classroom routine. In a recent study of sixth graders' reading preferences, an overwhelming 62% of students reported that they enjoy listening to the teacher read aloud (Ivey & Broaddus, 2001). Children's author Mem Fox (2001) and reading-aloud guru Jim Trelease (2006) both urge teachers to make time to read aloud every day because as students listen, they gain valuable experiences with books, enrich their background knowledge and vocabulary, and develop a love of reading. Reading aloud is an art; effective readers are familiar with the book they're reading, and they read fluently and with expression, changing the tone of their voices and using pauses to enhance students' listening experience.

Reading aloud has been an informal activity in most classrooms: Teachers pick up a book, read the title aloud, and begin reading while children listen quietly. Often young children sit in a group on the floor around the teacher, and older students sit attentively at their desks. The children are passive as they listen, but afterward, they become more engaged as they talk briefly about the story and perhaps participate in a follow-up activity. The focus is on the sharing of literature with little or no student involvement until after the reading is over. Researchers who have studied reading aloud, however, have concluded that children are better listeners when they are involved while the teacher is reading, not afterward (Dickinson & Tabors, 2001). This conclusion has led to the development of the interactive read-aloud procedure (Barrentine, 1996).

In an interactive read-aloud, teachers introduce the book and activate students' background knowledge before they begin to read. They model listening strategies and fluent oral reading as they read aloud, and they engage students while they're reading. Then after reading, they provide opportunities for students to respond to the book. The most important component, however, is how teachers involve students while they're reading aloud (Fisher, Flood, Lapp, & Frey, 2004). The steps in an interactive read-aloud are described on page 216.

One way that teachers engage students is to stop reading periodically to discuss what has just been read. What matters is when teachers stop reading: When they're reading stories aloud, it's more effective to stop at points where students can make predictions and suggest connections, after reading episodes that students might find confusing, and just before it becomes clear how the story will end. When they're reading poems, teachers often read the entire poem once, and then stop as they read the poem a second time for students to play with words, notice poetic

Laima Druskis/PH College

Using Listening Centers

These two first graders enjoy rereading a familiar story at the listening center. After their teacher reads aloud stories, she places two or more copies of the book at the listening center along with the tape she made as she read the book aloud. As students listen to the tape and follow along in the book, they notice high-frequency words, learn vocabulary, and gain valuable reading experience. Listening centers promote students' learning when teachers teach them how to work effectively in the center.

1 **Pick a book**   Teaches choose award-winning and other high-quality books that are appropriate for students and that fit into their instructional programs.

2 **Preview the book**   Teachers practice reading the book to ensure that they can read it fluently and to decide where to pause and engage the class with the text; they write prompts on self-stick notes to mark these pages. Teachers also think about how they will introduce the book and select difficult vocabulary words to highlight.

3 **Introduce the book**   Teachers activate students' background knowledge, set a clear purpose for listening, and preview the text.

4 **Read the book interactively**   Teachers read the book aloud, modeling fluent and expressive reading. They stop periodically to ask questions to focus students on specific points in the text and involve them in other activities.

5 **Involve students in after-reading activities**   Students participate in discussions and other types of response activities.

devices, and repeat favorite words and lines. Deciding how often to stop for discussion and knowing when to end the discussion and continue reading develop through practice and vary from one group of students to another. When they're reading informational books aloud, teachers stop to talk about big ideas as they're presented, briefly explain technical terms, and emphasize connections among the big ideas. Figure 7–2 presents additional ways to actively involve students with read-aloud books.

Choosing Books to Read Aloud. Guidelines for choosing stories to read aloud are simple: Choose books that you like and that you think will appeal to your students. Trelease (2006) makes these suggestions: Stories should be fast-paced to hook students' interest as quickly as possible; contain well-developed characters; include easy-to-read dialogue; and keep long descriptive passages to a minimum. Books that have received awards or other acclaim from teachers, librarians, and children make good choices. Two of the most prestigious awards are the Caldecott Medal and the Newbery Medal. Lists of outstanding books are prepared annually by the National Council of Teachers of English and other professional groups. In many states, children read and vote for books to receive recognition, such as the Buckeye Book Award in Ohio and the Sequoyah Book Award in Oklahoma. The International Reading Association sponsors a Children's Choices competition, in which children read and select their favorite books, and a similar Teachers' Choices competition; lists of these books are published annually in *The Reading Teacher*. Some of my favorite read-aloud stories are included in the booklist on page 217.

Teachers choose grade-appropriate books for read-alouds that are too difficult for students to read independently. The idea is that even if students can't read the words, they can understand the ideas presented in the book. This read-aloud strategy works for many students, but for others, it doesn't. For example, students may lack sufficient background knowledge on the topic or may be overwhelmed by unfamiliar

Booklist

RECOMMENDED READ-ALOUD STORIES

Kindergarten

McCloskey, R. (2001). *Make way for ducklings*. New York: Viking.

Sendak, M. (2003). *Where the wild things are*. New York: HarperCollins.

Grade 1

Brett, J. (1989). *The mitten*. New York: Putnam.

Rathmann, P. (1995). *Officer Buckle and Gloria*. New York: Putnam.

Grade 2

Meddaugh, S. (1995). *Hog-eye*. Boston: Houghton Mifflin.

Polacco, P. (1996). *Rechenka's eggs*. New York: Putnam.

Grade 3

MacLachlan, P. (2004). *Sarah, plain and tall*. New York: HarperCollins.

White, E. B. (2006). *Charlotte's web*. New York: HarperCollins.

Grade 4

Ryan, P. M. (2000). *Esperanza rising*. New York: Scholastic.

Cohen, B. (2005). *Molly's pilgrim*. New York: HarperCollins.

Grade 5

Curtis, C. P. (2000). *The Watsons go to Birmingham—1963*. New York: Delacorte.

Lowry, L. (2005). *Number the stars*. New York: Yearling.

Grade 6

Babbitt, N. (2002). *Tuck everlasting*. New York: Farrar, Straus & Giroux.

Paulsen, G. (2006). *Hatchet*. New York: Aladdin Books.

Grade 7

Cushman, K. (1994). *Catherine, called Birdy*. New York: HarperCollins.

Sachar, L. (1998). *Holes*. New York: Farrar, Straus & Giroux.

Grade 8

Lowry, L. (2006). *The giver*. New York: Delacorte.

Whelan, G. (2000). *Homeless bird*. New York: Scholastic.

FIGURE 7–2

Ways to Actively Involve Students With Books

Stories	• Make and revise predictions at pivotal points in the story • Share personal, world, and literary connections • Talk about what they're visualizing or how they're using other strategies • Draw a picture of a character or an event • Assume the persona of a character and share what the character might be thinking • Reenact a scene from the story
Poems	• Add sound effects • Mumble-read along with the teacher as the poem is read • Repeat lines after the teacher • Clap or snap fingers when they hear rhyming words, alliterations, onomatopoeia, or other poetic devices
Informational Books	• Ask questions or share information • Raise their hands when they hear specific information • Restate headings as questions • Take notes • Complete graphic organizers

vocabulary in the book. They may not listen strategically, or they may not be interested in the book.

Teachers can solve these problems. First, they can build background knowledge before reading by showing a video, reading a picture book, or sharing a story box of objects related to the book. At the same time they're building background knowledge, they introduce key vocabulary words, and while reading, they briefly explain unfamiliar words—sometimes providing a synonym is enough. In addition, struggling students may not know how to listen. It's important to teach listening strategies. Finally, struggling students often complain that a book is "boring," but what they generally mean is that they don't understand it. Making sure that students understand often takes care of their seeming lack of interest; however, if the book really doesn't interest students, teachers need to create interest by making connections with students' lives, showing the video version of the story, or asking students to assume a role as a character and dramatize events from the story. If none of these strategies work, then teachers should choose a different book to read.

It's not unusual for primary-grade students to listen to their teacher read aloud several books during the school day. If children are read to only once a day, they will listen to fewer than 200 books during the school year, and this isn't enough! More than 50,000 books are available for children, and reading aloud is an important way to share this literature with children. Older students should also listen to chapter books read aloud as part of literature focus units.

What About Rereading Books? Children—especially kindergartners and first graders—often beg to have familiar stories reread. Although it's important to share a wide variety of books with children, researchers have found that children benefit in specific ways from repeated readings (Yaden, 1988). Through repetition, children gain control over the parts of a story and are better able to synthesize those parts into a whole. The quality of children's responses to a repeated story changes, too.

Martinez and Roser (1985) examined young children's responses to stories and found that as stories became increasingly familiar, children's responses indicated a greater depth of understanding. They found that children talked almost twice as much about familiar books that had been reread many times as they did about unfamiliar books that had been read only once or twice. The form and focus of children's talk changed, too: Children tended to ask questions about unfamiliar stories, but they made comments about familiar ones. Children's talk about unfamiliar stories focused on characters; the focus changed to details and word meanings when they talked about familiar stories.

The researchers also found that children's comments after repeated readings were more probing and more specific, suggesting that they had greater insight into the story. Researchers investigating the value of repeated readings have focused mainly on preschool and primary-grade students, but rereading favorite stories and other books may have similar benefits for older students as well.

Benefits of Reading Aloud. It's easy to take reading aloud for granted, assuming that it's something teachers do for fun in between instructional activities. However, reading aloud to students is an important instructional activity with numerous benefits, including the following:

- Students' interest in reading is stimulated.
- Students' reading interests and their taste for quality literature are broadened.

- Students are introduced to the sounds of written language.
- Students' knowledge of vocabulary and sentence patterns is expanded.
- Students are introduced to books that are "too good to miss."
- Students listen to books that are too difficult for them to read on their own or that are "hard to get into."
- Students see their teachers model what capable readers do.
- Students' background knowledge is expanded.
- Students are introduced to genres and elements of text structure.

And, most important, students who regularly listen to stories read aloud are more likely to become lifelong readers.

Responding to Stories

In the vignette, Mr. Hernandez actively involved his second graders in listening by encouraging them to talk about the story as he read it aloud. Barrentine (1996) recommends that teachers invite brief conversations so that students can talk about their use of listening strategies, notice literary elements and other aspects of the story, and make predictions and connections. Sipe (2002) found that students make five types of responses as they interact with stories; Mr. Hernandez's second graders made these responses in the vignette:

Dramatizing. Students spontaneously act out the story in both nonverbal and verbal ways. Mr. Hernandez's second graders, for example, dramatized cutting strawberries and beating cream as their teacher read aloud.

Talking Back. Students talk back to the characters, giving them advice or criticizing and complimenting them. At the beginning of the story, for example, Mr. Hernandez's students tell the Rooster not to ask the cat, the dog, and the goose for help, and later in the story, they tell Iguana that he has the wrong kind of stick.

Critiquing/Controlling. Students suggest alternative plots, characters, or settings to personalize the story. For example, several of Mr. Hernandez's students suggest ways that Rooster could handle Pig more effectively.

Inserting. Students insert themselves or their friends into the story. One of Mr. Hernandez's students, for example, inserts Mr. Hernandez into the story and says that he is the team captain.

Taking Over. Students take over the text and manipulate it to express their own creativity. These responses are usually humorous and provide an opportunity for students to show off. For example, after Mr. Hernandez's students suggest several possible endings for the story after the pig eats the first strawberry shortcake, Larry gets a big laugh when he suggests a different ending using words from "Gingerbread Man."

Students make these types of responses when teachers encourage their active participation in the story, but the tricky part is to balance the time spent reading and talking.

Listening and Viewing

Students often view high-quality videos of children's literature as part of literature focus units and thematic units, and it's important that teachers take advantage of the unique capabilities of this technology. Teachers use videos in connection with books children are reading or books they're listening to the teacher read aloud. Teachers decide whether students view the video before or after reading, or how much of the video they watch, depending on the students' needs and interests. Those with limited background knowledge often benefit from viewing before reading or listening to the book read aloud, but for other students, watching a video before reading would curtail their interest in reading the book.

Students often make comparisons between the book and video versions of a story and choose the one they like better. Interestingly, less capable students who don't visualize the story in their minds often prefer the video version, whereas more capable listeners often prefer the book version because the video doesn't meet their expectations. They can also examine some of the conventions used in video productions, such as narration, music and sound effects, the visual representation of characters and the setting, the camera's perspective, and any changes from the book version. Guidelines for using videos in the classroom are listed in the LA Essentials box on page 221.

Teaching Aesthetic Listening

Listening is something most people take for granted. It's an invisible process by which spoken messages are received and converted to meaning in the mind (Lundsteen, 1979; National Communication Association, 1998). Children are often admonished to listen, but few teachers teach them how to improve their ability to listen. Instead, teachers usually assume that children already know how to listen. Also, some teachers feel that it's more important to spend instructional time on reading and writing instruction. Despite these concerns, most teachers agree that children need to more about how to listen because it's essential for learning (Opitz & Zbaracki, 2004).

When reading stories aloud, teachers have three responsibilities. First, they help students activate their background knowledge before reading. Students need to become actively involved in books they listen to read aloud, and the first step in active involvement is to connect the book to their background knowledge. Second, teachers model and teach aesthetic listening strategies as they read aloud and provide opportunities for students to practice using the strategies as they listen. And third, teachers provide opportunities for students to respond to the book after reading. Students need opportunities to share their ideas, ask questions, and bring closure to the listening experience.

Aesthetic Listening Strategies. Three of the most important strategies that students use for aesthetic listening are predicting, visualizing, and connecting.

🗩 **Predicting.** As students listen, they're predicting what will happen next, and they revise their predictions as they continue listening. When they read aloud, teachers encourage students to predict by stopping and asking them what they think will happen next.

🗩 **Visualizing.** Students create an image or picture in their minds while listening to a story that has strong visual images. They practice this strategy by closing their

GUIDELINES FOR USING VIDEOS IN THE CLASSROOM

- **Preview the Video**

  Before showing the video to students, teachers make sure it's suitable for them to view. It may be necessary to skip some portions because of excessive length or unsuitable content.

- **Plan How to Use the Video**

  Students who have little background knowledge on the topic or students for whom the sentence structure or vocabulary is difficult may benefit from viewing the video before reading or listening to the book read aloud.

- **Set the Purpose**

  Teachers explain the purpose for viewing the video and explain whether students should use primarily aesthetic, efferent, or critical listening.

- **Use the Pause Function**

  Teachers stop the video periodically for students to make predictions, reflect on their use of a listening strategy, talk about the video, or compare the book and video versions. When students are listening to an informational video, teachers can stop the video periodically to allow students to take notes.

- **Re-view the Video**

  Teachers consider showing the video more than once because re-viewing is as beneficial as rereading. Use the rewind function to show particular scenes twice during the first viewing, or show the video without interruption the first time and later play it a second time.

- **Vary the Procedure Used to Show Videos**

  Teachers sometimes show the beginning of a story on the videotape and then read aloud the entire book. Afterward, students can view the entire video. Or, teachers can alternate reading and viewing chapters of a longer book.

- **Compare the Author's and Camera's Views**

  Students can examine the impact of the narration, music and sound effects, the visual representation of the characters and setting, and camera angles.

- **Respond to the Video**

  Teachers provide opportunities for students to respond to videos after viewing. They can respond by participating in grand conversations or instructional conversations and writing in reading logs.

eyes, thinking about descriptive words and phrases, and trying to draw mental pictures while they're listening.

Connecting. Students make three types of connections when they are listening to a story read aloud. First, they make text-to-self connections between the story and events in their own lives. Next, they make text-to-world connections between the story and familiar current events. Third, they make text-to-text connections between the story and other stories they've read or television shows and movies they've watched. Teachers help students use this strategy by asking them to talk about connections they've made as they discuss the story.

The second graders in the vignette at the beginning of this chapter used these strategies as they listened to their teacher read aloud *Cook-a-Doodle-Doo!* (Stevens & Crummel, 1999). Mikey offered predictions spontaneously, and at key points in the story, Mr. Hernandez asked the children to make additional predictions. They made personal connections to their families' cooking experiences and literary connections to the "Little Red Hen" stories they had read. The children also made literary connections when they noticed the similarity between the names *Big Brown Rooster* and *Little Red Hen* and the "not I" refrain from "The Little Red Hen." The children used visualizing when they made character charts after listening to Mr. Hernandez read the story. Students don't always use every strategy as they listen to a story, but this story provided many opportunities, and Mr. Hernandez knew how to take advantage of them.

Minilessons. Researchers have repeatedly cited the need to teach listening strategies to help children become more effective listeners (Optiz & Zbaracki, 2004; Wolvin & Coakley, 1996). There are added benefits, too: Children use the same strategies when they're listening, reading, and viewing because these three language arts are receptive processes, and sometimes teachers are more successful when they teach strategies while students are listening to stories instead of when they're reading stories. Teachers teach minilessons to introduce, practice, and review strategies, as well as procedures, concepts, and skills related to aesthetic listening. See page 232 for a list of topics for minilessons related to aesthetic listening.

Assessing Students' Aesthetic Listening

Students need to learn how to listen aesthetically so that they can engage more fully in the lived-through experience of literature. Teachers assess whether students are listening aesthetically in several ways. First, they judge the predictions students make to see that they are actively involved in listening to and thinking about the story being read aloud. Teachers also listen to the comments students make as they talk about stories and read entries in students' reading logs to see whether they are using aesthetic listening strategies. Teachers can also check that students are transferring their use of these listening strategies to reading and viewing.

EFFERENT LISTENING

Efferent listening is practical listening to understand a message. The term *efferent*, first applied to language arts by Louise Rosenblatt (2005), means "carrying away." It's the most common type of listening students do in school. They listen efferently when teachers present information and give directions. Students may be learning about homonyms during language arts, for example, the water cycle during a science unit, or the Bill of Rights during a social studies unit. No matter the topic, teachers want students to remember the big ideas and understand the relationships among them. They can use these five techniques to improve students' listening:

- Activating students' background knowledge
- Setting a clear purpose for listening
- Using manipulatives
- Creating graphic organizers
- Having students take notes

Teachers make their oral presentations more like interactive read-alouds when they incorporate these techniques, and students' curiosity is piqued and they are likely to become more actively involved in listening.

Meeting the Needs of English Learners

Why Is Listening Crucial for English Learners?

Listening is a key to language development because children learn English as they listen to the teacher and classmates talk and read aloud.

Reason 1: Language Models

When teachers read aloud, the books provide language models. English learners acquire new vocabulary and more sophisticated language patterns and sentence structures through listening. Gibbons (2002) warns, however, that classrooms are noisy places and the background buzz may make it harder for English learners to hear, understand, and learn. Teachers can alleviate this problem by sitting English learners close to where they often talk and read to the whole class and by insisting that classmates be courteous listeners.

Reason 2: Expanding Knowledge

Students also develop background knowledge through listening. They learn new information and the vocabulary to express ideas, and they also make new connections between the ideas and past experiences. This contribution is especially important for children of poverty, including English learners, who have limited background knowledge.

Reason 3: Transfer to Reading

Listening is an important instructional tool because it's a receptive process, like reading. Students can transfer the listening strategies they learn to reading, and both listening and reading involve the active construction of meaning.

Effective listening can be very challenging for English learners because it depends on expectations and predictions about the content, language, and genre that listeners bring to the text (Rothenberg & Fisher, 2007). In addition, whether students are successful listeners depends on their background knowledge and familiarity with the topic teachers are talking or reading about.

Activate Background Knowledge. Teachers encourage students to activate background knowledge and build on that knowledge by having them explore the topic. They can brainstorm ideas while the teacher takes notes on chart paper, in list or cluster format. As students share ideas, the teacher asks them to elaborate, and the teacher clarifies any misconceptions. Or, students can quickwrite on the topic and then share their writing with the class. Teachers also use anticipation guides to stimulate students' interest in a topic and activate their background knowledge. They present a set of statements related to the topic, some of which are true and will be confirmed by the presentation, and others that are false and will be corrected by the presentation. Before the presentation, students read and discuss each statement and mark whether they think it's true or false. Then they listen to the presentation and mark each statement again after listening (Readence, Bean, & Baldwin, 2004). An eighth-grade anticipation guide on the Crusades is presented in Figure 7–3. Notice that students mark whether they agree or disagree before listening on the left side of the paper and after listening on the right side of the paper. The steps in preparing anticipation guides are shown in the Step by Step feature on page 225.

Set a Clear Purpose. Teachers explain the purpose for listening and tell students to listen efferently, to remember information. For example, their purpose might be to learn how to identify prefixes or to identify the reasons why pioneers traveled west in covered wagons.

Use Manipulatives. Teachers choose objects, pictures, and photos, or word cards for students to examine or use in activities during the presentation. Using manipulatives increases students' interest and makes abstract ideas more concrete.

Create Graphic Organizers. Teachers create diagrams using circles, boxes, lines, and arrows to show the relationships among the big ideas, and students complete the graphic organizers by adding words during the presentation.

FIGURE 7–3

An Eighth-Grade Anticipation Guide

Anticipation Guide on the Crusades

Before			After	
T	F		T	F
		1. The Crusaders wanted to go to the Holy Land to meet Jesus.		
		2. The Crusades took place between 1096 and 1270.		
		3. The Crusaders fought the Muslims to recapture the Holy Land.		
		4. Only noblemen and rich people were allowed to go on the Crusades.		
		5. The Crusaders traveled to the Holy Land for religious reasons.		
		6. Because of the Crusades, Europeans were introduced to many luxuries, including sugar, silk, and glass mirrors.		

-------- Anticipation Guides -------------

1 Identify several major concepts. Teachers consider their students' knowledge about the topic and any misconceptions students might have as they identify concepts related to their presentation.

2 Develop a list of three to six statements. Teachers write a statement about each major concept they identified on a chart, or individual copies can be made for each student. These statements should be general enough to stimulate discussion, present major concepts, and help clarify misconceptions.

3 Discuss the statements on the anticipation guide. Teachers introduce the anticipation guide and have students respond to the statements. Students think about the statements and mark whether they are true or false.

4 Listen to the presentation. Students listen to the oral presentation and think about information that relates to the statements on the anticipation guide.

5 Discuss the statements again. After listening, students reconsider their earlier responses to each statement and again mark whether the statements are true or false. Then students share their responses with the class. Sometimes they also revise the false statements to make them true.

◗ **Have Students Take Notes.** Students are more active listeners when they take notes to help them remember the big ideas while they listen to an oral presentation. Teachers introduce note taking by demonstrating the procedure. They set a clear purpose, and during the oral presentation, they stop periodically and ask students to identify the idea being presented and its relationship to other ideas that have been presented. Then teachers list students' responses on the chalkboard. Teachers often begin by writing notes in a list format, but the notes can also be written in an outline or diagram.

Upper-grade students often use a special kind of note taking in which they divide their papers into two columns, labeling the left column *Take Notes* and the right column *Make Notes*. They write notes in the left column, but, more important, they think about the notes, make connections, and personalize the notes in the right column (Berthoff, 1981). The right column should be more extensive than the left one because this column shows students' thinking. A fifth grader's note-taking and note-making sheet about illegal drugs is presented in Figure 7–4. The student's comments in the "Make Notes" column are especially interesting because they show the connections she was making.

Reading Aloud Informational Books

Teachers use the interactive read-aloud procedure to actively involve students in the informational books they're reading aloud. Informational books have the power to intrigue and excite students, and students use a combination of efferent and aesthetic listening because informational books provide both a literary and a learning experience. High-quality informational books cover a wide range of topics, including *Wildfire* (Morrison, 2006), which explains why forest fires have been increasing and how firefighters use cutting-edge technologies to control the devastation; *Mosquito Bite* (Siy, 2005), which presents photomicrograph close-ups of mosquito anatomy; *Reaching for the Moon* (Aldrin, 2005), which describes the author's lifelong interest in space and his history-making trip to the moon; *Now and Ben: The Modern Inventions of Benjamin Franklin* (Barretta, 2006), which humorously explains how 22 of his inventions are still used today; and *Aliens Are Coming! The True Account of the 1938 War of the Worlds Radio Broadcast* (McCarthy, 2006), which recounts the real-life panic that ensued when the radio play convinced many listeners there was a real alien invasion. Teachers often think about the instructional value of informational books when they read them aloud, but the books also captivate students' imaginations while they are listening. Guidelines for using informational books are listed in the LA Essentials box on page 227.

After reading, students need to talk about the book: They share interesting information, ask questions, clarify confusions, and respond to the listening experience. Teachers often have students complete graphic organizers, write in learning logs, and apply what they have learned. Students apply what they have learned as

---

FIGURE 7–4

A Fifth Grader's Note-Taking and Note-Making Sheet

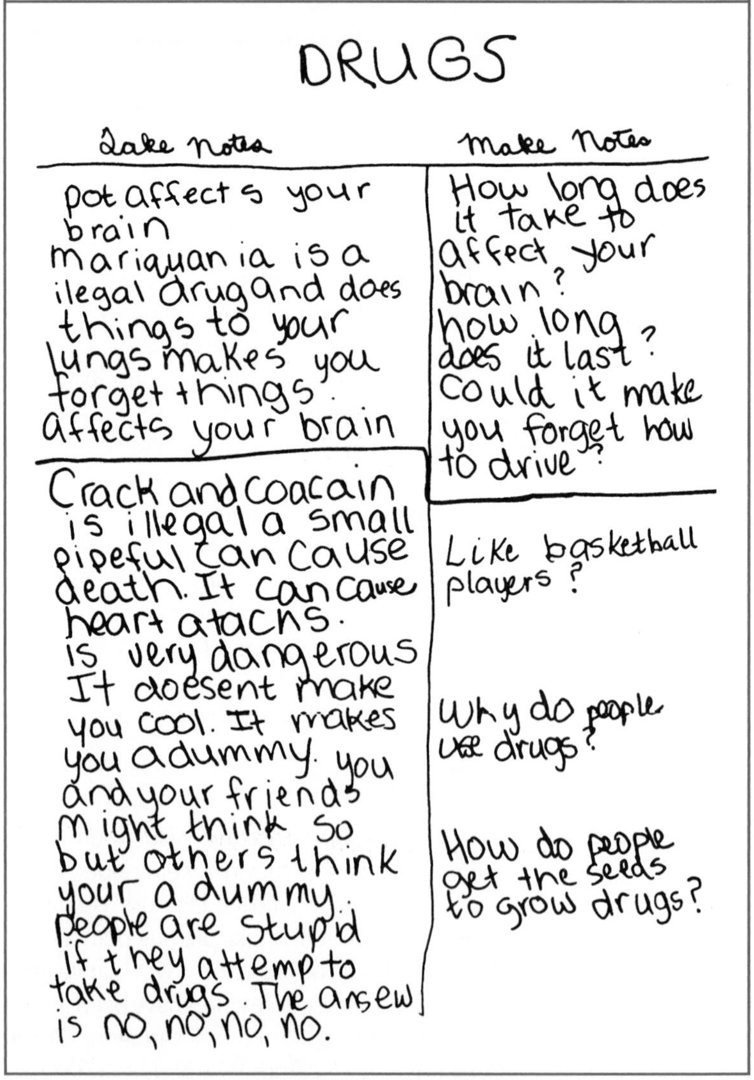

DRUGS

Take notes	Make Notes
pot affects your brain	How long does it take to affect your brain?
mariquania is a ilegal drug and does things to your lungs makes you forget things. affects your brain	how long does it last? Could it make you forget how to drive?
Crack and coacain is illegal a small pipeful can cause death. It can cause heart atachs. Is very dangerous It doesent make you cool. It makes you a dummy. you and your friends might think so but others think your a dummy. people are stupid if they attemp to take drugs. The ansew is no, no, no, no.	Like basketball players? Why do people use drugs? How do people get the seeds to grow drugs?

GUIDELINES FOR READING ALOUD INFORMATIONAL BOOKS

- **Choose High-Quality Books**

  Teachers choose high-quality informational books for thematic-unit text sets. Books should have visual appeal and relevance to the unit.

- **Actively Involve Children in the Reading Experience**

  Teachers increase children's involvement in the book when they ask questions and set purposes, use manipulatives and graphic organizers, and have students raise their hands when they hear important information or answers to questions that have been asked.

- **Point Out Features of Informational Books**

  As teachers read aloud, they point out the unique features of informational books, including the table of contents, glossary, illustrations and diagrams, and index, and they demonstrate how to use them.

- **Teach Efferent Listening Strategies**

  Teachers model and teach note taking and other efferent listening strategies when reading aloud informational books.

- **Use Graphic Organizers**

  Teachers give students copies of a chart to complete while they listen or draw a diagram on the chalkboard to organize students' thinking before reading.

- **Plan Oral Performances**

  Teachers and students adapt informational books for readers theatre performances, choral reading, puppet shows, and other presentations.

they create projects, including posters, oral reports, and found poems. They can also write their own informational books and create information quilts—like story quilts, but with facts students have learned written and illustrated on each square.

Teaching Efferent Listening

Teachers can improve students' efferent listening. They enhance students' interest in the topic and increase their active involvement during listening. They use minilessons to explain the differences between aesthetic and efferent listening and teach students how to use the efferent listening strategies.

Efferent Listening Strategies. Students use a variety of strategies as they listen efferently; some of the strategies are the same as for reading and viewing, and others are unique to efferent listening. The purpose of each strategy is to help listeners organize and remember the information. Four of the most important strategies that students use for efferent listening are organizing, summarizing, getting clues from the speaker, and monitoring.

◗ *Organizing* Informational presentations are usually organized in special ways called *expository text structures*. The five most common patterns are description, sequence, comparison, cause and effect, and problem and solution. Students learn to recognize these patterns and use them to understand and remember a speaker's message more easily. Speakers often use certain words to signal the organizational structures they are following; signal words include *first, second, third, next, in contrast,* and *in summary.* Students can learn to attend to these signals to identify the organizational pattern the speaker is using. To learn more about the expository text structures, turn to Chapter 10, "Reading and Writing Information."

Students often use graphic organizers to visualize the organization of oral presentations, informational videos, or informational books (Yopp & Yopp, 2006). When students listen to a presentation comparing amphibians and reptiles, for example, students make T-charts or Venn diagrams to organize the information. They can draw a two-column T-chart, labeling one column "Amphibians" and the other "Reptiles," then they write notes in the columns while they listen to the presentation or immediately after listening. A sixth grader's T-chart comparing amphibians and reptiles is shown in Figure 7–5.

FIGURE 7–5

A Sixth Grader's T-Chart Comparing Amphibians and Reptiles

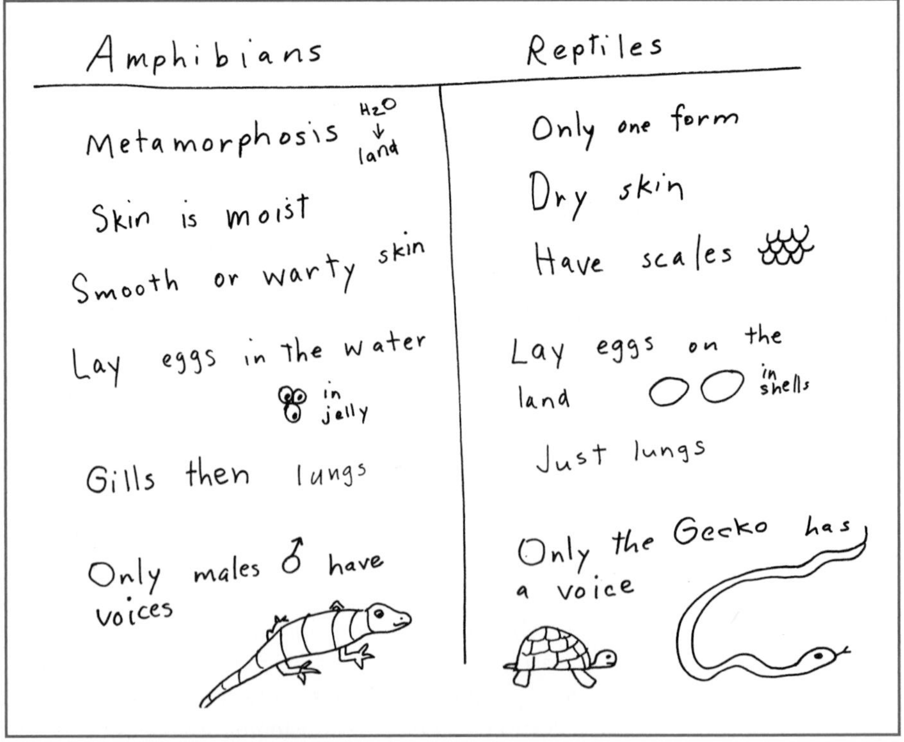

FIGURE 7–6

Cluster Diagram on Simple Machines

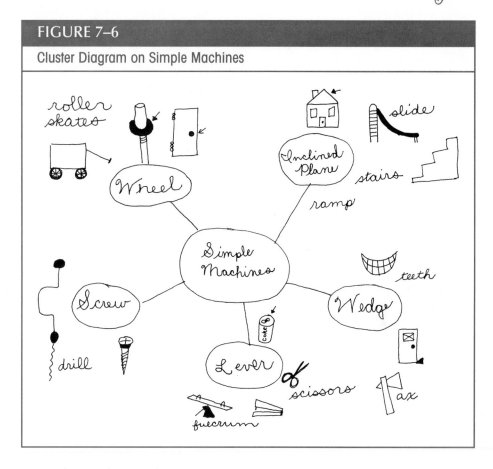

When students are listening to a presentation or an informational book that contains information on more than two or three categories, they can make a cluster diagram, write each category on a ray, and then add descriptive information. For example, when students are listening to a presentation on simple machines, they make a cluster with five rays, one for each type of simple machine. Then students add words and drawings to take notes about each type of simple machine. A fifth grader's cluster is shown in Figure 7–6.

🖉 *Summarizing* Speakers present several main ideas and many details during oral presentations, so students need to learn to focus on the main ideas in order to summarize; otherwise, they try to remember everything and quickly feel overwhelmed. Once students can identify the main ideas, they can chunk the details to the main idea.

When teachers introduce the summarizing strategy, they ask students to listen for two or three main ideas; they write these ideas on the chalkboard and draw boxes around them. Then teachers give an oral presentation, having students raise their hands when they hear the first main idea stated. Students then raise their hands when they hear the second main idea, and again for the third main idea. After students gain practice in detecting already-stated main ideas, teachers give a very brief presentation with one main idea and ask students to identify it. Once students can identify the main idea, teachers give longer oral presentations and ask students to identify two or three main ideas. A teacher might make these points when giving an oral presentation on simple machines:

There are five kinds of simple machines.
Simple machines are combined in specialized machines.

Machines make work easier.

Almost everything we do involves machines.

After students identify the main ideas during an oral presentation, they can chunk details to the main ideas. This hierarchical organization is the most economical way to remember information, and students need to understand that they can remember more information when they use the summarizing strategy.

Getting clues from the speaker Speakers use both visual and verbal clues to convey their messages and direct their listeners' attention. Visual clues include gesturing, writing or underlining important information on the chalkboard, and changing facial expressions. Verbal clues include pausing, raising or lowering the voice, slowing down speech to stress key points, and repeating important information. Surprisingly, many children are not aware of these attention-directing behaviors, so teachers must point them out. Once children are aware of these clues, they can use them to increase their understanding of a message.

Monitoring Students monitor whether they're understanding while they're actively involved in listening. It's an important strategy because students need to know when they're not listening successfully or when a listening strategy isn't working so that they can correct the situation. Students can use these self-questions as they begin to listen:

- Why am I listening to this message?
- Will I need to take notes?
- Does this information make sense to me?

These are possible questions to use as students continue listening:

- Is my strategy still working?
- Am I organizing the information effectively?
- Is the speaker giving me clues about the organization of the message?
- Is the speaker giving me nonverbal clues, such as gestures and facial expressions?

Monitoring is an important strategy for all sorts of language arts activities because students always need to be aware of whether what they're doing is effective and meets their purposes.

Minilessons. Because efferent listening is so important in school, teachers shouldn't assume that students already know how to listen to oral presentations of information. In addition to helping students with brainstorming ideas, using anticipation guides and graphic organizers, and note taking, teachers also teach minilessons about efferent listening. A list of minilesson topics for efferent listening is presented in the box on page 232, followed by a sample minilesson about getting clues from the speaker.

Assessing Students' Efferent Listening

Teachers often use objective tests to measure students' efferent listening. For example, if teachers have provided information about the causes of the American Revolution or the greenhouse effect, they can check students' understanding of the information and infer whether students listened. However, teachers should assess students' listening more directly. Specifically, they should check how well students understand efferent listening strategies and how they apply them when they're listening. Asking students to reflect on and talk about the strategies they use provides insights into students' thinking in a way that objective tests can't.

CRITICAL LISTENING

Students—even those in the primary grades—need to become critical listeners because they're exposed to persuasion and propaganda all around. Interpreting books and films requires critical thinking and listening. And social studies and science lessons on topics such as the Ku Klux Klan, illegal drugs, gangs, and global warming demand that students listen and think critically. Television commercials are another form of persuasion and source of propaganda, and because many commercials are directed at children, it is essential that they listen critically and learn to judge the advertising claims. For example, do the jogging shoes actually help you run faster? Will the breakfast cereal make you a better football player? Will a particular video game make you more popular?

Persuasion and Propaganda

There are three ways to persuade people. The first is by reason. We seek logical conclusions, whether from absolute facts or from strong possibilities; for example, we can be persuaded to practice more healthful living as the result of medical research. It's necessary, of course, to distinguish between reasonable arguments and illogical appeals. To suggest that diet pills will bring about extraordinary weight loss is illogical.

A second way is an appeal to character. We can be persuaded by what another person recommends if we trust that person. Trust comes from personal knowledge or the reputation of the person who is trying to persuade. We can believe what scientists say about the dangers of nuclear waste, but can we believe what a sports personality says about the taste of a particular brand of coffee?

The third way is by appealing to people's emotions. Emotional appeals can be as strong as intellectual appeals. We have strong feelings and concern for ourselves and other people and animals. Fear, a need for peer acceptance, and a desire for freedom of expression are all potent feelings that influence our opinions and beliefs.

Any of the three types of appeals can be used to try to persuade someone. For example, when a child wishes to convince her parents that her bedtime should be delayed by 30 minutes, she might argue that neighbors allow their children to stay up later—an appeal to character. It's an appeal to reason when the argument focuses on the amount of sleep a 10-year-old needs. And when the child announces that she has the earliest bedtime of anyone in her class and it makes her feel like a baby, the appeal is to emotion. The same three appeals apply to in-school persuasion. To persuade classmates to read a particular book in a book report "commercial," a student might argue that classmates should read the book because it's written by a favorite author (reason); because it's hilarious (emotion); or because it's the most popular book in the seventh grade and everyone else is reading it (character).

It's essential that students become critical consumers of commercials and advertisements because they're bombarded with them (Brownell, 2006; Lutz, 1997). Advertisers use appeals to reason, character, and emotion just as other persuaders

What Students Need to Learn About Listening

Topics

Procedures	Concepts	Strategies and Skills
Aesthetic Listening		
Listen to a story read aloud Listen to a poem read aloud Write a response in a reading log Choose favorite quotations from a story	**Aesthetic listening** Difference between aesthetic and efferent listening Concept of story	Activate background knowledge Predict Visualize Make connections
Efferent Listening		
Take notes Do note taking/note making Use graphic organizers Participate in instructional conversations	**Efferent listening** Organizational patterns of informational texts Features of informational books	Activate background knowledge Set purpose Organize ideas Summarize Monitor understanding Ask questions **Get clues from the speaker**
Critical Listening		
Analyze propaganda Create advertisements	Critical listening Types of persuasion Propaganda Deceptive language Propaganda devices	Evaluate the message Determine the speaker's purpose Recognize appeals Recognize deceptive language Identify propaganda devices

> If you'd like to learn more about teaching listening, visit MyEducationLab. To view sixth graders listening to their teacher read a novel aloud, look in the topic "Listening" and click on the video "Aesthetic Listening;" and to watch sixth graders listen while a classmate reads aloud a composition from the author's chair, go again to the topic "Listening" and click on the video "Efferent Listening."

Minilesson

Mrs. Rodriquez's Students Watch for Clues

1 Introduce the topic

Mrs. Rodriquez explains to her second graders that she often does some special things to get their attention and to tell them what information is most important when she teaches a lesson.

2 Share examples

Mrs. Rodriquez asks her students to watch her carefully as she begins a lesson about the body of an insect as part of a thematic unit on insects. She begins to speak, and she holds up three fingers as she explains that insects have three body parts. Next, she points to the three body parts on a nearby chart and names them, tapping each part with a pointer. Then she writes the names of the body parts on the chalkboard. Afterward, Mrs. Rodriquez asks children to recall what she did during the presentation, and they correctly point out the three clues she used.

3 Provide information

Mrs. Rodriquez explains to children that teachers or other presenters often use clues to help

listeners understand what is most important in a lesson. She explains that teachers use a variety of clues and asks her students to look for more clues as she continues the lesson. She demonstrates several more clues, including repeating an important fact and raising her voice for emphasis. Afterward, Mrs. Rodriquez asks the class to identify the clues.

4 Supervise practice

The next day, Mrs. Rodriquez presents a lesson comparing insects and spiders, and she asks children to watch for her clues and to raise their hands to indicate that they noticed them. Afterward, she reviews the clues she used. She repeats this step for several additional lessons about insects.

5 Reflect on learning

Mrs. Rodriquez and her second graders make a list of clues she uses during a lesson, and children draw pictures to illustrate each clue they add to the list. Then they post the list in the classroom.

do to promote products, ideas, and services; however, advertisers may also use propaganda to influence our beliefs and actions. Propaganda suggests something shady or underhanded. Like persuasion, propaganda is designed to influence people's beliefs and actions, but propagandists may use certain techniques to distort, conceal, and exaggerate. Two of these techniques are deceptive language and propaganda devices.

People seeking to influence us often use words that evoke a variety of responses. They claim that something is "improved," "more natural," or "50% better"—loaded words and phrases that are deceptive because they are suggestive. When a product is advertised as 50% better, for example, consumers need to ask, "50% better than what?" Advertisements rarely answer that question.

Doublespeak is another type of deceptive language characterized as evasive, euphemistic, confusing, and self-contradictory. It is language that only pretends to communicate (Lutz, 1997). Two kinds of doublespeak that children can understand are euphemisms and inflated language. Euphemisms are words or phrases (e.g., "passed away") that are used to avoid a harsh or distasteful reality, often out of concern for someone's feelings rather than to deceive. Inflated language includes words intended to make the ordinary seem extraordinary. Thus, car mechanics become "automotive internists," and used cars become "preowned" or even "experienced."

Students need to learn that people sometimes use words that only pretend to communicate; sometimes they use words to intentionally misrepresent, as when someone advertises a vinyl wallet as "genuine imitation leather" or a ring with a glass stone as a "faux diamond." When students can interpret deceptive language, they can avoid being deceived.

To sell products, advertisers use propaganda devices, such as testimonials, the bandwagon effect, and rewards. Six devices that students can identify are listed in Figure 7–7. Students can listen to commercials to find examples of each propaganda device and discuss the effect the device has on them. They can also investigate how the same devices vary in commercials directed toward youngsters, teenagers, and adults. For instance, a commercial for a snack food with a sticker or toy in the package will appeal to a youngster, and an advertisement for DVD player offering a factory rebate will appeal to an adult. The same propaganda device—a reward—is used in both ads. Propaganda devices can be used to sell ideas as well as products; public service announcements as well as political advertisements use these devices.

Critical listening strategies The most important strategy for critical listening is evaluating because students need to judge the message (Lundsteen, 1979). As they listen, students consider these questions simultaneously:

- What's the speaker's (or author's) purpose?
- Is there an intellectual appeal? a character appeal? an emotional appeal?
- Are propaganda devices being used?
- Are deceptive words or inflated language used?

As students listen to books read aloud, view commercials and advertisements, and listen to speakers, they ask themselves these questions in order to critically evaluate the message. They also use efferent listening strategies because critical listening is an extension of efferent listening.

FIGURE 7–7

Propaganda Devices

Device	Description
Glittering Generality	Propagandists use generalities such as "environmentally safe" to enhance the quality of a product. Even though the generality is powerful, listeners need to think beyond it to assess the product.
Name Calling	Persuaders try to pin a bad label on someone or something they want listeners to dislike, such as calling a person "unpatriotic." Listeners then consider the effect of the label.
Bandwagon	Advertisers claim that everyone is using their product; for example, "four of five physicians recommend this medicine." Listeners must consider whether everyone really does use this product.
Testimonial	Advertisers associate a product with an athlete or movie star. Listeners must consider whether the person offering the endorsement has the expertise to judge the quality of the product.
Card Stacking	Propagandists often use only items that favor one side of an issue; unfavorable facts are ignored. To be objective, listeners seek information about other viewpoints.
Rewards	Propagandists offer rewards for buying their products—children are lured by toys and adults by discounts or rebates. Listeners need to ask whether the reward makes the product worth buying.

Teaching Critical Listening

The steps in teaching students to be critical listeners are similar to those in teaching aesthetic and efferent listening strategies. In this teaching strategy, students view commercials to examine propaganda devices and persuasive language. Later, they can create their own commercials and advertisements. The steps are shown in the Step by Step feature on page 236.

Students use the same procedures and activities with advertisements they collect from magazines and product packages. Have them collect advertisements and display them on a bulletin board. They examine advertisements and then decide how the writer is trying to persuade them to purchase the product. Students can also compare the amount of space devoted to text and illustrations. Not surprisingly, toy advertisements feature large, colorful pictures and cosmetic advertisements feature pictures of beautiful women, but advertisements for medicines devote more space to text. Students may also point out sports stars and entertainment personalities in many advertisements. Even young children recognize intellectual, character, and emotional appeals in these advertisements. Students apply what they have learned about persuasion by creating advertisements. Figure 7–8 shows the "Wanted" poster a second grader made after reading *Sylvester and the Magic Pebble* (Steig, 2005), the story of a donkey who is lost after magically turning into a stone. The student featured a large picture of the missing donkey with an emotional appeal and a reward offer.

Creating Commercials and Advertisements

1 Introduce commercials. Talk about commercials, and ask students about familiar commercials. Videotape some commercials and share them with your class. Use these questions to probe students' thinking about persuasion and propaganda:

- What is the speaker's purpose?
- What are the speaker's credentials?
- Is there evidence of bias?
- Does the speaker use deceptive language?
- Does the speaker make sweeping generalizations or unsupported inferences?
- Do opinions predominate the talk?
- Does the speaker use any propaganda devices?
- Do you accept the message? (Devine, 1982, pp. 41–42)

2 Explain deceptive language. Introduce the propaganda devices, and view the commercials again, looking for examples of each device. Explain deceptive language, and view the commercials a third time to look for examples of doublespeak.

3 Analyze deceptive language. Have students work in small groups to critique a commercial as to type of persuasion, propaganda devices, and deceptive language. They might also want to test the claims made in the commercial.

4 Review concepts. Review the concepts about persuasion and propaganda introduced in the first three steps. It's often helpful for students to make charts about these concepts.

5 Provide practice. Have students work in small groups to critique a new set of videotaped commercials. Ask them to identify persuasion, propaganda devices, and deceptive language in them.

6 Create commercials. Have students apply what they have learned by creating their own products and writing and producing their own commercials to advertise them. Possible products include breakfast cereals, toys, beauty and diet products, and sports equipment. They might also create homework and house-sitting services to advertise, or they can choose community or environmental issues to campaign for or against.

Teaching With Trade Books. Many stories and informational books that teachers read aloud encourage critical thinking. Students use a combination of aesthetic and critical listening as they listen to stories such as *Flush* (Hiaasen, 2005) and *The True Story of the 3 Little Pigs!* (Scieszka, 1999). They use critical listening to evaluate the environmental theme and to determine whether the wolf's story is believable. When students listen to informational books such as *Rosa* (2005), in which Nikki Giovanni recounts Rosa Parks's act of civil disobedience, they confront important social issues. Through these activities, students think more deeply about

FIGURE 7–8

A Second Grader's "Wanted" Poster

controversial issues and challenge and expand their own beliefs. A list of recommended books that encourage critical listening is presented in the Booklist on page 238.

Minilessons. Teachers also teach minilessons to introduce, practice, and review procedures, concepts, and strategies and skills related to critical listening. See page 232 for a list of topics for minilessons on critical listening.

Assessing Students' Critical Listening

After teaching about persuasion and propaganda, teachers can assess students' knowledge of critical listening by having them view and critique commercials, advertisements, and other oral presentations. They can note the critical listening procedures, strategies, and skills their students use. A second way to assess students' understanding of critical listening is to have them develop their own commercials and advertisements. Critical listening goes beyond one unit, however, and is something that teachers should return to again and again during the school year.

Booklist

BOOKS THAT ENCOURAGE CRITICAL LISTENING

Avi. (2003). *Nothing but the truth.* New York: Orchard Books. (U)

Babbitt, N. (2002). *Tuck everlasting.* New York: Farrar, Straus & Giroux. (U)

Bunting, E. (1999). *Smoky night.* San Diego: Harcourt Brace. (M)

Cohen, B. (1998). *Molly's pilgrim.* New York: Lothrop, Lee & Shepard. (M)

Cowcher, H. (1990). *Antarctica.* New York: Farrar, Straus & Giroux. (P–M)

Creech, S. (2004). *Heartbeat.* New York: HarperCollins. (M–U)

Gantos, J. (2000). *Joey Pigza loses control.* New York: Farrar, Straus & Giroux. (M–U)

Giovanni, N. (2005). *Rosa.* New York: Henry Holt. (M)

Haddix, M. P. (1998). *Among the hidden.* New York: Aladdin Books. (U)

Hesse, K. (2001). *Witness.* New York: Scholastic. (U)

Hiaasen, C. (2002). *Hoot.* New York: Knopf. (M–U)

Hiaasen, C. (2005). *Flush.* New York: Knopf. (M–U)

Jeffers, S. (2002). *Brother eagle, sister sky.* New York: Dial Books. (M)

Lobel, A. (2004). *Potatoes, potatoes.* New York: Greenwillow. (P–M)

Naylor, P. R. (2000). *Shiloh.* New York: Aladdin Books. (M–U)

Scieszka, J. (1999). *The true story of the 3 little pigs!* New York: Viking. (P–M)

Spinelli, J. (1997). *Wringer.* New York: HarperCollins. (M–U)

Turner, A. (1987). *Nettie's trip south.* New York: Macmillan. (M)

Whelan, G. (2000). *Homeless bird.* New York: HarperCollins. (U)

Woodson, J. (2005). *Show way.* New York: Putnam. (M–U)

P = primary grades (K–2); M = middle grades (3–5); U = upper grades (6–8).

Review

Listening is the most basic and most used of the language arts. Despite its importance, listening instruction is often neglected because teachers assume that students already know how to listen. This chapter focused on four types of listening—discriminative, aesthetic, efferent, and critical—and you read about how to help students become more effective listeners. Here are the key concepts presented in this chapter:

- Students use discriminative listening as they develop phonemic awareness.
- Students listen aesthetically as teachers read stories aloud and while viewing puppet shows, plays, and movie versions of stories.
- Teachers use interactive read-alouds to share stories with students.
- Students are more successful listeners when they're responding to the stories that the teacher reads aloud.
- Students learn strategies to become more effective listeners.
- Students use efferent listening to remember information.
- Students are more effective listeners when they're actively involved in listening.
- Students use critical listening to evaluate a message.
- Students need to learn to listen critically because they are exposed to many types of persuasion.
- Students apply what they learn about persuasion as they create commercials and advertisements.

Professional References

Barrentine, S. J. (1996). Engaging with reading through inter-active read-alouds. *The Reading Teacher, 50,* 36–43.

Berthoff, A. E. (1981). *The making of meaning.* Montclair, NJ: Boynton/Cook.

Brownell, J. (2006). *Listening: Attitudes, principles, and skills.* Boston: Allyn & Bacon.

Devine, T. G. (1982). *Listening skills schoolwide: Activities and programs.* Urbana, IL: ERIC Clearinghouse on Reading and Communication Skills and the National Council of Teachers of English.

Dickinson, D. K., & Tabors, P. O. (2001). *Beginning literacy with language.* Baltimore: Brookes.

Fisher, D., Flood, J., Lapp, D., & Frey, N. (2004). Interactive read-alouds: Is there a common set of implementation practices? *The Reading Teacher, 58,* 8–17.

Fox, M. (2001). *Reading magic: Why reading aloud to our children will change their lives forever.* San Diego: Harcourt Brace.

Gibbons, P. (2002). *Scaffolding language, scaffolding learning: Teaching second language learners in the mainstream classroom.* Portsmouth, NH: Heinemann.

Ivey, G., & Broaddus, K. (2001). "Just plain reading": A survey of what makes students want to read in middle school classrooms. *Reading Research Quarterly, 36,* 350–377.

Lundsteen, S. W. (1979). *Listening: Its impact on reading and the other language arts* (Rev. ed.). Urbana, IL: National Council of Teachers of English.

Lutz, W. (1997). *The new doublespeak: Why no one knows what anyone's saying anymore.* New York: HarperCollins.

Martinez, M. G., & Roser, N. L. (1985). Read it again: The value of repeated readings during storytime. *The Reading Teacher, 38,* 782–786.

National Communication Association. (1998). *Competent communicators: K–12 speaking, listening, and media literacy standards and competencies.* Washington, DC: Author.

Opitz, M. F., & Zbaracki, M. D. (2004). *Listen hear! 25 effective comprehension strategies.* Portsmouth, NH: Heinemann.

Readence, J. E., Bean, T. W., & Baldwin, R. S. (2004). *Content area reading: An integrated approach* (8th ed.). Dubuque, IA: Kendall/Hunt.

Rosenblatt, L. (2005). *Making meaning with texts: Selected essays.* Portsmouth, NH: Heinemann.

Rothenberg, C., & Fisher, D. (2007). *Teaching English language learners: A differentiated approach.* Upper Saddle River, NJ: Merrill/Prentice Hall.

Sipe, L. R. (2002). Talking back and taking over: Young children's expressive engagement during storybook read-alouds. *The Reading Teacher, 55,* 476–483.

Trelease, J. (2006). *The read-aloud handbook* (6th ed.). New York: Penguin.

Wolvin, A. D., & Coakley, C. G. (1996). *Listening* (5th ed.). New York: McGraw-Hill.

Yaden, D. B., Jr. (1988). Understanding stories through repeated read-alouds: How many does it take? *The Reading Teacher, 41,* 556–560.

Yopp, H. K., & Yopp, R. H. (2006). *Literature-based reading activities* (4th ed.). Boston: Allyn & Bacon.

Children's Book References

Aldrin, B. (2005). *Reaching for the moon.* New York: Harper-Collins.

Barretta, G. (2006). *Now and Ben: The modern inventions of Benjamin Franklin.* New York: Holt.

Galdone, P. (2006). *The Little Red Hen.* New York: Clarion Books.

Giovanni, N. (2005). *Rosa.* New York: Henry Holt.

Hiaasen, C. (2005). *Flush.* New York: Knopf.

McCarthy, M. (2006). *Aliens are coming! The true account of the 1938 War of the Worlds radio broadcast.* New York: Knopf.

Morris, A. (1993). *Bread, bread, bread.* New York: Harper-Collins.

Morrison, T. (2006). *Wildfire.* Boston: Houghton Mifflin.

Pinkney, J. (2006). *The little red hen.* New York: Dial Books.

Scieszka, J. (1999). *The true story of the 3 little pigs!* New York: Viking.

Siy, A. (2005). *Mosquito bite.* Watertown, MA: Charlesbridge.

Steig, W. (2005). *Sylvester and the magic pebble.* New York: Simon & Schuster.

Stevens, J., & Crummel, S. S. (1999). *Cook-a-doodle-doo!* San Diego: Harcourt Brace.

chapter eight

Sustaining Talk in the Classroom

I n addition to guided reading lessons, the students in Mrs. Zumwalt's third-grade class participate in literature circles each day because she knows that these children need lots of reading practice and opportunities to talk about books. For 30 minutes each day, they read or talk about the easy chapter books they are reading in small groups. Most of her students are English learners who read a year below grade level, so Mrs. Zumwalt works hard to find easy-to-read chapter books that will interest them. The box on page 242 lists 20 of the books that Mrs. Zumwalt has in her classroom.

One small group of children is reading *The Cat's Meow* (Soto, 1997), the story of a white cat named Pip who speaks Spanish to Graciela, the little girl who owns him. Spanish words are included in the text. All but one of the children in this group speak Spanish at home, so they feel very comfortable with the inclusion of the Spanish words.

Yesterday, the five children in the group read the first chapter, and now they're talking about the story. Mrs. Zumwalt joins the group for a few minutes. The discussion focuses on whether the cat can really speak Spanish or whether it's just Graciela's imagination at work.

What can you learn by listening to students talk about a book?

What can you learn by listening to students talk about a book?

Teachers know that they can learn a great deal through observing students as they work, listening to students participate in discussions, and talking with students during conferences. As you read this vignette about a small group of third graders discussing a book they're reading, notice Armando's role in the discussion and how the children use talk to clarify their understanding. In addition, think about how they talk about their use of reading strategies.

Armando:	That girl knows Spanish, so it could be that she is just pretending. She really could be just thinking those Spanish words. And it says that her mom and dad are weird. Maybe she comes from a weird family. That's what I think.
Maricela:	I think Pip can speak Spanish, but she will just speak to that girl and no one else.
Marcos:	Yeah, I think Pip can talk in Spanish. That would be cool.
Ruben:	No, Armando. It's for real, man. The cat—what's his name?
Linda:	Pip, and she's a girl, not a boy.
Ruben:	Yeah, Pip. I think he, I mean she, can talk. And Linda, how do you know it's a girl cat?
Linda:	Look, I'll show you. (She turns to the first page of the first chapter, scanning for a word.) Look, on page 1, here it is. It says "looked at *her* empty bowl." Her. That's how I know.

Mrs. Zumwalt redirects the conversation and asks, "Do you think you'll find out for sure whether Pip can talk by the time you finish reading the book?" The children are sure they will find out. Then she asks them to consider possible story lines: "So, what do you think might happen in the story?"

Linda:	I think the story might be like the one about Martha the talking dog that we read last year. Martha got in trouble for talking too much so she stopped talking, but then at the end when some robbers came, she called the police and was a hero.
Mrs. Zumwalt:	I know that story! It's called *Martha Speaks,* right? (The children agree.)
Armando:	I don't think Pip will talk in front of anyone except for Graciela. Not that Juanita. Pip doesn't

---

Twenty Easy-to-Read Chapter Books

Bang-Campbell, M. (2002). *Little rat sets sail.* San Diego: Harcourt Brace.

Benchley, P. (1994). *Small wolf.* New York: HarperCollins.

Cazet, D. (2005). *The octopus.* New York: HarperCollins.

Coerr, E. (1993). *Chang's paper pony.* New York: HarperCollins.

Coerr, E. (1999). *Buffalo Bill and the Pony Express.* New York: HarperCollins.

Coerr, E. (1999). *The Josefina story quilt.* New York: HarperCollins.

Cushman, D. (2000). *Inspector Hopper.* New York: HarperCollins.

Dahl, R. (1999). *Esio trot.* New York: Puffin Books.

Danziger, P. (2006). *Amber Brown is not a crayon.* New York: Puffin Books.

Haas, J. (2001). *Runaway radish.* New York: Greenwillow.

Horowitz, R. (2001). *Breakout at the bug lab.* New York: Dial Books.

Laurence, D. (2001). *Captain and matey set sail.* New York: HarperCollins.

Livingstone, S. (2001). *Harley.* New York: North-South Books.

Lottridge, C. B. (2003). *Berta: A remarkable dog.* Toronto: Groundwood Books.

Lowry, L. (2002). *Gooney bird Greene.* Boston: Houghton Mifflin.

McDonald, M. (2002). *Judy Moody.* Cambridge, MA: Candlewick Press.

Rylant, C. (2005). *The high-rise private eyes: The case of the desperate duck.* New York: Greenwillow.

Seuling, B. (2001). *Robert and the great pepperoni.* Chicago: Cricket Books.

Turner, A. (1997). *Dust for dinner.* New York: HarperCollins.

Yee, W. H. (2005). *Upstairs mouse, downstairs mole.* Boston: Houghton Mifflin.

---

want to be sent to be in a circus because she's a freak. She wants to be a normal white cat. I think maybe it will stay her secret.

Ruben: I think people will find out about Pip and she will be famous. Then she'll win a million dollars on *Who Wants to Be a Millionaire?*

After everyone laughs at Ruben's comment, Mrs. Zumwalt asks about Juanita, and the children respond.

Armando: Juanita is the girl that Graciela talks to and tells that Pip can talk Spanish. She doesn't believe her, but she could still gossip about it at school.

Mrs. Zumwalt: Is Juanita a friend of Graciela's?

Linda: I think so.

Maricela: They play together.

Armando: No, I don't think they're friends. They just know each other and maybe they play together, but they are not friends. They don't act like friends.

Maricela: I think Graciela *wants* to be friends. That's what I think.

Mrs. Zumwalt moves the conversation around to Juanita because the children seemed unaware of her when Armando mentioned her and because she will figure prominently in the book. As several of the children suggested, people will find out about Pip the talking cat, and a big problem develops.

The children continue reading and talking about the book as they learn that Graciela's neighbor, Sr. Medina, is the one who taught Pip to speak Spanish. In Chapter 6, they read that Sr. Medina's nosy neighbor has called the television stations and told them about Pip and her special ability. During their discussion, the children talk about the television news crews coming to interview Sr. Medina and Pip. The children are angry that the neighbor called the television stations.

Linda:	It's not fair that that lady across the street was so nosy and she ruined everything. It got so bad that Sr. Medina had to move away.
Maricela:	I like that Graciela sprayed that lady with the hose and she got all wet. And Graciela called her a "sour old snoop." That's funny.
Mrs. Zumwalt:	In the book, it says that Graciela hoped the lady would "shrink into a puddle of nothing like the evil witch in *The Wizard of Oz*." What does that mean?
Armando:	That's what happened in *The Wizard of Oz*. I saw the movie so I know.
Ruben:	This chapter reminds me of when my neighbor's son got killed. His name was Manuel. He was 16, I think. He got killed by some gang bangers. They were in a car and they came by his house and they shot him. He was in the house and the bullet came in through the window. Then the ambulance came but he was dead. So the police came and they put up this yellow ribbon all around the house. My mom and dad made me stay in the house but I wanted to go outside and watch. Then the television reporters came and it was crowded with people. Just like in this chapter.
Marcos:	Sr. Medina had to move away and he took Pip with him.
Linda:	No, he didn't take Pip. She's Graciela's cat.
Marcos:	Look on page 69. It says, "He moved out last night and took his cat with him."
Linda:	Well, it's not *his* cat.

Mrs. Zumwalt asks the children to predict whether Graciela will get her cat back, and then they read the last chapter of the book and learn that Pip does come back, and now she's black, not white, and she speaks French, not Spanish! They talk about the ending.

Linda:	I'm happy. I knew Pip would come back. I would be so, so, so sad if anyone stole my cat.
Marcos:	I liked this book. It was funny.
Ruben:	I wish it would happen to me.
Maricela:	I would like to be Graciela.
Mrs. Zumwalt:	Why?
Maricela:	Well, her parents are weird; that's for sure. But, she does some interesting things. And I wish I had a cat who could talk to me in Spanish or in English.
Armando:	I liked the Spanish words. I'm going to write a story and put Spanish words in it. Those Spanish words made it fun to read this book.

Mrs. Zumwalt moves from group to group as they discuss the books they're reading. Her focus in these conversations is that children should use talk to deepen their comprehension. She watches to make sure that all children are participating and that the conversation explores important elements of plot, character, and theme. She asks questions to probe their thinking or redirect their attention. She also watches children's growing involvement with the story. Mrs. Zumwalt is pleased that Ruben became more involved with *The Cat's Meow*; after reading the first chapter, he didn't seem interested in the story, but by the end, he was hooked. Mrs. Zumwalt believes that it is the conversation that brings about the change.

---

*N*oted researcher Shirley Brice Heath (1983) explored the value of talk in classrooms and concluded that students' talk is an essential part of language arts and is necessary for academic success. Quiet classrooms were once considered the most conducive to learning, but research now emphasizes that talk is a necessary ingredient for learning. Talk is often thwarted in classrooms because of large class size and the mistaken assumption that silence facilitates learning; instead, teachers must make an extra effort to provide opportunities for students to use talk for both socialization and learning.

As you continue reading, you will learn ways to encourage talk in your classroom. Think about these questions as you read:

- ◆ How do students participate in conversations?
- ◘ How do students use talk to respond to literature?
- ◆ How do students use talk as a learning tool?
- ◗ What types of dramatic activities are appropriate for students?

CONVERSATIONS

Students get together to respond to literature they're reading, talk about each other's writing, work on projects, and share information they've learned. The most important feature of talk activities is that they promote higher-level thinking. Teachers take students' ideas seriously, and students are validated as thinkers (Nystrand, Gamoran, & Heck, 1993). As they converse with classmates, students use talk for different purposes: to control classmates' behavior, maintain social relationships, convey information, and share personal experiences and opinions.

Small-Group Conversations

Students learn and refine their strategies for conversing with classmates as they participate in small-group conversations (Kaufman, 2000). They learn how to begin conversations, take turns, keep the conversation moving forward, support comments and questions that classmates make, deal with conflicts, and bring the conversation to a close. And, they learn how powerful talk is in making meaning and creating knowledge. The characteristics of small-group conversations are listed in Figure 8–1.

To begin the conversation, students gather in groups at tables or other areas in the classroom, bringing with them any necessary materials. One student in each group begins the conversation with a question or comment; classmates then take turns making

FIGURE 8–1

Characteristics of Small-Group Conversations

- Each group has three to six members. These groups may be permanent, or they may be established for specific activities. It's important that group members be a cohesive group and courteous to and supportive of each other. Students in established groups often choose names for their groups.
- The purpose of the small-group conversation or work session is to develop interpretations and create knowledge.
- Students' talk is meaningful, functional, and genuine. Students use talk to solve problems and discover answers to authentic questions—questions that require interpretation and critical thinking.
- The teacher clearly defines the goal of the group work and outlines the activities to be completed. Activities require cooperation and collaboration and could not be done as effectively through independent work.
- Group members have assigned jobs. Sometimes students keep the same jobs over a period of time, and at other times, specific jobs are identified for a particular purpose.
- Students use strategies to begin the conversation, keep it moving forward and on task, and end it.
- Students feel ownership of and responsibility for the activities they are involved in and the projects they create.

comments and asking questions and support the other group members as they elaborate on and expand their comments. The tone is exploratory, and throughout the conversation, the group is progressing toward a common goal. The goal may be deepening students' understanding of a book they have read, responding to a question the teacher has asked, or creating a project. From time to time, the conversation slows down and there may be a few minutes of silence. Then a group member asks a question or makes a comment that sends the conversation in a new direction.

Students try to support one another in groups, and two of the most important ways they do this are by calling each other by name and maintaining eye contact. They also cultivate a climate of trust in the group by expressing agreement, sharing feelings, voicing approval, and referring to comments that group members made earlier. Conflict is inevitable, but students need to learn how to deal with it so that it doesn't get out of control. They learn to accept that there will be differing viewpoints and to make compromises. Cintorino (1993) reported that her eighth graders used humor to defuse disagreements in small-group conversations.

At the end of a conversation, students reach consensus and conclude that they have finished sharing ideas, explored all dimensions of a question, or completed a project. Sometimes they produce a product during the conversation; the product may be a brainstormed list, a chart, or something more elaborate, such as a set of puppets. Group members are responsible for collecting and storing materials they have used and for reporting on the group's work.

Students participate in small-group conversations as part of all four patterns of practice, as shown in the box on page 246. Teachers play an important role in making the conversations successful, beginning with creating a community of learners in the classroom so that students understand that they are responsible group members

How Small-Group Conversations Fit Into the Four Patterns of Practice

Literature Focus Units

Students often participate in small-group conversations as they talk about the book they're reading. They also work in small groups as they create projects during the applying stage.

Literature Circles

Literature circles are essentially small-group conversations. Students work in small groups as they read and respond to a book.

Reading and Writing Workshop

Students don't usually participate in small-group conversations during reading workshop because they are reading different books, but they do meet in small groups to share their rough drafts during writing workshop.

Thematic Units

Students often get into small groups to read an informational book or content-area textbook chapter and to work on projects. They also participate in small-group conversations to talk about their reading.

(Kaufman, 2000). Teachers create a climate of trust by demonstrating to students that they trust them and their ability to learn. Similarly, students learn to socialize with classmates and to respect one another as they work together in small groups.

Grand Conversations

To dig deeper into a story and deepen their comprehension, students talk about stories they are reading in literature focus units and literature circles; these conversations are often called *grand conversations* (Peterson & Eeds, 1990). They're different from traditional discussions because students take responsibility for their own learning as they voice their opinions and support their views with examples from the story. They talk about what puzzles them, what they find interesting, their personal connections to the story, and connections they see between this story and others they have read. Students also encourage their classmates to contribute to the conversation. Even though teachers often sit in on conversations as a participant, not as a judge, the talk is primarily among the students.

Teachers often use a combination of small-group and whole-class groupings for grand conversations, but they can be held with the whole class or in small groups. When students meet in small groups, they have more opportunities to talk, and when they meet as a class, there is a feeling of community. Young children usually meet as a class, but students participating in literature circles meet in small groups because they are reading different books. When the teacher is reading aloud a novel, students often meet first in small groups and then come together as a class to respond to the book.

Grand conversations have two parts. The first part is open-ended: Students talk about their reactions to the book, and their comments determine the direction of the conversation. Teachers do participate, however, and share their responses, ask questions, and provide information. In the second part, the teacher focuses students' attention on one or two aspects of the book that they did not talk about in the first part of the conversation. The steps are shown in the Step by Step feature below.

After the grand conversation, students often write in their reading logs, or write again if they wrote before the grand conversation. Then they continue reading the book if they have read only part of it. Both participating in grand conversations and writing entries in reading logs help students think about and respond to what they have read.

From their observational study of fifth and sixth graders conducting grand conversations, Eeds and Wells (1989) found that students extend their individual interpretations of books through talk and even create a better understanding of them. Students talk about their understanding of the story and can change their opinions after listening to classmates' alternative views. They share personal stories related to their reading in

Step by Step

------- Grand Conversations -------

1 **Read the book.**   Students read a picture book or a chapter in a novel or listen to the teacher read a story aloud.

2 **Prepare for the conversation.**   Students think about the story by drawing pictures or writing in reading logs. This step is especially important when students don't talk much because with this preparation, they are more likely to have ideas to share.

3 **Have small-group conversations.**   Students form small groups to talk about the story before getting together as a class. This step is optional and is generally used when students don't talk much.

4 **Begin the class conversation.**   Students form a circle for the class conversation so that everyone can see each other. Teachers begin by asking, "Who would like to begin?" or "What are you thinking about?" One student makes a comment, and classmates take turns talking about the idea that the first student introduced.

5 **Continue the class conversation.**   A student introduces a new idea, and classmates talk about it, making connections, providing details, and reading excerpts from the story to make a point. Students limit their comments to the idea being discussed, and after they finish discussing this idea, a new one is introduced. To ensure that everyone participates, teachers often ask students not to make more than three comments until everyone has spoken at least once.

6 **Ask questions.**   Teachers ask questions to direct students to an aspect of the story that has been missed; for example, they might focus on an element of story structure or the author's craft. Or, they may ask students to compare the books to the film version of the story, or to other books by the same author.

7 **Conclude the conversation.**   After all of the big ideas have been explored, teachers end the conversation by summarizing and drawing conclusions about the story.

8 **Reflect on the conversation.**   Students often write in reading logs to reflect on the ideas discussed in the grand conversation.

poignant ways that trigger other students to identify with them. Students also gain insights about how authors use the elements of story structure to develop their message.

Martinez and Roser (1995) researched the content of students' grand conversations, and they found that students often talk about story events and characters or explore the themes of the story but delve less often into the author's craft to explore the way he or she structured the book, the arrangement of text and illustrations on the page, or the author's use of figurative or repetitive language. The researchers called these three conversation directions *experience, message,* and *object.* They suggest that stories help to shape students' talk about books and that some books lend themselves to conversation about message and others to talk about experience or object. Stories with dramatic plots or stories that present a problem to which students can relate, such as *Chrysanthemum* (Henkes, 1991) and *The Tale of Despereaux* (DiCamillo, 2003), focus the conversation on the book as experience. Multilayered stories or books in which main characters deal with dilemmas, such as *Smoky Night* (Bunting, 1999) and *Princess Academy* (Hale, 2005), focus the conversation on the message. Books with distinctive structures or language features, such as *Flotsam* (Wiesner, 2006) and *Witness* (Hesse, 2001), focus the conversation on the object.

Drawing students' attention to the "object" is important because they apply what they've learned about the author's craft when they write their own stories. Students who know more about leads, pacing, figurative language, point of view, imagery, surprise endings, voice, and flashbacks write better stories than those who don't. One way teachers can help students examine the author's craft is through the questions they ask during grand conversations.

An additional benefit of grand conversations is that when students talk in depth about stories, their writing shows the same level of inferential comprehension

Gail E. Tompkins

Grand Conversation
These sixth graders are participating in a literature circle, and they meet with their teacher twice a week to talk about the novel they are reading. Their discussion is a grand conversation because it's authentic; the students share ideas, make connections, ask questions, offer predictions, and talk about the author's use of story elements and literary devices. Their teacher also participates in the grand conversation, modeling how to talk about literature, scaffolding students' comments, and asking questions to help them think more critically about the novel.

(Sorenson, 1993). Students seem to be more successful in grand conversations if they have written in reading logs first, and they are more successful in writing entries if they've talked about the story first.

Instructional Conversations

Instructional conversations provide opportunities for students to talk about the main ideas they are learning in thematic units; through these conversations, students enhance their academic language proficiency (Goldenberg, 1992/1993). As in grand conversations, students are active participants, sharing ideas and building on classmates' ideas with their own comments. Teachers are participants, too, making comments much as the students do, but they also clarify misconceptions, ask questions, and provide instruction.

Instructional conversations deepen students' content-area knowledge and develop their academic language proficiency in these ways:

- Students deepen their knowledge about the topic.
- Students use technical and precise vocabulary and more complex sentence structures to express the ideas being discussed.
- Students learn to provide support for the ideas they present with information found in informational books, content-area textbooks, and other resources in the classroom.
- Students ask inference and critical-level questions, those with more than one answer.
- Students participate actively and make comments that build on and expand classmates' comments.

Students use talk in instructional conversations to accomplish goals, learn information, and work out problems in thematic units. As they talk, students pose hypotheses, ask questions, provide information, and clarify ideas; recall ideas presented earlier; make personal, world, and literary connections; make inferences; and evaluate the text and the information presented in it (Roser & Keehn, 2002). In contrast to grand conversations about stories in which students use primarily aesthetic talk to create and deepen their interpretations, here students use primarily efferent talk to create knowledge and understand relationships among the big ideas they're learning.

Researchers have compared the effectiveness of small-group conversations with other instructional approaches and have found that students' learning is enhanced when they relate what they are learning to their own experiences—especially when they do so in their own words (Wittrock & Alesandrini, 1990). Similarly, Pressley (1992) reported that students' learning was promoted when they had opportunities to elaborate ideas through talk. The steps in an instructional conversation are explained in the Step by Step feature on page 250.

Instructional conversations are useful for helping students grapple with important ideas they are learning in social studies, science, and other content areas. When students are discussing literature, they use generally grand conversations, which facilitate response to literature. An exception is when students focus on analyzing plot, characters, theme, and other elements of story structure; then they are thinking efferently and are participating in an instructional conversation, not a grand conversation.

Instructional Conversations

1 Choose a focus.   Teachers choose a focus that's related to the goals of a thematic unit.

2 Present information.   Teachers present information or read an informational book or an excerpt from a content-area textbook in preparation for the discussion.

3 Prepare for the instructional conversation.   Sometimes teachers have students complete a graphic organizer together as a class or in small groups before beginning the conversation.

4 Have small-group conversations.   Sometimes students respond to a question in small groups before beginning the whole-class conversation.

5 Begin the conversation.   Teachers begin by asking a question related to the focus they identified in the first step. Students take turns sharing information, asking questions, and making connections. Teachers often write students' comments on chart paper in a list or create a graphic organizer.

6 Continue the conversation.   Teachers continue the conversations by asking additional questions, and students take turns responding to the questions and reexploring the big ideas.

7 Conclude the conversation.   Teachers bring the conversation to an end by reviewing the big ideas that were discussed using the charts they've developed.

8 Reflect on the conversation.   Students record the ideas discussed during the conversation by writing and drawing in learning logs.

TALK AS A LEARNING TOOL

Asking Questions

Asking and answering questions are common types of talk in classrooms. Researchers have found that teachers ask as many as 50,000 questions a year, whereas students ask as few as 10 (Watson & Young, 2003). The most common questions are literal questions, those that require simple recall, even though the most useful questions require students to analyze, interpret, evaluate, and offer opinions.

After reading *Amber Brown Is Not a Crayon* (Danziger, 2006), the story of two best friends and what happens as one of them moves to another state, a group of third graders in Mrs. Zumwalt's class wrote their own questions. The group spent a few minutes considering the questions and deciding which ones to actually use. Their questions included the following:

Why do you think Amber and Justin are best friends?
Do you think Mr. Cohn is sort of like Ms. Frizzle [in the Magic School Bus series]?
Do you think Mr. Cohn is a good teacher?

Meeting the Needs of English Learners

How Do English Learners Use Talk as a Learning Tool?

Talk facilitates learning for all students, but it's especially important for English learners who are struggling to learn English at the same time they're grappling with grade-level content-area learning (Gibbons, 2002; Rothenberg & Fisher, 2007). In addition, school is the only place where some English learners have opportunities to hear and speak English. How does talk facilitate learning? As they talk, students focus on the big ideas, questioning, clarifying, and elaborating their thinking. They organize these big ideas, relate them to their background knowledge, and practice using newly introduced vocabulary words. English learners benefit from daily opportunities to talk in large groups, in small groups, and one-on-one with a classmate or the teacher (Fay & Whaley, 2004).

English learners use talk as a learning tool in all four patterns of practice. In thematic unit, for example, students use talk as they are involved in meaningful oral, written, and visual activities and broaden their knowledge of the world. Teachers support English learners in these ways during thematic units and the other patterns of practice:

- Involve students in hands-on, active learning opportunities
- Have students work with classmates in small groups
- Link lessons to students' prior experiences, or build needed background knowledge
- Clarify meaning with objects, photos, and demonstrations
- Teach technical vocabulary related to the topic
- Use graphic organizers to emphasize the relationships among the big ideas
- Have students talk, read, create visuals, and write about the topic
- Teach students to recognize when they're confused and how to take action to solve the problem
- Demonstrate how to ask and answer higher-level questions
- Teach students how to listen to informational books and content-area textbooks
- Involve students in making small-group projects to demonstrate their learning

With these instructional supports in place, students are better able to learn age-appropriate content knowledge along with their classmates.

Did you know from the beginning that Justin was going to move away?
How can best friends fight and still be best friends?
Is Justin happy or sad about moving to Alabama?
Why is Amber so mean to Justin?
What do you think will happen to the friendship after Justin moves away?
Can they still be best friends after Justin moves away?

These questions involve higher-level thinking and delve into the "best friends" theme of the book. They require students to think deeply about the story and even to go back and reread portions to support their answers. If students are not going this deeply into a story, teachers should pose questions like these.

Questions can be grouped into three levels: literal, inferential, and critical. Literal or "on the page" questions have a single factual answer and can usually be answered with a few words or "yes" or "no." When the questions refer to a story or other book that students are reading, the answers are directly stated in the text. The second level of questions is inferential or "between the lines." To answer these questions, students synthesize information and form interpretations using both their background knowledge and clues in the text. The answers are implicitly stated in the text. The third, most complex level of questioning is critical or "beyond the page." These questions are open-ended; they require students to go beyond the text and think creatively and abstractly about global ideas, issues, and concerns. At this level, students apply information, make connections, evaluate and value the text, and express opinions. The LA Essentials box below reviews the three levels of questioning.

Teachers use these three levels of questions for different purposes. They use literal questions to check that students have basic information and understand the meaning of words. Literal questions are easy to ask and to answer, but, because they are the most frequently asked questions, teachers need to be careful not to use too many of them.

LEVELS OF QUESTIONING

Level	Category	Description
3	Critical or "Beyond the Page" Questions	Critical questions go beyond the text and focus on global issues, ideas, and problems. Often there are no correct answers. To answer these questions, students think creatively; make personal connections, world connections, and literary connections; evaluate the text; and express opinions.
2	Inferential or "Between the Lines" Questions	Inferential questions require analysis and interpretation. The answers are implicitly stated in the text. To answer these questions, students use a combination of background knowledge and clues in the text.
1	Literal or "On the Page" Questions	Literal questions are factual. The answers to these questions are stated explicitly in the text. Students answer these questions with "yes" or "no" or with a few words taken directly from the text.

To help students think more deeply and to challenge their thinking, teachers use inferential and critical questions. When they are talking about literature, teachers ask inferential questions to probe students' understanding of a story and make interpretations, and when they ask students to analyze the ideas, make comparisons, and summarize information. Teachers ask critical questions to challenge students' thinking to go beyond the story to make connections, evaluate the story, reflect on the overall theme, and delve into the author's craft. They ask critical questions during thematic units for similar purposes: to consider different viewpoints, examine issues, and draw conclusions.

Teachers commonly use the IRF (Initiate-Response-Feedback) cycle when they ask questions:

- *Initiate:* The teacher asks a question.
- *Response:* The student answers the question.
- *Feedback:* The teacher responds to the student's answer.

This cycle is teacher centered because teachers do most of the talking and control the flow of the conversation. It's the primary way teachers involve students in discussion; in fact, researchers report that more than half the instructional talk in classrooms occurs in IRF cycles (Watson & Young, 2003). Teachers often use this cycle for assessment, to check on students' attention and understanding rather than to promote learning. Even though the IRF cycle is common, it's less conducive to learning than other procedures that involve students in asking questions and doing more of the talk.

K-W-L Charts

Teachers use K-W-L charts (Ogle, 1989) to activate and build students' background knowledge during thematic units. The letters *K, W,* and *L* stand for "What I/We Know," "What I/We Want to Learn" or "What I/We Wonder," and "What I/We Learned." Students share what they know and ask questions about a topic, and teachers write students' comments and questions on a chart. Through this activity, students become curious and more engaged in the learning process, and teachers have opportunities to introduce complex ideas and technical vocabulary in a nonthreatening way.

Teachers divide a large chart into three columns and label them "K—What We Know," "W—What We wonder," and "L—What We learned." At the beginning of a unit, teachers introduce the chart and complete the first two columns as students think about the topic, share information, and ask questions. Then at the end of the unit, teachers complete the third column of the chart to summarize and review students' learning. The Step by Step box on page 258 lists the steps in the procedure.

Teachers direct, scribe, and monitor the development of the K-W-L chart, but it's the students' talk that makes this such a powerful activity. Students use talk to explore and question ideas as they complete the K and W columns and to share new knowledge as they complete the L column.

K-W-L charts are very adaptable; they can be used in several ways. Teachers can make class K-W-L charts with their students, students can work in small groups to make charts, and students can make individual charts in journals or on drawing paper. Class charts work best for younger children or for older students who have not made K-W-L charts before. Middle- and upper-grade students often work with classmates to make group charts on chart paper, or they can make individual K-W-L charts. Figure 8–2 shows a K-W-L chart that a second-grade class developed as they studied penguins, and

FIGURE 8–2

A Second-Grade Class's K-W-L Chart on Penguins

K What We Know	W What We Wonder	L What We Learned
Penguins are black and white.	Are penguins fish or birds?	Some penguins can swim real fast—25 miles an hour.
Penguins are good swimmers and divers.	Do penguins live in California?	They have feathers on their bodies.
We saw penguins at the zoo.	What do penguin babies look like?	Penguins live at the South Pole. It is called Antarctica.
They eat fish.	Do polar bears hunt and kill penguins?	They don't get cold because they have fat and feathers on their bodies to keep warm.
Penguins like to play on ice and snow.	Do penguins have enemies?	Penguins have flippers that look like little wings but they can't fly.
Penguins look funny when they walk on little feet.	Do penguins ever get cold?	The emperor penguin is the largest penguin. It's almost as big as us.
	How long do penguins live?	Babies hatch from eggs. They're chicks.
	Can you have a penguin for a pet?	The fathers care for eggs until they hatch.
		The penguin's enemies are leopard seals, killer whales, sharks, and people.

Figure 8–3 shows an individual K-W-L chart on spiders. The individual chart was made by folding a sheet of paper in half vertically. Next, the student cut three flaps and labeled them "K," "W," and "L," as shown in the top drawing in the figure. Then the student flipped up the flaps to write on the chart, as shown in the lower drawing.

Minilessons

So that children can grow in their knowledge of and use of academic language, Courtney Cazden (2001) challenges teachers to make changes in classroom language use and to incorporate more academic language. Finding ways to help all children develop academic language has become more urgent because of the enactment of the No Child Left Behind Act of 2001. It's essential that teachers set high standards for themselves and for their students. The activities they organize should challenge students to use higher-order thinking as they listen, talk, read, and write. Whether students use higher-order thinking is dependent on the level of questions teachers ask and on the types of activities in which students are involved. Teachers should incorporate academic language into their instruction, even with young children and English learners: Too often, in an attempt to be kind, they simplify the words and sentence structures they use. What happens,

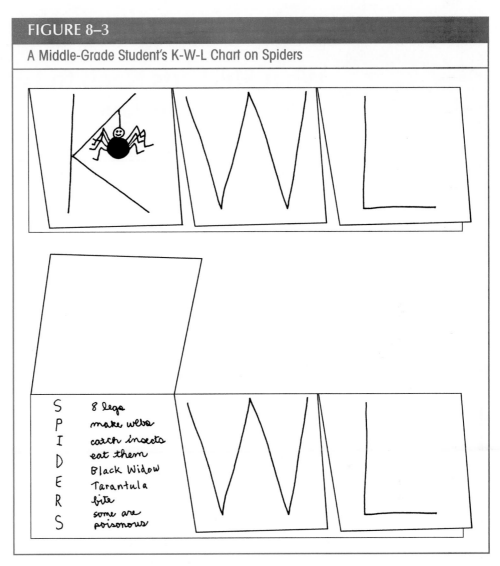

FIGURE 8–3

A Middle-Grade Student's K-W-L Chart on Spiders

S 8 legs
P make webs
I catch insects
D eat them
E Black Widow
R Tarantula
S bite
   some are
   poisonous

however, is that students don't have the opportunity to learn the technical vocabulary and sophisticated sentence patterns that are part of academic language.

Teachers teach minilessons about academic language and a variety of talk-related procedures, concepts, strategies, and skills. A list of minilesson topics related to talk is presented on page 256, along with a sample minilesson on how to sustain a conversation.

Oral Reports

Learning how to prepare and present an oral report is an important efferent talk activity for middle- and upper-grade students. However, students are often assigned an oral report without any guidance about how to prepare and give one. Too many students simply copy the report verbatim from an encyclopedia and then read it aloud. The result is that students learn to fear speaking in front of a group rather than gain confidence in their oral language abilities.

What Students Need to Learn About Talk

Topics

Procedures	Concepts	Strategies and Skills
Begin a conversation	Academic language	Refer to previous comments
Take turns	Higher-level questions	Extend a comment
Sustain a conversation	Roles of speakers and listeners	Call classmates by name
End a conversation	Small-group conversations	Look at classmates while speaking
Tell a story		Vary tone of voice
Make K-W-L charts	**Grand conversations**	Vary pace of speech
Present an oral report	**Instructional conversations**	Ask questions
Conduct an interview	Levels of questions	Express a viewpoint
Participate in a debate	Interviews	Maintain the audience's interest
Create a puppet	Oral presentations	Present main ideas coherently
Perform a puppet show	Debates	
Write a script		

I invite you to learn more about sustaining talk in the classroom by visiting MyEducationLab. To see sixth graders participate in a grand conversation, go to the topic "Talking" and click on the video "Grand Conversations," and to watch fourth graders participate in an instructional conversation, go to the topic "Talking" and click on the video "Instructional Conversations."

Minilesson

Ms. Shapiro Teaches Her Second Graders About Sustaining Conversations

1 Introduce the topic

Ms. Shapiro explains to her second graders that she wants them to think about how they behave during grand conversations. She asks them to observe a grand conversation that she has planned with four students in the class. "We will be doing some good things to help the conversation and some bad things that hurt the conversation," she says. "Watch carefully so you will notice them."

2 Share examples

Ms. Shapiro and four chidlren have a grand conversation about a familiar story, *Hey, Al* (Yorinks, 1986). She chose a familiar story so that students could focus on the conversation itself and not get caught up in the story. The students participating in the conversation take turns making comments, but they don't expand on each other's comments, nor do they call each other by name or look at classmates as they are talking. Also, some children are looking away from the group as though they are not listening.

3 Provide information

Ms. Shapiro's students are eager to identify the strengths and weaknesses of the grand conversation they have observed. The "good things" were that "everyone talked about the story and nothing else" and "everybody was nice." The

"bad things" included that "some people didn't pay attention and look at the person talking," "some people didn't say other people's names," and "some people just said things but they didn't go next to what other people said." Ms. Shapiro agrees that the children have identified the problems, and she explains that she's seen some of these same problems in their conversations. Together they make a chart of "Good Things to Do in a Grand Conversation."

4 Supervise practice

Ms. Shapiro's students participate in grand conversations as part of literature circles and after she reads a book aloud to the class. She explains that she will observe their grand conversations to make sure they are doing all the good things they listed on their chart. For the next 2 weeks, Ms. Shapiro briefly reviews the chart with them before each grand conversation and takes a few minutes afterward to talk about the changes in behavior she has observed.

5 Reflect on learning

After 2 weeks of practice, Ms. Shapiro brings the children together to talk about their grand conversations, and she asks the second graders which of the good things from the chart they're doing better now. The children mention various points and conclude that their grand conversations have improved.

-------- K-W-L Charts --------

1 Create a large chart. Teachers post a large sheet of paper on the classroom wall, divide it into three columns, and label the columns *K* (or "What We *Know*"), *W* (or "What We *Wonder*"), and *L* (or "What We *Learned*").

2 Complete the K column. At the beginning of the thematic unit, teachers have students brainstorm what they know about the topic and then record their responses in this column. If students suggest any incorrect information, teachers help them reword the information as a question and add it to the W column.

3 Complete the W column. Teachers write the questions that students ask in the W column. They continue to add questions to the W column throughout the unit.

4 Complete the L column. At the end of the unit, students reflect on what they've learned, and then teachers record this information in the L column. Teachers don't expect students to answer each of the questions posted in the W column; instead, students focus on the most important and interesting information they've learned.

Students prepare and give reports about topics they are studying in social studies and science. Giving a report orally helps students to learn about topics in specific content areas as well as to develop their speaking abilities. Students need more than just an assignment to prepare a report for presentation on a particular date; they need to learn how to prepare and present an oral report. The steps in giving reports are listed in the Step by Step feature on the next page.

Students are usually the audience for the oral reports, and members of the audience have responsibilities: They should be attentive, listen to the speaker, ask questions, and applaud the speaker. Sometimes they also provide feedback to speakers about their presentations using a checklist or rubric, but at other times, students self-assess the process they used to prepare and give their presentations. The Weaving Assessment Into Practice feature on page 260 presents a self-assessment rubric developed by a fourth-grade class; it lists questions about the students' preparation for the presentation and about the presentation itself.

Interviews

Almost all students see interviews on television news programs and are familiar with the interviewing techniques reporters use. Interviewing is an exciting language arts activity that helps students refine questioning skills and use oral and written language for authentic purposes. Interviewing is an important language tool that can be integrated effectively in literature focus units and thematic units. As part of a unit on school, for example, a class of first graders invited the local high school principal to visit their class to be interviewed. The principal, who had been blinded several years earlier, brought his guide dog with him. The children asked him questions about how visually impaired people manage everyday tasks as well as how he performed his job as a principal. They also asked questions about his guide dog. After the interview, students drew pictures and wrote summaries of the interview. A first grader's report is shown in Figure 8–4.

One way to introduce interviewing is to watch interviews conducted on a television newscast and discuss what the purpose of the interview is, what a reporter does before and after an interview, and what types of questions are asked. Interviewers use a variety of questions, some to elicit facts and others to probe for feelings and opinions, but all questions are open-ended. Rarely do interviewers ask questions that require only a *yes* or *no* answer.

Interviewing involves far more than simply conducting the actual interview. Students prepare for the interview by generating a list of questions and follow up after the interview by using what they have learned in some way. For example, they might write a biography about the person who was interviewed or use the information in a report they're writing.

Hot Seat. Children assume the persona of a character from a story or biography they're reading and sit in the "hot seat" to be interviewed by classmates. It's called the "hot seat" because they're expected to respond to their classmates' questions. Students aren't intimidated by the activity; in fact, in most classrooms, it's very popular. Students are usually eager for their turn to sit in the hot seat. They answer the

---

Oral Reports

1 Choose a topic.   Students begin by brainstorming a list of possible topics related to the thematic unit, and then each student chooses a topic for the report. Next, students inventory, or think over, what they know about their topic and decide what they need to learn about it. Teachers often help students identify several key questions to focus the report.

2 Gather and organize information.   Students gather information to answer the key questions using a variety of resources, including informational books, content-area textbooks, the Internet, and encyclopedias. In addition, students can view videotapes and interview people in the community who have special expertise on the topic.

3 Develop the report.   Students review the information they have gathered and decide how best to present it so that the report will be both interesting and well organized. Students can transfer the notes they want to use for their reports from the cluster or data chart onto note cards. Only key words—not sentences or paragraphs— should be written on the cards.

4 Create visuals.   Students develop visuals, such as charts, diagrams, maps, pictures, models, and time lines. Visuals provide a crutch for the speaker and add an element of interest for the listeners.

5 Rehearse the presentation.   Students choose an interesting fact to begin their presentation, review key points, and read over their note cards; however, they don't read the report verbatim from the note cards. Then they rehearse their presentations.

6 Give the presentation.   Before the presentations begin, teachers teach minilessons on the characteristics of successful presentations. For instance, speakers should talk loudly enough for all to hear, look at the audience, keep to the key points, refer to note cards for important facts, and use the visuals they have prepared.

FIGURE 8–4

A First Grader's Interview Report

Mr. Kirtley came down. We asked him questions. He answered them. He is blind. His dog's name is Milo.

Weaving Assessment Into Practice

A SELF-ASSESSMENT RUBRIC FOR ORAL REPORTS

Name _____   Date _____

Topic _____

	no	1	2	3	4	yes
1. Did you collect enough information on a cluster or data chart?		—	—	—	—	
2. Did you make a useful chart or visual to show during your presentation?		—	—	—	—	
3. Did you rehearse your presentation?		—	—	—	—	
4. Did you speak loudly so everyone could hear?		—	—	—	—	
5. Did you look at the audience?		—	—	—	—	
6. Did you use your visuals?		—	—	—	—	
7. Did you make your main points?		—	—	—	—	
8. How pleased were you with your report?		—	—	—	—	
9. How did the audience respond?		—	—	—	—	

questions they're asked from the viewpoint of the character; through this activity, they deepen their comprehension as well as their classmates'. The steps in the procedure are listed in the box below. Students often wear a costume they've created when they assume the character's persona and share information about the character with classmates. They also collect objects and make artifacts to share.

Debates

Students participate in debates when they are excited about an issue and when most of the students have taken positions on one side of the issue or the other. Students can debate issues related to social studies and science topics, community issues, and current events. Middle- and upper-grade students can also debate topics related to books they are reading. For example, after reading *Tuck Everlasting* (Babbitt, 2002), they might debate whether people should live forever. Books that spark debates are listed in the Booklist on page 262. Students have strong feelings about the issues raised in many of these books, and debating provides a forum for thinking about important issues.

As they participate in debates, students learn how to use oral language to persuade their classmates. They must be able to articulate their viewpoints clearly, use information and emotional appeals to support their viewpoints, and think on their feet to respond to the opposing team's questions. The steps in a debate are listed in the Step by Step feature on page 262.

Students who are not participating in the debate often assess their classmates' performance in the debate and determine the winning team. The students can develop an assessment form and award points to each team based on the effectiveness of the team's arguments and manner of presentation.

-------- Hot Seat --------

1 Learn about the character.   Students prepare for the hot seat activity by reading a story or a biography to learn about the character they will impersonate.

2 Create a costume.   Students design a costume appropriate for the character. In addition, they often collect objects or create artifacts to use in their presentation.

3 Prepare opening remarks.   Students think about the most important things they'd like to share about the character and plan what they will say at the beginning of the activity.

4 Introduce the character.   The student sits in front of classmates in a chair designated as the "hot seat," tells a little about the character he or she is role-playing using a first-person viewpoint (e.g., "I was the first person to step onto the moon's surface"), and shares artifacts.

5 Ask questions.   Classmates ask thoughtful, higher-level questions to learn more about the character, and the student remains in the role to answer them.

6 Summarize the ideas.   The student doing the role play selects a classmate to summarize the important ideas that have been presented and adds any big ideas that the classmate doesn't mention.

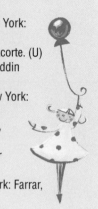

Booklist

BOOKS THAT SPARK DEBATES

Avi. (2003). *Nothing but the truth.* New York: Orchard Books. (U)

Babbitt, N. (2002). *Tuck everlasting.* New York: Farrar, Straus & Giroux. (U)

Bunting, E. (1997). *A day's work.* New York: Clarion Books. (M)

Bunting, E. (1999). *Smoky night.* San Diego: Harcourt Brace. (M)

Clements, A. (1998). *Frindle.* New York: Aladdin Books. (M–U)

Curtis, C. P. (2000). *The Watsons go to Birmingham—1963.* New York: Delacorte. (M–U)

Fox, P. (2003). *One-eyed cat.* New York: Simon & Schuster. (M–U)

Gantos, J. (2000). *Joey Pigza loses control.* New York: Farrar, Straus & Giroux. (U)

Haddix, M. P. (1998). *Among the hidden.* New York: Aladdin Books. (U)

Lowry, L. (2005). *Number the stars.* New York: Yearling. (M–U)

Lowry, L. (2006). *The giver.* New York: Delacorte. (U)

Naylor, P. R. (2000). *Shiloh.* New York: Aladdin Books. (M)

Ryan, P. M. (1998). *Riding Freedom.* New York: Scholastic. (M–U)

Sachar, L. (1998). *Holes.* New York: Farrar, Straus & Giroux. (U)

Staples, S. F. (1989). *Shabanu: Daughter of the wind.* New York: Knopf. (U)

Steig, W. (1990). *Doctor DeSoto.* New York: Farrar, Straus & Giroux. (M)

P = primary grades (K–2); M = middle grades (3–5); U = upper grades (6–8).

Debates

1 Identify a topic. The class decides on an issue, clarifies it, and identifies positions that support or oppose the issue.

2 Prepare for the debate. Students form supporting and opposing teams. Then students in each team prepare for the debate by deciding on their arguments and how they will respond to the other team's arguments.

3 Conduct the debate. A podium is set up in the front of the classroom, and the teacher initiates the debate by asking a student from the supporting side to state that position on the issue. After this opening statement, a student on the opposing side makes a statement. From this point, students take turns going to the podium and speaking in support of or in opposition to the issue. Students who have just made a statement are often asked a question before a student for the other side makes a return statement.

4 Conclude the debate. After students on both sides have presented their viewpoints, one member from each team makes a final statement to sum up that team's position.

THE POWER OF DRAMA

Drama provides a medium for students to use language—both verbal and nonverbal—in a meaningful context. Drama is not only a powerful form of communication but also a valuable way of knowing. When students participate in dramatic activities, they interact with classmates, share experiences, and explore their own understanding.

According to Dorothy Heathcote, a highly acclaimed British drama teacher, drama "cracks the code" so that the message can be understood (Wagner, 1999). Drama has this power for three reasons: It involves a combination of logical and creative thinking, it requires active experience, and it integrates the language arts. Research confirms that drama has a positive effect on both students' oral language development and their literacy learning (Wagner, 2003). Too often, however, teachers ignore drama because it seems unimportant compared to reading and writing.

Dramatic activities range from quick improvisations that are student centered to polished theatrical performances that are audience centered. Instead of encouraging students to be spontaneous and use drama to explore ideas, theatrical performances require that students memorize lines and rehearse their presentations. Our focus here is on student-centered dramatizations that are used to enhance learning.

Improvisation

Students step into someone else's shoes and view the world from that perspective as they reenact stories. These activities are usually quick and informal because the emphasis is on learning, not performance. Students assume the role of a character and then role-play as the teacher narrates or guides the dramatization. Students usually don't wear costumes, and there's little or no rehearsal; it's the spontaneity that makes improvisation so effective.

Students often reenact stories during literature focus units. Sometimes they dramatize episodes while they are reading to examine a character, understand the sequence of events, or clarify a misunderstanding. As students dramatize an episode, teachers often direct the class's attention by asking questions, such as "What's (character's name) thinking?" and "Why is (character's name) making him do this?" For example, while seventh graders read *Holes* (Sachar, 2002), the story of a boy named Stanley Yelnats who is sent to a juvenile detention center for a crime he didn't commit, they often reenact Stanley digging a hole on his first day at Camp Green Lake to analyze the effect the experience had on him. Later, as they continue reading, they focus on pivotal points in the story: when Stanley finds the small gold lipstick tube while he's digging a hole, when he claims he stole a bag of sunflower seeds and is taken to the Warden's office, when he escapes from the camp and meets up with another escaped boy nicknamed "Zero," and finally, when the two boys return to camp and find the "treasure" suitcase. Through these improvisations, students understand individual episodes better as well as the overall structure of the story.

At other times, students, especially young children, dramatize an entire story after they finish reading it or listening to the teacher read it aloud. Teachers often break stories into three parts—beginning, middle, and end—to organize the dramatization and provide more opportunities for children to participate in the activity. Through improvisation, children review and sequence the events in a story and develop their concept of story. Folktales, such as *One Grain of Rice: A Mathematical Folktale* (Demi, 1997) and *The Empty Pot* (Demi, 1996), are easy for younger children to dramatize.

Process Drama

British educator Dorothy Heathcote has developed an imaginative and spontaneous dramatic activity called *process drama* to help students explore stories they're reading, social studies topics, and current events (Tierney & Readence, 2005; Wagner,

1999). Teachers create an unscripted dramatic context about a story episode or a historical event, and the students in the class assume roles to experience and reflect on the episode or event (Schneider & Jackson, 2000).

For example, if the class is studying the Underground Railroad, the teacher might create a dramatic context on the moment when the escaped slaves reach the Ohio River. They'll be safe once they cross the river, but they're not safe yet. It's important that the teacher focuses on a particular critical moment—one that is tension filled or that creates challenges. Most of the students would play the role of escaped slaves, but others would be conductors guiding the slaves to safety or the Quakers who risked their lives to hide the slaves. Either the teacher or other students would be bounty hunters or plantation owners trying to capture the escaped slaves.

With everyone participating in a role, the class dramatizes the event, examining the critical moment from their viewpoint. The teacher moves the action forward by recounting the event and asking questions. After reliving the experience, students reflect on it by writing a simulated journal entry or a simulated letter; they write in the persona of their character, sharing information about the experience and reflecting on it. Afterward, students step out of their roles to discuss the experience and share what they have learned. The steps in process drama are summarized in the Step by Step box below.

Process drama goes beyond improvisation: Not only do the students reenact the episode or event, but they explore the topic from the viewpoint of their character as they respond to the teacher's questions and when they write simulated journal entries or letters. The discussion that follows the reenactment also deepens students' understanding. Heathcote believes that process drama is a valuable activity because it stimulates students' curiosity and makes them want to read books and learn more about historical or current events.

Process Drama

1 Set the purpose.   Teachers identify the purpose for the dramatic activity.

2 Create the dramatic context.   Teachers explain the dramatic context for the activity, and everyone assumes a role. Sometimes teachers share artifacts they have collected that relate to the characters and the event.

3 Dramatize the event.   Students participate in the dramatization, staying in the role of the character they have chosen and building on the experience. Teachers create tension or present a challenge during the dramatization.

4 Ask questions.   Teachers ask questions or they invite students to ask questions about the dramatic context, and then students respond to them, usually from the viewpoint of their characters.

5 Prompt reflection.   Students write simulated journal entries or letters in the persona of their characters. They include details and insights they've gained through the dramatization.

6 Discuss the activity.   Teachers and students talk about the dramatization, reflecting on the experience and sharing their writing to gain new insights about the event.

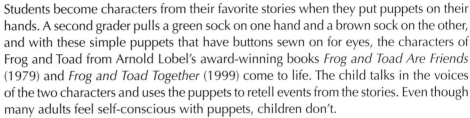

Playing With Puppets

Students become characters from their favorite stories when they put puppets on their hands. A second grader pulls a green sock on one hand and a brown sock on the other, and with these simple puppets that have buttons sewn on for eyes, the characters of Frog and Toad from Arnold Lobel's award-winning books *Frog and Toad Are Friends* (1979) and *Frog and Toad Together* (1999) come to life. The child talks in the voices of the two characters and uses the puppets to retell events from the stories. Even though many adults feel self-conscious with puppets, children don't.

Students can create puppet shows with commercially manufactured puppets, or they can construct their own. When students create their own puppets, they are limited only by their imaginations, their ability to construct things, and the materials at hand. Simple puppets provide students with the opportunity to develop both creative and dramatic ability. The simpler the puppet, the more is left to the imagination of the audience and the puppeteer. Six kinds of hand and finger puppets that students can make are shown in Figure 8–5.

After students have made their puppets, they can create and perform puppet shows almost anywhere; they don't even need a script or a stage. Several students can sit together on the floor holding their puppets and invent a story that they tell to other classmates who sit nearby, listening intently. Or, students can make a stage from an empty appliance packing crate and climb inside to present their puppet show. What matters is that students can use their puppets to share a story with an appreciative audience. Simple puppets provide children with the opportunity to develop both creative and dramatic ability.

Theatrical Productions

Scripts are a unique written language form that students need opportunities to explore. Scriptwriting often grows out of informal dramatic activities. Soon students recognize the need to write notes when they prepare for plays, puppet shows, readers theatre, and other dramatic productions. This need provides the impetus for introducing students to the unique dramatic conventions and for encouraging them to write scripts to present as theatrical productions.

Scriptwriting. Once students want to write scripts, they'll recognize the need to add the structures unique to dramatic writing to their repertoire of written language conventions. Students begin by examining scripts. It's especially effective to have them compare narrative and script versions of the same story; for example, Richard George has adapted two of Roald Dahl's fantastic stories, *Charlie and the Chocolate Factory* (2004) and *James and the Giant Peach* (2007), into scripts. Then students discuss their observations and compile a list of the unique characteristics of scripts. An upper-grade class compiled the list of unique dramatic conventions presented in Figure 8–6.

The next step is to have students apply what they have learned about scripts by writing a class collaboration script. The whole class develops a script by adapting a familiar story. As the script is being written, the teacher refers to the chart of dramatic conventions and asks students to check that they are using these conventions. Collaborative writing affords unique teaching opportunities and needed practice for students before they must write individually. After the script is completed, students produce it as a puppet show or play.

Once students are aware of the dramatic conventions and have participated in writing a class collaboration script, they can write scripts individually or in small

FIGURE 8–5

Types of Puppets

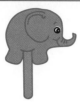

Stick Puppets
Attach pictures students have drawn or pictures cut from magazines to sticks, tongue depressors, or popsicle sticks to make these simple puppets.

Paper Bag Puppets
Place the puppet's mouth at the fold of the paper bag and draw or paint on faces, add clothes and yarn for hair, and attach arms and legs.

Cylinder Puppets
Paint faces on cardboard tubes, add yarn for hair, and decorate with clothing. Insert fingers in the bottom of the tube to manipulate the puppet.

Cup Puppets
Glue facial features, hair, wings, and other decorations on a styrofoam cup. Then attach a stick or heavy-duty straw to the inside of the cup as the handle.

Paper Plate Puppets
Use crayons or paint to make a face on the paper plate and add junk materials for decorations. Tape a stick or ruler to the back of the plate as the handle.

Finger Puppets
Draw, color, and cut out small figures, add tabs to either side of the figure and tape the tabs together to fit around a finger. Or, cut the finger section from a glove and add decorations.

groups. Students often adapt familiar stories for their first scripts; later, they will want to create original scripts. An excerpt from "The Lonely Troll," a script written by a small group of sixth graders, appears in Figure 8–7 as an example of the type of scripts older students can compose. Although most of the scripts they write are narrative, students also create biographical scripts about famous people or informational scripts about science or social studies topics.

Producing Video Scripts. Students use a similar approach in writing scripts that will be videotaped, but they must now consider the visual component of the film as well as the written script. They often compose their scripts on storyboards, which focus their attention on the camera's view and how the story they are creating will be filmed (Cox, 1985). Storyboards—sheets of paper divided into three sections—are used to sketch in scenes. Students place a series of three or four large squares in a row down the center of the paper, with space for dialogue and narration on the left and shooting directions

FIGURE 8–6

An Upper-Grade-Class List of Dramatic Conventions

Everything You Ever Wanted to Know About Scripts

1. Scripts are divided into acts and scenes.
2. Scripts have four parts:
   a. a list of characters (or cast)
   b. the setting at the beginning of each act or scene
   c. stage directions written in parentheses
   d. dialogue
3. The dialogue carries the action.
4. Descriptions and other information are set apart in the setting or in stage directions.
5. Stage directions give actors important information about how to act and how to feel.
6. The dialogue is written like this:
   Character's Name: Dialogue
7. Sometimes a narrator is used to quickly fill in parts of the story.

FIGURE 8–7

An Excerpt From a Script Written by Upper-Grade Students

The Lonely Troll

NARRATOR: Once upon a time, in a far, far away land, there was a troll named Pippin who lived all alone in his little corner of the woods. The troll hated all the creatures of the woods and was very lonely because he didn't have anyone to talk to since he scared everyone away. One day, a dwarf named Sam wandered into Pippin's yard and . . .

PIPPIN: Grrr. What are you doing here?

SAM: Ahhhhh! A troll! Please don't eat me!

PIPPIN: Why shouldn't I?

SAM: (Begging) Look, I'm all skin and bones. I won't make a good meal.

PIPPIN: You look fat enough for me. (Turns to audience) Do you think I should eat him? (Sam jumps off stage and hides in the audience.)

PIPPIN: Where did he go? (Pippin jumps off stage and looks for Sam. When he finds Sam, he takes him back on stage, laughing; then he ties Sam up.) Ha, ha, ha. Boy, that sure did tire me out. (Yawn) I'll take a nap. Then I'll eat him later. (Pippin falls asleep. Lights dim. Sam escapes and runs behind a tree. Lights return, and Pippin wakens.)

PIPPIN: (To audience) Where's my breakfast? (Sam peeps out from behind a tree and cautions the audience to be quiet.) Huh? Did someone say he was behind that tree? (Points to tree. Pippin walks around. Sam kicks him in the rear. Pippin falls and is knocked out.)

SAM: I must get out of here, and warn the queen about this short, small, mean, ugly troll. (Sam leaves. Curtains close.)

NARRATOR: So Sam went to tell Queen Muffy about the troll. Meanwhile, in the forest, Pippin awakens, and decides to set a trap for Sam. (Open curtains to forest scene, showing Pippin making a box trap.)

on the right. Cox compares storyboards to road maps because they provide directions for filming the script. The scene renderings and the shooting directions help students tie the dialogue to the visual images that will appear on the videotape.

The script can be produced several ways—as a live-action play, as a puppet show, or through animation. After writing the script on the storyboards or transferring a previously written script to storyboards, students collect or construct the props they will need to produce the script. They design a backdrop and collect clothes for costumes. Teachers should encourage students to keep the production details simple. Students should also print the title and credits on large posters to appear at the beginning of the film. After several rehearsals, the students film the script using a video camera.

Review

Talk is a valuable instructional tool. Children talk about stories they're reading and information they're learning in thematic units. They learn and use academic language as they participate in conversations, give oral reports, and participate in other types of talk activities. Here are the key points in this chapter:

- Academic language, the language of schooling, is more cognitively demanding and decontextualized than social language.
- Questions can be classified as literal, inferential, or critical.
- Students use K-W-L charts to talk about what they are learning in a thematic unit.
- Students participate in small-group conversations as part of all four instructional patterns.
- Students use talk to respond to stories in grand conversations.
- Students participate in instructional conversations to discuss what they're learning in thematic units.
- Students share what they've learned and develop presentational skills when they give oral reports.
- Students develop their abilities to persuade when they participate in debates.
- Students use improvisation and process drama as a tool for learning.
- Students integrate the language arts when they write scripts and present them as plays or videos.

Professional References

Cazden, C. D. (2001). *Classroom discourse: The language of teaching and learning* (2nd ed.). Portsmouth, NH: Heinemann.

Cintorino, M. A. (1993). Getting together, getting along, getting to the business of teaching and learning. *English Journal, 82,* 23–32.

Cox, C. (1985). Filmmaking as a composing process. *Language Arts, 62,* 60–69.

Eeds, M., & Wells, D. (1989). Grand conversations: An exploration of meaning construction in literature study groups. *Research in the Teaching of English, 23,* 4–29.

Fay, K., & Whaley, S. (2004). *Becoming one community: Reading and writing with English language learners.* Portland, ME: Stenhouse.

Gibbons, P. (2002). *Scaffolding language, scaffolding learning: Teaching second language learners in the mainstream classroom.* Portsmouth, NH: Heinemann.

Goldenberg, C. (1992/1993). Instructional conversations: Promoting comprehension through discussion. *The Reading Teacher, 46,* 316–326.

Heath, S. B. (1983). Research currents: A lot of talk about nothing. *Language Arts, 60,* 999–1007.

Kaufman, D. (2000). *Conferences and conversations: Listening to the literate classroom.* Portsmouth, NH: Heinemann.

Martinez, M. G., & Roser, N. L. (1995). The books make a difference in story talk. In N. L. Roser & M. G. Martinez (Eds.), *Book talk and beyond: Children and teachers respond to literature* (pp. 32–41). Newark, DE: International Reading Association.

Nystrand, M., Gamoran, A., & Heck, M. J. (1993). Using small groups for response to and thinking about literature. *English Journal, 82,* 14–22.

Ogle, D. M. (1989). The know, want to know, learn strategy. In K. D. Muth (Ed.), *Children's comprehension of text: Research into practice* (pp. 205–223). Newark, DE: International Reading Association.

Peterson, R., & Eeds, M. (1990). *Grand conversations: Literature groups in action.* New York: Scholastic.

Pressley, M. (1992). Encouraging mindful use of prior knowledge: Attempting to construct explanatory answers facilitates learning. *Educational Psychologist, 27,* 91–109.

Roser, N. L., & Keehn, S. (2002). Fostering thought, talk, and inquiry: Linking literature and social studies. *The Reading Teacher, 55,* 416–426.

Rothenberg, C., & Fisher, D. (2007). *Teaching English learners: A differentiated approach.* Upper Saddle River, NJ: Merrill/Prentice Hall.

Schneider, J. J., & Jackson, S. A. W. (2000). Process drama: A special space and place for writing. *The Reading Teacher, 54,* 38–51.

Sorenson, M. (1993). Teach each other: Connecting talking and writing. *English Journal, 82,* 42–47.

Tierney, R. J., & Readence, J. E. (2005). *Reading strategies and practices: A compendium* (6th ed.). Boston: Allyn & Bacon.

Wagner, B. J. (1999). *Dorothy Heathcote: Drama as a learning medium* (Rev. ed.). Portsmouth, NH: Heinemann.

Wagner, B. J. (2003). Imaginative expression. In J. Flood, D. Lapp, J. R. Squire, & J. M. Jensen (Eds.), *Handbook of research on teaching the English language arts* (2nd ed., pp. 1008–1025). Mahwah, NJ: Erlbaum.

Watson, K., & Young, B. (2003). Discourse for learning in the classroom. In S. Murphy, & C. Dudley-Marling (Eds.), *Literacy through language arts: Teaching and learning in context* (pp. 39–49). Urbana, IL: National Council of Teachers of English.

Wittrock, M. C., & Alesandrini, K. (1990). Generation of summaries and analogies and analytic and holistic abilities. *American Research Journal, 27,* 489–502.

Children's Book References

Babbitt, N. (2002). *Tuck everlasting.* New York: Farrar, Straus & Giroux.

Bunting, E. (1999). *Smoky night.* San Diego: Harcourt Brace.

Danziger, P. (2006). *Amber Brown is not a crayon.* New York: Puffin Books.

Dahl, R. (2004). *Charlie and the chocolate factory.* New York: Knopf.

Dahl, R. (2007). *James and the giant peach.* New York: Puffin Books.

Demi. (1996). *The empty pot.* New York: Henry Holt.

Demi. (1997). *One grain of rice: A mathematical folktale.* New York: Scholastic.

DiCamillo, K. (2003). *The tale of Despereaux.* Cambridge, MA: Candlewick Press.

Hale, S. (2005). *Princess academy.* New York: Bloomsbury.

Henkes, K. (1991). *Chrysanthemum.* New York: Greenwillow.

Hesse, K. (2001). *Witness.* New York: Scholastic.

Lobel, A. (1979). *Frog and Toad are friends.* New York: HarperCollins.

Lobel, A. (1999). *Frog and Toad together.* New York: HarperCollins.

Meddaugh, S. (1995). *Martha speaks.* Boston: Houghton Mifflin.

Sachar, L. (2002). *Holes.* Austin, TX: Holt, Rinehart & Winston.

Soto, G. (1997). *The cat's meow.* New York: Scholastic.

Wiesner, D. (2006). *Flotsam.* New York: Clarion Books.

Yorinks, A. (1986). *Hey, Al.* New York: Farrar, Straus & Giroux.

chapter nine

Reading and Writing Stories

M rs. Ochs teaches a literature focus unit on *Number the Stars* (Lowry, 2005), a Newbery award–winning story of two girls, one Christian and one Jewish, set in Denmark during World War II. In her unit, she wants to help her fifth-grade students use their knowledge of genre and story structure to deepen their comprehension of the story. She rereads the story, analyzes the elements of story structure in the book, and considers how she wants to teach the unit. She makes the chart shown on page 272.

To begin the unit, Mrs. Ochs asks about friendship: "Would you help your friend if he or she needed help?" The students talk about friendship and what it means to them. They agree that they would help their friends in any way they could—helping them get medical treatment if they were ill, and sharing their lunch if they were hungry, for example. One student volunteers that he is sure that his mom would let his friend's family stay at his house if the friend's house burned down. Then Mrs. Ochs asks, "What if your friend asked you to hold something for him or her, something so dangerous that 60 years ago you could be imprisoned or killed for having it?" Many say they would, but doubt they would ever be called to do that. Then she shows them a broken Star of David necklace, similar to the one on the cover of *Number the Stars*, and one student says, "You're talking about the Nazis and the Jews in World War II."

How can teachers facilitate students' comprehension of stories?

Teachers include activities at each stage of the reading process in literature focus units to ensure that everyone comprehends what they're reading. This attention to comprehension is essential because when students don't understand what they are reading, the experience has been wasted. As you read this vignette, notice how Mrs. Ochs involves her fifth graders in language arts activities to deepen their understanding of World War II and facilitate their comprehension of *Number the Stars*.

The prereading stage continues for 2 more days as students share what they know about the war, and Mrs. Ochs presents information, reads several picture-book stories about the war, and shows a video.

Mrs. Ochs reads the first chapter of *Number the Stars* aloud to students as they follow along in individual copies of the book. She almost always starts a book this way because she wants to get all students off to a good start and because so many concepts and key vocabulary words are introduced in the beginning of a book. After the first chapter, students continue reading the second chapter. Most of the students read independently, but some read with buddies, and Mrs. Ochs continues reading with a group of the six lowest readers.

Then Mrs. Ochs brings the class together for a grand conversation. The students make connections between the information they have learned about World War II and the story events. Mrs. Ochs reads aloud *The Yellow Star: The Legend of King Christian X of Denmark* (Deedy, 2000), a picture-book story about the Danish king who defies the Nazis, because the king is the focus of the second chapter. The students predict that the Nazis will take Ellen and her family to a concentration camp even though Annemarie and her family try to hide them. After the grand conversation, the students write in reading logs. For this entry, Mrs. Ochs asks students to write predictions about what will happen in the story based on what they know about World War II and what they read in the first two chapters.

Mrs. Ochs continues having the students read and respond to the chapters. Some students read independently, but many of them form reading groups so that they can read and talk about the story as they are reading. Mrs. Ochs continues reading with the lowest readers. The whole class comes together after reading each day to talk about the story in a grand conversation. Afterward, they write in journals.

During the grand conversations, Mrs. Ochs probes students' understanding of the story and asks them to think about the role in the story of plot, characters, setting, and other elements of story structure. Mrs. Ochs has taught the students about the elements,

Mrs. Ochs's Story Analysis

Element	Story Analysis	Teaching Ideas
Plot	The beginning is before Ellen goes into hiding; the middle is while Ellen is hiding; and the end is after Ellen and her family leave for the safety of Sweden. The problem is saving Ellen's life.	Build background knowledge about World War II, the Nazis, Jews and the holocaust, and Resistance fighters before reading. There are many details, so it is important to focus on the problem and how to solve it.
Characters	Annemarie and Ellen are the main characters, and through their actions and beliefs, readers learn that these two girls are much more alike than different. They're both courageous, one because she has to be, the other because she chooses to be.	Even though one girl is Christian and one is Jewish, the girls are more alike than they are different. Use a Venn diagram to emphasize this point. Students might make open-mind portraits from one girl's viewpoint.
Setting	The story is set in Denmark during World War II. The setting is integral to the plot and based on actual events, including fishermen ferrying Jews to safety in Sweden.	Use maps of Europe to locate the setting of the story. Students can draw maps and mark story locations, and they can also mark the spread of the German (and Japanese) forces during the war on a world map.
Point of View	The story is limited omniscient. It is told from the third-person viewpoint, and readers know only what Annemarie is thinking.	Have students retell important events from one of the girls' perspectives or from the parents' or the Nazis' viewpoints.
Theme	This story deals with courage and bravery: the Jews, the fishermen, the Resistance fighters, King Christian X and Danes who wore six-pointed, yellow stars on their clothes, and Annemarie and her family. One theme is that people choose to be courageous when they see others mistreated.	Ask students to focus on the theme as they talk in grand conversations and collect favorite quotes from the story. Students might also read about other people who have been courageous to examine the qualities of courage.

so they are able to apply their knowledge to the story they are reading. One day, she asks about the conflict situation in the story. At first the students say that the conflict is between people—Nazis and Danes—but as they continue talking, they realize that the conflict is not between individual people, but within society.

Another day, Mrs. Ochs talks about the setting. She asks if this story could have happened in the United States. At first the students say no, because the Nazis never invaded the United States, and they use maps to make their point. But as they continue to talk, students broaden their discussion to the persecution of minorities and conclude that persecution can happen anywhere. They cite two examples—the mistreatment of Native Americans and internment of Japanese Americans during World War II.

During the grand conversation after students finish reading *Number the Stars,* Mrs. Ochs asks about the theme. "Did Lois Lowry have a message in her book? What do you think about the theme?" Several students comment that the theme was that the Nazis were bad people. Others said "innocent people get killed in wars" and "peace is better than war." To move the students forward in their thinking, Mrs. Ochs suggests that one theme is about courage or being brave. She reads two sentences from the book: "That's all that *brave* means—not thinking about the dangers. Just thinking about what you must do" (p. 123). The students agree that both girls and their families were brave. Mrs. Ochs asks students to think back through the story and help her brainstorm a list of all the times they were brave. They brainstormed more than 30 instances of bravery!

Mrs. Ochs and her students continue their discussion about the theme for several more days. Finally, she asks them, "Do you think you're brave? Would you be brave if you were Annemarie or Ellen?" They talk about war and having to be brave in a war. "What about Ellen?" Mrs. Ochs asks. "Did she *have* to be brave?" The students agree that she did. "But what about Annemarie? Couldn't she and her family have stayed safely in Copenhagen?" The students are surprised at first by the question, but through their talk, they realize that Annemarie, her family, and the other Resistance fighters had chosen to be brave.

As the students read *Number the Stars,* Mrs. Ochs also involves them in several exploring-stage activities focusing on the story structure. They mark areas of Nazi and Japanese occupation on world maps and draw maps of Denmark. To compare Annemarie and Ellen, they make Venn diagrams and conclude that the girls are more alike than they are different; one student's Venn diagram is shown here. They also make open-mind portraits of one of the girls, showing what the girl is thinking at several pivotal points in the story. The cover and one page from one student's open-mind portrait of Ellen are shown on page 274.

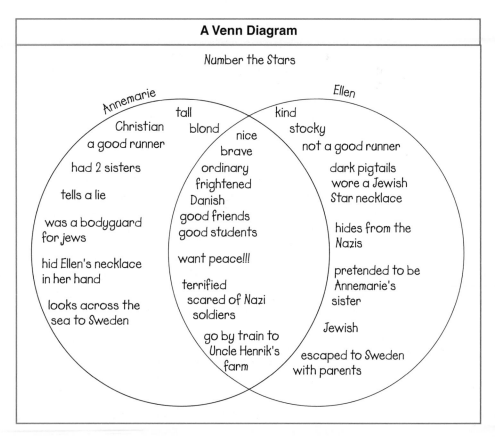

A Venn Diagram

Number the Stars

Annemarie   Ellen

tall   kind
Christian   blond   nice   stocky
a good runner   brave   not a good runner
had 2 sisters   ordinary
                           frightened   dark pigtails
tells a lie   Danish   wore a Jewish
                         good friends   Star necklace
was a bodyguard   good students
for jews   hides from the
                         want peace!!!   Nazis
hid Ellen's necklace
in her hand   terrified   pretended to be
                         scared of Nazi   Annemarie's
looks across the   soldiers   sister
sea to Sweden
                         go by train to   Jewish
                         Uncle Henrik's
                         farm   escaped to Sweden
                                         with parents

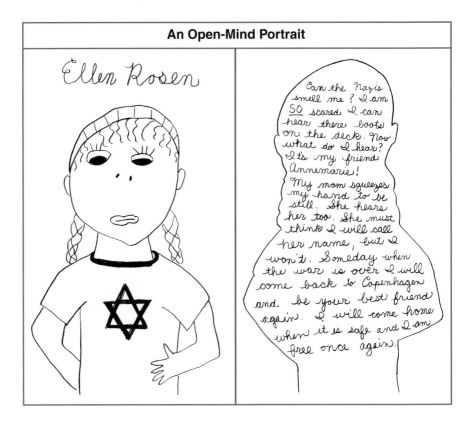

The students plan an applying-stage activity after the great-grandfather of one of the students comes for a visit. This student brings his great-grandfather to school to talk about his remembrances of World War II, and then the students decide to each interview a great-grandparent or an elderly neighbor who was alive during the war. They develop this set of interview questions:

- What did you do during the war?
- How old were you?
- Were you on the home front or the war front?
- Did you know about the Holocaust then?
- What do you remember most from World War II?

Then each student conducts an interview and writes an essay about the person's wartime experiences using the writing process. They word-process their essays so that they have a professional look. Here is one student's essay:

My great-grandfather Arnold Ott was in college at the time the war started. All of a sudden after Pearl Harbor was attacked, all his classmates started to join the army. He did also and became an engineer that worked on B-24 and B-25 bombers. The military kept sending him to different schools so he would be able to fix all the bombers. He never had to fight because of that. He earned some medals, but he said the real ones were only given to those who fought. He said that he was glad that he did not fight because he had friends that never came back.

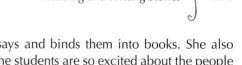

Then Mrs. Ochs duplicates the essays and binds them into books. She also makes extra copies for the interviewees. The students are so excited about the people they interviewed and the essays they wrote that they decide to have a party. They invite the interviewees and introduce them to their classmates, and they ask the interviewees to autograph the essays they've written about them.

---

*S*tories give meaning to the human experience, and they're a powerful way of knowing and learning. Preschoolers listen to family members tell and read stories aloud, and they have developed an understanding or concept about stories by the time they come to school. Students refine this knowledge as they read and write stories. Many educators, including Jerome Bruner (1986), recommend using stories as a way into literacy.

Students write stories about events in their lives, such as a birthday party, a fishing trip, or a car accident; retell familiar stories, including "Gingerbread Man"; and write sequels for favorite stories. The stories that students write reflect what they've read. De Ford (1981) and Eckhoff (1983) found that when students read stories in traditional basal reading textbooks, they write stories that reflect the short, choppy linguistic style of the textbooks, but when students read trade-book stories, their writing reflects the more sophisticated language structures and literary style of the trade books. Dressel (1990) also found that the quality of fifth graders' writing was dependent on the quality of the stories they read or listened to someone read aloud, regardless of their reading levels.

As you read this chapter, think about these questions:

- How do students develop a concept of story?
- What kinds of reading activities are available for students?
- What kinds of writing activities are available for students?
- How do students read and write stories as part of the four instructional patterns?

CHILDREN'S CONCEPT OF STORY

Researchers have documented that children's concept of story begins in the preschool years (Applebee, 1978). Children acquire this concept of story gradually, by listening to stories read to them, by reading stories themselves, and by telling and writing stories. Not surprisingly, older children have a better understanding of story structure than do younger children. Similarly, the stories older children tell and write are increasingly more complex; the plot structures are more tightly organized, and the characters are more fully developed. Yet, Applebee found that by the time children who have been read to begin kindergarten, they have already developed a basic concept of what a story is, and these expectations guide them in responding to stories and telling their own stories. He found, for example, that kindergartners could use three story markers: "Once upon a time . . . " to begin a story; the past tense in telling a story; and formal endings such as "The End" or " . . . and they lived happily ever after."

Meeting the Needs of English Learners

How Do Teachers Scaffold English Learners' Knowledge of Stories?

When English learners understand about how stories are structured, their comprehension improves, and they're better able to write well-crafted, entertaining stories. Three ways that teachers help English learners learn about stories are through providing opportunities for students to do extensive reading, teaching them about the elements of story structure, and nurturing their responses to literature.

Extensive Reading

All students need daily opportunities to enjoy good literature. Teachers regularly read stories to students using interactive read-aloud procedures, and students read stories themselves as they participate in guided reading, literature circles, and reading workshop. As they listen and read, students expand their background knowledge, build their vocabularies, and become more interested in literature. It's essential that teachers put together a large collection of multicultural books at a variety of reading levels that their students will find interesting. Students need to know how to select books at their reading levels; if older students read at lower levels, then books at those levels need to be age-appropriate.

Elements of Story Structure

To deepen their understanding of stories, English learners need to learn about the elements of story structure (Peregoy & Boyle, 2005). They will acquire some basic understanding about the structure of stories through reading, but they also need direct instruction about the story elements. In addition to minilessons, English learners benefit from activities that include nonverbal components. Graphic organizers, such as diagrams of the beginning, middle, and end of a story or an open-mind portrait, help students visually represent the structure of a story. Dramatic activities are also useful: To examine the plot of story, students can reenact beginning, middle, and end events; to explore a character, they can participate in a hot seat activity; and to understand the importance of setting, they can draw a setting map.

Response to Literature

English learners negotiate meaning through social interaction, just like their classmates do (Samway & McKeon, 1999). As they share their own reactions to a story and listen to their classmates' ideas about plot, characters, and setting, they deepen their comprehension. It's important that English learners know how to talk about the stories they're reading and that they're able to apply what they've learned about story structure through conversation. They need to learn how to reflect on stories they're reading, write in reading logs, and participate in grand conversations in small, comfortable groups with their classmates.

Because stories are often at the center of the language arts program, it's crucial that English learners develop their knowledge of stories so that they can read and write them more successfully.

Students' concept of story plays an important role in their comprehension of the stories they read, and it is just as important in their writing (Golden, Meiners, Lewis, 1992; Rumelhart, 1975). Story meaning is dynamic, growing continuously in readers' minds, and as they respond to and explore stories they are reading and writing, students learn about elements of story structure.

Elements of Story Structure

Stories have unique structural elements that distinguish them from other forms of literature. In fact, the structure of stories is quite complex—plot, characters, setting, and other elements interact to produce a story. Authors manipulate the elements to make their stories complex and interesting. The five most important elements of story structure are *plot, characters, setting, point of view*, and *theme*. In the following sections, you'll read about each element and how students examine the element using familiar and award-winning trade books.

Plot. The sequence of events involving characters in conflict situations is the *plot*. The plot is based on the goals of one or more characters and the processes they go through to attain these goals (Lukens, 2006). The main characters want to achieve a goal, and other characters are introduced to oppose the main characters or prevent them from being successful. The story events are put in motion by characters as they attempt to overcome conflict, reach their goals, and solve their problems.

The most basic aspect of plot is the division of the main events of a story into three parts—beginning, middle, and end. Upper-grade students may substitute the terms *introduction, development* or *complication,* and *resolution.* In *The Tale of Peter Rabbit* (Potter, 2002), for instance, one can easily pick out the three story parts: As the story begins, Mrs. Rabbit sends her children out to play after warning them not to go into Mr. McGregor's garden; in the middle, Peter goes to Mr. McGregor's garden and is almost caught; then Peter finds his way out of the garden and gets home safely—the end of the story. Students can cluster the beginning-middle-end of a story using words or pictures, as the cluster for *The Tale of Peter Rabbit* in Figure 9–1 shows.

Specific information is included in each story part. In the beginning, the author introduces the characters, describes the setting, and presents a problem. Together, the characters, setting, and events develop the plot and sustain the theme throughout the story. In the middle, the author adds to events presented in the beginning, with each event preparing readers for what comes next. Conflict heightens as the characters face roadblocks that keep them from solving their problems. Seeing how the characters tackle these problems adds suspense to keep readers interested. In the end, the author reconciles all that has happened in the story, and readers learn whether the characters' struggles are successful. Recommended stories exemplifying plot and other elements of story structure are presented in the Booklist on page 279.

The plot is developed through the problem that's introduced in the beginning of a story, expanded in the middle, and finally resolved at the end. Plot development involves four components:

- **A Problem.** A problem is presented at the beginning of a story.
- **Roadblocks.** In the middle of the story, characters face roadblocks in attempting to solve the problem.

FIGURE 9–1

A Beginning-Middle-End Cluster for *The Tale of Peter Rabbit*

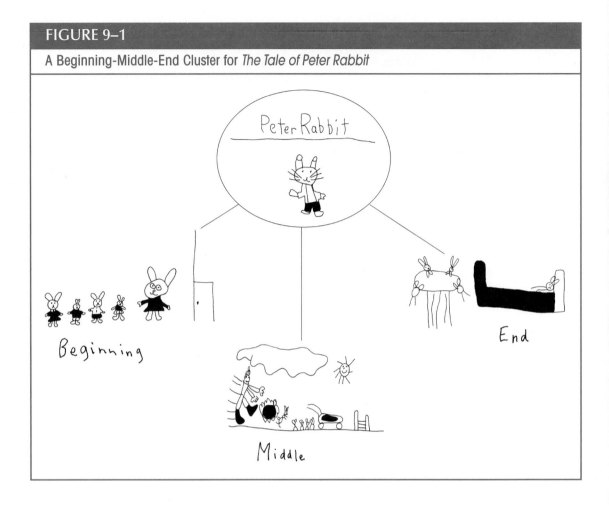

- **The High Point.** The high point in the action occurs when the problem is about to be solved. It separates the middle and end of the story.
- **Solution.** The problem is solved and the roadblocks are overcome at the end of the story.

The problem is introduced at the beginning of the story, and the main character is faced with trying to solve it. The problem determines the conflict. For example, the problem in Hans Christian Andersen's heartfelt story *The Ugly Duckling* (Pinkney, 1999) is that the big, gray duckling does not fit in with the other ducklings, and conflict develops between the ugly duckling and the other ducks.

After the problem has been introduced, authors use conflict to throw roadblocks in the way of an easy solution. As characters remove one roadblock, the author devises another to further thwart the characters. Postponing the solution by introducing road-blocks is the core of plot development. In *The Ugly Duckling,* the first conflict comes in the yard when the ducks make fun of the main character. The conflict is so great that the duckling goes out into the world and spends a miserable, cold winter in the marsh.

The high point of the action occurs when the solution of the problem hangs in the balance. Tension is high, and readers continue reading to learn whether the main characters solve the problem. With *The Ugly Duckling,* readers are relieved that the duckling has survived the winter, but tension continues because he's still an outcast. Then he flies to a pond and sees some beautiful swans. He flies near to them even though he expects to be scorned.

As the story ends, the problem is solved and the goal is achieved. When he joins the other swans at the garden pond, they welcome him. He sees his reflection in the water and realizes that he is no longer an ugly duckling. Children come to feed the swans and praise the new swan's beauty. The young swan is happy at last!

Students make a chart called a *plot profile* to track the tension in a story (Johnson & Louis, 1987). Figure 9–2 presents a plot profile for *Stone Fox* (Gardiner, 2003), a story about a boy who wins a dogsled race to save his grandfather's farm. A class of fourth graders met in small groups to talk about each chapter, and after these discussions, the whole class came together to decide how to mark the chart. At the end of the story, students analyzed the chart and rationalized the tension dips in Chapters 3 and 7: They decided that the story would be too stressful without these dips. Also, students were upset about the abrupt ending to the story and wished the story had continued a chapter or two longer so that their tension would have been reduced.

Booklist

STORIES EXEMPLIFYING THE STORY ELEMENTS

Plot

Bunting, E. (1999). *Smoky night.* San Diego: Harcourt Brace. (P–M)

Dahl, R. (2004). *Charlie and the chocolate factory.* New York: Knopf. (M)

Sachar, L. (1998). *Holes.* New York: Farrar, Straus & Giroux. (U)

Soto, G. (1993). *Too many tamales.* New York: Putnam. (P)

Characters

Avi. (2005). *Poppy.* New York: HarperCollins. (M)

Cushman, K. (1994). *Catherine, called Birdy.* New York: HarperCollins. (U)

Henkes, K. (1991). *Chrysanthemum.* New York: Greenwillow. (P)

Spinelli, J. (2002). *Maniac Magee.* New York: Scholastic. (U)

Setting

Curtis, C. P. (2000). *The Watsons go to Birmingham—1963.* New York: Delacorte. (M–U)

Lowry, L. (2006). *The giver.* New York: Delacorte. (U)

Hale, S. (2005). *Princess academy.* New York: Bloomsbury. (M–U)

Whelan, G. (2000). *Homeless bird.* New York: Scholastic. (U)

Point of View

Babbitt, N. (2002). *Tuck everlasting.* New York: Farrar, Straus & Giroux. (U)

Creech, S. (2000). *The wanderer.* New York: Scholastic. (M–U)

Meddaugh, S. (1995). *Hog-eye.* Boston: Houghton Mifflin. (P)

Ryan, P. M. (2000). *Esperanza rising.* New York: Scholastic. (M)

Theme

Avi. (2003). *Nothing but the truth: A documentary novel.* New York: Orchard Books. (U)

Hesse, K. (2001). *Witness.* New York: Scholastic. (U)

Pinkney, J. (1999). *The ugly duckling.* New York: Morrow. (P)

White, E. B. (2006). *Charlotte's web.* New York: HarperCollins. (M)

P = primary grades (K–2); M = middle grades (3–5); U = upper grades (6–8).

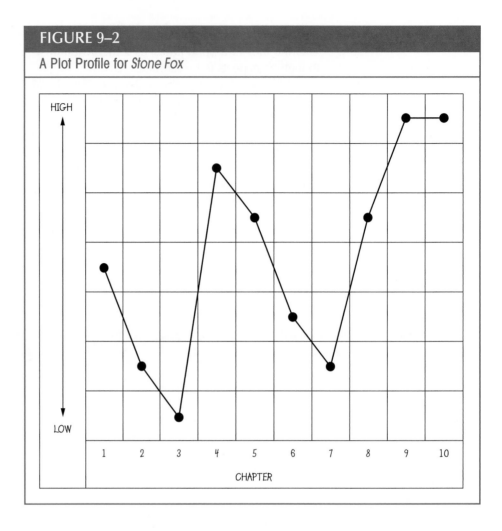

FIGURE 9–2

A Plot Profile for *Stone Fox*

Characters. Characters, the people or personified animals who are involved in the story, are often the most important element of story structure because many stories are centered on a character. In *Catherine, Called Birdy* (Cushman, 1994), for example, the story focuses on Birdy and her determination to outwit her father and not be married off to a revolting, shaggy-bearded suitor. Usually, one or two well-rounded characters and several supporting characters are created in a story. Fully developed main characters have many personality traits, both good and bad—that is to say, they have all the characteristics of real people, and it's essential to understand these traits to comprehend a story. Smith (2005) emphasizes that teachers should introduce their students to character-rich stories. The Booklist on page 279 includes stories with fully developed main characters.

Birdy is the main character in *Catherine, Called Birdy,* and readers get to know her as a real person. Although she is shaped by the culture of medieval England, she challenges the traditional role of "a lady" and is determined to marry someone she cares for, not some rich lord of her father's choosing. Through Birdy's journal entries, readers learn about her activities at the manor, how she helps her mother care for sick and injured people, and her beliefs and superstitions. Readers view events in the story through her eyes and sense her wit as she recounts her daily activities. In

contrast, the author tells us little about the supporting characters in the story: Birdy's parents, her brothers, the servants, and the peasants who live and work on her father's lands.

Characters are developed in four ways—through appearance, action, dialogue, and monologue. Authors present the characters to involve readers in the story's experiences. Similarly, readers notice these four types of information as they read in order to understand the characters. Authors generally provide some physical description of the characters when they are introduced. Readers learn about characters by the description of their facial features, body shapes, habits of dress, mannerisms, and gestures. Little emphasis is placed on Birdy's appearance, but Birdy writes that she is unattractive. She squints because of poor eyesight and describes herself as tanned and with gray eyes. She often blackens her teeth and crosses her eyes to make herself more unattractive when her father introduces her to potential suitors.

The second way to learn about characters is through their actions, and what a character does is often the best way to know about him or her. Birdy writes about picking fleas off her body, making soap and remedies for the sick, doctoring with her mother, keeping birds as pets, traveling to a fair and to a friend's castle, and learning how to sew and embroider. She tells how she prefers being outside and how she sneaks away to visit the goat-boy and other friends who work at the manor.

Dialogue is the third way characters are developed. What characters say is important, but so is how they speak. The register of the characters' language is determined by the social situation: A character might speak less formally with friends than with respected elders or characters in positions of authority. The geographic location of the story, the historical period, and the characters' socioeconomic status also determine how characters speak. The language in Birdy's journal entries is often archaic:

> *"Mayhap I could be a hermit." (p. 130)*
>
> *"I am full weary tonight . . . " (p. 131)*
>
> *"Corpus bones. I utterly loathe my life." (p. 133)*

Authors also provide insight into characters by revealing their thoughts through monologue. Birdy shares her innermost thoughts in her journal. Readers know how she attempts to thwart her father's plans to marry her off to a rich lord, her worries about her mother's miscarriages, her love for the goat-boy, and her guilt over meddling in Uncle George's love life.

As students examine the main character of a story, they draw conclusions about his or her defining traits. Birdy, for example, is witty, defiant, determined, clever, kindhearted, and superstitious. Teachers work with students to develop a list of character traits, and then students write about one or more of the traits, providing examples from the story to show how the character exemplified the trait. Students can write about character traits in a reading log entry or make a chart. Figure 9–3 shows an eighth grader's chart about Birdy's character traits. Another way students can examine characters and reflect on story events from the character's viewpoint is to draw open-mind portraits, as Mrs. Ochs's students did in the vignette at the beginning of the chapter. These portraits have two parts: The face of the character is on one page, and his or her mind is on the second page. The two pages are stapled together, with the mind page under the face page.

FIGURE 9–3

An Eighth Grader's Character Traits Chart

Will the Real Birdy Please Stand Up?

Trait	Explanation
Defiant	Birdy is defiant because she does not obey her parents. She doesn't want to marry any of the rich men that her father wants her to marry. She does not want to do the needlework that her mother wants her to do. Because she is rebellious, disobedient, and obstinate, she is defiant.
Kindhearted	Birdy is very kindhearted. She is compassionate to the servants and the peasants who are her friends. She treats them like they are as good as her. She is humane because she is like a doctor making medicines and treating sick people. Birdy has a charitable manner; therefore she is kindhearted.
Clever	Birdy is a clever girl. She manages to get rid of her suitors with ingenious plans. She avoids her mother because she is quick-witted. She is smart for someone in the Middle Ages, but not for someone now. She can even read and write which is unusual for a girl back then. Because she gets her way most of the time, I think she is clever.

Setting. In some stories, the setting is barely sketched; these settings are *backdrop settings*. The setting in many folktales, for example, is relatively unimportant, and these tales may simply use the convention "Once upon a time . . ." to set the stage. In other stories, the setting is elaborated and is integral to the story's effectiveness. These settings are *integral settings* (Lukens, 2006). Stories with integral settings are included in the Booklist on page 279. The setting is specific, and authors take care to ensure the authenticity of the historical period or geographic location in which the story is set. Four dimensions of setting are location, weather, time period, and time.

Location is an important dimension in many stories. For example, the Boston Public Garden in *Make Way for Ducklings* (McCloskey, 2001) and the Alaskan North Slope in *Julie of the Wolves* (George, 2005) are integral to the effectiveness of those stories. The settings are artfully described and add something unique to the story. In contrast, many stories take place in predictable settings that do not contribute to their effectiveness.

Weather is a second dimension of setting and, like location, is crucial in some stories. A rainstorm is essential to the plot development in *Bridge to Terabithia* (Paterson, 2006), but at other times, weather isn't mentioned because it doesn't affect the outcome of the story. Many stories take place on warm, sunny days. Think about the impact weather can have on a story; for example, what might have happened if a snowstorm had prevented Little Red Riding Hood from reaching her grandmother's house?

The third dimension of setting is the time period, an important element in stories set in the past or future. If *The Witch of Blackbird Pond* (Speare, 2003) were set in a different era, for example, it would lose much of its impact. Today, few people would believe that Kit Tyler is a witch. In stories that take place in the future, such as *A Wrinkle in Time* (L'Engle, 2007), things are possible that are not possible today.

The fourth dimension, time, includes both time of day and the passage of time. Most stories ignore time of day, except for scary stories that take place after dark. In nighttime stories, time is a more important dimension than in stories that take place during the day, because night makes things scarier. Many short stories span a brief period of time, often less than a day, and sometimes less than an hour. Other stories, such as *Charlotte's Web* (White, 2006) and *The Ugly Duckling* (Pinkney, 1999), span a long enough period for the main character to grow to maturity.

Students can draw maps to show the setting of a story; these maps may show the path a character traveled or the passage of time in a story. Figure 9–4 shows a setting map for *Number the Stars* (Lowry, 2005) that indicates where the families lived in Copenhagen, their trip to a fishing village in northern Denmark, and the ship they hid away on for the trip to Sweden.

FIGURE 9–4

A Setting Map for *Number the Stars*

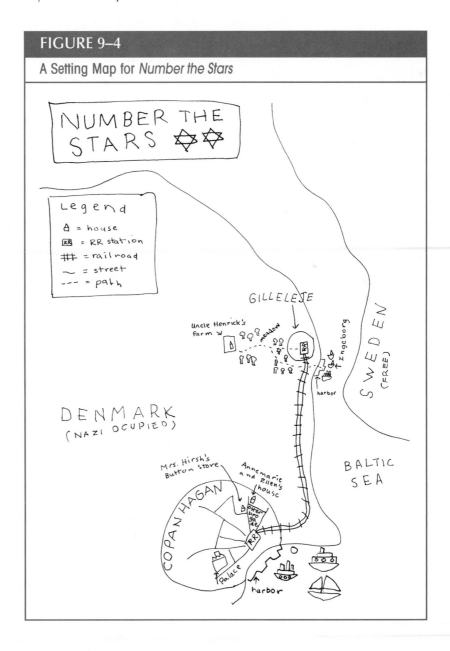

Point of View. Stories are written from a particular viewpoint, and this focus determines to a great extent readers' understanding of the characters and the events of the story. The four points of view are first-person viewpoint, omniscient viewpoint, limited omniscient viewpoint, and objective viewpoint (Lukens, 2006). The Booklist on page 279 includes stories written from different viewpoints.

The first-person viewpoint tells a story through the eyes of one character using the first-person pronoun *I*. In this point of view, the reader experiences the story as the narrator tells it. The narrator, usually the main character, speaks as an eyewitness to and a participant in the events. For example, in *Shiloh* (Naylor, 2000), Marty tells how he works for Judd Travers in order to buy the puppy Travers has mistreated, and in *Abuela* (Dorros, 1991) and the sequel, *Isla* (Dorros, 1995), a girl describes magical flying adventures with her grandmother. Many children's books are written from the first-person viewpoint, and the narrator's voice is usually very effective. However, one limitation is that the narrator must remain an eyewitness.

In the omniscient viewpoint, the author is godlike, knowing all. The author tells readers about the thought processes of each character without worrying about how the information is obtained. Most stories told from the omniscient viewpoint are chapter books, because revealing the thought processes of each character makes a story longer. One notable exception is *Doctor De Soto* (Steig, 1990), a picture-book story about a mouse dentist who outwits a fox with a toothache. Steig lets readers know that the fox wants to eat the dentist as soon as his toothache is cured and that the mouse dentist is planning to trick the fox.

The limited omniscient viewpoint is used so that readers can know the thoughts of one character. The story is told in the third person, and the author concentrates on the thoughts, feelings, and significant past experiences of the main character or another important character. Many stories are told from this viewpoint. Lois Lowry uses this viewpoint in *The Giver* (2006). She concentrates on the main character, Jonas, using his thoughts to explain the "perfect" community to readers. Later in the story, Jonas's thoughts reveal his growing dissatisfaction with the community and his decision to escape with the baby Gabriel.

In the objective viewpoint, readers are eyewitnesses to the story and are confined to the immediate scene. They learn only what they can see and hear, without knowing what any character thinks. Many folktales, such as *The Three Little Pigs* (Galdone, 2006) and *The Little Red Hen* (Pinkney, 2006), are told from this viewpoint. Other picture-book stories, such as *Martha Speaks* (Meddaugh, 1992), are also told from this viewpoint. The focus is on recounting events, not on developing the personalities of the characters.

Most teachers postpone introducing the four viewpoints until the upper grades, but younger children can experiment with point of view to understand how the author's viewpoint affects a story. One way to demonstrate point of view is to contrast *The Three Little Pigs* (Galdone, 2006), the traditional version told from an objective viewpoint, with *The True Story of the 3 Little Pigs!* (Scieszka, 1999), a self-serving narrative told by Mr. A. Wolf from a first-person viewpoint. In this satirical retelling, the wolf tries to explain away his bad image. Even first graders are struck by how different the two versions are and how the narrator filters the information.

Theme. The underlying meaning of a story is the *theme*, and it embodies general truths about human nature (Lehr, 1991). It usually deals with the characters' emotions and values. Themes can be stated either explicitly or implicitly. Explicit themes are stated openly and clearly in the story. Lukens (2006) uses *Charlotte's Web* to point out how one theme of friendship—the giving of oneself for a friend—is expressed as an explicit theme:

> Charlotte has encouraged, protected, and mothered Wilbur, bargained and sacrificed for him, and Wilbur, the grateful receiver, realizes that "Friendship is one of the most satisfying things in the world." And Charlotte says later, "By helping you perhaps I was trying to lift up my life a little. Anyone's life can stand a little of that." Because these quoted sentences are exact statements from the text they are called explicit themes. (p. 94)

Implicit themes are suggested rather than explicitly stated in the story. They are developed as the characters attempt to overcome the obstacles that prevent them from reaching their goals. The theme emerges through the thoughts, speech, and actions of the characters as they seek to resolve their conflicts. Lukens also uses *Charlotte's Web* to illustrate implicit themes:

> Charlotte's selflessness—working late at night to finish a new word, expending her last energies for her friend—is evidence that friendship is giving oneself. Wilbur's protection of Charlotte's egg sac, his sacrifice of first turn at the slops, and his devotion to Charlotte's babies—giving without any need to stay even or to pay back—leads us to another theme: True friendship is naturally reciprocal. As the two become fond of each other, still another theme emerges: One's best friend can do no wrong. In fact, a best friend is sensational! Both Charlotte and Wilbur believe in these ideas; their experiences verify them. (p. 95)

Charlotte's Web has several friendship themes, one explicitly stated and others inferred from the text. Stories generally have more than one theme, and their themes generally cannot be articulated with a single word. Friendship is a multidimensional theme. Teachers can ask questions during conversations about literature to guide students' thinking as they work to construct a theme (Au, 1992). Students must go beyond one-word labels in describing the theme and construct their own ideas about it.

Sketch-to-stretch is a visually representing activity that moves students beyond literal comprehension to think more deeply about the theme of a story (Harste, Short, & Burke, 1988; Whitin, 1996). Students work in small groups or individually to draw pictures or diagrams to represent what the story means to them, not pictures of their favorite character or episode. In their sketches, students use lines, shapes, colors, symbols, and words to express their interpretations and feelings. Because students work in a social setting with the support of classmates, they share ideas, extend their understanding, and generate new insights. Students make sketch-to-stretch drawings in reading logs or on posters. The steps in sketch-to-stretch are given in the Step by Step feature on page 286.

Students need many opportunities to experiment with this activity before they can think symbolically. It's helpful to introduce this teaching strategy through a minilesson and draw several sketches together as a class before students do their own sketches. As they create symbolic illustrations of books, students probe their understanding of the story and what it means to them (Whitin, 2002). *The Ballad of Lucy Whipple* (Cushman, 1996), for example, is the story of a girl who reluctantly comes with her family to Lucky Diggins, California, during the 1849 Gold Rush. Even though she wants nothing more than to return home to Massachusetts, Lucy makes a new home for herself and finally becomes a "happy citizen" (p. 187) in Lucky Diggins. Figure 9–5 shows a fourth grader's sketch-to-stretch drawing about *The Ballad of Lucy Whipple* that reflects the "home" theme.

In a yearlong study of two seventh-grade language arts classes, Whitin (1996) found that students' use of sketching helped deepen their understanding of theme; however, she warns that some upper-grade students view this strategy as an easy form of response and suggests that teachers clarify this misconception early in the school year. Students explored new avenues of expression, such as using color to signify meaning and pie charts to signify feelings. Whitin also had her students write reflections to accompany the sketches.

Students also examine the theme as they create quilts. As students design class quilts, the symbols, colors, and quotes they choose reflect their understanding of theme. For example, after reading *Chrysanthemum* (Henkes, 1991), the story of a little girl mouse who is made fun of at school because of her name, and discussing the theme of the story, a second-grade class made a names quilt using construction paper. They decided to emphasize the importance of honoring one another's names in their quilt. The children researched their names, and then each child wrote his or her name and its meaning in a square for the quilt. The teacher also added a square about her first name, and because one more square was needed to finish the quilt, one child made a square about Chrysanthemum, the mouse in the story, and her name. They placed the squares next to each other, and

---

-------- Sketch-to-Stretch --------

1 **Read a story.**   Students read a story or several chapters of a longer book.

2 **Discuss the story.**   Students discuss the story in a grand conversation and talk about ways to symbolize the theme using lines, colors, shapes, and words.

3 **Draw sketches.**   Students draw sketches that reflect what the story means to them. Rather than drawing a picture of their favorite part, they focus on using symbols to represent what the story means to them.

4 **Share the sketches.**   Students meet in small groups to share their sketches and talk about the symbols they used. Teachers encourage classmates to study each student's sketch and tell what they think he or she is trying to convey.

5 **Share some sketches with the class.**   Each group chooses one sketch to share with the class.

FIGURE 9–5

A Fourth Grader's Sketch-to-Stretch Drawing for *The Ballad of Lucy Whipple*

around the outside border of the quilt they wrote "Our names are very important to us. We never make fun of anyone's name. Everyone has a beautiful and special name with a story behind it."

Genres

Stories can be categorized in different ways, one of which is according to genres (Buss & Karnowski, 2000). Three broad categories are *folklore, fantasies*, and *realism*. Traditional stories, including fables, fairy tales, myths, and legends, are folklore. Many of these stories, such as "Gingerbread Man," "The Tortoise and the Hare," and "Cinderella," were told and retold for centuries before they were written down. Fantasies are make-believe stories. They may be set in imaginary worlds or in future worlds where characters do impossible things. In some fantasies, such as *Bunnicula: A Rabbit-Tale of Mystery* (Howe & Howe, 2006), animals can talk, and in others, the characters travel through time. In *King of Shadows* (Cooper, 1999), for instance, modern-day Nat Field travels to London as part of a drama troupe to perform in the newly built replica of the famous Globe Theatre. After arriving in England, Nat goes to bed ill and awakens after being transported back 400 years to Elizabethan times to perform in the original Globe Theatre with William Shakespeare. Realistic stories, in contrast, are believable. Some stories take place in the past, such as *Crispin: The Cross of Lead* (Avi, 2002), set in medieval England, and *Rodzina* (Cushman, 2003), an orphan train story set in the 1800s. Other stories are set in the contemporary world, such as *Joey Pigza*

Conferencing With Students
This teacher asks students to think about the elements of story structure in the stories they are reading. Students come together to talk about how the author of their particular book crafted the story using plot, characters, setting, point of view, and theme. This conversation is more than a check to make sure students understand what they are reading; it's important because students deepen their comprehension and gain new insights as they think and talk about the story.

Loses Control (Gantos, 2000) and *Amber Brown Is Not a Crayon* (Danziger, 2006). Figure 9–6 presents an overview of the story genres. Poetry, biography, and nonfiction are genres, too, and you will learn more about them in upcoming chapters.

Some researchers are currently looking at genres in a much broader way: They have moved beyond the idea of genres as simply categories of children's literature to examine the different patterns or genres of text that young children interact with at home or at school. These genres include magazines, lists, recipes, children's books, workbooks, newspapers, and letters and greeting cards. Through their examination of young children's interaction with genres, Duke and Purcell-Gates (2003) concluded that during the preschool years, children develop the understanding that texts have different patterns or genres. Duke and Kays (1998) also found that kindergartners demonstrate their knowledge of genres when they vary how they pretend-read unfamiliar wordless books—these young children pretend-read information books differently than stories. These studies suggest that students come to school with a concept of genre and that through reading and writing experiences and minilessons, they refine and apply their understanding of genres.

Literary Devices

Authors use literary devices to make their writing more vivid and memorable. Without these devices, writing can be dull (Lukens, 2006). A list of six literary devices that students learn about is presented in Figure 9–7. Imagery is probably the most commonly used literary device; many authors use imagery as they paint rich word pictures that bring their characters and settings to life. Authors use metaphors and similes to compare one thing to another, personification to endow animals and

objects with human qualities, and hyperbole to exaggerate or stretch the truth. They also create symbols as they use one thing to represent something else. In Chris Van Allsburg's *The Wretched Stone* (1991), for example, the glowing stone that distracts the crew from reading, from spending time with their friends, and from doing their jobs symbolizes television or computers. For students to understand the theme of the story, they need to recognize symbols. The author's style conveys the tone or overall feeling in a story. Some stories are humorous, some are uplifting celebrations of life, and others are sobering commentaries on society.

FIGURE 9–6

Story Genres

Category	Genre	Description and Examples
Folklore	Fables	Brief tales told to point out a moral. For example: *Aesop's Fables* (Pinkney, 2000) and *Head, Body, Legs: A Story From Liberia* (Paye & Lippert, 2002).
	Folk- and Fairy Tales	Stories in which heroes and heroines demonstrate virtues to triumph over adversity. For example: *Beautiful Blackbird* (Bryan, 2003), *The Girl Who Spun Gold* (Hamilton, 2000), and *The Sleeping Beauty* (Hyman, 2000).
	Myths	Stories created by ancient peoples to explain natural phenomena. For example: *King Midas: The Golden Touch* (Demi, 2002), *A Gift From Zeus: Sixteen Favorite Myths* (Steig, 2001), and *The Star-Bearer: A Creation Myth From Ancient Egypt* (Hofmeyr, 2001).
	Legends	Stories, including tall tales, that recount the courageous deeds of people as they struggled against each other or against gods and monsters. For example: *Mystic Horse* (Goble, 2003), *Mike Fink* (Kellogg, 1998), *The Boy Who Drew Cats* (Hodges, 2002), and *Master Man: A Tall Tale of Nigeria* (Shepard, 2001).
Fantasy	Modern Literary Tales	Stories written by modern authors that exemplify the characteristics of folk-tales. For example: *The Runaway Tortilla* (Kimmel, 2000), *Gingerbread Baby* (Brett, 1999), and *Sylvester and the Magic Pebble* (Steig, 2006).
	Fantastic Stories	Imaginative stories that explore alternate realities and contain one or more elements not found in the natural world. For example: *Princess Academy* (Hale, 2005) and *Charlotte's Web* (White, 2006).
	Science Fiction	Stories that explore scientific possibilities. For example: *Commander Toad in Space* (Yolen, 1980), *The Giver* (Lowry, 2006), and *Stinker From Space* (Service, 1988).
	High Fantasy	These stories focus on the conflict between good and evil and often involve quests. For example: *The Lion, the Witch and the Wardrobe* (Lewis, 2005) and *Harry Potter and the Chamber of Secrets* (Rowling, 1999).
Realism	Contemporary Stories	Stories that portray the real world and contemporary society. For example: *Hatchet* (Paulsen, 2006), *Joey Pigza Loses Control* (Gantos, 2000), and *Locomotion* (Woodson, 2003).
	Historical Fiction	Realistic stories set in the past. For example: *The Watsons Go to Birmingham—1963* (Curtis, 2000), *Sarah, Plain and Tall* (MacLachlan, 2004), and *A Single Shard* (Park, 2001).

FIGURE 9–7

Literary Devices

Comparison	Authors compare one thing to another. When the comparison uses the word *like* or *as*, it's a simile; when the comparison is stated directly, it's a metaphor. For example, "the ocean is like a playground for whales" is a simile; "the ocean is a playground for whales" is a metaphor. Metaphors are stronger comparisons because they're more direct.
Hyperbole	Authors use hyperbole when they overstate or stretch the truth to make obvious and intentional exaggerations. "It's raining cats and dogs" and "my feet are killing me" are two. American tall tales also have rich examples of hyperbole.
Imagery	Authors use descriptive or sensory words and phrases to create imagery or a picture in the reader's mind. Sensory language stirs the reader's imagination. Instead of saying "the kitchen smelled good as Grandmother cooked Thanksgiving dinner," authors create imagery when they write "the aroma of a turkey roasting in the oven filled Grandmother's kitchen on Thanksgiving."
Personification	Authors use personification when they attribute human characteristics to animals or objects. For example, "the moss crept across the sidewalk" is personification.
Symbolism	Authors often use a person, place, or thing as a symbol to represent something else. For example, a dove symbolizes peace, the Statue of Liberty symbolizes freedom, and books symbolize knowledge.
Tone	Authors create an overall feeling or effect in the story through their choice of words and use of other literary devices. For example, *Bunnicula: A Rabbit-Tale of Mystery* (Howe & Howe, 2006) and *Catherine, Called Birdy* (Cushman, 1994) are humorous stories, and *Babe the Gallant Pig* (King-Smith, 2005) and *Sarah, Plain and Tall* (MacLachlan, 2004) are uplifting, feel-good stories.

Young children focus on events and characters as they read and discuss a story, but gradually students become more sophisticated readers. They learn to notice both what the author says and how he or she says it. Teachers facilitate students' growth in reading and evaluating stories by directing their attention to literary devices and the author's style during the responding and exploring stages of the reading process.

Teaching Students About Stories

The most important way that students refine their concept of story is by reading and writing stories, but teachers help students expand their concepts through a variety of activities. As they talk about stories during grand conversations, teachers often draw students' attention to theme and other elements of story structure, genres, and literary devices. And as students develop open-mind portraits, beginning-middle-end clusters, and other diagrams and charts, they're examining stories more closely. In addition, teachers teach minilessons that focus on story elements, genres, and literary devices.

Minilessons. Teachers adapt the teaching strategy set out in Chapter 2 to teach minilessons about story structure, genres, and literary devices as well as other procedures, concepts, and strategies and skills related to reading and writing stories. A list of topics for minilessons about stories is presented on pages 292 and 293, as well as a minilesson that a second-grade teacher taught on theme.

Minilessons about story structure, genres, and literary devices are usually taught during the exploring stage of the reading process, after students have had an opportunity to read and respond to a story and share their reactions. This sequence is important because students need to understand the events of the story before they try to analyze the story at a more abstract level.

READING STORIES

Students read stories as they participate in literature focus units, literature circles, reading workshop, and thematic units, and as they read stories, their concept of story informs and supports their reading. Teachers provide guidance and support for students as they participate in a variety of reading activities, including guided reading and readers theatre, and they can assess students' comprehension through retelling stories.

Guided Reading

Teachers scaffold students' reading to enable them to develop and use reading strategies and skills in guided reading (Fountas & Pinnell, 1996, 2001). This type of reading is teacher directed and is usually done in small groups with students who read at the same level or who use similar reading strategies and skills. Teachers listen to individual students read during guided reading, noticing how they use meaning, structure, and phonological cues. When a student makes an error, the teacher quickly determines the source of the error and decides what type of immediate instruction or other support to use so that the student can be successful (Schwartz, 2005). Teachers often use guided reading with young children and with other students who need direct instruction.

Selections used for guided reading should be written at students' instructional reading levels, that is, slightly beyond their ability to read the text independently, or at their level of proximal development. They usually read the selection silently so if the selection is too difficult, shared reading is a better procedure. If the selection is too easy, then independent reading is a better choice because teacher support isn't needed. Teachers often group and regroup students for guided reading so that the book selected is appropriate for all students in a group. The steps in guided reading are shown in the Step by Step feature on page 294.

Readers Theatre

Readers theatre is a dramatic presentation of a story by a group of readers. Stories are usually rewritten as scripts, and students each assume a role and read that character's lines. Students develop reading fluency and increased motivation for reading through

What Students Need to Learn About Stories

Topics

Procedures	*Concepts*	*Strategies and Skills*
Make a beginning-middle-end cluster	**Concept of story**	Visualize
Make a setting map		Predict and confirm
Make a plot profile	Beginning-middle-end	Empathize with characters
Make an open-mind portrait	Plot	Identify with characters
Do a sketch-to-stretch drawing	Characters	Write dialogue for characters
Design a story quilt	Setting	**Rereading**
Do a readers theatre presentation	**Theme**	**Re**tell a story
Use the Goldilocks strategy	Point of view	Respond to stories
Participate in SSR	Genres	Monitor understanding
Make a class collaboration book	Literary devices	Connect to one's own life
Write an innovation	Metaphor	Connect to the world
Write a sequel	Simile	Connect to previously read literature
Write original stories		Value the story
		Evaluate the story

To investigate about how students learn about stories, please visit MyEducationLab. You can watch second graders use their knowledge of story structure as they "read" a wordless book by going to the topic "Viewing" and clicking on the video "Concept of Story," or see an eighth-grade teacher review story structure by going to the topic "Reading" and clicking on the video "Literary Elements." And if you'd like to see second graders rereading a story, go again to the topic "Reading" and click on the video "Rereading."

Minilesson

Mrs. Levin's Second Graders Learn About Theme

1 Introduce the topic

Mrs. Levin's second-grade class has just read *Martha Speaks* (Meddaugh, 1992), the story of a talking dog. Mrs. Levin rereads the last paragraph of the story, which exemplifies the theme, and says, "I think this is what the author, Susan Meddaugh, is trying to tell us—that sometimes we should talk and sometimes we should be quiet. What do you think?" The children agree, and Mrs. Levin explains that the author's message or lesson about life is called the *theme*.

2 Share examples

Mrs. Levin shows the class *Little Red Riding Hood* (Galdone, 1974), a story they read earlier in the year, and after briefly reviewing the story, she asks children about the theme of this story. One child quickly responds, "I think the author means that you shouldn't talk to strangers." Another child explains, "Little Red Riding Hood's mom probably tried to teach her to not talk to strangers but Little Red Riding Hood must have forgotten because she talked to the wolf and he was like a stranger." It is a message every child has heard, but they agree that they, too, sometimes forget, just like Little Red Riding Hood.

3 Provide information

The next day, Mrs. Levin shares three other familiar books and asks children to identify the theme. The first book is *The Three Bears* (Galdone, 1972), and children easily identify the "don't intrude" theme. The second book is *Chrysanthemum* (Henkes, 1991), the story of a young mouse named Chrysanthemum who doesn't like herself after her classmates make fun of her name. The children identify two variations of the theme: "you should be nice to everyone and not hurt their feelings," and "kids who aren't nice get in trouble." The third book is *Miss Nelson Is Missing!* (Allard, 1977), the story of a sweet teacher who transforms herself into a mean teacher after her students refuse to behave. The children identify the theme as "teachers are nice when you behave but they are mean when you are bad."

4 Supervise practice

Mrs. Levin asks children to choose one of the five stories they have examined and to draw pictures showing the theme. For example, they could draw a picture of Martha using the telephone to report burglars in the house or a picture of themselves ringing the doorbell at a friend's house. Mrs. Levin walks around as children work, helping them add titles to their pictures that focus on the theme of the story.

5 Reflect on learning

Children share their pictures with the class and explain how they illustrate the theme of the various stories.

Step by Step

---- Guided Reading ----

1 Choose a book.   Teachers choose a book that students in a small group can read with 90–94% accuracy and collect copies of the book for each student in the group.

2 Introduce the book.   Teachers show the cover, reading the title and author's name, and activate students' background knowledge on a related topic. They use key vocabulary words as they talk about the book but don't directly teach them. Students also "picture walk" through the book, examining the illustrations.

3 Have students read the book.   Teachers have students read the book independently and ask individual students to take turns reading aloud. They help individual students decode unfamiliar words, deal with unfamiliar sentence structures, and comprehend ideas whenever assistance is needed.

4 Respond to the book.   Students talk about the book and relate it to others they have read, as in a grand conversation.

5 Teach concepts.   Teachers teach a comprehension strategy or a phonics skill, review vocabulary words, or examine an element of story structure.

6 Provide opportunities for independent reading.   Teachers have students reread the book several more times to develop fluency. They often place the book in students' book baskets so they can reread it independently.

---

this dramatic activity (Black & Stave, 2007; Worthy & Prater, 2002). The reader's responsibility is to interpret a story without using much action. Students may stand or sit, but they must carry the whole communication of the plot, characterization, mood, and theme through their voices, gestures, and facial expressions.

A few collections of readers theatre scripts are available for young children, including *Getting Ready to Read With Readers Theatre* (Barchers & Pfeffinger, 2007) and *Nonfiction Readers Theatre for Beginning Readers* (Fredericks, 2007). However, very few quality scripts are available for older students, so they usually prepare their own scripts from books they have read, such as *Amber Brown Is Not a Crayon* (Danziger, 2006) and *The Giver* (Lowry, 2006). Karen Hesse's *Witness* (2001), a story told from multiple voices, is very powerful when performed as a readers theatre presentation. Students begin by reading the book and thinking about its theme, characters, and plot. Next, they choose an episode to script, make copies of it, and use felt-tip pens to highlight the dialogue. They then adapt the scene by adding narrators' lines to bridge gaps, set the scene, and summarize. Students assume roles and read the script aloud, revising and experimenting with new text until they are satisfied with the script. The final version is typed, duplicated, and stapled into booklets. The steps in developing readers theatre performances are shown in the Step by Step feature on the next page.

Independent Reading

One way to provide daily opportunities for recreational reading is what Stephen Krashen (1993) calls *free voluntary reading* (FVR). Researchers have confirmed again and again that children, including English learners, who do more reading become more capable readers (Cohen, 1999; Krashen, 1993, 2001). Two ways to provide independent reading at school are Sustained Silent Reading and reading workshop. No matter which program teachers use to provide students with independent reading, these guidelines are followed:

- Students choose the books they read.
- Students have access to a large collection of books from which to choose those they want to read and are able to read.
- Students have daily uninterrupted time to read.
- Students have a comfortable, quiet location in which to read.
- Students receive encouragement from their teachers.

The Goldilocks Strategy. Students need to learn to choose books for independent reading that they really can read. Ohlhausen and Jepsen (1992) developed a strategy for choosing books called the "Goldilocks strategy." These teachers developed three categories of books—"too easy," "too hard," and "just right" using "The Three Bears" folktale as their model. The books in the "too easy" category were books students had read before or could read fluently. "Too hard" books were unfamiliar and confusing, and books in the "just right" category were interesting and had just a few unfamiliar words. The books in each category vary according to the students' reading levels. This approach was developed with second graders, but the categorization scheme can work at any grade level. Figure 9–8 presents a chart developed by a third-grade class about choosing books for independent reading using the Goldilocks strategy.

Readers Theatre

1 Select a script.   Teachers select a script for students to use, or they work with students to craft a script from a familiar picture-book story or an episode from a chapter book.

2 Rehearse the performance.   Students choose their parts and read through the script once or twice. Then they stop to talk about the story and deepen their understanding of the characters they're playing. They decide how to use their voices, gestures, and facial expressions to interpret the characters and read the script one or two more times, striving for accurate pronunciation, strong voice projection, and appropriate inflection.

3 Decide on props.   Students often collect props and prepare simple costumes to enhance their presentation, but students shouldn't get so involved in props that it interferes with the interpretive quality of the reading.

4 Stage the performance.   Students usually do the readers theatre performance at the front of the classroom. They stand or sit in a row and read their lines, staying in position throughout the performance. If readers are sitting, they may stand to read their lines; if they are standing, they may step forward to read. The emphasis isn't on production quality; rather, it's on the interpretive quality of the readers' voices and expressions.

FIGURE 9–8

A Third-Grade Chart Applying the Goldilocks Strategy

How to Choose the Best Books for YOU

"Too Easy" Books

1. The book is short.
2. The print is big.
3. You have read the book before.
4. You know all the words in the book.
5. The book has a lot of pictures.
6. You are an expert on this topic.

"Just Right" Books

1. The book looks interesting.
2. You can decode most of the words in the book.
3. Mrs. Donnelly has read this book aloud to you.
4. You have read other books by this author.
5. There's someone to give you help if you need it.
6. You know something about this topic.

"Too Hard" Books

1. The book is long.
2. The print is small.
3. There aren't many pictures in the book.
4. There are a lot of words that you can't decode.
5. There's no one to help you read this book.
6. You don't know much about this topic.

Sustained Silent Reading. In Sustained Silent Reading (SSR), students read independently for 10 to 15 minutes or more in books they've chosen themselves that are at their reading level, and teachers model independent reading at the same time (Pilgreen, 2000). Children don't write book reports, and teachers don't keep records of which books children read; instead, the emphasis is on reading for pleasure. This popular reading activity goes by a variety of names, including "drop everything and read" (DEAR), "sustained quiet reading time" (SQUIRT), and "our time to enjoy reading" (OTTER). In contrast, reading workshop is different; it's not a short block of time. Students usually spend more time reading, and students participate in other types of activities (Atwell, 1998). Students conference with the teacher about books they're reading, and they share the books they've read with the class. The teacher's role is different, too, because teachers monitor and assess students' reading during reading workshop.

Teachers often have concerns that students won't use the reading time productively or that they'll always choose books that are too easy for them, but that doesn't seem to be the case (Von Sprecken & Krashen, 1998). Most students actually read during SSR, and students' reading tastes do mature gradually.

Responding to Stories

When you're reading a novel, do you imagine yourself as one of the characters? Do you laugh out loud or cry while you're reading? Do you wish the story wouldn't end because you're enjoying it so much? If so, it's because you're having a dynamic engagement with literature. This powerful feeling of pleasure and desire to do more reading is reader response, and it's what teachers want their students to experience. Marjorie Hancock (2004) describes response to literature as "the unique interaction that occurs within the mind and heart of the individual reader through the literature event" (p. 9).

The three components of response are the reader, the text, and the context for response (Galda, 1988). Readers bring their background knowledge, past literary experiences, ability to use reading strategies and skills, and desire to read to the reading experience; these characteristics are part of the reason why students' responses are unique and personal. Text characteristics are topic, genre, structural patterns, and literary elements, and students' awareness of these characteristics affects their comprehension. The context is the setting for the response. Students' responses reflect their sociocultural background, their family's income level, their religious beliefs, and the classroom climate. When teachers involve students with literature through literature focus units, literature circles, and reading workshop, they provide opportunities for response and celebrate students' responses. Not surprisingly, children respond differently than when teachers don't highlight literature in their language arts programs.

Many of the responses that students make are spontaneous, but others are planned by teachers. For example, kindergartners laugh (spontaneous response) while listening to their teacher read Thacher Hurd's hilarious picture book, *Moo Cow Kaboom!* (2003). In the story, Moo Cow is cownapped by a space cowboy named Zork and taken to Planet 246 for the InterGalactic Rodeo. Afterward, children take turns dressing up as Farmer George (wearing a nightshirt), Moo Cow (wearing a cow mask), and Zork (wearing a black cowboy hat) while classmates become a cast of supporting characters to reenact the story. This is a planned response. As eighth graders read *Crispin: The Cross of Lead* (Avi, 2002), the story of Crispin, a 13-year-old peasant boy who is falsely accused of being a thief and declared a "wolf's head" (which gives everyone in the country permission to kill him on sight), they compare Crispin's life to their own and comment on their compassion for him. This is a spontaneous response. Students also make entries in their reading logs to explore the ideas in the story and make connections to what they're learning about the Middle Ages—a planned response. And when students reach the end of the story, where Crispin redeems himself, they cheer loudly. This is another spontaneous response.

Spontaneous responses are those that students make without prompting by the teacher. They make these responses because the story is so engaging. Young children, for example, clap their hands and tap their feet to the rhythm of Bill Martin and John Archambault's *Chicka Chicka Boom Boom* (1989) and chant along as the teacher reads and rereads the book. They spot the dangers facing two bugs named Frieda and Gloria in the illustrations in *Absolutely Not!* (McElligott, 2004) and call out warnings to the bugs. Older students take action in their own neighborhood after reading Paul Fleischman's *Seedfolks* (2004), a timeless story about a blighted community that's transformed after a girl plants some seeds and her neighbors are stirred to take action.

Janet Hickman (1980) examined young children's spontaneous responses and classified a variety of response behaviors, including the following:

- Children laugh, chant repetitive phrases, stretch to see illustrations, and clap with pleasure as they listen to the teacher read aloud.
- Children touch books as they browse in the classroom library, examine books in book baskets on their desks, and self-select books to read.
- Children eagerly talk about books, sharing discoveries and making connections.
- Children pretend to be characters and reenact stories.
- Children draw pictures of characters and events in the book.
- Children write their own books, often using the book as a model.

When children respond to books without being prompted by the teachers, their responses genuinely reflect their attention, understanding, and interest in the book.

Teachers plan responses that are appropriate for the books that students are reading, and it's possible to design responses that address any of the language arts, as shown in the LA Essentials box on the next page. Students often listen to a book on tape, view the film version of a story, or examine the illustrations in a picture book. They talk about the story in a grand conversation, tell sequels, perform puppet shows, and dramatize the story while their classmates watch. They read other books by the same author. They write in reading logs and write sequels, letters to the author, or books using the story as a model. They also make Venn diagrams, posters, open-mind portraits, and sketch-to-stretch drawings.

When children participate in reader response activities, they grow as readers. Researchers report that students become more interested in books, and their reading abilities improve (Spiegel, 1998). In particular, they deepen their understanding of reading as a process, apply reading strategies that they're learning, grow in their appreciation of literary quality, and assume responsibility for learning. Another benefit is that students are more likely to become lifelong readers because of these successful reading experiences.

Retelling Stories

Students often retell familiar stories they've read or watched on television, and when they retell a story, students organize the information they remember and provide a personalized summary (Hoyt, 1999). Teachers can capitalize on students' interest in retelling stories and use it to assess their comprehension. Retelling is an authentic assessment tool because it's similar to the language arts activities that take place in classrooms every day (McKenna & Stahl, 2003). As they listen to students retell a story, teachers use a scoring sheet or rating scale to evaluate the cohesiveness and completeness of the retellings. This activity is especially valuable for English learners because teachers can assess both students' comprehension and their oral language fluency (O'Malley & Pierce, 1996).

WAYS TO RESPOND TO STORIES

Listening

- Listen to the story on tape
- Listen to classmates talk in a grand conversation

Talking

- Participate in a grand conversation
- Retell stories
- Perform a puppet show
- Reenact a story
- Sit on the hot seat and be interviewed as a character

Reading

- Read sequels
- Read other books by the same author
- Read more about the topic
- Research the author

Writing

- Write in reading logs
- Write a retelling
- Write a new version or a sequel
- Write a poem about the story or the character
- Write a letter to the author

Viewing

- Watch film versions of stories
- Examine illustrations in picture books

Visually Representing

- Create an open-mind portrait of a character
- Draw a diagram about the story
- Make puppets of characters
- Dramatize the story

Once you begin listening to students retell stories, you'll notice that the ones who understand a story retell it differently than those who don't. Capable readers' retellings make sense: Their retellings reflect the organization of the story, and they incorporate all of the important story events. In contrast, less capable readers often recall events haphazardly or omit important events, especially those in the middle of the story.

Three Children's Retellings. A first-grade teacher reads aloud *Hey, Al* (Yorinks, 1986), the award-winning picture-book story about Al, a hardworking janitor, and his loyal dog, Eddie, who yearn for a better life. At the beginning of the story, Al is discouraged because he has to work so hard, and then a bird offers him an easy life. Al accepts the bird's offer, and in the middle of the story, the bird flies Al and Eddie to an island paradise where they have a wonderful time—until they start turning into birds. They escape and fly toward their home in the city. Al reaches home safely, but Eddie almost drowns. At last Al and Eddie are reunited, and they realize that it's up to them to make their own happiness. After the teacher finishes reading the story, the children draw pictures of their favorite parts and talk about the story in a grand conversation. Afterward, the first graders individually retell the story to her, but they aren't prompted to add more information. Here are three children's retellings:

◆ *Retelling #1. The story is about Al and Eddie. A bird took them to Hawaii and they had a lot of fun there. They were swimming and playing a lot. Then they came back home because they didn't like being birds.*

◆ *Retelling #2. Al and Eddie are at the island. They like it and they are changing into birds. They have wings and feathers and stuff that made them look funny. That makes them scared so they fly back to their old home. I think Eddie crashed into the ocean and drowned. So Al buys a new dog and they have lots of fun together.*

◆ *Retelling #3. This man named Al and his puppy called Eddie wanted more excitement so they went to an island. It was wonderful at first, but then they started changing into birds and they hated that. They wanted to go back home. They started flying home, and they were fly- ing, and they were changing back into their real selves. Al made it home, but Eddie almost drowned because he was smaller. All in all, they did learn an important lesson: You should be happy with yourself just the way you are.*

These three retellings show children's differing levels of comprehension. The first child's brief retelling is literal: It includes events from the beginning, middle, and end of the story, but it lacks an interpretation. Many details are missing; in fact, this child doesn't mention that Al's a man (or a janitor) or that Eddie's a dog. Even though the second retelling is longer than the first one, it shows only partial comprehension. It's incomplete because it lacks a beginning: This child focuses most of the retelling on the middle and misunderstands the end of the story because Eddie doesn't drown. With some prompting from the teacher, this child might have added more informa- tion about the beginning of the story or corrected the ending. The third child's retelling, in contrast, is quite complete. This child retells the beginning, middle, and

-------- Retelling Stories --------

1 **Introduce the story.** The teacher introduces the story by reading the title, examining the cover of the book, or talking about a topic related to the story. The teacher also explains that students will be asked to retell the story afterward.

2 **Read the story.** Students read the story or listen to the teacher read it aloud.

3 **Discuss the story.** Students and the teacher talk about the story, sharing ideas and clarifying confusions. (This step is optional, but discussing the story usually improves students' retellings.)

4 **Create a graphic organizer.** Students can create a graphic organizer or a series of drawings to guide the retelling. (This step is optional, too, but it's especially helpful for students who have difficulty retelling stories.)

5 **Have a student retell the story.** The teacher asks students to individually retell the story in their own words, and usually asks prompting questions to elicit more information:

- What happened next?
- Where did the story take place?
- What did the character do next?
- How did the story end?
- What was the author's message?

6 **Mark the scoring guide.** The teacher scores the retelling using a scoring guide as the student retells the story.

end of the story and explains the characters' motivation for going to the island. Most important, this child establishes a purpose for the story by explaining its theme—making your own happiness.

After examining the strengths and weaknesses of each retelling, teachers can use what they learn to plan instruction. For example, the first child might benefit from learning to add more details in a retelling, and the second one needs to learn more about organizing the retelling into beginning, middle, and end parts. They both need to learn more about how to recognize the theme of a story. Because the third child's retelling was so complete, this child might be interested in reading more challenging stories where the theme is less obvious.

Guidelines for Retelling. Teachers sit one-on-one with individual students in a quiet area of the classroom and ask them to retell a familiar story. While the student is retelling, teachers use a scoring sheet to mark the components that the student includes in the retelling. If the student hesitates or doesn't finish retelling the story, teachers ask questions, such as "What happened next?" The steps in the procedure are explained in the Step by Step box above.

Weaving Assessment Into Practice

RETELLING STORIES SCORING GUIDE

Name _Cassie_   Date _Mar. 10_

Book _Ruby Lu, Brave and True_

4	__ Names and describes all characters.
	__ Includes specific details about the setting.
	__ Explains the problem.
	__ Describes attempts to solve the problem.
	__ Explains the solution.
	__ Identifies the theme.

③	✓ Names all characters and <u>describes</u> some of them. _P_
	__ Identifies more than one detail about the setting (location, weather, time).
	✓ Recalls events in order.
	✓ Identifies the problem. _P_
	✓ Includes the beginning, <u>middle</u>, and end. _P_

2	__ Names all characters.
	✓ Mentions the setting.
	__ Recalls most events in order.
	__ Includes the beginning and end.

1	__ Names some characters.
	__ Recalls events haphazardly.
	__ Includes only beginning or end.

P = prompted

Teachers can't assume that students already know how to retell stories, even though many do. Through a series of minilessons on retelling strategies and demonstrations of the procedure, students will understand what's expected of them. They need to practice retelling stories before they'll be good at it. They can retell stories with a classmate and to their parents at home. Students who continue to have difficulty retelling stories may need to learn more about story structure, especially beginning, middle, and end. It's often helpful to have them draw pictures to scaffold their retellings. As their comprehension improves, so will their retelling abilities.

Judging Students' Retellings. Most students enjoy retelling stories, and their rubric scores provide a useful measure of their comprehension. A rubric for scoring third graders' retellings is shown in the Weaving Assessment Into Practice box above. Some students, however, are shy or uncomfortable talking with teachers, so their scores may underestimate how well they comprehend (McKenna & Stahl, 2003). The same is true for English learners.

WRITING STORIES

As students read and talk about stories, they learn how writers craft stories. They also draw from stories they've read as they create their own stories, intertwining several story ideas and adapting story elements and genres to meet their own needs (Atwell, 1998). Cairney (1990) found that students weave bits of the stories they've read into the stories they write; they share their compositions, and then bits of these compositions make their way into classmates' compositions. Students make intertextual links in different ways:

- Use specific story ideas without copying the plot
- Copy the plot from a story, but add new events, characters, and settings
- Use a specific genre they have studied for a story
- Use a character borrowed from a story read previously
- Write a retelling of the story
- Incorporate content from an informational book into a story
- Combine several stories into a new story

The first two strategies were the ones most commonly used in Cairney's study of sixth graders. The next-to-the-last strategy was used only by less capable readers, and the last one only by more capable readers.

When students write stories, they incorporate what they have learned about stories, and they use the writing process to draft and refine their stories. They write stories as part of literature focus units, during thematic units, and in writing workshop. Stories are probably the most complex writing form that students use. It is difficult—even for adults—to craft well-formed stories incorporating plot and character development and other elements of story structure.

Writing Retellings of Stories

Students often write retellings of stories they've read and enjoyed. As they retell a story, they internalize the structure of the story and play with the language the author used. Sometimes students work together to write a collaborative retelling, and at other times, they write their own individual retellings. Students can work together as a group to write or dictate the retelling, or they can divide the story into sections or chapters and have each student or pair of students write a small part. Then the parts are compiled. A class of second graders worked together to dictate their retelling of *I, Doko: The Tale of a Basket* (Young, 2004), which they published as a big book.

Page 1: *I am a basket, and my name is Doko. A good man named Yeh-yeh bought me at a market many years ago.*

Page 2: *Yeh-yeh's wife used to carry her precious baby inside me. I was a safe basket.*

Page 3: *In the blink of an eye the baby grew and became a boy. I was always with him and I helped him carry the wood for the cooking fire. I was a protective basket.*

Page 4: *Then a bad time came and Yeh-yeh's wife died. Yeh-yeh put her dead body in my basket, and I carried her to the grave. I was a trusted basket.*

Page 5: *By now the boy was all grown up and he got married. I got a good scrubbing before the wedding, and I got to carry the bride's presents to her new home. I was a handsome basket.*

Page 6: *Next the boy and his wife had a baby. They called him Wangal and I carried him in my basket. I was a proud basket.*

Page 7: *Finally Yeh-yeh got old and so did I. We stayed home by the fire, and Yeh-yeh told me wonderful stories. I was a listening basket.*

Page 8: *One day Yeh-yeh let the fire go out of the fireplace and almost burned down the house. People said it was time to get rid of Yeh-yeh. They told Yeh-yeh's son to take him to the temple steps and leave him there for the priests to take care of. I was a worried basket.*

Page 9: *The next day Yeh-yeh's son put the old man in my basket to take him to the temple steps, but Wangal said something very important. He said, "Don't forget to bring Doko back home because I will need it to get rid of you when you get old." That made Yeh-yeh's son understand that he was doing something very bad. I was a sad basket.*

Page 10: *Yeh-yeh's son learned a good lesson: He learned to respect old people and not want to get rid of them. So Yeh-yeh lived at home with his son and Wangal and me for many happy years. I was a respectful basket.*

As the second graders dictated the retelling, their teacher wrote it on chart paper. Then they read the story over several times, making revisions. Next, the children divided the text into sections for each page. Then they recopied the text onto each page for the big book, drew pictures to illustrate each page, and added a cover and a title page. Children also wrote their own books, including the major points at the beginning, middle, and end of the story.

Sometimes students change the point of view in their retellings and tell the story from a particular character's viewpoint. A fourth grader wrote this retelling of "Goldilocks and the Three Bears" from Baby Bear's perspective:

One day mom got me up. I had to take a bath. I hate to take baths, but I had to. While I was taking my bath, Mom was making breakfast. When I got out of the tub breakfast was ready. But Dad got mad because his breakfast porridge was too hot to eat. So Mom said, "Let's go for a walk and let it cool." I thought, "Oh boy, we get to go for a walk!" My porridge was just right, but I could eat it later.

When we got back our front door was open. Dad thought it was an animal so he started to growl. I hate it when Dad growls. It really scares me. Anyway, there was no animal anywhere so I rushed to the table. Everybody was sitting down to eat. I said, "Someone ate my porridge." Then Dad noticed someone had tasted his porridge. He got really mad.

Then I went into the living room because I did not want to get yelled at. I noticed my rocking chair was broken. I told Dad and he got even madder.

Then I went into my bedroom. I said, "Someone has been sleeping in my bed and she's still in it." So this little girl with long blond hair raises up and starts to scream. Dad plugged his ears. She jumped up like she was scared of us and ran out of the house. We never saw that little girl again.

Writing Innovations

Many stories have a repetitive pattern or refrain, and students can use this structure to write their own stories. As part of a literature focus unit, a first-grade class read *If You Give a Mouse a Cookie* (Numeroff, 1985) and talked about the circular structure of the story: The story begins with giving a mouse a cookie and ends with the mouse getting a second cookie. Then the first graders wrote stories about what they would do if they were given a cookie. A child named Michelle drew the circle diagram shown in Figure 9–9 to organize her story, and then she wrote this story, which has been transcribed into conventional English spelling:

If you gave Michelle a cookie she would probably want some pop. Then she would want a napkin to clean her face. That would make her tired and she would go to bed to take a nap. Before you know it, she will be awake and she would like to take a swim in a swimming pool. Then she would watch cartoons on T.V. And she would be getting hungry again so she would probably want another cookie.

FIGURE 9–9

A Circle Diagram for *If You Give Michelle a Cookie*

Judith Viorst's *Alexander and the Terrible, Horrible, No Good, Very Bad Day* (1987) is a more sophisticated pattern story. After reading the book, students often write about their own bad days. A fifth grader named Jacob wrote his version, entitled "Jacob and the Crummy, Stupid, Very Bad Day":

> *One day I was riding my bike and I fell off and broke my arm and sprained my foot. I had to go to the hospital in an ambulance and get my arm set in a cast and my foot wrapped up real tight in a bandage. I knew it was going to be a crummy, stupid, very bad day. I think I'll swim to China.*
>
> *Then I had to go to the dentist with my sister Melissa. My sister had no cavities, but guess who had two cavities. I knew it was going to be a crummy, stupid, very bad day. I think I'll swim to China.*
>
> *My mom felt bad for me because it was such a bad day so she went and bought me a present—two Nintendo games. But my sister started fighting with me and my mom blamed me for it even though it wasn't my fault. So my mom took the games away. I wonder if there are better sisters in China?*
>
> *Then I went outside and found out that someone had stolen my bike. It was gone without a trace. It really was a crummy, stupid, very bad day. Now I am going to swim to China for sure.*

Writing Sequels

Students often choose to write sequels as projects during literature focus units. For example, after reading *The Sign of the Beaver* (Speare, 2005), students can write sequels in which Matt and Attean meet again. They write additional adventures about the boa constrictor after reading *The Day Jimmy's Boa Ate the Wash* (Noble, 1992). Many stories lend themselves to sequels, and students enjoy extending a favorite story.

Writing Genre Stories

During some literature focus units, students read books and learn about a particular genre, such as folktales, historical fiction, myths, or fables. After learning about the genre, they try their hand at writing stories that incorporate its characteristics. After reading gingerbread man stories, a class of kindergartners dictated this story, which their teacher wrote on chart paper. Interestingly, the children asked their teacher to write the story in two columns. In the left column, the teacher wrote the story, and in the right column, she wrote the refrain:

THE RUNAWAY HORSE

Once upon a time	*Run, run,*
there was a horse.	*as fast as you can,*
He jumped over the	*you can't catch me!*
stable gate and ran away.	
He meets a farmer.	*Run, run,*
The farmer chases him	*as fast as you can,*
but the horse runs	*you can't catch me!*
as fast as the wind.	
The horse meets a dog.	*Run, run,*

The dog chases him.	*as fast as you can,*
The horse runs	*you can't catch me!*
as fast as the wind.	
Then the horse meets a fox.	*Snip, snap, snout,*
And the fox gobbles him up.	*This tale is told out.*

A seventh-grade class read and examined myths and compared myths from various cultures. Then they applied what they had learned about myths in this class collaboration myth, "Suntaria and Lunaria: Rulers of the Earth," about the origin of the sun and the moon:

> *Long ago when gods still ruled the earth, there lived two brothers, Suntaria and Lunaria. Both brothers were wise and powerful men. People from all over the earth sought their wisdom and counsel. Each man, in his own way, was good and just, yet the two were as different as gold and coal. Suntaria was large and strong with blue eyes and brilliantly golden hair. Lunaria's hair and eyes were the blackest black.*
>
> *One day Zeus, looking down from Mount Olympus, decided that Earth needed a ruler—someone to watch over his people whenever he became too tired or too busy to do his job. His eyes fell upon Suntaria and Lunaria. Both men were wise and honest. Both men would be good rulers. Which man would be the first ruler of the earth?*
>
> *Zeus decided there was only one fair way to solve his problem. He sent his messenger, Postlet, down to earth with ballots instructing the mortals to vote for a king. There were only two names on the ballot—Suntaria and Lunaria.*
>
> *Each mortal voted and after the ballots were placed in a secure box, Postlet returned them to Zeus. For seven years Zeus and Postlet counted and recounted the ballots. Each time they came up with the same results: 50% of the votes were for Suntaria and 50% were for Lunaria. There was only one thing Zeus could do. He declared that both men would rule over the earth.*
>
> *This is how it was, and this is how it is. Suntaria still spreads his warm golden rays to rule over our days. At night he steps down from his throne, and Lunaria's dark, soft night watches and protects us while we dream.*

The students incorporated three characteristics of myths in their story. First, their myth explained a phenomenon that has more recently been explained scientifically. Second, the setting is backdrop and barely sketched, and finally, the characters in their myth are heroes with supernatural powers.

Writing Original Stories

Students move into writing original stories through writing personal narratives and writing retellings of familiar stories they've read, movies and television programs they've watched, and video games they've played. Their first stories are typically action-driven. Jorgensen (2001) explains that many children's stories resemble a fast-paced television commercial: There's action, more action, and still more action; sometimes with a high point, but other times without one. Other young writers' stories lack focus; they're either endless conversations or a series of unrelated events.

In contrast, more knowledgeable writers craft character-driven stories that exemplify these characteristics:

- The plot is logical with a beginning, middle, and end, and the focus is on the conflict between the characters.
- The characters seem like real people: They come to life through their appearance, dialogue, and actions.
- The setting is carefully described so that readers can visualize it, and it's usually important to the story.
- The narrator's viewpoint is consistent throughout the story.
- A worthwhile theme or message is expressed through the story's characters and events.

Students learn to write more effective stories by examining the elements of story structure, reading lots of stories, and writing stories themselves.

Students' stories represent a variety of genres, especially realistic stories based on events drawn from their own lives and fantasy stories describing imaginary worlds, talking animals, and events that couldn't really happen in today's world. Books, such as the Harry Potter series (Rowling, 2007), give students ideas for their fantasies. Increasingly, both boys and girls include violence in their stories, and it's essential that teachers set guidelines to avoid offensive language and gratuitous bloodthirstiness and brutality.

Karen Jorgensen (2001) taught her fifth graders to write well-crafted stories through a writing workshop approach she calls "fiction workshop." They spend time writing stories independently, and they also conference with classmates and the teacher to get feedback on their stories. When students finish writing a story, they publish it by making a book and reading it to classmates. Then they ceremoniously place the book in the classroom library. She also teaches minilessons about the elements of story structure and how to solve common fiction-writing problems, such as an ineffective setting and excessive dialogue.

Assessing Students' Stories

Teachers consider four components in assessing students' stories: their knowledge of the elements of story structure, their application of the elements in writing, their use of the writing process, and the quality of the finished stories. Determining whether students learned about the element and applied what they learned in their stories is crucial in assessing their stories. Consider the following points:

- Can the student define or identify the characteristics of the element?
- Can the student explain how the element was used in a particular story?
- Did the student apply the element in the story he or she has written?

The quality of students' stories is difficult to measure. Students who write high-quality and interesting stories use the story structure, genre, and literary devices to their advantage. The assessment and grading of students' stories, however, should reflect more than simply the quality of the finished product; they should reflect all four components of students' involvement with stories.

Review

Students develop their concept of stories as they learn about story structure, genres, and literary devices. Students apply this knowledge as they read and write stories. Here are the key concepts presented in this chapter:

- Students acquire a concept of story by reading and writing stories and by learning about story structure, genres, and literary devices.
- Stories have unique structural elements that distinguish them from other forms of writing: plot, characters, setting, point of view, and theme.
- Stories can be categorized according to genres, such as fairy tales and science fiction, and each genre has distinguishing characteristics.
- Literary devices, including comparison, hyperbole, imagery, personification, symbolism, and tone, make stories more vivid and memorable.
- Teachers use guided reading to teach reading to small groups of students who read at the same level.
- As students perform readers theatre presentations, they demonstrate their interpretations of a story.
- Teachers promote reading through free voluntary reading.
- When students respond to literature in both spontaneous and planned ways, their comprehension and interest in reading are enhanced.
- Students retell stories to demonstrate their comprehension.
- Students use intertextuality as they incorporate ideas from the stories they have read into the stories they write.

Professional References

Applebee, A. N. (1978). *The child's concept of story: Ages 2 to 17.* Chicago: University of Chicago Press.

Atwell, N. (1998). *In the middle: New understandings about writing, reading, and learning.* Portsmouth, NH: Heinemann.

Au, K. H. (1992). Constructing the theme of a story. *Language Arts, 69,* 106–111.

Barchers, S. I., & Pfeffinger, C. R. (2007). *Getting ready to read with readers theatre.* Portsmouth, NH: Teacher Ideas Press.

Black, A., & Stave, A. M. (2007). *A comprehensive guide to readers theatre.* Newark, DE: International Reading Association.

Bruner, J. (1980). *Actual minds, possible worlds.* Cambridge, MA: Harvard University Press.

Buss, K., & Karnowski, L. (2000). *Reading and writing literary genres.* Newark, DE: International Reading Association.

Cairney, T. (1990). Intertextuality: Infectious echoes from the past. *The Reading Teacher, 43,* 478–484.

Cohen, K. (1999). Reluctant eighth grade readers enjoy Sustained Silent Reading. *California Reader, 33*(1), 22–25.

De Ford, D. (1981). Literacy: Reading, writing, and other essentials. *Language Arts, 58,* 652–658.

Dressel, J. H. (1990). The effects of listening to and discussing different qualities of children's literature on the narrative writing of fifth graders. *Research in the Teaching of English, 24,* 397–414.

Duke, N. K., & Kays, J. (1998). "Can I say 'Once upon a time'?": Kindergarten children's developing knowledge of information book language. *Early Childhood Research Quarterly, 13,* 295–318.

Duke, N. K., & Purcell-Gates, V. (2003). Genres at home and at school: Bridging the known to the new. *The Reading Teacher, 57,* 30–37.

Eckhoff, B. (1983). How reading affects children's writing. *Language Arts, 60,* 607–616.

Fountas, I. C., & Pinnell, G. S. (1996). *Guided reading: Good first teaching for all children.* Portsmouth, NH: Heinemann.

Fountas, I. C., & Pinnell, G. S. (2001). *Guided readers and writers, grades 3–6.* Portsmouth, NH: Heinemann.

Fredericks, A. D. (2007). *Nonfiction readers theatre for beginning readers.* Portsmouth, NH: Teacher Ideas Press.

Galda, L. (1998). Readers, texts, and contexts: A response-based view of literature in the classroom. *The New Advocate, 1,* 92–102.

Golden, J. M., Meiners, A., & Lewis, S. (1992). The growth of story meaning. *Language Arts, 69,* 22–27.

Hancock, M. R. (2004). *A celebration of literature and response: Children, books, and teachers in K–8 classrooms* (2nd ed.). Upper Saddle River, NJ: Merrill/Prentice Hall.

Harste, J. C., Short, K. G., & Burke, C. (1988). *Creating classrooms for authors: The reading-writing connection.* Portsmouth, NH: Heinemann.

Hickman, J. (1980). Children's responses to literature: What happens in the classroom. *Language Arts, 57,* 524–529.

Hoyt, L. (1999). *Revisit, reflect, retell: Strategies for improving reading comprehension.* Portsmouth, NH: Heinemann.

Johnson, T. D., & Louis, D. R. (1987). *Literacy through literature.* Portsmouth, NH: Heinemann.

Jorgensen, K. (2001). *The whole story: Crafting fiction in the upper elementary grades.* Portsmouth, NH: Heinemann.

Krashen, S. (1993). *The power of reading: Insights from the research.* Englewood, CO: Libraries Unlimited.

Krashen, S. (2001). More smoke and mirrors: A critique of the National Reading Panel report on fluency. *Phi Delta Kappan, 83,* 119–123.

Lehr, S. S. (1991). *The child's developing sense of theme: Responses to literature.* New York: Teachers College Press.

Lukens, R. J. (2006). *A critical handbook of children's literature* (8th ed.). New York: Allyn & Bacon.

McKenna, M., & Stahl, S. (2003). *Assessment for reading instruction.* New York: Guilford Press.

Ohlhausen, M. M., & Jepsen, M. (1992). Lessons from Goldilocks: "Somebody's been choosing my books but I can make my own choices now!" *The New Advocate, 5,* 31–46.

O'Malley, J. M., & Pierce, L. V. (1996). *Authentic assessment for English language learners: Practical approaches for teachers.* Reading, MA: Addison-Wesley.

Peregoy, S. F., & Boyle, O. F. (2005). *Reading, writing, and learning in ESL: A resource book for K–12 teachers* (4th ed.). Boston: Allyn & Bacon.

Pilgreen, J. (2000). *The SSR handbook: How to organize and maintain a Sustained Silent Reading program.* Portsmouth, NH: Heinemann.

Rumelhart, D. (1975). Notes on a schema for stories. In D. G. Bobrow (Ed.), *Representation and understanding: Studies in cognitive science* (pp. 99–135). New York: Academic Press.

Samway, K. D., & McKeon, D. (1999). *Myths and realities: Best practices for language minority students.* Portsmouth, NH: Heinemann.

Schwartz, R. M. (2005). Decisions, decisions: Responding to primary students during guided reading. *The Reading Teacher, 58,* 436–443.

Smith, K. (2005). Enhancing the literature experience through deep discussions of character. In N. L. Roser & M. G. Martinez (Eds.), *What a character! Character study as a guide to literary meaning making in grades K–8* (pp. 124–132). Newark, DE: International Reading Association.

Spiegel, D. L. (1998). Reader response approaches and the growth of readers. *Language Arts, 76,* 41–48.

Von Sprecken, D., & Krashen, S. (1998). Do students read during sustained silent reading? *California Reader, 32*(1), 11–13.

Whitin, P. E. (1996). Exploring visual response to literature. *Research in the Teaching of English, 30,* 114–140.

Whitin, P. E. (2002). Leading into literature circles through the sketch-to-stretch strategy. *The Reading Teacher, 55,* 444–450.

Worthy, J., & Prater, K. (2002). "I thought about it all night": Readers theatre for reading fluency and motivation. *The Reading Teacher, 50,* 204–212.

Children's Book References

Allard, H. (1977). *Miss Nelson is missing!* Boston: Houghton Mifflin.

Avi. (2002). *Crispin: The cross of lead.* New York: Hyperion Books.

Brett, J. (1999). *Gingerbread baby.* New York: Putnam.

Bryan, A. (2003). *Beautiful blackbird.* New York: Atheneum.

Cooper, S. (1999). *King of shadows.* New York: Aladdin Books.

Curtis, C. P. (2000). *The Watsons go to Birmingham—1963.* New York: Delacorte.

Cushman, K. (1994). *Catherine, called Birdy.* New York: HarperCollins.

Cushman, K. (1996). *The ballad of Lucy Whipple.* New York: Clarion Books.

Cushman, K. (2003). *Rodzina.* New York: Clarion Books.

Danziger, P. (2006). *Amber Brown is not a crayon.* New York: Puffin Books.

Deedy, C. A. (2000). *The yellow star: The legend of King Christian X of Denmark.* Atlanta: Peachtree.

Demi. (2002). *King Midas: The golden touch.* New York: McElderry.

Dorros, A. (1991). *Abuela.* New York: Dutton.

Dorros, A. (1995). *Isla.* New York: Dutton.

Fleischman, P. (2004). *Seedfolks.* New York: HarperTrophy.

Galdone, P. (1972). *The three bears.* New York: Clarion Books.

Galdone, P. (1974). *Little red riding hood.* New York: McGraw-Hill.

Galdone, P. (2006). *The three little pigs.* New York: Clarion Books.

Gantos, J. (2000). *Joey Pigza loses control.* New York: Farrar, Straus & Giroux.

Gardiner, J. R. (2003). *Stone Fox.* New York: HarperTrophy.

George, J. C. (2005). *Julie of the wolves.* New York: HarperTrophy.

Gobel, P. (2002). *Mystic horse.* New York: HarperCollins.

Hamilton, V. (2000). *The girl who spun gold.* New York: Scholastic.

Henkes, K. (1991). *Chrysanthemum.* New York: Morrow.

Hesse, K. (2001). *Witness.* New York: Scholastic.

Hodges, M. (2002). *The boy who drew cats.* New York: Holiday House.

Hofmeyr, D. (2001). *The star-bearer: A creation myth from ancient Egypt.* New York: Farrar, Straus & Giroux.

Howe, D., & Howe, J. (2006). *Bunnicula: A rabbit-tale of mystery.* New York: Aladdin Books.

Hurd, T. (2003). *Moo cow kaboom!* New York: HarperCollins.

Hyman, T. S. (2000). *The sleeping beauty.* Boston: Little, Brown.

Kellogg, S. (1998). *Mike Fink.* New York: Aladdin Books.

Kimmel, E. A. (2000). *The runaway tortilla.* Delray Beach, FL: Winslow Press.

King-Smith, D. (2005). *Babe the gallant pig.* New York: Random House.

L'Engle, M. (2007). *A wrinkle in time.* Shoreham, VT: Square Fish.

Lewis, C. S. (2005). *The lion, the witch and the wardrobe.* New York: HarperCollins.

Lowry, L. (2005). *Number the stars.* New York: Yearling.

Lowry, L. (2006). *The giver.* Boston: Delacorte.

MacLachlan, P. (2004). *Sarah, plain and tall.* New York: HarperCollins.

Martin, B., Jr., & Archambault, J. (1998). *Chicka chicka boom boom.* New York: Simon & Schuster.

McCloskey, R. (2001). *Make way for ducklings.* New York: Viking.

McElligott, M. (2004). *Absolutely not!* New York: Walker.

Meddaugh, S. (1992). *Martha speaks.* Boston: Houghton Mifflin.

Naylor, P. R. (2000). *Shiloh.* New York: Aladdin Books.

Noble, T. H. (1992). *The day Jimmy's boa ate the wash.* New York: Dial Books.

Numeroff, L. J. (1985). *If you give a mouse a cookie.* New York: HarperCollins.

Park, L. S. (2001). *A single shard.* New York: Clarion Books.

Paterson, K. (2006). *Bridge to Terabithia.* New York: Harper-Collins.

Paulsen, G. (2006). *Hatchet.* New York: Aladdin Books.

Paye, W., & Lippert, M. H. (2002). *Head, body, legs: A story from Liberia.* New York: Holt.

Pinkney, J. (1999). *The ugly duckling.* New York: Morrow.

Pinkney, J. (2000). *Aesop's fables.* New York: North-South.

Pinkney, J. (2006). *The little red hen.* New York: Dial Books.

Potter, B. (2002). *The tale of Peter Rabbit.* New York: Warne.

Rowling, J. K. (1999). *Harry Potter and the chamber of secrets.* New York: Scholastic.

Rowling, J. K. (2007). *Harry Potter and the deathly hallows.* New York: Scholastic.

Scieszka, J. (1999). *The true story of the 3 little pigs!* New York: Viking.

Sendak, M. (2003). *Where the wild things are.* New York: HarperCollins.

Service, P. (1988). *Stinker from space.* New York: Scribner.

Shepard, A. (2001). *Master man: A tall tale of Nigeria.* New York: HarperCollins.

Speare, E. G. (2003). *The witch of Blackbird Pond.* Boston: Houghton Mifflin.

Speare, E. G. (2005). *The sign of the beaver.* New York: Yearling.

Steig, W. (1990). *Doctor De Soto.* New York: Farrar, Straus & Giroux.

Steig, J. (2001). *A gift from Zeus: Sixteen favorite myths.* New York: HarperCollins.

Steig, W. (2006). *Sylvester and the magic pebble.* New York: Aladdin Books.

Yolen, J. (1980). *Commander Toad in space.* New York: Coward, McCann.

Yorinks, A. (1986). *Hey, Al.* New York: Farrar, Straus & Giroux.

Young, E. (2004). *I, Doko: The tale of a basket.* New York: Philomel.

Van Allsburg, C. (1991). *The wretched stone.* Boston: Houghton Mifflin.

Viorst, J. (1987). *Alexander and the terrible, horrible, no good, very bad day.* New York: Atheneum.

White, E. B. (2006). *Charlotte's web.* New York: HarperCollins.

Woodson, J. (2003). *Locomotion.* New York: Putnam.

chapter ten

Reading and Writing Information

Mrs. LaRue's kindergartners are studying fish. The thematic unit began when the teacher brought in two goldfish to be class pets. The children were excited and immediately named them; they named the orange one Goldie and the white one Moon. So that the children would know how to care for them, the teacher read aloud *Pet Fish* (Nelson, 2002). After listening to the book, the class wrote about their new pets using interactive writing. The children usually write one sentence on chart paper, but because they had more to write, they wrote the first sentence interactively and then Mrs. LaRue wrote their dictated sentences. Here's their completed chart about "Our New Pets":

> *We have 2 goldfish named Goldie and Moon. We will take good care of them. We will feed them goldfish food and keep their bowl clean. We will look at them but not touch them.*

They posted the chart near the fish bowl and reread it each day. With practice, the children learned to pick out some familiar words on the chart, such as *we, good, goldfish, Goldie,* and *Moon.*

Can kindergartners read and write information?

Some teachers think that stories are more appropriate for young children and that reading and writing information should be postponed until the middle grades. Nothing could be further from the truth! Many kindergartners, especially boys, are very curious about science topics. In fact, they prefer to read and write about information. As you read this vignette, notice how Mrs. La Rue's students listened to informational books read aloud and wrote their own informational books.

Mrs. LaRue began a K-W-L chart at the beginning of the unit to record what the children knew about fish and what they wanted to learn. Looking for answers to their questions helped direct the children's attention as they participated in unit-related activities. Today, they are completing the right column of the chart about what they have learned. They have learned so much information to list on the chart that it takes Mrs. LaRue 30 minutes to write their dictated sentences. The completed chart is shown on page 314.

Mrs. LaRue has a text set of stories and informational books about fish that she has been reading aloud to the kindergartners, and she uses the books as springboards to language arts activities. The children are curious about the parts of a fish, so Mrs. LaRue shows them an illustration of a goldfish in *Fish: Pet Care Guides for Kids* (Evans & Caras, 2001), and they identify the fish's body parts—mouth, eyes, scales, gills, fins, tail. Afterward, she draws a picture of goldfish on chart paper, and the children use interactive writing to label the parts. Later, many of the children draw or paint their own pictures of fish, and Mrs. LaRue helps them label two or more body parts on their pictures.

Each day, Mrs. LaRue reads a story or informational book about fish. The kindergartners' favorite book is *The Rainbow Fish* (Pfister, 2002), the story of a vain and selfish fish who learns the value of friendship. The children talk about this book in a grand conversation, and later they draw pictures about their favorite part of the story and dictate a sentence for Mrs. LaRue to add to their pictures. The children share their pictures from the author's chair, and then the teacher binds the pictures into a book that's placed in the classroom library for children to "read."

The next day, this question is posted on their sign-in chart: *What did the rainbow fish learn?* The children choose from among these three answers: *To be selfish. To be a friend. To look pretty.* Mrs. LaRue reads the three possible answers to the first few children who ar-rive in the classroom, and then they read them to the next group and so on until everyone has signed in. The teacher uses the sign-in chart to check her students' comprehension as well as to take attendance and encourage socialization and sharing.

The children learn more about fish at learning centers. They spend 30 minutes each day working at centers. Mrs. LaRue has set up these eight centers in the classroom:

Science center   Children use magnifying glasses to observe the goldfish and draw pictures of them in their science journals. Charts about fish and several informational books about fish are also available for children to examine.

Book-making center   After reading Lois Ehlert's *Fish Eyes: A Book You Can Count On* (2001), the children make their own fish counting books. Some kindergartners make books to count to 5, and others with more interest in writing and knowledge about numbers make books to count to 10. They use a familiar sentence starter, "I see . . . ," and Mrs. LaRue has introduced the words *big* and *little*. Children choose a word card with one of the words to add to their sentence. They write the other words themselves with the assistance of a parent volunteer. One page from a child's book is shown in the box on the next page.

The Kindergartners' K-W-L Chart About Fish		
What We Know About Fish	What We Wonder About Fish	What We Learned About Fish
Fish live in water.	Are sharks fish?	Sharks are fish.
Fish can swim.	How does a fish breathe underwater?	Eels are fish.
Tuna is a fish.	How long does a fish live?	Sea horses are fish, too.
My Grandpa likes to fish.	Why don't fish have arms and legs?	Whales are not fish.
There are different kinds of fish.	Are whales fish?	Jellyfish and starfish are not fish either.
Fish are slippery if you hold them.	Where do fish live?	Fish breathe through gills.
You can eat fish.	Do fish sleep?	Fish live any place there is water.
Fish are pretty.	What do they eat?	Fish eat little animals they find in the water.
	Can fish hear me talk?	Fish eyes don't have eyelids.
		Fish swim by moving their tails.
		Fish will die if they are not in the water because they cannot breathe.
		Fish hatch from eggs in the water.
		Fish have all the colors of the rainbow.
		Fishes' skin is covered with scales.
		Yes, fish can hear.

A Page From a Child's Fish Counting Book

Listening center Children listen to cassette tapes of Dr. Seuss's *One Fish Two Fish Red Fish Blue Fish* (1960) and *Fish Is Fish* (Lionni, 2005) and follow along in individual copies of the books.

Storytelling center Children use storyboards (pictures from the story backed with cardboard and laminated) from *The Rainbow Fish* (Pfister, 2002) and puppets of the rainbow fish and other fish to retell the story and create new adventures for the rainbow fish.

Sequencing center Kindergartners arrange a set of life-cycle photos in order from egg to adult fish.

Sorting center Children sort picture cards of fish and other water animals and place the cards with pictures of fish in one pocket chart labeled "Fish," and pictures of other animals in the "Not Fish" pocket chart. Fish pictures include goldfish, swordfish, trout, shark, eel, catfish, and seahorse; other animal pictures include dolphin, octopus, crab, turtle, whale, jellyfish, lobster, sea otter, and starfish. Mrs. LaRue introduced this center after teaching that fish have backbones and breathe with gills. The children practiced identifying and sorting the picture cards with the teacher before working at the center.

Word work center Mrs. LaRue teaches phonemic awareness, phonics, and spelling lessons here. The children read and recite rhymes about fish, match objects that rhyme, such as *fish* and *dish,* and sort pictures and objects that begin with /f/, such as a fish, a fan, and a feather. They also write letters and words on dry-erase boards as Mrs. LaRue teaches handwriting skills at the same time she is teaching phonics and spelling.

Library center Children look at fish books from the text set. Each day, a fifth-grade student comes to help out at the center. This student rereads one of the books Mrs. LaRue has already read to interested children while other kindergartners look at books independently.

The highlight of the unit is the day that the children take a field trip to a nearby aquarium to observe the fish they've been learning about. Mrs. LaRue takes many photos with her digital camera, and when they get back to school, she prints out copies of the photos for the children to examine and talk about. Then each child chooses one photo to use in making a square for their fish quilt. They glue their photos to the center of 8 by 8-inch squares of light blue construction paper and add a sentence under the photo. Joshua dictates, "Sharks are very dangerous!" Miriam dictates, "I saw lots of shiny sardine fish." Anthony writes, "Jellyfish are beautiful but they're not fish." Some children dictate their sentence for Mrs. LaRue to write, and others write interactively with her assistance. Because these sentences will be read and reread, Mrs. LaRue emphasizes that they should be written with "grown-up" spelling so that everyone can read them. Finally, the kindergartners help the teacher place the photo squares on a bulletin board that she has covered with wrapping paper decorated with fish. They add a title: Our Field Trip to the Aquarium. The finished product is a paper quilt.

Now the unit is coming to an end. After finishing the K-W-L chart, the children work on their culminating project—a collaborative book about fish. Each child dictates one fact about fish, and Mrs. LaRue types their facts on the computer. Children then add a picture to illustrate their fact. Malisa's page is shown in the box below. The teacher compiles the pages, adds a cover, laminates the pages, and binds the book together. Everyone eagerly watches as Mrs. LaRue shares the book with the class, clapping with excitement after each page is read. The book is added to their classroom library, and children take turns checking out the book and taking it home to share with their families. Mrs. LaRue included three blank pages at the back of the book, and families write notes to the class on these pages, congratulating them on making such an informative book. These kindergartners are proud authors!

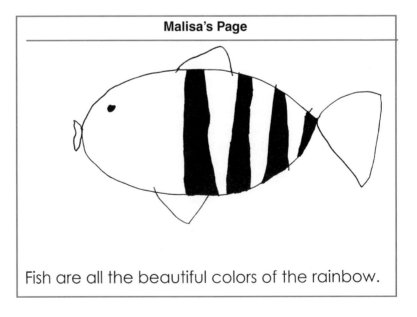

Malisa's Page

Fish are all the beautiful colors of the rainbow.

*C*hildren are curious about the world—why the dinosaurs became extinct, Neil Armstrong's moon landing, differences between warm- and cold-blooded animals, how to decipher secret codes, threats to the rain forest, why snakes shed their skins, and how skyscrapers are built—and nonfiction books provide this information. Years ago, most nonfiction books were written for children in grades 4–8, but now they're available for everyone, including emergent and struggling readers (Palmer & Stewart, 2003). Because so many high-quality nonfiction books are available today, teachers are stocking their classroom libraries with them, and they're incorporating more nonfiction into their instruction.

Research suggests that children understand and want to write informational texts (Palmer & Stewart, 2003; Read, 2001; Robb, 2004). Students often assume the efferent stance as they read informational books to locate facts, but they don't always do so (Rosenblatt, 2005). Many times, they pick up an informational book to check a fact, and then they continue reading—aesthetically, now—because they are fascinated by what they are reading. They get carried away in the book, just as they do when reading stories. At other times, students read books about topics they're interested in, and they read aesthetically, engaging in the lived-through experience of reading and connecting what they are reading to their own lives and prior reading experiences. Students also write informational books to share their excitement about what they're learning (Stead, 2002). The nonfiction trade books they have read serve as models for their writing, and they organize the information that they present using the same types of patterns or structures used in informational books (Freeman, 1991).

This chapter focuses on expository text, the type of writing used in informational books. As you continue reading, think about these questions:

- How do teachers develop students' knowledge about expository text?
- How can teachers facilitate students' reading of informational books?
- How can teachers facilitate students' writing of various types of informational texts, including reports and biographies?

LEARNING ABOUT INFORMATIONAL BOOKS

Children read informational books to explore the world. These books blend textual and visual information, and because they're visually appealing, children often pick them up to look at the photos and graphic presentations of information. They get excited about reading nonfiction books, and the good news is that they're able to understand these texts as well as they do stories (Kristo & Bamford, 2004). Informational books are more than just collections of facts, and once children start reading, they get interested in the topic and continue reading. They broaden their background knowledge through reading nonfiction books and become interested in learning more about content-area topics (Moss & Hendershot, 2002).

Types of Informational Books

If you browse in a children's bookstore or school library, you'll notice how many different types of nonfiction books there are. The simplest way to classify them is that books about specific people are biographies and autobiographies: Biographies are accounts of a person's life written by someone else, such *as Leonardo: Beautiful Dreamer* (Byrd, 2003), and autobiographies are written by the featured person. Many authors of children's books, including Gary Paulsen (1999, 2001), Stan and Jan Berenstain (2002), Tomie dePaola (2006), Lois Lowry (1998), and Dick King-Smith (2002), have written autobiographies that appeal to children who enjoy their books. In addition, many upper-grade students read Francisco Jiménez's moving books about his family's experiences as migrant farm workers, *The Circuit* (1997) and *Breaking Through* (2001). Other books about animals, places, and things are referred to simply as nonfiction. Figure 10–1 lists the types of informational books.

Many nonfiction books are concept books—they explore a topic, such as *Hurricanes* (Simon, 2003) or *Mosque* (Macaulay, 2003). When the concept is explored mainly using photos, the book is a photo essay. Others are arranged in special ways. For example, in alphabet books, such as *America: A Patriotic Primer* (Cheney, 2002), the information is organized around key words beginning with each letter of the alphabet. Information is organized sequentially in how-to books, and the question-and-answer format is used in others, including . . . *If You Lived When There Was Slavery in America* (Kamma, 2004). Journals and collections of letters, such as *Searching for Anne Frank: Letters From Amsterdam to Iowa* (Rubin, 2003), are informational books, too.

Multigenre Books Present Information Using More Than One Genre. The Magic School Bus series of science-related books, including *The Magic School Bus in the Rain Forest* (Cole, 1998), and the social studies–related books in the Ms. Frizzle's Adventures series, including *Ms. Frizzle's Adventures: Medieval Castle* (Cole, 2003), are the best-known multigenre books. The main text is presented as a narrative, and the side panels and other special boxes provide additional information. This information is presented as questions and answers, notes, and brief reports written by Ms. Frizzle's students as well as charts, maps, and other diagrams. *The 5,000-Year-Old Puzzle: Solving a Mystery of Ancient Egypt* (Logan, 2002) presents information about the discovery of King Tut's tomb through journal entries, photos, maps, postcards, sidebars, and newspaper articles. By using a combination of genres, the author and illustrator provide multiple viewpoints and enrich their presentation of information in the book. In *Leonardo: Beautiful Dreamer* (Byrd, 2003), boxes with notes, explanations, and excerpts from Leonardo da Vinci's own notes amplify the text. Multigenre books are richly layered texts, often presented in picture-book form. Because of the complexity of the page layout, Chapman and Sopko (2003) compare reading multigenre books to peeling an onion. They recommend that teachers read such books three or four times over a period of several days so that students can fully comprehend and appreciate them. First, they suggest taking a picture walk to examine the illustrations. Then teachers read the book, focusing on the informational text, and for the second reading, they focus on the narrative text. Finally, they focus on the sketches and borders. Of course, the number of rereadings depends on the students' interests and the complexity of the book.

Differences Between Stories and Informational Books. Stories and informational books are different; they're written and read differently. It's important that children learn about these differences so that they can recognize whether a book is a story or nonfiction in order to read it effectively. To examine these differences, pick up a story and a nonfiction book on the same topic; Mary Pope Osborne's popular Magic Tree House series, for example, includes both stories and accompanying nonfiction research

FIGURE 10–1

Types of Informational Books

Type	Description	Examples
Concept books	A topic is delineated using a combination of text and illustrations.	Ballard, C. (2004). *How we use water.* Cambridge, MA: Candlewick Press. (P–M) McWhorter, D. (2004). *A dream of freedom: The civil rights movement from 1954 to 1968.* New York: Scholastic. (U)
Photo essays	A photo display with minimal accompanying text.	Goodman, S. E. (2004). *Skyscraper: From the ground up.* New York: Knopf. (M) Sobol, R. (2004). *An elephant in the backyard.* New York: Dutton. (P–M)
Alphabet books	Facts are presented in alphabetical order.	Grodin, E. (2004). *D is for democracy: A citizen's alphabet.* Chelsea, MI: Sleeping Bear Press. (M)
Directions	The steps in making or doing something are described.	LaFosse, M. G. (2004). *Origami activities: Asian arts and crafts for creative kids.* North Clarendon, VT: Tuttle. (M–U)
Question-and-answer books	A question-and-answer format is used to share information.	Crisp, M. (2004). *Everything dolphin: What kids really want to know about dolphins.* Minnetonka, MN: NorthWord. (M)
Biographies	An account of a person's life, written by someone else.	Krull, K. (2004). *The boy on Fairfield Street: How Ted Geisel grew up to become Dr. Seuss.* New York: Random House. (M) Robinson, S. (2004). *Promises to keep: How Jackie Robinson changed America.* New York: Scholastic. (M–U)
Autobiographies	An account of a person's life, written by that person.	Weber, E. N. R. (2004). *Rattlesnake mesa: Stories from a Native American childhood.* New York: Lee & Low. (U)
Journals, letters, and speeches	A collection of documents.	Al-Windawi, T. (2004). *Thura's diary: My life in wartime Iraq.* New York: Viking. (U)
Reference books	A comprehensive collection of articles on a topic.	Ransford, S. (2004). *The Kingfisher illustrated horse and pony encyclopedia.* Boston: Kingfisher. (M–U)
Blended story/informational books	A book that combines narrative and expository elements.	Warren, A. (2004). *Escape from Saigon: How a Vietnam War orphan became an American boy.* New York: Farrar, Straus & Giroux. (U)

P = primary grades (K–2); M = middle grades (3–5); U = upper grades (6–8).

guides. The differences are easy to pick out when you read *Hour of the Olympics* (Osborne, 1998) and *Ancient Greece and the Olympics* (Osborne, 2004). Here is a list of differences that a class of fourth graders noticed after reading these two books:

- Informational books are true, but stories are invented.
- You can start reading anywhere in an informational book, but you read stories from beginning to end.

- Informational books have photos and drawings, but stories just have drawings.
- Informational books have a table of contents, but only some stories have it.
- Informational books have indexes at the back, but stories don't.
- Informational books have extra things: notes in the margin, highlighted words, pronunciation guides, and diagrams with labels.
- At the end of informational books, the author tells you how to learn more.

As they examine informational books, children learn how to use the special features to enhance their comprehension. They learn to use an index to locate specific information, to use diagrams and margin notes to learn more about topics presented in the regular text, and to notice the vocabulary terms that are highlighted in the text.

Why Use Informational Books? According to Kristo and Bamford (2004), the most compelling reason for using informational books is the impact that they have on students. As they read and listen to the teacher read informational books, students expand their background knowledge and enrich their vocabulary. Many of the words they're learning are academic English. The students often become more interested in reading and learning through nonfiction. Teachers notice that they participate more actively in class projects and show initiative in researching topics. More than just learning facts, students are often more motivated and better prepared for school success when they read informational books.

Expository Text Structures

Informational books are organized in particular ways called *expository text structures*. Five of the most common organizational patterns are *description, sequence, comparison, cause and effect,* and *problem and solution* (Meyer & Freedle, 1984). Figure 10–2 gives an overview of these patterns and lists informational books illustrating each one. Some informational books are organized around a single pattern, but often they use a combination of patterns. Gail Gibbons's picture book *Owls* (2006), for example, is basically a book that describes owls, their behavior, and their habitat (descriptive), but the book also includes information on their life cycle (sequence), different species (comparison), and environmental hazards threatening some species (cause and effect).

    🖘 *Description* Writers describe a topic by listing characteristics, features, and examples in this organizational pattern. Phrases such as *for example* and *characteristics are* cue this structure. When students delineate any topic, such as tigers, submarines, or Alaska, they use description.

    🖘 *Sequence* Writers list items or events in numerical or chronological order in this pattern. Cue words include *first, second, third, next, then,* and *finally.* Students use sequence to write directions for completing a math problem, the stages in an animal's life cycle, or events in a biography.

    🖘 *Comparison* Writers explain how two or more things are alike or different in this structure. *Different, in contrast, alike, same as,* and *on the other hand* are cue words and phrases that signal this structure. When students compare and contrast book and video versions of a story, reptiles and amphibians, or life in ancient Greece with life in ancient Egypt, they use this organizational pattern.

    🖘 *Cause and effect* Writers describe one or more causes and the resulting effect or effects in this pattern. *Reasons why, if . . . then, as a result, therefore,* and *because* are words and phrases that cue this structure. Explanations of why dinosaurs

FIGURE 10–2

The Expository Text Structures

Structure	Description	Examples
Description	A topic is delineated using attributes and examples.	Arnosky, J. (2002). *All about frogs.* New York: Scholastic. (P–M) Gibbons, G. (2007). *Vegetables we eat.* New York: Holiday House. (P) Simon, S. (2000). *Gorillas.* New York: HarperCollins. (M–U)
Sequence	Steps, events, or directions are presented in numerical or chronological order.	Hibbert, C. (2004). *The life of a grasshopper.* Chicago: Raintree. (P–M) Steltzer, U. (1995). *Building an igloo.* New York: Holt. (P–M) Zemlicka, S. (2004). *From fruit to jelly.* Minneapolis: Lerner. (P)
Comparison	Two or more things are compared or contrasted.	Markle, S. (1993). *Outside and inside trees.* New York: Bradbury Press. (M) Robinson, F. (1995). *Solid, liquid, or gas?* Chicago: Childrens Press. (P) Spier, P. (1991). *We the people.* New York: Doubleday. (M–U)
Cause and effect	Causes and the resulting effects are described.	Heller, R. (1999). *The reason for a flower.* New York: Grosset & Dunlap. (M) Lauber, P. (1995). *Who eats what? Food chains and food webs.* New York: HarperCollins. (M) Pfeffer, W. (2004). *Wiggling worms at work.* New York: HarperCollins. (P–M)
Problem and solution	A problem and one or more solutions are presented. Also includes question-and-answer format.	Allen, T. B. (2004). *George Washington, spymaster: How the Americans outspied the British and won the Revolutionary War.* Washington, DC: National Geographic Association. (M–U) Geisert, B. (1995). *Haystack.* Boston: Houghton Mifflin. (P) Schanzer, R. (2003). *How Ben Franklin stole the lightning.* New York: HarperCollins. (M)

became extinct, the effects of pollution on the environment, or the causes of the Civil War use the cause-and-effect pattern.

> ❧ ***Problem and solution*** Writers present a problem and offer one or more solutions in this expository structure. A variation is the question-and-answer format, in which the writer poses a question and then answers it. Cue words and phrases include *the problem is, the puzzle is, solve,* and *question . . . answer.* Students use this structure when they write about why money was invented, saving endangered animals,

and building dams to stop flooding. They often use the problem-solution pattern in writing advertisements and in other persuasive writing.

Graphic organizers can help students organize and visually represent ideas for the five organizational patterns. Students might use a cluster for description, a Venn diagram or T-chart for comparison, or a series of boxes and arrows for cause and effect (Yopp & Yopp, 2005). Most of the research on expository text structures has focused on older students' use of these patterns in reading; however, children also use the patterns and cue words in their writing (Raphael, Englert, & Kirschner, 1989).

Even though the expository text structures are used with informational texts, some books that are classified as stories also involve sequence, cause and effect, or one of the other expository text structures. Teachers can point out these structures or use graphic organizers to help students look more closely at the story. The popular *The Very Hungry Caterpillar* (Carle, 2002), for example, involves two sequences: Eric Carle uses sequence to show the development of the caterpillar from egg to butterfly and to list what the caterpillar ate each day. In *The Blue and the Gray* (2001), a story about the construction of a modern interracial community on the site of a Civil War battlefield, Eve Bunting contrasts the misery of the war with the harmony of the neighborhood. Bunting's Caldecott Medal book about the riots in Los Angeles, *Smoky Night* (1999), demonstrates cause and effect. Anger causes the riots, and the riots bring hope and understanding.

Teaching Students About Informational Books

Teachers infuse informational books into their classrooms and incorporate them into instruction throughout the school day. They read aloud informational books and often pair them with stories or with content-area textbooks. Teachers also teach students how to read and understand nonfiction and about the unique structures and features of these books.

Scott Cunningham/Merrill

Graphic Organizers

These second graders are working with their teacher to create a cluster to record information they are learning during a unit on animals. They are beginning the cluster after reading a book about different types of animal homes, and as they continue to read books and learn more about animal homes, they will add more information to the cluster. Later they will use the information on the cluster to make posters and write reports. Clusters and other graphic organizers are important note-taking tools for all students, even primary-grade students.

How to Read Informational Books. To take full advantage of informational books, students need to know how to read them and how to use their special features to locate information, how to read pages that combine textual and visual information, and how to use text structure to comprehend and remember what they've read. Kristo and Bamford (2004) call this "navigating" informational books. Teachers teach students how to navigate informational books through minilessons and demonstrations as they read books aloud.

Reading nonfiction begins in kindergarten; it shouldn't be postponed until students are older. Young children can distinguish fact from fiction and learn information from informational books that teachers read aloud (Richgels, 2002). Primary-grade teachers often use informational big books for read-alouds, and children are actively engaged in the reading experience. They listen intently, ask questions, share experiences, and notice nonfiction features in the text. In addition, the collections of leveled books that teachers use in guided reading in the primary grades include many nonfiction titles.

Teachers use the same reading process to read stories, informational books, and poems, but some of the activities vary because informational books are different from other types of texts and place different demands on readers. When students read informational books, activating and building their background knowledge and introducing key vocabulary words become more important. Teachers often spend more time during the prereading stage to ensure that students are prepared to begin reading. Students also examine the special features of nonfiction texts so that they're prepared to use the features as comprehension aids while they're reading.

During reading, the focus is on helping students identify and remember the big ideas. Sometimes students read an informational book one section at a time. They turn the heading of the section into a question to set a purpose for reading, and then they read to find the answer. Students often stop to discuss each section of text after they've read it, rather than reading the entire book before talking about it. Their discussions are instructional conversations, not grand conversations.

After reading, the focus is on deepening students' understanding of the big ideas. They reread sentences with the big ideas, add vocabulary to the word wall, complete graphic organizers to emphasize the relationships among the big ideas, draw visual representations of the big ideas, and create projects to apply what they've learned.

Examining Expository Text Structures. Just as teachers teach students about the elements of story structure, they point out how authors structure informational books. When students recognize the five expository text structures in books they are reading, they are better able to comprehend what they are reading, and when they structure their own informational writing according to these structures, the writing is easier to understand. Research over the past 20 years has confirmed the importance of teaching students to recognize expository text structures as an aid to reading comprehension and to improve writing effectiveness (Harvey, 1998; Robb, 2003).

Many informational books are clearly organized using one of the expository text structures, and students can identify the pattern because it is signaled by the title, topic sentences, or cue words. Other books, however, use a combination of two or more structures or may have no apparent structure at all. Sometimes the title of a book incorrectly signals an organizational pattern. When the book doesn't have a clear structure or falsely signals a structure, students are likely to have trouble

Planning for Instruction

What Students Need to Learn About Informational Books

Topics

Procedures	Concepts	Strategies and Skills
Expository Text Structures Topics		
Make clusters	Description	Vary reading according to purpose
Make Venn diagrams	Sequence	Locate information in resources
Make flowcharts	Comparison	Interpret information
	Cause and effect	Identify expository text structures
	Problem and solution	Note cue words
		Use graphic organizers
Report-Writing Topics		
Read charts, diagrams, and maps	Reports versus stories	Design questions
Make K-W-L charts	Alphabet books	Gather information
Draw clusters	Introductions	Organize information
Draw diagrams	Big ideas	Take a stand
Write data charts	Conclusions	Summarize
	Transitions	
Draw time lines		
Make cubes		

 I invite you to learn more about reading and writing information by visiting MyEducationLab. To see how first graders create a chart about the ocean food chain, go to the topic "Visually Representing" and click on the video "Graphic Organizers."

comprehending and remembering big ideas. Whenever there isn't a clear structure, teachers should provide one through the purpose they set for reading the book.

As teachers share informational books with students, they teach them to identify the expository text structures. Being able to identify the expository structures is not the goal, but when students recognize how a text is structured, they're better able to comprehend what they're reading. Similarly, students learn to diagram each expository text structure using a specific graphic organizer so they'll be able to use

Minilesson

Mr. Uchida Teaches His Fifth Graders How to Write Data Charts

1 Introduce the topic

Mr. Uchida's fifth graders are preparing to write state reports. They have each chosen a state to research, and they developed a list of five research questions:

Who are the people in the state?
What are the physical features of the state?
What are the key events in the state's history?
What is the economy of the state?
What places should you visit in the state?

Mr. Uchida explains that students need to collect information to answer each of these five questions, and he has a neat tool to use to collect the data: It's called a *data chart*.

2 Share examples

Mr. Uchida shares three sample data charts that his students made to collect information for their state reports last year. He unfolds the large sheets of white construction paper that have been folded into many cells or sections. Each cell is filled with information. The students examine the data charts and read the information in each cell.

3 Provide information

Mr. Uchida folds a clean sheet of construction paper into four rows and five columns to create 20 cells. Then he unfolds the paper, shows it to the students, and counts the 20 cells. He explains how he folded the paper and traces over the folded lines so that students can see the cells.

Then he writes the five research questions in the cells in the top row. He explains that students will write the information they locate to answer each question in the cells under that question. He demonstrates how to paraphrase information and take notes in the cells.

4 Supervise practice

Mr. Uchida passes out large sheets of white construction paper and assists students as they divide the sheet into 20 cells and write the research questions in the top row. Then the fifth graders begin to take notes using resources they have collected. Mr. Uchida circulates in the classroom, helping students to locate information and take notes.

5 Reflect on learning

After several days, Mr. Uchida brings the class together to check on the progress students are making with their data charts. Students show their partially completed charts and talk about their data collection. They ask what to do when they can't find information or when the information won't all fit into one box. Several students comment that they know how they will use their data charts when they begin writing their reports: They will use all the information in one column for one chapter of the report. They are amazed to have made this discovery!

the structure to help them pick out the main ideas when they are reading. This knowledge pays off as well when students are writing: They apply what they have learned as they organize their writing.

Minilessons. Teachers present minilessons about the five expository text structures and show students how to use the organizational patterns to improve their reading comprehension as well as to organize their writing. A list of minilesson topics related to expository text structures is presented on the preceding page.

RESEARCHING AND WRITING REPORTS

Isn't researching too difficult for children? Not according to Paula Rogovin (2001), who points out that children are naturally inquisitive. They enthusiastically pursue special interests and show genuine engagement with learning as they participate in research workshop. They identify an important question that drives the research (McMackin & Siegel, 2002). Asking and answering questions seem to be as empowering for children as for adults and help children become more thoughtful adults. As children explore topics they're passionate about and search for answers to questions that puzzle them, they learn the inquiry process. Their understanding of the world deepens as they uncover answers, write reports, and share what they've learned with classmates (Harvey, 1998).

Visual Reports

Students can report the answers they've found in charts, maps, flowcharts, and other diagrams (Stead, 2006). Visual reports are used when the information can be presented more effectively through a diagram than through a written report. Formats for visual reports include clusters, diagrams, data charts, maps, time lines, and cubes. Moline (1995) explains that visual presentations are sophisticated, multilayered reports. At first thought, these formats might seem easier to produce than written reports, but if they are done properly, they're just as challenging.

The diagrams used for visual reports can be used as learning tools as well as for reports. When students make a flowchart in their learning logs, for example, they are using the flowchart as a graphic organizer to better understand a concept they're learning. Students' diagrams are quickly sketched when they are being used as part of the learning process. In contrast, when students use diagrams for visual reports, they use the writing process to draft, revise, edit, and make a final copy. As reports, visual reports are as formal as other types of reports.

As students develop their visual reports, they consider the layout, how the words and drawings are integrated, and the typography, the type styles they use to communicate meaning (Moline, 1995). As they plan their layout, students consider the arrangement of the diagram on the page; the use of lines, boxes, and headings to organize information; and the drawings and colors to highlight key points. Students also consider how they use type styles: They might print some words in all capital letters or highlight key terms, or they might choose a type style for the title that emphasizes the concept. For example, when students make a visual report on ancient Egypt, they use a type style that resembles hieroglyphics for the title. Word processing programs allow students to experiment with a variety of fonts and to use italics and boldface to add emphasis.

Two types of visual reports are *clusters* and *cubes*. Clusters are weblike diagrams that students use to gather and organize information (Bromley, Irvin-Devitis, Hires, 1999; Rico, 1983). The topic is written in a circle centered on a sheet of paper or poster. Main ideas are written on rays drawn out from the circle, and branches with details and examples are added to complete each main idea.

Two clusters are presented in Figure 10–3. The top cluster was developed by a sixth-grade teacher during a thematic unit on birds. The purpose of the cluster was to assist students in categorizing birds such as cardinals, penguins, vultures,

How Do English Learners Use Writing as a Learning Tool?

Writing is a learning tool for all students, and it's an essential tool for helping English learners remember the big ideas and important details that they've read in informational books. Students are more apt to understand connections among big ideas when they write about them, both in learning logs and through projects. Peregoy and Boyle (2005) recommend that teachers have English learners use writing to facilitate learning in these ways: write in learning logs, conduct research, and create projects. They've found that even young English learners can use writing as a learning tool and to report their learning.

Writing in Learning Logs

As English learners make entries in learning logs, they use the technical vocabulary that teachers have introduced and posted on word walls. They learn the meanings of these words and how to spell them. They practice stringing words together and manipulating sentences to clarify and extend the meaning. As they write, students summarize the big ideas they're learning, make connections to their background knowledge and personal experiences, and think about ways to apply the information. Sometimes students self-select topics for journal entries, but teachers often provide prompts to direct students' attention to the big ideas and technical vocabulary words.

Conducting Research

English learners often participate in small groups to conduct research on nonfiction topics related to thematic units. Like their classmates, English learners should select and shape their own research topics. They work together to learn about a topic using informational books, the Internet, and other classroom resources. The benefit of working together with their classmates is that English learners can share the work and learn from each other. Students use writing as they take notes and record information on graphic organizers and drawings.

Creating Projects

English learners create projects to share the results of their research. They can work with classmates to create traditional written reports, but multigenre reports are often more successful because they integrate written and visual reports of information. Peregoy and Boyle (2005) suggest that English learners create photo essays by organizing a set of photographs into a useful sequence and adding captions. Or, students can draw a series of pictures and use them in creating a pictorial essay. Afterward, students do brief oral presentations to share their projects with classmates.

All three of these ways to use writing as a learning tool are effective because they encourage students to think about the big ideas they're studying. As an added benefit, teachers can monitor students' writing to assess what they understand.

FIGURE 10–3

Two Clusters About Birds

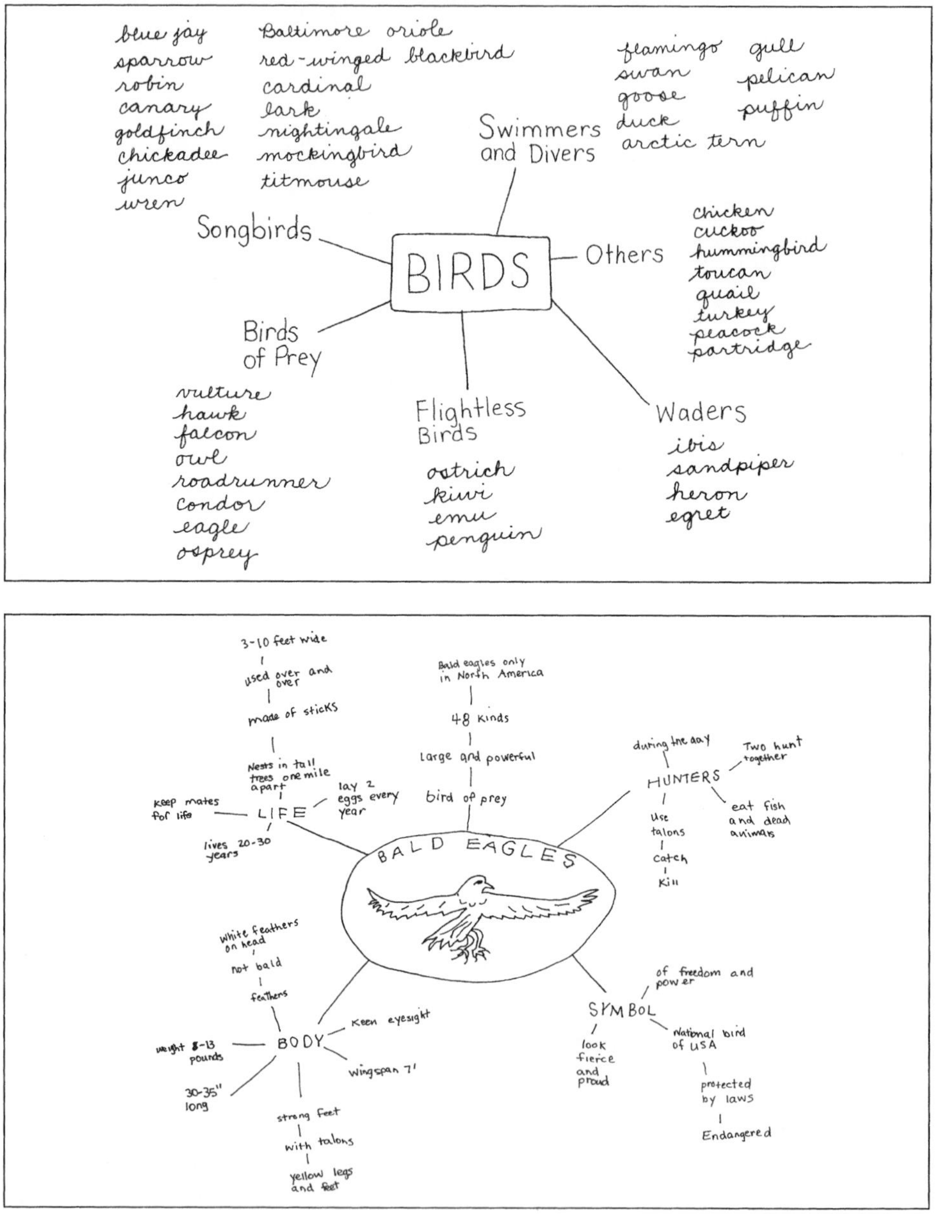

Songbirds: blue jay, sparrow, robin, canary, goldfinch, chickadee, junco, wren, Baltimore oriole, red-winged blackbird, cardinal, lark, nightingale, mockingbird, titmouse

Swimmers and Divers: flamingo, swan, goose, duck, arctic tern, gull, pelican, puffin

Others: chicken, cuckoo, hummingbird, toucan, quail, turkey, peacock, partridge

Birds of Prey: vulture, hawk, falcon, owl, roadrunner, condor, eagle, osprey

Flightless Birds: ostrich, kiwi, emu, penguin

Waders: ibis, sandpiper, heron, egret

BIRDS

BALD EAGLES

LIFE: 3-10 feet wide, used over and over, made of sticks, Nests in tall trees one mile apart, keep mates for life, lives 20-30 years, lay 2 eggs every year

Bald eagles only in North America, 48 kinds, large and powerful, bird of prey

HUNTERS: during the day, Two hunt together, eat fish and dead animals, use talons, catch, kill

BODY: white feathers on head, not bald, feathers, weight 8-13 pounds, 30-35" long, strong feet with talons, yellow legs and feet, keen eyesight, wingspan 7'

SYMBOL: of freedom and power, National bird of USA, look fierce and proud, protected by laws, Endangered

chickens, and ducks. As the class talked about the categories, students wrote the names of examples beside each category to complete the cluster. Later in the unit, students each chose one bird to research, and then they presented the results of their research in cluster form. The bottom cluster presents the results of one student's research on bald eagles. The information in the cluster is divided into four categories: life, hunters, symbol, and body; other, more general, information is listed at the top of the figure.

Cubing is a useful procedure for thematic units; middle- and upper-grade students can cube topics such as Antarctica, the United States Constitution, tigers or other endangered animals, the Underground Railroad, and the Nile River. In cubing, students explore a topic they have studied from six dimensions or viewpoints (Neeld, 1990). The name *cubing* comes from the fact that cubes have six sides and students explore the topic from six perspectives in this activity:

🖋 *Description.* Students describe the topic, including its colors, shapes, and sizes.

🖋 *Comparison.* Students compare the topic to something else. They consider how it is similar to or different from this other thing.

🖋 *Association.* Students associate the topic to something else and explain why the topic makes them think of this other thing.

🖋 *Analysis.* Students analyze the topic and tell how it is made or what it is composed of.

🖋 *Application.* Students apply the topic and tell how it can be used or what can be done with it.

🖋 *Argumentation.* Students argue for or against the topic. They take a stand and list reasons to support it.

The steps in cubing are described in the Step by Step feature below.

What's especially valuable about cubing is that students apply the information they've been learning about a topic in new ways as they analyze, associate, and consider the other perspectives. Figure 10–4 presents a cubing written by small groups of fifth graders at the end of a thematic unit on the American Revolution.

--- Cubing ---

Step by Step

1 Choose a topic. Students choose a familiar topic related to a social studies or science unit.

2 Examine the topic from each perspective. Students divide into six small groups, and each group examines the topic from one of the perspectives.

3 Draft a paragraph. Students brainstorm ideas and use them to develop a paragraph that explores the perspective.

4 Share drafts with the class. Students read their paragraphs to the class, and classmates react to the ideas and novel connections they've made and suggest possible revisions.

5 Revise and edit the paragraphs. Students revise, edit, and then make a final copy of their paragraphs.

6 Construct the cube. Students attach the final copies of their paragraphs to a box or cube.

7 Display the cube. Students display the cube in the classroom.

FIGURE 10–4

A Cubing on the American Revolution

Describe	The American Revolution was fought from 1775 to 1783 between Britain's Lobster Backs and the young American patriots. From the first major battle of Bunker Hill in 1775 to the battle of Yorktown in 1781, there were many hardships and deaths. The brave Americans continued on in spite of Britain's better supplied army because they wanted freedom, justice, and independence from King George.
Compare	The American Revolution and the Civil War were alike in many ways. They were both fought on American soil. Both wars were fought for people's rights and freedoms. With families fighting against families, these wars were very emotional. The winning side of each war had commanding generals who became presidents of the United States: George Washington and Ulysses S. Grant. The soldiers in the war rallied to the song "Yankee Doodle."
Associate	We celebrate the American Revolution on the 4th of July with fireworks and parades. Fireworks are spectacular things for spectacular days! Rockets shoot into the air like cannonballs! Great big booms and sparkles fall from the sky as people celebrate! Parades remind us of soldiers marching into battle led by flutes, drums, and flags! The 4th of July is a celebration of history.
Analyze	The American Revolution began when King George taxed the colonists too much and did not ask them if they wanted to pay or not. In five years, the Stamp Act, the Townsend Act, the Quartering Act, and the Intolerable Acts were forced on the colonists. This money was to pay for the French and Indian War. This made the colonists angry. One time the colonists dressed up like Indians and threw tea into the Boston Harbor. King George kept on pushing until the colonists revolted and started a war.
Apply	The most important outcome of the American Revolution was the beginning of our 200-year-old country. We enjoy the freedom of speech, religion, and the press. The Constitution grants us a lot of other freedoms, too. This living document has given us the opportunity to be anything we want to be.
Argue for	If we had not fought and won the American Revolution, there would be no United States of America. We would not have the right to speak our minds. We might all have to go to the same church. We would not have freedom or equality. There would be no Liberty Bell or Statue of Liberty. Although war is scary, painful, and violent, if we had the chance to go back, we would go and fight with all our might. We would rather do math problems all day than be ruled by a king.

"All About . . ." Books

Children write or dictate "All About . . . " books on a single topic. Usually one piece of information and an illustration appear on each page. A second grader wrote the "All About . . . " book, "Snowy Thoughts," shown in Figure 10–5, as part of a unit on the four seasons. Even though the child omitted some capital letters and punctuation

FIGURE 10–5

A Second Grader's "All About . . ." Book

John - David

Snowy Thoughts

the best thing about Snow is a Snon man

When it stats to Snow I think about having a snow ball fight

When its Snowing I like to play With my brother.

My favorite Swon-day food is hot sup.

marks and used invented spelling for a few words in his book, the information can be easily deciphered.

Young children can dictate reports to their teacher, who serves as scribe to record them. After listening to a guest speaker, viewing a film, or reading several books about a particular topic, kindergartners and first graders can dictate brief reports. A class of kindergartners compiled this book-length report on police officers:

Page 1: *Police officers help people who are in trouble. They are nice to kids. They are only mean to robbers and bad people. Police officers make people obey the laws. They give tickets to people who drive cars too fast.*

Page 2: *Men and women can be police officers. They wear blue uniforms like Officer Jerry's. But sometimes police officers wear regular clothes when they work undercover. They wear badges on their uniforms and on their hats. Officer Jerry's badge number is 3407. Police officers have guns, handcuffs, whistles, sticks, and two-way radios. They have to carry all these things.*

Page 3: *Police officers drive police cars with flashing lights and loud sirens. The cars have radios so the officers can talk to other police officers at the police station. Sometimes they ride on police motorcycles or on police horses or in police helicopters or in police boats.*

Page 4: *Police officers work at police stations. The jail for the bad people that they catch is right next door. One police officer sits at the radio to talk to the police officers who are driving their cars. The police chief works at the police station, too.*

Page 5: *Police officers are your friends. They want to help you so you shouldn't be afraid of them. You can ask them if you need some help.*

Page 6: *How We Learned About Police Officers for Our Report*

    1. We read these books:
       Police *by Ray Broekel*
       What Do They Do? Policemen and Firemen *by Carla Greene*
    2. We interviewed Officer Jerry.
    3. We visited the police station.

The teacher read two books aloud to the children, and Officer Jerry visited the classroom and talked to the class about his job. The children also took a field trip to the police station. The teacher took photos of Officer Jerry, his police car, and the police station to illustrate the report. With this background, the children and the teacher together developed a cluster with these five main ideas: what police officers do, what equipment police officers have, how police officers travel, where police officers work, and police officers are your friends. The children added details to each main idea until each one developed into one page of the report. The background of experiences and the clustering activity prepared children to compose their report. After they completed the report, included a bibliography called "How We Learned About Police Officers for Our Report," and inserted the photographs, it was ceremoniously presented to the school library to be enjoyed by all students in the school.

Collaborative Reports

An effective way to introduce report writing is to write a collaborative report. The teacher presents a broad "umbrella" topic, and then students brainstorm subtopics and identify questions related to them. Students choose questions, and those who are interested in the same questions gather in small groups to work together. Before they begin working, however, the teacher chooses one of the questions that no one chose and the class researches that question and writes the answer collaboratively. Then the groups work together to research their questions and write their sections of the report. Afterward, the teacher collects the completed sections, compiles them, and makes copies for each student. The steps are listed in the Step by Step feature below.

A class of second graders researched crabs as part of a thematic unit about the seashore. First they wrote this chapter as a collaborative report:

How Are Crabs Like Us?

We don't look anything like crabs, but we are alike in some ways. The most important thing is that crabs and people are both alive. Crabs eat, but they eat different food than we do. Crabs have arms but they look different. They have pincers instead of fingers. They have legs, but they have 6 more legs than we do. We can walk, run, and swim, and that's what crabs can do.

Collaborative Reports

1 Choose a question. Teachers identify an "umbrella" topic, and then students identify related questions to research.

2 Model how to write a section. The teacher chooses a different question to research and works with students to gather information, organize it in a graphic organizer, and write the section of the report on chart paper. Often the teacher takes the students' dictation to speed up the process.

3 Gather and organize information. Students working in small groups research their questions using books, the Internet, and other resources. They take notes and organize the information in a graphic organizer.

4 Write the sections. Students write and refine their sections using the writing process. Then the class comes together and reads the entire report aloud, checking for errors or redundancies. Finally, students word-process the final copy of their sections.

5 Compile the report. Students compile their sections, and as a class, they design the cover, make the title page and table of contents, and compile the bibliography.

6 Publish the report. The teacher duplicates and binds a copy for each student.

Then the second graders divided into small groups and wrote answers to these questions:

Where Do Crabs Live?

Crabs live in lots of different places. Some crabs live in shallow pools. They also like to live under the sand and in the ocean. Each place is just perfect for the crabs to live and grow.

How Do Crabs Move?

Crabs have eight legs. There are four on each side. We think that so many legs probably makes it hard to move. Crabs don't walk or run like we do. They actually move sideways.

Do You Know Why Crabs Have Pincers?

Crabs have two claws called pincers. They use their pincers to catch food, and they use their pincers to fight predators like seagulls. The pincers are powerful.

How Do Crabs Grow?

Crabs have hard shells. They grow and grow inside their shells. When they outgrow their shells, crabs shed it and grow a new one.

Can Crabs Grow New Legs?

Yes! Crabs really can grow new legs. They can get new claws and new antennas, too. So if an animal bites off their leg, crabs grow new ones. They are small at first but they keep growing until they are normal. It's just remarkable!

Students can organize reports in a variety of formats—formats they see used in informational books. One possibility is a question-and-answer format; another possibility is an alphabet book. A group of fourth-grade students wrote an alphabet book about the California missions, with one page for each letter of the alphabet. The "U" page appears in Figure 10–6.

Individual Reports

After students learn to conduct research and share what they learn in a collaborative report, they're ready to write individual reports. Writing an individual report is similar to writing a collaborative report, except that students assume the entire responsibility themselves. To begin, students identify several research questions or an umbrella question with several subtopics, and then they research the answers. Each question and answer usually becomes a chapter in the report. Students use a variety of techniques as they conduct research: They interview experts, collect data through surveys, conduct experiments, make observations, consult Internet sources, and read

FIGURE 10–6

The "U" Page From an Alphabet Book on California Missions

Some of the Indians thought life was UNBEARABLE at the missions. They thought this because they couldn't hunt or do the things they were used to. Once they were at the missions they couldn't leave. They were sometimes beaten if they did.

informational books (Kristo & Bamford, 2004). They learn to choose the techniques that are most appropriate for their questions (Harvey, 1998).

As students consult the books and other resources, they collect lots of information that they need to remember. Students often use self-stick notes to mark important information in books as they're reading. Then they go back and write short phrases, usually paraphrasing the information, on note cards, or they complete graphic organizers. They don't try to take notes about everything they read, only about the big ideas. In addition, they're careful not to get distracted by other interesting information in the resources they're reading.

Next, students need to create categories to organize it. Choosing an appropriate organizational structure is important because it's reflected in the students' writing. The structure also influences which information is most important. Sometimes students complete graphic organizers, design charts, or write informal outlines.

As students begin to draft, they write sentences and paragraphs to present the information they collected. They also think about which special features to include to aid readers, such as chapter titles and headings. As they write, they summarize and synthesize the big ideas, being careful to distinguish between fact and opinion. They write leads to engage readers and summarize the big ideas in the conclusion. Students also create visuals to display other information, and sometimes they identify additional information to highlight in sidebars (Kristo & Bamford, 2004).

When students revise their rough drafts, their first concern is whether they've answered their questions. They share their rough drafts with classmates and get feedback on how well they're communicating. They also double-check their notes to ensure the accuracy of their information and statistics, add details, revise their leads, and check transitions. Next, students finish the writing process by editing their reports to correct misspelled words, capitalization and punctuation errors, and nonstandard English usage.

Students usually word-process the final copies of their reports, and they carefully format them, taking advantage of what they know about nonfiction features. They include a title page, a table of contents, chapter titles, illustrations with captions, photos downloaded from the Internet, a bibliography, and an index. They compile the pages and bind them into a book or display them on a chart. The steps in writing individual reports are reviewed in the Step by Step feature below.

A fourth-grade class began a unit on birds by brainstorming questions they wanted to answer. The teacher encouraged them to search for answers in the books they had checked out of the school and community libraries and during an interview with an ornithologist from the local zoo. Once they learned the answers to their

-------- Individual Reports --------

1 Choose a topic. Students choose a topic for a report that's related to a thematic unit, hobby, or other interest.

2 Design research questions. Students brainstorm a list of questions related to the topic that they'd like to research. They review the list, combine some questions, delete others, and finally arrive at four to six questions that they think they can answer and that will be interesting to readers.

3 Gather and organize information. Students read books, consult Internet sources, and use other resources to gather information, and then they use graphic organizers to organize information they've collected.

4 Draft the report. Students write a rough draft using the information they've gathered. Each research question becomes a section or a chapter in students' reports.

5 Revise and edit the report. Students meet in writing groups to share their rough drafts, and then they make revisions based on the feedback they receive from their classmates. Afterward, they proofread and correct mechanical errors in their reports.

6 Publish the report. Students recopy their reports in book format and add illustrations, a title page, a table of contents, and bibliographic information.

FIGURE 10–7

An Excerpt From a Fourth Grader's Report on Egrets

How to Recognize an Egret!

An egret is a bird with white feathers. Some egrets have black and red feathers but the egrets around Marysville are white. They have very long necks and long beaks because they stick their heads under water to catch fish. An egret can be from 20 to 41 inches tall. When they are just standing, they look like in the picture but when they are flying their wing spand can stretch to one-and-a-half feet.

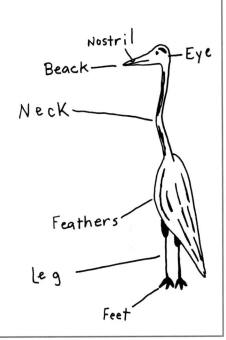

questions, the students were eager to share their new knowledge and decided to write reports and publish them as books. Each student's book began with a table of contents and contained four or five chapters, a glossary, a bibliography, and an index. An excerpt from a fourth grader's book on egrets is presented in Figure 10–7. The text was word processed, and then the student added the illustrations.

Multigenre Projects

A new approach to report writing is the multigenre project (Allen, 2001; Romano, 2000), in which students explore a topic through several genres. Tom Romano (1995) explains, "Each genre offers me ways of seeing and understanding that others do not" (p. 109). Grierson, Anson, and Baird (2002) explain that "research comes alive when students explore a range of alternate genres instead of writing the traditional research report" (p. 51). Students collect a variety of informational materials, including books, textbooks, Internet articles, charts, diagrams, and photos, and then they study the materials. Students write several pieces, including essays, letters, journal entries, stories, and poems; collect photos, charts, and other visual representations; and compile them in a book or display them on a poster. For example, for a multigenre project on the planet Mars, students might include the following pieces:

- An informational essay describing the planet
- A data chart comparing Mars to other planets taken from an informational book students have read

- A photograph of the planet downloaded from the NASA website
- A found poem about Mars with words and phrases taken from a book students have read
- A simulated journal written from the perspective of an astronaut who is exploring the planet

Through these five pieces, students present different kinds of information about the planet, and the project is much more complete than it would have been with just one genre. The LA Essentials box on the next page lists different genres that can be used for multigenre projects.

Teaching Students to Write Reports

For students to become capable researchers, teachers need to establish a climate of inquiry in their classrooms and teach students how to conduct research and write reports. They scaffold students' first report-writing experiences to help them develop the knowledge, strategies, and skills to be successful. Perry and Drummond (2002) describe this process as moving from teacher-regulated to student self-regulated report writing. They have identified these characteristics of classrooms that promote responsible, independent writers:

- The classroom is a community of learners where students collaborate and cooperate with classmates.
- Students are involved in meaningful research activities that require them to think strategically and reflectively.
- Students increasingly assume responsibility for their learning by making choices, dealing constructively with challenges, and evaluating their work.
- The evaluation emphasizes both research and the writing process that students use as well as the quality of their finished products.
- The teacher scaffolds students' learning by providing direct instruction about doing research, modeling the process, having students do research in groups, and gradually releasing responsibility to the students to work independently.

It's essential that teachers establish a climate of inquiry in their classrooms and teach students how to conduct research and write reports rather than just assigning students to write reports as homework. Nor is it enough for students to complete one research project during the school year.

The Inquiry Process. Inquiry is a way of learning (Berghoff, Egawa, Harste, & Hoonan, 2000). Students use the inquiry process as they ask questions and collect information to answer their questions in preparation for writing reports and sharing learning (McMackin & Siegel, 2002). Here are the steps:

1. *Questioning:* Students identify a question that interests them to research.
2. *Planning:* Students think about how they will be able to find answers to their questions. They identify people to interview, plan surveys and observations, and locate books, magazine articles, and Internet resources to use.
3. *Collecting:* Students gather information from a variety of resources and organize the information using a graphic organizer or outline.
4. *Synthesizing:* Students combine the big ideas to create a coherent report or other project.

GENRES FOR MULTIGENRE PROJECTS

Bibliography	Students list the resources they consulted in preparing the paper or poster or list suggested readings related to a topic.
Biographical sketch	Students write a biographical sketch of a person related to the topic being studied.
Cartoons	Students draw a cartoon or copy a published cartoon from a book or Internet article.
Clusters	Students draw clusters or other diagrams to display information concisely.
Cubes	Students examine a topic from six perspectives.
Data charts	Students create a data chart to list and compare information.
Found poems	Students collect words and phrases from a book or article and arrange them to make a poem.
Graffiti	Students write words and draw designs to represent the topic visually.
Letters	Students write simulated letters or make copies of real letters related to the topic.
Lifelines	Students draw lifelines and mark important dates related to a person's life.
Maps	Students make copies of actual maps or draw maps related to the topic.
Newspaper articles	Students make copies of actual newspaper articles or write simulated articles related to the topic.
Open-mind portraits	Students draw open-mind portraits of people related to the topic.
Photos	Students download photos from the Internet or make copies of photos in books.
Quotes	Students collect quotes about the topic from materials they are reading.
Simulated journals	Students write simulated-journal entries from the viewpoint of a person related to the topic.
Sketch-to-stretch	Students make sketch-to-stretch drawings to emphasize the theme or key points related to the topic.
Stories	Students write stories related to the topic.
Time lines	Students draw time lines to sequence events related to the topic.
Venn diagrams	Students draw Venn diagrams to compare the topic with something else.
Word wall	Students make an alphabetized word wall of key words related to the topic.

5. *Evaluating:* Students examine their reports to judge the accuracy of their information, the completeness of their answers, and the effectiveness of their writing.
6. *Reporting:* Students share their completed reports with classmates and other audiences.

This process, which is similar to the writing process, nurtures students' curiosity, promotes questioning, and develops students' ownership of their research projects.

Plagiarism isn't a big problem when students use the inquiry process, but they still need to understand what plagiarism is and why it's wrong. Students are less likely to plagiarize because they've collected information to answer questions that they care about, and because they have developed their compositions step by step—from prewriting and drafting to revising and editing. The two best ways to avoid having students copy from another source and pass it off as their own are to teach the inquiry process and to have students write reports at school using the writing process rather than assigning reports as homework.

Research Workshop. Research workshop is a 60- to 90-minute period where students identify questions and conduct research to find answers to the questions they've posed. It's a unique combination of reading workshop and writing workshop that can fit into all the patterns of practice, as shown in the box below. Sometimes students choose questions that interest them; at other times, research workshop is connected to thematic units. In this case, the teacher identifies an umbrella topic, and students choose subtopic questions. In addition to providing a large chunk of time for students to read, research, and write, teachers teach minilessons on research procedures and model how to do research as the class works together on collaborative projects. At the end of the workshop, students come together as a class to share what they've been working on and what they've learned.

When Rogovin (2001) conducts research workshops, she chooses broad topics, such as people at work or immigration, for her students to study, and then they choose subtopics, ask questions, and do research in small groups. The students collect information and share what they've learned by writing reports and giving oral

How Research Workshop Fits Into the Four Patterns of Practice

Literature Focus Units

After the students read a featured book during a literature focus unit, they may then participate in research workshop to learn more about the historical period in which the book was set or another related topic.

Literature Circles

Research workshop doesn't fit into literature circles, but after students read an informational book during a literature circle, they may decide to form an inquiry group to learn more about the topic.

Reading and Writing Workshop

Research workshop fits naturally because it's a combination of reading and writing workshop. Students read books to find answers to their questions and then share what they've learned by writing reports and other books.

Thematic Units

Students often use research workshop to delve more deeply into topics related to thematic units. They conduct research to find answers to questions and then write reports to share what they've learned.

presentations. Christine Duthie (1996) also has her primary-grade students conduct research during their writing workshop periods.

Minilessons. Teachers teach minilessons about nonfiction writing and to prepare students for writing reports (Portalupi & Fletcher, 2001). Students learn how to pose questions, search for answers, and share what they've learned. A list of minilesson topics related to report writing is presented on page 324. Included with the list is a description of Mr. Uchida's minilesson on data charts.

Assessing Students' Reports

Students need to understand what they're expected to do when they're asked to write a report and how they'll be assessed. Many teachers distribute a checklist before students begin working so that they can take responsibility for completing the assignment. The checklist for an individual report might include these observable behaviors and products:

- Identify four or five questions to research.
- Use a graphic organizer to gather and organize information to answer each question.
- Write a rough draft with a section or a chapter to answer each question.
- Meet in writing groups to get feedback about your rough draft.
- Make at least three changes in your rough draft.
- Complete an editing checklist with a partner.
- Add a bibliography.
- Write the final copy.

The checklist can be simpler or more complex, depending on students' ages and experiences. Students staple the checklist to the inside cover of the folder in which they keep all the work for the project and check off each requirement as they complete it.

Other teachers use rubrics. Sometimes they use commercially prepared rubrics, but it's more effective when teachers create a rubric with students before they begin to work. This way they'll know what's expected of them. The focus of the rubric is whether students answered their research questions clearly and completely. Teachers often specify these points in the rubric:

- Ideas are fully developed.
- Details elaborate ideas.
- Organization clarifies ideas.
- Transitions between paragraphs are effective.
- Style is captivating.
- Mechanics are used appropriately.

Sometimes teachers use the rubric to provide feedback during revising and editing as well as after the report has been completed.

LIFE STORIES

Children often wonder what it would be like to be someone else—an Olympic athlete, a test pilot, a knight in shining armor, a dancer, or the president, for example. One of the best ways to learn about other people's lives is by reading biographies and autobiographies. There are so many life-story books available today that children can read about a wide range of contemporary and historical personalities, including Mohammed, Annie Oakley, J. K. Rowling, Dizzy Gillespie, Harriet Tubman, and Houdini. At the same time children are reading about these people's lives, they also are learning about personal qualities such as courage and determination that they can apply to their own lives to help them reach their dreams and deal with the realities of both success and failure. As they read life stories and listen to them read aloud, children learn about this genre and examine its structure. These books also serve as models for children's own writing.

Reading Biographies

Authors use several approaches in writing biographies (Fleming & McGinnis, 1985). The most common approach is historical: The writer focuses on dates and events and presents them chronologically. Many biographies that span the person's entire life follow this pattern, including *Theodore Roosevelt: Champion of the American Spirit* (Kraft, 2003) and *Martin's Big Words: The Life of Dr. Martin Luther King, Jr.* (Rappaport, 2001).

Next is the sociological approach, in which the writer describes life during a historical period, providing information about family life, food, clothing, education, economics, transportation, and so on. For instance, in *Woody Guthrie: Poet of the People* (Christensen, 2001), readers learn about the hard life many Americans faced during the Depression as they learn about the folk legend.

A third approach is psychological: The writer focuses on conflicts the central figure faces. Conflicts may be with oneself, others, nature, or society. The psychological approach has many elements in common with stories and is most often used in shorter autobiographies and biographies that revolve around particular events or phases in the person's life. One example is *John Muir: America's First Environmentalist* (Lasky, 2006), which describes Muir's reverence for the natural world and his drive to preserve it.

Biographies are accounts of a person's life written by someone else, and autobiographies are written by the featured person himself or herself. Contemporary biographies are written about a living person, whereas historical biographies are about people who are no longer alive. To make the account as accurate and authentic as possible, writers consult a variety of sources of information during their research. The best source, of course, is the biography's subject, and writers can learn many things about the person through an interview. Other primary sources include diaries and letters, photographs, mementos, historical records, and recollections of people who know the person. Examples of secondary sources are books and newspaper articles written by someone other than the biographical subject.

Recommended autobiographies and biographies appear in the Booklist on the next page . These life stories feature well-known people such as astronauts, prophets, and entertainers, as well as "common" people who have endured hardship and shown exceptional courage.

Booklist

LIFE STORIES

Autobiographies

Aldrin, B. (2005). *Reaching for the moon*. New York: HarperCollins. (P–M)

dePaola, T. (2006). *I'm still scared: The war years*. New York: Putnam. (P)

Fletcher, R. (2005). *Marshfield dreams: When I was a kid*. New York: Henry Holt. (M)

Gantos, J. (2002). *Hole in my life*. New York: Farrar, Straus & Giroux. (M–U)

Kimmel, E. A. (2005). *Tuning up: A visit with Eric A. Kimmel*. Katonah, NY: Richard C. Owen.

Jiménez, F. (2001). *Breaking through*. Boston: Houghton Mifflin. (M–U)

Ma, Y. (2005). *The diary of Ma Yan: The struggles and hopes of a Chinese schoolgirl*. New York: HarperCollins. (U)

Numeroff, L. (2003*). If you give an author a pencil*. Katonah, NY: Richard C. Owen. (P)

Russo, M. (2005). *Always remember me*. New York: Atheneum. (M-U)

Steig, W. (2003). *When everybody wore a hat*. New York: HarperCollins. (P–M)

Biographies

Cohn, A. L., & Schmidt, S. (2002). *Abraham Lincoln*. New York: Scholastic. (P–M)

Demi. (2003). *Muhammad*. New York: McElderry. (M)

Fleischman, S. (2006). *Escape! The story of the great Houdini*. New York: Greenwillow. (M–U)

Freedman, R. (2002). *Confucius: The golden rule*. New York: Scholastic. (M–U)

Mitchell, D. (2006). *Liftoff: A photobiography of John Glenn*. Washington, DC: National Geographic Society. (M–U)

Pinkney, A. D. (2002). *Ella Fitzgerald: The tale of a vocal virtuosa*. New York: Hyperion Books. (P–M)

Poole, J. (2005). *Joan of Arc*. New York: Knopf. (M–U)

St. George, J. (2004). *You're on your way, Teddy Roosevelt*. New York: Philomel. (M)

Weatherford, C. B. (2006). *Moses: When Harriet Tubman led her people to freedom*. New York: Hyperion Books. (P–M)

Winter, J. (2006). *Dizzy*. New York: Scholastic. (P–M)

Teaching Students to Write Autobiographies

When students write autobiographies, they relive and document their lives, usually in chronological order. They describe the memorable events that are important to know about in order to understand them. Autobiographical writing grows out of children's personal journal entries and "All About Me" books that they write in kindergarten and first grade. Students' own experiences and memories are their primary sources of information for writing.

"Me" Boxes. One way for students to focus on their own lives is to make a "me" box (Duthie, 1996). Students collect objects and pictures representing events in their lives, their families, their hobbies, and special accomplishments. Next, they write explanations to accompany each object. Then students decorate the outside of a shoe box, coffee can, or other container and put all the objects in it. They can use the same approach to make character boxes about a character in a book they are reading or about a historical figure as part of a biography project.

Lifeline Clotheslines. Another way students gather and organize information for an autobiography is to collect objects that symbolize their life and hang them on a lifeline clothesline (Fleming & McGinnis, 1985). Next, they write briefly about each object, explaining what the object is and how it relates to their lives, and then they add their explanations to the clothesline, too.

"All About Me" Books. Children in kindergarten and first grade often compile "All About Me" books. These autobiographies usually list information such as the child's birthday, family members, friends, and favorite activities, with drawings as well as text. Figure 10–8 shows two pages from a first grader's "All About Me" book. To write these books, the children first decide on a topic for each page; then, after brainstorming possible ideas for the topic, they draw a picture and write about it. Children may also need to ask their parents for information about their birth and events during their preschool years.

Teaching Students to Write Biographies

When students study someone else's life in preparation for writing a biography, they need to become personally involved in the project (Zarnowski, 1988). There are several ways to engage students in biographical study, that is, to help them walk in the subject's footsteps. For contemporary biographies, meeting and interviewing the

FIGURE 10–8

Two Pages From a First Grader's "All About Me" Book

This is me wen I'm five. I'm reading a book. My mom comes in and puts out my cloths for me to wear but I didn't wat to wear them. I became very picky about my cloths my dad said.

This is my Grammy's house. I have my own room in it. Sometimes I sleep on the love seat. I like to see papa. Sometimes my papa takes me fishing. I love to go fishing. My Grammy makes me feel special.

person are best; for other projects, students read books about the person, view videos, dramatize events from the person's life, and write about the person. An especially valuable activity is writing simulated journals, in which students assume the role of the person they are studying and write journal entries just as that person might have.

Students write biographies about living people they know personally as well as about famous personalities. In contrast to the primary sources available for gathering information about local people, students may have to depend on secondary sources (e.g., books, magazines, newspapers, Internet sources) for information about well-known and geographically more distant people. Sometimes, however, students can write letters to well-known personalities or perhaps arrange conference telephone calls.

Lifelines. Students sequence the information they gather—about either their life or someone else's—on a lifeline, a person's time line. This activity helps students identify and sequence milestones and other events. They can use the information on the lifeline to identify topics for a biography.

Biography Boxes. Students can make biography boxes similar to "me" boxes. They begin by identifying items that represent the person, then collect them and put them in a box they have decorated. They also write papers to put with each object, explaining its significance to the person. A fifth grader created a biography box for Paul Revere and decorated it with aluminum foil, explaining that it looked like silver and Paul Revere was a silversmith. Inside the box, he placed the following items:

- A spoon (to represent his career as a silversmith)
- A toy horse (to represent his famous midnight ride)
- A tea bag (to represent his involvement in the Boston Tea Party)
- A copy of Longfellow's poem "The Midnight Ride of Paul Revere"
- An advertisement for Revere pots and pans (along with an explanation that Paul Revere is credited with inventing the process of layering metals)
- A portrait of the patriot
- Photos of Boston, Lexington, and Concord that were downloaded from the Internet
- A lifeline the student had drawn marking important events in Paul Revere's life

The student wrote a card describing the relationship of each object to Paul Revere and attached it to the item.

Biography Posters. Students present the information they've learned about the subject of their biography project on a poster. Posters can include a portrait of the person and information about the person's life and accomplishments. Students in an eighth-grade class made a biography quilt with paper squares, and each square was modeled after the illustrations in *My Fellow Americans,* by Alice Provensen (1995). One student's square about Martin Luther King Jr. is presented in Figure 10–9. This student drew a portrait of the civil rights leader set in Washington, D.C., on August 28, 1963, the day he delivered his famous "I Have a Dream" speech. The student also added well-known sayings and other phrases related to Martin Luther King Jr. around the outside.

FIGURE 10–9

A Biography Poster About Martin Luther King Jr.

Multigenre Biography Projects. Students write and draw a variety of pieces about a person to create a multigenre biography, which is like a multigenre report. Students collect and create some of the following items for a multigenre biography:

lifeline	*collection of objects*
quotations	*simulated journal*
photographs	*found poem or other poem*
open-mind portrait	*story*
report	*poster*

Each item is a complete piece by itself and contributes to the overall impact of the biography. Students compile their biographies on posters or in notebooks.

A seventh-grade class created multigenre biographies. To begin, students read a biography and located additional information about the person from two other sources. Then they created the following pieces for their biography project:

- A lifeline: Students made a lifeline of the person's life, indicating the dates of the person's birth and death and at least 10 key events in his or her life.
- A simulated journal: Students wrote 10 entries spanning the person's entire life.
- An open-mind portrait: Students drew a portrait of the person and on separate pages showed what the person was thinking about three key events in his or her life.
- Quotes: Students collected at least three quotes that best illustrated how the person spoke or what he or she believed.
- A heart map: Students drew a heart and filled it with pictures and words representing things that really mattered to the person.

Figure 10–10 presents excerpts from a seventh grader's multigenre biography project on Maya Angelou.

Assessing Students' Life Stories

Students need to know the requirements for their autobiography or biography project, as well as how they will be assessed or graded. A checklist for an autobiography might include the following components:

- Make a lifeline showing at least one important event for each year of your life.
- Draw a cluster showing at least three main-idea topics and at least five details for each topic.
- Write a rough draft with an introduction, three or more chapters, and a conclusion.
- Meet in a writing group to share your autobiography.
- Make at least three changes in your rough draft.
- Complete an editing checklist with a partner.
- Write a final copy with photos or drawings as illustrations.
- Compile your autobiography as a book.
- Decorate the cover.

The checklist for a biography might include the following requirements:

- Learn about the person's life from at least three sources (including Internet websites as well as books).
- Make a lifeline listing at least 10 important events.
- Write at least 10 simulated-journal entries as the person you are studying.
- Make a cluster with at least three main-idea topics and at least five details for each topic.
- Write a rough draft with at least three chapters and a bibliography.
- Meet in a writing group to share your biography.
- Make at least three changes in your rough draft.
- Complete an editing checklist with a partner.
- Recopy the biography.

FIGURE 10–10

Excerpts From a Seventh Grader's Multigenre Biography Project on Maya Angelou

Maya Angelou

In Maya's Heart

- The pineapple expresses Maya's love for pineapples.
- Ms. Flowers is the woman who gave Maya her first book of poetry.
- Mother Dear is Maya's mother and even though she didn't really raise her, Maya looked up to her.
- Bailey was Maya's brother and they had a strong bond being that they were only one year apart in age.
- Guy is her son and her entire life.

Dear Diary,
One night I was scared and momma let me sleep in the bed with her and Mr. Freeman. Then when momma left early to run an errand, I felt a strange pressure on my left leg. I knew it wasn't a hand because it was much too soft. I was afraid to move and I didn't budge. Mr. Freeman's eyes were wide open with both hands above the covers. He then said, "Stay right here, Rite, I'm not gonna hurt you." I really wasn't afraid, a little curious, but not afraid. Then he left and came back with a glass of water and poured it on the bed. He said, "see how you done peed in the bed." Afterwards, I was confused and didn't understand why Mr. Freeman had held me so gently, then accused me of peeing in the bed.　　　　Marguerite

Dear Diary,
While I was sitting talking to Miss Glory, Mrs. Cullinan called for someone. She said, "Mary P." We didn't know who she was calling, but my name is Marguerite. Now I settled for Margaret, but Mary was a whole nother name. Bailey told me bout Whites and how they felt like they had the power to shorten our names for their convenience. Miss Glory told me her name used to be Hallelujah and Mrs. Cullinan shortened it to Glory. Mrs. Cullinan sent me on an errand, which was a good idea because I was upset and anything was bound to come out of my mouth at the time.
　　　　　　　　　　Marguerite

Dear Diary,
Graduation day was a big event in Stamps. The high school seniors received most of the glory. I'm just a twelve year old 8th grader. I'm pretty high-ranked in my class along with Henry Reed. Henry is also our class valedictorian. The tenth grade teacher helped him with his speech. Momma was even going to close the store. Our graduation dresses are a lemon yellow, but momma added ruffles and cuffs with a crocheted collar. She added daisy embroideries around the trim before she considered herself finished. I just knew all eyes were going to be on me when graduation day came.
　　　　　　　　　　Marguerite

Quotes

"Cleanliness is next to Godliness."

"God blessed everyone with an intelligent mind. Only we can decide how we use it."

Students keep the checklist in their project folders and check off each item as it is completed; at the end of the project, they submit the folders to be assessed or graded. Teachers can award credit for each item on the checklist, as discussed in the section on assessing students' research reports. This approach helps students assume greater responsibility for their own learning and gives them a better understanding of why they receive a particular grade.

Review

Recent research suggests that reading and writing information may be as important for kindergarten through eighth-grade students as reading and writing stories. Students enjoy reading informational books, and they learn This knowledge about text structure supports students' reading and writing. Students write a variety of reports of information, including visual reports, collaborative books, and individual reports. Students also read biographies and autobiographies, and they write their own life stories. Here are some of the important concepts presented in this chapter:

- Students read informational books to learn information, and they write informational books to share information with others.
- Students may use either efferent or aesthetic reading when reading informational books, depending on their purpose for reading.
- Informational writing is organized into five expository text patterns: description, sequence, comparison, cause and effect, and problem and solution.
- Students use their knowledge of expository text structures when reading and writing informational books.
- Students create visual reports using clusters, diagrams, flowcharts, data charts, maps, time lines, and cubes.
- Students write collaborative reports to learn how to write reports before writing individual reports.
- Students prepare multigenre projects using a combination of reports, stories, poems, photographs and other illustrations, and other materials.
- Students make boxes, lifelines, and posters to document events in their own lives and in other people's lives.
- Students write autobiographies about events in their own lives and write biographies about both historical and contemporary personalities.
- Students use the writing process to write reports, autobiographies, and biographies.

Professional References

Allen, C. A. (2001). *The multigenre research paper: Voice, passion, and discovery in grades 4–6.* Portsmouth, NH: Heinemann.

Berghoff, B., Egawa, K. A., Harste, J. C., & Hoonan, B. T. (2000). *Beyond reading and writing: Inquiry, curriculum, and multiple ways of knowing.* Urbana, IL: National Council of Teachers of English.

Bromley, K., Irwin-Devitis, L., & Hires, D. (1999). *Graphic organizers.* New York: Scholastic.

Chapman, V. G., & Sopko, D. (2003). Developing strategic use of combined-text trade books. *The Reading Teacher, 57,* 236–239.

Duthie, C. (1996). *True stories: Nonfiction literacy in the primary classroom.* York, ME: Stenhouse.

Fleming, M., & McGinnis, J. (Eds.). (1985). *Portraits: Biography and autobiography in the secondary school.* Urbana, IL: National Council of Teachers of English.

Freeman, E. B. (1991). Informational books: Models for student report writing. *Language Arts, 68,* 470–473.

Grierson, S. T., Anson, A., & Baird, J. (2002). Exploring the past through multigenre writing. *Language Arts, 80,* 51–59.

Harvey, S. (1998). *Nonfiction matters: Reading, writing, and research in grades 3–8.* York, ME: Stenhouse.

Kristo, J. V., & Bamford, R. A. (2004). *Nonfiction in focus.* New York: Scholastic.

McMackin, M. C., & Siegel, B. S. (2002). *Knowing how: Researching and writing nonfiction, 3–8.* Portland, ME: Stenhouse.

Meyer, B. J., & Freedle, R. O. (1984). Effects of discourse type on recall. *American Educational Research Journal, 21,* 121–143.

Moline, S. (1995). *I see what you mean: Children at work with visual information.* York, ME: Stenhouse.

Moss, B., & Hendershot, J. (2002). Exploring sixth graders' selection of nonfiction trade books. *The Reading Teacher, 56,* 6–17.

Neeld, E. C. (1990). *Writing* (3rd ed.). Glenview, IL: Scott Foresman.

Palmer, R. G., & Stewart, R. A. (2003). Nonfiction trade book use in primary grades. *The Reading Teacher, 57,* 38–48.

Peregoy, S. F., & Boyle, O. F. (2005). *Reading, writing, and learning in ESL: A resource book for K–12 teachers* (4th ed.). Boston: Allyn & Bacon.

Perry, N., & Drummond, L. (2002). Helping young students become self-regulated researchers and writers. *The Reading Teacher, 56,* 298–310.

Portalupi, J., & Fletcher, R. (2001). *Nonfiction craft lessons: Teaching information writing K–8.* York, ME: Stenhouse.

Raphael, T. E., Englert, C. S., & Kirschner, B. W. (1989). Acquisition of expository writing skills. In J. M. Mason (Ed.), *Reading and writing connections* (pp. 261–290). Boston: Allyn & Bacon.

Read, S. (2001). "Kid mice hunt for their selfs": First and second graders writing research. *Language Arts, 78,* 333–342.

Richgels, D. J. (2002). Informational texts in kindergarten. *The Reading Teacher, 55,* 586–595.

Rico, G. L. (1983). *Writing the natural way.* Los Angeles: Tarcher.

Robb, L. (2003). *Teaching reading in social studies, science, and math.* New York: Scholastic.

Robb, L. (2004). *Nonfiction writing: From the inside out.* New York: Scholastic.

Rogovin, P. (2001). *The research workshop: Bringing the world into your classroom.* Portsmouth, NH: Heinemann.

Romano, T. (1995). *Writing with passion: Life stories, multiple genres.* Portsmouth, NH: Boynton/Cook.

Romano, T. (2000). *Blending genre, altering style: Writing multigenre papers.* Portsmouth, NH: Boynton/Cook.

Rosenblatt, L. M. (2005). *Making meaning with texts: Selected essays.* Portsmouth, NH: Heinemann.

Stead, T. (2002). *Is that a fact? Teaching nonfiction writing K–3.* Portland, ME: Stenhouse.

Stead, T. (2006). *Reality checks: Teaching reading comprehension with nonfiction K–5.* Portland, ME: Stenhouse.

Yopp, H. K., & Yopp, R. H. (2005). *Literature-based reading activities* (4th ed.). Boston: Allyn & Bacon.

Zarnowski, M. (1988, February). The middle school student as biographer. *Middle School Journal, 19,* 25–27.

Children's Book References

Berenstain, S., & Berenstain, J. (2002). *Down a sunny dirt road.* New York: Random House.

Bunting, E. (1999). *Smoky night.* San Diego: Harcourt Brace.

Bunting, E. (2001). *The blue and the gray.* New York: Scholastic.

Byrd, R. (2003). *Leonardo: Beautiful dreamer.* New York: Dutton.

Carle, E. (2002). *The very hungry caterpillar.* New York: Puffin Books.

Cheney, L. (2002). *America: A patriotic primer.* New York: Simon & Schuster.

Christensen, B. (2001). *Woody Guthrie: Poet of the people.* New York: Knopf.

Cole, J. (1998). *The magic school bus in the rain forest.* New York: Scholastic.

Cole, J. (2003). *Ms. Frizzle's adventures: Medieval castle.* New York: Scholastic.

dePaola, T. (2006). *I'm still scared: A 26 Fairmount Avenue book.* New York: Putnam.

Ehlert, L. (2001). *Fish eyes: A book you can count on.* New York: Red Wagon Books.

Evans, M., & Caras, R. A. (2001). *Fish: Pet care guides for kids.* New York: Dorling Kindersley.

Gibbons, G. (2006). *Owls.* New York: Holiday House.

Jiménez, F. (1997). *The circuit.* Albuquerque: University of New Mexico Press.

Jiménez, F. (2001). *Breaking through.* Boston: Houghton Mifflin.

Kamma, A. (2004). *. . . If you lived when there was slavery in America.* New York: Scholastic.

King-Smith, D. (2002). *Chewing the cud: An extraordinary life remembered by the author of* Babe: The gallant pig. New York: Knopf.

Kraft, B. H. (2003). *Theodore Roosevelt: Champion of the American spirit.* New York: Clarion Books.

Lasky, K. (2006). *John Muir: America's first environmentalist.* Cambridge, MA: Candlewick Press.

Lionni, L. (2005). *Fish is fish.* New York: Scholastic.

Logan, C. (2002). *The 5,000-year-old puzzle: Solving a mystery of ancient Egypt.* New York: Farrar, Straus & Giroux.

Longfellow, H. W. (1996). *Hiawatha.* New York: Puffin Books.

Longfellow, H. W. (2000). *The midnight ride of Paul Revere.* Washington, DC: National Geographic Society.

Lowry, L. (1998). *Looking back: A book of memories.* Boston: Houghton Mifflin.

Macaulay, D. (2003). *Mosque.* Boston: Houghton Mifflin.

Moore, C. (1998). *The night before Christmas.* New York: Putnam.

Nelson, R. (2002). *Pet fish.* Minneapolis: Lerner.

Osborne, M. P. (1998). *Hour of the Olympics.* New York: Random House.

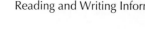

Osborne, M. P. (2004). *Ancient Greece and the Olympics.* New York: Random House.

Paulsen, G. (1999). *My life in dog years.* New York: Yearling.

Paulsen, G. (2001). *Guts: The true stories behind Hatchet and the Brian books.* New York: Delacorte.

Pfister, M. (2002). *The rainbow fish.* New York: North-South Books.

Provensen, A. (1995). *My fellow Americans: A family album.* San Diego: Browndeer Press.

Rappaport, D. (2001). *Martin's big words: The life of Dr. Martin Luther King, Jr.* New York: Hyperion Books.

Rubin, S. G. (2003). *Searching for Anne Frank: Letters from Amsterdam to Iowa.* New York: Abrams.

Seuss, Dr. (1960). *One fish two fish red fish blue fish.* New York: Random House.

Simon, S. (2003). *Hurricanes.* New York: HarperCollins.

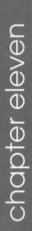
Reading and Writing Poetry

Mrs. Harris holds a weeklong poetry workshop in her sixth-grade classroom several times each year. It lasts 2 hours each day; the first hour is devoted to reading poetry and the second to writing poetry. Her students read and respond to poems during the reading workshop component and write poems during the writing workshop component. Her schedule is shown in the box on page 354.

During class meetings this week, Mrs. Harris draws students' attention to poetic devices. On Monday, she asks students to think about their favorite poems. What makes a poem a good poem? She reads aloud some favorite poems, and the students mention these poetic elements: rhyme, alliteration, repetition, and onomatopoeia, which they call "sound effects."

On Tuesday, Mrs. Harris focuses on metaphors and similes. She reads aloud these poems from *The Random House Book of Poetry for Children* (Prelutsky, 2000): "The Toaster," "Steam Shovel," "The Dandelion," and "The Eagle." She reads each poem aloud to students, and they notice these comparisons: The toaster is compared to a dragon, the steam shovel to a dinosaur, the dandelion to a soldier, and the eagle's dive to a bolt of lightning. The next day, students come to the class meeting to share poems they have found that have comparisons. Their classmates identify the comparisons. After they discuss the poems, Mrs. Harris explains the terms *metaphor*

How does poetry fit into the four patterns of practice?

Teachers incorporate poetry into all four instructional patterns. They share poems with students on topics related to literature focus units and thematic units, and in literature circles and reading workshops, students read books of poetry as well as other books. Students write poems as projects, and once students learn how to write poetry, they often choose to do so during writing workshop. As you continue reading, notice how Mrs. Harris adapts reading and writing workshop for her poetry workshop.

and *simile* and asks students to classify the comparisons in the poems they've shared.

On Thursday, Mrs. Harris reads aloud "The Night Is a Big Black Cat" (Prelutsky, 2000), a brief, four-line poem comparing night to a black cat, the moon to the cat's eye, and the stars to mice she is hunting in the sky. The students draw pictures illustrating the poem and add the lines or paraphrases of the lines to their pictures. One student's drawing is shown on page 355. On Friday, students finish their pictures and share them with the class.

Mrs. Harris points out the poetry section of the classroom library that's been infused with 75 more books of poetry. Students select books of poetry from the library to read during the independent reading time. Next, she introduces some recently published books about poetry. *Love That Dog* (Creech, 2001), *Locomotion* (Woodson, 2003), and *A Bird About to Sing* (Montenegro, 2003) are stories written in poetic form about how children use poetry to write about their feelings. She also shares Janet Wong's book of poetry with advice about writing poems, *You Have to Write* (2002), and three informational books, *Poetry Matters: Writing a Poem From the Inside Out* (Fletcher, 2002), *A Kick in the Head: An Everyday Guide to Poetic Forms* (Janeczko, 2005), and *Troy Thompson's Excellent Peotry* [sic] *Book* (Crew, 1998), books about how to write poetry. She has several copies of each book, and students choose one to read during the week.

During independent reading time, students also read poems and pick their favorites to share with classmates. They list the books they read in their poetry folders. They also choose their three favorite poems, and Mrs. Harris makes copies of them for their poetry folders. For each poem, students write a brief reflection explaining why they like the poem, mentioning poetic elements whenever possible in their explanations.

After reading, students get into small groups to share their favorite poems, and they rehearse the poem they'll read to the whole class. Five or six students read one poem aloud each day. During a previous poetry workshop, Mrs. Harris taught the students how to read poetry expressively, or as she says, "like a

---

Poetry Workshop Schedule

15 minutes	**Class Meeting** Mrs. Harris leads a whole-class meeting to give a book talk on a new poetry book, talk about a poet, read several favorite poems using choral reading, or talk about a difficult or confusing poem.
30 minutes	**Independent Reading** Students choose books of poetry from the classroom library and read poems independently. As they read, students choose favorite poems and mark them with small self-stick notes.
15 minutes	**Sharing** Students form small groups and share favorite poems with class mates. Then several students read their favorite poems aloud to the whole class. They rehearse before reading to the class and try to "read like a poet" with good expression.
15 minutes	**Minilesson** Mrs. Harris teaches minilessons on poetry-writing strategies, such as how to use poetic devices, how to arrange the lines of a poem on a page, and how to use "unwriting" to revise poems. She also introduces and reviews poetry formulas during minilessons.
45 minutes	**Writing** Students write lots of rough-draft poems and choose the ones they like best to take through the writing process and publish. Students meet in revising groups and editing conferences with Mrs. Harris and classmates as they polish their poems. On Friday, the students have a poetry reading and they read aloud one of the poems they have written.

---

poet." They know how to vary the speed and loudness of their voices, how to emphasize the rhyme or other important words, and how to pause at the ends of lines or within lines. Mrs. Harris expects her students to apply what they've learned when they read poetry aloud.

During the writing workshop minilessons this week, Mrs. Harris focuses on "unwriting," a strategy students use to revise their poems. On Monday, she shares the rough draft of a color poem she's written, which she displays on an overhead projector. She explains that she thinks it has too many unnecessary words and asks the students to help her unwrite it. The students make suggestions, and she crosses out words and substitutes stronger words for long phrases. Together they revise the poem to make it tighter. Mrs. Harris explains that poems are powerful because they say so much using only a few words and encourages students to use unwriting as they revise their poems.

On Tuesday and Wednesday, Mrs. Harris shares students' rough-draft poems, which she has copied onto transparencies. Then students suggest ways to unwrite their classmates' poems using the same procedure they used on Monday.

Several students ask to learn more about limericks, so on Thursday, Mrs. Harris reviews the limerick form and shares limericks from a book in the classroom library and other limericks that her students wrote in previous years. Then on Friday, students

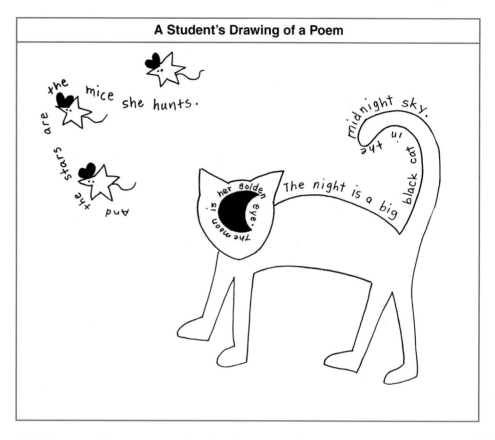

A Student's Drawing of a Poem

divide into small groups to try their hand at writing limericks. Mrs. Harris moves from group to group, providing assistance as needed. Afterward, they share their limericks with classmates.

Mrs. Harris's students keep writing notebooks in which they record collections of words, quotes from books they've read, interesting sentences and descriptions, lists of writing topics, and rough drafts of stories, poems, and other writings. They also have a paper describing the different types of poems that Mrs. Harris has taught them. During the independent writing time, they often use ideas, words and sentences, or even rough-draft poems in their writing notebooks. Students write lots of rough drafts and then choose the most promising ones to take through the writing process and publish. During the week, they meet in revising groups and editing conferences with Mrs. Harris and a small group of classmates. During the first half of the writing time, Mrs. Harris holds a revising group, and during the second half, she holds an editing group. Students sign up for the groups in advance. They keep all their drafts of the poems they publish to document their use of the writing process and to trace the development of their poems.

On the last day of the poetry workshop, the students type final copies of their poems, which they contribute to the class book of poetry that Mrs. Harris compiles. The students move their desks into a circle and have a poetry reading. They read around, each taking a turn to read aloud one of the poems he or she has written.

Mrs. Harris posts the schedule for poetry workshop in the classroom so that students know what they're doing during the 2-hour time block. She also sets out her expectations for students at the beginning of the poetry workshop: They are to read and write lots of poems. She wants them to choose at least three favorite poems from the ones that they read and to take at least one poem that they write through the writing process. She passes out copies of the grading sheet they'll use that week, and they place them in their writing folders. This way students know from the first day of the workshop what they're expected to accomplish. A copy of Mrs. Harris's poetry workshop grading sheet is shown here.

Poetry Workshop Grading Sheet

Name _____   Date _____

Student's Check   Teacher's Grade

_____ 1. Read lots of poems. Keep a list of poetry books that you read. (15)   _____

_____ 2. Make copies of three favorite poems and write why you like the poems. (15)   _____

_____ 3. Read one poem aloud to the class. Be sure to read like a poet. (10)   _____

_____ 4. Write rough drafts of at least five poems. (25)   _____

_____ 5. Take one poem through the writing process to publication. (15)   _____

_____ 6. Read one of your poems during the poetry reading on Friday. (10)   _____

_____ 7. Other (10)   _____

    Draw a "night cat" picture.

    Write a limerick in a small group.

As students complete the assignments, they add checkmarks in the lefthand column. After they finish the unit, they turn in their writing folders with the grading sheet and the papers they completed during the workshop. Mrs. Harris reviews their assignments and awards points to determine the grade using a 100-point grading scale.

Poetry **"brings sound and sense together in words and lines,"** according to Donald Graves, "ordering them on the page in such a way that both the writer and reader get a different view of life" (1992, p. 3). Our concept of poetry has broadened to include songs and raps, word pictures, memories, riddles, observations, questions, odes, and rhymes. Adult and child poets write about every imaginable subject—grasshoppers, fire trucks, boa constrictors, spaghetti and meatballs, Jupiter, and grandfathers. These poems tell stories, create images and moods, make us laugh or cry, develop our sense of wonder, and show us the world in a new way (Cullinan, Scala, & Schroder, 1995; Glover, 1999).

In an article in *Language Arts*, Lisa Siemens (1996) describes how her primary-grade students are immersed in reading and writing poetry. She makes poetry the core of her language arts program, and her students respond enthusiastically. She shares three of her students' descriptions of poetry. One child writes:

> *A poem is like a big green dragon waiting to blow fire at the knight who seeks the treasure. (p. 239)*

Another child shares:

> *Poems are words that you feel and mumble jumble words too, also words that float around in your head. (p. 239)*

A third child explains:

> *I think poetry is when you wake up and see the sun racing above from the clouds. Poetry is when sunlight and moon shines up together. Poetry is when you go to Claude Monet's garden for the first time and everything is breathtaking. That is what I think poetry is. (p. 239)*

With the current emphasis on standards, poetry is sometimes considered to be a frill, but for these young children, it's essential! Other teachers, too, know that reading and writing poetry can be an effective way to meet content-area standards (Holbrook, 2005).

The focus of this chapter is on involving students with poetry. As you read, think about these questions:

- How do teachers encourage students to play with words and express ideas using figurative language?
- How do students read and respond to poems?
- What kinds of poems do students write?
- How can teachers incorporate poetry activities into the four patterns of practice?

PLAYING WITH WORDS

As children experiment with words, they create images, play with words, and evoke feelings. They laugh with language, experiment with rhyme, and invent new words. These activities provide a rich background of experiences for reading and writing poetry, and children gain confidence in choosing the "right" word to express an idea, emphasizing the sounds of words, and expressing familiar ideas with fresh comparisons. The Booklist on page 358 presents a collection of wordplay books.

Laughing With Language

As children learn that words have the power to amuse, they enjoy reading, telling, and writing riddles and jokes. Geller (1985) researched children's humorous language and identified two stages of riddle play: Primary-grade children experiment with the riddle form and its content, and beginning in third or fourth grade, students explore the paradoxical constructions in riddles. Riddles are written in a question-and-answer format,

Booklist

WORDPLAY BOOKS

Agee, J. (1994). *Go hang a salami! I'm a lasagna hog! and other palindromes.* New York: Farrar, Straus & Giroux. (U)

Agee, J. (2002). *Palindromania!* New York: Farrar, Straus & Giroux. (M–U)

Bayer, J. (1992). *A my name is Alice.* New York: Dial Books. (P–M)

Carroll, L. (2003). *Jabberwocky.* Cambridge, MA: Candlewick Press. (M–U)

Cerf, B. (1999). *Riddles and more riddles.* New York: Random House. (P)

Cobb, R. (2006). *Tongue twisters to tangle your tongue.* London: Marion Boyars. (M)

Cole, J. (1994). *Why did the chicken cross the road?* New York: HarperCollins. (P–M)

Eiting, M., & Folsom, M. (2005). *Q is for duck: An alphabet guessing game.* New York: Clarion Books. (P–M)

Ernst, L. C. (2004). *The turn-around, upside-down alphabet book.* New York: Simon & Schuster. (P)

Gwynne, F. (2005). *A chocolate moose for dinner.* New York: Aladdin Books. (M–U)

Gwynne, F. (2006). *The king who rained.* New York: Aladdin Books. (M–U)

Hall, K., & Eisenberg, L. (2002). *Kitty riddles.* New York: Puffin. (P)

Schwartz, A. (1992). *Busy buzzing bumblebees and other tongue twisters.* New York: HarperCollins. (P–M)

Terban, M. (1992). *Funny you should ask: How to make up jokes and riddles with wordplay.* New York: Clarion Books. (M–U)

Terban, M. (1997). *Time to rhyme: A rhyming dictionary.* Honesdale, PA: Wordsong. (M)

Terban, M. (2007). *Eight ate: A feast of homonym riddles.* New York: Clarion Books. (P–M)

Terban, M. (2007). *In a pickle and other funny idioms.* New York: Clarion Books. (M)

Wilbur, R. (2006). *Opposites, more opposites, and a few differences.* San Diego: Harcourt. (M–U)

P = primary grades (K–2); M = middle grades (3–5); U = upper grades (6–8)

but young children at first may only ask questions, or ask questions and offer unrelated answers. As they gain experience, children learn to provide questions and give related answers, and their answers may be either descriptive or nonsensical. Here is an example of a descriptive answer:

> *Why did the turtle go out of his shell?*
> *Because he was getting too big for it.*

A nonsensical answer might involve an invented word. For example:

> *Why did the cat want to catch a snake?*
> *Because he wanted to turn into a rattlecat. (Geller, 1981, p. 672)*

Children's riddles seem foolish by adult standards, but wordplay is an important precursor to creating true riddles.

Riddles depend on using metaphors and on manipulating words with multiple meanings or similar sounds. The Opies (1967) identified five riddle strategies that children learn to use:

- Using multiple referents for a noun: What has an eye but cannot see? A needle.
- Combining literal and figurative interpretations for a single phrase: Why did the kid throw the clock out the window? Because he wanted to see time fly.
- Shifting word boundaries to suggest another meaning: Why did the cookie cry? Because its mother was a wafer (away for) so long.

- Separating a word into syllables to suggest another meaning: When is a door not a door? When it's ajar (a jar).
- Creating a metaphor: What are polka dots on your face? Pimples.

Children begin riddle play by telling familiar riddles and reading riddles written by others, and soon they're composing their own by adapting riddles they've read and turning jokes into riddles. A third grader wrote this riddle using two meanings for Milky Way:

> *Why did the astronaut go to the Milky Way?*
> *Because he wanted a Milky Way Bar.*

A fifth grader wrote this riddle using the homophones *hair* and *hare:*

> *What is gray and jumpy and on your head? A gray hare!*

The juxtaposition of words is important in many jokes and riddles.

Creating Word Pictures

Children create word pictures by arranging words to make a picture. These word pictures can be single-word pictures or a string of words or a sentence arranged in a picture. Figure 11–1 shows two word pictures. In the box on the left, the word *nervous* is written concretely, and on the right, descriptive sentences about an ice cream cone have been arranged in that shape. An asterisk indicates where to start reading the sentence picture. To make word pictures, students sketch a picture. Next, they place a second sheet of paper over the drawing and replace all or most of the lines with descriptive words so that the arrangement, size, and intensity of the letters illustrate the meaning.

Experimenting With Rhyme

Because of their experience with Dr. Seuss stories and nursery rhymes, children enjoy creating rhymes. When it comes naturally, rhyme adds a delightful quality to children's writing, but when it is equated with poetry, it can get in the way of wordplay and vivid images. The following three-line poem, "Thoughts After a 40-Mile Bike Ride," shows a fifth grader's effective use of rhyme:

> My feet
> And seat
> Are beat.

A small group of first graders created their own version of *Oh, A-Hunting We Will Go* (Langstaff, 1991). They identified the refrain (lines 1, 2, and 5) and added their own rhyming couplets. Here is an excerpt:

> Oh, a-hunting we will go,
> a-hunting we will go.
> We'll catch a little bear
> and curl his hair,
> and never let him go.
> Oh, a-hunting we will go,
> a-hunting we will go.
> We'll catch a little bug
> and give him a big hug
>
> and never let him go.
> Oh, a-hunting we will go,
> a-hunting we will go.
> We'll catch a little bunny
> and fill her full of honey,
> and never let her go.
> Oh, we'll put them in a ring
> and listen to them sing
> and then we'll let them go.

FIGURE 11–1

Students' Word Pictures

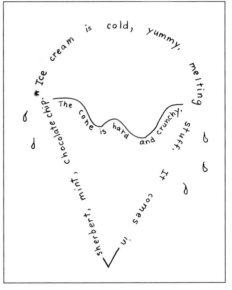

The first graders wrote this collaboration with the teacher taking dictation on a large chart. Next, each child chose a stanza to copy and illustrate. The pages were collected and compiled to make a book. Finally, they shared the book with their classmates, with each child reading aloud his or her own page.

Hink-pinks are short rhymes that take the form of an answer to a riddle or describe something. These rhymes are composed with two one-syllable rhyming words; they're called *hinky-pinkies* when two two-syllable words are used, and *hinkity-pinkities* with two three-syllable words (Geller, 1981). Here are two examples:

Ghost
White
Fright

What do you call an astronaut?
A sky guy.

Poetic Devices

Poets choose words carefully. They craft powerful images when they use unexpected comparisons, repeat sounds within a line or stanza, imitate sounds, and repeat words and phrases; these techniques are *poetic devices*. As students learn about them, they appreciate the poet's ability to manipulate an element in poems they read and apply it in their own writing (Cullinan et al., 1995). The terminology is also helpful when students talk about poems they've read and in writing groups when they want to compliment classmates on the use of a device or suggest that they try a particular element when they revise their writing.

🖉 *Comparison* One way to describe something is to compare it to something else. Students compare images, feelings, and actions to other things using two types of comparisons—*similes* and *metaphors*. A simile is an explicit comparison of one thing to another—a statement that one thing is like something else. Similes are signaled by the use of *like* or *as*. In contrast, a metaphor compares two things by implying that one is something else, without using *like* or *as*. Differentiating between the two terms is less important than using comparisons to make writing more vivid; for example, children can compare anger to an occurrence in nature. Using a simile, they might say, "Anger is like a thunderstorm, screaming with thunder-feelings and lightning-words." Or, as a metaphor, they might say, "Anger is a volcano, erupting with poisonous words and hot-lava actions."

Students begin by learning traditional comparisons and idioms, and they learn to avoid stale comparisons, such as "high as a kite," "butterflies in your stomach," and "light as a feather." Then they invent fresh, unexpected comparisons. A sixth grader uses a combination of expected and unexpected comparisons in this poem, "People":

> People are like birds
> who are constantly getting their feathers ruffled.
> People are like alligators
> who find pleasure in evil cleverness.
> People are like bees
> who are always busy.
> People are like penguins
> who want to have fun.
> People are like platypuses—unexplainable!

✍ *Alliteration* Alliteration is the repetition of the initial consonant sound in consecutive words or in words in close proximity. Repeating the initial sound makes poetry fun to read, and children enjoy reading and reciting alliterative verses, such as *A My Name Is Alice* (Bayer, 1992) and *The Z Was Zapped* (Van Allsburg, 1998). After reading one of these books, children can create their own versions. A fourth-grade class created its own version of Van Allsburg's book, which they called *The Z Was Zipped*. Students divided into pairs, and each pair composed two pages for the class book. Students illustrated their letter on the front of the paper and wrote a sentence on the back to describe their illustration, following Van Allsburg's pattern. Two pages from the book are shown in Figure 11–2. Before reading the sentences, examine the illustrations and try to figure out the sentences. These are the students' alliterative sentences:

> *The D got dunked by the duck.*
> *The T was totally terrified.*

Tongue twisters are an exaggerated type of alliteration in which every word (or almost every word) in the twister begins with the same letter. Dr. Seuss compiled an easy-to-read collection of tongue twisters for primary-grade students in *Oh Say Can You Say?* (2004). *Tongue Twisters to Tangle Your Tongue* (Cobb, 2006) and *Alison's Zinnia* (Lobel, 1996) are two good books of tongue twisters for middle-grade students. Practice with tongue twisters and alliterative books increases children's awareness of the poetic device in poems they read and write. Few students consciously think about adding alliteration to a poem they are writing, but they get high praise in writing groups when classmates notice an alliteration and compliment the writer on it.

✍ *Onomatopoeia* Onomatopoeia is a device in which poets use sound words to make their writing more sensory and more vivid. Sound words (e.g., *crash, slurp, varoom, meow*) sound like their meanings. Two books of sound words are *Slop Goes the Soup: A Noisy Warthog Word Book* (Edwards, 2001) and *Achoo! Bang! Crash! The Noisy Alphabet* (MacDonald, 2003). Children can compile a list of sound words they find in stories, poems, and wordplay books and display the list on a classroom chart or in their language arts notebooks to refer to when they write their own poems.

In *Wishes, Lies, and Dreams* (2000), Kenneth Koch recommends having children write noise poems that include a noise or sound word in each line. These first poems often sound contrived (e.g., "A dog barks bow-wow"), but the experience helps children learn to use onomatopoeia, as this poem, "Elephant Noses," dictated by a kindergartner, illustrates:

ELEPHANT NOSES

Elephant noses	Big noses
Elephants have big noses	Elephants have big noses
Big noses	through which they drink
	SCHLURRP

Repetition Repetition of words and phrases is another device writers use to structure their writing as well as to add interest. Poe's use of the word *nevermore* in "The Raven" is one example, as is the Gingerbread Boy's boastful refrain in "Gingerbread Boy." In this riddle, a fourth grader uses a refrain effectively:

I am a little man standing all alone	What to call this little man
In the deep, dark wood.	Standing all alone
I am standing on one foot	In the deep, dark wood.
In the deep, dark wood.	Who am I?
Tell me quickly, if you can,	(Answer: a mushroom)

FIGURE 11–2

Two Pages From a Fourth-Grade Class Book of Alliterations

READING POEMS

Children have a natural affinity to verse, songs, riddles, jokes, chants, and puns. Preschoolers are introduced to poetry when their parents repeat Mother Goose rhymes, read *The House at Pooh Corner* (Milne, 2001) and the Dr. Seuss books, and sing songs to them. And, children often create jump-rope rhymes and other ditties on the playground.

Types of Poems

Poems for children assume many different forms. The most common type of poetry is rhymed verse, such as Christina Rossetti's "Who Has Seen the Wind" and John Ciardi's "Mummy Slept Late and Daddy Fixed Breakfast" (Prelutsky, 2000). Poems that tell a story are narrative poems; examples are Clement Moore's *The Night Before Christmas* (1998) and Henry Wadsworth Longfellow's "Hiawatha" (1996). A Japanese form, haiku, is popular in anthologies of poetry for children. Haiku is a three-line poem that contains just 17 syllables. Because of its brevity, it has been considered an appropriate form of poetry for children to read and write. Free verse has lines that don't rhyme, and rhythm is less important than in other types of poetry; images take on greater importance in free-form verse. Carl Sandburg's "Fog" and William Carlos Williams's "This Is Just to Say" (Prelutsky, 2004) are two examples of free verse. Other forms of poetry include limericks, a short, five-line, rhymed verse form popularized by Edward Lear (1995), and concrete poems, which are arranged on the page to create a picture or an image. These forms are summarized in Figure 11–3.

There are three types of poetry books. A number of picture-book versions of single poems (in which each line or stanza is illustrated on a page) are available, such as *The Midnight Ride of Paul Revere* (Longfellow, 2001). Others are specialized collections, either written by a single poet or related to a single theme, such as dinosaurs or Halloween. Comprehensive anthologies are the third type, and they feature 50 to 500 or more poems arranged by category. One of the best anthologies is *The Random House Book of Poetry for Children* (Prelutsky, 2000). Poetry books representing each type are included in the Booklist on page 365.

Children have definite preferences about which poems they like best. Fisher and Natarella (1982) surveyed the poetry preferences of first, second, and third graders; Terry (1974) investigated fourth, fifth, and sixth graders' preferences; and Kutiper (1985) researched seventh, eighth, and ninth graders' preferences. The results of the three studies are important for teachers to consider when they select poems. The most popular forms of poetry were limericks and narrative poems; least popular were haiku and free verse. In addition, children preferred funny poems, poems about animals, and poems about familiar experiences; they disliked poems with visual imagery and figurative language. The most important elements were rhyme, rhythm, and sound. Primary-grade students preferred traditional poetry, middle graders preferred modern poetry, and upper-grade students preferred rhyming verse. The researchers found that children in all three studies liked poetry, enjoyed listening to poetry read aloud, and could give reasons why they liked or disliked particular poems.

Researchers have also used school library circulation figures to examine children's poetry preferences. Kutiper and Wilson (1993) found that the humorous poetry of Shel Silverstein (2004) and Jack Prelutsky (1984) was the most popular. Both poets

FIGURE 11–3

Forms of Poetry

Type	Description	Examples
Rhymed verse	Poems with a rhyme scheme so that some lines end with the same sound.	Kirk, D. (2003). *Dogs rule!* New York: Hyperion Books. (M) Shields, C. D. (2003). *Almost late to school: And more school poems.* New York: Dutton. (P–M)
Free verse	Poems that don't rhyme; images take on greater importance.	Medina, J. (2004). *The dream on Blanca's wall. Poems in English and Spanish.* Honesdale, PA: Boyds Mills Press. (M–U) Wong, J. S. (2002). *You have to write.* New York: McElderry. (M)
Haiku	Japanese three-line nature poems containing 17 syllables.	Mannis, C. D. (2002). *One leaf rides the wind: Counting in a Japanese garden.* New York: Viking. (P) Prelutsky, J. (2004). *If not for the cat.* New York: Greenwillow. (P)
Limerick	A five-line, rhymed verse form popularized by Edward Lear.	Ciardi, J. (1992). *The hopeful trout and other limericks.* Boston: Houghton Mifflin. (M–U) Livingston, M. C. (1991). *Lots of limericks.* New York: McElderry. (M)
Concrete	Poems arranged on the page to create a picture or image.	Janeczko, P. B. (2001). *A poke in the I: A collection of concrete poems.* Cambridge, MA: Candlewick Press. (M–U) Roemer, H. B. (2004). *Come to my party and other shape poems.* New York: Holt. (P–M)
Acrostic	Lines in a poem arranged so the first letter of each line spells a word when read vertically.	Powell, C. (2003). *Amazing apples.* New York: Whitman. (P–M) Schnur, S. (2001). *Summer: An alphabet acrostic.* New York: Clarion Books. (P–M)

use rhyme and rhythm effectively in their humorous narrative poems about familiar, everyday occurrences; these are the same qualities that children liked in the earlier poetry preference studies.

Reading and Responding to Poems

In her poem "How to Eat a Poem," Eve Merriam (American Poetry and Literacy Project, 2006) provides useful advice for students who are reading poems: She compares reading a poem to eating a piece of fruit and advises biting right in and letting the juice run down your chin. The focus is on enjoyment: Children read poems and listen to them read aloud because they're pleasurable activities. With so many poems available for children today, it's easy to find poems that appeal to every child and poems that teachers like, too. Guidelines for reading and responding to poems are presented in the LA Essentials feature on page 366.

How to Read a Poem. Poetry is intended to be shared orally because the words and phrases lose much of their music when they're read with the eyes and not with the voice. As teachers and students read poems aloud, they read expressively, stressing and elongating words, adjusting reading speeds, and using musical instruments or props to accompany the reading (Elster & Hanauer, 2002). Readers consider these four aspects of expressive reading:

- Tempo—how fast or slowly to read the lines
- Rhythm—which words to stress or say loudest

- Pitch—when to raise or lower the voice
- Juncture—when and how long to pause

Students experiment with tempo, rhythm, pitch, and juncture as they read poems in different ways and learn how to vary their reading to make their presentations more interpretive. They also learn that in some poems, reading speed may be more important and that in others, pausing is more important. These considerations reinforce the need to rehearse a poem several times before reading it aloud for classmates.

Making Sense of Poems. Some poems are very approachable, and students grasp their meaning during the first reading. For example, Jack Prelutsky's poem "The New Kid on the Block" (1984) is about a bully, and in the last line of the poem, students learn that the bully is a girl. What a kicker! Students laugh as they realize that they'd assumed the bully was a boy. They reread the poem to figure out how the poet set

---

Booklist

POETRY BOOKS

Picture-Book Versions of Single Poems

Bates, K. L. (2003). *America the beautiful.* New York: Putnam. (M)

Carroll, L. (2003). *Jabberwocky.* Cambridge, MA: Candlewick Press. (M–U)

Frost, R. (2002). *Birches* (E. Young, Illus.). New York: Henry Holt. (U)

Hoberman, M. A. (2003). *The lady with the alligator purse.* Boston: Little, Brown. (P)

Howitt, M. (2002). *The spider and the fly.* New York: Simon & Schuster. (P)

Thayer, E. L. (2000). *Casey at the bat: A ballad of the republic sung in the year 1888.* (C. Bing, Illus.). New York: Handprint Books. (M–U)

Specialized Collections

Adoff, J. (2002). *Song shoots out of my mouth: A celebration of music.* New York: Dutton. (U)

Carlson, L. M. (Ed.). (1998). *Sol a sol: Bilingual poems.* New York: Henry Holt. (P–M)

Demi. (1994). *In the eyes of the cat: Japanese poetry for all seasons.* New York: Henry Holt. (M)

Fleischman, P. (2004). *Joyful noise: Poems for two voices.* New York: HarperCollins. (M–U)

Florian, D. (2003). *Bow wow meow meow: It's rhyming cats and dogs.* San Diego: Harcourt Brace. (P)

Herrera, J. F. (1998). *Laughing out loud, I fly.* New York: HarperCollins. (M–U)

Hopkins, L. B. (Ed.). (2002). *Hoofbeats, claws and rippled fins: Creature poems.* New York: HarperCollins. (P)

Kennedy, X. J. (2002). *Exploding gray: Poems to make you laugh.* Boston: Little, Brown. (M–U)

Kuskin, K. (2003). *Moon, have you met my mother? The collected poems of Karla Kuskin.* New York: HarperCollins. (M)

Myers, W. D. (2003). *blues journey.* New York: Holiday House. (M–U)

Prelutsky, J. (2006). *Behold the bold umbrellaphant.* New York: Greenwillow. (M)

Swados, E. (2002). *Hey you! C'mere: A poetry slam.* New York: Scholastic. (M–U)

Comprehensive Anthologies

Hall, D. (2001). *The Oxford illustrated book of American children's poems.* New York: Oxford University Press. (P–M–U)

Prelutsky, J. (Compiler). (2000). *The Random House book of poetry for children.* New York: Random House. (P–M–U)

GUIDELINES FOR READING POEMS

- **Reading Aloud**

  Read poetry aloud, not silently, in order to appreciate the cadence of the words. Even if students are reading independently, they should speak each word, albeit softly or in an undertone.

- **Expression**

  Teach students how to read a poem expressively, how to emphasize the rhythm and feel of the words, and where to pause.

- **Song Tunes**

  Have children sing poems to familiar tunes, such as "Twinkle, Twinkle Little Star" or "I've Been Working on the Railroad," that fit the line structure of the poem.

- **Rehearsal**

  Have readers rehearse poems several times before reading aloud so that they can read fluently and with expression. In other words, encourage students to read "poetically."

- **Poetry Books**

  Include a collection of poetry books in the classroom library for children to read during reading workshop and other independent reading times.

- **Memorization**

  Rarely assign students a particular poem to memorize; rather, encourage students who are interested in learning a favorite poem to do so and to share it with class members.

- **Author Units**

  Teach author units to focus on a poet, such as Dr. Seuss, Jack Prelutsky, or Gary Soto. Have students read the poet's poems and learn about his or her life through biographies and Internet resources.

- **Display Poems**

  Copy and display poems on chart paper or on sentence strips in pocket charts for students to read and enjoy.

them up, and they pick out the words in the poem that created the image of a boy bully in their minds. As they talk about the poem, students discuss their assumptions about bullies and point out words in the text that led them astray. Some students also insist that the poet used the words *and boy* as an interjection early in the poem to intentionally mislead them.

Other poems are more difficult to understand. It might be helpful to think that understanding a poem is like peeling an onion. It requires multiple readings (Wood, 2006). From the first reading, students come away with an initial impression. Words and images stick in their minds: They giggle over silly rhymes, repeat alliterations and refrains, and ask questions about things that puzzle them.

Students' comprehension grows as they explore the poem. In the primary grades, students often explore poems together as a class, but Dias (1996) recommends that older students work in small groups to reread and talk about a poem. At this point, it's important that students remain flexible and recognize that a fuller meaning is possible. They reread the poem, drawing on their personal experiences and their knowledge of poetry to look for clues to meaning. Sometimes they wonder about the title of the poem and why the poet chose it. They also identify favorite lines, divide the poem into parts to understand its organization, examine line breaks, or discuss one of these points:

- Structure of the poem
- Order of words in a line
- Rhythm and rhyme
- Shape of the poem
- Imagery in the poem

They share their ideas, and as they listen to classmates' comments, their understanding grows. Teachers support students as they delve into a poem; they don't simply tell them what it means. They do provide information and ask questions to nudge students toward becoming independent, responsible readers. Poems often mean different things to students because they approach the poem with individual background knowledge and past experiences. Even so, a poem can't mean just anything; students' interpretations must be supported by the words in the text.

Gail E. Tompkins

Reading Poems

These children are rereading a poem their teacher recently introduced to the class. Through this reading practice, these first graders learn high-frequency words and develop reading fluency as well as an awareness of various poetic devices. After reading the poem, the children take the sentence strips out of the pocket chart, shuffle them, and then resequence them on the chart. Sometimes they decide that they prefer their new arrangement to the poet's. In another week of practice, their teacher will cut apart the words on each strip, and children can again practice resequencing the words in each line.

Performing Poems. Students share their understanding of a poem as they perform it for classmates. One way is using choral reading, in which students take turns reading a poem together. Students arrange the poem for choral reading so that individual students, pairs of students, and small groups read particular lines or stanzas. Here are four possible arrangements:

Echo Reading. The leader reads each line, and the group repeats it.

Leader and Chorus Reading. The leader reads the main part of the poem, and the group reads the refrain or chorus in unison.

Small-Group Reading. The class divides into two or more groups, and each group reads one part of the poem.

Cumulative Reading. One student or one group reads the first line or stanza, and another student or group joins in as each line or stanza is read so that a cumulative effect is created.

Then students rehearse their parts and, finally, they read the poem as an oral presentation. Students also can add props or play music in the background to enhance their presentation. The procedure for choral reading is shown in the Step by Step feature below.

Spanish speakers enjoy reading poems that incorporate some Spanish words, such as Gary Soto's *Neighborhood Odes* (2005) and Juan Felipe Herrera's *Laughing Out Loud, I Fly* (1998). The Spanish words are translated in a glossary, so even non-Spanish speakers can understand the poems. Other books of poetry are bilingual; the poems are printed side by side in Spanish and English, such as *Sol a Sol: Bilingual Poems* (Carlson, 1998), *Poems to Dream Together/Poemas para Soñar Juntos* (Alarcón, 2005), and *The Tree Is Older Than You Are* (Nye, 1998). Students can read these poems in either language, or alternate reading one line in English and the next in Spanish.

Choral Reading

1 Select a poem. Teachers choose a poem and copy it onto a chart or make multiple copies for students to read.

2 Create the arrangement. Teachers work with students to decide how to read the poem. They divide the poem into parts and identify who will read each part. Then the teacher adds marks to the chart, or students mark their copies so that they can follow the arrangement.

3 Rehearse the poem. Teachers read the poem with students several times at a natural speed, pronouncing words carefully. Individual students and small groups are careful to read only their own parts.

4 Perform the poem. Students read the poem expressively, following the arrangement they have rehearsed. Teachers often tape-record students' reading so that they can listen to their presentation.

5 Revise the arrangement. Teachers work with students to fine-tune the arrangement to make it more effective, or they create another arrangement and perform it again.

FIGURE 11–4

Ways to Respond to a Poem

Oral Activities

- Read the poem expressively to classmates.
- Sing the poem.
- Arrange the poem for choral reading and have classmates read it aloud.

Reading and Writing Activities

- Choose a favorite line and use it in a poem the student is writing.
- Read other poems written by the same poet.
- Write a poem on the same topic or following the format of the poem the student has read.
- Research the poet by reading a biography and consulting Internet resources.

Visual Activities

- Dramatize the poem with classmates as a tape recording of the poem is played aloud.
- Draw or paint a picture of an image the poem brings to mind and write a favorite line or two from the poem on the picture.
- Write the poem on sentence strips and then "build" the poem, sequencing the strips in a pocket chart.
- Make a picture book with lines or a stanza of the poem written on each page and illustrated.
- "Can," "box," or "bag" the poem by decorating a container and inserting a copy of the poem and two related items.

Response Activities. As children read poems or listen to them read aloud, they participate spontaneously in response actions: They move their bodies, tap their feet, or clap to the poem's rhythm, and they often repeat words, rhymes, and refrains, savoring the word choice and rhyme. Teachers also plan response activities that involve oral, reading and writing, and visual activities to enhance students' appreciation of the poems they're reading. Some activities are listed in Figure 11–4.

One way students explore a poem is by sequencing the lines. Teachers copy the lines of the poem on long strips of chart paper, and students sequence the lines in a pocket chart or by lining up around the classroom. Through this sequencing activity, students investigate the syntactic structure of poems and get ideas for poems they write.

A second way children respond to poems is by singing them. They pick a tune that fits the rhythm of the poem and sing it instead of reading it. Many teachers report that children quickly memorize poems when they sing them again and again. Alan Katz's hilarious book *Take Me Out of the Bathtub and Other Silly Dilly Songs* (2001) shows children how to fit new words to familiar tunes.

Children can celebrate a favorite poem by creating a class collaboration book of the poem. They each prepare one page by writing a line or stanza of the poem on it and then add an illustration to complement the text. One student also makes a cover for the book with the title of the poem and the poet's name. The teacher compiles the pages and binds the book, and then the book is placed in the classroom library. Children enjoy rereading their illustrated version of the poem. A page from a third-grade class book illustrating Shel Silverstein's "Hug O' War" (2004) is shown in Figure 11–5.

FIGURE 11–5

An Excerpt From a Third-Grade Book Illustrating Shel Silverstein's "Hug O' War"

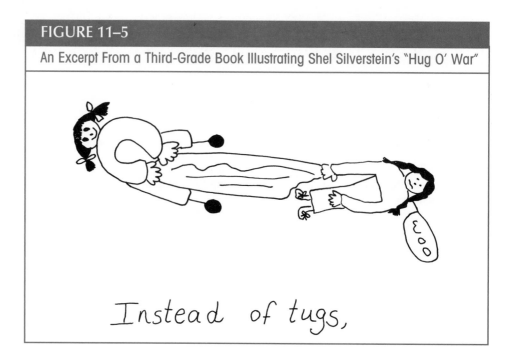

Instead of tugs,

Writing is another way students respond to poems. They can write new poems following the format of the poem they've read. In this poem, a second grader uses "My Teacher" (Dakos, 1995) as a model:

MY MOM

She loves to exercise at the gym
And watch romantic movies
And eat Mexican food
And get flowers painted on her nails

And sing in the choir at church
And most of all
ME!

Students also write poems by choosing a favorite line from a poem and incorporating it in a poem they write.

What About Memorizing Poems? Memorization is a useful mental exercise, but it's probably not a good idea to assign a particular poem for students to learn. Children vary in their poetry preferences, and requiring them to memorize a poem that they don't like risks killing their interest in poetry. A better approach is to encourage students who are interested in memorizing a favorite poem to do so and then recite it for the class; soon memorizing poems will become a popular response activity. In addition, as children rehearse for choral reading presentations, they often memorize the poem without even trying.

Teaching Minilessons. Teachers present minilessons to teach students about how to read and respond to poems. Minilessons cover procedures, concepts, and strategies and skills related to reading poetry. They also teach students to identify and appreciate comparisons, alliteration, and other types of wordplay in poems. A list of topics for minilessons is presented on page 372. Also included is a minilesson about how to read a poem expressively.

Assessing Students' Experiences With Poems

Teachers assess students' experiences with poetry in several ways. They observe students as they participate in poetry-reading activities, and they keep anecdotal notes of students as they read and respond to poems and share poems they like with classmates. Teachers can also conference with students and ask them about favorite poems to assess their interest in poetry. Students can write reflections about their learning and work habits during the poetry activities, and these reflections provide valuable assessment information.

WRITING POEMS

Children can write poetry! They write funny verses, vivid word pictures, powerful comparisons, and expressions of deep sentiment. The key to successful poetry is poetic formulas, which serve as scaffolds, or temporary writing frameworks, so that students focus on ideas rather than on the mechanics of writing poems (Cecil, 1997). In some formula poems, students begin each line with particular words, as with color poems; in some, they count syllables, as in haiku; and in others, they follow rhyming patterns, as in limericks. Many types of poetry do not use rhyme, and rhyme is the sticking point for many would-be poets. In searching for a rhyming word, children often create inane verse, for example:

> I see a funny little goat
> Wearing a blue sailor's coat
> Sitting in an old motorboat.

Of course, children should be allowed to write rhyming poetry, but rhyme should never be imposed as a criterion for acceptable poetry. Children should use rhyme when it fits naturally into their writing. When children write poetry, they are searching for their own voices, and they need freedom to do that.

Five types of poetic forms are formula poems, free-form poems, syllable- and word-count poems, rhymed poems, and model poems. They're discussed in the upcoming sections, and students' poems illustrate each poetic form. Kindergartners' and first graders' poems may seem little more than lists of sentences compared with the more sophisticated poems of older students, but the range of poems shows how students in kindergarten through eighth grade grow in their ability to write poetry.

What Students Need to Learn About Poetry

Topics

Procedures	Concepts	Strategies and Skills
Reading Poetry		
Read a poem expressively	Poetry	Vary tempo
Do choral reading	Rhymed verse	Emphasize rhythm
Share poems	Narrative poems	Vary pitch
Respond to poems	Free verse	Stress juncture
Do a project	Concrete poems	
Compile an anthology	Poetic elements	
	Information about poets	
Writing Poetry Topics		
Write formula poems	Poetic forms	Use poetic forms
Write preposition poems		Create sensory images
Craft found poem		Paint word pictures
Write free-form poems		Unwrite
Design concrete poems		Use model poems
Write word-count poems		Write rhymes
Write limericks		Punctuate poems
Write model poems		Capitalize poems
		Arrange poems on the page

If you'd like to learn more about teaching poetry, visit MyEducationLab. To watch first graders perform a choral reading presentation of a poem, go to the topic "Reading" and click on the video "Choral Reading."

Formula Poems

The poetic forms may seem like recipes, but they're not intended to be followed rigidly (Janeczko, 2005). Rather, they provide a scaffold, organization, or skeleton for students' poetry-writing activities. After collecting words, images, and comparisons through brainstorming or another prewriting strategy, students craft their poems, choosing words and arranging them to create a message. Meaning is always most important, and form follows the search for meaning.

Minilesson

Mr. Johnston Teaches His Third Graders How to Read Poems Expressively

1 Introduce the topic

Mr. Johnston places a transparency of "A Pizza the Size of the Sun" by Jack Prelutsky (1996) on the overhead projector and reads it aloud in a monotone voice. He asks his third graders if he did a good job reading the poem, and they tell him that his reading was boring.

2 Share examples

Mr. Johnston asks what he could do to make his reading better, and they suggest that he read with more expression. He asks the children to tell him which words he should read more expressively and marks their changes on the transparency. He reads the poem again, and the children agree that it is better. Then they suggest he vary his reading speed, and he marks their changes on the transparency. He reads the poem a third time, incorporating more changes. The children agree that his third reading is the best!

3 Provide information

Mr. Johnston praises his students for their suggestions; they did help him make this reading better. Then he asks what he can do to make his

reading more interesting, and they make these suggestions:

- Read some parts loud and some parts soft.
- Read some parts fast and some parts slow.
- Change your voice for some words.

4 Supervise practice

Mr. Johnston divides the class into small groups and passes out transparencies of other poems. Children in each group decide how to read the poem and mark parts they will read in special ways. Mr. Johnston circulates around the classroom as children work, providing assistance as needed. Then children display their poems on the overhead projector and read them aloud with expression.

5 Reflect on learning

Mr. Johnston asks the third graders to talk about what they have learned. One child explains that there are two ways of reading: One is boring and the other is fun. They have learned how to read the fun way so that they can share their enjoyment of poems with others.

Poet Kenneth Koch (2000) developed some simple formulas that make it easy for nearly every student to become a successful poet. These formulas call for students to begin every line the same way or to insert a particular kind of word in every line. The formulas use repetition, a stylistic device that is more effective for young poets than rhyme. Some forms may seem more like sentences than poems, but the dividing line between poetry and prose is a blurry one, and these poetry experiences help students move toward poetic expression.

Meeting the Needs of English Learners

Shouldn't English Learners Be Doing Something More Important Than Reading and Writing Poetry?

You might argue that there is so much language arts instruction that English learners need that they don't have time for poetry, but that's just plain wrong. Poetry offers English learners a unique opportunity for success, and when they're successful, their self-confidence increases, and they're more willing to take risks with other language arts activities.

There are specific benefits for reading, too. Students develop reading fluency and learn vocabulary words as they practice reading a favorite poem in preparation for choral reading performance (Peregoy & Boyle, 2005). Students refine their oral language and presentational skills as they read and respond to poetry: They might memorize a favorite poem and recite it expressively, adding background music or pictures to accompany it. Or, they might share a poem written in their native language and then translate it for the class.

There are benefits for writing as well. Many English learners have difficulty with long writing assignments. Because poems are short, they're often easier to write. English learners' poems are usually better organized than other compositions because they structure their writing with familiar poetic forms, and the quality of their poems is often remarkable. They draw images with words, combine words in fresh, unexpected ways, and create a strong voice through their writing; in fact, students often surprise themselves with the poems they write.

"I Wish . . ." Poems. Students begin each line of their poems with the words "I wish" and complete the line with a wish (Koch, 2000). In a second-grade class collaboration, children simply listed their wishes:

> I wish I had all the money in the world.
> I wish I was a star fallen down from Mars.
> I wish I were a butterfly.
> I wish I were a teddy bear.
> I wish I had a cat.
> I wish I were a pink rose.
> I wish it wouldn't rain today.
> I wish I didn't have to wash a dish.
> I wish I had a flying carpet.
> I wish I could go to Disney World.
> I wish school was out.
> I wish I could go outside and play.

After this experience, students choose one of their wishes and expand on the idea in another poem. Brandi expanded her wish this way:

> I wish I were a teddy bear
> Who sat on a beautiful bed
> Who got a hug every night
> By a little girl or boy

Maybe tonight I'll get my wish
And wake up on a little girl's bed
And then I'll be as happy as can be.

Color Poems. Students begin each line of their poems with a color. They can use the same color in each line or choose a different color (Koch, 2000). For example, a class of seventh graders wrote about yellow:

Yellow is shiny galoshes
splashing through mud puddles.
Yellow is a street lamp
beaming through a dark, black night.
Yellow is the egg yolk
bubbling in a frying pan.
Yellow is the lemon cake
that makes you pucker your lips.
Yellow is the sunset
and the warm summer breeze.
Yellow is the tingling in your mouth
after a lemon drop melts.

Students can also write more complex poems by expanding each idea into a stanza, as this poem about black illustrates:

Black is a deep hole
sitting in the ground
waiting for animals
that live inside.
Black is a beautiful horse
standing on a high hill
with the wind
swirling its mane.
Black is a winter night sky
without stars
to keep it
company.
Black is a panther
creeping around a jungle
searching for
its prey.

Yellow Elephant: A Bright Bestiary (Larios, 2006) is one source of color poems, and *Hailstones and Halibut Bones* (O'Neill, 1990) is another. However, poets often use rhyme as a poetic device so it's important to emphasize that students' poems need not rhyme.

Five-Senses Poems. Students write about a topic using the five senses. These poems are usually five lines long, with one line for each sense, as this poem, "Being Heartbroken," written by a sixth grader, demonstrates:

Sounds like thunder and lightning
Looks like a carrot going through a blender

Tastes like sour milk
Feels like a splinter in your finger
Smells like a dead fish
It must be horrible!

It is often helpful to have students develop a five-senses cluster and collect ideas for each sense before beginning to write. Then they select the most vivid idea for each sense to use in a line of the poem.

"If I Were …" Poems. Students write about how they would feel and what they would do if they were something else—a Tyrannosaurus rex, a hamburger, or sunshine (Koch, 2000). They begin each poem with "If I were" and tell what it would be like to be that thing. Students can also write poems from the viewpoint of a book character. Fifth graders, for example, wrote this short poem after reading *Number the Stars* (Lowry, 2005):

If I were Annemarie,   I would lie if I had to.
I'd be brave.   If I were Annemarie,
I'd hide my friends,   I'd be brave.
and trick those Nazi soldiers.

Comparison Poems. Students compare something to something else and then expand on the comparison in the rest of the poem (Koch, 2000). A third grader wrote this poem after brainstorming a list of possible explanations for thunder:

Thunder is a brontosaurus sneezing,
that's all it is.
Nothing to frighten you—
just a dinosaur with a cold.

This child's comparison is a metaphor. She could have written "Thunder is like a brontosaurus sneezing," a simile, but her metaphor is a much stronger comparison.

"I Am …" Poems. Children write "I Am … " poems from the viewpoint of a book character or historical figure. They use repetition by beginning and ending each stanza with "I am" and beginning the lines in between with "I." First graders wrote this class collaboration poem after reading *Where the Wild Things Are* (Sendak, 2003), the story of a boy who imagines that he travels to the land of the wild things after being sent to his bedroom for misbehaving:

I am Max   But I got homesick
wearing my wolf suit   so I sailed home.
and making mischief.   I am Max,
I turned into a Wild Thing.   a hungry little boy
I became the king of the Wild Things.   who wants his mommy.

Preposition Poems. Students begin each line of their poems with a preposition. This pattern often produces a delightful poetic effect. A seventh grader wrote this preposition poem about Superman:

Within the city   Through the walls
In a phone booth   Until the crime
Into his clothes   Among us
Like a bird   Is defeated!
In the sky

It's helpful to have a list of prepositions available for students to refer to when they write preposition poems. Students may find that they need to ignore the formula for a line or two to give the content of their poems top priority, or they may mistakenly begin a line with an infinitive (e.g., *to say*) rather than a preposition. These forms provide a structure for students' writing that should be adapted as necessary.

Acrostic Poems. Students write acrostic poems using key words. They choose a key word and write it vertically on a sheet of paper. Then they create lines of poetry, each one beginning with a letter of the word they've written (Janeczko, 2005). Students can use their names during a unit on autobiography or names of characters during a literature focus unit. For example, after reading *Officer Buckle and Gloria* (Rathmann, 1995), the story of a police officer and his dog who give safety speeches at schools, a group of first graders wrote this acrostic using the dog's name, Gloria, as the key word:

Gloria
Loves to do tricks.
Officer Buckle tells safety
Rules at schools.
I wish I had
A dog like Gloria.

Other children composed this acrostic using the same key word:

Good dog Gloria
Likes to help
Officer Buckle teach safety
Rules to boys and girls.
I promise to remember
All the lessons.

Free-Form Poems

Students choose words to describe something and put the words together to express a thought or tell a story, without concern for rhyme or other arrangements. The number of words per line and the use of punctuation vary. In the following poem, an eighth grader poignantly describes loneliness concisely, using only 15 well-chosen words:

A lifetime
Of broken dreams
And promises
Lost love
Hurt
My heart
Cries
In silence

Students can use several methods for writing free-form poems: They can select words and phrases from brainstormed lists and clusters, or they can write a paragraph and then "unwrite" it to create the poem by deleting unnecessary words. They arrange the remaining words to look like a poem.

Concrete Poems. Students create concrete poems through art and the careful arrangement of words on a page (Fletcher, 2002). Words, phrases, and sentences can

---

FIGURE 11–6

Students' Concrete Poems

---

be written in the shape of an object, or word pictures can be inserted within poems written left to right and top to bottom (Janeczko, 2005). Concrete poems are extensions of the word pictures discussed earlier. Two concrete poems are shown in Figure 11–6. In "Ants," the words *ants, cake,* and *frosting* create the image of a familiar picnic scene, and in "Cemetery," repetition and form create a reflection of peace. Three books of concrete poems are *Meow Ruff: A Story in Concrete Poetry* (Sidman, 2006), *Technically, It's Not My Fault: Concrete Poems* (Grandits, 2004), and *A Poke in the I* (Janeczko, 2001).

Found Poems. Students create poems by culling words from other sources, such as stories, songs, and informational books (Fletcher, 2002). They collect words and phrases and then arrange them to make a poem (Janeczko, 2005). A sixth grader wrote this poem after reading *Hatchet* (Paulsen, 2006), the story of a boy who survives for months in the wilderness after his plane crashes:

> He was 13.
> Always started with a single word:
> Divorce.
> An ugly word,
> A breaking word, an ugly breaking word.
> A tearing ugly word that meant fights and yelling.
> Secrets.
> Visitation rights.
> A hatchet on his belt.
> His plane.
> The pilot had been sighted.
> He rubbed his shoulder.
> Aches and pains.

A heart attack.
The engine droned.
A survival pack which had emergency supplies.
Brian Robeson
Alone.
Help, p-l-e-a-s-e.

When they write found poems, students experiment with more sophisticated words and language structures than they might write themselves, and they also document their understanding of the stories and other texts they've read.

Poems for Two Voices.

A unique type of free verse is poems for two voices. These poems are written in two columns, side by side, and the columns are read together by two readers or groups of readers: one reader reads the left column, and the other reads the right column. Sometimes readers alternate when they read, but when readers both have words—either the same words or different words—written on the same line, they read them simultaneously so that the poem sounds like a musical duet. Two books of poems for two readers are Paul Fleischman's *I Am Phoenix: Poems for Two Voices* (1985), which is about birds, and the Newbery Medal–winning *Joyful Noise: Poems for Two Voices* (2004), which is about insects. And, if two voices aren't enough, Fleischman has also written *Big Talk: Poems for Four Voices* (2000).

Lorraine Wilson (1994) suggests that topics with contrasting viewpoints are the most effective. Students can also write poems from two characters' viewpoints. For example, after reading *Officer Buckle and Gloria* (Rathmann, 1995), a second-grade class wrote this poem for two voices. The voice on the left is Officer Buckle's and the voice on the right is Gloria the dog's:

I am Officer Buckle	
	I am Gloria,
	a police dog in the K-9.
I teach safety tips	I teach safety tips
to boys and girls.	to boys and girls.
I say,	
"Keep your shoelaces tied."	
	I do a trick.
I say,	
"Do not go swimming	
during electrical storms."	
	I do a trick.
I say,	
"Stay away from guns."	
	I do a trick.
Bravo!	Bravo!
Everyone claps.	Everyone claps.
Do the kids love me?	
	Yes, they do.
No, the kids love you more.	
	The kids love both of us.
We're buddies!	We're buddies!
Always stick with your buddy.	Always stick with your buddy.

Syllable- and Word-Count Poems

Haiku and other syllable- and word-count poems provide a structure that helps students succeed in writing; however, the need to adhere to these poems' formulas may restrict freedom of expression. In other words, the poetic structure may both help and hinder. The exact syllable counts force students to search for just the right words to express their ideas and feelings and provide a valuable opportunity for them to use thesauri and dictionaries.

Haiku. The most familiar syllable-count poem is *haiku* (high-KOO), a Japanese poetic form consisting of 17 syllables arranged in three lines of 5, 7, and 5 syllables. Haiku poems deal with nature and present a single, clear image. Haiku is a concise form, much like a telegram. A fourth grader wrote this haiku poem about a spider web she saw one morning:

> Spider web shining
> Tangled on the grass with dew
> Waiting quietly.

Books of haiku to share with students include *Cool Melons—Turn to Frogs!* (Gollub, 1998), *Fold Me a Poem* (George, 2005), and *In the Eyes of the Cat: Japanese Poetry for All Seasons* (Demi, 1994). The photographs and artwork in these trade books may give students ideas for illustrating their haiku poems.

Cinquain. A cinquain (SIN-cane) is a five-line poem containing 22 syllables in a 2-4-6-8-2 syllable pattern. They usually describe something but may also tell a story. This is the formula:

Line 1: a one-word subject with two syllables
Line 2: four syllables describing the subject
Line 3: six syllables showing action
Line 4: eight syllables expressing a feeling or an observation about the subject
Line 5: two syllables describing or renaming the subject

A seventh-grade student wrote this cinquain poem:

> Wrestling
> skinny, fat
> coaching, arguing, pinning
> trying hard to win
> tournament

If you compare this poem to the cinquain formula, you'll notice that some lines are short a syllable or two. The student bent some of the guidelines in choosing words to create a powerful image of wrestling; however, the message of the poem is always more important than adhering to the formula.

Diamante. Iris Tiedt (2002) invented the *diamante* (dee-ah-MAHN-tay), a seven-line contrast poem written in the shape of a diamond. This poetic form helps students apply their knowledge of opposites and parts of speech. The formula is as follows:

Line 1: one noun as the subject
Line 2: two adjectives describing the subject

Line 3: three participles (ending in -*ing*) telling about the subject

Line 4: four nouns (the first two related to the subject and the second two related to the opposite)

Line 5: three participles telling about the opposite

Line 6: two adjectives describing the opposite

Line 7: one noun that is the opposite of the subject

A third-grade class wrote this diamante poem about the stages of life:

Baby

wrinkled tiny

crying wetting sleeping

rattles diapers money house

caring working loving

smart helpful

Adult

The students created a contrast between *baby,* the subject represented by the noun in the first line, and *adult,* the opposite in the last line. This contrast gives students the opportunity to play with words and apply their understanding of opposites. The third word in the fourth line, *money,* begins the transition from *baby* to its opposite, *adult.*

Rhymed Verse Forms

Several rhymed verse forms, such as limericks and clerihews, can be used effectively with middle- and upper-grade students. However, it is important that teachers try to prevent the forms and rhyme schemes from restricting students' creative and imaginative expression.

Limericks. The limerick is a form of light verse that uses both rhyme and rhythm. The poem consists of five lines; the first, second, and fifth lines rhyme, and the third and fourth lines rhyme with each other and are shorter than the other three (Janeczko, 2005). The last line often contains a funny or surprise ending, as in this limerick written by an eighth grader:

There once was a frog named Pete
Who did nothing but sit and eat.
He examined each fly
With so careful an eye
And then said, "You're dead meat."

Writing limericks can be a challenging assignment for many upper-grade students, but middle-grade students can also be successful with this poetic form, especially if they write a collaborative poem first.

Limericks are believed to have originated in Limerick, Ireland, and were first popularized by Edward Lear (1812–1888). Poet X. J. Kennedy (1999) describes limericks as the most popular type of poem in the English language and recommends introducing students to limericks by reading aloud some of Lear's verses so they can appreciate the rhythm of the verse. Two collections of Lear's limericks are *Daffy Down Dillies: Silly Limericks by Edward Lear* (Lear, 1995) and *Lots of Limericks* (Livingston,

1991). Children also enjoy the playfulness of John Ciardi's verses in *The Hopeful Trout and Other Limericks* (1992).

Clerihews. *Clerihews* (KLER-i-hyoos), four-line rhymed verses that describe a person (Janeczko, 2005). They're named for Edmund Clerihew Bentley (1875–1956), a British detective writer who invented the form. This is the formula:

> Line 1: the person's name
> Line 2: the last word rhymes with the last word in the first line
> Lines 3 and 4: the last words in these lines rhyme with each other

Clerihews can be written about anyone—historical figures, characters in stories, and even the students themselves. A sixth grader wrote this clerihew about Albert Einstein:

> Albert Einstein
> His genius did shine.
> Of relativity and energy did he dream
> And scientists today hold him in high esteem.

Model Poems

Students model their poems on poems composed by adult poets, as Kenneth Koch suggested in *Rose, Where Did You Get That Red?* (1990). In this approach, students read a poem and write their own, using some of the words and the theme expressed in the model poem. For other examples of model poems, see Paul Janeczko's *Poetry From A to Z: A Guide for Young Writers* (1994) and Nancy Cecil's *For the Love of Language* (1994).

Apologies. Using William Carlos Williams's "This Is Just to Say" as the model, children write a poem in which they apologize for something they are secretly glad they did (Koch, 1990). Middle- and upper-grade students are familiar with offering apologies and enjoy writing humorous apologies. A seventh grader wrote this apology poem, "The Truck," to his dad:

> Dad,   I knew it
> I'm sorry   was wrong.
> that I took   But . . .
> the truck   the exhilarating
> out for   motion was
> a spin.   AWESOME!

Apology poems don't have to be humorous; they may be sensitive, genuine apologies, as another seventh grader's poem, "Open Up," demonstrates:

> I didn't   a death
> open my   had caused.
> immature eyes   Forgive me,
> to see   I misunderstood
> the pain   your anguished
> within you   broken heart.

Invitations. Students write poems in which they invite someone to a magical, beautiful place full of sounds and colors and where all kinds of marvelous things happen.

The model is Shakespeare's "Come Unto These Yellow Sands" (Koch, 1990). A seventh grader wrote this invitation poem, "The Golden Shore":

> Come unto the golden shore
> Where days are filled with laughter,
> And nights filled with whispering winds.
> Where sunflowers and sun
> Are filled with love.
> Come take my hand
> As we walk into the sun.

Teaching Students to Write Poems

Students use what they have learned about poetry through reading poems and mini-lessons as they write poems. Too often they have misconceptions that interfere with their ability to write poems. It's important that teachers help students develop a concept of poetry and experiment with poetic elements as they begin writing poems.

Introducing Students to Writing Poetry. One way to introduce students to writing poetry is to read excerpts from the first chapter of *Anastasia Krupnik* (Lowry, 1995), in which 10-year-old Anastasia, the main character, is excited when her teacher, Mrs. Westvessel, announces that the class will write poems. Anastasia works at home for eight nights to write a poem. Lowry does an excellent job of describing how poets search long and hard for words to express meaning and the delight that comes when they realize their poems are finished. Then Anastasia and her classmates bring their poems to class to read aloud. One student reads his four-line rhymed verse:

> I have a dog whose name is Spot.
> He likes to eat and drink a lot.
> When I put water in his dish,
> He laps it up just like a fish. (p. 10)

Anastasia is not impressed. She knows the child who wrote the poem has a dog named Sputnik, not Spot! But Mrs. Westvessel gives it an A and hangs it on the bulletin board. Soon it is Anastasia's turn, and she is nervous because her poem is very different. She reads her poem about tiny creatures that move about in tidepools at night:

> hush   hush   the sea-soft night is aswim
>   with wrinklesquirm creatures
>   listen (!)
> to them   move   smooth   in the moistly dark
>   here in the   whisperwarm   (pp. 11–12)

In this free-form poem without rhyme or capital letters, Anastasia has created a marvelous picture with invented words. Regrettably, Mrs. Westvessel has an antiquated view that poems should be about only serious subjects, be composed of rhyming sentences, and use conventional capitalization and punctuation. She doesn't understand Anastasia's poem and gives her an F because she didn't follow directions.

Although this first chapter presents a depressing picture of teachers and their lack of knowledge about poetry, it's a dramatic introduction about what poetry is and what it isn't. After reading excerpts from the chapter, develop a chart with your students comparing what poetry is in Mrs. Westvessel's class and what poetry is in your class. A seventh-grade class developed the chart in Figure 11–7

After this introduction to writing poetry, teachers teach minilessons about the poetic formulas and how to write poems, and they provide opportunities for students to write poems. Jack Prelutsky's *Read a Rhyme, Write a Rhyme* (2005) also provides "poemstarts" to help children start writing their own poems. A list of guidelines for writing poetry is shown in the LA Essentials box on the next page.

Minilessons. Teachers use minilessons to introduce students to poetic forms and write collaborative poems for practice before students write poems independently. Class collaborations are crucial because they are a practice run for students who aren't sure what to do. The 5 minutes it takes to write a class collaboration poem can be the difference between success and failure for students. Teachers also teach other topics related to writing poetry. They teach minilessons on the poetic elements and how to incorporate them into the poems that students write, how to arrange lines of poetry for the greatest impact, and how to punctuate and capitalize poems, for example. A list of topics for minilessons related to writing poetry is presented on page 372

Teaching minilessons about writing poetry is important; it is not enough simply to provide opportunities for students to experiment with poetry. Georgia Heard (1999) emphasizes the importance of teaching students about line breaks and white space on the page. Young children often write poems with the same page arrangement as stories, but as they experiment with line breaks, they shape their poems to emphasize rhythm and rhyme, images, and poetic elements. Students learn that the way the lines are broken affects both how the poem looks and how it sounds when read aloud.

FIGURE 11–7

A Comparison Chart Created After Reading *Anastasia Krupnik*

Rules About Writing Poetry

Mrs. Westvessel's Rules	Our Rules
1. Poems must rhyme.	1. Poems do not have to rhyme.
2. The first letter in each line must be capitalized.	2. The first letter in each line does not have to be capitalized.
3. Each line must start at the left margin.	3. Poems can take different shapes and be anywhere on a page.
4. Poems must have a certain rhythm.	4. You hear the writer's voice in a poem—with or without rhythm.
5. Poems should be written about serious things.	5. Poems can be about anything—serious or silly things.
6. Poems should be punctuated like other types of writing.	6. Poems can be punctuated in different ways or not be punctuated at all.
7. Poems are failures if they don't follow these rules.	7. There are no real rules for poems, and no poem is a failure.

GUIDELINES FOR WRITING POEMS

- **Concept of Poetry**

  Explain what poetry is and what makes a good poem. Too often, students assume that all poems must rhyme, are written on topics such as love and flowers, must be punctuated in a particular way, or have other restrictions.

- **Poetry Books**

  Set out books of poetry in a special section of the classroom library. Students learn about poetry through reading, and some poems can serve as models for the poems they write.

- **Model Poems**

  Encourage students to write poems that model or incorporate a line from a poem they've read.

- **Formulas**

  Teach students 5 to 10 poetic formulas so that they have options when they write poems. At the same time, it's important that students know that they can break the formulas in order to express themselves more effectively.

- **Class Collaboration Poems**

  Write a collaborative poem with students to ensure that everyone understands how to write a poem before they write poems on their own.

- **Minilessons**

  Present minilessons on poetic devices, formulas, and other topics.

- **Wordplay**

  Encourage students to play with words, invent new words, and create word pictures as they write poems.

- **Anthologies**

  Create a class anthology of students' poems, and make copies of the anthology for each student. Students can also make collections of the poems they've written.

Publishing Students' Poems. Students use the writing process to draft and refine their poems; the final stage of the writing process is publishing. It's important because it brings closure to the writing process, and students are motivated by sharing and by receiving their classmates' approval. They also collect ideas they can use in their own writing as they listen to and read their classmates' poems. Students share their poetry in two ways—by reading it aloud to classmates and by sharing written copies of their poems for classmates to read.

The most common way that students share their poems is by reading them aloud—and with expression—from the author's chair. Classmates listen and then offer compliments about what they liked about the poem—word choice, topic, or poetic element. Another way that students share their poems with classmates is through a read-around, as Mrs. Harris's students did in the vignette at the beginning of the chapter.

Students compile their poems into anthologies that they place in the classroom library for classmates to read. Teachers also display copies of students' poems, often accompanied by an illustration, on a wall of the classroom and then have a gallery walk for students to read and respond to the poems. If there isn't enough classroom space to display the students' work, teachers can post them in the hallway or on students' desks. Students move from poem to poem and read and respond using small self-stick notes that they attach to the edge of the student's paper. The steps in conducting a gallery walk are shown in the Step by Step feature below. This activity is quick; it can be completed much more quickly than if each student were to share his or her poem in front of the class.

-------- Gallery Walks --------

1 Display the work.   Students post their work on classroom walls or place it on desks so classmates can read it.

2 Provide comment sheets.   Teachers give students small self-stick notes on which to write comments about each student's work. Students will attach notes with their comments to the edge of classmates' work.

3 Give directions.   Teachers explain the purpose of the gallery walk, how to view and/or read the work, and what comments to make to classmates. Teachers also set time limits and direct students to visit three, five, eight, or more students' work, if there isn't time to read everyone's work.

4 Model behavior.   The teacher models how to view, read, and respond during the gallery walk using one or two students' work as examples.

5 Direct the flow of traffic.   Teachers direct students as they move around the classroom, making sure that everyone's work is read and that comments are supportive and useful.

6 Bring closure.   Students move to their own work and look at the comments, questions, or other responses they've received. One or two students may share their responses or comment on the gallery walk experience.

Incorporating Poetry Into the Patterns of Practice. Teachers share poems and invite students to write poems as part of most of the patterns of practice. It's easy to find poems to accompany most featured books for literature focus units and topics for thematic units, and many students often choose to write poetry, when they're given a choice. The box below shows how poetry fits into the four patterns of practice. Teachers can also create a poetry workshop as Mrs. Harris did in the vignette at the beginning of the chapter.

Assessing the Poems Students Write

Donald Graves (1992) recommends that teachers focus on the passion and wonder in students' writing and on their unique ability to make the common seem uncommon. Teachers notice the specific details, strong images, wordplay, comparisons, onomatopoeia, alliteration, and repetitions of words and lines that students incorporate in their poems. Assessing the quality of students' poems is especially difficult, because poems are creative combinations of wordplay, poetic forms, and poetic devices. Instead of trying to give a grade for quality, teachers can ask these questions:

- Has the student experimented with the poetic form presented in a minilesson?
- Has the student used the process approach in writing, revising, and editing the poem?
- Has the student used wordplay or another poetic device in the poem?

Teachers also ask students to assess their own poems. Students choose their best efforts and poems that show promise. They can explain which writing strategies they used in particular poems and which poetic forms they used.

How Poetry Fits Into the Four Patterns of Practice

Literature Focus Units

Teachers often share poems in conjunction with featured books, and students often choose to write poems as projects during the extending stage of the reading process.

Literature Circles

Poetry isn't used very often in literature circles, but sometimes students do choose to read books of poetry in a literature circle.

Reading and Writing Workshop

Sometimes students choose books of poetry to read during reading workshop, especially when teachers frequently read poetry aloud to students. Many students write poems during writing workshop, especially when they've learned to use various poetic formulas.

Thematic Units

Teachers and students often read aloud poems related to the thematic unit, and they also write poems. Sometimes they use the poems they've read as models, incorporate a line from a familiar poem, or choose a formula they've learned for the poems they write.

Review

Students read and respond to poems, and they write their own poems. They participate in wordplay activities and read and write poetry as part of the four patterns of practice. Here are some of the important concepts about reading and writing poetry presented in this chapter:

- Wordplay activities with riddles, comparisons, rhyme, and other poetic devices provide the background of experiences students need for reading and writing poetry.
- Three types of poetry books published for children are picture-book versions of single poems, specialized collections of poems, and comprehensive anthologies of poems.
- Students have definite opinions about the types of poems they like best.
- Poems should be read aloud and with expression.
- Tempo, rhythm, pitch, and juncture are four considerations when reading poetry aloud.
- Choral reading is an effective way for students to perform a poem.
- Students participate in oral, reading and writing, and visual response activities to explore favorite poems.
- Students can write poems successfully using poetic formulas in which they begin each line with particular words, count syllables, or create word pictures.
- Because rhyme is a sticking point for many, students should be encouraged to experiment with other poetic elements in their writing.
- Reading and writing poetry aren't frills; they're an important part of the language arts program.

Professional References

Cecil, N. L. (1994). *For the love of language: Poetry for every learner*. Winnipeg, MB: Peguis.

Cullinan, B. E., Scala, M. C., & Schroder, V. C. (1995). *Three voices: An invitation to poetry across the curriculum*. York, ME: Stenhouse.

Dias, P. X. (1996). *Reading and responding to poetry: Patterns in the process*. Portsmouth, NH: Boynton/Cook.

Elster, C. A., & Hanauer, D. I. (2002). Voicing texts, voices around texts: Reading poems in elementary school classrooms. *Research in the Teaching of English, 37,* 89–134.

Fisher, C. J., & Natarella, M. A. (1982). Young children's preferences in poetry: A national survey of first, second, and third graders. *Research in the Teaching of English, 16,* 339–354.

Fletcher, R. (2002). *Poetry matters: Writing a poem from the inside out*. New York: HarperCollins.

Geller, L. G. (1981). Riddling: A playful way to explore language. *Language Arts, 58,* 669–674.

Geller, L. G. (1985). *Word play and language learning for children*. Urbana, IL: National Council of Teachers of English.

Glover, M. K. (1999). *A garden of poets: Poetry writing in the elementary classroom*. Urbana, IL: National Council of Teachers of English.

Graves, D. H. (1992). *Explore poetry*. Portsmouth, NH: Heinemann.

Heard, G. (1999). *Awakening the heart: Exploring poetry in elementary and middle school*. Portsmouth, NH: Heinemann.

Holbrook, S. (2005). *Practical poetry: A nonstandard approach to meeting content-area standards*. Portsmouth, NH: Heinemann.

Janeczko, P. B. (2005). *A kick in the head: An everyday guide to poetic forms*. Cambridge, MA: Candlewick Press.

Koch, K. (2000). *Wishes, lies, and dreams.* New York: Harper-Perennial.

Koch, K. (1990). *Rose, where did you get that red?* New York: Vintage.

Kutiper, K. (1985). *A survey of the poetry preferences of seventh, eighth, and ninth graders.* Unpublished doctoral dissertation, University of Houston.

Kutiper, K., & Wilson, P. (1993). Updating poetry preferences: A look at the poetry children really like. *The Reading Teacher, 47,* 28–35.

Opie, I., & Opie, P. (1967). *The lore and language of school children.* Oxford: Oxford University Press.

Peregoy, S. F., & Boyle, O. F. (2005). *Reading, writing, and learning in ESL: A resource book for K–12 teachers* (4th ed.). Boston: Allyn & Bacon.

Siemens, L. (1996). "Walking through the time of kids": Going places with poetry. *Language Arts, 73,* 234–240.

Terry, A. (1974). *Children's poetry preferences: A national survey of upper elementary grades* (NCTE Research Report No. 16). Urbana, IL: National Council of Teachers of English.

Tiedt, I. (2002). *Tiger lilies, toadstools, and thunderbolts: Engaging K–8 students with poetry.* Newark, DE: International Reading Association.

Wilson, L. (1994). *Write me a poem: Reading, writing, and performing poetry.* Portsmouth, NH: Heinemann.

Wood, J. R. (2006). *Living voices: Multicultural poetry in the middle school classroom.* Urbana, IL: National Council of Teachers of English.

Children's Book References

Alarcón, F. X. (2006). *Poems to dream together/poemas para soñar juntos.* New York: Greenwillow.

American Poetry and Literacy Project. (2006). *How to eat a poem: A smorgasbord of tasty and delicious poems for young readers.* Mineola, NY: Dover.

Bayer, J. (1992). *A my name is Alice.* New York: Dial Books.

Carlson, L. M. (Ed.). (1998). *Sol a sol: Bilingual poems.* New York: Henry Holt.

Ciardi, J. (1992). *The hopeful trout and other limericks.* Boston: Houghton Mifflin.

Cobb, R. (2006). *Tongue twisters to tangle your tongue.* London: Marion Boyars.

Creech, S. (2001). *Love that dog.* New York: HarperCollins.

Crew, G. (1998). *Troy Thompson's excellent peotry [sic] book.* Victoria, Australia: Lothian.

Dakos, K. (1995). *Mrs. Cole on an onion roll and other school poems.* New York: Aladdin Books.

Demi. (1994). *In the eyes of the cat: Japanese poetry for all seasons.* New York: Henry Holt.

Edwards, P. D. (2001). *Slop goes the soup: A noisy warthog word book.* New York: Hyperion Books.

Fleischman, P. (1985). *I am phoenix: Poems for two voices.* New York: HarperCollins.

Fleischman, P. (2000). *Big talk: Poems for four voices.* Cambridge, MA: Candlewick Press.

Fleischman, P. (2004). *Joyful noise: Poems for two voices.* New York: HarperCollins.

Fletcher, R. (2002). *Poetry matters: Writing a poem from the inside out.* New York: HarperCollins.

George, K. O. (2005). *Fold me a poem.* San Diego: Harcourt.

Grandits, J. (2004). *Technically it's not my fault: Concrete poems.* New York: Clarion Books.

Gollub, M. (1998). *Cool melons—turn to frogs!* New York: Lee & Low.

Herrera, J. F. (1998). *Laughing out loud, I fly.* New York: HarperCollins.

Janeczko, P. B. (1994). *Poetry from A to Z: A guide for young writers.* New York: Bradbury Press.

Janeczko, P. B. (2001). *A poke in the I.* Cambridge, MA: Candlewick Press.

Katz, A. (2001). *Take me out of the bathtub and other silly dilly songs.* New York: McElderry.

Kennedy, X. J., & Kennedy, D. M. (1999). *Knock at a star: A child's introduction to poetry* (rev. ed.). Boston: Little, Brown.

Langstaff, J. (1991). *Oh, a-hunting we will go.* New York: Aladdin Books.

Larios, J. (2006). *Yellow elephant: A bright bestiary.* San Diego: Harcourt.

Lear, E. (1995). *Daffy down dillies: Silly limericks by Edward Lear.* Honesdale, PA: Wordsong.

Livingston, M. C. (1991). *Lots of limericks.* New York: McElderry.

Lobel, A. (1996). *Alison's zinnia.* New York: Greenwillow.

Longfellow, H. W. (1996). *Hiawatha.* New York: Puffin Books.

Longfellow, H. W. (2001). *The midnight ride of Paul Revere* (C. Bing, Illus.). New York: Handprint Books.

Lowry, L. (1995). *Anastasia Krupnik.* New York: HarperCollins.

Lowry, L. (2005). *Number the stars.* New York: Yearling.

MacDonald, R. (2003). *Achoo! Bang! Crash! The noisy alphabet.* New York: Roaring Brook Press.

Milne, A. A. (2001). *The house at Pooh Corner.* New York: Dutton.

Montenegro, L. N. (2003). *A bird about to sing.* Boston: Houghton Mifflin.

Moore, C. C. (1998). *The night before Christmas.* New York: Putnam.

Nye, N. S. (1998). *The tree is older than you are.* New York: Simon & Schuster.

O'Neill, M. (1990). *Hailstones and halibut bones: Adventures in color.* Garden City, NJ: Doubleday.

Paulsen, G. (2006). *Hatchet.* New York: Aladdin Books.

Prelutsky, J. (1984). *The new kid on the block*. New York: Greenwillow.

Prelutsky, J. (1996). *A pizza the size of the sun*. New York: Greenwillow.

Prelutsky, J. (Sel.). (2000). *The Random House book of poetry for children*. New York: Random House.

Prelutsky, J. (2005). *Read a rhyme, write a rhyme*. New York: Knopf.

Rathmann, P. (1995). *Officer Buckle and Gloria*. New York: Putnam.

Sendak, M. (2003). *Where the wild things are*. New York: HarperCollins.

Seuss, Dr. (2004). *Oh say can you say?* New York: Beginner Books.

Sidman, J. (2006). *Meow ruff: A story in concrete poetry*. Boston: Houghton Mifflin.

Silverstein, S. (2004). *Where the sidewalk ends*. New York: HarperCollins.

Soto, G. (2005). *Neighborhood odes*. San Diego: Harcourt.

Van Allsburg, C. (1998). *The Z was zapped*. Boston: Houghton Mifflin.

Wong, J. S. (2002). *You have to write*. New York: McElderry.

Woodson, J. (2003). *Locomotion*. New York: Putnam.

chapter twelve

Learning to Spell Conventionally

The 28 students in Mr. Martinez's fourth-grade classroom participate in a 30-minute spelling lesson sandwiched between reading and writing workshop. During this time, the teacher assigns spelling words, and students practice them for the Friday test. Mr. Martinez uses the words from a textbook spelling program, and each week's list of words focuses on a topic—*r*-controlled vowels or compound words, for example. Mr. Martinez introduces the topic through a series of lessons a week in advance so that his students will understand the topic and be familiar with the words before they study them for the spelling test.

During the first semester, students studied vowel patterns (e.g., *strike, each*), *r*-controlled vowels (e.g., *first*), diphthongs (e.g., *soil*), more sophisticated consonant spellings (e.g., *edge, catch*), words with silent letters (e.g., *climb*), and homophones (e.g., *one–won*). Now in the second semester, they are learning two-syllable words. They've studied compound words (e.g., *headache*) and words with inflectional suffixes (e.g., *get–getting*), and now the topic is irregular verbs. It's a difficult topic because students need to know the verb forms as well as how to spell the words.

Because the students' spelling levels range from second to sixth grade, Mr. Martinez has divided them into three groups. Each month, the groups choose

How can teachers incorporate textbooks into their spelling programs?

Teaching spelling is more than having students memorize a list of words and take a test on Friday. Students need to learn spelling concepts—not just practice words—in order to become competent spellers. Also, a single list of words usually isn't appropriate for everyone. As you read this vignette about Mr. Martinez's spelling program, notice how he teaches spelling concepts, incorporates the textbook's weekly lists of spelling words, and takes into account students' levels of spelling development.

new food-related names for themselves. This month, the names are types of pizza; earlier in the year, they chose fruit names, Mexican food names, vegetable names, cookie names, and snack names. Of course, at the end of the month, they sample the foods. Mr. Martinez calls these food names his "secret classroom management tool" because students behave and work hard in order to participate in the tasting.

Students in the Pepperoni Pizza group spell at the second-grade level, and they're studying *r*-controlled vowels. They have already studied two-letter spelling patterns, and now they are learning three-letter patterns. This week, the focus is on *ear* and *eer* patterns. Students in the Sausage Pizza group are at and almost at grade level; they're reviewing ways to spell /ou/. Students in the Hawaiian Pizza group are above-grade-level spellers; they're studying Latin root words and examining noun and verb forms of these words. This week's focus is spelling /shun/. Mr. Martinez meets with each group twice a week, and each group has a folder of activities to work on between meetings. Some of these group meetings are held during the spelling period (usually on Thursdays), and others are squeezed into reading and writing workshop. The teacher also encourages students to look for words they're studying in the books they're reading and to use them in their writing. They bring their examples to share at these meetings.

This week's spelling list is shown on page 394. The irregular verbs in the "All Pizzas" column are taken from the spelling textbook. All students study the words in the "All Pizzas" column, and students in each group also study their own list of words. Students study between 15 and 20 words each week, and they spell 15 words on the Friday test. When they are studying more than 15 words, as they are this week, students don't know which words will be on the test, but the asterisks in the box indicate which words Mr. Martinez plans to use.

Mr. Martinez and his students are involved in three types of activities during the 30-minute

This Week's Spelling List			
All Pizzas	Pepperoni Pizzas	Sausage Pizzas	Hawaiian Pizzas
*forget	*year	*smooth	educate
*forgot	fear	*group	*education
*forgotten	deer	soup	observe
*know	beard	*moving	*observation
*knew	*cheer	wood	admit
*known	*hear	would	*admission
*throw			
*threw			
*thrown			
*break			
*broke			
*broken			

* = words on the spelling test

spelling period: He teaches lessons on the weekly topic, students study words for the weekly spelling test, and they meet in small groups to study other spelling topics. Here is the schedule:

Monday	15 min.	Introduce the topic for the week
	15 min.	Have students take the pretest and self-check it
Tuesday	20 min.	Teach a lesson on the week's topic
	10 min.	Have students practice spelling words
Wednesday	15 min.	Teach a lesson on the week's topic
	15 min.	Have students take the practice test and self-check it
Thursday	20 min.	Work with small groups on other spelling topics
	10 min.	Have students practice spelling words
Friday	10 min.	Give spelling test
	20 min.	Review topic for the week and/or meet with small groups

This is the fourth week that Mr. Martinez has been teaching verbs. During the first week, students brainstormed verbs and Mr. Martinez listed them on one of four charts: verbs that don't change form (e.g., *set, hurt*), regular verbs (e.g., *walk–walked*), irregular verbs with three forms (e.g., *do–did–done*), and irregular verbs with two forms (e.g., *sell–sold*). The students reviewed verbs that don't change form and regular verbs whose past and past participle forms are created by adding *-ed*. That week, students were tested on words with inflectional suffixes, the topic taught the previous week. Regular verbs were tested the week after they were taught. For the next 2 weeks, students studied irregular verbs with three forms; because it was a difficult concept for many of the students, Mr. Martinez took 2 weeks to teach it. Students sorted the words into present, past, and past participle columns, practiced spelling the words on dry-erase boards, and created posters using the words in sentences. One student chose *eat–ate–eaten* and wrote this paragraph:

> *I like to EAT m & ms. They are my favorite candy. I ATE a whole bag of m & ms yesterday. Now I have a stomachache because I have EATEN too much candy.*

The students created their posters during writing workshop. They used the writing process to draft and refine their sentences, word-processed them, enlarged them to fit their posters, and printed them out. After sharing them during a spelling lesson, the students posted them on a wall in the classroom.

This week, the focus changes to irregular verbs with two forms, such as *sleep–slept, leave–left,* and *buy–bought.* On Monday, they review the list of verbs they created several weeks ago that is shown below. Mr. Martinez observes that students are already familiar with these irregular verbs; the only difficult one is *wind–wound.* The students know the nouns *wind* and *wound,* but not the verbs *wind* and *wound.* Mr. Martinez explains each word:

Wind (noun; pronounced with a short i): air in motion

Wind (verb; pronounced with a long i): to coil or wrap something or to take a bending course

Wound (verb—past tense of wind; the ou is pronounced as in cow): having coiled or wrapped something or to have taken a bending course

Wound (noun; the ou is pronounced as in moon): an injury

He sets out these objects to clarify the words: a small alarm clock to wind, a map showing a road that winds around a mountain, wind chimes to show the wind's motion, a skein of yarn to wind, and an elastic bandage to wind around a wound. The students examine each item and talk about how it relates to one or more of the words. Clayton explains the bandage and manages to include all four words:

> *OK. Let's say it is a* windy *day. The* wind *could blow you over and you could sprain your ankle. I know because it happened to me. A sprain is an injury like a* wound *but there's no blood. Well, then you get a bandage and you put it around your ankle like this [he demonstrates as he talks]: You* wind *it around and around to give your ankle some support. Now [he says triumphantly], I have* wound *the bandage over the* wound.

Irregular Verbs With Two Forms

*sleep–slept	meet–met	*leave–left	*bring–brought
shine–shone	fight–fought	*wind–wound	*buy–bought
*catch–caught	pay–paid	mean–meant	hang–hung
bleed–bled	*teach–taught	creep–crept	*build–built
dig–dug	tell–told	*think–thought	sell–sold
make–made	keep–kept	*sweep–swept	say–said

* = word (past-tense form) on next week's spelling list

On Tuesday, the students play the "I'm thinking of . . . " game to practice the words on the Irregular Verbs With Two Forms chart. They are familiar with the game and eager to play it. Mr. Martinez begins, "I'm thinking of a word where you delete one vowel to change the spelling from present to past tense." The students identify *bleed–bled* and *meet–met*. Next, he says, "I'm thinking of a word where you add one letter to the present-tense verb to spell the past-tense form," and the students identify *mean–meant*.

Then the students take turns being the leader. Simone begins, "I'm thinking of a word where you change one vowel for the past tense." The students identify *dig–dug, hang–hung,* and *shine–shone*. Next, Erika says, "I'm thinking of a word where you change one consonant to make past tense," and the students answer *build–built* and *make–made*. Joey offers, "I'm thinking of a verb where you change the *i* to *ou* to get the past tense." The students identify four pairs: *wind–wound, think–thought, bring–brought,* and *fight–fought*. Then, Camille says, "I'm thinking of a verb where you take away an *e* and add a *t* to make the past tense," and the students reply *keep–kept, sweep–swept, sleep–slept,* and *creep–crept*. The students continue the game until they have practiced all the verbs.

Today Mr. Martinez distributes dry-erase boards to the class. He says the past-tense form of an irregular verb, and students write both the present- and past-tense forms, without looking at the chart, unless they need help: *slept, taught, paid, bought, built,* and *left*. Many of the words he chooses are the ones that will be on next week's spelling list, but he also includes other words from the list. After they write each pair of words, the students hold up their boards so that Mr. Martinez can check their work. When necessary, he reviews how to form a letter or points out an illegible letter.

After 15 minutes of practice, the students return to their desks to take the practice test on this week's words. Mr. Martinez reads the list aloud while the students write using blue pens, and then he places a transparency with the words on the overhead projector so students can check their own tests. The students put away their blue pens and get out red pens to check their papers, so cheating is rarely a problem. Mr. Martinez walks around the classroom to monitor students' progress.

Spelling is a tool for writers that allows them to communicate** conventionally with readers. As Graves explains: "Spelling is for writing. Children may achieve high scores on phonic inventories or weekly spelling tests, but the ultimate test is what the child does under 'game conditions,' within the process of moving toward meaning" (1983, pp. 193–194). Rather than equating spelling instruction with weekly spelling tests, students need to learn to spell words conventionally so that they can communicate effectively through writing. English spelling is complex, and attempts to teach spelling through weekly lists have not been very successful. Many students spell the words correctly on the weekly test, but they continue to misspell them in their writing.

As you continue reading this chapter, consider these questions:

- How do children learn to spell?
- How can teachers determine students' level of spelling development?
- How should spelling be taught?
- How can teachers make weekly spelling tests more effective?

STUDENTS' SPELLING DEVELOPMENT

The alphabetic principle suggests a one-to-one correspondence between phonemes and graphemes, but English spelling is phonetic only about half the time. Other spellings reflect the language from which a word was borrowed. For example, *alcohol,* like most words beginning with *al-*, is an Arabic word, and *homonym,* like most words with *y* where *i* would work, is a Greek word. Other words are spelled to reflect semantic relationships, not phonological ones. The spelling of *national* and *nation* and of *grade* and *gradual* indicates related meanings even though there are vowel or consonant changes in the pronunciations of the word pairs. If English were a purely phonetic language, it would be easier to spell, but at the same time, it would lose much of its sophistication.

Students learn to spell the phonetic elements of English as they learn about phoneme-grapheme correspondences, and they continue to refine their spelling knowledge through reading and writing. Children's spelling reflects their growing awareness of English orthography, and they move from using scribbles and single letters to represent words through a series of stages until they adopt conventional spellings.

What Is Invented Spelling?

Children create unique spellings, called *invented spellings*, based on their knowledge of English orthography. Charles Read (1975), one of the first researchers to study preschoolers' efforts to spell words, discovered that they used their knowledge of phonology to invent spellings. These children used letter names to spell words, such as U (*you*) and R (*are*), and they used consonant sounds rather consistently: GRL (*girl*), TIGR (*tiger*), and NIT (*night*). The preschoolers used several unusual but phonetically based spelling patterns to represent affricates: They spelled *tr* with *chr* (e.g., CHRIBLES for *troubles*) and *dr* with *jr* (e.g., JRAGIN for *dragon*), and they substituted *d* for *t* (e.g., PREDE for *pretty*). Words with long vowels were spelled using letter names: MI (*my*), LADE (*lady*), and FEL (*feel*). The children used several ingenious strategies to spell words with short vowels. The 3-, 4-, and 5-year-olds rather consistently selected letters to represent short vowels on the basis of place of articulation in the mouth. Short *i* was represented with *e* as in FES (*fish*), short *e* with *a* as in LAFFT (*left*), and short *o* with *i* as in CLIK (*clock*). These spellings may seem odd to adults, but they are based on phonetic relationships. The children often omitted nasals within words (e.g., ED for *end*) and substituted *-eg* or *-ig* for *-ing* (e.g., CUMIG for *coming* and GOWEG for *going*). Also, they often ignored the vowel in unaccented syllables, as in AFTR (*after*) and MUTHR (*mother*).

These children developed strategies for their spellings based on their knowledge of the phonological system and of letter names, their judgments of phonetic similarities and differences, and their ability to abstract phonetic information from letter names. Read suggested that from among the many phonetic properties in the phonological system, children abstract certain phonetic details and preserve others in their invented spellings.

Stages of Spelling Development

Based on Read's seminal work, other researchers began to systematically study how children learn to spell. After examining students' spelling errors and determining that their errors reflected their knowledge of English orthography, Bear, Invernizzi, Templeton, and Johnston (2007b) identified these five stages of spelling development that students move through as they learn to read and write: emergent spelling, letter-name spelling, within-word spelling, syllables and affixes spelling, and derivational relations spelling. The characteristics of each of the stages are summarized in this LA Essentials box on page 399.

As they continued to study students' spelling development, Bear and his colleagues also noticed three principles of English orthography that children master as they move through the stages of spelling development:

- Alphabetic Principle: Letters represent sounds.
- Pattern Principle: Letters are combined in predictable ways to spell sounds.
- Meaning Principle: Related words have similar spellings even when they are pronounced differently.

Young children focus on the alphabetic principle as they learn to represent sounds with letters. They pronounce words and record letters to represent sounds they hear, spelling *are* as *r* and *bed* as *bad,* for example. Children learn the pattern principle next, as they study phonics. They learn to spell consonant and vowel patterns; for example, they learn to spell the /k/ at the end of short-vowel words with *ck* so that they spell *luck* correctly, not as *luk*, and they learn the CVCe pattern, as in *shine*. They also learn the pattern for adding inflectional suffixes, so that they spell the plural of *baby* as *babies*, not *babys*. The third principle is meaning; students learn, for example, that the words *oppose* and *opposition* are related in both spelling and meaning. Once students understand this principle, they are less confused by irregular spellings because they don't expect words to be phonetically regular.

Emergent Spelling. Children string scribbles, letters, and letterlike forms together, but they don't associate the marks they make with any specific phonemes. Emergent spelling represents a natural, early expression of the alphabet and other concepts about writing. Children may write from left to right, right to left, top to bottom, or randomly across the page. Some emergent spellers have a large repertoire of letterforms to use in writing, whereas others repeat a small number of letters over and over. Children use both upper- and lowercase letters, but they show a distinct preference for uppercase letters. Toward the end of this stage, children are beginning to discover how spelling works and that letters represent sounds in words. This stage is typical of preschoolers, ages 3 to 5. During the emergent stage, children learn these concepts:

- The distinction between drawing and writing
- The formation of upper- and lowercase letters
- The direction of writing on a page
- Some letter-sound matches

CHARACTERISTICS OF THE STAGES OF SPELLING DEVELOPMENT

Stage 1: Emergent Spelling

Children string scribbles, letters, and letterlike forms together, but they do not associate the marks they make with any specific phonemes. This stage is typical of 3- to 5-year-olds who learn these concepts:

- The difference between drawing and writing
- The direction of writing on a page
- Some letter-sound matches
- The formation of letters

Stage 2: Letter-Name Spelling

Children represent phonemes in words with letters. At first, their spellings are quite abbreviated, but they learn to use consonant blends and digraphs and short-vowel patterns to spell words. Spellers are 5- to 7-year-olds who learn these concepts:

- The alphabetic principle
- Short vowel sounds
- Consonant sounds
- Consonant blends and digraphs

Stage 3: Within-Word Spelling

Students learn long-vowel patterns and *r*-controlled vowels, but they may confuse spelling patterns and spell *meet* as *mete* and reverse the order of letters, such as *form* for *from* and *gril* for *girl*. Spellers are 7- to 9-year-olds who learn these concepts:

- Long-vowel spelling patterns
- Complex consonant patterns
- *r*-controlled vowels
- Diphthongs

Stage 4: Syllables and Affixes Spelling

Students learn to spell multisyllabic words. They also add inflectional endings, use apostrophes in contractions, and differentiate between homophones, such as *your–you're*. Spellers are often 9- to 11-year-olds who learn these concepts:

- Inflectional endings
- Homophones
- Syllabication
- Possessives

Stage 5: Derivational Relations Spelling

Students explore the relationship between spelling and meaning and learn that words with related meanings are often related in spelling despite sound changes (e.g., *wise–wisdom*). They also learn Latin and Greek root words and derivational affixes (e.g., *amphi-, -tion*). Spellers are 11- to 14-year-olds who learn these concepts:

- Consonant and vowel alternations
- Greek affixes and root words
- Latin affixes and root words
- Etymologies

Adapted from Bear, Invernizzi, Templeton, & Johnston, 2007b.

Letter-Name Spelling. Children learn to represent phonemes in words with letters, indicating that they have a rudimentary understanding of the alphabetic principle—that a link exists between letters and sounds. Spellings are quite abbreviated and represent only the most prominent features in words. Examples of stage 2 spelling are DA (*day*), KLZ (*closed*), BAD (*bed*), and CLEN (*clean*). Many children continue to write mainly with capital letters. These spellers use a letter-name strategy: They slowly pronounce words they want to write, listening for familiar letter names and sounds. Spellers at this stage are 5- to 7-year-olds. During the letter-name stage, children learn the following concepts:

- The alphabetic principle
- Consonant sounds
- Short vowel sounds
- Consonant blends and digraphs

Within-Word Spelling. Children's understanding of the alphabetic principle is further refined in this stage as they learn how to spell long-vowel patterns, diphthongs and the less common vowel patterns, and *r*-controlled vowels (Henderson, 1990). Examples of within-word spelling include LIEV (*live*), SOPE (*soap*), HUOSE (*house*), and BERN (*burn*). Children experiment with long-vowel patterns and learn that words such as *come* and *bread* are exceptions that don't fit the vowel patterns. Children may confuse spelling patterns and spell *meet* as METE, and they reverse the order of letters, such as FORM for *from* and GRIL for *girl*. They also learn about complex consonant sounds, including *-tch* (*match*) and *-dge* (*judge*), and about diphthongs (*oi/oy*) and other less common vowel patterns, including *au* (*caught*), *aw* (*saw*), *ew* (*sew, few*), *ou* (*house*), and *ow* (*cow*). Children also become aware of homophones and compare long- and short-vowel combinations (*hop–hope*) as they experiment with vowel patterns. Spellers at this stage are typically 7- to 9-year-olds, and they learn these spelling concepts:

- Long-vowel spelling patterns
- *r*-controlled vowels
- More complex consonant patterns
- Diphthongs and other less common vowel patterns

Syllables and Affixes Spelling. The focus in this stage is on syllables and the spellings used where two syllables join together. Students apply what they have learned about one-syllable words to multisyllabic words, and they learn to break words into syllables. They learn about inflectional endings (*-s, -es, -ed,* and *-ing*) and rules about consonant doubling, changing the final *y* to *i*, or dropping the final *e* before adding an inflectional suffix. They also learn about homophones, compound words, possessives, and contractions, as well as some of the more common derivational prefixes and suffixes. Examples of syllables and affixes spelling include EAGUL (*eagle*), MONY (*money*), GETING (*getting*), BABYIES (*babies*), THEIR (*there*), CA'NT (*can't*), and BE CAUSE (*because*). Spellers in this stage are generally 9- to 11-year-olds. Students learn about these concepts during the syllables and affixes stage of spelling development:

- Inflectional endings (*-s, -es, -ed, -ing*)
- Syllabication
- Contractions

- Homophones
- Possessives

Derivational Relations Spelling. Students explore the relationship between spelling and meaning during the derivational relations stage, and they learn that words with related meanings are often related in spelling despite changes in vowel and consonant sounds (e.g., *wise–wisdom, sign–signal, nation–national*) (Templeton, 1983). Examples of spelling errors include CRITISIZE (*criticize*), APPEARENCE (*appearance*), and COMMITTE or COMMITEE (*committee*). The focus in this stage is on morphemes, and students learn about Greek and Latin root words and affixes. They also begin to examine etymologies and the role of history in shaping how words are spelled. They learn about eponyms (words from people's names), such as *maverick* and *sandwich*. Spellers at this stage are 11- to 14-year-olds. Students learn these concepts at this stage of spelling development:

- Consonant alternations (e.g., *soft–soften, magic–magician*)
- Vowel alternations (e.g., *please–pleasant, define–definition, explain–explanation*)
- Greek and Latin affixes and root words
- Etymologies

Teachers do many things to scaffold students' spelling development as they move through the stages of spelling development, and the kind of support they provide depends on students' stage of development. As young children scribble, for example, teachers encourage them to use pencils, not crayons, for writing, to differentiate between drawing and writing. Letter-name spellers notice words in their environment, and teachers help children use these familiar words to choose letters to represent the sounds in the words they are writing. As students enter the syllables and affixes stage, teachers teach syllabication rules, and in the derivational relations stage, they teach students about root words and the variety of words created from a single Latin or Greek root word. For example, from the Latin root word *-ann* or *-enn,* meaning "year," students learn these words: *annual, centennial, biannual, millennium, anniversary, perennial,* and *sesquicentennial.* Figure 12–1 presents a list of guidelines for supporting students' spelling development at each stage.

Analyzing Students' Spelling Development

Teachers analyze the spelling errors in students' compositions by classifying them according to the five stages of spelling development. This analysis will provide information about the student's current level of spelling development and the kinds of errors he or she makes. Knowing the stage of a student's spelling development helps teachers determine the appropriate type of instruction.

A personal journal entry written by Marc, a first grader, is presented in the Weaving Assessment Into Practice feature on page 403. He reverses *d* and *s,* and these two reversals make his writing more difficult to decipher. Here is Marc's composition using conventional spelling:

> *Today a person at home called us and said that a bomb was in our school and made us go outside and made us wait a half of an hour and it made us waste our time on learning. The end.*

FIGURE 12–1

Ways to Support Students' Spelling at Each Stage of Development

Stage 1: Emergent Spelling
Allow the child to experiment with making and placing marks on the paper.
Suggest that the child write with a pencil and draw with a crayon.
Model how adults write.
Point out the direction of print in books.
Encourage the child to notice letters in names and environmental print.
Ask the child to talk about what he or she has written.

Stage 2: Letter-Name Spelling
Sing the ABC song and name letters of the alphabet with children.
Show the child how to form letters in names and other common words.
Demonstrate how to say a word slowly, stretch it out, and isolate beginning, middle, and ending sounds in the word.
Use Elkonin boxes to segment words into beginning, middle, and ending sounds.
Post high-frequency words on a word wall.
Teach lessons on consonants, consonant digraphs, and short vowels.
Write sentences using interactive writing.

Stage 3: Within-Word Spelling
Teach lessons on long-vowel spelling rules, vowel digraphs, and *r*-controlled vowels.
Encourage students to develop visualization skills in order to recognize whether a word "looks" right.
Teach students to spell irregular high-frequency words.
Focus on silent letters in one-syllable words (e.g., *k*now, li*gh*t).
Have students sort words according to spelling patterns.
Have students make words using magnetic letters and letter cards.
Introduce proofreading so students can identify and correct misspelled words in compositions.
Write sentences using interactive writing.

Stage 4: Syllables and Affixes Spelling
Teach how to divide words into syllables and the rules for adding inflectional endings.
Teach schwa sounds and spelling patterns (e.g., *handle*).
Teach homophones, contractions, compound words, and possessives.
Sort two-syllable words and homophones.
Have students make words using letter cards.
Teach proofreading skills, and encourage students to proofread all writings.

Stage 5: Derivational Relations
Teach root words and derivational affixes.
Make clusters with a root word in the center and related words on rays.
Teach students to identify words with English, Latin, and Greek spellings.
Sort words according to roots or language of origin.
Have students check the etymologies of words in a dictionary.

Marc was writing about a traumatic event, and it was appropriate for him to use invented spelling in his journal entry. Primary-grade students should write using invented spelling, and correct spelling is appropriate when the composition will "go public." Prematurely differentiating between "kid" and "adult" spelling interferes with children's natural spelling development and makes them dependent on adults to supply the adult spelling.

Weaving Assessment Into Practice

AN ANALYSIS OF A FIRST GRADER'S SPELLING

Tobay a perezun at home kob
uz anb seb that a bome wuz in
or skuwl anb mab uz go at zib
anb makbe uz wat a haf uf
a awr anb it mab uz wazt on
time on loren ee ing.

THE eNb

Emergent	Letter-Name	Within-Word	Syllables and Affixes	Derivational Relations
	KOB/called	BOME/bomb	TO BAY/today	
	SEB/said	OR/our	PEREZUN/person	
	WUZ/was	SKUWL/school	MAKBE/maked	
	MAB/made	AT SIB/outside		
	WAT/wait	UF/of		
	HAF/half	AWR/hour		
	MAB/made	OR/our		
	WAZT/waste	LORENEEING/learning		

Data Analysis		Conclusions
Emergent	0	Marc's spelling is at the Letter-Name and Within-Word stages. From his misspellings, he is ready for the following instruction:
Letter-Name	8	
Within-Word	8	• high-frequency words
Syllables and Affixes	3	• CVCe spellings
Derivational Relations	0	• r-controlled vowels
Correctly spelled words	22	• compound words
Total words in sample	41	He also reverses b/d and s/z.

Spelling can be categorized on a chart, also shown in the feature on page 403, to gauge students' spelling development and to anticipate upcoming changes in their spelling strategies. Teachers write the stages of spelling development across the top of the chart and list each misspelled word in the student's composition under one of the categories, ignoring proper nouns. When teachers are scoring young children's spellings, they often ignore capitalization errors and poorly formed or reversed letters, but when scoring older students' spellings, these errors are considered.

Perhaps the most interesting thing about Marc's writing is that he spelled half the words correctly even though at first reading it might seem that he spelled very few words correctly. Marc wrote this paper in January of his first-grade year, and his spellings are typical of first graders. Of his misspellings, eight were categorized as letter-name spelling, and another eight were within-word spellings. This score suggests that he is moving into the within-word stage.

Marc is clearly using a sounding-out strategy, which is best typified by his spelling of the word *learning*. His errors suggest that he is ready to learn CVCe and other long-vowel spelling patterns and *r*-controlled vowels. Marc spells some high-frequency words phonetically, so he would benefit from more exposure to high-frequency words, such as *was* and *of*. He also spelled *today* and *outside* as separate words, so he is ready to learn about compound words.

Marc pronounced the word MAKBE as "maked," and the DE is a reversal of letters, a common characteristic of within-word spelling. Based on this categorization of Marc's spelling errors, he would benefit from instruction on high-frequency words, the CVCe long-vowel spelling pattern, *r*-controlled vowels, and compound words. His teacher should also monitor his *b/d* and *s/z* reversal problem to see if it disappears with more writing practice. It is important, of course, to base instructional recommendations on more than one writing sample. Teachers should look at three or more samples to be sure the recommendations are valid.

Older students' spelling can also be analyzed the same way. Fifth-grade Eugenio wrote the "Why My Mom Is Special" essay shown in the Weaving Assessment Into Practice feature on the next page. Eugenio is Hispanic; his native language is Spanish, but he's now fully proficient in English. His writing is more sophisticated than Marc's, and the spelling errors he makes reflect both his use of longer, more complex words and his pronunciation of English sounds.

All but one of Eugenio's spelling errors are classified at either the within-word stage or the syllables and affixes stage. His other error, classified at the letter-name stage, is probably an accident because when he was asked, he could spell the word correctly.

Eugenio's within-word stage errors involve more complex consonant and vowel spelling patterns. Eugenio has moved beyond spelling *because* as BECUZ, but he still must learn to replace the *u* with *au* and the *z* with *s*. His spelling of *shoes* as SHOSE is interesting because he has reversed the last two letters. He doesn't recognize that, however, when he is questioned. Instead, his focus is on representing the /sh/ and the /oo/ sounds correctly. His spelling of both *school* and *career* seem to be influenced by his pronunciation. The /sh/ sound is difficult for him, as it is for many children whose first language is Spanish, and he doesn't recognize that *school* begins with /sk/, not /sh/. Eugenio pronounces the first syllable of *career* as he spelled it, and he explains that it's a hard word but it looks right to him. These comments suggest that Eugenio understands that spelling has both phonetic and visual properties. In the word *policeman,* Eugenio used *s* rather than *ce* to represent the /s/. Even though it is

Weaving Assessment Into Practice

AN ANALYSIS OF A FIFTH GRADER'S SPELLING

My mom is special to me. She gave me everething when I was small. When she gets some mony she byes me pizza. My mom is specil to me becuze she taks me anywhere I want to get some nike shose. She byes me some.

My mom changed my life. She is so nice and loveble. She cares what I am doing in shool. She cares about my grades. I will do anything for mom. I would get a ceriar. Maybe I could be a polisman. That is why I think she is so nice.

Emergent	Letter-Name	Within-Word	Syllables and Affixes	Derivational Relations
	TAKS/takes	BECUZE/because	SPECIL/special	
		SHOSE/shoes	EVERETHING/everything	
		SHOOL/school	MONY/money	
		CERIAR/career	BYES/buys	
		POLISMAN/policeman	SPECIL/special	
			BYES/buys	
			LOVEBLE/lovable	

Data Analysis		Conclusions
Emergent	0	Eugenio's spelling is at the syllables and affixes stage. Based on this sample, this instruction is suggested:
Letter-Name	1	
Within-Word	5	• dividing words into syllables
Syllables and Affixes	7	• compound words
Derivational Relations	0	• using y at the end of 1- and 2-syllable words
Correctly spelled words	82	• homophones
Total words in sample	95	• suffixes

a compound word, this word is classified at this level because the error has to do with spelling a complex consonant sound.

The largest number of Eugenio's spelling errors fall into the syllables and affixes stage. Most of his errors at this stage deal with spelling multisyllabic words. In SPECIL, Eugenio has misspelled the schwa sound, the vowel sound in unaccented syllables of multisyllabic words. In *everything,* Eugenio wrote *e* instead of *y* at the end of *every.* What he did not understand is that the long *e* sound at the end of a two-syllable word is usually represented by *y.* Eugenio spelled *money* as MONY. It's interesting that he used *y* to represent the long *e* sound here, but in this case, *ey* is needed. BYES for *buys* is a homophone error, and all homophone errors are classified as this stage even though they are one-syllable words. Eugenio's other spelling error at this stage is LOVEBLE. Here he added the suffix *-able* but misspelled it. He wasn't aware that he added a suffix. When he was asked about it, he explained that he sounded it out and wrote the sounds that he heard. It is likely that he also knows about the *-ble* end-of-word spelling pattern because if he had spelled the suffix phonetically, he probably would have written LOVEBUL.

Even though Eugenio has a number of errors at both the within-word and syllables and affixes stages, his spelling can be classified at the syllables and affixes stage because most of his errors are at that stage. Based on this one writing sample, it appears that he would benefit from instruction on dividing words into syllables, compound words, using *y* at the end of one- and two-syllable words, homophones, and suffixes. These instructional recommendations should not be based on only one writing sample; they should be validated by examining several writing samples.

TEACHING SPELLING

Conventional spelling is often considered to be the hallmark of an educated person. Parents say that they view spelling as critically important, citing the relationship between reading and spelling, the need for students to be conventional spellers to be successful in the job market and in higher education, and the negative effect incorrect spellings have on compositions as reasons for its importance (Chandler & the Mapleton Teacher-Research Group, 2000). However, Bean and Bouffler (1997) claim that "standard spelling has assumed an importance beyond the function it plays in written language" (p. 67).

The goal of spelling instruction is to help students develop what Gentry (1997) and Turbill (2000) call a *spelling conscience*—a desire to spell words conventionally. Two dimensions of a spelling conscience are understanding that standard spelling is a courtesy to readers and developing the ability to proofread to spot and correct misspellings. Spelling is important to effective writing, but it's a means to an end, not the end in itself. Dull, uninspired writing, not matter how well spelled, has little communicative effect.

The question is how to best teach spelling because we know that reliance on spelling textbooks and rote memorization of words is inadequate. The widely held assumption that children learn how to spell through weekly spelling tests has been challenged by research (Rymer & Williams, 2000). Studies raise questions about the transfer of spelling skills learned through weekly spelling tests to students' writing. There's more to the development of conventional spellers than rote memorization of about a thousand words between first and eighth grades.

Meeting the Needs of English Learners

How Do Teachers Teach Spelling to English Learners?

English learners move through the same five stages of spelling development that native English speakers do (Bear, Helman, Templeton, Invernizzi, & Johnston, 2007a). How quickly and easily they learn to spell English words depends on what they already know about how words are spelled. Students have more orthographic knowledge when their home language is similar to English, when they are literate in their home language, and when their parents are literate.

Bear and his colleagues (2007a) recommend that in addition to determining students' level of spelling development, teachers do the following as they plan spelling instruction for English learners:

◆ *Compare oral languages.* Teachers analyze the sounds and grammar structures used in students' native language and compare them to English because it's important to point out the similarities and differences to make it easier for students to learn English words.

◆ *Compare written languages.* Teachers examine the writing system—including its characters or letters and directionality—in students' native language, investigate how sounds are spelled and other spelling patterns, and compare them to English in order to explain the similarities and differences to students as they learn to spell English words.

◆ *Investigate students' language and literacy experiences.* Teachers learn about students' levels of experience using their own language and English because students come to school with a range of language and literacy experiences, and they use what they know about their native language as they learn to speak, read, and write in English.

With this information, teachers set goals for their English learners, taking into account that students' differing levels of language and literacy experiences will affect their success, and plan spelling activities to support students as they become more conventional spellers.

The best way to teach spelling to English learners is through a combination of explicit and systematic instruction, opportunities to practice new spelling concepts through word-study activities, and authentic opportunities for students to apply what they're learning about spelling through writing. First, teachers teach minilessons on spelling concepts that are appropriate for students' level of spelling development, taking care to point out similarities and differences between students' home language and English. They emphasize the pronunciation of English words because the way students pronounce a word often influences their spelling. If the words are unfamiliar to students, teachers explain their meaning and model how to use them in English sentences. Next, they involve students in interactive writing activities and have them work in small groups to participate in word-study activities, including making words and word sorts. Third, teachers involve students in a wide variety of reading and writing activities every day so that they can apply their spelling knowledge. Just like their classmates, English learners write books and other compositions in writing

workshop, read and discuss books with classmates in literature circles, and create projects as part of literature focus units and thematic units.

Weekly spelling tests aren't generally considered to be a good way to teach spelling, and they're even less effective for English learners. These students need to learn the sound, pattern, and meaning layers of words rather than simply memorize the sequence of letters in words. The words on a grade-level spelling list may be too difficult for English learners who might not be familiar with the words or understand their meaning. When teachers have to use weekly spelling tests, they should select several words from grade-level lists and others that are more appropriate for students' developmental level, including some high-frequency words.

Components of the Spelling Program

A comprehensive spelling program has a number of components, including reading and writing opportunities, making-words activities, proofreading, and using the dictionary. These components are summarized in the LA Essentials box on the next page.

◆ *Daily writing opportunities* Providing daily opportunities for students to write is an essential component of an effective spelling program. Students who write daily use their knowledge of English orthography to invent spellings for unfamiliar words, and in the process they move closer and closer toward conventional spelling (Hughes & Searle, 2000). When they write, students predict spellings using their developing knowledge of sound-symbol correspondences and spelling patterns. When students use the writing process to develop and polish their writings, emphasis on conventional spelling belongs in the editing stage. Through the process approach, students learn to recognize spelling for what it is—a courtesy to readers. As they write, revise, edit, and share their writing with genuine audiences, students understand that they need to spell conventionally so that their audience can read their compositions.

◆ *Daily reading opportunities* Reading plays an enormous role in students' learning to spell (Hughes & Searle, 1997). As they read, students store the visual shapes of words. The ability to recall how words look helps students decide when a spelling they are writing is correct. When students decide that a word doesn't look right, they can rewrite the word several ways until it does look right, ask the teacher or a classmate who knows the spelling, or check the spelling in a dictionary.

◆ *Word walls* One way to direct students' attention to words in books they're reading or in thematic units is through the use of word walls. Students and the teacher choose words to write on word walls, large sheets of paper hanging in the classroom. Then students refer to these word walls for word-study activities and when they are writing. Seeing the words posted on word walls, clusters, and other charts in the classroom and using them in their writing help students learn to spell the words. Teachers also hang word walls with high-frequency words (Cunningham, 2004). Researchers have identified the most commonly used words and recommend that children learn to spell 100 to 500 of these words because of their usefulness. The 100 most frequently used words represent more than 50% of all the words children and adults write (Horn, 1926)! Figure 12–2 lists the 100 most frequently used words, and Figure 12–3 presents a

COMPONENTS OF A COMPREHENSIVE SPELLING PROGRAM

Writing
Students write informally in journals and use the writing process to draft, revise, and edit writing every day.

Reading
Students develop visual images of words as they read a variety of books each day.

Word Walls
Students and the teacher post high-frequency words, words related to books they are reading, and words related to thematic units in alphabetized sections on word walls in the classroom.

Making Words
Students participate in making-words activities in which they arrange letter cards to spell increasingly longer and more complex words.

Word Sorts
Students sort word cards into two or more categories to focus on particular spelling patterns.

Proofreading
Students learn to proofread their own compositions to locate and then correct spelling errors.

Dictionaries
Students learn to use dictionaries to locate the spellings of unknown words.

Spelling Options
Students explore the variety of ways phonemes are spelled in English in order to know options they have for spelling sounds in words.

Root Words and Affixes
Students learn about root words and affixes and use that knowledge to spell multisyllabic words.

Spelling Strategies
Students learn strategies, including "think it out," to spell unknown words.

FIGURE 12–2

The 100 Most Frequently Used Words

A	B	C	D	E
a and	back	came	day	
about are	be	can	did	
after around	because	could	didn't	
all as	but		do	
am at	by		don't	
an			down	

F	G	H	I	J
for	get	had his	I into	just
from	got	have home	if is	
		he house	in it	
		her how		
		him		

K	L	M	N	O
know	like	man	no	of our
	little	me	not	on out
		mother	now	one over
		my		or

P	QR	S	T	U
people		said	that think	up
put		saw	the this	us
		school	them time	
		see	then to	
		she	there too	
		so	they two	
		some	things	

V	W	X	Y	Z
very	was when		you	
	we who		your	
	well will			
	went with			
	were would			
	what			

FIGURE 12–3

100 High-Frequency Words for Older Students

A	B	C	D	E
a lot	beautiful	caught	decided	either
again	because	certain	desert–dessert	embarrassed
all right	belief	close–clothes	different	enough
although	believe	committee	discussed	especially
another	beneath	complete	doesn't	etc.
anything	between			everything
around	board–bored			everywhere
	breathe			excellent
	brought			experience

F	G	H	I	J
familiar		hear–here	immediately	
favorite		heard–herd	interesting	
field		height	it's–its	
finally		herself		
foreign		himself		
friends		humorous		
frighten		hungry		

K	L	M	N	O
knew–new	language	maybe	necessary	once
know–no	lying		neighbor	ourselves
knowledge				

P	QR	S	T	U
particular	quiet–quite	safety	their–there–they're	until
people	really	school	themselves	usually
piece–peace	receive	separate	though	
please	recommend	serious	thought	
possible	remember	since	threw–through	
probably	restaurant	special	throughout	
	right–write	something	to–two–too	
		success	together	

V	W	X	Y	Z
	weight		your–you're	
	were			
	we're			
	where			
	whether			
	whole–hole			

second list of 100 useful words for students in the middle and upper grades. Some teachers type the alphabetized word list on small cards—personal word walls—that students keep at their desks to refer to when they write (Lacey, 1994).

◆ *Making words* Students arrange and rearrange a group of letter cards to spell words (Cunningham & Cunningham, 1992). Primary-grade students can use the letters *s, p, i, d, e,* and *r* to spell *is, red, dip, rip, sip, side, ride,* and *ripe.* With the letters *t, e, m, p, e, r, a, t, u, r,* and *e,* a class of fifth graders spelled these words:

> *2-letter words:* at, up
> *3-letter words:* pet, are, rat, eat, ate, tap, pat
> *4-letter words:* ramp, rate, pare, pear, meat, meet, team, tree
> *5-letter word:* treat
> *6-letter words:* temper, tamper, mature, repeat, turret
> *7-letter words:* trumpet, rapture
> *8-letter words:* repeater
> *9-letter words:* temperate, trumpeter

The procedure for making words is explained in the Step by Step feature below.

Teachers often introduce making words as a whole-class lesson and then set the cards and the word list in a center for students to use again independently or in small groups. Teachers can use almost any words for making-words activities, but words related to literature focus units and thematic units work best.

Making Words

1 Make letter cards. Teachers prepare a set of small letter cards with multiple copies of each letter, especially common letters such as *a, e, i, r, s,* and *t.* They print the lowercase letter form on one side of the letter cards and the uppercase form on the reverse. They store the cards with each letter separately in plastic trays or plastic bags.

2 Choose a word. Teachers choose a word or spelling pattern to use in the word-making activity, and they have a student distribute the needed letter cards to individual students or to small groups of students.

3 Name the letter cards. Teachers ask students to name the letter cards and to arrange consonants in one group and vowels in another.

4 Make words. Students use the letter cards to spell words containing two, three, four, five, and six or more letters and then list the words they've spelled on a chart. Teachers monitor students' work and encourage them to fix any misspelled words.

5 Share words. Teachers have students identify two-letter words they made with the letter cards and continue to report longer and longer words until they identify the chosen word using every single letter card. After students share all of the words, teachers suggest any words they missed and point out recently taught spelling patterns and other concepts.

Making Words

These second graders use small plastic letters to spell words. They benefit more by manipulating plastic letters than by writing lists of words—because making words is a fun activity and students actually do spell more words this way than through traditional spelling activities. Through making words, children examine spelling patterns and practice spelling high-frequency words. When teachers participate by asking children to switch letters or substitute one letter for another, they take advantage of teachable moments.

◆ *Word sorts* Students use word sorts to compare and contrast spelling patterns as they sort a pack of word cards. Teachers prepare word cards for students to sort into two or more categories according to vowel patterns, affixes, root words, or another spelling concept (Bear et al., 2007b). Sometimes teachers tell students what categories to, making the sort a closed sort; at other times, students determine the categories themselves, making the sort an open sort. Students can sort word cards and then return them to an envelope for future use, or they can glue the cards onto a sheet of paper. Figure 12–4 shows a word sort for *r*-controlled vowels. In this sort, students work in small groups to pronounce the words and sort them according to how the *r*-controlled vowel is spelled.

◆ *Proofreading* Proofreading is a special kind of reading that students use to locate misspelled words and other mechanical errors in their rough drafts. As students learn about the writing process, they are introduced to proofreading. In the editing stage, they receive more in-depth instruction about how to use proofreading to locate spelling errors and then correct these misspelled words (Wilde, 1996). Through a series of minilessons, students can proofread sample student papers and mark misspelled words. Then, working in pairs, students can correct the misspelled words.

Proofreading is introduced in the primary grades. Young children and their teachers proofread class collaboration and dictated stories together, and students can be encouraged to read over their own compositions and make necessary corrections soon after they begin writing. In this way, students accept proofreading as a natural part of both spelling and writing. Proofreading activities are more valuable for teaching spelling than dictation activities, in which teachers dictate sentences for students

FIGURE 12–4

A Word Sort on *r*-Controlled Vowels

ar	are	air	ar + e	others
shark	hare	chair	large	are
yard	square	stairs	carve	heart
jar	bare	flair		their
sharp		hair		there
hard		pair		bear

to write and correctly capitalize and punctuate. Few people use dictation in their daily lives, but students use proofreading skills every time they polish a piece of writing.

◆ *Dictionaries* Students need to learn how to locate the spelling of unknown words in the dictionary. Of the approximately 750,000 entry words in an unabridged dictionary, students typically learn to spell 3,000 through weekly spelling tests by the end of eighth grade—leaving 747,000 words unaccounted for! Obviously, students must learn how to locate the spellings of some additional words. Although it is relatively easy to find a "known" word in the dictionary, it is hard to locate an unfamiliar word, so students need to learn what to do when they don't know how to spell a word. One approach is to predict possible spellings for unknown words, then check the most probable spellings in a dictionary. This procedure involves six steps:

1. Identify root words and affixes.
2. Consider related words (e.g., *medicine–medical*).
3. Determine the sounds in the word.

4. Generate a list of possible spellings.
5. Select the most probable alternatives.
6. Consult a dictionary to check the correct spelling.

The fourth step, during which students develop a list of possible spellings using their knowledge of both phonology and morphology, is undoubtedly the most difficult. Phoneme-grapheme relationships may rate primary consideration in generating spelling options for some words; root words and affixes or related words may be more important in determining how other words are spelled.

◆ *Spelling options* In English, there are alternative spellings for many sounds because so many words borrowed from other languages retain their native spellings. There are many more options for vowel sounds than for consonants. Even so, there are four spelling options for /f/ (*f, ff, ph, gh*). Spelling options sometimes vary according to position in a syllable or word. For example, *ff* and *gh* are used to represent /f/ only at the end of a syllable or word, as in *cuff* and *laughter.* Common spelling options for phonemes are listed in Figure 12–5.

Teachers point out spelling options as they write words on word walls and when students ask about the spelling of a word. They can also use a series of minilessons to teach upper-grade students about these options. During each minilesson, students focus on one phoneme, such as /f/ or /ar/, and as a class or small group develop a list of the various ways the sound is spelled in English, giving examples of each spelling. A sixth-grade chart on long *i* is presented in Figure 12–6 with lists of one-syllable and multisyllable words. The location of the long *i* sound in the word is also marked on the chart.

◆ *Root words and affixes* Students learn about roots and affixes as they read and spell longer, multisyllabic words. Teaching root words helps students unlock meaning when they read and spell the words correctly when they write. Consider the Latin root word *terra,* meaning "earth." Middle- and upper-grade students learn to read and spell these *terra* words and phrases: *terrarium, all-terrain vehicles, subterranean, territory, terrace,* and *terrier dogs.* Lessons about root words merge instruction about vocabulary and spelling.

Children learn to spell inflectional suffixes, such as the plural -*s* marker and the past-tense -*ed* marker, in the primary grades, and in the middle and upper grades, they learn about derivational prefixes and suffixes and how they affect meaning. They learn to recognize the related forms of a root word, for example: *educate, uneducated, educator, education, educational.*

Students also learn rules for spelling suffixes. For example, the -*able* suffix is added to *read* to spell *readable,* but the -*ible* suffix is added to *leg-* (a Latin root word that is not a word in English) to spell *legible.* The rule is that -*able* is added to complete words and -*ible* is added to word parts. In other words, such as *lovable,* the final *e* in *love* is dropped before adding -*able* because *a* serves the same function in the word, and in *huggable,* the *g* is doubled before adding -*able* because the *u* in *hug* is short. Through a combination of wide reading and minilessons, students learn about root words and affixes, and they use this knowledge to expand their vocabularies.

◆ *Spelling strategies* Students use strategies to spell unfamiliar words (Laminack & Wood, 1996). Novice spellers often use a "sound-it-out" strategy for spelling, but because English isn't a completely phonetic language, this strategy is only somewhat effective. Students identify many of the sounds they hear in a word, but they can't spell

FIGURE 12–5

Common Spelling Options for Phonemes

Sound	Spellings	Examples	Sound	Spellings	Examples
long a	a-e	date	short oo	oo	book
	a	angel		u	put
	ai	aid		ou	could
	ay	day		o	woman
ch	ch	church	ou	ou	out
	t(u)	picture		ow	cow
	tch	watch	s	s	sick
	ti	question		ce	office
long e	ea	each		c	city
	ee	feel		ss	class
	e	evil		se	else
	e-e	these		x(ks)	box
	ea-e	breathe	sh	ti	attention
short e	e	end		sh	she
	ea	head		ci	ancient
f	f	feel		ssi	admission
	ff	sheriff	t	t	teacher
	gh	cough		te	definite
	ph	photograph		ed	furnished
j	ge	strange		tt	attend
	g	general	long u	u	union
	j	job		u-e	use
	dge	bridge		ue	value
k	c	call		ew	few
	k	keep	short u	u	ugly
	ck	black		o	company
l	l	last		ou	country
	ll	allow	y	y	yes
	le	automobile		i	onion
m	m	man	z	z	zoo
	me	come		s	present
	mm	comment		se	applause
n	n	no		ze	gauze
	ne	done	syllabic l	le	able
long o	o	go		al	animal
	o-e	note		el	cancel
	ow	own		il	civil
	oa	load	syllabic n	en	written
short o	o	office		on	lesson
	a	all		an	important
	au	author		in	cousin
	aw	saw		contractions	didn't
oi	oi	oil		ain	certain
	oy	boy	r-controlled	er	her
long oo	u	cruel		ur	church
	oo	noon		ir	first
	u-e	rule		or	world
	o-e	lose		ear	heard
	ue	blue		our	courage
	o	to			
	ou	group			

FIGURE 12–6

Sixth Graders' Chart of Spelling Options for Long *i*

Spelling	Examples	Location		
		Initial	Medial	Final
i	child, climb, blind, wild, hire		x	
	idea, Friday, microwave, lion, gigantic, rhinoceros, variety, triangle, siren, liar, rabbi	x	x	x
i-e	smile, bride, drive, write		x	
	criticize, impolite, beehive, paradise, valentine, capsize, ninety, sniper, united, decide		x	x
ie	pies, lie, die		x	x
	untie			x
ei	none			
	feisty, seismograph		x	
igh	high, sight, knight, bright		x	x
	knighthood, sunlight		x	
eigh	height		x	
	none			
y	why, my, by, try, fly			x
	July, nylon, crying, xylophone, unicycle, notify, dynamite, skyscraper, hydrogen		x	x
y-e	byte, types, hype, rhyme		x	x
	paralyze, stylist		x	x
ye	dye, rye			x
	goodbye			x
eye	eye			x
	eyeball, eyelash	x		
ui	none			
	guidance		x	
ui-e	guide			x
	none			
uy	guy, buy			x
	buyer		x	

unpronounced letters or spelling patterns (e.g., SIK–sick, BABES–*babies*). The "think-it-out" strategy is much more effective. Students who have more knowledge about spelling will sound the word out and then think about what they know about English spelling patterns and meaning relationships among words to create a more conventional spelling. Specifically, they do the following:

- Break the word into syllables
- Sound out each syllable
- Add affixes to root words
- Look at the word to see if it looks correct
- Generate possible spellings based on spelling patterns and meaning relationships if the word doesn't look correct
- Choose the best alternative

Students also use other spelling strategies: They learn to proofread to identify and correct spelling errors in their writing. They also learn two ways to find the correct spelling of a word. First, they locate words they want to spell on word walls and other charts in the classroom; and second, they find the spelling of unfamiliar words in a dictionary.

Minilessons

Teachers teach students about spelling procedures, concepts, and strategies and skills during minilessons. A list of topics for spelling minilessons is presented on pages 420–421, along with a second-grade teacher's minilesson on the "think it out" strategy.

Weekly Spelling Tests

Many teachers question the use of spelling tests to teach spelling, because research on children's spelling development suggests that spelling is best learned through reading and writing (Gentry & Gillet, 1993; Wilde, 1992). In addition, teachers complain that lists of spelling words are unrelated to the words students are reading and writing, and that the 30 minutes of valuable instructional time spent each day in completing spelling textbook activities is excessive. Weekly spelling tests, when they are used, should be individualized so that children learn to spell the words they need for their writing.

In an individualized approach to spelling instruction, students choose the words they will study, and many of the words they choose are words they use in their writing projects. Students study five to eight words during the week using a specific study strategy. This approach places more responsibility on students for their own learning, and when students have responsibility, they tend to perform better. The guidelines for using individualized spelling tests are provided in the LA Essentials feature on page 422.

Teachers develop a weekly word list of 25 to 50 words of varying levels of difficulty from which students select words to study. Words for the master list are drawn from words students needed for their writing projects during the previous week, high-frequency words, and words related to literature focus units and thematic units ongoing in the classroom. Words from spelling textbooks can also be added to the list, but they should never make up the entire list. The master word list can be used for minilessons during the week. Students can look for phoneme-grapheme correspondences, add words to charts of spelling options, and note root words and affixes.

On Monday, the teacher administers the pretest using the master list of words, and students spell as many of the words as they can. Students correct their own pretests, and from the words they misspell, each student chooses 5 to 10 words to study. They make two copies of their study list. Students number their spelling words using the numbers on the master list to make it easier to take the final test on Friday. Students keep one copy of the list to study, and the teacher keeps the second copy.

Researchers have found that the pretest is a critical component in learning to spell. The pretest eliminates words that students already know how to spell so that they can direct their study toward words that they don't know yet. More than half a century ago, Ernest Horn recommended that the best way to improve students' spelling was for them to get immediate feedback by correcting their own pretests. His advice is still sound today.

Students spend approximately 5 to 10 minutes studying the words on their study lists each day during the week. Research shows that instead of busywork activities, such as using their spelling words in sentences or gluing yarn in the shape of the words, it is more effective for students to use this strategy for practicing spelling words:

1. Look at the word and say it to yourself.
2. Say each letter in the word to yourself.
3. Close your eyes and spell the word to yourself.
4. Write the word, and check that you spelled it correctly.
5. Write the word again, and check that you spelled it correctly.

This strategy focuses on the whole word rather than breaking it apart into sounds or syllables. During a minilesson at the beginning of the school year, teachers explain how to use the strategy, and then they post a copy of the strategy in the classroom. In addition to this word-study strategy, sometimes students trade word lists with a partner on Wednesday or Thursday and give each other a practice test.

A final test is administered on Friday. The teacher reads the master list, and students write only those words they have practiced during the week. To make it easier to administer the test, students first list the numbers of the words they have practiced from their study lists on their test papers. Any words that students misspell should be included on their lists the following week.

This individualized approach is recommended instead of a textbook approach. Typically, textbooks are arranged in weeklong units, with lists of 10 to 20 words and practice activities that often require at least 30 minutes per day to complete. Research indicates that only 60 to 75 minutes per week should be spent on spelling instruction, however; greater periods of time do not result in improved spelling ability (Johnson, Langford, & Quorn, 1981). Moreover, many textbook activities focus on language arts skills that are not directly related to learning to spell.

The words in each unit are often grouped according to spelling patterns or phonetic generalizations, even though researchers question this approach unless teachers teach students about the pattern and provide practice activities, as Mr. Martinez did in the vignette at the beginning of the chapter. Otherwise, students

What Students Need to Learn About Spelling

Topics

Procedures	Concepts	Strategies and Skills
Locate words on a word wall	Alphabetic principle	Invent spellings
Locate words in a dictionary	"Kid" or invented spelling	Use placeholders
Use a thesaurus	Homophones	Sound it out
Do making words	Root words and affixes	**Think it out**
	Spelling options	
Do word sorts	High-frequency words	Visualize words
Study a spelling word	Contractions	Spell by analogy
Analyze spelling errors	Compound words	Apply affixes
	Possessives	Proofread
		Apply capitalization rules

I invite you to learn more about spelling by visiting MyEducationLab. To see how third graders participate in a making-words activity, go to the topic "Language Tools" and click on the video "Making Words."

Minilesson

Mrs. Hamilton Teaches the "Think It Out" Strategy to Her Second Graders

1 Introduce the topic

Mrs. Hamilton asks her second graders how to spell the word *because*, and they suggest these options: *beecuz, becauz, becuse,* and *becuzz*. She asks the children to explain their spellings. Aaron explains that he sounded the word out and heard *bee* and *cuz*. Molly explains that she knows there is no *z* in *because* so she spelled it *becuse*. Other students explain that they say the word slowly, listening for all the sounds, and then write the sounds they hear. Mrs. Hamilton explains that this is a good first-grade strategy, but now she is going to teach them an even more important second-grade strategy called "think it out."

2 Share examples

Mrs. Hamilton asks the class to observe as she spells the word *make*. She says the word slowly and writes *mak* on the chalkboard. Then she explains, "I sounded the word out and wrote the sounds I heard, but I don't think the word is spelled right because it looks funny." The children agree and eagerly raise their hands to supply the right answer. "No," she says, "I want to 'think it out.' Let's see. Hmmm. Well, there are vowel rules. The *a* is long so I could add an *e* at the end of the word." The students clap, happy that she has figured out the spelling of the word. She models the process two more times, spelling *great* and *running*.

3 Provide information

Mrs. Hamilton shares a chart she has made with the steps in the "think it out" strategy:

1. Sound the word out and spell it the best you can.
2. Think about spelling rules to add.
3. Look at the word to see if it looks right.
4. If it doesn't look right, try to change some letters, ask for help, or check the dictionary.

The children talk about how Mrs. Hamilton used the strategy to spell *make, great,* and *running*.

4 Supervise practice

Mrs. Hamilton passes out dry-erase boards and pens for the children to use as they practice the strategy. They write *time, what, walked, taking, bread,* and *people* using the "think it out" strategy. As they move through each step, they hold up their boards to show Mrs. Hamilton their work.

5 Reflect on learning

Mrs. Hamilton ends the minilesson by asking children what they learned, and they explain that they learned the grown-up way to spell words. They explain the steps this way: First they sound it out, then they look it out, and then they think it out.

INDIVIDUALIZED SPELLING TESTS

Master List
Teachers prepare a master list of 20–50 words, depending on students' grade level and the range of spelling levels in the classroom. Words on the list are drawn from spelling textbooks, words students misspell in their writing, and spelling skills being taught.

Pretest
On Monday, students take a pretest of the 20–50 words on the master list, and they self-correct their pretests immediately afterward using red pens.

Words to Study
Students choose 5 to 10 words to study from the words they misspelled on the pretest.

Study Lists
Students make two study lists, one to take home and one to use at school.

Study Strategy
Students use an effective strategy to study the words each day during the week. They study their spelling words this way rather than by writing sentences or stories using the words.

Practice Test
Students work with a partner to give each other a practice test during the week to check their progress in learning to spell the words.

Posttest
On Friday, students take a posttest of the words they have practiced. Teachers collect the tests and grade them themselves.

Next Week's Words
Teachers make a list of words that students misspell to include on their master list for the following week.

memorize the rule or spelling pattern and score perfectly on the spelling test but later are unable to choose among spelling options in their writing. For example, after learning the *i-e* vowel rule and the *-igh* spelling pattern in isolation, students are often stumped about how to spell a word such as *light*. They have learned two spelling options for /i/, *i-e* and *-igh,* and *lite* is an option, one they often see in their environment. Instead of organizing words according to phonetic generalizations and spelling rules, teachers should teach minilessons and point out the rules as they occur when writing words on word walls.

Assessing Students' Progress in Spelling

Grades on weekly spelling tests are the traditional measure of progress in spelling, and the individualized approach to spelling instruction provides this convenient way to assess students. This method of assessing student progress is somewhat deceptive, however, because the goal of spelling instruction is not simply to spell words correctly on weekly tests but to use the words, spelled conventionally, in writing. Samples of student writing should be collected periodically to determine whether words that were spelled correctly on tests are being spelled correctly in writing projects. If students are not applying in their writing what they have learned through the weekly spelling instruction, they may not have learned to spell the words after all.

When students perform poorly on spelling tests, consider whether faulty pronunciation or poor handwriting is to blame. Ask students to pronounce words they habitually misspell to see if their pronunciation or dialect differences may be contributing to spelling problems. Students need to recognize that pronunciation does not always predict spelling. For example, in some parts of the United States, people pronounce the words *pin* and *pen* as though they were spelled with the same vowel, and sometimes we pronounce *better* as though it were spelled *bedder* and *going* as though it were spelled *goin'*. Also, ask students to spell orally the words they misspell in their writing to see whether handwriting difficulties are contributing to spelling problems. Sometimes a minilesson on how to connect two cursive letters (e.g., *br*) or a reminder about the importance of legible handwriting will solve the problem.

It is essential that teachers keep anecdotal information and samples of students' writing to monitor their overall progress in spelling. Teachers can examine error patterns and spelling strategies in these samples. Checking to see if students have spelled their spelling words correctly in writing samples provides one type of information, and examining writing samples for error patterns and spelling strategies provides additional information. Fewer misspellings do not necessarily indicate progress, because to learn to spell, students must experiment with spellings of unfamiliar words, which will result in errors from time to time. Students often misspell a word by misapplying a newly learned spelling pattern. The word *extension* is a good example: Middle-grade students spell the word EXTENSHUN, then change their spelling to EXTENTION after they learn the suffix *-tion*. Although they are still misspelling the word, they have moved from using sound-symbol correspondences to using a spelling pattern—from a less sophisticated spelling strategy to a more sophisticated one.

Students' behavior as they proofread and edit their compositions also provides evidence of spelling development. They should become increasingly able to spot misspelled words in their compositions and to locate the spelling of unknown words in a dictionary. It is easy for teachers to calculate the number of spelling errors students have identified in proofreading their compositions and to chart students' progress in learning to spot errors. Locating errors is the first step in proofreading; correcting the errors is the second step. It is fairly simple for students to correct the spelling of known words, but to correct unknown words, they must consider spelling options and predict possible spellings before they can locate the words in a dictionary. Teachers can document students' growth in locating unfamiliar words in a dictionary by observing their behavior when they edit their compositions.

Teachers can use the writing samples they collect to document children's spelling development. They can note primary-grade students' progression through the stages of invented spelling by analyzing writing samples using a chart such as the ones in the Weaving Assessment Into Practice Features on pages 403 and 405 to determine a general stage of development. Students in the middle and upper grades can use this chart to analyze their own spelling errors.

Review

Spelling is a language tool, and through instruction in spelling, students learn to communicate more effectively. Most students learn to spell conventionally before they enter high school. Here are the key concepts discussed in this chapter:

- Students move through a series of five stages of spelling development.
- In the first stage, emergent spelling, students string scribbles, letters, and letterlike forms together with little or no understanding of the alphabetic principle.
- In the second stage, letter-name spelling, students learn to represent phonemes in the beginning, middle, and end of words with letters.
- In the third stage, within-word spelling, students learn to spell long-vowel patterns, *r*-controlled vowels, and complex consonant combinations.
- In the fourth stage, syllables and affixes, students learn to spell two-syllable words and add inflectional endings.
- In the fifth stage, derivational relations, students learn that multisyllabic words with related meanings are often related in spelling despite changes in vowel and consonant sounds.
- Teachers can analyze students' misspellings to determine their stage of spelling development and plan appropriate instruction.
- Spelling instruction includes daily opportunities to read and write, word walls, word-making and word-sort activities, proofreading, dictionary use, and instruction in spelling options, root words and affixes, and other spelling concepts.
- Teachers teach minilessons about strategies for spelling unfamiliar words as well as other spelling procedures, concepts, and strategies and skills.
- Weekly spelling tests, when they are used, should be individualized so that students learn to spell words they don't already know how to spell.

Professional References

Bean, W., & Bouffler, C. (1997). *Read, write, spell.* York, ME: Stenhouse.

Bear, D. R., Helman, L., Templeton, S., Invernizzi, M., & Johnston, F. (2007a). *Words their way with English learners.* Upper Saddle River, NJ: Merrill/Prentice Hall.

Bear, D. R., Invernizzi, M., Templeton, S., & Johnston, F. (2007b). *Words their way: Word study for phonics, vocabulary, and spelling instruction* (4th ed.). Upper Saddle River, NJ: Merrill/Prentice Hall.

Chandler, K., & the Mapleton teacher-research group. (2000). Squaring up to spelling: A teacher-research group surveys parents. *Language Arts, 77,* 224–231.

Cunningham, P. M. (2004). *Phonics they use: Words for reading and writing* (4th ed.). Boston: Allyn & Bacon.

Cunningham, P. M., & Cunningham, J. W. (1992). Making words: Enhancing the invented spelling-decoding connection. *The Reading Teacher, 46,* 106–115.

Gentry, J. R. (1997). *My kid can't spell! Understanding and assessing your child's literacy development.* Portsmouth, NH: Heinemann.

Gentry, J. R., & Gillet, J. W. (1993). *Teaching kids to spell.* Portsmouth, NH: Heinemann.

Graves, D. H. (1983). *Writing: Teachers and children at work.* Portsmouth, NH: Heinemann.

Henderson, E. H. (1990). *Teaching spelling* (2nd ed.). Boston: Houghton Mifflin.

Horn, E. (1926). *A basic writing vocabulary.* Iowa City: University of Iowa Press.

Hughes, M., & Searle, D. (1997). *The violent "e" and other tricky sounds: Learning to spell from kindergarten through grade 6.* York, ME: Stenhouse.

Hughes, M., & Searle, D. (2000). Spelling and "the second 'R.'" *Language Arts, 77,* 203–208.

Johnson, T. D., Langford, K. G., & Quorn, K. C. (1981). Characteristics of an effective spelling program. *Language Arts, 58,* 581–588.

Lacey, C. (1994). *Moving on in spelling: Strategies and activities for the whole language classroom.* New York: Scholastic.

Laminack, L. L., & Wood, K. (1996). *Spelling in use: Looking closely at spelling in whole language classrooms.* Urbana, IL: National Council of Teachers of English.

Read, C. (1975). *Children's categorization of speech sounds in English* (NCTE Research Report No. 17). Urbana, IL: National Council of Teachers of English.

Rymer, R., & Williams, C. (2000). "Wasn't that a spelling word?" Spelling instruction and young children's writing. *Language Arts, 77,* 241–249.

Templeton, S. (1979). Spelling first, sound later: The relationship between orthography and higher order phonological knowledge in older students. *Research in the Teaching of English, 13,* 255–265.

Turbill, J. (2000). Developing a spelling conscience. *Language Arts, 77,* 209–217.

Wilde, S. (1992). *You kan red this! Spelling and punctuation for whole language classrooms, K–6.* Portsmouth, NH: Heinemann.

Wilde, S. (1996). A speller's bill of rights. *Primary Voices K–6, 4,* 7–10.

chapter thirteen

Language Tools: Grammar and Handwriting

Mr. Keogh's fifth graders are reading *Poppy* (Avi, 1995), the story of a little deer mouse named Poppy who outwits Mr. Ocax, a great horned owl. Mr. Keogh introduced the novel to the class, and they read the first chapter together. Then the students continued reading and talking about the book in small groups that operate like literature circles. The teacher brings the class back together for grammar activities and other exploring-stage activities.

The students list important words from the story on the word wall posted in the classroom after reading each chapter or two, and as the words are listed, the teacher asks them to identify their parts of speech. Even though the book is rich with adverbs, few are chosen for the word wall, so Mr. Keogh begins adding some, such as *profoundly, sufficiently,* and *ravenously.*

For the first grammar activity, Mr. Keogh has students work in small groups to list 10 nouns, 10 adjectives, 10 verbs, and 10 adverbs from the word wall. The teacher walks around the classroom, monitoring students' progress and referring them to the

How can teachers teach grammar as part of literature focus units?

Traditionally, teachers taught grammar by having their students complete exercises in a textbook. The problem was that students didn't apply what they were practicing orally or in writing. A newer approach is to teach grammar more authentically through books students are reading and through their writing. The focus on grammar fits into the exploring stage of the reading process and the editing stage of the writing process. In this vignette, you'll see how Mr. Keogh incorporates grammar instruction into a literature focus unit.

novel to see how a word was used or to the dictionary to check the part of speech. Some of the words are tricky because they are written in isolation on the word wall. An example is *fake*. It can be used in two ways: as an adjective in *the fake owl* and as a noun in *it was a fake*. Mr. Keogh allows the students to list it either way, but they have to be able to defend their choice. This activity serves as a good review.

Next, Mr. Keogh creates a word-sort activity using words from the groups' lists. Students cut the word cards apart and sort them into noun, adjective, verb, and adverb categories. Pairs of students practice several times before they glue the cards down. One student's completed word sort is shown on page 428.

The next day, the students create sentences using one or more words from each category on their word sort; they can also add words to complete the sentences. The first sentences they create, *Mr. Ocax shrieked furiously from the abandoned tree* and *Mr. Ocax shrieked harshly under the crescent moon,* are predictable. Mr. Keogh encourages the fifth graders to experiment with more creative ways to use the words, the way Avi did in *Poppy*. The students work with partners to create these sentences:

> *Delicate little Poppy swiveled nervously on one foot, searching the sky for Mr. Ocax.*

> *Harshly Mr. Ocax snatched the appetizing little mouse named Poppy from the slippery moss-covered rock.*

They write their sentences on sentence strips and post them in the classroom to reread. The next day, Mr. Keogh has them reread the sentences and mark the nouns with green crayons and the verbs with blue crayons.

After this review of the parts of speech, Mr. Keogh changes his focus to sentences. He has created a pack of word and phrase cards to use in reviewing simple sentences, sentence fragments, and compound sentences. He also includes *as* and *when* cards in the pack so his students can build complex sentences, even though they are not expected to learn this concept in fifth grade. Students cut apart a sheet of cards to use in making sentences about Mr. Ocax. A copy of the sheet of cards is shown on page 429.

First, the fifth graders use the cards to create these simple sentences:

The great horned owl ruled Dimwood Forest.

He swiveled his head from right to left.

The great horned owl smiled into the night air.

Soundlessly, the great horned owl soared into the night air.

With his piercing gaze, Mr. Ocax ruled Dimwood Forest triumphantly.

After they create each sentence, Mr. Keogh asks them to identify the subject and the verb. To simplify the process, students color their subject cards green and their verb cards blue. They continue to sort the cards and identify the adverbs and prepositional phrases and the one conjunction card in the pack.

The students save their packs of cards in small, self-sealing plastic bags, and they continue this activity the next day. Mr. Keogh asks them to use the *and* card in their sentences, and they create these sentences with compound predicates:

Mr. Ocax swiveled his head from right to left and surveyed Dimwood Forest.

The great horned owl called a long, low cry of triumph, spread his wings, and soared back into the air.

The students identify the subjects and verbs in the sentences to figure out that these sentences have compound predicates. They try to make a sentence with a compound subject but find that they can't with the word cards they have.

Next, Mr. Keogh asks them to craft compound sentences using two subjects and two verbs, and they arrange these sentences:

The great horned owl called a long, low cry of triumph, and he soared soundlessly into the night air.

Mr. Ocax surveyed Dimwood Forest triumphantly, and he smiled.

Grammar Word Sort			
Nouns	Adjectives	Verbs	Adverbs
Mr. Ocax	crescent	shrieked	enormously
whirligig	charred	hunched	cautiously
dignity	appetizing	roosting	furiously
Poppy	motionless	luxuriating	harshly
porcupine	perplexed	saunter	desperately
notion	porcupine-quill	surveyed	deftly
Ereth	wary	skittered	stately
privacy	abandoned	swiveling	profoundly
effrontery	delicate	plunged	nervously
camouflage	fake	snatch	entirely

Cards for Making Sentences			
spread his wings	on a branch	triumphantly	with his piercing gaze
soundlessly	a long, low cry of triumph	surveyed	called
from right to left	and	of an old charred oak	he
back into the air	perched	Mr. Ocax	into the night air
swiveled his head	when	smiled	Dimwood Forest
ruled	the great horned owl	as	soared

After they share each sentence, Mr. Keogh asks the students to identify the subjects and verbs. Several students make additional word cards so that they can create the compound sentences they want:

> The great horned owl spread his wings, and he flew up high into the night sky.

> Mr. Ocax blinked his large round eyes, and he watched a little mouse named Poppy.

"Let's make some even more interesting sentences," Mr. Keogh suggests as he asks them to use the *as* or *when* cards in their sentences. They create these complex sentences:

> Mr. Ocax smiled triumphantly as he ruled Dimwood Forest.

> As the great horned owl called a long, low cry of triumph, he perched on a branch of an old charred oak.

> Mr. Ocax smiled as he soundlessly spread his wings and soared back into the air.

The students identify the subjects and verbs in the sentences, and at first they assume the sentences are compound sentences. Mr. Keogh explains that these sentences are called *complex sentences*: They have one independent clause and one dependent clause. He explains that the clauses beginning with *as* or *when* are called *dependent clauses* because they cannot stand alone as sentences. The students color these two cards red so that they will stand out in a sentence.

Several days later, Mr. Keogh repeats the process with a pack of cards with words and phrases about Poppy. The students practice arranging the cards to make simple, compound, and complex sentences, and they keep a list of the sentences they make in their reading logs.

For one of the projects at the end of the book, the students write a character sketch about Mr. Ocax or Poppy. Mr. Keogh explains that in a character sketch, students do three things:

- Describe what the character looks like
- Describe what the character did
- Identify one character trait the character exemplified, such as being smart, brave, or determined

This writing project grows out of the grammar activities. The students are encouraged to use words they've been arranging as well as other words from the word wall in their character sketches. They don't plagiarize because they're using newly learned words and phrases from charts in the classroom in their writing. Here is Darla's character sketch about Poppy; the underlined words and phrases in her writing came from the novel and were collected on charts or sentence strips posted in the classroom:

> Poppy was a _dainty_ little girl mouse. She looked like a mouse. Her fur was _orange-brown_, and she had a _plump belly_ that was white. She had _a tiny nose, pink toes_, and a very long _tail_. On her nose was a scar made by a _great horned owl_ named Mr. Ocax. Her _ears were long_, and _her eyes were dark, almost round_.

> Mr. Ocax _ruled_ over the entire _territory_ where Poppy lived. He controlled them _with pure power and fury_. They had to get his _permission_ to do anything or else they were his _dinner_. He said he protected them from the _vicious_ porcupine who lived in Dimwood Forest, but he was lying. One day Poppy met Ereth, the porcupine. He told her that he eats bark, not mice. Mr. Ocax had to stop Poppy or she would tell everyone that he was _a liar and a bully_. He would not be _king_ anymore. Many times the owl tried to catch Poppy, but she always escaped. Then he tricked her and caught her. _Bravely_ she stuck her _porcupine-quill_ sword into his _left claw_. That's how she escaped. Mr. Ocax was not so lucky. His flying was _totally out of control_ because of the pain in his claw, and he _slammed into the salt lick_. It was the violent death he deserved.

> Poppy was a brave little mouse. I think she was a hero. That might surprise you because she _was trembling with fear_ every time she confronted the owl who _looked like death_ to her. What she did was she pretended to be brave. To be a coward was bad. She said it is _hard to be brave, but harder to be a coward_. She risked her life, but now her whole family was safe.

Through these grammar activities, Darla's writing has become stronger with more sophisticated language and sentence patterns.

---

*C*hildren learn the structure of the English language—its grammar—intuitively as they learn to talk; the process is an unconscious one, and they have almost completed it by the time they enter kindergarten. The purpose of grammar instruction, then, is to make this intuitive knowledge about the English language explicit and to provide labels for words within sentences, parts of sentences, and types of sentences. Children speak the dialect that their parents and community members speak. Dialect, whether Standard English or nonstandard English, is informal and differs to some degree from the written Standard English, or book language, that students will read and write in school (Edelsky, 1989; Pooley, 1974).

Handwriting is a tool for writers. Students need to develop legible and fluent handwriting so that they can communicate their ideas effectively though writing. Although nearly everyone would agree that the message is more than the formation of letters, handwriting instruction can't be ignored. Donald Graves (1994) urges teachers to keep handwriting in perspective and to remember that it is a tool, best taught and applied through authentic writing activities.

As you read this chapter, think about the role of grammar and handwriting in the language arts program. Use these questions to guide your reading:

- What are the components of grammar?
- How should teachers teach grammar concepts?
- How does children's handwriting develop?
- How do teachers teach and assess handwriting?

GRAMMAR

Grammar is probably the most controversial area of language arts. Teachers, parents, and the community disagree about the content of grammar instruction, how to teach it, and when to begin teaching it. Some people believe that formal instruction in grammar is unnecessary—if not harmful—during the elementary grades; others believe that grammar instruction should be a key component of language arts instruction. Before getting into the controversy, let's clarify the terms *grammar* and *usage*. *Grammar* is the description of the syntax or structure of a language and prescriptions for its use (Weaver, 1996). It involves principles of word and sentence formation. In contrast, *usage* is correctness, or using the appropriate word or phrase in a sentence. It is the socially preferred way of using language within a dialect. *My friend, she; the man brung;* and *hisself* are examples of Standard English usage errors that students sometimes make.

Grammar Concepts

The five most common types of information about grammar that students learn are parts of speech, parts of sentences, types of sentences, capitalization and punctuation, and usage. These components are summarized in the LA Essentials box on page 432.

Parts of Speech. Grammarians have sorted words into eight groups, called *parts of speech*: nouns, pronouns, verbs, adjectives, adverbs, prepositions, conjunctions, and interjections. Words in each group are used in essentially the same way in all sentences. Consider this sentence: *Hey, did you know that it rains more than 200 days a year in a tropical rain forest and that as much as 240 inches of rain fall each year?* All eight parts of speech are represented in this sentence. *Rain forest, days, year, inches,* and *rain* are nouns, and *you* and *it* are pronouns. *Tropical* is an adjective describing *rain forest,* and *each* is an adjective describing *year.* The verbs are *did know, rains,* and

COMPONENTS OF GRAMMAR INSTRUCTION

Parts of Speech

The eight parts of speech are nouns, pronouns, adjectives, verbs, adverbs, prepositions, conjunctions, and interjections. Students learn to identify the parts of speech in order to understand the role of each in a sentence.

Parts of Sentences

Simple sentences can be divided into the subject and the predicate. The subject is the noun or pronoun and words or phrases that modify it, and the predicate is the verb and the words or phrases that modify it. Students learn to identify subjects and predicates to check for subject-verb agreement and to determine sentence types.

Types of Sentences

Sentences can be classified according to structure and purpose. The structure of a sentence may be simple, compound, complex, or compound-complex, according to the number and type of clauses. The purpose of a sentence can be to make a statement (declarative sentence), ask a question (interrogative sentence), make a command (imperative sentence), or express strong emotion or surprise (exclamatory sentence). Students learn to recognize the structure and purposes of sentences.

Capitalization and Punctuation

Capitalization and punctuation marks signal the structure of a sentence. The first word and other important words in the sentence are capitalized, and some punctuation marks indicate internal sentence structure whereas others mark the end of a sentence. Students learn to use capital letters and punctuation marks to indicate the structure of the sentences they write.

Usage

Standard English is used by educated people in speaking and writing; however, many people speak dialects, or nonstandard varieties of English. Children come to school speaking the language used by their families, and those children who speak nonstandard varieties learn Standard English through reading and writing activities.

fall. More than is an adverb modifying *200 days,* and *as much as* is an adverb modifying *240 inches;* they both answer the question "how much." *Of* and *in* are prepositions, and they introduce prepositional phrases. The conjunction *and* joins the two dependent clauses. The first word in the sentence, *hey,* is an interjection, and it's set off with a comma. Figure 13–1 presents an overview of the eight parts of speech.

Parts of a Sentence. A sentence is made up of one or more words to express a complete thought and, to express the thought, must have a subject and a predicate

---

FIGURE 13–1

The Eight Parts of Speech

Part of Speech	Definition	Examples	
Noun	A word used to name something—a person, a place, or a thing. A proper noun names a particular person, place, or thing and is capitalized. In contrast, a common noun doesn't name a particular person, place, or thing and isn't capitalized.	United States Kleenex pilot	sandwich courage
Pronoun	A word used in place of a noun.	I me	you who
Adjective	A word used to describe a noun or a pronoun. Adjectives are common or proper, and proper adjectives are capitalized. Some words can be either adjectives or pronouns; they are adjectives if they come before a noun and modify it, and they're pronouns if they stand alone.	the fastest	American slippery-fingered
Verb	A word used to show action or state of being. A verb's form varies depending on its number (singular or plural) and tense (present, past, future). Some verbs are auxiliary, or helping, verbs; they are used to help form some tenses or voice. Voice is either active or passive.	eat think will have	saw is can would
Adverb	A word used to modify a verb, an adjective, or another adverb. An adverb tells how, when, where, why, how often, and how much.	quickly outside loudly	now well
Preposition	A word or group of words used to show position, direction, or how two words or ideas are related to each other.	at to between	with from
Conjunction	A word used to connect words and groups of words. These are the three types: coordinating conjunctions, which connect equivalent words, phrases, or clauses; correlative conjunctions, which are used in pairs; and subordinating conjunctions, which connect two clauses that are not equally important.	and or because	but either-or when
Interjection	A word or phrase used to express strong emotion and set off by commas or an exclamation point.	wow hey	How are you? Cool, dude!

(one-word sentences have understood subjects—"Help!"—or predicates—"You!"). The subject names who or what the sentence is about, and the predicate includes the verb and anything that completes or modifies it. In a simple sentence with one subject and one predicate, everything that is not part of the subject is part of the predicate. Consider this sentence about the rain forest: *Most rain forests are found in warm, wet climates near the equator.* The subject is *most rain forests,* and the rest of the sentence is the predicate.

Types of Sentences. Sentences are classified in two ways. First, they're classified according to structure, or how they're put together. The structure may be simple, compound, complex, or compound-complex, according to the number and type of clauses in the sentence. A clause consists of a subject and a predicate, and there are two types of clauses. If the clause presents a complete thought and can stand alone, it's an independent clause. If the clause isn't a complete thought and can't stand alone as a sentence, it's a dependent clause because it depends on the meaning expressed in the independent clause. An example of an independent clause is *Tropical rain forests are the most complex ecosystems on earth,* and an example of a dependent clause is *Because tropical rain forests are the most complex ecosystems on earth.* This dependent clause can't stand alone as a sentence; it must be attached to an independent clause. For example: *Because tropical rain forests are the most complex ecosystems on earth, scientists are interested in studying them.* The independent clause, which could stand alone as a sentence, is *scientists are interested in studying them.*

A simple sentence contains only one independent clause, and a compound sentence has two or more independent clauses. A complex sentence contains one independent clause and one or more dependent clauses. A compound-complex sentence has two or more independent clauses and one or more dependent clauses. Can you identify which of these sentences are simple, compound, complex, and compound-complex?

Although a tropical rain forest is a single ecosystem, it is composed of four layers.
The tallest trees in the rain forest grow to be about 300 feet tall, and they form the top, emergent layer.
The next level is the canopy, and it is alive with activity as hummingbirds, woodpeckers, tree frogs, and monkeys go from flower to flower and branch to branch.
Vines, ferns, and palms grow in the understory.
Few flowers bloom in the understory because sunlight does not shine through the leaves of the canopy.
The bottom layer is the forest floor; mosses, fungi, and other parasitic plants grow here.

The fourth sentence is simple, the second and sixth sentences are compound, the first and fifth sentences are complex, and the third sentence is compound-complex.

Second, sentences are classified according to their purpose or the type of message they contain. Sentences that make statements are declarative, those that ask questions are interrogative, those that make commands are imperative, and those that communicate strong emotion or surprise are exclamatory. The purpose of a sentence is often signaled by the punctuation mark placed at the end of the sentence. Declarative sentences and some imperative sentences are marked with periods, interrogative sentences are marked with question marks, and exclamatory sentences and some imperative sentences are marked with exclamation points.

Capitalization and Punctuation. Students learn that capital letters divide sentences and signal important words within sentences (Fearn & Farnan, 1998). Consider how the use of capital letters affects the meaning of these three sentences:

They were going to the white house for dinner.

They were going to the White house for dinner.

They were going to the White House for dinner. (Wilde, 1992, p. 18)

Capital letters also express loudness of speech or intensity of emotion because they stand out visually.

Children often begin writing during the preschool years using only capital letters; during kindergarten and first grade, they learn the lowercase forms of letters. They learn to capitalize *I,* the first word in a sentence, and names and other proper nouns and adjectives. By sixth grade, the most common problem is overcapitalization, or capital-izing too many words in a sentence, as in this example: *If the Tropical Rain Forest is destroyed, the Earth's climate could get warmer, and this is known as the Greenhouse Effect.* This problem persists into adolescence because students have trouble differenti-ating between common and proper nouns (Shaughnessy, 1977). Too often, students assume that important words in the sentence should be capitalized.

It's a common assumption that punctuation marks signal pauses in speech, but punctuation plays a greater role than that, according to Sandra Wilde (1992).

Linda Peterson/Merrill

Learning Centers

These first graders experiment with end-of-sentence punctuation marks at a learning center. The sentences they're working with were written during a minilesson several days ago. As they work collaboratively to identify the punctuation marks, reread the sentences, and choose the appropriate punctuation marks, they are learning more than they would by working individually to complete a worksheet. Teachers can make the center activities self-checking, too, so that students will know immediately if they're correct, and can get help from classmates or the teacher if they aren't correct.

Punctuation marks both signal grammatical boundaries and express meaning; some punctuation marks indicate sentence boundaries as well. Periods, question marks, and exclamation points mark sentence boundaries and indicate whether a sentence makes a statement, asks a question, or expresses an exclamation. In contrast, commas, semicolons, and colons mark grammatical units within sentences.

Quotation marks and apostrophes express meaning within sentences. Quotation marks are used most often to indicate talk, but a more sophisticated use is to express irony, as in *My son "loves" to wash the dishes*. Apostrophes are used in contractions to join two words and in possessive nouns to show relationships. Consider the different meanings of these phrases:

> The monkey's howling (and it's running around the cage).
>
> The monkey's howling (annoyed us; we wanted to kill it).
>
> The monkeys' howling (annoyed us; we wanted to kill them).
>
> (We listened all night to) the monkeys howling. (Wilde, 1992, p. 18)

Researchers have documented that learning to use punctuation is a developmental process. Beginning in the preschool years, children notice punctuation marks and learn to discriminate them from letters (Clay, 1991). In kindergarten and first grade, children are formally introduced to the end-of-sentence punctuation marks, and they learn to use them conventionally about half the time (Cordeiro, Giacobbe, & Cazden, 1983). Many beginning writers use punctuation marks in more idiosyncratic ways, such as between words and at the end of each line of writing, but over time, children's usage becomes more conventional. English learners exhibit similar developmental patterns.

Usage. Children come to school speaking dialects or varieties of English that their parents speak, and when these dialects differ from Standard English, they're called *nonstandard English*. Children may use double negatives rather than single negatives, so that they say *I ain't got no money* instead of *I don't have any money*. Or they may use objective pronouns instead of subjective pronouns so that they say *Me and him have dirt bikes* instead of *He and I have dirt bikes*.

Students who speak nonstandard English learn Standard English as an alternative to the forms they already know. Rather than trying to substitute standard forms for students' nonstandard forms, teachers explain that Standard English is the language of school. It is the language used in books, and students can easily locate Standard English examples in books they are reading. Calling Standard English "book language" also helps to explain the importance of proofreading to identify and correct usage errors in students' writing. Figure 13–2 lists 10 types of usage errors that older students can learn to correct.

Teaching Grammar

For many years, grammar was taught using language arts textbooks. Students read rules and definitions, copied words and sentences, and marked them to apply the concepts presented in the text, but this type of activity often seemed meaningless to students. Researchers suggest that integrating grammar study with reading and writing produces the best results (Beers, 2001; Weaver, McNally, & Moerman, 2001). They view grammar

FIGURE 13–2

Ten Usage Errors That Middle- and Upper-Grade Students Can Correct

Irregular Verb Forms

Students form the past tense of irregular verbs as they would a regular verb; for example, some students might use *catch + ed* to make *catched* instead of *caught,* or *swim + ed* to make *swimmed* instead of *swam.*

Past-Tense Forms

Students use present-tense or past-participle forms in place of past-tense forms, such as *I ask* for *I asked, she run* for *she ran,* or *he seen* for *he saw.*

Nonstandard Verb Forms

Students use *brung* for *brought* or *had went* for *had gone.*

Double Subjects

Students use both a noun and a pronoun in the subject, such as *My mom she.*

Nonstandard Pronoun Forms

Students use nonstandard pronoun forms, such as *hisself* for *himself, them books* for *those books*, and *hisn* for *his*

Objective Pronouns for the Subject

Students use objective pronouns instead of subjective pronouns in the subject, such as *Me and my friend went to the store* or *Her and me want to play outside.*

Lack of Subject-Verb Agreement

Students use *we was* for *we were* and *he don't* for *he doesn't.*

Double Negatives

Students use two negatives when only one is needed; for example, *I don't got none* and *Joe don't have none.*

Confusing Pairs of Words

Some students confuse word pairs, such as *learn–teach, lay–lie,* and *leave–let.* They might say *I'll learn you to read,* instead of *I'll teach you to read, go lay down* instead of *go lie down,* and *leave me do it* instead of *let me do it.* Other confusing pairs include *bring–take, among–between, fewer–less, good–well, passed–past, real–really, set–sit, than–then, who–which–that, who–whom, it's–its,* and *your–you're.*

***I* as an Objective Pronoun**

Students incorrectly use *I* instead of *me* as an objective pronoun, saying or writing *It's for Bill and I* instead of *It's for Bill and me.*

Adapted from Pooley, 1974, and Weaver, 1996.

as a language tool and recommend integrating grammar instruction with reading and writing. Guidelines for teaching grammar are listed in the LA Essentials box on page 438. In the vignette at the beginning of the chapter, Mr. Keogh followed many of these recommendations as he taught grammar as part of a literature focus unit.

Why Teach Grammar? Teachers, parents, and the community at large cite many reasons for teaching grammar. First, using Standard English is the mark of an educated person, and students should know how to use it. Many teachers feel that

GUIDELINES FOR TEACHING GRAMMAR

- **Minilessons**

  Teachers teach minilessons on grammar concepts and have students locate examples of the grammar concepts they're learning in books they're reading and in their writing.

- **Concept Books**

  Teachers share concept books when students are studying parts of speech, and students also create their own grammar concept books.

- **Sentence Collection**

  Students collect favorite sentences from books they're reading and use the sentences for grammar activities.

- **Sentence Manipulation**

  Students use sentences from books they're reading for sentence unscrambling, sentence imitating, sentence combining, and sentence expanding activities.

- **New Versions of Books**

  Young children write innovations, or new versions of books, using sentence patterns in books they have read.

- **Posters**

  Students make grammar posters to visually represent parts of speech, sentence types, and other grammar conepts they're learning.

- **Proofreading**

  Students need to learn to proofread so that they can locate and correct grammar and usage errors in their own writing.

- **Standard English Alternative**

  Teachers explain that Standard English is the language of school and is one way of speaking and writing. It is important that students understand that the purpose of grammar instruction is to expand their repertoire of language options, not to replace their home language.

teaching grammar will help students understand sentence structure and form sentences to express their thoughts. Another reason is that parents expect that grammar will be taught, and teachers must meet these expectations. Other teachers explain that they teach grammar to prepare students for the next grade or for instruction in a foreign language. Others pragmatically rationalize grammar instruction because it is a part of norm-referenced achievement tests mandated by state departments of education.

Conventional wisdom is that knowledge about grammar and usage should improve students' oral language and writing, but research for more than 75 years hasn't confirmed this assumption. In 1936, for example, the National Council of Teachers of English (NCTE) passed a resolution against the formal teaching of grammar, and based on their review of research conducted before 1963, Braddock, Lloyd-Jones, and Schoer concluded that "the teaching of formal grammar has a negligible or, because it usually displaces some instruction and practice in actual composition, even a harmful effect on the improvement of writing" (1963, pp. 37–38). Since then, other studies have reached the same conclusion, and the NCTE resolution has been reaffirmed again and again (Hillocks & Smith, 2003).

Despite the controversy about teaching grammar and its value for students, grammar is a part of the language arts program and will undoubtedly remain so for some time. Given this fact, it is only reasonable that grammar should be taught in the most beneficial manner possible.

Teaching Grammar Through Reading. Students learn about the structure of the English language through reading. They learn more sophisticated academic language, a more formal register than they speak, and sophisticated ways of phrasing ideas and arranging words into sentences. Students often read sentences that are longer than the ones they speak and learn new ways to string words into sentences. In *Chrysanthemum* (Henkes, 1991), the story of a mouse named Chrysanthemum who loves her name until she starts school and is teased by her classmates, the author uses a combination of long and short sentences very effectively: "Chrysanthemum could scarcely believe her ears. She blushed. She beamed. She bloomed" (n.p.).

Students read sentences exemplifying all four sentence types in many books. One example is the Caldecott Medal–winning *Officer Buckle and Gloria* (Rathmann, 1995), the story of a police officer and his dog, Gloria. "Officer Buckle loved having a buddy" and "That night Officer Buckle watched himself on the 10 o'clock news" (n.p.) are statements, or declarative sentences. "How about Gloria?" and "Could she come?" (n.p.) are questions, or interrogative sentences. Officer Buckle's safety tips, such as "Keep your shoelaces tied" and "Do not go swimming during electrical storms!" (n.p.), are imperative sentences. The children loved Gloria and her tricks, and they cheered, "Bravo!" (n.p.)—an example of an exclamation, or exclamatory sentence.

Students read simple, compound, complex, and compound-complex sentences in books. On the first page of *The Giver* (Lowry, 2006), for instance, there are examples of simple, compound, and complex sentences:

Simple Sentence: *"But the aircraft a year ago had been different."*
Compound Sentence: *"It was almost December, and Jonas was beginning to be frightened."*
Complex Sentence: *"Frightened was the way he had felt a year ago when an unidentified aircraft had overflown the community twice."*

Meeting the Needs of English Learners

What's the Best Way to Teach Grammar to English Learners?

The goal of grammar instruction is to increase students' ability to structure and manipulate sentences and to expand their repertoire of sentence patterns. Teaching grammar is a controversial issue, and it is especially so for English learners, but learning Standard English is crucial for these students' success in school.

Correcting Students' Grammar Errors

The best way to promote students' language development is to encourage all students to talk freely in the classroom. In the past, researchers have recommended that teachers not correct students' talk so as not to embarrass them; however, teachers are now finding that many English learners want to be corrected so that they can learn to speak Standard English correctly in order to do well in school (Scarcella, 2003).

The same is true with writing. During the editing stage of the writing process, teachers teach proofreading and help students identify and correct grammar and usage errors. After teachers explain grammar concepts in minilessons, students should become responsible for identifying and correcting the errors themselves.

Teaching Grammar Concepts

Teachers also provide direct instruction about grammar concepts through minilessons for English learners and other students who don't speak and write Standard English. The rationale for providing direct instruction is that many English learners haven't been successful in acquiring Standard English through naturalistic approaches alone.

Topics for Minilessons

The best way to choose minilesson topics is to identify the kinds of errors students are making and then teach lessons on those topics. Also, teachers choose topics from state and district-level curriculum guides. Here are 10 of the most common topics:

Plurals	Prepositions
Verb tenses	Possessives
Irregular verbs	Negatives
Contractions	Comparatives
Subject-verb agreement	Articles

Teachers use the same approach for grammar minilessons that they use for other types of lessons.

Learning to speak, read, and write Standard English takes time, and it's unrealistic to assume that students will learn a grammar topic through a single minilesson. What's important is that teachers regularly teach Standard English to their English learners and expect them to assume responsibility for learning it.

And on the second page, there's an example of a compound-complex sentence: "His parents were both at work, and his little sister, Lily, was at the Childcare Center where she spent her after-school hours."

One way to help students focus on sentences in stories is sentence collecting (Speaker & Speaker, 1991). Students collect favorite sentences and share them with classmates. They copy the sentences on chart paper or on long strips of tagboard and post them in the classroom. Students and the teacher talk about the merits of each sentence, focus on word choice, and analyze the sentence types. Sometimes students also cut the words in the sentences apart and rebuild them, either in the author's original order or in an order that appeals to them.

Teaching the Parts of Speech. Students learn about parts of speech through reading and writing activities as well as through minilessons. They can locate examples of the parts of speech in books they're reading and experiment with words to see how the parts of speech are combined to form sentences. They read grammar concept books, including the popular books by author-illustrator Ruth Heller, and make their own books, too. These activities are described in the following sections.

♦ *Collecting parts of speech* Students work in small groups to identify words representing one part of speech or all eight parts of speech from a book they are reading. A group of fifth graders identified words representing the parts of speech in Van Allsburg's popular book *The Polar Express* (2005):

- Nouns: *train, children, Santa Claus, elves, pajamas, roller coaster, conductor, sleigh, hug, clock, Sarah*
- Pronouns: *we, they, he, it, us, you, his, I, me*
- Verbs: *filled, ate, flickered, raced, were, cheered, marched, asked, pranced, stood, shouted*
- Adjectives: *melted, white-tailed, quiet, no, first, magical, cold, dark, polar, Santa's*
- Adverbs: *soon, faster, wildly, apart, closer, alone*
- Prepositions: *in, through, over, with, of, in front of, behind, at, for, across, into*
- Conjunctions: *and, but*
- Interjections: *oh, well, now*

After identifying the parts of speech, teachers can make word cards and have students sort the words according to the part of speech. Because some words, such as *melted* and *hug,* can represent more than one part of speech, depending on how the word is used in a sentence, teachers must choose words for this activity carefully or use the words in a sentence on the word card so that students can classify them correctly.

After collecting words representing one part of speech from books they are reading or from books they have written, students can create a book using some of these words. Figure 13–3 shows the cover and a page from an alphabet book focusing on adjectives that second graders developed.

♦ *Reading and writing grammar concept books* Students examine concept books that focus on one part of speech or another grammar concept. For example, Brian Cleary describes adjectives and lists many examples in *Hairy, Scary, Ordinary: What Is an Adjective?* (2000). After students read the book and identify the adjectives, they can make posters or write their own books about the parts of speech. Useful books for teaching parts of speech are listed in the Booklist on page 444.

FIGURE 13–3

An Excerpt From a Second-Grade Class Book on Adjectives

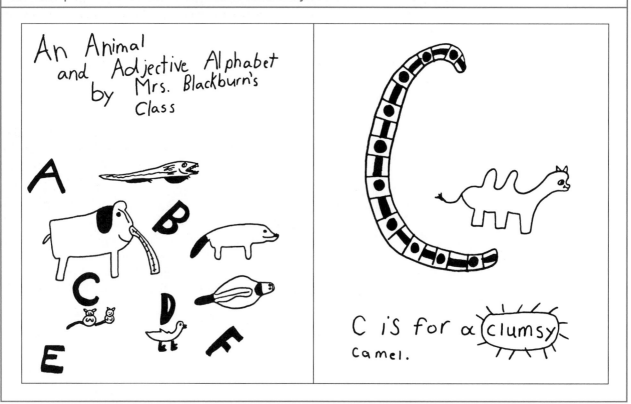

Students in an eighth-grade class divided into small groups to read Ruth Heller's books about parts of speech, including *Up, Up and Away: A Book About Adverbs* (1991), *Mine, All Mine: A Book About Pronouns* (1997), *Behind the Mask: A Book of Prepositions* (1995), and *Merry-Go-Round: A Book About Nouns* (1990). After reading one of her books, students made a poster with information about the parts of speech, which they presented to the class. The students' poster for adverbs is shown in Figure 13–4. Later, students divided into small groups to do a word sort. In this activity, students cut apart a list of words and sorted them into groups according to the part of speech. All the words had been taken from posters that students created, and they could refer to the posters if needed.

Teaching Students to Manipulate Sentences. Students experiment with or manipulate sentences when they rearrange words and phrases in a sentence, combine several sentences to make a single, stronger sentence, or write sentences based on a particular sentence pattern. Through these activities, students learn about the structure of sentences and experiment with more sophisticated sentences than they might otherwise write.

Primary-grade students often create new books or "innovations" using the sentence structure in repetitive books. For example, young children write their own versions of *Brown Bear, Brown Bear, What Do You See?* (Martin, 2007) and the sequel, *Polar*

Bear, Polar Bear, What Do You Hear? (Martin, 1992). Similarly, middle-grade students write new verses following the rhyming pattern in Laura Numeroff's *Dogs Don't Wear Sneakers* (1993) and the sequel, *Chimps Don't Wear Glasses* (1995). Third graders used Numeroff's frame to write verses, including this verse that rhymes *TV* and *bumblebee:*

Ducks don't have tea parties,
Lions don't watch TV,
And you won't see a salamander
being friends with a bumblebee.

Older students often choose a favorite sentence from a book they're reading and imitate its structure by plugging in new words, a procedure Stephen Dunning calls "copy changes" (Dunning & Stafford, 1992). For example, eighth graders chose sentences from *The Giver* (Lowry, 2006) for copy changes. One original sentence was "Dimly, from a nearly forgotten perception as blurred as the substance itself, Jonas recalled what the whiteness was" (p. 175). A student created this sentence using the sentence frame: "Softly, from a corner of the barn as cozy and warm as the kitchen, the baby kitten mewed to its mother."

FIGURE 13–4

An Eighth-Grade Poster on Adverbs

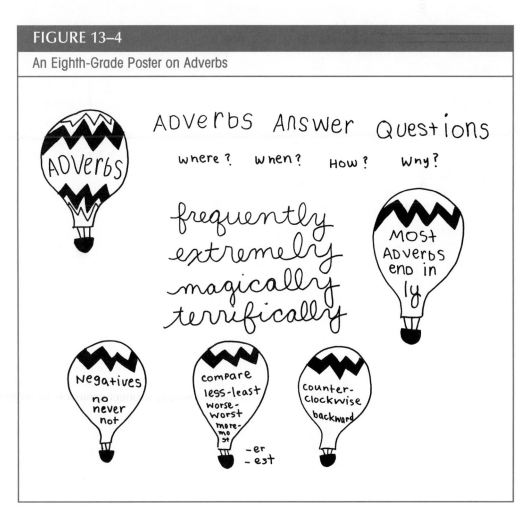

Booklist

GRAMMAR CONCEPT BOOKS

Nouns

Cleary, B. P. (1999). *A mink, a fink, a skating rink: What is a noun?* Minneapolis: Carolrhoda. (M)

Heller, R. (1990). *Merry-go-round: A book about nouns.* New York: Grosset & Dunlap. (M–U)

Terban, M. (1986). *Your foot's on my feet! and other tricky nouns.* New York: Clarion Books. (M)

Pronouns

Cleary, B. P. (2004). *I and you and don't forget who: What is a pronoun?* Minneapolis: Carolrhoda. (M)

Heller, R. (1997). *Mine, all mine: A book about pronouns.* New York: Grosset & Dunlap. (M–U)

Adjectives

Cleary, B. P. (2000). *Hairy, scary, ordinary: What is an adjective?* Minneapolis: Carolrhoda. (M)

Heller, R. (1989). *Many luscious lollipops: A book about adjectives.* New York: Grosset & Dunlap. (M–U)

Verbs

Cleary, B. P. (2001). *To root, to toot, to parachute: What is a verb?* Minneapolis: Carolrhoda. (M)

Heller, R. (1988). *Kites sail high: A book about verbs.* New York: Grosset & Dunlap. (M–U)

Schneider, R. M. (1995). *Add it, dip it, fix it: A book of verbs.* Boston: Houghton Mifflin. (M)

Adverbs

Cleary, B. P. (2003). *Dearly, nearly, insincerely: What is an adverb?* Minneapolis: Carolrhoda. (M)

Heller, R. (1991). *Up, up and away: A book about adverbs.* New York: Grosset & Dunlap. (M–U)

Prepositions

Cleary, B. P. (2002). *Under, over, by the clover: What is a preposition?* Minneapolis: Carolrhoda. (M)

Heller, R. (1995). *Behind the mask: A book of prepositions.* New York: Grosset & Dunlap. (M–U)

Conjunctions

Heller, R. (1998). *Fantastic! Wow! And unreal! A book about interjections and conjunctions.* New York: Penguin. (M–U)

Interjections

Heller, R. (1998). *Fantastic! Wow! And unreal! A book about interjections and conjunctions.* New York: Penguin. (M–U)

P = primary grades (K–2); M = middle grades (3–5); U = upper grades (6–8)

Killgallon (1997, 1998) recommends that teachers help students examine how authors write sentences through four types of activities: sentence unscrambling, sentence imitating, sentence combining, and sentence expanding. Sentence imitating is like the innovations and copy changes discussed earlier. Through sentence manipulation, students learn new syntactic structures and practice ways to vary the sentences they write. These four types of sentence manipulation are summarized in Figure 13–5.

◆ *Sentence unscrambling* Teachers choose a sentence from a book students are reading and divide it into phrases. They present the phrases in a random order,

FIGURE 13–5
Killgallon's Four Types of Sentence Manipulation

Sentence Unscrambling
Teachers choose a long sentence from a book students are reading and break it into phrases. Then students reassemble the sentence to examine how the author structures sentences. Sometimes students duplicate the author's sentence, but other times, they create an original sentence that they like better.

Sentence Imitating
Teachers choose a sentence with an interesting structure to imitate from a book students are reading. Then students create a new sentence on a new topic that imitates the structure and style of the original sentence.

Sentence Combining
Teachers choose a conceptually dense sentence from a book students are reading and break the sentence into three or more simple sentences. Then students combine and embed the simple sentences to re-create the author's original sentence. They compare their sentence with the original sentence.

Sentence Expanding
Teachers choose a sentence from a book students are reading and shorten the sentence to make an abridged version. Then students expand the abridged sentence, trying to re-create the author's original sentence, or write a new sentence, trying to match the author's style.

Adapted from Killgallon, 1997, 1998.

and students unscramble the sentence and rearrange the phrases, trying to duplicate the author's original order. Then students compare their rearrangement with the author's. Sometimes they discover that they've created a new sentence that they like better. Here's a sentence from E. B. White's *Charlotte's Web* (2006), broken into phrases and scrambled:

> in the middle of the kitchen
> teaching it to suck from the bottle
> a minute later
> with an infant between her knees
> Fern was seated on the floor

Can you unscramble the sentence? Here's the original: "A minute later Fern was seated on the floor in the middle of the kitchen with an infant between her knees, teaching it to suck from the bottle" (pp. 6–7).

◆ *Sentence imitating* Students choose a sentence from a book they are reading and then write their own sentence imitating the structure of the one they've chosen. Here's an original sentence from *Charlotte's Web:* "Avery noticed the spider web, and coming closer, he saw Charlotte" (p. 71). Can you create a sentence on a new topic that imitates E. B. White's sentence structure, especially the "and coming closer" part? A class of sixth graders created this imitation: *The fox smelled the poultry, and coming closer, he saw five juicy chickens scratching in the dirt.* Here's another sentence from *Charlotte's Web:* "His medal still hung from his neck; by looking out of the corner of his eye he could still see it" (p. 163). Sixth graders also created this imitation: *The message was still stuck in the keyhole; using a magnifying glass the little mouse could still read those awful words.*

◆ *Sentence combining* Students combine and rearrange words in sentences to make the sentences longer and more conceptually dense (Strong, 1996). The goal of sentence combining is for students to experiment with different ways to join and embed words. Teachers choose a sentence from a book students are reading and break it into short, simple sentences. Then students combine the sentences, trying to recapture the author's original sentence. Try your hand at combining these short sentences that were taken from a more complex sentence in *Charlotte's Web*:

> No one ever had such a friend.
> The friend was so affectionate.
> The friend was so loyal.
> The friend was so skillful.

Here is the original sentence: "No one ever had such a friend—so affectionate, so loyal, and so skillful" (p. 173). You might wonder whether the *and* before *so skillful* is necessary. Students often wonder why E. B. White added it.

◆ *Sentence expanding* Teachers choose a rich sentence from a book students are reading and present an abridged version. Then students expand the sentence, taking care that the words and phrases they add blend in with the author's sentence. Here's an abridged sentence from *Charlotte's Web*:

> There is no place like home. . . .

This is the original: "There is no place like home, Wilbur thought, as he placed Charlotte's 514 unborn children carefully in a safe corner" (p. 172). A sixth grader wrote this expansion: *There is no place like home, like his home in the barn, cozy and warm straw to sleep on, the delicious smell of manure in the air, Charlotte's egg sac to guard, and his friends Templeton, the goose, and the sheep nearby.* Even though it is not the same as E. B. White's sentence, the student's sentence retains the character of White's writing style.

Minilessons Teachers teach minilessons on grammar topics. They explain grammar concepts, have students make charts and posters, and involve them in examining sentences in books they're reading and in writing their own sentences. Finally, students apply what they're learning in their own writing.

Teachers identify topics for grammar minilessons in two ways. They identify concepts by examining students' writing and noting what types of grammar errors they're making. Teachers also choose topics from state standards for their grade level. A list of minilesson topics is presented in the Planning for Instruction feature on pages 454 and 455.

Assessing Students' Knowledge About Grammar Teachers might think about administering a test to assess students' knowledge of grammar, but the best gauge is how they arrange words into sentences as part of genuine writing projects. As teachers examine students' compositions, they note errors, plan and teach minilessons based on these observed needs, note further errors, plan and teach other minilessons, and so on.

HANDWRITING

The goal in handwriting instruction is to help students develop legible forms to communicate effectively through writing. The two most important criteria in determining quality in handwriting are legibility (the writing can be easily and quickly read) and fluency (the writing can be easily and quickly written). Even though a few students take great pleasure in developing flawless handwriting skills, most feel that handwriting instruction is boring and unnecessary. It's imperative, therefore, to convey to students the importance of developing legible handwriting. Writing for genuine audiences is the best way to convey the importance of legibility. A letter sent to a favorite author that is returned by the post office because the address is not decipherable or a child's published hardcover book that sits unread on the library shelf because the handwriting is illegible makes clear the importance of legibility. Illegible writing means a failure to communicate—a harsh lesson for a writer!

Handwriting Forms

Two forms of handwriting are currently used in elementary schools: manuscript, or printing, and cursive, or connected writing. These are illustrated in Figure 13–6. Typically, young children use the manuscript form, and they switch to cursive handwriting in third grade. In the upper grades, students use both handwriting forms.

Manuscript Handwriting. Until the 1920s, students learned only cursive handwriting. Marjorie Wise is credited with introducing the manuscript form for young children in 1921 (Hildreth, 1960). Manuscript handwriting is considered better for young children because they lack the eye–hand coordination necessary for cursive handwriting. In addition, manuscript handwriting is similar to the type style in primary-level reading textbooks. Only two lowercase letters, *a* and *g*, are usually different in typed and handwritten forms. The similarity may actually facilitate young children's introduction to reading because it simplifies letter recognition (Adams, 1990).

Despite its advantages, the manuscript form has been criticized. A major complaint is the reversal problem caused by some similar lowercase letters; *b* and *d* are particularly confusing. Detractors also argue that using both the manuscript and cursive forms requires teaching students two totally different kinds of handwriting within several years. They also complain that the "circle and sticks" style of manuscript handwriting requires frequent stops and starts, thus inhibiting a smooth and rhythmic flow of writing.

Cursive Handwriting. When most people think of handwriting, the cursive or connected form comes to mind. The letters in cursive handwriting are joined together to form a word with one continuous movement. Children often view cursive handwriting as the grown-up type. Primary-grade students often attempt to imitate this form by connecting the manuscript letters in their names and other words before they are taught how to form and join the letters. Awareness of cursive handwriting and interest in imitating it are indicators that children are ready for instruction.

D'Nealian Handwriting. D'Nealian handwriting is an innovative manuscript and cursive handwriting program developed by Donald Neal Thurber, a teacher in Michigan, to mitigate some of the problems associated with the traditional manuscript

FIGURE 13–6

Manuscript and Cursive Handwriting Forms

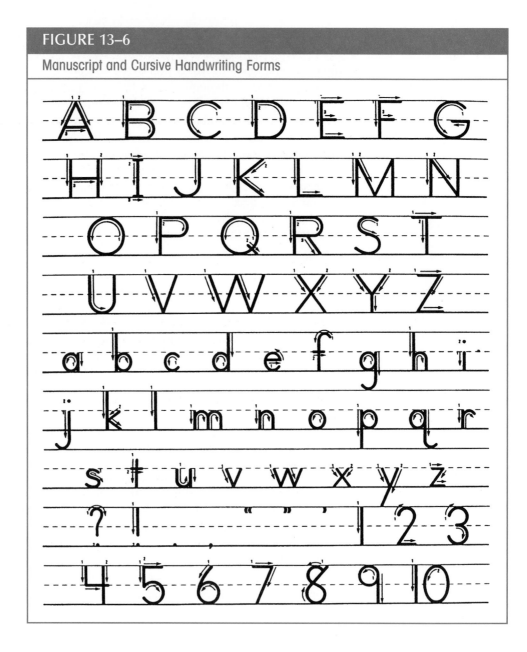

form. D'Nealian manuscript uses the same basic letter forms that students will need for cursive handwriting, as well as the slant and rhythm required for cursive. In the manuscript form, letters are slanted and formed with a continuous stroke; in the cursive form, the letters are simplified, without the flourishes of traditional cursive. Both forms were designed to increase legibility and fluency and to ease the transition from manuscript to cursive handwriting. Another advantage is that the transition from manuscript to cursive involves adding only connective strokes to most manuscript letters. Only five letters—*f, r, s, v,* and *z*—are shaped differently in the cursive form. The D'Nealian handwriting forms are shown in Figure 13–7. Research has not yet documented that D'Nealian is better than the traditional manuscript form even though many teachers prefer it (Graham, 1992).

FIGURE 13–6   (Continued)

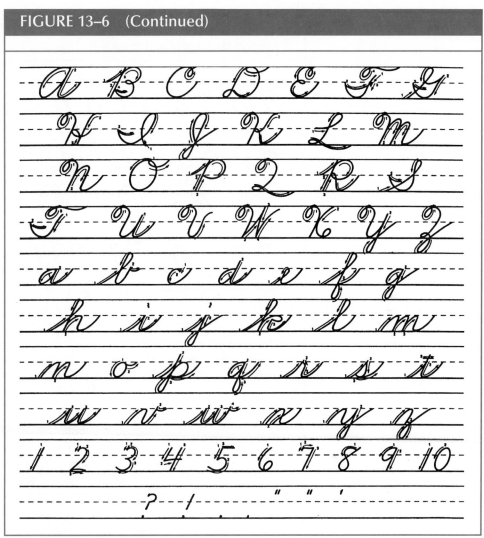

Used with permission of the publisher, Zaner-Bloser, Inc., Columbus, OH, copyright 2003. From *Handwriting: A Way to Self-Expression,* by Clinton Hackney.

Children's Handwriting Development

Young children enter kindergarten with different backgrounds of handwriting experience. Some 5-year-olds have never held a pencil, whereas others have written cursivelike scribbles or manuscript-letter-like forms. Some preschoolers have learned to print their names and some other letters. Handwriting in kindergarten typically includes three types of activities: stimulating children's interest in writing, developing their ability to hold writing instruments, and printing letters of the alphabet. Adults are influential role models in stimulating children's interest in writing. They record children's talk and write labels on signs. They can also provide paper, pencils, and pens so that children can experiment with writing. Children learn to hold a pencil by

FIGURE 13–7

D'Nealian Manuscript and Cursive Handwriting Forms

D'Nealian manuscript and cursive alphabets and numbers from D'NEALIAN HANDWRITIING. Copyright © 2008 by Pearson Education, Inc. D'Nealian Handwriting is a registered trademark of Donald Neal Thurber. Reprinted by permission.

watching adults and through numerous opportunities to experiment with pencils, paintbrushes, and crayons. Instruction is necessary so that children don't learn bad habits that later must be broken. They often devise bizarre ways to form letters when they haven't been shown how to form them, and these bad habits can cause problems as children need to develop greater writing speed.

Formal handwriting instruction begins in first grade. Students learn how to form manuscript letters and space between them, and they develop skills related to the six elements of legibility (see pp. 452 and 456). A common handwriting activity requires students to copy short writing samples from the chalkboard, but this type of activity is not recommended. For one thing, young children have great difficulty with far-to-near copying; a piece of writing should be placed close to the child for copying. Children can recopy interactive writing compositions and Language Experience stories, but other types of copying should be avoided. It's far better for children to create their own writing than to copy words and sentences they may not even be able to read!

Special pencils and handwriting paper are often provided for handwriting instruction. Kindergartners and first graders have commonly been given "fat" beginner pencils because it has been assumed that these pencils are easier for young children to hold; however, most children prefer to use regular-sized pencils that older students and adults use. Moreover, regular pencils have erasers! Research now indicates that beginner pencils aren't better than regular-sized pencils for young children (Graham, 1992). Likewise, there's no evidence that specially shaped pencils and small writing aids that slip onto pencils to improve children's grips are effective.

Students' introduction to cursive handwriting typically occurs in the first semester of third grade. Parents and students often attach great importance to the transition from manuscript to cursive, thus adding unnecessary pressure for the students. Beverly Cleary's *Muggie Maggie* (1990) describes the pressure some children feel. The time of transition is usually dictated by tradition rather than by sound educational theory. All students in a school or school district are usually introduced to cursive handwriting at the same time, regardless of their interest in making the change.

Some students indicate an early interest in cursive handwriting by trying to connect manuscript letters or by asking their parents to demonstrate how to write their names. Because of individual differences in motor skills and levels of interest in cursive writing, it's better to introduce some students to cursive handwriting in first or second grade while providing other students with additional time to refine their manuscript skills. These students then learn cursive handwriting in third or fourth grade.

The practice of changing to cursive handwriting only a year or two after children learn the manuscript form is receiving increasing criticism. The argument has been that students need to learn cursive handwriting as early as possible because of their growing need for handwriting speed. Because of its continuous flow, cursive handwriting was thought to be faster to write than manuscript; however, research suggests that manuscript handwriting can be written as quickly as cursive handwriting (Jackson, 1971). The controversy over the benefits of the two forms and the best time to introduce cursive handwriting is likely to continue.

Students are introduced to the cursive handwriting form in third grade. Usually, the basic strokes that make up the letters (e.g., slant stroke, undercurve, downcurve) are taught first. Next, the lowercase letters are taught in isolation, and then the connecting strokes are introduced. Uppercase letters are taught later because they are used far less often and are more difficult to form. Which cursive letters are most difficult? The lowercase *r* is the most troublesome letter. The other lowercase letters students frequently form incorrectly are *k, p,* and *z.*

Cursive handwriting does not replace manuscript handwriting. Students continue to use manuscript handwriting part of the time. Because manuscript handwriting is easier for them to form and to read, many students often continue to use the manuscript form when they're writing informally, saving cursive handwriting for projects and final copies of their writing. Teachers need to review both forms periodically. By this time, too, students have firmly established handwriting habits, both good and bad. Now the emphasis is on helping students diagnose and correct their handwriting trouble spots so that they can develop a legible and fluent handwriting style. Older students both simplify their letterforms and add unique flourishes to their handwriting to develop their own trademark styles. A review of the sequence of handwriting development is presented in the LA Essentials box on the next page.

Teaching Handwriting

Handwriting is best taught in separate periods of direct instruction and teacher-supervised practice. As soon as skills are taught, students should apply them in real-life writing activities; busywork assignments, such as copying sentences from the chalkboard, aren't effective. Moreover, students often develop poor handwriting habits or learn to form letters incorrectly if they practice without direct supervision. It's much more difficult to correct bad habits and errors in letter formation than to teach correct handwriting in the first place.

Elements of Legibility. For students to develop legible handwriting, they need to know what qualities or elements determine legibility and then to analyze their own handwriting according to these elements (Hackney, 2003). Here are the six elements of legible handwriting:

◆ *Letter Formation.* Letters are formed with specific strokes. Letters in manuscript handwriting are composed of vertical, horizontal, and slanted lines plus circles or parts of circles. The letter *b,* for example, is composed of a vertical line and a circle, and *M* is composed of vertical and slanted lines. Cursive letters are composed of slanted lines, loops, and curved lines. The lowercase cursive letters *m* and *n,* for instance, are composed of a slant stroke, a loop, and an undercurve stroke. An additional component in cursive handwriting is the connecting stroke used to join letters.

◆ *Size and Proportion.* Students' handwriting gradually becomes smaller, and the proportional size of uppercase to lowercase letters increases. First graders' uppercase manuscript letters are twice the size of their lowercase letters. When second- and third-grade students begin cursive handwriting, the proportional size of letters remains 2:1; later, the proportion increases to 3:1 for middle- and upper-grade students.

◆ *Spacing.* Students should leave adequate space between letters in words and between words in sentences. Spacing between words in manuscript handwriting should equal one lowercase letter *o,* and spacing between sentences should equal two lowercase *o*'s. The most important aspect of spacing within words in cursive handwriting is consistency. To correctly space between words, the writer makes the beginning stroke of the new word directly below the end stroke of the preceding word. Spacing between sentences should equal one uppercase letter *O,* and the indent for a new paragraph should equal two uppercase letter *O*'s.

SEQUENCE OF HANDWRITING DEVELOPMENT

Handwriting Before First Grade

Teachers teach basic handwriting skills during kindergarten.

- Children learn how to hold a pencil.
- Children learn to form upper- and lowercase letters.
- Children learn to write their names and other common words.

Handwriting in the Primary Grades

Primary-grade students develop legible manuscript handwriting.

- Children learn to form upper- and lowercase manuscript letters and space between letters.
- Children often use "fat" beginner pencils even though research does not support this practice.
- Children use wide, lined paper with a dotted midline to guide them in forming lowercase letters.

Transition to Cursive Handwriting in the Middle Grades

Teachers teach students to both read and write cursive handwriting because it is a new writing system.

- Students are introduced to cursive handwriting in third grade.
- Students learn to read cursive writing.
- Students learn to form upper- and lowercase letters and to join letters.

Handwriting in the Upper Grades

Teachers expect students to use both manuscript and cursive handwriting in daily writing activities.

- Students have learned both manuscript and cursive handwriting forms.
- Students develop their own trademark styles.
- Students vary the legibility and neatness of their handwriting for private and public writing.

What Children Need to Learn About Language Tools

Topics

Procedures	*Concepts*	*Strategies and Skills*
Grammar		
Unscramble sentences	Parts of speech	Rearrange sentences
Imitate sentences	Subject and predicate	Vary sentence length
Combine sentences	Simple sentences	
Expand sentences	Compound sentences	**Proofread to locate usage errors**
	Complex sentences	
	Punctuation	
	Capitalization	
Handwriting		
Grip a pencil	Legibility	Determine purpose of handwriting
Space between letters	Manuscript handwriting	Choose manuscript or cursive
Write manuscript letters	Cursive handwriting	Apply elements of legibility
		Personalize handwriting
Write cursive letters		
Self-assess handwriting problems		

If you'd like to learn more about teaching grammar and handwriting, visit MyEducationLab. To view third graders expanding sentences, go to the topic "Language Tools" and click on the video "Expanding Sentences," and to see a student-teacher conference on writing mechanics, go to the topic "Language Tools" and click on the video "Proofreading."

Minilesson

Ms. Thomas Teaches Her First Graders Manuscript-Letter Formation

1 Introduce the topic

Ms. Thomas brings her first graders together on the rug for handwriting practice and passes out a small dry-erase board, pen, and eraser to each child. They begin by rereading the class news chart that they wrote the day before using interactive writing. Ms. Thomas explains that she wants to practice three lowercase letters—*m, n,* and *u*—that the children had difficulty writing the previous day.

2 Share examples

Ms. Thomas rereads the chart and asks children to point out the three letters when they notice them in the class news chart. She asks one child to underline each word the children point out. They mention these words: *and, made, not, when, never, some, then, you, your,* and *wanted.* After reading the entire chart, the children agree that these letters are important because they are used so often in their writing.

3 Provide information

Ms. Thomas demonstrates how to form each of the letters by writing the letter on a dry-erase board and verbalizing the strokes she's making.

Then the children practice writing the letters on their boards as Ms. Thomas observes them. She assists several children in holding their pencils correctly, and she demonstrates again for several children who are continuing to have trouble writing the letters.

4 Supervise practice

Once she is satisfied that each child can form the three letters and differentiate among them, Ms. Thomas asks children to write several of the underlined words on their dry-erase boards as she observes. She provides immediate feedback to those who are not forming the letters correctly or who make the letters too large.

5 Reflect on learning

After this brief review, Ms. Thomas asks children to remember what they learned about forming these letters when they are writing. The children name all the occasions they have during the day to remember how to form the letters when they are writing—when they write books at the writing center, when they write in journals, and when they do interactive writing.

◆ *Slant.* Letters should be consistently parallel. Letters in manuscript handwriting are vertical, and in the cursive form, letters slant slightly to the right. To ensure the correct slant, right-handed students tilt their papers to the left, and left-handed students tilt their papers to the right.

◆ *Alignment.* For proper alignment in both manuscript and cursive handwriting, all letters should be uniform in size and consistently touch the baseline.

◆ *Line quality.* Students should write at a consistent speed and hold their writing instruments correctly and in a relaxed manner to make steady, unwavering lines of even thickness.

Correct letter formation and spacing receive the major focus in handwriting instruction. Although the other four elements usually receive less attention, they are important in developing legible handwriting.

Minilessons. Handwriting is best taught in minilessons. Brief lessons and practice sessions taught several times a week are more effective than a single, lengthy period weekly or monthly. Regular handwriting instruction is necessary when teaching the manuscript form in kindergarten and first grade and the cursive form in third grade. In the upper grades, instruction focuses on specific handwriting problems that students demonstrate and periodic reviews of both handwriting forms. A list of mini-lesson topics is presented in the box on page 454, and a sample lesson on teaching manuscript-letter formation in first grade is also shown.

Research has shown the importance of the teacher's active involvement in handwriting instruction and practice. Observing "moving" models—that is, having students watch the teacher write the handwriting sample—is of far greater value than copying models that have already been written (Wright & Wright, 1980). Moving models are possible when the teacher circulates around the classroom, stopping to demonstrate a procedure, strategy, or skill for one student and moving to assist another; circling incorrectly formed letters and marking other errors with a red pen on completed handwriting sheets is of little value.

Working With Left-Handed Writers. Approximately 10% of the U.S. population is left-handed, and two or three students in most classrooms are left-handed. Until 1950 or so, teachers insisted that left-handed students use their right hands for handwriting because left-handed writers were thought to have inferior handwriting skills. Parents and teachers are more realistic now and accept children's natural tendencies for left- or right-handedness.

Most young children develop handedness—the preference for using either the right or left hand for fine-motor activities—by age 5. Teachers must help those children who haven't developed handedness to consistently use one hand for handwriting and other fine-motor activities. Teachers observe the child's behavior and hand preference over a period of days and note which hand he or she uses in activities such as building with blocks, throwing balls, cutting with scissors, holding a paintbrush, manipulating clay, and pouring water. Teachers may find that a child uses both hands interchangeably. For example, a child may first reach for several blocks with one hand and then reach for the next block with the other. During drawing activities, the child may switch hands every few minutes. In this situation, the teacher asks the child's parents to observe his or her behavior at home, noting hand preferences when the child eats, brushes teeth, turns on the television, opens drawers, and so on. Then the teacher, the child, and the child's parents confer and—based on the results of joint observations, the handedness of family members, and the child's wishes—make a tentative decision about hand preference. At school, teacher and child will work closely together so that the child uses the chosen hand. As long as the child continues to use both hands interchangeably, neither hand will develop the prerequisite fine-motor control for handwriting.

Teaching handwriting to left-handed students isn't simply the reverse of teaching handwriting to right-handed students: Left-handed students have unique handwriting problems, so special adaptations of the procedures for teaching right-handed students are necessary. In fact, many of the problems that left-handed students have can actually be made worse by using the procedures designed for right-handed writers (Harrison, 1981). Special adjustments are necessary to enable left-handed students to write legibly, fluently, and with less fatigue.

The basic difference between right- and left-handed writing is physical orientation: Right-handed students pull their arms toward their bodies as they write, whereas left-handed writers push away. As left-handed students write, they move their left hand across what they have just written, often covering it. Consequently, many children adopt a "hook" position to avoid covering and smudging what they have written. Because of their different physical orientation, left-handed writers need to make three major types of adjustments:

Holding Pencils. Left-handed writers should hold pencils an inch or more farther back from the tip than right-handed writers do. This change helps them see what they have just written and avoid smearing their writing. Left-handed writers need to work to avoid hooking their wrists: They should keep their wrists straight and elbows close to their bodies to avoid the awkward hooked position. Practicing handwriting on the chalkboard is one way to help them develop a more natural style.

Tilting Paper. Left-handed students should tilt their writing papers slightly to the right, in contrast to right-handed students, who tilt their papers to the left. Sometimes it is helpful to place a piece of masking tape on the student's desk to indicate the proper amount of tilt.

Slanting Letters. Whereas right-handed students are encouraged to slant their cursive letters to the right, left-handed writers often write vertically or even slant their letters slightly backward. Some handwriting programs recommend that left-handed writers slant their cursive letters slightly to the right as right-handed students do, but others advise teachers to permit any slant between vertical and 45 degrees to the left of vertical.

Correcting Handwriting Problems Students use the six elements of legibility to diagnose their handwriting problems. Primary-grade students, for example, can check to see that they have formed a particular letter correctly, that the round parts of letters are joined neatly, and that slanted letters are joined in sharp points. Older students can examine a piece of handwriting to see if their letters are consistently parallel and if the letters touch the baseline consistently. A checklist for evaluating manuscript handwriting is shown in the Weaving Assessment Into Practice feature on page 458. Checklists can also be developed for cursive handwriting. It is important to involve students in developing the checklists so that they appreciate the need to make their handwriting more legible.

Another reason students need to diagnose and correct their handwriting problems is that handwriting quality influences teacher evaluation and grading. Researchers have found that teachers consistently grade papers with better handwriting higher than those with poor handwriting, regardless of the content (Graham, 1992). Children aren't too young to learn that poor or illegible handwriting may lead to lower grades.

Weaving Assessment Into Practice

A CHECKLIST FOR ASSESSING MANUSCRIPT HANDWRITING

Name _____

Writing Project_____

Date _____

_____ 1. Did I form my letters correctly?
          Did I start my line letters at the top?
          Did I start my circle letters at 1:00?
          Did I join the round parts of the letters neatly?
          Did I join the slanted strokes in sharp points?

_____ 2. Did my lines touch the midline or top line neatly?

_____ 3. Did I space evenly between letters?

_____ 4. Did I leave enough space between words?

_____ 5. Did I make my letters straight up and down?

_____ 6. Did I make all my letters sit on the baseline?

Keyboarding: An Alternative to Handwriting

To become efficient computer users, students need to develop keyboarding skills so they can use the computer more easily for word processing, to write e-mail messages, and to create HyperStudio® projects. Keyboarding is also faster than writing by hand: By sixth or seventh grade, students can learn to type 20 to 25 words per minute, but they handwrite only 10 to 15 words in the same amount of time (National Business Education Association, 1997).

Informal keyboarding instruction begins in the primary grades. Students become familiar with the keyboard and learn basic hand positioning. They learn to keep their right hand on the right side of the keyboard and their left hand on the left side. They learn simple keyboarding skills, such as keeping their fingers on the home-row keys (*asdfghjkl;*) and typing with more than one finger. Students also learn proper posture: They sit directly in front of the computer and keep their feet on the floor.

In third or fourth grade, students receive formal keyboarding lessons. Through a series of lessons, they learn touch typing and to look mainly at the screen rather than at their fingers while typing. It is crucial that students develop good touch-typing skills and avoid bad habits that inhibit efficient use of the keyboard. Students often practice keyboarding using AlphaSmart™ or another portable keyboard because a full computer is not needed. Guidelines for teaching keyboarding skills are presented in the LA Essentials box on the next page.

Students can learn keyboarding through teacher-directed lessons or using software packages. The Kid Keys® software package, which is recommended for primary students, includes lessons on becoming familiar with the letter positions on the keyboard and games using keyboarding skills to make music. The Mavis Beacon Teaches Typing® software package is recommended for students in third grade and above; the lessons teach fundamental keyboarding skills at several levels of difficulty and offer

GUIDELINES FOR SUCCESSFUL KEYBOARDING

- **Body Position**

  Students sit up straight and directly in front of the keyboard, aligning the center of their bodies with the *j* key.

- **Foot Position**

  Students keep their feet flat on the floor, about a hand span's distance apart.

- **Back Position**

  Students keep their backs straight and lean slightly forward.

- **Arm Position**

  Students keep their arms and shoulders relaxed and their elbows close to the body.

- **Wrist Position**

  Students keep their wrists straight.

- **Home-Row Keys**

  Students anchor their fingers on the home-row keys (*asdfghjkl;*). They use their thumbs to press the space bar and their little fingers to press the shift and return keys.

- **Finger Position**

  Students keep their fingers in a well-curved position and use a snap stroke to press the keys.

- **Touch Typing**

  Students learn touch typing and other special computer-related keyboard features.

- **Eye Position**

  Students keep their eyes on the screen or the text they are typing onto the computer.

- **Speed and Accuracy**

  Students develop typing speed and accuracy through practice and using the computer for authentic writing activities.

National Business Education Association, 1997.

games to reinforce the skills. Even though voice-recognition systems may someday replace the need for computer keyboards, keyboarding skills are still essential.

Review

Grammar and handwriting are language tools. *Grammar* is the description of the structure of a language and the principles of word and sentence formation. Even though grammar is a controversial topic, the position in this text is that grammar should be taught within the context of authentic reading and writing activities. Handwriting is a tool for writers, and students learn both manuscript and cursive handwriting. The emphasis in handwriting instruction is on legibility rather than on imitating handwriting models perfectly; students need to learn how to write so that their writing can be easily read. Here are the key concepts discussed in this chapter:

- Grammar is the structure of language, whereas usage is the socially accepted way of using words in sentences.
- Teaching grammar is a controversial topic, but teachers are expected to teach grammar even though research hasn't documented its usefulness.
- Grammar should be taught in the context of reading and writing activities.
- Teachers use sentences from books students are reading and from students' own writing for grammar instruction.
- Teachers deal with students' usage errors more effectively as part of the editing stage of the writing process than by correcting their oral language.
- Students learn two handwriting forms—manuscript and cursive—within several years.
- D'Nealian handwriting simplifies students' transition from manuscript to cursive handwriting.
- The six elements of handwriting are letter formation, size and proportion, spacing, slant, alignment, and line quality.
- The most important component of handwriting instruction is that the teacher demonstrate handwriting and provide feedback during the lesson.
- Students learn keyboarding as an alternative to handwriting.

Professional References

Adams, M. J. (1990). *Beginning to read: Thinking and learning about print*. Cambridge, MA: MIT Press.

Beers, K. (2001). Contextualizing grammar. *Voices From the Middle, 8*(3), 4.

Braddock, R., Lloyd-Jones, R., & Schoer, L. (1963). *Research in written composition*. Champaign, IL: National Council of Teachers of English.

Clay, M. M. (1991). *Becoming literate: The construction of inner control*. Portsmouth, NH: Heinemann.

Cordeiro, P., Giacobbe, M. E., & Cazden, C. (1983). Apostrophes, quotation marks, and periods: Learning punctuation in the first grade. *Language Arts, 60,* 323–332.

Dunning, S., & Stafford, W. (1992). *Getting the knack: 20 poetry writing exercises*. Urbana, IL: National Council of Teachers of English.

Edelsky, C. (1989). Putting language variation to work for you. In P. Rigg & V. G. Allen (Eds.), *When they don't all speak English: Integrating the ESL student into the regular classroom* (pp. 96–107). Urbana, IL: National Council of Teachers of English.

Fearn, L., & Farnan, N. (1998). *Writing effectively: Helping children master the conventions of writing*. Boston: Allyn & Bacon.

Graham, S. (1992). Issues in handwriting instruction. *Focus on Exceptional Children, 25,* 1–14.

Graves, D. H. (1994). *A fresh look at writing.* Portsmouth, NH: Heinemann.

Hackney, C. (2003). *Handwriting: A way to self-expression.* Columbus, OH: Zaner-Bloser.

Harrison, S. (1981). Open letter from a left-handed teacher: Some sinistral ideas on the teaching of handwriting. *Teaching Exceptional Children, 13,* 116–120.

Hildreth, G. (1960). Manuscript writing after sixty years. *Elementary English, 37,* 3–13.

Hillocks, G., Jr., & Smith, M. W. (2003). Grammar and literacy learning. In J. Flood, D. Lapp, J. R. Squire, & J. M. Jensen (Eds.), *Handbook of research on teaching the English language arts* (2nd ed., pp. 721–737). Mahwah, NJ: Erlbaum.

Jackson, A. D. (1971). *A comparison of speed and legibility of manuscript and cursive handwriting of intermediate grade pupils.* Unpublished doctoral dissertation, University of Arizona. *Dissertation Abstracts, 31,* 4384A.

Killgallon, D. (1997). *Sentence composing for middle school.* Portsmouth, NH: Heinemann.

Killgallon, D. (1998). Sentence composing: Notes on a new rhetoric. In C. Weaver (Ed.), *Lessons to share: On teaching grammar in context* (pp. 169–183). Portsmouth, NH: Heinemann.

National Business Education Association. (1997). *Elementary/middle school keyboarding strategies guide* (2nd ed.). Reston, VA: Author.

Pooley, R. C. (1974). *The teaching of English usage.* Urbana, IL: National Council of Teachers of English.

Scarcella, R. C. (2003). *Accelerating academic English: A focus on the English learner.* Oakland: Regents of the University of California.

Shaughnessy, M. P. (1977). *Errors and expectations: A guide for teachers of basic writing.* New York: Oxford University Press.

Speaker, R. B., Jr., & Speaker, P. R. (1991). Sentence collecting: Authentic literacy events in the classroom. *Journal of Reading, 35,* 92–95.

Strong, W. (1996). *Writer's toolbox: A sentence-combining workshop.* New York: McGraw-Hill.

Thurber, D. N. (1999). *D'Nealian handwriting (grades K–8).* Glenview, IL: Scott, Foresman.

Weaver, C. (1996). *Teaching grammar in context.* Portsmouth, NH: Heinemann.

Weaver, C., McNally, C., & Moerman, S. (2001). To grammar or not to grammar: That is *not* the question! *Voices From the Middle, 8*(3), 17–33.

Wilde, S. (1992). *You kan red this! Spelling and punctuation for whole language classrooms, K–6.* Portsmouth, NH: Heinemann.

Wright, C. D., & Wright, J. P. (1980). Handwriting: The effectiveness of copying from moving versus still models. *Journal of Educational Research, 74,* 95–98.

Children's Book References

Avi. (1995). *Poppy.* New York: Orchard Books.

Cleary, B. (1990). *Muggie Maggie.* New York: Morrow.

Cleary, B. P. (2000). *Hairy, scary, ordinary: What is an adjective?* Minneapolis: Carolrhoda.

Heller, R. (1990). *Merry-go-round: A book about nouns.* New York: Grosset & Dunlap.

Heller, R. (1991). *Up, up and away: A book about adverbs.* New York: Grosset & Dunlap.

Heller, R. (1995). *Behind the mask: A book of prepositions.* New York: Grosset & Dunlap.

Heller, R. (1997). *Mine, all mine: A book about pronouns.* New York: Grosset & Dunlap.

Henkes, K. (1991). *Chrysanthemum.* New York: Greenwillow.

Lowry, L. (2006). *The giver.* New York: Delacorte.

Martin, B., Jr. (1992). *Polar bear, polar bear, what do you hear?* New York: Holt.

Martin, B., Jr. (2007). *Brown bear, brown bear, what do you see?* New York: Holt.

Numeroff, L. J. (1993). *Dogs don't wear sneakers.* New York: Simon & Schuster.

Numeroff, L. J. (1995). *Chimps don't wear glasses.* New York: Simon & Schuster.

Rathmann, P. (1995). *Officer Buckle and Gloria.* New York: Putnam.

Van Allsburg, C. (2005). *The polar express.* Boston: Houghton Mifflin.

White, E. B. (2006). *Charlotte's web.* New York: HarperCollins.

chapter fourteen

Putting It All Together

Mrs. McNeal's first graders are studying the solar system. At the beginning of the thematic unit, the children listed what they knew about the planets on a K-W-L chart, and at the end of the unit, they'll finish the chart by adding what they've learned. A word wall also went up at the beginning of the unit, and children added the names of the planets, *astronaut, moon, ring, asteroid, alien, comet,* and other new words to the word wall. They also added small illustrations to make identifying the words easier.

Each morning, the first graders sign in when they arrive in the classroom. Mrs. McNeal makes daily sign-in sheets on a large sheet of drawing paper by writing a unit-related question at the top of the paper and two or three possible answers at the bottom. The children read the question and possible answers and sign in by writing their names in a column above the answer they think is correct. Today's question is *What makes the moon shine?* These are three possible answers: *The sun makes it shine, It has its own light,* and *The earth makes it shine.* Most of the students think that it has its own light, but they aren't sure. The purpose of the question is to pique the children's interest before reading, and Mrs. McNeal reads aloud Gail Gibbons's *The Moon Book* (1997). They learn, of course, that the moon reflects the sun's light.

*H*ow do students use the six language arts during thematic units?

Students use the six language arts as tools for learning and to document their learning during thematic units. For example, they talk and listen as they participate in discussions, read text sets of books, write in learning logs and create reports, view photos and maps, and make posters. As you continue reading, notice how Mrs. McNeal provides opportunities for her students to use the language arts as they learn about the solar system.

Mrs. McNeal has been reading aloud stories, informational books, and poems from a text set of books about the solar system. After they read a book, the children have been writing paragraphs to define and explain concepts they are learning. They choose the three most important pieces of information, arrange them into sentences, and combine the sentences to make a paragraph. Here are several of their paragraphs:

Moon
The moon is a ball of rock. It goes around the earth. It has no air or atmosphere.

Asteroids
Asteroids are chunks of rock and metal. They orbit around the sun. Many asteroids are in the asteroid belt between Mars and Jupiter.

The Inner Planets
The inner planets are Mercury, Venus, Earth, and Mars. They are closest to the sun. All four are made of rock.

The children write the paragraphs on chart paper using interactive writing, and Mrs. McNeal supervises their work, making corrections and teaching spelling, capitalization, and punctuation skills as needed. It's important that the paragraphs are written conventionally because they're posted in the classroom for children to read and reread.

The first graders participate in other unit-related activities at eight centers that Mrs. McNeal has set up in her classroom. They participate in all of the centers, with certain ones assigned each day. They go to some centers only once a week and others, such as the research center, more often. Here are the centers:

◆ *Art center* Students use paint to create a map of the solar system with a parent volunteer's assistance at this center. They dip nine round sponges of varying sizes (one for the sun and eight for the planets) into paint and stamp them on a wide sheet of construction paper. After the paint dries, the students label the planets, add moons, rings, and the asteroid belt using marking pens.

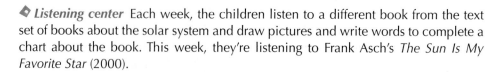

◆ *Listening center* Each week, the children listen to a different book from the text set of books about the solar system and draw pictures and write words to complete a chart about the book. This week, they're listening to Frank Asch's *The Sun Is My Favorite Star* (2000).

◆ *Writing center* The students make a pattern book based on Pat Hutchins's *Rosie's Walk* (1968), a story the first graders know well. Mrs. McNeal writes one line on each page of the book, omitting the last word or phrase. She compiles the pages and binds the book together so that all children have to do is supply the underlined word or phrase and add an illustration to complete the page. Here is Jacky's completed book:

> *My star and I traveled through <u>space</u>*
> *Across the <u>clouds</u>*
> *Around the <u>moon</u>*
> *Over the <u>stars</u>*
> *Past the <u>space shuttle</u>*
> *Under the <u>meteors</u>*
> *Through the <u>milky way</u>*
> *And I got back in time for my <u>birthday</u>.*

The underlined words are the ones that Jacky chose for her book. After she finished her book, she put it in her personal box of books to read and reread at home and during the first 10 minutes of the school day.

◆ *Word wall center* Children use a pointer to reread the words on the solar system word wall. Then they participate in other activities, including writing the words on dry-erase boards, spelling them with magnetic letters, and matching word cards to pictures.

◆ *Research center* Children write and illustrate books about the solar system at the research center. Every other day, Mrs. McNeal focuses on one of the planets and records information about it on a large data chart hanging on the wall next to the center. The completed data chart is shown on the next page. Then children each write a paragraph-long report about the planet that contains three facts. They refer to the chart as they write their reports, and through this activity, they are practicing what they've been learning about writing paragraphs with three facts. Alex's report about Jupiter is shown in the box on page 466. He has incorporated three facts from the data chart, and most of the words are spelled correctly because he could check the spellings on the data chart.

◆ *Computer center* Children use the Internet to check the NASA website for photos of the planets taken by Voyager and other spacecraft, and the National Geographic site for a virtual tour of the solar system. Mrs. McNeal has bookmarked these two sites, and children navigate the World Wide Web with the assistance of a Tech Liaison from the local high school.

◆ *Library center* Children read books from the solar system text set at this center. They are especially interested in reading and rereading the leveled books and in poring over the photos in the informational books.

Data Chart on the Planets

Planet	Where is it?	How big is it?	Does it have moons or rings?	Is it hot or cold?	What does it look like?	Is there life?	Other facts
Mercury	first, closest to the sun	second smallest	no	roasting hot or freezing cold	dry, airless, rocky, lots of craters	no	about the size of our moon
Venus	second	about the size of earth	no	hotter than an oven	thick, yellow clouds and tall mountains	no	air is poisonous, easiest planet to see in the sky
Earth	third	a middle-sized planet	1 moon	just right for life	made of rock and mostly covered with oceans	yes	we live here
Mars	fourth	half the size of earth	2 tiny moons	colder than earth	red dirt desert and pink sky	no	nickname is the Red Planet because of rusty iron in the soil
Jupiter	fifth, outside the asteroid belt	biggest planet, the "king"	16 moons 2 rings	cold	giant ball of gas, has a great red spot, covered with clouds	no	all the other planets could fit inside it
Saturn	sixth	second biggest planet	17 moons thousands of rings	very cold	giant ball of gas, covered with clouds	no	most beautiful planet
Uranus	seventh	third biggest planet	15 moons 10 rings	freezing cold	giant ball of gas, bluish-green color	no	lies on its side, spins differently
Neptune	eighth	fourth biggest planet	8 moons 4 rings	freezing cold	giant ball of gas, also bluish-green color, has a great dark spot	no	takes a rocket 8 years to go from Neptune to the sun

◆ *Poetry center* Children reread poems about the sun, moon, and planets written on chart paper that they have practiced reading as a class. They also take the poems written on sentence strips out of pocket charts and rearrange the lines to create new versions. This is a popular center because one child gets to pretend to be Mrs. McNeal and use a pointer to direct the other children in the group as they read the poems.

Mrs. McNeal has a magnetized dry-erase board that she uses to direct children to centers, and they check off the centers they complete on a chart hanging near the board so that Mrs. McNeal can keep track of their work. At the end of each week, children are expected to have completed six of the eight centers, including the art, writing, and research centers.

As they approach the end of the unit, Mrs. McNeal brings the class together to talk about their final project to extend their learning and demonstrate all they have learned. They talk about several possibilities, but they decide to invite their parents to come to the classroom on Friday afternoon to listen to oral presentations about the planets and to see their work. They divide into groups of two or three, and each group chooses one planet to report on. They make posters with drawings of the planet and three facts about it. They check the information on the data chart and practice what

---

Alex's Report

Jupiter is a giant ball of gas. It is outside the asroid belt. Did you no all the other planets could fit inside it?

2 rings

16 moons

---

they will say. They also ask Mrs. McNeal to take the parents on a tour of the class-room, showing them their books, charts, centers, and other activities. Many parents, grandparents, and friends come to the after-school presentation, and they're im-pressed with all that their children have learned, especially the new information that the NASA spacecraft have discovered.

---

*T*eachers often search for the one best way to develop units or design language arts instruction, but there isn't one best way. Instead, teachers pick and choose from thou-sands of books, activities, and assignments as they plan literature focus units, litera-ture circles, reading and writing workshop, and thematic units. In this text, you've read about these components of language arts instruction:

- Creating a community of learners
- The reading and writing processes
- Language arts procedures, concepts, strategies, and skills
- Word walls and vocabulary activities
- Journals and other ways to use writing as a learning tool
- Three purposes for listening

- Grand conversations and other talk and drama activities
- Language arts centers
- Reading and writing stories and learning about the structure of stories
- Reading and writing information and learning about expository text structures
- Reading and writing poetry and learning about poetic forms and stylistic devices
- Spelling, handwriting, and grammar

Teachers pick and choose among these components as they plan for instruction. Choosing to have students write in reading logs or create a story quilt is not necessarily better than having them write sequels or collect sentences from a book to examine sentence structure. Teachers begin with frameworks for the three instructional approaches and then select literature, activities, and assignments based on their instructional goals and beliefs about how children learn.

As teachers gain experience developing units, they often go beyond the "What shall I do with this book?" or "What shall I teach in this unit?" questions to think about the choices they make as they plan instruction and teach (McGee & Tompkins, 1995). Teachers need to think about why students should choose many of the books they read and why skill and strategy instruction should be taught in context. Through this reflection, teachers realize how theories about how children learn, along with their instructional goals, provide the foundation for language arts instruction.

As you continue reading, think about how you will organize for language arts instruction and how you will design literature focus units, literature circles, reading and writing workshop, and thematic units. Consider these key points:

- ◆ How do teachers design, teach, and assess literature focus units?
- ▣ How do teachers organize, monitor, and assess literature circles?
- ◆ How do teachers set up, manage, and assess reading and writing workshop?
- ◢ How do teachers develop, teach, and assess thematic units?

LITERATURE FOCUS UNITS

Teachers plan literature focus units featuring popular and award-winning stories for children and adolescents. Some literature focus units feature a single book, either a picture book or a chapter book, whereas others feature a text set of books for a genre unit or an author study unit. During these units, students move through the five stages of the reading process as they read and respond to stories, learn reading and writing strategies and skills, and engage in language arts activities.

How to Develop a Literature Focus Unit

Teachers develop a literature focus unit through an eight-step series of activities, beginning with choosing the literature for the unit, continuing to identify and schedule activities, and ending with deciding how to assess students' learning. Whether or not teachers are using trade books, they develop a unit using the steps outlined in the LA Essentials box on page 468 and described more fully in the following sections. Teachers need to make the plans themselves because they're the ones who best know their students, the standards their students are expected to meet, the reading materials they have available, the time available for the unit, the skills and strategies their students need to learn, and the language arts activities they want to use.

Literature focus units featuring a picture book are usually completed in 1 week, and units featuring a chapter book are completed in 2, 3, or 4 weeks. Genre and author units may last 2, 3, or 4 weeks. Rarely, if ever, do literature focus units continue for more than a month. When teachers drag a unit out for 6 weeks, 2 months, or longer, they risk killing students' interest in the particular book or, worse yet, their love of literature.

STEPS IN DEVELOPING A LITERATURE FOCUS UNIT

1. Book Selection
Select the book to be featured in the literature focus unit, obtain a class set of books, and collect a text set of related books.

2. Instructional Focus
Identify the focus for the unit and the standards to address during the unit.

3. Strategies and Skills
Choose the language arts strategies and skills related to the standards to teach during the unit.

4. Reading Process Activities
Plan activities representing all five stages of the reading process.

5. Grouping Patterns
Coordinate whole-class, small-group, and individual grouping patterns with the activities.

6. Technology Resources
Locate technology resources related to the featured book.

7. Assessment
Plan how students' work will be assessed, and make an assignment checklist or other grading sheet.

8. Schedule
Create a time schedule and lesson plans.

Step 1: Select the Featured Book. Teachers begin by selecting the featured book for the literature focus unit. The book may be a story—either a picture book or a chapter book—or an informational book. The reading materials should be high-quality literature and should often include multicultural selections. Sometimes teachers select several related books representing the same genre for a genre study or books written by the same author for an author study. Teachers collect multiple copies of the book or books for the unit. In some school districts, class sets of selected books are available for teachers; however, in other school districts, teachers have to request that administrators purchase multiple copies of books or buy them themselves, often through book clubs.

Once the book (or books) is selected, teachers collect related books for the text set, including other versions of the same story, other books written by the same author, books with the same theme or representing the same genre, or related informational books or books of poetry. Teachers collect one or more copies of each book for the text set, which they place on a special shelf or in a crate in the library center. At the beginning of the unit, teachers introduce the books in the text set and encourage students to read them during independent reading time.

Step 2: Identify the Instructional Focus. Teachers identify the instructional focus for the unit by matching the book's strengths with the language arts standards they'll teach. Some standards, such as interpreting words with multiple meanings, can be taught using almost any book, but others, such as comparing and contrasting tales from different cultures, are book-specific. Teachers also identify standards that focus on listening, talking, writing, and other language arts to teach as students participate in the unit. For example, when teachers plan to read the featured book aloud, they identify listening comprehension standards to address, and when students will write sequels to the story, teachers identify standards dealing with the writing process and writing mechanics to teach. Teachers identify what they want students to know and be able to do at the end of the unit, and then these standards become the focus of both instruction and assessment.

Step 3: Specify Language Arts Strategies and Skills to Teach. Teachers review the standards they've selected and decide which strategies and skills to teach using the featured book. Sometimes the standard specifies the strategies and skills, but at other times, teachers analyze the standard to determine which ones their students need to learn. In addition, teachers consider students' observed needs. Sometimes they plan minilessons to teach strategies and skills directly, but at other times, they plan to model how to use the strategies and skills as they read aloud or to ask students to share how they use the strategies and skills during grand conversations.

Step 4: Plan Reading Process Activities. After determining the instructional focus, including the strategies and skills they plan to teach, teachers decide which activities to include in the unit. The activities they choose need to fit into the five stages of the reading process. Questions teachers can ask themselves at each stage of the reading process are listed in Figure 14–1. Teachers also make sure that students have opportunities to engage in listening, talking, reading, writing, viewing, and visually representing activities during the literature focus unit. Of course, not all six language arts fit into every unit, but for most units they do.

Step 5: Coordinate Grouping Patterns With Activities. Teachers think about how to incorporate whole-class, small-group, buddy, and individual activities into their unit plans. It's important that students have opportunities to read and write

---

FIGURE 14–1

Questions to Use in Developing Literature Focus Units

Prereading
- What background knowledge do students need before reading?
- What key concepts and vocabulary should I teach before reading?
- How will I introduce the story and stimulate students' interest for reading?
- How will I assess students' learning?

Reading
- How will students read this story?
- What reading strategies and skills will I model or ask students to use?
- How can I make the story more accessible for less capable readers and English learners?

Responding
- Will students write in reading logs? How often?
- Will students participate in grand conversations? How often?
- What scenes from the book will students want or need to dramatize?

Exploring
- What words might be added to the word wall?
- What vocabulary activities might be used?
- Will students reread the story?
- What skill and strategy minilessons might be taught?
- How can I focus students' attention on words and sentences in the book?
- How will books from the text set be used?
- What information can I share about the author, illustrator, or genre?

Applying
- What projects might students choose to pursue?
- How will books from the text set be used?
- How will students share projects?

---

independently as well as to work with small groups and to come together as a class. Small groups are especially effective for English learners because they feel more comfortable in these settings, and classmates help to clarify confusions and support their learning (Brock & Raphael, 2005).

Step 6: Locate Technology Resources. Teachers locate technology resources to use in the unit, including Internet sites with author information and information on related topics, CD-ROM and video versions of stories for students to view and compare to the book version, and audiotapes of stories to use at listening centers. Teachers also plan how they will use computers for writing and researching projects and digital cameras for photographic essays related to the unit.

Step 7: Plan for Assessment. Teachers plan for two types of assessment—assessment of students' learning and monitoring of students' work during the unit. Teachers provide opportunities for students to pursue authentic assessment projects that are based on standards and that show the relationship between instruction and assessment rather than paper-and-pencil tests. Students usually choose the projects they'll create to demonstrate their learning, and they often get involved in the assessment process when they self-assess their work and what they've learned.

Teachers often use unit folders to monitor students' work. Students keep all work, reading logs, reading materials, and related materials in the folder, which makes the unit easier for both students and teachers to manage. Teachers also plan ways to monitor students' work at centers during a literature focus unit. The Weaving Assessment Into Practice feature on page 472 shows a centers assessment checklist prepared in booklet form for a first-grade unit on *The Mitten* (Brett, 1989). Students color in the mitten on each page as they complete work at the center.

Teachers also plan ways to document students' learning and to assign grades. One form of record keeping is an assignment checklist. This sheet is developed with students and distributed at the beginning of the literature focus unit. Students keep track of their work during the unit and sometimes negotiate to change the sheet as the unit evolves. They keep the lists in unit folders, and they mark off each item as it is completed. At the end of the unit, students turn in their completed assignment checklist and other completed work.

An assignment checklist for an upper-grade literature focus unit on *The Giver* (Lowry, 2006b), a story about a "perfect" community that isn't, is presented in the Weaving Assessment Into Practice feature below. Although this list doesn't

Weaving Assessment Into Practice

AN UPPER-GRADE ASSIGNMENT CHECKLIST FOR *THE GIVER*

Name _____

Student's Check		Points
_____	1. Read The Giver. (20)	_____
_____	2. Write at least ten entries in your reading log. Use a double-entry format with quotes and your connections. (20)	_____
_____	3. Participate in small-group grand conversations. (5)	_____
_____	4. Create a storyboard. Chapter # _____ (5)	_____
_____	5. Make an open-mind portrait of Jonas with four mind pages. (5)	_____
_____	6. Write an essay about the theme of the book. (10)	_____
_____	7. Choose and analyze ten words from the word wall according to prefix, root word, and suffix. (5)	_____
_____	8. Read one book from the text set. Write a brief summary in your reading log and compare what you learned about societies with The Giver. (5)	_____
	Title _____	
	Author _____	
_____	9. Make a square for the class story quilt. (5)	_____
_____	10. Create a project and share it with the class. (20)	_____
	Project _____	_____
	Date shared _____	

Total _____

A CENTERS ASSESSMENT BOOKLET FOR A UNIT ON *THE MITTEN*

"The Mitten"

Centers Booklet

Retelling Center

Use puppets and pictures to tell "The Mitten" story.

Word Work Center

Make words using magnetic letters.

Listening Center

Listen to other books by Jan Brett.

Writing Center

Write books about "The Mitten" or books about the animals in the story.

Reading Center

Compare the three "The Mitten" stories and pick your favorite one.

Knitting Center

Learn to knit with Tasha's mom.

Sorting Center

Sort the phonics objects and word cards into buckets.

include every activity students are involved in, it does list the activities and other assignments that the teacher holds students accountable for. Students complete the checklist on the left side of the sheet and add titles of books and other requested information. The teacher awards points (up to the number listed in parentheses) on the lines on the right side of the sheet, and totals the number of points on the bottom of the page. Then the total score can be translated into a letter grade or other type of grade.

Step 8: Create a Time Schedule. Teachers create a time schedule that allows students sufficient time to move through the five stages of the reading process and to complete the activities planned for the focus unit. Literature focus units require large blocks of time each day, at least 2 hours, in which students read, listen, talk, and write about the featured book.

A Primary-Grade Literature Focus Unit on _The Mitten_

Jan Brett's _The Mitten_ (1989), a cumulative picture-book story about a series of animals that climb into a mitten that a little boy has dropped in the snow on a cold winter day, is the featured selection in literature focus units taught in many primary-grade classrooms. A planning cluster for a literature focus unit on _The Mitten_ is shown in Figure 14–2. Teachers use the big book version of _The Mitten_ to introduce the unit and to examine Brett's innovative use of borders. Children retell the story with the teacher's collection of stuffed animals and puppets representing the animals in the story—a mole, a rabbit, a hedgehog, an owl, a badger, a fox, a bear, and a mouse. They read the story several times—in small groups with the teacher, with partners, and independently. The teacher also reads aloud several other versions of the story, such as _The Woodcutter's Mitten_ (Koopmans, 1990) and _The Mitten_ (Tresselt, 1989), and children make a chart to compare the versions. The teacher presents minilessons on phonemic awareness and phonics skills, creates a word wall, and involves the children in word-study activities. They participate in sequencing and writing activities and learn about knitting from a parent volunteer. The teacher also sets out a text set of other books by Jan Brett and reads some of the books aloud. As their application project, children divide into small groups to research one of the animals mentioned in the story. Fifth graders work with the primary-grade students as they research the animals and share what they learn on large posters.

An Upper-Grade Literature Focus Unit on _The Giver_

Upper-grade students spend 3 or 4 weeks reading, responding to, exploring, and applying their understanding of Lois Lowry's Newbery Medal book, _The Giver_ (2006b). Lowry creates a "perfect" community in which the people are secure but regulated. Jonas, the main character, is chosen to be a leader in the community, but he rebels against the society and escapes. To introduce this book, teachers might connect the book to the United States Constitution and the Bill of Rights, or discuss the problems in U.S. society today and ask students to create a perfect society. Or, students might think about how their lives would be different in a world without colors, like Jonas's.

Students can read the story together as a class, in small groups with the teacher or in literature study groups, with buddies, or independently. Students come together to

FIGURE 14–2

A Planning Cluster for a Primary-Grade Unit on *The Mitten*

Word Wall

A	acorn	M	meadow mouse
B	Baba		mitten
	badger		mole
	bear		muzzle
	bear's nose	N	Nicki
	big kickers	O	owl
	borders	PQ	prickles
C	commotion	RS	sheep
	cozy		snowshoe rabbit
D	diggers		stretched
	drowsy		swelled
E	enormous sneeze		swooped down
F	fox	T	trotted
G	glinty talons		tunneling along
	glove	UV	Ukraine
	grandmother	WX	whiskers
HIJ	hedgehog		wool
K	knitted		wriggled
L	lumbered by	YZ	yarn

Other Books by Jan Brett

Armadillo rodeo. (1995). New York: Putnam.
Berlioz the bear. (1991). New York: Putnam.
Gingerbread baby. (1999). New York: Putman.
Goldilocks and the three bears. (1987). New York: Putnam.
The hat. (1997). New York: Putnam.
The owl and the pussycat. (1991). New York: Putnam.
Town mouse, country mouse. (1994). New York: Putnam.
Trouble with trolls. (1992). New York: Putnam.

Big Book

Introduce the story using the big book version of the book (published by Scholastic) and shared reading.

Author Study

- Read other books by Jan Brett.
- Visit her website at www.JanBrett.com.
- Examine Brett's use of borders in her books and have students create borders in the books they write.
- Write letters to the author.

Compare Versions of the Story

Read these versions and make a chart to compare them with Brett's version:

Koopmans, L. (1990). *The woodcutter's mitten.* New York: Crocodile Books.
Tresselt, A. (1989). *The mitten.* New York: HarperTrophy.

The Mitten

Vocabulary Activities

- Post an alphabetized word wall.
- Make colorful word posters in the shape of a mitten.
- Sort words according to "mitten" and "animal" categories or using phonics categories.

Sequencing Activities

- Sequence events using storyboards cut from two copies of the book, backed with cardboard and laminated.
- Dramatize the story with puppets or stuffed animals.
- Create a circle diagram of the story. Have students draw pictures of each event and post them in a circle, beginning and ending with the grandmother.

Research

- Research the animals in the story.
- Create a semantic feature analysis to compare the animals.
- Write a class book about one of the animals.
- Research sheep, wool, and yarn using these books:

Fowler, A. (1993). *Woolly sheep and hungry goats.* Chicago: Children's Press.
Mitgutsch, A. (1975). *From sheep to scarf.* Minneapolis: Carolrhoda.

Writing Activities

- Write a class collaboration retelling of the story.
- Create a found poem using words and phrases from the book.
- Write letters to the author.
- Create a story quilt with a mitten design on each square and a sentence about the book.

discuss the story in grand conversations and deal with the complex issues presented in the book in both small groups and whole-class discussions. They also write in reading logs. Teachers identify skills and strategies to model during reading and to teach in minilessons. Students write important words from the story on the word wall and engage in a variety of vocabulary activities. They also learn about the author and examine the story structure in the book. After reading, they can do a choral reading, create a story quilt, compare U.S. society with the society described in the book, and create other projects. Figure 14–3 shows a planning cluster for *The Giver.*

LITERATURE CIRCLES

Students divide into small groups, and they read and respond to a self-selected book together during a literature circle (Daniels, 2001; Evans, 2001; Frank, Dixon, & Brandts, 2001). Students read independently, and then they come together to participate in grand conversations to discuss the book. They also write in reading logs and sometimes create projects related to the book. For students to be successful in literature circles, a community of learners is essential. Students need to develop responsibility, learn how to work in a small group with classmates, and participate in group activities.

How to Organize for Literature Circles

Teachers move through a series of steps as they prepare for literature circles. Even though students assume leadership roles and make a number of decisions as they participate in literature circles, the success depends on the teacher's planning and the classroom community that has been created. The LA Essentials box on page 477 outlines the steps in organizing literature circles.

Step 1: Choose Books. Teachers choose five, six, or seven books and then collect six copies of each one. To introduce the books, teachers give a book talk about each one, and students sign up for the book they want to read. One way to do this is to set each book on the chalk tray and have students sign their names on the chalkboard above the book they want to read. Or, teachers can set the books on a table and place a sign-up sheet beside each one. Students take time to preview the books, and then they select the book they want to read. Once in a while, students don't get to read their first-choice book, but they can always read it later during another literature circle or during reading workshop.

Traditionally, students read stories during literature circles, but teachers have found that students also enjoy reading informational books (Heller, 2006/2007; Stein & Beed, 2004). Students read and discuss nonfiction much like they do stories, talking about what they liked about the book as well as the big ideas and what they learned. In fact, teachers report that literature circles are an effective way to increase students' interest in informational books.

Step 2: Identify Strategies and Skills. Teachers identify the reading and literary response standards to address as students participate in literature circles, and then they decide which strategies and skills to emphasize. Sometimes the standard specifies the strategies and skills, but at other times, teachers analyze the standard to determine which ones their students need to learn. Teachers plan to emphasize

FIGURE 14–3

A Planning Cluster for an Upper-Grade Unit on *The Giver*

Introducing the Book

- Read the book when studying ancient civilizations and focus on the traits of a civilization.
- Discuss the problems in U.S. society, and ask students to create a perfect society.
- Create a world with no colors.
- Share objects from a book box, including an apple, a bicycle, a sled, the number 19, a stuffed bear or other "comfort object," and a kaleidoscope of colors.

Story Structure Activities

- Create a set of storyboards, one for each chapter, with a good title for the chapter, a picture, and a summarizing paragraph.
- Create a plot diagram to graph the highs and lows of the book.
- Make an open-mind portrait with several mind pages to track Jonas's thinking through the book.
- Compare Jonas's character to Kira's in Lowry's *Gathering Blue* (2000a) or that of another familiar character.
- Draw a setting map of the story.
- Analyze the theme of the book and create a story quilt to represent it.

Vocabulary Activities

- Post an alphabetized word wall in the classroom, and have students make individual word walls.
- Draw word clusters.
- Sort words according to "Jonas," "Giver," and "Community" categories.
- Teach minilessons on dividing long words into syllables or identifying root words and affixes (e.g., *obediently, distrustful, apprehensive*).
- Teach minilessons on etymology (e.g., English, Latin, and Greek words).
- Collect powerful sentences and write them on sentence strips.

The Giver

Comparing Societies

Students read a book about U.S. democratic society and compare it with the perfect society in *The Giver*.

Cowman, P. (1995). *Strike! The bitter struggle of American workers from colonial times to the present.* New York: Millbrook.

Fleming, R. (1995). *Rescuing a neighborhood: The Bedford-Stuyvesant Volunteer Ambulance Corps.* New York: Walker.

Haskins, J. (1993). *The march on Washington.* New York: HarperCollins.

Hoose, P. (1993). *It's our world, too! Stories of young people who are making a difference.* New York: Joy Street.

Meltzer, M. (1990). *Crime in America.* New York: Morrow.

Author Information

- Collect information about Lois Lowry, including "Newbery Acceptance" by Lois Lowry, published in the July/August 1994 issue of *Horn Book* (pp. 414–422).
- Read other books in the series, including *Gathering Blue* (2006a) and *The Messenger* (2006c).
- Read Lowry's autobiography, *Looking Back: A Book of Memories* (2000).
- Write letters to the author.

Grand Conversations

- Have students share their ideas about the chapters they have read.
- Have students choose an appropriate title for the chapter.
- Have students share favorite sentences from the chapter.
- Have students make predictions about the next chapter.

Word Wall

A	anguished	PQ	permission
	assignment		precision
B	bicycle		punishment
CD	ceremony	R	Receiver
	community		regret
EF	Elders		released
	elsewhere		ritual
GH	Gabe	S	sameness
	guilt		stirrings
I	ironic		successor
JK	Jonas	T	transgression
L	luminate		transmit
M	memories		tunic
N	Nurturer	UV	
O	obediently	WX	
	obsolete	YZ	yearning

Reading Log

- Keep a simulated journal, written from Jonas's viewpoint, after reading each chapter.
- Write a double-entry journal with quotes from the story in one column and personal connections or predictions in the other column.

Writing Projects

- Write found poems, "I Am" poems, or other poems.
- Write an essay comparing Jonas's society with ours.
- Write a reaction to this quote: "The greatest freedom is the freedom of choice."
- Write a simulated letter from one character to another in the story.
- Write a prequel or a sequel to the story.

STEPS IN ORGANIZING LITERATURE CIRCLES

1. Books
Choose six or seven titles and collect five or six copies of each book for students to read.

2. Strategies and Skills
Identify the standards to address and the language arts strategies and skills related to the standards to teach.

3. Groups
Organize the circles by giving book talks and having students sign up for the book they want to read.

4. Roles
Decide on roles for group members and clearly explain the responsibilities of each role.

5. Schedule
Set the schedule for literature circles and have students in each small group decide how they will schedule reading, discussion, and other work times.

6. Grand Conversations
Conduct grand conversations to monitor students' reading, and support students as they respond to and deepen their understanding of the book.

7. Reading Logs
Set guidelines for how often students will write in reading logs and the types of entries they will make.

8. Assessment
Plan ways to monitor students as they read and respond to the book in small groups.

particular strategies and skills as they determine which roles students will assume or plan questions for grand conversations and reading log entries. They also think about how they can model the use of strategies and skills as they interact with the students in the literature circles.

Step 3: Organize the Circles or Groups. The books in the text set often vary in length and difficulty, but students are not placed in groups according to their reading levels. Students choose the books they want to read and, as they preview the books, they consider how good a fit the book is, but that's not their only consideration: They often choose to read the book they find most interesting or the one their best friend has chosen. Students can usually manage whatever book they choose because of support and assistance from their group and through plain and simple determination. Once in a while, teachers counsel students to choose another book or provide an additional copy of the book to practice at home or to read with a tutor at school.

Step 4: Decide on Roles for Group Members. Teachers decide how to structure the literature circles and what roles students will assume. Sometimes students in a group choose their own group leader, or a natural leader emerges when they first get together; however, at other times, teachers identify the group leader. In addition to the leadership role, each group member assumes a role, and students also select these during the first meeting of the group. When teachers have students assume roles, they must clearly outline the responsibilities of each group member. Teachers often spend a great deal of time at the beginning of the school year teaching students how to fulfill the responsibilities of each role.

Students assume roles to facilitate the group's understanding of the book they're reading: One student becomes the Passage Master, and other group members assume the roles of Word Wizard, Connector, Summarizer, Artist, and Investigator. When students are reading informational books, some roles remain the same, but teachers and students create other roles that focus on the unique characteristics of nonfiction. Stien and Beed's (2004) students added a Timeline Traveler, who creates a timeline of historical events, and a Fantastic Fact Finder, who shares interesting facts; and when students read biographies, an additional role was Vital Statistics Collector, who shares personal information about the person being profiled.

Some teachers continue to have students use the same roles for each literature circle during the school year, but others find that after students learn to use each of the roles they can assume them flexibly as they read and think about the book. One way to do this is by "tabbing" (Stien & Beed, 2004): Teachers pass out packs of small self-stick notes, and students use them to make notes applying what they've learned about the different roles as they read. On some notes, students ask a question, choose an interesting passage to read aloud, note an interesting word to look up in the dictionary, or jot a personal, world, or text connection, for example.

Step 5: Set the Schedule. Teachers set a time schedule for the literature circle, and then each small group of students decides how to use the time to read the book and participate in grand conversations. During group meetings, teachers often participate in grand conversations and add their ideas to the discussion. They also monitor that students are completing their reading assignments and fulfilling the responsibilities of their roles. While the teacher meets with one group, the other groups read independently or participate in other activities.

Step 6: Conduct Grand Conversations. Students alternate reading and discussing the book in grand conversations. At the beginning of the literature circle, students decide how often to meet for grand conversations and how much of the book to read before each discussion. Sometimes teachers participate in the conversations and sometimes they don't. When the teachers are participants, they participate as fellow readers who share joys and difficulties, insights and speculations. They also help students develop literary insights by providing information, asking insightful questions, and guiding students to make comments.

Step 7: Write in Reading Logs. Students often write in reading logs as part of literature circles. Teachers make decisions about the types of entries they want students to make as they read. Sometimes students write entries in their logs after each chapter, and at other times, they write once a week. Students may write their reactions to the chapters they have read or write about issues that arose during the grand conversation. They may also write predictions, collect vocabulary words, and record powerful sentences from the book in their journals. Depending on the complexity of the book and the issues the teacher wants students to think about, the teacher may ask students to respond to a question after reading a particular chapter.

Step 8: Plan for Assessment. The assessment focuses on students' comprehension of the book they've read and their participation in the literature circle. The standards that teachers select guide the assessment. When teachers choose a standard that focuses on analyzing the theme of the story, for example, they check students' reading logs and listen to their comments in grand conversations. Teachers also plan how they will assess students' participation in the literature circle. Most teachers observe students as they move around the classroom and participate in grand conversations. Many teachers also use an assignment sheet to assess students' work. A fifth-grade grading sheet is shown in the Weaving Assessment Into Practice feature on page 480.

READING AND WRITING WORKSHOP

Nancie Atwell (2007) introduced reading workshop as an alternative to traditional reading instruction. In reading workshop, students read books that they choose themselves and respond to them through writing in reading logs and conferencing with teachers and classmates. This approach represents a change in what we believe about how children learn and how literature is used in the classroom. Atwell developed reading workshop with her middle school students, but it has been adapted and used successfully at every grade level, first through eighth. There are several versions of reading workshop, but they usually contain these components: reading, sharing, minilessons, and reading aloud to students (Serafini, 2001).

Writing workshop is similar to reading workshop, except that the focus is on writing. Students write on topics that they choose themselves, and they assume ownership of their writing and learning (Atwell, 1998; Calkins, 1994; Fletcher & Portalupi, 2001). At the same time, the teacher's role changes from that of being a provider of knowledge to that of serving as a facilitator and guide. The classroom becomes a community of writers who write and share their writing. There is a spirit of pride and acceptance in the classroom.

ASSESSMENT CHECK

Name _____   **Book** _____

Circle Members

1. _____   3. _____   5. _____

2. _____   4. _____   6. _____

Write a schedule of your activities. What was your role?

M	T	W	T	F

M	T	W	T	F

M	T	W	T	F

Reflect on your work in this literature circle. Score yourself, and then write about your work on the back of this sheet.

1. Read the book. | A | B | C | D |

2. Complete your group role. | A | B | C | D |

3. Participate in grand conversations. | A | B | C | D |

4. Write in your reading log. | A | B | C | D |

5. Make a group project. | A | B | C | D |

6. Share your project. | A | B | C | D |

Writing workshop is a 60- to 90-minute period scheduled each day. During this time, students are involved in three components: writing, sharing, and minilessons. Sometimes a fourth activity, reading aloud to students, is added to writing workshop when it's not used in conjunction with reading workshop.

Establishing a Workshop Environment

Teachers begin to establish the workshop environment in their classroom from the first day of the school year by providing students with choices, time to read and write, and opportunities for response (Overmeyer, 2005). Through their interactions with students, the respect they show to students, and the way they model reading and writing, teachers establish the classroom as a community of learners.

Teachers develop a schedule for reading and writing workshop with time allocated for each component, or they alternate between the two types of workshops. They allot as much time as possible in their schedules for students to read and write. After developing the schedule, teachers post it in the classroom, talk about the activities, and discuss their expectations with students. Teachers teach the workshop procedures and continue to model them as students become comfortable with the routines (Kaufman, 2001). As students share what they're reading and writing at the end of workshop sessions, their enthusiasm grows and the workshop approaches are successful.

Students keep two folders—one for reading workshop and one for writing workshop. In the reading workshop folder, students keep a list of books they've read, notes from minilessons, reading logs, and other materials. In the writing workshop folder, they keep all rough drafts and other compositions. They also keep a list of all compositions, topics for future pieces, and notes from minilessons. They also keep language arts notebooks in which they jot down images, impressions, dialogue, and experiences that they can build on for writing projects (Calkins, 1991).

How to Set Up a Reading Workshop

Teachers move through a series of steps as they set up their classroom, prepare students to work independently in the classroom, and provide instruction. These steps are summarized in the LA Essentials box on page 482.

Step 1: Collect Books for Reading Workshop. Students read all sorts of books during reading workshop, including stories, informational books, and books of poetry. Most of their reading materials are selected from the classroom library, but students also bring books from home and borrow others from the public library, the school library, and classmates. Students read many award-winning books, but they also read series of popular books and technical books related to their hobbies and special interests. These books are not necessarily the same ones that teachers use for literature focus units, but students often choose to reread books they read earlier in the school year or during the previous year in literature focus units and literature circles. Teachers need to have literally hundreds of books in their class libraries, including books written at a range of reading levels, in order to meet the needs of English learners, advanced readers, and struggling readers.

Teachers introduce students to the books in the classroom library so that they can more effectively choose books to read during reading workshop. The best way

STEPS IN SETTING UP A READING WORKSHOP

1. Books
Collect a wide variety of books at varying reading levels for students to read, including stories, informational books, poems, and other resources, and place them on a special shelf in the classroom library.

2. Workshop Procedures
Teach reading workshop procedures so that students know how to choose and respond to books, participate in conferences, and share books they've read. Reading workshop operates much more smoothly when students are familiar with the procedures.

3. Minilessons
Teach minilessons on topics drawn from standards as well as other strategies and skills that students are using but confusing.

4. Read-Aloud Books
Choose read-aloud books to introduce students to new genres, authors, literary elements, or series stories that they might want to continue reading on their own.

5. Schedule
Design a reading workshop schedule that incorporates reading, sharing, minilessons, and reading aloud to students.

6. Conferences
Plan a schedule for conferences so that you can talk with students individually or in small groups about the books they're reading, and monitor their comprehension.

7. Assessment
Monitor students' work and assess their reading with state-of-the-class charts, observations, and conferences.

to preview books is using a very brief book talk to interest students in the book. In book talks, teachers tell students a little about the book, show the cover, and perhaps read the first paragraph or two (Prill, 1994/1995). Teachers also give book talks to introduce text sets of books, and students give book talks as they share books they have read with the class during the sharing part of reading workshop.

Step 2: Teach Reading Workshop Procedures.
Students need to learn how to choose books, write responses to books they are reading, share books they have finished reading, and conference with the teacher, as well as other procedures related to reading workshop. Some of these procedures need to be taught before students begin reading workshop, and others can be introduced and reviewed as minilessons during reading workshop.

Step 3: Teach Minilessons.
Minilessons are an important part of reading workshop because the workshop approach is more than reading practice. Instruction is important, and minilessons are the teaching step. Teachers present minilessons on reading workshop procedures and on reading concepts, strategies, and skills. They identify topics for minilessons based on the standards they are addressing and students' observed needs. Teachers use examples from books students are reading, and students are often asked to reflect on their own reading processes.

Step 4: Choose Books to Read Aloud to Students.
When teachers include the reading-aloud component with reading workshop, they carefully choose the books they will read. These books may be more difficult than those students can read independently, or they may be chosen to introduce students to a genre, an author, or a literary element. Sometimes teachers read aloud the first book in a series and then invite students to continue reading the sequels themselves. Teachers choose books to read aloud for a variety of specific instructional purposes.

Step 5: Design a Schedule for Reading Workshop.
Teachers examine their daily schedule, consider the other language arts activities in which their students are involved, decide how much time is available for reading workshop, and allocate time to each of the reading workshop components. Some teachers make reading and writing workshop their entire language arts program. They begin by reading aloud a book, chapter by chapter, to the class and talking about the book in a grand conversation for the first 30 minutes of reading workshop. During this time, teachers focus on modeling reading strategies and talking about elements of story structure. For the next 45 to 50 minutes, students read self-selected books independently. The teacher conferences with small groups of students as they read and presents minilessons to small groups of students as needed. Then students spend the next 15 to 20 minutes writing about their reading in reading logs. Sharing is held during the last 15 minutes, and students do book talks about books they have finished reading.

Other teachers coordinate reading workshop with literature focus units. For example, they decide to allocate one hour to reading workshop at the beginning of their language arts block. Students begin with 30 minutes of independent reading and then use the next 10 minutes to share books they have finished reading with the class. The last 20 minutes are used for a minilesson. Then students move into a literature focus unit for the next 90 minutes. In some classrooms, teachers alternate reading and writing workshop, either by month or by grading period.

Step 6: Plan for Conferencing. During reading workshop, students are reading independently, and teachers must find ways to monitor their progress. Many teachers begin each reading period by moving around the classroom to check that students have chosen books and are reading purposefully and then use the rest of the reading period for individual and small-group conferences. Teachers create conference schedules and meet with students on a regular basis, usually once a week, to talk about their reading and reading skills and strategies, listen to them read excerpts aloud, and make plans for the next book. Teachers take notes during these conferences in folders they keep for each student.

Step 7: Plan for Assessment. Teachers use a classroom chart to monitor students' work on a daily basis. At the beginning of reading workshop, students or the teacher records on a class chart what book students are reading and the activity in which they are currently involved. Atwell (1998) calls this chart "the state of the class." Teachers can review students' progress and note which students need to meet with the teacher or receive additional attention. When students fill in the chart themselves, they develop responsibility for their actions and a stronger desire to accomplish tasks they set for themselves.

To monitor primary-grade students, teachers often use a pocket chart and have children place a card in their pocket, indicating whether they are reading or responding during reading workshop or at which stage of the writing process they are working during writing workshop.

Teachers take time during reading workshop to observe students as they interact and work together in small groups. Researchers who have observed in reading and writing workshop classrooms report that some students, even as young as first graders, are excluded from group activities because of gender, ethnicity, or socioeconomic status (Henkin, 1995; Lensmire, 1992). The socialization patterns in classrooms seem to reflect society's patterns. Henkin recommends that teachers be alert to the possibility that boys might share books only with other boys or that some students won't find anyone willing to be their editing partner. If teachers see instances of discrimination in their classrooms, they should confront them directly and work to foster a classroom environment where students treat each other equitably.

How to Set Up a Writing Workshop

As teachers set up a writing workshop classroom, they collect writing supplies and materials for making books for the writing center. They set out different kinds of paper—some lined and some unlined—and various writing instruments, including pencils and red and blue pens. Bookmaking supplies include cardboard, contact paper, cloth, and wallpaper for book covers; stencils; stamps; art supplies; and a saddleback stapler and other equipment for binding books. Teachers also set up a bank of computers with word-processing programs and printers or arrange for students to have access to the school's computer lab. Teachers encourage students to use the classroom library, and many times, students' writing grows out of favorite books they've read.

Teachers also think about the classroom arrangement. Students sit at desks or tables arranged in small groups as they write. The teacher circulates around the classroom, conferencing briefly with students, and the classroom atmosphere is free enough that students converse quietly with classmates and move around the classroom to collect materials at the writing center, assist classmates, or share ideas. There is space for students to meet for writing groups, and often a sign-up sheet for writing groups is posted in the classroom. A table is available for the teacher to meet with individual students or small groups for conferences, writing groups, proofreading, and minilessons.

In addition to collecting supplies and arranging the classroom, teachers need to prepare students for writing workshop and make plans for the instruction. The steps in setting up a writing workshop are summarized in the LA Essentials box on page 486.

Step 1: Teach the Stages of the Writing Process. Teachers often begin writing workshop by teaching or reviewing the five stages of the writing process, setting guidelines for writing workshop, and taking students through one writing activity together.

Step 2: Teach Writing Workshop Procedures. Teachers need to explain how students will meet in groups to revise their writing, how to sign up for a conference with the teacher, how to proofread, how to use the publishing center, and other procedures used in writing workshop (Ray & Laminack, 2001). A set of guidelines for writing workshop that one seventh-grade class developed is presented in Figure 14-4.

Step 3: Identify Topics for Minilessons. As with reading workshop, teachers teach minilessons during writing workshop related to the standards they've identified. Teachers present minilessons on procedures related to writing workshop and writing concepts, skills, and strategies that students can apply in their own writing. Other topics for minilessons come from teachers' observations of students as they write and the questions students ask.

Teachers also share information about authors and how they write during minilessons. For students to think of themselves as writers, they need to know what writers do. Each year, there are more autobiographies written by authors. For example, Tomie dePaola has written a popular series of autobiographical picture-book stories for young children, including *Things Will NEVER Be the Same* (2003), and Lois Lowry has written *Looking Back: A Book of Memories* (2000). Each chapter focuses on a memory prompted by a photo; this is a format students can imitate when they write autobiographies. A number of well-known authors and illustrators are profiled in the Meet the Author series published by Richard C. Owen, including *Can You Imagine*, by Patricia McKissack (1997), *If You Give an Author a Pencil*, by Laura Numeroff (2003), *From Paper Airplanes to Outer Space*, by Seymour Simon (2000), and *Firetalking*, by Patricia Polacco (1994). Students like these picture-book autobiographies because they provide interesting information, and the authors come to life through the color photographs on each page. They can be read aloud to primary students, and older students can read them independently. Video productions about authors and illustrators are also available. For example, in the 27-minute video *Eric Carle: Picture Writer* (1993), Eric Carle demonstrates how he uses paint and collage to create the illustrations for his popular picture books.

Step 4: Design a Writing Workshop Schedule. An important instructional decision that teachers make is how to organize their daily schedule and what portion of the language arts block to allocate to reading and writing workshop. Some teachers

STEPS IN SETTING UP A WRITING WORKSHOP

1. Writing Process
Teach the stages of the writing process so that students understand how to develop and refine a composition.

2. Workshop Procedures
Teach writing workshop procedures so that students know how to meet in revising groups, sign up for conferences, and publish their writing, for example. For students to be successful, it's essential that they know the procedures they will be expected to use.

3. Minilessons
Identify topics for minilessons to teach during writing workshop while anticipating that other topics will arise from strategies and skills that students are using but confusing.

4. Schedule
Design a writing workshop schedule that includes writing, sharing, and teaching minilessons. Consistency is important so that students know what is expected of them and can develop a routine.

5. Conferences
Plan how you will conference in small groups and individually with students so that you can monitor their work, provide feedback about their writing, and assess their progress.

6. Sharing
Include opportunities for students to share their published writing with classmates.

7. Assessment
Plan to monitor and assess students' work using state-of-the-class reports, conferences, writing-process checklists, and rubrics.

make reading and writing workshop the focus of their language arts program. During the writing workshop portion, students move through the writing process as they write on self-selected topics for 45 or 50 minutes. The teacher meets with small groups of students or with individual students as they draft, revise, and edit their compositions during this writing time. Next, teachers use a 15- to 30-minute block of time for minilessons during which they present minilessons on writing workshop procedures and writing concepts, skills, and strategies to the whole class, small groups of students, or individual students as needed. Sharing is held during the last 15 minutes, and students read their finished compositions aloud to classmates, often sitting in the author's chair.

Other teachers coordinate writing workshop with literature focus units. For example, they may allocate the last hour of their language arts block for reading and writing workshop, and alternate reading workshop and writing workshop by month or by grading period. Another way some teachers allocate time for writing workshop is during the last week of a literature focus unit, when students are developing a writing project. For example, in the literature focus unit on *The Mitten* discussed earlier

FIGURE 14–4
A Seventh-Grade Class's Guidelines for Writing Workshop

Ten Writing Workshop Rules

1. Keep everything in your writing folder.
2. Write rough drafts in pencil.
3. Double-space all rough drafts so you will have space to revise, and only write on one side of a page.
4. Revise in blue ink.
5. Edit in red ink.
6. Show your thinking and never erase except on the final copy.
7. Don't throw anything away—keep everything.
8. Date every piece of writing.
9. Keep a record of the compositions you write in your writing folder.
10. Work hard!

in this chapter, primary-grade students use a writing workshop approach as they re-search one of the animals mentioned in the story and create posters to share what they learn.

Step 5: Plan for Conferencing. Teachers conference with students as they write (Calkins, Hartman, & White, 2005). Many teachers prefer moving around the class-room to meet with students rather than having the students come to a table to meet with them because too often, a line forms as students wait to meet with the teacher, and students lose precious writing time. Some teachers move around the classroom in a regular pattern, meeting with one-fifth of the students each day. In this way, they can talk with every student during the week.

Other teachers spend the first 15 to 20 minutes of writing workshop stop-ping briefly to check on 10 or more students each day. Many use a zigzag pattern to get to all parts of the classroom each day. These teachers often kneel down be-side each student, sit on the edge of the student's seat, or carry their own stool to each student's desk. During the 1- or 2-minute conferences, teachers ask students what they are writing, listen to students read a paragraph or two, and then ask what they plan to do next. Then these teachers use the remaining time during writing workshop to conference more formally with students who are revising and editing their compositions. Students often sign up for these conferences. Teachers make comments to find strengths, ask questions, and discover possibilities during these revising conferences. Some teachers like to read the pieces themselves, whereas others like to listen to students read their papers aloud. As they interact with students, teachers model the kinds of responses that students are learning to give to each other.

As students meet to share their writing during revising and editing, they continue to develop their sense of community. They share their rough drafts with classmates in writing groups composed of four or five students. In some classrooms, teachers join in the writing groups whenever they can, but students normally run the groups themselves. They take turns reading their rough drafts to one another and listen as their classmates offer compliments and suggestions for revision. In other classrooms, students work with one partner to edit their writing, and they often use red pens.

After proofreading their drafts with a classmate and then meeting with the teacher for a final editing, students make the final copy of their writing. Students often want to put their writing on the computer so that their final copy will appear professional. Many times, students compile their final copy to make a book during writing workshop, but sometimes they attach their writing to artwork, make a poster, write a letter that is mailed, or perform a script as a skit or puppet show. Not every piece is published, however. Sometimes students decide not to continue with a piece of writing; they file the piece in their writing folders and start some-thing new.

Step 6: Include Sharing. For the last 10 to 15 minutes of writing workshop, students gather together as a class to share their new publications and make other, related announcements. Younger students often sit in a circle or gather together on a rug for sharing time. If an author's chair is available, each student sits in the special chair to read his or her composition. After reading, classmates clap and offer

Weaving Assessment Into Practice

AN EXCERPT FROM A FIFTH-GRADE STATE-OF-THE-CLASS CHART

Names	10/18	10/19	10/20	10/21	10/22	10/25	10/26	10/27
Antonio	4 5	5	5	6	7	8	8	8 9
Bella	2	2	2 3	2	2	4	5	6
Charles	8 9 1	3 1	1	2	2 3	4	5	6 7
Dina	6	6	6	7 8	8	9 1	1	2 3
Dustin	7 8	8	8	8	8	8	9 1	1
Eddie	2 3	2	2 4	5 6	8	9 1	1 2	2 3
Elizabeth	7	6	7	8	8	8	9	1 2
Elsa	2	3	4 5	5 6	6 7	8	8	9 1

Code:

1 = Prewrite	4 = Writing Group	7 = Conference
2 = Draft	5 = Revise	8 = Make Final Copy
3 = Conference	6 = Edit	9 = Publish

compliments. They may also make other comments and suggestions, but the focus is on celebrating completed writing projects, not on revising the composition to make it better. Classmates help celebrate after the child shares by clapping, and perhaps the best praise is having a classmate ask to read the newly published book.

Step 7: Plan for Assessment. Teachers monitor students' work in several ways. They monitor students' progress from day to day with a state-of-the-class report; an excerpt from a fifth-grade writing workshop chart is shown in the Weaving Assessment Into Practice feature above. Teachers can also use the chart to award weekly effort grades, to have students indicate their need to conference with the teacher, or to have students announce that they are ready to share their writing. Teachers also develop checklists with which students keep track of their work and monitor their application of strategies and skills that are being taught. In addition, teachers use rubrics to assess the quality of students' published compositions.

THEMATIC UNITS

Thematic units are interdisciplinary units that integrate reading and writing with social studies, science, and other curricular areas (Kucer, Silva, & Delgado-Larocco, 1995). Students take part in planning the thematic units and identifying some of the questions they want to explore and activities that interest them

(Lindquist & Selwyn, 2000). Students are involved in authentic and meaningful learning activities, not simply reading chapters in content-area textbooks in order to answer the questions at the end of the chapter. Textbooks might be used as a resource, but only as one of many available resources. Students explore topics that interest them and research answers to questions they have posed and are genuinely interested in answering. They share their learning at the end of the unit and are assessed on what they have learned as well as on the processes they used in learning and working in the classroom.

How to Develop a Thematic Unit

To begin planning a thematic unit, teachers choose the general topic and then identify three or four big ideas that they want to develop through the unit. The goal of a thematic unit is not to teach a collection of facts, but to help students grapple with several big understandings (Tunnell & Ammon, 1993). Next, teachers identify the resources that they have available for the unit and develop their teaching plan. Ten steps in developing a thematic unit are summarized in the LA Essentials box on the next page.

Step 1: Collect a Text Set. Teachers collect stories, poems, informational books, magazines, newspaper articles, and reference books for the text set related to the unit. The text set is placed in the special area for unit materials in the classroom library. Teachers plan to read some books aloud to students, students will read some independently, and they will read others together as shared or guided reading. These materials can also be used for minilessons, to teach students about strategies and skills. Other books can be used as models or patterns for writing projects. Teachers also copy some poems on charts to share with students or arrange a bulletin-board display of the poems.

Step 2: Set Up a Listening Center. Teachers select recordings to accompany stories or informational books or create their own tapes so that absent students can catch up on a book being read aloud day by day. Also, the recordings can be used to provide additional reading experiences for students who listen to a recording when they read or reread a story or informational book.

Step 3: Coordinate Content-Area Textbook Readings. Sometimes content-area textbooks are used as the entire instructional program in social studies or science, but that's not a good idea (Robb, 2003). Textbooks typically only survey topics; other instructional materials are needed to provide depth and understanding. Students need to read, write, and discuss topics. It's most effective to use the reading process and then extend students' learning with projects. Developing thematic units and using content-area textbooks as one resource are a much better idea. Tierney and Pearson (1992) recommend that teachers shift from teaching *from* textbooks to teaching *with* textbooks and incorporate other types of reading materials and activities into thematic units.

Step 4: Locate Technology Resources. Teachers plan the videotapes, CD-ROMs, charts, time lines, maps, models, posters, and other displays to be used in connection with the unit. Children view videos and explore Internet sites to provide background knowledge about the unit, and other materials are used in teaching the big ideas.

STEPS IN DEVELOPING A THEMATIC UNIT

1. Text Set
Collect a text set of books to use in the unit. Set the books out on a special shelf in the classroom library.

2. Listening Center
Set up a listening center and collect recordings of various books in the text set.

3. Textbooks
Coordinate content-area textbook reading with other activities in the unit.

4. Technology Resources
Locate Internet and other technology resources and plan ways to integrate them into the unit.

5. Word Walls
Identify potential words for the word wall and activities to teach those words.

6. Learning Logs
Plan how students will use learning logs as a tool for learning.

7. Strategies and Skills
Identify language arts strategies and skills to teach.

8. Talk and Visually Representing Activities
Plan ways to involve students in talk activities, such as instructional conversations and oral presentations, and in visually representing activities, such as graphic organizers and quilts.

9. Projects
Brainstorm possible projects students can create to apply their learning, but usually allow students some choice in which projects they develop.

10. Assessment
Plan ways to monitor and assess students' learning with assignment checklists, rubrics, and other assessment tools.

Materials can be viewed or displayed in the classroom, and students can make other materials during the thematic unit.

Step 5: Identify Potential Words for the Word Wall. Teachers preview books in the text set and identify potential words for the word wall. This list is useful in planning vocabulary activities, but teachers don't use their word lists simply for the classroom word wall. Students and the teacher develop the classroom word wall together as they read and discuss the big ideas and other information related to the unit.

Step 6: Consider How Students Will Use Learning Logs. Teachers plan for students to keep learning logs in which they take notes, write questions, make observations, clarify their thinking, and write reactions to what they're learning during thematic units. They also write quickwrites and make clusters to explore what they're learning.

Step 7: Identify Strategies and Skills. Teachers identify the language arts standards they will address and plan minilessons to teach strategies and skills, such as expository text structures, how to locate information, report writing, and interviewing techniques. Minilessons are taught so that students can apply what they are learning in unit activities.

Step 8: Plan Talk and Visually Representing Activities. Students use talk and visually representing to learn during the thematic unit and to demonstrate their learning. These are possible activities:

- Give oral reports.
- Interview someone with special expertise related to the unit.
- Participate in a debate related to the unit.
- Create charts and diagrams to display information.
- Role-play a historical event.
- Assume the role of a historical figure.
- Participate in a readers theatre presentation of a story or poem.
- Tell or retell a story, biography, or event.
- Use a puppet show to tell a story, biography, or event.
- Make a quilt with information or vocabulary related to the unit.
- Write and perform a skit or play.

Step 9: Brainstorm Possible Projects. Teachers think about possible projects students may choose to develop to apply and personalize their learning during thematic units. This advance planning makes it possible for teachers to collect needed supplies and to have suggestions ready to offer to students who need assistance in choosing a project. Students work on projects independently or in small groups and then share them with the class at the end of the unit. Projects involve one or more of the six language arts. Here are some suggestions:

- Read a biography related to the unit.
- Create a poster to illustrate a big idea.

Weaving Assessment Into Practice

AN ASSIGNMENT CHECKLIST FOR A MIDDLE-GRADE THEMATIC UNIT ON FLIGHT

Name _____ Date _____

	Excellent	Good	Fair	Poor
1. Make a K-W-L chart on flight.	____	____	____	____
2. Read five books on flight and write a note card on each one.	____	____	____	____
3. Write 10 pages in your learning log.	____	____	____	____
4. Make a word wall on flight with 50 words.	____	____	____	____
5. Make a cluster about birds.	____	____	____	____
6. Make a time line about flight.	____	____	____	____
7. Write a compare-contrast essay on birds and airplanes.	____	____	____	____

_____ Prewriting
_____ Drafting
_____ Revising
_____ Editing
_____ Publishing

8. Make a report poster on flight. Choose four ways
to share information.   ____   ____   ____   ____

____ report   ____ diagram   ____ photo
____ poem   ____ picture   ____ quote
____ story   ____ Internet   ____ other

- Write and mail a letter to get information related to the unit.
- Write a story related to the unit.
- Perform a readers theatre production, puppet show, or other dramatization.
- Write a poem, song, or rap related to the unit.
- Write an "All About . . ." book or a report about one of the big ideas.
- Create a commercial or advertisement related to the unit.
- Create a tabletop display or diorama about the unit.

Step 10: Plan for Assessment. Teachers consider how they will monitor and assess students' learning as they make plans for activities and assignments. In this way, teachers can explain to students at the beginning of the thematic unit how they will be assessed and can check that their assessment will emphasize students' learning of the big ideas. An assignment checklist for a unit about flight for middle-grade students is shown in the Weaving Assessment Into Practice feature on this page.

FIGURE 14–5

Guidelines for Using Content-Area Textbooks

Comprehension Aids
Teach students how to use the comprehension aids in content-area textbooks, including chapter overviews; headings that outline the chapter; helpful graphics, such as maps, charts, tables, graphs, diagrams, photos, and drawings; technical words defined in the text; end-of-chapter summaries; and review questions.

Questions
Divide the reading of a chapter into sections. Before reading each section, have students turn the section heading into a question and read to find the answer to the question. As they read, have students take notes about the section, and then after reading, answer the question they created from the section heading.

Expository Text Structures
Teach students about expository text structures and assist them in identifying the patterns used in the reading assignment, especially cause and effect or problem and solution, before reading.

Vocabulary
Introduce only the key terms as part of a presentation or discussion before students read the textbook assignment. Present other vocabulary during reading, if needed, and after reading, develop a word wall with all important words.

Big Ideas
Have students focus on the big ideas instead of trying to remember all the facts or other information.

Content-Area Reading Techniques
Use content-area reading techniques, such as PReP, exclusion brainstorming, and anticipation guides, to help students identify and remember big ideas after reading.

Headings
Encourage students to use headings and subheadings to select and organize relevant information. The headings can be used to create a graphic organizer.

Listen-Read-Discuss Format
Use a listen-read-discuss format. First, the teacher presents the big ideas orally, and then the students read and discuss the chapter. Or, have students read the chapter as a review activity rather than as the introductory activity.

Using Content-Area Textbooks

Content-area textbooks are often difficult for students to read—more difficult, in fact, than many informational books. One reason textbooks are difficult is that they mention many topics briefly without developing any of them. A second reason is that content-area textbooks are read differently than stories. Teachers need to show students how to approach content-area textbooks and teach them how to use specific expository-text reading strategies and procedures to make comprehension easier. Figure 14–5 presents guidelines for using content-area textbooks.

Teachers can make content-area textbooks more readable and show students ways to remember what they've read (Robb, 2003). Some activities are used before reading and others after reading: the before-reading activities help students activate prior knowledge, set purposes for reading, or build background knowledge, and the after-reading activities help them identify and remember big ideas and details. Other activities are used when students want to locate specific information. Here are some activities to make content-area textbooks more readable:

◈ *Preview.* Teachers introduce the reading assignment by asking students to note main headings in the chapter and then skim or rapidly read the chapter to get a general idea about the topics covered.

◈ *Prereading Plan (PReP).* Teachers introduce a big idea discussed in the reading assignment and ask students to brainstorm words and ideas related to the idea before reading (Langer, 1981).

◈ *Anticipation Guides.* Teachers present a set of statements on the topic to be read. Students agree or disagree with each statement and then read the assignment to see if they were right (Head & Readence, 1992).

◈ *Exclusion Brainstorming.* Teachers distribute a list of words, most of which are related to the key concepts to be presented in the reading assignment. Teachers ask students to circle the words that are related to a key concept and then read the assignment to see if they circled the right words (Johns, Van Leirsburg, & Davis, 1994).

◈ *Graphic Organizers.* Teachers distribute a cluster, map, or other graphic organizer with the big ideas marked. Students complete the graphic organizer by adding details after reading each section.

◈ *Note Taking.* Students develop an outline by writing the headings and then take notes after reading each section.

◈ *Scanning.* Students reread quickly to locate specific information.

Students in the upper grades also need to learn how to use the SQ3R study strategy, a five-step technique in which students survey, question, read, recite, and review as they read a content-area reading assignment. This study strategy was devised in the 1930s and has been researched and thoroughly documented as a very effective technique when used properly (Anderson & Armbruster, 1984; Caverly & Orlando, 1991). Teachers introduce the SQ3R study strategy and provide opportunities for students to practice each step. At first, students can work together as a class as they use the technique with a text the teacher is reading aloud. Then they can work with partners and in small groups before using the strategy independently. Teachers need to emphasize that if students simply begin reading the first page of the assignment without doing the first two steps, they won't be able to remember as much of what they read. Also, when students are in a hurry and skip some of the steps, the technique will not be as successful.

A Middle-Grade Thematic Unit on Flight

Middle-grade students connect science and language arts in a thematic unit on flight. To begin the unit, students and the teacher create a K-W-L chart and students write facts about how birds and airplanes fly, space flight, and famous aviators. They also identify questions they will investigate during the unit. The teacher sets out a text set of stories, poems, and informational books about flight for the students to read. Some of the books are on tape or CD, which students can listen to at the listening center. Students list important words about flight on a word wall and participate in a variety of vocabulary activities. Students research flight-related questions using books and Internet resources and through interviews with a pilot, flight attendant, astronaut or other knowledgeable person. Students present oral reports or prepare multigenre papers to share what they learn. A planning cluster for a thematic unit on flight is presented in Figure 14–6.

FIGURE 14–6

A Planning Cluster for a Middle-Grade Thematic Unit on Flight

Books

Bellville, C. W. (1993). *Flying in a hot air balloon.* Minneapolis: Carolrhoda.

Bernhard, E. (1994). *Eagles: Lions of the sky.* New York: Holiday House.

Borden, L. (1998). *Good-bye, Charles Lindbergh: Based on a true story.* New York: McElderry.

Busby, P. (2003). *First to fly: How Wilbur and Orville Wright invented the airplane.* New York: Crown.

Johnston, S. A. (1995). *Raptor rescue: An eagle flies free.* New York: Dutton.

Kalman, B. (1998). *How birds fly.* New York: Crabtree.

Lopez, D. (1995). *Flight.* New York: Time-Life.

Maynard, C. (1995). *Airplane.* London: Dorling Kindersley.

Peters, L. W. (1994). *This way home.* New York: Holt.

Ryan, P. M. (1999). *Amelia and Eleanor go for a ride: Based on a true story.* New York: Scholastic.

Weiss, H. (1995). *Strange and wonderful aircraft.* Boston: Houghton Mifflin.

Yolen, J. (2003). *My brothers' flying machine: Wilbur, Orville, and me.* Boston: Little, Brown.

Word Wall

AB	airflow	H	helicopters
	airfoil	I	instruments
	airplane	JK	jet
	airport		jet stream
	altitude	L	landing
	Amelia Earhart		lift
	astronauts	MNO	migration
	aviation	PQ	passengers
	aviator		pilot
C	Charles Lindbergh		pitch
	Chuck Yeager		propeller
	controls	RS	roll
D	drag		rudder
E	engine	TUV	takeoff
F	FAA		thrust
	flapping wings		tilt
	flight attendant	WX	weight
	flightless		wing
	flyways		Wright brothers
	fuselage	YZ	yaw
G	glide		

Charts and Diagrams

• Make a time line of the history of flight.
• Draw diagrams of birds' wings or airplanes.
• Make a Venn diagram comparing birds and airplanes.
• Make a data chart of information about animals that fly, including birds, bats, insects, and fish.

Multigenre Projects

• Prepare a multigenre project about flight.
• Prepare a multigenre biography of an aviator, such as Chuck Yeager, Charles Lindbergh, or Amelia Earhart.

Vocabulary Activities

• Post words on an alphabetized word wall hanging in the classroom.
• Use words on the word wall for a minilesson on dividing words into syllables.
• Make word clusters and hang them on airplane and bird mobiles.

Flight

K-W-L Charts

• Post a K-W-L chart on the wall and complete the sections together as a class.
• Have students make individual flip book K-W-L charts.

Interviews

• Interview a pilot, flight attendant, astronaut, zookeeper, ornithologist, or someone else knowledgeable about flight.
• Participate in an on-line interview of a pilot or astronaut.

Learning Logs

• Have students keep learning logs with notes, drawings, maps, diagrams, vocabulary words, and other information.

Internet

• Have students use yahooligans.com or another search engine designed for children to learn about flight on the Internet.
• Have students participate in an on-line interview of a pilot, astronaut, or other person involved with flight.

Oral Presentations

• Have students present oral reports about an airplane, bird, or aviator.
• Have students do an oral presentation of a poem from Fleischman, P. (1985). *I am Phoenix: Poems for two voices.* New York: HarperCollins.

Review

Designing language arts instruction that reflects the theory and research about language and how children learn is an important responsibility. Teachers follow a series of steps to develop literature focus units, literature circles, reading and writing workshop, and thematic units. Here are 10 key concepts presented in this chapter:

- Teachers develop literature focus units featuring award-winning and other high-quality books that students could not read independently.
- Teachers develop activities using all five stages of the reading process for literature focus units.
- Teachers organize for literature circles so that students can read and respond to self-selected books in small groups.
- Teachers create a community of learners so that students can work successfully in small groups.
- Teachers organize reading and writing workshop with plenty of time for reading and writing, and they present minilessons on procedures, strategies, and skills.
- Teachers provide opportunities for students to read and write independently during reading and writing workshop.
- Teachers can adapt and combine the patterns of practice to fit the needs of their students and their curriculum.
- Teachers focus on several big ideas as they develop thematic units.
- Content-area textbooks can be used as one resource in thematic units, but they should never be the only books that students read.
- Teachers design assignment checklists that students complete to document their learning during thematic units.

Professional References

Anderson, T. H., & Armbruster, B. B. (1984). Studying. In P. D. Pearson, R. Barr, M. L. Kamil, & P. Mosenthal (Eds.), *Handbook of reading research* (pp. 657–679). New York: Longman.

Atwell, N. (1998). *In the middle: New understandings about writing, reading, and learning.* Portsmouth, NH: Heinemann.

Atwell, N. (2007). *The reading zone.* New York: Scholastic.

Brock, C. H., & Raphael, T. E. (2005). *Windows to language, literacy, and culture: Insights from an English-language learner.* Newark, DE: International Reading Association.

Calkins, L. M. (1991). *Living between the lines.* Portsmouth, NH: Heinemann.

Calkins, L. M. (1994). *The art of teaching writing* (2nd ed.). Portsmouth, NH: Heinemann.

Calkins, L., Hartman, A., & White, Z. R. (2005). *One-to-one: The art of conferencing with young writers.* Portsmouth, NH: Heinemann.

Carle, E. (1993). *Eric Carle: Picture writer* (videotape). New York: Philomel.

Caverly, D. C., & Orlando, V. P. (1991). Textbook study strategies. In D. C. Caverly & V. P. Orlando (Eds.), *Teaching reading and study strategies at the college level* (pp. 86–165). Newark, DE: International Reading Association.

Daniels, H. (2001). *Literature circles: Voice and choice in book clubs and reading groups.* York, ME: Stenhouse.

Evans, K. S. (2001). *Literature discussion groups in the intermediate grades: Dilemmas and possibilities.* Newark, DE: International Reading Association.

Fletcher, R., & Portalupi, J. (2001). *Writing workshop: The essential guide.* Portsmouth, NH: Heinemann.

Frank, C. R., Dixon, C. N., & Brandts, L. R. (2001). Bears, trolls, and pagemasters: Learning about learners in book clubs. *The Reading Teacher, 54,* 448–462.

Head, M. H., & Readence, J. E. (1992). Anticipation guides: Meaning through prediction. In E. K. Dishner, T. W. Bean, J. E. Readence, & D. W. Moore (Eds.), *Reading in the content areas* (2nd ed., pp. 229–234). Dubuque, IA: Kendall/Hunt.

Heller, M. F. (2006/2007). Telling stories and talking facts: First graders' engagements in a nonfiction book club. *The Reading Teacher, 60,* 358–369.

Henkin, R. (1995). Insiders and outsiders in first-grade writing workshops: Gender and equity issues. *Language Arts, 72,* 429–434.

Johns, J. L., Van Leirsburg, P., & Davis, S. J. (1994). *Improving reading: A handbook of strategies.* Dubuque, IA: Kendall/Hunt.

Kaufman, D. (2001). Organizing and managing the language arts workshop: A matter of motion. *Language Arts, 79,* 114–123.

Kucer, S. B., Silva, C., & Delgado-Larocco, E. L. (1995). *Curricular conversations: Themes in multilingual and monolingual classrooms.* York, ME: Stenhouse.

Langer, J. A. (1981). From theory to practice: A prereading plan. *Journal of Reading, 25,* 152–157.

Lensmire, T. (1992). *When children write.* New York: Teachers College Press.

Lindquist, T., & Selwyn, D. (2000). *Social studies at the center: Integrating kids, content, and literacy.* Portsmouth, NH: Heinemann.

McGee, L. M., & Tompkins, G. E. (1995). Literature-based reading instruction: What's guiding the instruction? *Language Arts, 72,* 405–414.

Overmeyer, M. (2005). *When writing workshop isn't working: Answers to ten tough questions, grades 2–5.* York, ME: Stenhouse.

Prill, P. (1994/1995). Helping children use the classroom library. *The Reading Teacher, 48,* 363–364.

Ray, K. W., & Laminack, L. L. (2001). *The writing workshop: Working through the hard parts (and they're all hard parts).* Urbana, IL: National Council of Teachers of English.

Robb, L. (2003). *Teaching reading in social studies, science, and math.* New York: Scholastic.

Serafini, F. (2001). *Creating space for readers.* Portsmouth, NH: Heinemann.

Stien, D., & Beed, P. L. (2004). Bridging the gap between fiction and nonfiction in the literature circle setting. *The Reading Teacher, 57,* 510–518.

Tierney, R. J., & Pearson, P. D. (1992). Learning to learn from text: A framework for improving classroom practice. In E. K. Dishner, T. W. Bean, J. E. Readence, & D. W. Moore (Eds.), *Reading in the content areas: Improving classroom instruction* (2nd ed., pp. 85–99). Dubuque, IA: Kendall/Hunt.

Tunnell, M. O., & Ammon, R. (Eds.). (1993). *The story of ourselves: Teaching history through children's literature.* Portsmouth, NH: Heinemann.

Children's Book References

Asch, F. (2000). *The sun is my favorite star.* New York: Scholastic.

Brett, J. (1989). *The mitten.* New York: Putnam.

dePaola, T. (2003). *Things will NEVER be the same.* New York: Putnam.

Gibbons, G. (1997). *The moon book.* New York: Holiday House.

Hutchins, P. (1968). *Rosie's walk.* New York: Macmillan.

Koopmans, L. (1990). *The woodcutter's mitten.* New York: Crocodile Books.

Lowry, L. (2000). *Looking back: A book of memories.* New York: Delacorte.

Lowry, L. (2006a). *Gathering blue.* New York: Delacorte.

Lowry, L. (2006b). *The giver.* New York: Delacorte.

Lowry, L. (2006c). *The messenger.* New York: Delacorte.

McKissack, P. (1997). *Can you imagine.* Katonah, NY: Richard C. Owen.

Numeroff, L. (2003). *If you give an author a pencil.* Katonah, NY: Richard C. Owen.

Polacco, P. (1994). *Firetalking.* Katonah, NY: Richard C. Owen.

Simon, S. (2000). *From paper airplanes to outer space.* Katonah, NY: Richard C. Owen.

Tresselt, A. (1989). *The mitten.* New York: HarperTrophy.

NAME INDEX

Abodeep, T. L., 59
Ada, A. F., 202
Adams, M. J., 119, 120, 123, 124
Afflerbach, P. P., 52
Ahlberg, A., 186
Ahlberg, J., 186
Akhavan, N., 162, 163
Alarcón, F. X., 368
Aldrin, B., 225
Alesandrini, K., 249
Allard, H., 293
Allen, C. A., 337
Allen, J., 83, 162
Angelillo, J., 87
Angelou, M., 347, 348
Anson, A., 337
Applebee, A. N., 275
Archambault, J., 297
Areglado, N., 58
Arya, P., 64
Ashton-Warner, S., 130
Atwell, N., 43, 44, 46, 296, 303
Au, K. H., 285
August, D., 163
Avi, 287, 297
Aylesworth, J., 101

Babbitt, N., 34–35, 43, 261
Baird, J., 337
Baldwin, R. S., 224
Ball, E., 119
Bamford, R. A., 317, 320, 323, 335, 336
Barchers, S. I., 294
Barnes, D., 84
Baron, A., 129
Barone, D. M., 112
Barrentine, S. J., 215, 219
Barretta, G., 225–226
Baugh, A. C., 147
Baumann, J. F., 172
Bauserman, K. L., 23
Bayer, J., 361
Bean, T. W., 224

Bean, W., 406
Bear, D. R., 167, 397–398, 399n, 407
Beck, I., 120, 145, 162, 163, 165
Bell, L., 120
Bennett-Armistead, V. S., 113, 115
Bentley, E. C., 382
Berenstain, J., 318
Berenstain, S., 318
Berghoff, B., 338
Berglund, R. L., 169
Berthoff, A. E., 188, 220
Beverly, L., 47, 84, 86
Bewell, D., 188
Blachman, B., 119
Blachowicz, C., 79, 164
Black, A., 294
Blanton, W. E., 74
Bogner, K., 23
Bouffler, C., 406
Boyd-Batstone, P., 55
Boyle, O. F., 163, 197, 276, 327, 374
Brett, J., 101, 129, 132, 289
Britton, J., 86, 180
Broaddus, K., 214
Brock, C. H., 14
Bromley, K., 79, 158, 326
Brown, M. W., 47
Brown, V., 43
Brownell, J., 221
Bruchac, J., 191–192
Bruner, J., 8, 275
Bryan, A., 289
Bunting, E., 200, 248, 322
Burgess, T., 86
Burke, C., 114, 285
Burns, S., 112
Buss, K., 287
Butler, A., 102
Butterworth, C., 72
Button, K., 134
Byrd, R., 318

Cable, T., 147
Cairney, T., 303
Calkins, L. M., 46, 89, 90, 91
Cambourne, B., 22n
Canalis, J., 20
Caras, R. A., 313
Carle, E., 59, 124, 128, 132, 322
Carlo, M. S., 163
Carlson, L. M., 368
Casbergue, R. M., 132
Caserta-Henry, C., 129
Caxton, W., 148
Cazden, C., 16, 254
Cecil, N. L., 371, 382
Chandler, K., 406
Chang-Wells, G. L., 20
Chapman, V. G., 318
Cheney, L., 318
Chhabra, V., 30
Christensen, B., 342
Christie, J., 113
Ciardi, J., 363, 382
Cintorino, M. A., 245
Clay, M. M., 112, 114
Cleary, B., 37, 200
Cleary, L. M., 7
Cleland, J., 56, 60
Clemmons, J., 58
Clymer, T., 123, 125n
Coakley, C. G., 213
Cobb, C., 64
Cobb, R., 361
Cohen, K., 295
Cohle, D. M., 44
Cole, H., 127
Cole, J., 142, 318
Collom, S., 134
Compton-Lilly, C., 30
Cooper, D., 58
Cooper, S., 287
Courtney, A. M., 59
Cox, C., 266, 268
Crawford, L., 198

Creech, S., 68, 69, 353
Crew, G., 353
Cronin, D., 129
Crummel, S. S., 101, 208–212, 222
Culham, R., 97, 100, 102
Cullinan, B. E., 360
Cummins, J., 15
Cunningham, J. W., 412
Cunningham, P. A., 126
Cunningham, P. M., 408, 412
Curtis, C. P., 18, 289
Cushman, K., 100, 142, 191, 195,
    280–281, 286, 287, 290

Dahl, K. L., 126
Dahl, R., 37, 265
Dakos, K., 370
Daniels, H., 43, 46
Danziger, P., 68–70, 250, 288, 294
D'Aoust, C., 58
Day, J., 43
Dean, D., 25
Deedy, C. A., 271
De Ford, D., 275
Demi, 263, 289, 380
dePaola, T., 318
Devine, T. G., 236
Dias, P. X., 367
DiCamillo, K., 248
Dickinson, D. K., 215
Dill, M., 58
Ditzel, R. J., 128, 132
Dolezal, S. E., 23
Dorn, L. J., 28–29
Dorros, A., 284
Dorsey-Gaines, C., 113
Dowhower, S. L., 82
Dressel, J. H., 275
Dressler, C., 163
Drummond, L., 338
Duke, N. K., 113, 115, 288
Durrell, D. D., 123
Duthie, C., 341, 343
Dwyer, J., 24
Dyson, A. H., 8, 95

Eckhoff, B., 275
Edmunds, K. M., 23
Edwards, P. D., 100, 362
Eeds, M., 78, 79, 246, 247
Egawa, K. A., 338
Ehlert, L., 129, 314
Ellis, D., 18, 38
Elster, C. A., 364
Englert, C. S., 322

Evans, K. S., 44
Evans, M., 313

Faigley, L., 90
Fawson, P. C., 129
Fay, K., 251
Ferrell, R., 60
Ferruggia, A., 128
Finch, M., 186
Fisher, B., 76, 126
Fisher, C. J., 363
Fisher, D., 215, 223, 251
Fisher, P., 79, 164
Fitzgerald, J., 102, 162, 163
Flavell, J. H., 6, 7
Fleischman, P., 298, 379
Fleming, D., 127
Fleming, M., 342, 344
Fletcher, R., 26, 46, 47, 341, 353,
    377, 378
Flint, A. S., 19
Flood, J., 215
Flower, L., 84
Foss, A., 18
Fountas, I. C., 76, 291
Fox, M., 214
Frank, A., 17, 180
Fraustino, L. R., 191
Fredericks, A. D., 294
Freebody, P., 18
Freedle, R. O., 320
Freeman, E. B., 317
Freire, P., 17
French, M. P., 169
Freppon, P. A., 126
Frey, N., 215
Furgerson, P., 134

Galda, L., 297
Galdone, P., 127, 129–130, 208,
    284, 293
Gallagher, M., 84
Gambrell, L. B., 28
Gamoran, A., 244
Gantos, J., 287–288, 289
Garan, E., 30
Gardiner, J. R., 37, 279, 280
Gardner, H., 80
Geller, L. G., 357, 358, 360
Gentry, J. R., 406, 418
George, J. C., 282
George, K. O., 380
George, R., 265
Gibbons, G., 320
Gibbons, P., 223, 251

Gill, R. S., 55
Gillet, J. W., 47, 84, 86, 418
Gillon, G. T., 120
Giovanni, N., 18, 236
Giroux, H., 17
Glover, M. K., 356
Goble, P., 289
Golden, J. M., 277
Goldenberg, C., 249
Gollub, M., 380
Goodman, Y. M., 52, 54
Grandits, J., 378
Graves, D. H., 25, 47, 55, 60, 84, 86,
    91, 95, 356, 386, 396
Graves, M. F., 150, 162, 163, 164
Gregory, K., 192
Greisman, J., 155
Grierson, S. T., 337
Griffin, P., 112
Griffith, F., 119
Griffith, P. L., 120
Gwynne, F., 157

Hale, S., 72, 248, 289
Hall, N., 198
Halliday, M. A. K., 9
Hamilton, V., 289
Hanauer, D. I., 364
Hancock, M. R., 186, 297
Hanna, J. S., 117
Hanna, P. R., 117
Hansen, J., 95
Harris, T., 128
Harste, J., 25, 114, 285, 338
Hartman, A., 90
Harvey, S., 323, 326, 335
Hayes, J. R., 84
Heard, G., 384
Heath, S. B., 113, 244
Heathcote, D., 263–264
Heck, M. J., 244
Heffernan, L., 47
Heide, A., 25
Heimlich, J. E., 169
Heller, R., 168
Helman, L., 407
Hendershot, J., 317
Henderson, E. H., 400
Henkes, K., 248, 286, 293
Herrera, J. F., 368
Hesse, K., 248, 294
Hiaasen, C., 236
Hickman, J., 298
Hiebert, E. H., 52
Hill, B. C., 44

Hires, D., 326
Hodges, M., 289
Hodges, R. E., 117
Hofmeyr, D., 289
Holbrook, S., 357
Holdaway, D., 75, 126, 128
Hook, J. N., 148
Hoonan, B. T., 338
Horn, E., 408, 419
Howe, D., 287, 290
Howe, J., 287, 290
Hoyt, L., 298
Hughes, C., 120
Hughes, M., 408
Hurd, T., 297
Hutchins, P., 121, 129
Hyman, T. S., 289
Hymes, D., 30

Inches, A., 119
Inhelder, B., 6
International Reading Association, 112
Invernizzi, M., 114, 167, 397–398, 399n, 407
Irwin, J. W., 83
Irwin-Devitis, L., 326
Ivey, G., 214

Jackson, S. A. W., 264
Janeczko, P. B., 353, 372, 377, 378, 381, 382
Jepsen, M., 295
Jiménez, F., 318
Johnson, M. J., 134
Johnson, N. J., 44
Johnson, T. D., 279, 419
Johnston, F., 167, 397–398, 399n, 407
Jorgensen, K., 308
Juel, C., 126

Kalan, R., 127
Kame'enui, E. J., 172
Kamma, A., 318
Karelitz, E. B., 95
Karnowski, L., 287
Kasza, K., 139
Katz, A., 369
Kaufman, D., 244, 246
Kays, J., 288
Keehn, S., 249
Kellogg, S., 289
Kennedy, X. J., 381
Kimmel, E. A., 289
King, M. L., Jr., 17, 345, 346
King-Smith, D., 290, 318

Kirschner, B. W., 322
Klesius, J. P., 120
Koch, K., 362, 373, 374, 375, 376, 382, 383
Kraft, B. H., 342
Krashen, S., 294, 295, 297
Kristo, J. V., 317, 320, 323, 335, 336
Kucan, L., 145, 163, 165
Kutiper, K., 363

Lacey, C., 412
Lane, B., 90
Langer, J. A., 86
Langford, K. G., 419
Langstaff, J., 359
Lapp, D., 215
Larios, J., 375
Lasky, K., 342
Lasse, L., 58
Lear, E., 363, 381
Lehr, S. S., 284
L'Engle, M., 36, 282
Lewis, C. S., 188, 190, 289
Lewis, S., 277
Lewison, M., 19
Lindquist, T., 47
Lionni, L., 315
Lippert, M. H., 289
Lippman, D. N., 163
Lively, T. J., 163
Livingston, M. C., 381
Loban, W., 26
Lobel, A., 265, 361
Logan, C., 318
Lomax, R. G., 120
Longfellow, H. W., 345, 363
Louis, D. R., 279
Lowry, L., 60, 74, 188, 189, 270–273, 283, 284, 289, 294, 318, 376, 383, 384
Luke, A., 18
Lukens, R. J., 277, 282, 284, 288
Lundsteen, S. W., 220, 234
Luongo-Orlando, K., 43
Lutz, W., 221, 234
Lyon, G. R., 30

Macaulay, D., 142, 318
MacDonald, R., 362
Macedo, D., 17
MacLachlan, P., 37, 201, 289, 290
Macon, J. M., 188
Mapleton Teacher-Research Group, 406
Martens, P., 64
Martin, B., Jr., 47, 127, 297

Martin, N., 86
Martinez, M. G., 218, 248
Mazzoni, S. A., 28
McCarthy, M., 226
McCloskey, R., 282
McElligott, M., 297
McGee, L. M., 117, 120, 182
McGinnis, J., 342, 344
McGlaughlin, B., 163
McKenna, M., 298, 302
McKeon, C. A., 200
McKeon, D., 14, 276
McKeown, M. G., 145, 163, 165
McLellan, J., 43
McLeod, A., 86
McMackin, M. C., 326, 338
Meddaugh, S., 284, 293
Medvic, E. F., 76, 126
Meiners, A., 277
Merriam, E., 364
Meyer, B. J., 320
Miller, P. H., 6, 7
Miller, S. A., 6, 7
Mills, H., 124
Milne, A. A., 363
Moats, L., 112
Mohan, L., 23
Moline, S., 25, 48, 326
Montenegro, L. N., 353
Moore, C. C., 363
Moorman, G. B., 74
Morgan, K., 84
Morris, A., 208
Morrison, T., 225
Morrow, L. M., 6, 8, 112
Moses, A. M., 113, 115
Moss, B., 317
Moss, L., 168
Moss, M., 195
Most, B., 119
Muhammad, R. J., 7
Murray, D. H., 84

Nagda, A. W., 202
Nagy, W. E., 12
Nash, M. F., 185
Natarella, M. A., 363
Nathenson-Mejia, S., 11, 55
National Association for the Education of Young Children, 112
National Communication Association, 220
National Council of Teachers of English (NCTE), 18–19, 216, 439
National Reading Panel, 30, 82, 112

Naylor, P. R., 37, 38, 59, 284
NCTE Elementary Section Steering Committee, 18–19
Neeld, E. C., 329
Nelson, R., 312–313
Noble, T. H., 306
Noe, K. L. S., 44
Novinger, S., 30
Numeroff, L. J., 108, 109, 110, 305
Nye, N. S., 368
Nystrand, M., 244

Ogle, D. M., 253
Ohlhausen, M. M., 295
O'Keefe, T., 124
Oldfather, P., 23
Olson, M., 119
O'Malley, J. M., 298
O'Neill, M., 375
Opie, I., 358
Opie, P., 358
Opitz, M. F., 77, 220, 222
Osborne, M. P., 318, 319

Palmer, R. G., 317
Papandropoulou, I., 114
Pardo, L. W., 84
Paris, S. G., 24, 27
Park, L. S., 289
Paterson, K., 176–179, 282
Paulsen, G., 289, 318, 378
Paye, W., 289
Pearson, P. D., 84, 102
Peregoy, S. F., 163, 197, 276, 327, 374
Perfitti, C., 120
Perl, S., 84
Perry, N., 338
Peterson, R., 78, 79, 246
Pfeffinger, C. R., 294
Pfister, M., 313
Piaget, J., 6
Pierce, L. V., 298
Pilgreen, J., 296
Pinkney, J., 127, 208, 278, 283, 284, 289
Pinnell, G. S., 76, 291
Pittelman, S. D., 169
Platt, R., 142
Poe, E. A., 362
Portalupi, J., 26, 46, 47, 341
Porter, C., 56, 60
Potter, B., 277
Prater, K., 294
Prelutsky, J., 352–353, 363, 365–366, 373, 384

Pressley, M., 23, 84
Provensen, A., 345
Pulver, R., 101
Purcell-Gates, V., 288

Quorn, K. C., 419

Raphael, L. M., 23
Raphael, T. E., 14, 322
Rappaport, D., 342
Rasinski, T. V., 82
Rathmann, P., 377, 379
Read, C., 397
Read, S., 317
Readence, J. E., 224, 263
Reutzel, D. R., 129
Reyes, M. de la Luz, 185
Rhodes, L. K., 55
Richgels, D. J., 117, 182, 323
Rico, G. L., 326
Rief, L., 47
Robb, L., 317, 323
Robinson, A., 198
Roehrig, A. D., 23
Rogovin, P., 326
Romano, T., 337
Roop, P., 201
Rosen, H., 86
Rosenblatt, L. M., 25, 72, 78, 213, 222, 317
Roser, N. L., 218, 248, 249
Rossetti, C., 363
Rothenberg, C., 223, 251
Routman, R., 91
Rowling, J. K., 37, 289, 308
Rubin, S. G., 318
Rudorf, E. H., 117
Rumelhart, D., 277
Ryan, P. M., 97
Rymer, R., 406

Sachar, L., 35–36, 100, 263
Samway, K. D., 14, 47, 276
Sandburg, C., 363
Scala, M. C., 360
Schickedanz, J. A., 132
Schneider, J. J., 264
Schroder, V. C., 360
Schulze, A. C., 104, 131
Schwartz, A., 119
Schwartz, D. M., 129
Schwartz, R. M., 291
Scieszka, J., 236, 284
Searle, D., 408
Seidler, A., 119

Selwyn, D., 47
Sendak, M., 2, 376
Service, P., 289
Seuss, Dr., 127, 315, 361
Shakespeare, W., 148, 383
Shanahan, T., 30, 104
Shefelbine, J., 120, 126
Shepard, A., 289
Short, K. G., 285
Sidman, J., 363, 369, 370, 378
Siegel, B. S., 326, 338
Siemens, L., 357
Silverstein, S., 363, 369, 370
Simon, S., 318
Sinclair, H., 114
Skillings, M. J., 60
Slepian, J., 119
Sly, A., 225
Smith, F., 91
Smith, K., 280
Snow, C. E., 13, 83, 112, 163
Sobel, J., 128
Soffos, C., 28–29
Sommers, N., 87
Sopko, D., 318
Sorenson, M., 249
Soto, G., 240, 244, 368
Sowell, J., 152
Spandel, V., 97, 100
Speare, E. G., 38, 282, 306
Spiegel, D. L., 43, 298
Spinelli, J., 37
Stahl, S., 12, 83, 298, 302
Stanovich, K. E., 112
Stauffer, R. G., 130
Stave, A. M., 294
Stead, T., 317, 326
Steig, J., 289
Steig, W., 235, 284, 289
Stephens, D., 124
Stevens, J., 101, 208–212, 222
Stevenson, V., 146
Stewart, R. A., 317
Stilborne, L., 25
Sulzby, E., 112, 114
Sumara, D., 20, 22
Sweet, A. P., 83
Swift, K., 44

Taback, S., 129
Tabors, P. O., 215
Taylor, D., 76, 113
Teale, W. H., 112
Templeton, S., 113, 167, 397–398, 399n, 401, 407

Terban, M., 160, 168
Terry, A., 363
Tiedt, I., 380
Tierney, R. J., 52, 102, 104, 263
Tomlinson, C. A., 49
Tompkins, G. E., 127, 134, 146, 161
Towle, W., 44
Tracey, D. H., 6, 8
Trachtenburg, R., 128
Trapani, I., 128
Treiman, R., 123
Trelease, J., 214, 216, 222
Turbill, J., 22n, 102, 406
Turner, A., 202
Turner, J. C., 24

Valencia, R. R., 31
Valencia, S. W., 52
Van Allsburg, C., 154, 155, 289, 361
Van Gogh, V., 180
Van Sluys, K., 19
Venezky, R. L., 117
Villarreal, B. J., 31
Vinci, Leonardo da, 179
Viorst, J., 306
Vogt, M. E., 188
Von Sprecken, D., 297
Vukelich, C., 113
Vygotsky, L. S., 8, 167

Wagner, B. J., 263–264
Walker, L., 20, 22
Wasik, B. A., 24
Watson, K., 250, 253
Weaver, C., 91
Webeler, M. B., 127
Weinhold, K., 84
Wells, D., 247
Wells, G., 20
Whaley, S., 251
Whatley, A., 20
Whelan, G., 18
White, C. E., 163
White, E. B., 283, 285, 289
White, T. G., 152
White, Z., 90
Whitin, P. E., 24, 285, 286
Wiesner, D., 248
Wilde, S., 413, 418
Williams, C., 406
Williams, S., 127
Williams, T. L., 25
Williams, W. C., 363, 382
Wilson, L., 379
Wilson, P., 64, 363
Wink, J., 17
Witte, S., 90
Wittels, H., 155
Wittrock, M. C., 249

Wolk, S., 18
Wolvin, A. D., 213
Wong, J. S., 353
Wong-Fillmore, L., 13
Wood, A., 129, 161
Wood, J. R., 366
Wood, K. D., 74
Woodson, J., 289, 353
Woodward, V. A., 114
Worthy, J., 294
Wright, J. W., 13
Wylie, R. E., 123

Yaden, D. B., Jr., 79, 113, 146, 161, 218
Yanagihara, A., 152
Yolen, J., 289
Yopp, H. K., 119, 120, 121, 228, 322
Yopp, R. H., 228, 322
Yorinks, A., 257, 300
Young, B., 250, 253
Young, E., 303

Zamowski, M., 344
Zbaracki, M. D., 220, 222
Zebroski, J. T., 8
Zielonka, P., 120

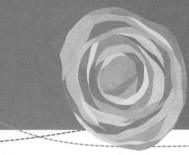

SUBJECT INDEX

Absolutely Not! (McElligott), 297
Abuela (Dorros), 284
Academic language
   developing, 16, 254–255
   minilessons and, 254–255
   sentence structure in, 14
   social language vs., 13, 14
   vocabulary used in, 14
Accommodation, 6
*Achoo! Bang! Crash! The Noisy
   Alphabet* (MacDonald), 362
Acrostic poems, 364, 377
Action, as narrative lead, 38
Adjectives, 431, 433, 442, 444
Adverbs, 433, 443, 444
Advertising
   creating, 236
   critical listening to, 231, 234
Aesop's Fables (Pinkney), 289
Aesthetic appreciation, of competent
   language users, 19
Aesthetic listening, 213–222
   assessing, 222
   interactive read-alouds and, 214–219
   minilesson on, 222
   responding to stories and, 219
   strategies for, 220, 222
   teaching, 220, 222
   viewing videos and, 220, 221
   what children need to learn
     about, 232
Aesthetic reading, 72
Affixes
   defined, 150
   root words and, 150–154, 409, 415
   spelling and, 398–399, 400–401,
     402, 409, 415
   with words with multiple
     meanings, 158
African Americans, growth of
   population of, 14
*Alexander and the Terrible, Horrible,
   No Good, Very Bad Day*
   (Viorst), 306

*Aliens Are Coming! The True Account
   of the 1938 War of the Worlds
   Radio Broadcast* (McCarthy), 226
Alignment, in handwriting, 456
"All about . . ." books, 330–332
"All about Me" books, 344
Alliteration, 361, 362
Alphabet, concepts about, 115–119
Alphabet books, 118, 319
Alphabetic principle, 116–117,
   399, 400
Amber Brown Goes Fourth (Danziger),
   68–70
Amber Brown Is Not a Crayon
   (Danziger), 250, 288, 294
Amelia's Notebook (Moss), 195
America: A Patriotic Primer
   (Cheney), 318
Analysis
   in cubing, 329, 339
   semantic feature, 165, 169, 170
   of spelling development, 401–406
   story, 272
Anastasia Krupnik (Lowry), 383, 384
Ancient Greece and the Olympics
   (Osborne), 319
Anecdotal notes, 54–55
Anglo-Saxons, 146–147, 161
Anne Frank: The Diary of a Young Girl
   (Frank), 17
Anticipation guides, 224, 225, 495
Antonyms, 154–155
Apologies, 382
Apostrophes, 436
Appearance, of characters, 281
Applying, in reading process, 73, 80,
   81, 83, 103, 110, 470
Argumentation, 329
Art center, 463
Artist, 478
Asian Americans, growth of population
   of, 14
Assessment, 52–64
   of aesthetic listening, 222

   authentic, 39, 52, 53
   of community of learners, 22
   of critical listening, 237
   of efferent listening, 230–231
   evaluation vs., 64
   grades and, 60–64
   guidelines for, 53
   integrating with instruction, 53
   of journal entries, 196
   of letter writing, 203, 206
   of life stories, 347–348
   of literature circles, 477, 479, 480
   monitoring and, 52–56
   plan for, 470–471
   of poetry, 386–387
   portfolios for, 56–60
   of progress in spelling, 423–424
   purposes of, 52
   in reading workshops, 482, 484
   of reports, 63, 260, 341
   rubrics and, 60, 62–64
   self-assessment, 52, 53, 59, 260
   of story retelling, 302
   of students' experiences with
     poems, 371
   of students' knowledge about
     grammar, 446
   of students' stories, 308
   tests and, 64. *See also* Testing
   in thematic units, 491, 493
   tools for, 53
   of vocabulary knowledge,
     173–174
   weaving into practice, 54
   in writing workshops, 486, 489
Assessment conferences, 56
Assignment checklists, 60, 61, 471,
   473, 493
Assimilation, 6, 14
Association, 329
Audience
   of letter writing, 196, 198
   sense of, 86
   of writing, 86, 95

Authentic assessment, 39
  guidelines for, 53
  purposes of, 52
Author(s)
  examining craft of, 79
  letters to, 200–201
Author's chair, 38, 47, 95
Autobiographies, 342, 343–344,
  347–348

Babe the Gallant Pig (King-Smith), 290
Backdrop settings, 282
Background knowledge
  activating, 26, 27, 73–74, 224
  of English learners, 51, 223
  expanding, 223
  responding to stories and, 297
  socioeconomic status and, 145–146
Ballad of Lucy Whipple, The
  (Cushman), 286, 287
Bandwagon effect, 234, 235
Barnyard Banter (Fleming), 127
Basic Interpersonal Conversational
  Skills (BICS), 15. *See also* Social
  language
Beautiful Blackbird (Bryan), 289
Beginning reading, 126
Beginning writing, 132
*Behind the Mask: A Book of
  Prepositions* (Heller), 442
BFG, The (Dahl), 37
Bibliography, 339
Big books, 128–129
Big Talk: Poems for Four Voices
  (Fleischman), 379
Biographical sketch, 339
Biographies, 342, 343, 344–348
Biography boxes, 345
Biography posters, 345, 346
BISC. *See* Basic Interpersonal
  Conversational Skills (BICS)
Blending, 26, 27
Blue and the Gray, The (Bunting), 322
Book(s)
  "All about . . . ," 330–332
  "All about Me," 344
  alphabet, 118, 319
  benefits of rereading, 218
  big, 128–129
  blended story/informational, 319
  choosing to read aloud, 216–218,
    482, 483
  concept, 319, 438, 441–442, 444
  in developing a literature focus unit,
    468, 469, 473

easy-to-read, 242
encouraging critical listening
  with, 238
about history of English, 149
including letters, 203
informational, 225–227, 317–325
of life stories, 343
for literature circles, 475, 477
for literature focus units, 42
multigenre, 318
of poetry, 363, 365, 385
predictable, 126–128
question-and-answer, 319
for reading workshop, 481,
  482, 483
reference, 156, 319, 409, 414–415
sparking debates with, 262
with stories exemplifying story
  elements, 279
teaching critical listening with,
  236–237
trade, 236–237
traveling bags of, 129–130
ways to involve students with,
  215–216, 217
in which characters and historical
  personalities keep journals,
  195–196
about words, 168, 171, 358
Book discussion conferences, 56, 288
Book groups. *See* Literature circles
Book-making center, 314, 315, 484
Borrowed words, 161–162
Bound morphemes, 10, 12
Boy Who Drew Cats, The (Hodges),
  289
Brain, 6
Brainstorming, 273
  exclusion, 495
  as language arts strategy, 26, 27
  for projects during thematic units,
    492–493
Bread, Bread, Bread (Morris), 208
Breadwinner, The (Ellis), 18, 38
Breaking Through (Jiménez), 318
Bridge to Terabithia (Paterson), 282
*Brown Bear, Brown Bear, What Do You
  See?* (Martin), 47, 442
Buddy journals, 197
Buddy reading, 74, 75, 76–77
  with cross-age reading buddies,
    129
  of dialogue journals, 185
Bunnicula: A Rabbit-Tale of Mystery
  (Howe & Howe), 287, 290

Business letters, 199, 201
*Busy Buzzing Bumblebees and Other
  Tongue Twisters* (Schwartz), 119

*Cache of Jewels and Other Collective
  Nouns, A* (Heller), 168
CALP. *See* Cognitive Academic
  Language Proficiency (CALP)
Can You Imagine (McKissack), 485
Capitalization, 432, 435
  in effective writing, 101
  syntactic system and, 11
Card(s)
  for making sentences, 427–429
  word, 166
Card stacking, 235
Cartoons, 339
Castle (Macaulay), 142
*Castle Diary: The Journal of Tobias
  Burgess* (Platt), 142
Category systems, 6
Catherine, Called Birdy (Cushman),
  100, 142, 191, 195, 280–281, 290
Catherine: The Great Journey
  (Gregory), 192
Cat's Meow, The (Soto), 240–244
Cause and effect, 228, 320–321, 322
Centers
  for emergent literacy, 109, 111
  for English learners, 51
  for informational reading and
    writing, 314–315
  for learning, 435
  for literacy play, 114–115, 116
  setting up, 49
  types of, 111, 116, 314–315
  for unit-related activities,
    463–466
Centers assessment booklet, 472
Character(s)
  actions of, 281
  appeal to, 231
  appearance of, 281
  dialogue of, 281
  in stories, 272, 280–282
  talking back to, 219
Character sketch, 430
Character traits, 281, 282
Charlie and the Chocolate Factory
  (Dahl), 265
Charlotte's Web (White), 283, 285,
  289, 445–446
Charts
  comparison, 384
  data, 325, 339, 465

K-W-L, 253–254, 255, 258, 313, 314, 316, 462
T-charts, 228, 322
Checklists
for assessing manuscript handwriting, 457, 458
for assessing pen pal letters, 206
assignment, 60, 61, 471, 473, 493
for editing, 92, 93
for monitoring, 55–56
Chicka Chicka Boom Boom (Martin & Archambault), 297
Chimps Don't Wear Glasses (Numeroff), 443
Chocolate Moose for Dinner, A (Gwynne), 157
Choice(s)
in community of learners, 21–22
differentiating instruction and, 49
Choral reading, 368, 372
Chrysanthemum (Henkes), 248, 286, 293, 439
Cinquain, 380
Circle diagram, 305
Circuit, The (Jiménez), 318
Clara Caterpillar (Edwards), 100
Classroom communities. *See* Community of learners
Classroom observations, 52, 54
Clauses
dependent, 429
independent, 434
Clerihews, 382
Click, Clack, Moo: Cows That Type (Cronin), 129
Clues, 230, 233
Cluster diagram, 229, 322, 326, 328–329, 339, 474, 496
Coaching, 29
Cock-a-Doodle-Moo! (Most), 119
Cognates, 163
Cognitive Academic Language Proficiency (CALP), 15
Cognitive structure, 6
Collaborative exploration, 19
Collaborative poems, 385
Collaborative reports, 333–334, 335
Colon, 436
Color poems, 375
"Come Unto These Yellow Sands" (Koch), 383
Comma, 436
Commander Toad (Yolen), 289
Commercials
creating, 236

critical listening to, 231, 234
Communication, creative, 19
Communicator, teacher as, 50
Community of learners. *See also* Students
characteristics of, 20, 21–22
creating, 20–22
for English learners, 51
Comparison, 228, 290, 320, 321, 322, 329, 360–361
Comparison chart, 384
Comparison poems, 376
Competent language users, characteristics of, 19–20
Complex sentences, 429
Compliments, in writing groups, 88, 89
Compound-complex sentence, 434, 439, 441
Compound predicates, 429
Compound sentences, 429, 434
Comprehension
facilitating, 271
reading process and, 83–84
Comprehension center, 111
Comprehension skills, 28, 29
Computer center, 464
Concept books, 319, 438, 441–442, 444
Concept entries, 188
Concrete poems, 363, 364, 377–378
Conferences
for monitoring, 55, 56
for reading workshops, 482, 484
about story structure, 288
types of, 56
with writing groups, 90–91
for writing workshops, 486, 488
Conflict
between characters, 37
within characters, 35
in small-group conversations, 245
in stories, 277
Conjunctions, 433, 444
Connecting
as aesthetic listening strategy, 222
as language arts strategy, 26, 27
Connector, 45, 478
Consonant(s), 122
Consonant blends, 122
Consonant digraphs, 122
Constructivist theory, 6
Contemporary stories, 287–288, 289
Conventions
dramatic, 267
in writing, 101

Conversations, 244–250
beginning, 244–245
grand. *See* Grand conversations
instructional, 249–250, 256
small-group, 244–246
sustaining, 256–257
Cook-a-Doodle-Doo! (Stevens & Crummel), 208–212, 222
Cool Melons—Turn to Frogs (Gollub), 380
Coordinator, teacher as, 50
Courtesy letters, 198
Creative communication, by competent language users, 19
Crispin: The Cross of Lead (Avi), 287, 297
Critical listening, 213, 214, 231–238
assessing, 237
books that encourage, 238
to persuasion and propaganda, 231, 234, 235
strategies for, 234
teaching, 235–237
what children need to learn about, 232
Critical literacy, 16–18
Critical pedagogy theory, 17
Critical questions, 252
Critiquing, 219
Cross-age reading buddies, 129
Cubing, 326, 329–330, 339
Cue, 230
Cueing systems. *See* Language systems
Cultural diversity
dialects and, 13
of English learners, 14–16
language learning and, 9–18
among students, 13–16
Cultural pluralism, 14
Cumulative reading, 368
Cumulative sequence, 127, 128
Cup puppets, 266
Cursive handwriting, 447, 449, 451–452, 453
CVCe pattern rule, 124, 125
CVC pattern rule, 124, 125
Cylinder puppets, 266

Data charts, 325, 339, 465
Day Jimmy's Boa Ate the Wash, The (Noble), 306
Dear Mr. Henshaw (Cleary), 200
DEAR (Drop Everything and Read) time, 76, 296
Dear Whiskers (Nagda), 202

Debates, 261–262
Deceptive language, 234, 236
Declarative sentence, 434
Demographic changes in population, 14
Demonstrations, to community of
    learners, 21
Dependent clause, 429
Derivational relations spelling, 399,
    401, 402
Description, 228, 320, 321, 322, 329
Diagnostician, teacher as, 50
Diagrams
    circle, 305
    cluster, 229, 322, 326, 328–329,
        339, 474, 496
    of story structure, 276
    Venn, 228, 273, 322, 339
    in visual reports, 326
Dialects, 13, 431, 436
Dialogue
    character development and, 281
    as narrative lead, 38
Dialogue journals, 181, 184–185
Diamante, 380–381
Dictation, from children, 131, 312,
    332, 414
Dictionaries, 155, 163, 165
    list of, 156
    in spelling program, 409, 414–415
Diphthongs, 123, 392, 400
Direct instruction, 49, 164
Discriminative listening, 213, 214
Discussion director, 45
Disequilibrium, 6–7
Distance, from writing, 91
Diversity. *See* Cultural diversity
D'Nealian handwriting, 447–448, 450
Doctor De Soto (Steig), 284
Dogs Don't Wear Sneakers
    (Numeroff), 443
Don't Forget the Bacon!
    (Hutchins), 121
Double-entry journals, 181, 188, 190
Double negatives, 437
Doublespeak, 234
Double subjects, 437
Draft(s)
    of poem, 355
    rereading, 88
Drafting
    for English learners, 94
    in writing process, 85, 86–87, 103
Drama, 262–268
    improvisation, 263
    playing with puppets, 265, 266

process, 263–264
    theatrical productions, 265–268
Dramatic conventions, 267
Dramatizing
    in literature focus units, 263
    stories, 219
    words, 167
Drop Everything and Read (DEAR)
    time, 76, 296
Dry-erase boards, 118

*Eating the Alphabet: Fruits and
    Vegetables from A to Z* (Ehlert), 129
Echo reading, 368
Editing
    checklist for, 92, 93
    for English learners, 94
    in writing process, 85, 91–93,
        94, 103
Editing conferences, 56
Efferent listening, 213, 214, 222–231
    assessing, 230–231
    minilesson on, 230
    strategies for, 228–230
    teaching, 227–230
    techniques for improving, 223–225
    what children need to learn
        about, 232
Efferent reading, 72
Elaborating, 7
E-mail messages, 200
Emergent literacy, 108–139
    age of, 111–112
    centers for, 109, 111
    defined, 126
    emergent writing and, 131–138
    minilessons for, 137, 139
    phonemic awareness and, 109,
        119–120
    phonics and, 109, 119, 120–126
    predictable books and, 126–128
    shared reading and, 126–130
    teacher support for, 109
    what students need to learn
        about, 138
Emergent spelling, 398, 399–400, 402
Emergent writing, 131–138
Emotional appeals, 231
Empty Pot, The (Demi), 263
Engagement, for community of
    learners, 21
English
    history of, 146–149
    as language source of words, 143,
        150, 151

Middle, 147–148
    Modern, 148
    nonstandard, 13, 16, 436
    Old, 146–147, 154, 157
    Standard, 13, 16–17, 436
    two types of proficiency in, 15
English learners, 14–16
    adapting instruction for, 51, 94
    developing vocabularies of,
        162–163
    extensive reading and, 276
    grammar of, 197
    importance of listening for, 223
    journals and, 185, 197
    poetry and, 374
    scaffolding knowledge of stories, 276
    spelling of, 197
    supporting language development
        of, 16
    talk as learning tool, 251
    teaching grammar to, 440
    teaching spelling to, 407–408
    types of English proficiency of, 15
    writing as learning tool of, 327
Environmental print, 114, 117, 118
Equilibration, 6–7
Equilibrium, 7
Errors
    correcting, 91–92, 93
    grammar, 440
    spelling, 404, 406
Esperanza Rising (Ryan), 97
Etymology, 149. *See also* Word history
Euphemisms, 234
Evaluating
    assessing vs., 64
    in inquiry process, 338
    as language arts strategy, 26, 27
Evaluator, teacher as, 50
Everyday language. *See* Social language
Exclamation point, 436
Exclamatory sentence, 434
Explicit theme, 285
Exploring
    emergent literacy and, 109
    in reading process, 73, 79, 83, 103,
        109, 110, 470
    using word walls for, 166
Expository text structures, 228,
    320–322, 323–325
Expressive reading, 364–365, 372, 373

Fables, 287, 289
Facilitator, teacher as, 50
Fading, 29

Fairy tales, 287, 289
Fantasies, 287, 289
Fantastic Fact Finder, 478
Fiction. *See* Stories
Fiction workshop, 308
Figurative language, 158–161,
  352–353
Finger puppets, 266
Firetalking (Polacco), 485
First-person viewpoint, 284
First Thesaurus, A (Wittels &
  Greisman), 155
Fish: Pet Care Guides for Kids (Evans &
  Caras), 313
Fish Eyes: A Book You Can Count On
  (Ehlert), 314
Fish Is Fish (Lionni), 315
Five-senses poems, 375–376
*5,000-Year-Old Puzzle: Solving a
  Mystery of Ancient Egypt*
  (Logan), 318
Flotsam (Wiesner), 248
Fluency
  reading process and, 82
  of sentences, 100–101
Fluent reading, 82, 126
Fluent writing, 132
Flush (Hiaasen), 236
"Fog" (Sandburg), 363
Folders. *See* Work folders
Fold Me a Poem (George), 380
Folklore, 287, 289
Formula poems, 372–377
Found poems, 179, 339, 378–379
Free-form poems, 377–379, 383
Free morphemes, 10, 12
Free verse, 363
Free voluntary reading (FVR), 294–295
French, as language source of words,
  143, 158
Friendly letters, 198–201
Friendship themes, 285
Frog and Toad Are Friends (Lobel), 265
Frog and Toad Together (Lobel), 265
From Paper Airplanes to Outer Space
  (Simon), 485
FVR (free voluntary reading), 294–295

Gallery walks, 387
Gender differences, 17
Genres
  multigenre biographies, 347, 348
  multigenre informational books, 318
  of stories, 287–288, 289, 306–307
  writing, 86, 87

Germanic languages, as language
  source of words, 147
Gift from Zeus: Sixteen Favorite Myths
  (Steig), 289
Gingerbread Baby (Brett), 129, 130, 289
Gingerbread Boy, The (Galdone), 127,
  129–130
Girl Who Spun Gold, The
  (Hamilton), 289
Giver, The (Lowry), 74, 188, 189, 284,
  289, 294, 439, 443, 471, 473,
  475, 476
Glittering generality, 235
Goldilocks strategy, 295, 296
Grading, 60–64
  of journal entries, 196
  reading logs and, 179
Grading sheets, 61, 356, 480
Graffiti, 339
Grammar, 426–446
  assessing students' knowledge
    about, 446
  concepts of, 431–436, 440
  defined, 11
  in effective writing, 101
  of English learners, 197
  errors in, 440
  guidelines for teaching, 438
  minilessons on, 438, 440, 446
  parts of speech and, 431–433,
    441–442
  purpose of instruction on, 430–431
  reasons for teaching, 17, 437, 439
  syntactic system and, 11
  teaching, 431, 432, 436–446
  what children need to learn
    about, 454
Grammar posters, 438
Grammar word sort, 428
Grand conversations, 69, 78–79, 109,
  246–249, 256
  benefits of, 248–249
  defined, 246
  in literature circles, 248, 477, 479
  parts of, 246–247
  reading stories and, 271–273
  steps in, 247
  traditional discussions vs., 246
Granny Torrelli Makes Soup (Creech),
  68, 69
Graphemes, 9, 10, 11, 116–117
Graphic organizers, 224, 226, 228,
  276, 322, 495
Great Gilly Hopkins, The (Paterson),
  176–179

Greek, as language source of words,
  143, 146, 148, 150, 151, 161
Grocery store center, 115, 116
Guided reading, 74, 75, 76, 77,
  291, 294

Haiku, 363, 364, 371, 380
Hailstones and Halibut (O'Neill), 375
Hairdresser center, 116
*Hairy, Scary, Ordinary: What Is an
  Adjective?* (Cleary), 441
Handwriting, 431, 447–460
  correcting problems in, 457
  cursive, 447, 449, 451–452, 453
  development of, 449–452, 453
  D'Nealian, 447–448, 450
  elements of legibility of, 452, 456
  formal instruction in, 451–452
  forms of, 447–449
  illegible, 447
  keyboarding as alternative to,
    458–460
  of left-handed writers, 456–457
  manuscript, 447, 448, 451, 457, 458
  minilessons on, 455, 456
  teaching, 452–457
  what children need to learn
    about, 454
*Harry Potter and the Chamber of
  Secrets* (Rowling), 289
Harry Potter and the Goblet of Fire
  (Rowling), 37
Hatchet (Paulsen), 289, 378–379
Head, Body, Legs: A Story from Liberia
  (Paye & Lippert), 289
Hey, Al (Yorinks), 257, 300
High-frequency words, 3, 109, 111,
  404, 408, 410–411
High point, of story, 278–279
High-stakes testing, preparing students
  for, 30, 31
High-utility phonics concepts,
  123–124, 126
Hink-pinks, 360
Hispanic Americans, 14, 15
Historical fiction, 287, 289
Holes (Sachar), 35–36, 100, 263
Homeless Bird (Whelan), 18
Homograph(s), 157
Homographic homophones, 157
Homonyms, 156–157, 397
Homophones, 156–157, 392, 398
Hop on Pop (Seuss), 127
Hot seat, 259, 261
Hour of the Olympics (Osborne), 318

Housekeeping center, 115
How Much Is a Million? (Schwartz), 129
"How to Eat a Poem" (Merriam), 364
"Hug O' War" (Silverstein), 369, 370
Hungry Thing, The (Slepian & Seidler), 119
Hurricanes (Simon), 318
Hyperbole, 289, 290

I, Doko: The Tale of a Basket (Young), 303
I Am Phoenix: Poems for Two Voices (Fleischman), 379
"I Am . . . " poems, 376
Ideas
    effective writing and, 97, 101
    of English learners, 197
    gathering and organizing, 86
    identifying, 26, 27
    vocabulary and, 197
Idiom(s), 158–160
Idiom poster, 160
"If I Were . . . " poems, 376
If You Give a Mouse a Cookie (Numeroff), 108–110, 305
If You Give a Mouse a Muffin (Numeroff), 108, 110
If You Give an Author a Pencil (Numeroff), 485
If You Give a Pig a Pancake (Numeroff), 108
. . . If You Lived When There Was Slavery in America (Kamma), 318
If You Take a Mouse to School (Numeroff), 108
If You Take a Mouse to the Movies (Numeroff), 108
Illustrator, 45, 200–201
Imagery, 288, 290
Immersion responses, 186, 187
Immigrants. *See* Cultural diversity
Imperative sentence, 434
Implicit theme, 285
Important Book, The (Brown), 47
Improvisation, 263
In a Pickle and Other Funny Idioms (Terban), 160
Independent clause, 434
Independent reading, 74, 75, 76, 77, 294–297, 354
Indirect instruction, 49, 164
Individual reports, 334–337
Inferencing, 26, 27
Inferential questions, 252
Inflated language, 234

Inflections, 148
Informational books, 317–325
    expository text structures of, 228, 320–322, 323–325
    how to read, 323
    minilessons on, 325, 341
    multigenre, 318
    reading aloud, 225–227
    reasons for using, 320
    stories vs., 318–320
    teaching students about, 322–325
    types of, 317–320
    what students need to learn about, 324
Informational reading
    autobiographies, 342, 343–344, 347–348
    biographies, 342, 343, 344–348
    centers for, 314–315
    example of, 312–316
    how to read, 323
    for kindergartners, 313
Informational writing, 87. *See also* Report(s)
    autobiographies, 343–344
    biographies, 344–348
    centers for, 314–315
    for kindergartners, 313
    life stories, 341–348
Information-processing theory, 6, 7
Initiate-Response-Feedback (IRF) cycle, 253
Innovations on text, 305–306
Inquiry process, 338, 340
Instruction
    adapting for English learners, 51
    differentiating, 49, 51
    direct, 49, 164
    indirect, 49, 164
    integrating with assessment, 53
    organizing for, 35, 69
Instructional conversations, 249–250, 256
Instructor, teacher as, 50
Integral settings, 282
Interactive read-alouds, 214–219
    choosing books for, 216–218
    steps in, 216
Interactive writing, 134–137
Interjection, 433, 444
Interpretation, by competent language users, 19
Interrogative sentence, 434
Interviews, 258–261, 274–275
Invented spelling

in beginning writing, 132
    defined, 397
    phonological system and, 11
Investigator, 45, 478
Invitations, 382–383
Involvement responses, 186, 187
IRF (Initiate-Response-Feedback) cycle, 253
Isla (Dorros), 284
It's Not My Fault: Concrete Poems (Grandits), 378
I Walk in Dread: The Diary of Deliverance Trembley (Fraustino), 191
I Went Walking (Williams), 127
"I Wish . . . " poems, 374–375

Jackalope (Stevens & Crummel), 101
Jack's Garden (Cole), 127
James and the Giant Peach (Dahl), 265
Joey Pigza Loses Control (Gantos), 287–288, 289
John Muir: America's First Environmentalist (Lasky), 342
Jolly Postman, or Other People's Letters, The (Ahlberg & Ahlberg), 186
Journal(s), 180–196
    assessing entries in, 196
    books in which characters and historical personalities keep, 195–196
    buddy, 197
    dialogue, 181, 184–185
    double-entry, 181, 188, 190
    English learners and, 185, 197
    language arts notebooks, 181, 188, 190
    learning logs, 181, 190–191, 192, 193, 491, 492
    minilessons on, 196
    monitored, 196
    patterns of practice and, 194
    personal, 181, 182–184
    prediction, 188
    privacy and, 183
    private, 196
    purposes of, 180
    reading logs. *See* Reading logs
    reading questions for, 70–71
    shared, 196
    simulated, 181, 191–194, 339
    teaching students to write in, 194–196
    topics for entries, 183
    types of, 181

what students need to learn about, 204
as writing genre, 87
Journal of Jesse Smoke: A Cherokee Boy (Bruchac), 191–192
Joyful Noise: Poems for Two Voices (Fleischman), 379
Julie of the Wolves (George), 282
Jump, Frog, Jump! (Kalan), 127
Juncture, 365

Keyboarding, 458–460
Key words, 118
Kick in the Head: An Everyday Guide to Poetic Forms (Janeczko), 353, 372, 377, 378, 381
Kid writing, 132–134, 135
King Arthur, 146
King Midas: The Golden Touch (Demi), 289
King of Shadows (Cooper), 287
King Who Rained, The (Gwynne), 157
K-W-L charts, 253–254, 255, 258, 313, 314, 316, 462

Language(s)
academic. *See* Academic language
deceptive, 234, 236
figurative, 158–161, 352–353
inflated, 234
laughing with, 357–359
playing with, 26, 27
social, 13, 14
social action and, 17
uses of, 13, 17, 19
Language arts
avoidance of, 24
cultural and linguistic differences and, 18
integrating, 49, 51
learning, 9, 18–31
relationships among, 26
six modes of, 3, 24–26
skills in, 26–30
strategies for, 26, 27, 28–30
Language Arts (journal), 357
Language arts instruction
components of, 466–467
goals of, 30–31
teachers' roles during, 50
Language arts notebooks, 181, 188, 190
Language development, of English learners, 16
Language Experience Approach (LEA)
defined, 130

drawback of, 130–131
emergent reading and, 126, 130–131
steps in, 131
Language models, 223
Language skills, 28, 29
Language source of words, 143
Language systems, 9–13
English learners and, 15
phonological, 9–11
pragmatic, 10, 13
semantic, 10, 12
syntactic, 10, 11–12
Language users, competent, 19–20
Latin, as language source of words, 143, 146, 148, 150, 151, 161
Layout, of diagrams, 326
LEA. *See* Language Experience Approach (LEA)
Leader and chorus reading, 368, 372
Learners. *See* Community of learners; Students
Learning, 6–9
contexts for, 162
of language arts, 9, 18–31
motivation for, 23–24
process of, 6–7
social contexts of, 8–9
strategies for, 7–8
Learning centers, 435
Learning logs, 39, 48, 190–191, 192, 193, 327, 491, 492
Left-handed writers, 456–457
Legends, 287, 289
Legibility, 452, 456
Leonardo: Beautiful Dreamer (Byrd), 318
Letter(s)
of alphabet, magnetic, 118
in multigenre projects, 339
as writing genre, 87
Letter books, 118
Letter containers, 118
Letter formation, 452
Letter frames, 118
Letter names, 117–119
Letter-name spelling, 398, 400, 402
Letter posters, 118
Letter sorts, 118
Letter stamps, 118
Letter writing, 180, 196–206
assessment of, 203, 206
audience of, 196, 198
to authors and illustrators, 200–201
business letters, 199, 201
courtesy letters, 198
e-mail messages, 200

forms for, 199
friendly letters, 198–201
minilessons on, 202, 205
pen pal letters, 198, 206
simulated letters, 201, 205
steps in, 202
teaching, 202
what students need to learn about, 204
Library center, 315, 353, 464, 484
Lifeline(s), 339, 345
Lifeline clotheslines, 344
Life stories, 341–348
Limericks, 354–355, 363, 364, 371, 381–382
Limited omniscient viewpoint, 284
Linguistic differences, 13–16
Lion, the Witch, and the Wardrobe, The (Lewis), 188, 190, 289
Listening, 208–238
aesthetic, 213–222, 232
characteristics of good listeners, 59
critical, 213, 214, 231–238
discriminative, 213, 214
efferent, 213, 214, 222–231, 232
importance to English learners, 223
key concepts about, 24
manipulatives and, 224
minilessons on, 222, 230, 233, 237
notetaking for, 224–225, 226
purposes of, 213, 224
during reading aloud, 209, 214–219
to students talk, 241
techniques for improving, 223–225
to videos, 220, 221
what children need to learn about, 232
Listening center, 111, 215, 315, 464, 490, 491
Literacy. *See also* Emergent literacy
concept of, 112
critical, 16–18
fostering young children's interest in, 113–126
Literacy play center, 114–115
Literal questions, 252
Literary connections, 186, 187
Literary devices, 288–290
Literature, response to, 276
Literature circles, 35, 39, 43–44
assessing, 477, 479, 480
choosing books for, 475, 477
components of, 44
grading sheet for, 480

grand conversations in, 248, 477, 479
identifying strategies and skills for, 475, 477, 478
journals and, 194
organizing, 475, 477–479
poetry and, 387
reading logs in, 477, 479
reading process and, 80
research workshop and, 340
roles for members of, 45, 478
schedule for, 36–37, 477, 478
small-group conversations and, 246
strengths and limitations of, 40
talking in, 240–244
types of reading and, 77
vocabulary and, 165
writing process and, 96
Literature focus units, 35–36, 39, 41–43
books for, 42
components of, 43
developing, 467–475
dramatizing stories in, 263
emergent literacy and, 109, 110
journals and, 194
organizing using reading process, 69–71
outline for, 110
poetry and, 387
reading process and, 80
research workshop and, 340
schedule for, 36, 468, 473
small-group conversations and, 246
strengths and limitations of, 40
teaching grammar as part of, 427
types of reading and, 77
vocabulary and, 165
writing process and, 96
Little Pigeon Toad, A (Gwynne), 157
Little Red Hen, The (Galdone), 208
Little Red Hen, The (Pinkney), 127, 208, 284
Little Red Riding Hood (Galdone), 293
Location, of stories, 282
Locomotion (Woodson), 289, 353
Looking Back: A Book of Memories (Lowry), 485

Magic School Bus in the Rain Forest, The (Cole), 318
Magnetic letters, 118
Make-believe stories, 287, 289
Make Way for Ducklings (McCloskey), 282
Manager, teacher as, 50
Maniac Magee (Spinelli), 37

Manipulatives, for listening, 224
Manuscript handwriting, 447, 448, 451, 457, 458
Maps
in multigenre projects, 339
setting, 276, 283
word, 165, 167, 168
Martha Speaks (Meddaugh), 284, 293
Martin's Big Words: The Life of Dr. Martin Luther King, Jr. (Rappaport), 342, 345, 346
Master list of spelling words, 422
Master Man: A Tall Tale of Nigeria (Shepard), 289
Mathematics, in daily schedule, 36
Math learning log, 190, 191
Meaning. *See also* Semantic system
context clues to, 163
literal vs. figurative, 158
multiple, 12, 158, 159, 163
shades of, 12, 155
of words, 12, 150–162
Meaning principle of spelling, 399
"Me" boxes, 343
Mechanics, 91, 101
Medical center, 116
Meow Ruff: A Story in Concrete Poetry, A (Sidman), 378
Merriam-Webster Children's Dictionary, 155
Merry-Go-Round: A Book about Nouns (Heller), 442
Metalinguistics, 113
Metaphor, 160–161, 288, 352–353, 358, 361
Middle Ages, and word history, 143–144
Middle English, 147–148
Midnight Ride of Paul Revere, The (Longfellow), 345
Mike Fink (Kellogg), 289
Mine, All Mine: A Book about Pronouns (Heller), 442
Minilesson(s)
academic language and, 254–255
for English learners, 51
exploring through, 79
on grammar, 438, 440, 446
on handwriting, 455, 456
identifying topics for, 485
on informational books, 325, 341
on journal writing, 196
on letter writing, 202, 205
on listening, 222, 230, 233, 237
in literature focus unit, 43

on poetry, 354, 370–371, 373, 384, 385
on predicting, 139
in reading workshops, 46, 482, 483
on reports, 341
on revising, 99
on root words, 173
on spelling, 418, 421
on stories, 291, 293
on sustaining conversations, 257
on theme, 293
on vocabulary, 142–144, 169, 171, 172, 173
on word history, 142–143
in writing workshops, 47, 485
for young children, 137, 139
Minilesson conferences, 56
Miss Nelson Is Missing! (Allard), 293
Mitten, The (Brett), 132, 471–472, 473, 474
Mitten, The (Tresslt), 473
Modeling, 29, 50, 134
Model poems, 382–383, 385
Modern English, 148
Monitored journals, 196
Monitoring, 7
anecdotal notes for, 54–55
assessment and, 52–56
checklists for, 55–56
classroom observations for, 52, 54
conferences for, 55, 56
as efferent listening strategy, 230
of English learners, 51
as language arts strategy, 26, 27
Monologue, 281
Moo Cow Kaboom! (Hurd), 297
Moon Book, The (Gibbons), 462–464
Morphemes, 10, 12
Morphology, 163
Mosque (Macaulay), 318
Mosquito Bite (Sly), 225
Motivation, 23–24
Ms. Frizzle's Adventures: Medieval Castle (Cole), 142, 318
Muggie Maggie (Cleary), 451
Multigenre biographies, 347, 348
Multigenre books, 318
Multigenre projects, 337–338, 339
Multiple intelligences, theory of, 80
Multiple meanings of words, 12, 158, 159, 163
Multisyllabic spelling, 398–399, 400–401, 402
"Mummy Slept Late and Daddy Fixed Breakfast" (Prelutsky), 363

My Fellow Americans: A Family Album (Provensen), 345
Mystic Horse (Goble), 289
Myths, 287, 289

Name calling, 235
Narrative leads, 38
Narrative poems, 363, 364
National Council of Teachers of English (NCTE), 18–19, 216, 439
Native Americans, words borrowed from, 161–162
NCLB Act. *See* No Child Left Behind (NCLB) Act of 2001
Neighborhood Odes (Soto), 368
Nettie's Trip South (Turner), 202
New Kid on the Block, The (Prelutsky), 365–366
Newspaper articles, 339
"Night Is a Big Black Cat, The" (Prelutsky), 353
No Child Left Behind (NCLB) Act of 2001
    developing academic language and, 16, 254–255
    emergent literacy and, 112
    language arts instruction and, 30
Nonfiction. *See* Informational reading
Nonstandard forms of English, 13, 16, 436
Nonverbal cues, 26, 27
Norman Conquest, 147, 154, 161
Northwest Regional Educational Laboratory, 97
Notebooks
    language arts, 181, 188, 190
    poetry, 355
    writing, 355
Notetaking, 39
    for developing outline, 495
    for listening, 224–225, 226
Nouns, 431, 433, 444
Novels, number read during school year, 36. *See also* Stories
Now and Ben: The Modern Inventions of Benjamin Franklin (Barretta), 225–226
Number the Stars (Lowry), 60, 61, 270–273, 283

Objective pronoun, 436, 437
Objective viewpoint, 284
Observations, 52, 54
Officer Buckle and Gloria (Rathmann), 377, 379, 439

Oh, A-Hunting We Will Go (Langstaff), 359
Oh Say Can You Say? (Seuss), 361
Old Black Fly (Aylesworth), 101
Old English, 146–147, 154, 157
Omniscient viewpoint, 284
Onomatopoeia, 361–362
On-the-spot conferences, 56
Open-mind portraits, 274, 281, 339
Oral language
    critical literacy and, 17
    of English learners, 51
    phonemic awareness activities and, 120
Oral reports, 255, 258, 259, 260
Organization, and effective writing, 97, 100, 101
Organizer, teacher as, 50
Organizing, 7
    as efferent listening strategy, 228–229
    for instruction, 35, 69
    as language arts strategy, 26, 27
    literature circles, 475, 477–479
    literature focus units, 69–71
Original stories, writing, 307–308
Orthography, 120, 399
Owls (Gibbons), 320

Page layout, 101
Paper bag puppets, 266
Paper plate puppets, 266
Paragraphing, 101
Paraphrasing, 353
Parents, vocabulary level of, 146
Participant, teacher as, 50
Parts of sentences, 432, 433–434
Parts of speech, 431–433, 441–442
Passage master, 45, 478
Pattern(s), sequential, 128
Pattern Fish (Harris), 121
Pattern principle of spelling, 399
Patterns of practice, 35, 40–48. *See also individual patterns*
    in daily schedule, 36–39
    how vocabulary fits into, 165
    journals and, 194
    overview of, 40, 41
    poetry and, 353, 386, 387
    reading process and, 80
    research workshop and, 340

small-group conversations and, 246
strengths and limitations of, 40, 41
teachers' role in, 48–51
types of reading and, 77
writing process and, 96
Pen pal letters, 198, 206
Period, 436
Personal expression, of competent language users, 19
Personal journals, 181, 182–184
Personal writing, 176–207
    in journals. *See* Journal(s)
    in letters. *See* Letter writing
    in reading logs, 176–179, 181, 185–188, 189
    what students need to learn about, 204
Personification, 288–289, 290
Persuasion, critical listening to, 231, 234, 235
Persuasive writing, 87
Pet Fish (Nelson), 312–313
Phonemes, 9, 10, 11
    correspondence with graphemes, 116–117
    phonemic awareness and, 119
    spelling options for, 416
Phonemic awareness
    defined, 10
    developing, 119–126
    emergent literacy and, 109, 119–120
    types of activities for, 121
    word work center and, 315
Phonics, 10, 11
    defined, 120
    emergent literacy and, 109, 119, 120–126
    teaching, 120
    word identification and, 82
    word work center and, 315
Phonics center, 111
Phonics generalizations, 123–126
Phonological awareness, 10
Phonological system, 9–11
Phonology, 120
Photographs, 339
Picture-book versions of single poems, 363, 365
Pitch, in expressive reading, 365
Pizza the Size of the Sun, A (Prelutsky), 373
Planned response, 297
Planning
    for assessment, 470–471
    in inquiry process, 338

Play, literacy, 114–115
Plot, 272, 277–280
Plot development, 277–278
Plot profile, 279, 280
Poetic devices, 360–362
Poetry, 87, 352–388
  acrostic, 364, 377
  apologies, 382
  assessing, 386–387
  assessing students' experiences
    with, 371
  children's preferences in, 363–364
  cinquain, 380
  clerihews, 382
  collaborative, 385
  color, 375
  comparison, 376
  concrete, 363, 364, 377–378
  creating word pictures in, 359, 360
  diamante, 380–381
  drafts of, 355
  drawing of, 355
  English learners and, 374
  five-senses, 375–376
  formula, 372–377
  found, 179, 339, 378–379
  free-form, 377–379, 383
  free verse, 363
  haiku, 363, 364, 371, 380
  hink-pinks, 360
  "I Am . . . ," 376
  "If I Were . . . ," 376
  invitations, 382–383
  "I Wish . . . ," 374–375
  limericks, 354–355, 363, 364, 371,
    381–382
  making sense of, 365–367
  memorizing, 366, 370
  minilessons on, 354, 370–371, 373,
    384, 385
  model, 382–383, 385
  patterns of practice and, 353,
    386, 387
  performing, 368
  preposition, 376–377
  publishing, 386
  reading, 363–371
  reading aloud, 366
  responding to, 364–371
  rhymed verse, 363, 364, 381–382
  rhyme in, 359–360, 363, 364
  sequencing lines in, 369
  sharing, 354
  singing, 369
  syllable- and word-count, 380–381

  with two voices, 379
  types of, 363–364
  what students need to learn
    about, 372
  wordplay and, 357–362, 385
  writing, 354, 355–357, 371–387
Poetry books, 363, 365, 385
Poetry center, 465–466
Poetry notebooks, 355
Poetry workshops, 353–357
  grading sheet for, 356
  schedule for, 354, 355–356
Point of view, of stories, 272, 284,
  304–305
Poke in the I, A (Janeczko), 378
*Polar Bear, Polar Bear, What Do You
  Hear?* (Martin), 127, 442–443
Polar Express, The (Van Allsburg), 441
Poppy (Avi), 426–430
Population, demographic changes in, 14
Portfolios, 56–60
  benefits of, 56–57
  collecting work in, 58–59
  showcasing, 60
  work folders vs., 58–59
Positive focus, 53
Posters
  biography, 345, 346
  grammar, 438
  idiom, 160
  letter, 118
  word, 167
Post office center, 116
Posttest, 422
Practice tests, 31, 422
Pragmatic system, 10, 13
Predicates, 429, 434
Predictable books, 126–128
Predicting, 7
  as aesthetic listening strategy,
    220, 222
  as language arts strategy, 26, 27
  minilesson on, 139
  about stories, 209
Prediction journal, 188
Prefixes, 150
Preposition, 433, 444
Prepositional phrases, 433
Preposition poems, 376–377
Prereading, 73–74, 83, 103, 110,
  270–271, 470
Prereading conferences, 56
Prereading plan (PReP), 495
Pretests, 419, 422
Prewriting, 84–86, 94, 103

Prewriting conferences, 56
Princess Academy (Hale), 72, 248, 289
Print, environmental, 114, 117, 118
Print skills, 28, 29
Privacy, 183
Private journals, 196
Problem, in story, 277, 278
Problem and solution, 228, 321–322
Procedure entries, 188
Process drama, 263–264
Projects
  for applying stage of reading
    process, 81
  as component of literature circles, 43
  as component of literature focus
    unit, 43
  for English learners, 327
  incorporating, 51
  multigenre, 337–338, 339
  in thematic units, 48, 491, 492–493
Pronoun(s), 431, 433
  books on, 444
  nonstandard forms of, 437
Proofreaders' marks, 92
Proofreading
  as language arts strategy, 26, 27
  with partners, 38
  in spelling program, 409, 413–414
  teaching grammar and, 438
  in writing process, 91–92
  in writing workshops, 488
Propaganda devices, 231, 234, 235
Publishing
  for English learners, 94
  poetry, 386
  in writing process, 85, 93–95, 103
*Punching the Clock: Funny Action
  Idioms* (Terban), 160
Punctuation, 432, 435–436
  in effective writing, 101
  syntactic system and, 11
Punctuation marks, 435–436
Punctuation Takes a Vacation
  (Pulver), 101
Puppets, 265, 266
Purpose(s)
  of assessment, 52
  of listening, 213, 224
  setting, 26, 27, 74
  for writing, 86

Question(s)
  critical ("beyond the page"), 252
  inferential ("between the lines"), 252
  literal ("on the page"), 252

as narrative lead, 38
in writing groups, 88, 89
Question-and-answer books, 319
Questioning, 250–253
  in inquiry process, 338
  as language arts strategy, 26, 27
  levels of, 252
Question mark, 436
Quick as a Cricket (Wood), 161
Quickwriting, 35
Quilt center, 111
Quotation mark, 436
Quotes, 339

Rainbow Fish, The (Pfister), 313
Ralph the Mouse (Cleary), 37
*Random House Book of Poetry for
  Children* (Prelutsky), 352–353, 363
Reaching for the Moon (Aldrin), 225
Read-alouds, 74, 75, 77–78
  benefits of, 218–219
  booklist for, 217
  choosing books for, 216–218,
    482, 483
  informational books, 225–227
  interactive, 214–219
  listening during, 209, 214–219
  of poetry, 366
  steps in, 216
Read a Rhyme, Write a Rhyme
  (Prelutsky), 384
Readers theatre, 291, 294, 295
Reading
  aesthetic, 72
  beginning, 126
  buddy. *See* Buddy reading
  as component of literature circles, 43
  as component of literature focus
    unit, 43
  as component of reading
    workshop, 46
  critical literacy and, 18
  cumulative, 368
  echo, 368
  efferent, 72
  emergent. *See* Emergent literacy
  expressive, 364–365, 372, 373
  extensive, for English learners, 276
  fluent, 82, 126
  guided, 74, 75, 76, 77, 291, 294
  independent, 74, 75, 76, 77,
    294–297, 354
  key concepts about, 25
  leader and chorus, 368, 372
  model of, 18

planning for, 74
poetry, 363–371
in reading process, 73, 74–78, 83,
  103, 110, 470
setting purposes for, 74
small-group, 368
stories, 291–302
teaching grammar through,
  439–441
in thematic units, 48
types of, 74–75
what's important in, 80–84
Reading center, 111
Reading comprehension, 145
Reading logs, 35, 70, 78, 181, 185–188
  grades and, 179
  grand conversations and, 247
  in literature circles, 477, 479
  response patterns to, 186, 187
  sample entries from, 189
  sharing, 177
  simulated entries in, 177–179
  topics for entries, 176, 177, 178
  traveling bags of books and, 129, 130
  of young children, 186–187
Reading process, 72–84
  applying in, 73, 80, 81, 83, 103,
    110, 470
  defined, 71
  exploring in, 73, 79, 83, 103, 109,
    110, 470
  to organize literature focus units,
    69–71
  patterns of practice and, 80
  prereading in, 73–74, 83, 103, 110,
    270–271, 470
  reading in, 73, 74–78, 83, 103,
    110, 470
  responding in, 73, 78–79, 83, 103,
    110, 470
  stages of, 72–73
  teaching, 80–84
  what students need to learn
    about, 98
  writing process and, 71–72, 102–104
Reading Teacher, The (journal), 216
Reading workshops, 35, 39, 44,
  479–484
  activity sheet for, 57
  assessment in, 482, 484
  books for, 481, 482, 483
  components of, 46
  conferences for, 482, 484
  establishing environment for, 481
  folders for, 481

journals and, 194
minilessons in, 46, 482, 483
poetry and, 387
procedures for, 482, 483
reading process and, 80
research workshop and, 340
schedules for, 46, 482, 483
setting up, 481–484
small-group conversations
  during, 246
strengths and limitations of, 41
types of reading and, 77
vocabulary in, 165
writing process and, 96
Reading-writing connection,
  195–196, 202
Realistic stories, 287–288, 289
Red Fox Dances (Baron), 129
Reference books, 156, 319, 409,
  414–415. *See also* Dictionaries;
  Thesaurus
Reference skills, 28, 29
Reflective interpretation, 19
Rehearsal, 7
Repetition
  as poetic device, 362
  in predictable books, 127, 128
Report(s)
  assessing, 63, 260, 341
  collaborative, 333–334, 335
  individual, 334–337
  interview, 258, 260
  minilessons on, 341
  oral, 255, 258, 259, 260
  researching and writing, 326–341
  teaching students to write, 338–341
  visual, 326–330
Reporting, in inquiry process, 338
Rereading, 79, 88, 218
Research, for English learners, 327
Research center, 464
Researching and writing reports. *See*
  Report(s)
Research projects, 81
Research workshops, 340–341
Responding
  of community of learners, 21
  as component of literature circles, 43
  as component of literature focus
    unit, 43
  as component of reading
    workshop, 46
  context for, 297
  to literature, 276
  planned, 297

to poetry, 364–371
in reading process, 73, 78–79, 83, 103, 110, 470
spontaneous, 297–298
to stories, 219, 297–298, 299
writing in reading logs, 78
Response activities, 369–370
Response behaviors, 298
Response patterns, 186, 187
Responsibility, 21
Restaurant center, 116
Retelling stories, 2–3, 4, 109, 298
assessing, 302
children's, 300–301
guidelines for, 301–302
steps in, 301
writing, 303–305
Revising
as language arts strategy, 26, 27
minilesson on, 99
in writing groups, 90
in writing process, 85, 87–88, 94, 103
Revising conferences, 56
Rewards, 234, 235
Rhyme, 127–128
experimenting with, 359–360
in poetry, 359–360, 363, 364
Rhymed verse, 363, 364, 381–382
Rhyming words, 119, 123
Rhythm, 127–128, 364
Riddles, 357–359
Rime, 123, 124
Risk taking, 21
Rodzina (Cushman), 287
Role-play, 263–264. *See also* Drama
Root words, 150–152
affixes and, 150–154, 409, 415
identifying, 26, 27
minilesson on, 173
in spelling program, 409, 415
suffixes and, 38, 150–154, 415
Rosa (Giovanni), 18, 236
Rose, Where Did You Get That Red? (Koch), 382, 383
Rosie's Walk (Hutchins), 129, 464
Rough draft, rereading, 88
Rubrics
assessment and, 60, 62–64
writing, 62, 64
Runaway Tortilla, The (Kimmel), 289

Sarah, Plain and Tall (MacLachlan), 37, 201, 289, 290
Saving Shiloh (Naylor), 38
Scaffold, 8

Scaffolding, 29, 84, 276, 291
Scanning, 495
Schedule(s)
for daily instruction, 36–39
for literature circles, 36–37, 477, 478
for literature focus unit, 36, 468, 473
for poetry workshop, 354, 355–356
for practice tests, 31
for reading and writing workshop, 46, 482, 483
for writing workshop, 36, 46, 47, 485, 486, 487–488
Schemata, 6
Scholastic Children's Thesaurus, 155, 156
Scholastic Dictionary of Idioms, Phrases, Sayings, and Expressions (Terban), 160
Schwa, 123
Science, 36
Science center, 314
Science fiction, 289
Science log, 190, 192
Scripts, producing, 266–268
Scriptwriting, 265–266
Sea Horse: The Shyest Fish in the Sea (Butterworth), 72
Searching for Anne Frank: Letters from Amsterdam to Iowa (Rubin), 318
Seedfolks (Fleischman), 298
Segmentation, 26, 27, 121
Self-assessment, 52, 53
involving students in, 59
for oral reports, 260
Semantic feature analysis, 165, 169, 170
Semantics, 10
Semantic system, 10, 12
Semicolon, 436
Sentence(s)
cards for making, 427–429
classifying, 434
complex, 429
compound, 429, 434
compound-complex, 434, 439, 441
declarative, 434
exclamatory, 434
imperative, 434
interrogative, 434
manipulating, 438, 442–444, 445
parts of, 432, 433–434
simple, 434
types of, 432, 434
unscrambling, 444–446
Sentence collecting, 438, 441
Sentence combining, 445, 446

Sentence expanding, 445, 446
Sentence fluency, 100–101
Sentence imitating, 445–446
Sentence structure, 14, 15
Sequels, writing, 306
Sequence
cumulative, 127, 128
in informational books, 320, 321, 322
of lines in poems, 369
as organizing pattern, 228
Sequencing center, 315
Sequential patterns, 128
Setting(s), of stories, 272, 282–283
Setting map, 276, 283
Setting purposes
as language arts strategy, 26, 27
in prereading, 74
Shared journals, 196
Shared reading, 74, 75–76, 77, 126–130
big books and, 128–129
with cross-age reading buddies, 129
emergent literacy and, 126–130
predictable books and, 126–128
steps in, 127
with traveling bags of books, 129–130
Sharing
in literature circles, 44
poetry, 354
in reading workshops, 46
in writing groups, 89–91
in writing process, 89–91, 95
in writing workshops, 486, 488–489
Shiloh (Naylor), 37, 59, 284
Shiloh Season (Naylor), 38
Shiver Me Letters: A Pirate ABC (Sobel), 128
Shoo Fly! (Trapani), 128
Signal words, 228
Sign of the Beaver, The (Speare), 38, 306
Silly Sally (Wood), 129
Simile, 160–161, 288, 353, 361
Simple sentence, 434
Simulated journals, 181, 191–194, 339
Simulated letters, 201, 205
Single Shard, A (Park), 289
Sketch-to-stretch, 285–286, 287, 339
Skill(s)
comprehension, 28, 29
language, 28, 29
in language arts, 26–30
for literature circles, 475, 477, 478
print, 28, 29

reference, 28, 29
study, 28, 29
for thematic units, 491, 492
Skill entries, 188
Slant, in handwriting, 456, 457
Sleeping Beauty, The (Hyman), 289
*Slop Goes the Soup: A Noisy Warthog
    Word Book* (Edwards), 362
Small group(s), differentiating
    instruction in, 49
Small-group conversations, 244–246
Smoky Night (Bunting), 200, 248, 322
Social contexts of learning, 8–9
Social language, 13, 14, 15
Social studies, 36, 38–39
Socioeconomic status (SES), 145–146
Solution, in story, 278, 279. *See also*
    Problem and solution
Some Smug Slug (Edwards), 100
Sorting center, 315
Sound, as narrative lead, 38
Sound-addition activities, 121
Sound-blending activities, 121
Sounding-out spelling strategy, 404, 415
Sound-isolation activities, 121
Sound-matching activities, 121
Sound-substitution activities, 121
Sound-symbol correspondences, 122
Spacing, in handwriting, 452
Speech, parts of, 431–433, 441–442
Spelling, 392–424
    assessing progress in, 423–424
    derivational relations, 399, 401, 402
    emergent, 398, 399–400, 402
    of English learners, 197
    invented, 11, 132, 397
    letter-name, 398, 400, 402
    minilessons on, 418, 421
    multisyllabic, 398–399, 400–401,
        402
    phonics and, 120
    strategies for, 409, 415, 418
    teaching, 406–424
    teaching to English learners,
        407–408
    textbooks for, 393, 418–419
    what students need to learn about,
        420
    within-word, 398, 400, 402, 404
    word work center and, 315
    writing and, 101, 396, 408
Spelling conscience, 406
Spelling development, 397–406
    analyzing, 401–406
    evidence of, 423–424

stages of, 397–399
Spelling errors, 404, 406
Spelling options, 409, 415, 416–417
Spelling program, 408–418
Spelling tests, 418–423
Spontaneous response, 297–298
SQ3R study strategy, 495
SQUIRT (sustained quiet reading
    time), 296
SSR (Sustained Silent Reading),
    296–297
Standard English, 13, 16–17, 436
Standards for the English Language Arts
    (National Council of Teachers of
    English and the International
    Reading Association), 24
*Star-Bearer: A Creation Myth from
    Ancient Egypt* (Hofmeyr), 289
Stick puppets, 266
Stinker from Space (Service), 289
Stone Fox (Gardiner), 37, 279, 280
Stories
    assessing, 308
    children's concept of, 275–291, 292
    dramatizing, 219
    endings of, 5
    facilitating comprehension of, 271
    genres of, 287–288, 289, 306–307
    grand conversations about, 271–273
    informational books vs., 318–320
    literary devices used in, 288–290
    minilessons on, 291, 293
    in multigenre projects, 339
    plot of, 272, 277–280
    predicting, 209
    reading, 291–302
    realistic, 287–288, 289
    responding to, 219, 297–298, 299
    retelling of, 2–3, 4, 109, 298,
        300–302
    scaffolding English learners'
        knowledge of, 276
    setting of, 272, 282–283
    teaching students about, 290–291
    theme of, 272–273, 284–287
    what students need to learn
        about, 292
    writing, 87, 303–308
Story analysis, 272
Storyboards, 266, 268, 315
Story elements, 279
Story quilts, 227, 286–287
Story structure
    conferences about, 288
    elements of, 276, 277–287

Storytellers, characteristics of, 59
Storytelling center, 315
Strategic language use, 19
Strategic readers, 84
Strategies
    for aesthetic listening, 220, 222
    for critical listening, 234
    for efferent listening, 228–230
    Goldilocks, 295, 296
    for language arts, 26, 27, 28–30
    for learning, 7–8
    for literature circles, 475, 477, 478
    for spelling, 409, 415, 418
    for thematic units, 491, 492
    word-learning, 163, 164, 165
Strategy entries, 188
Students. *See also* Community of
    learners
    choices of, 21–22
    conferences with, 55, 288
    cultural diversity among, 13–16
    inserting themselves into
        stories, 219
    involving in self-assessment, 59
    motivation of, 23–24
    risk taking by, 21
    ways to involve with books,
        215–216, 217
Study lists, 422
Study skills, 28, 29
*Stuffed Animals Get Ready for Bed,
    The* (Inches), 117
Subject, double, 437
Subjective pronoun, 436
Subject-verb agreement, 437
Suffixes
    defined, 150
    root words and, 38, 150–154, 415
    spelling, 415
Suggestions, in writing groups,
    88, 89
Summarizer, 45, 478
Summarizing
    as efferent listening strategy,
        229–230
    as language arts strategy, 26, 27
Sun Is My Favorite Star, The
    (Asch), 464
Superdupers! Really Funny Real Words
    (Terban), 168
Sustained quiet reading time
    (SQUIRT), 296
Sustained Silent Reading (SSR),
    296–297
Syllable-count poems, 380–381

Syllables and affixes spelling, 398–399, 400–401, 402, 409, 415
Sylvester and the Magic Pebble (Steig), 235, 289
Symbolism, 290
Synonyms, 143, 154–155
Syntactic system, 10, 11–12
Syntax, 10
Synthesizing, in inquiry process, 338

Tabbing, 478
Taking over text, 219
Tale of Despereaux, The (DiCamillo), 248
Tale of Peter Rabbit, The (Potter), 277, 278
Talk and drama projects, 81
Talking, 240–268
  debates, 261–262
  grand conversations. *See* Grand conversations
  instructional conversations, 249–250
  interviews, 258–261, 274–275
  key concepts about, 24
  K-W-L charts and, 253–254, 255, 258, 313, 314, 316
  as learning tool, 250–262
  listening to, 241
  in literature circles, 240–244
  oral reports, 255, 258, 259, 260
  questioning, 250–253
  small-group conversations, 244–246
  in thematic units, 491, 492
  what students need to learn about, 256–257
Talking back to characters, 219
T-charts, 228, 322
Teachers' roles
  in creating community of learners, 20–22
  in language arts instruction, 50
  as motivators, 23–24
  in patterns of practice, 48–51
  as scaffold, 8
  in supporting language development in English learners, 16
Teaching
  behaviors in, 23, 29
  types of, 49
Tea party, 165, 168
Technology resources, locating, 470, 490, 491, 492
Tempo, 364

Testimonials, 234, 235
Testing
  assessment and, 64
  conditions of, 31
  graphing results of, 31
  high-stakes, 30, 31
  pretests and, 419, 422
  of spelling, 418–423
  untimed and timed, 31
Test-taking strategies, 31
Textbooks
  content-area, 494–495
  in spelling programs, 393, 418–419
  in thematic units, 490, 491
Text set, for thematic unit, 490, 491
Text structures, expository, 228, 320–322, 323–325
Theatrical productions, 265–268
Thematic units, 35, 39, 47–48, 489–496
  activities in, 48
  assessment in, 491, 493
  in daily schedule, 36, 38–39
  defined, 489
  developing, 490–493
  journals and, 194
  poetry and, 387
  projects in, 48, 491, 492–493
  reading process and, 80
  research workshop and, 340
  small-group conversations and, 246
  strategies and skills for, 491, 492
  strengths and limitations of, 41
  textbooks in, 490, 491
  text set for, 490, 491
  types of reading and, 77
  using six language arts during, 463
  visual representations in, 48, 491, 492
  vocabulary and, 165
  writing process and, 96
Theme
  minilesson about, 293
  of stories, 272–273, 284–287
Theodore Roosevelt: Champion of the American Spirit (Kraft), 342
There Was an Old Lady Who Swallowed a Fly (Taback), 129
Thesaurus, 155
  list of, 156
  using, 143
Things Will NEVER Be the Same (dePaola), 485
"This Is Just to Say" (Williams), 363, 382
Thought, as narrative lead, 38

Three Bears, The (Galdone), 293
Three Billy Goats Gruff, The (Finch), 186
Three Little Pigs, The (Galdone), 284
Time
  for community of learners, 22
  in stories, 282–283
Time lines, 339
Timeline Traveler, 478
Tone, 290
Tongue twisters, 361
Topics
  choosing, 85
  for personal journals, 183
  for reading logs, 176, 177, 178
Trade books, teaching critical listening with, 236–237
Traveling bags of books, 129–130
Triangulation, 64
True Story of the 3 Little Pigs! (Scieszka), 236, 284
Trust, and persuasion, 231
Tuck Everlasting (Babbitt), 34–35, 43, 261
Type style, 326

Ugly Duckling, The (Pinkney), 278, 283
Umbrella, The (Brett), 101
Up, Up and Away: A Book about Adverbs (Heller), 442
Usage, 432, 436, 437. *See also* Grammar

Venn diagrams, 228, 273, 322, 339
Verb(s), 431
  books on, 444
  irregular forms of, 437
  nonstandard forms of, 437
  past-tense forms of, 437
Verbal cues, 230
Very Hungry Caterpillar, The (Carle), 124, 128, 132, 322
Video(s), 220, 221
Video scripts, producing, 266–268
Viewers, characteristics of, 59
Viewing, key concepts about, 25
Viewing projects, 81
Viewpoint, of stories, 272, 284, 304–305
Visual cues, 230
Visualizing
  as aesthetic listening strategy, 220, 222
  as language arts strategy, 26, 27
Visual reports, 326–330
Visual representations

for applying stage of reading
   process, 81
for English learners, 51
key concepts about, 25
in thematic units, 48, 491, 492
Visual system. *See* Phonological
   system
Vital Statistics Collector, 478
Vocabulary
   assessing knowledge of, 173–174
   direct vs. indirect instruction
      in, 164
   of English learners, 162–163, 197
   ideas and, 197
   minilessons on, 142–144, 169, 171,
      172, 173
   reading comprehension and, 145
   reading process and, 82–83
   in social vs. academic language, 14
   socioeconomic status and, 145–146
   what students need to learn
      about, 172
   word-learning strategies for, 163,
      164, 165
   word-study activities for, 143
   word walls for, 4, 71, 79, 109,
      142, 144, 164, 165, 166–167,
      339, 408, 409, 412, 426, 462,
      491, 492
Voice, 100, 101
Vowel(s), 122–123
Vowel combinations, 122–123
Vowel sounds, 122

Watsons Go to Birmingham—1963
   (Curtis), 18, 289
Weather, in stories, 282
Where the Sidewalk Ends (Silverstein),
   363, 369, 370
Where the Wild Things Are (Sendak),
   2, 376
"Who Has Seen the Wind"
   (Rossetti), 363
Wildfire (Morrison), 225
Wishes, Lies, and Dreams (Koch), 362,
   373, 374, 375, 376
Witch of Blackbird Pond, The
   (Speare), 282
Within-word spelling, 398, 400,
   402, 404
With Love, Little Red Hen (Ada), 202
Witness (Hesse), 248, 294
Wolf's Chicken Stew, The (Kasza), 139
Woodcutter's Mitten, The
   (Koopmans), 473

Woodie Guthrie: Poet of the People
   (Christensen), 342
Word(s), 142–174
   antonyms, 154–155
   books about, 168, 171, 358
   borrowed, 161–162
   choosing to teach, 165–166
   classifying, 165
   concept of, 114
   confusing pairs of, 437
   dramatizing, 167
   focusing on, 79
   high-frequency, 3, 109, 111, 404,
      408, 410–411
   key, 118
   language source of, 143
   making, 412, 413
   meanings of, 12, 150–162
   multiple meanings of, 12, 158,
      159, 163
   reviewing, 3
   rhyming, 119, 123
   root, 26, 27, 38, 150–152, 173,
      409, 415
   signal, 228
   sources of, 117
   synonyms, 143, 154–155
   teaching about, 162–174
   useful, 163, 165
Word cards, 166
Word chains, 165, 168
Word choice, 100, 101
Word consciousness, 114
Word-count poems, 380–381
Word forms, 12
Word history, 146–149
   books about, 149
   language source in, 143
   learning about, 148–149
   on Middle ages, 143–144
   minilesson on, 142–143
Word identification
   reading process and, 82, 83
   of root words, 26, 27
Word knowledge
   continuum of, 162, 164
   differences in, 145–146
   socioeconomic status and, 145–146
Word-learning strategies, 163,
   164, 165
Word maps, 165, 167, 168
Word order, 11
Word pictures, 359, 360
Wordplay, 71, 171, 357–362, 385
Word posters, 167

Word sorts, 165, 167–168, 169, 409,
   413, 414, 428
Word-study activities, 167–169
Word wall(s), 4, 71, 79, 109, 142, 144,
   164, 165, 166–167, 339, 408, 409,
   412, 426, 462, 491, 492
Word wall center, 464
Word wizard, 45, 478
Word work, 36, 38
Word work center, 315
Work folders
   portfolios vs., 58–59
   for reading and writing
      workshops, 481
Workshops. *See* Poetry workshops;
   Reading workshops; Research
   workshops; Writing workshops
Worrywarts, The (Edwards), 100
Wretched Stone, The (Van Allsburg),
   154, 155, 289
Wrinkle in Time, A (L'Engle), 36, 282
Writers, characteristics of, 59
Writing
   audience of, 86, 95
   beginning, 132
   collaborative reports, 333–334, 335
   conventions in, 101
   critical literacy and, 18
   effective, 97, 100–102
   emergent, 131–138
   final copies of, 94–95
   fluent, 132
   form of, 86
   gathering and organizing ideas
      for, 86
   getting distance from, 91
   individual reports, 334–337
   informational, 87
   innovations on text, 305–306
   interactive, 134–137
   introducing young children to,
      132–134
   key concepts about, 25
   kid, 132–134, 135
   as learning tool, 327
   multigenre projects, 337–338, 339
   original stories, 307–308
   personal. *See* Personal writing
   persuasive, 87
   poetry, 354, 355–357, 371–387
   purpose for, 86
   reports, 326–341
   sequels, 306
   spelling and. *See* Spelling
   stories, 87, 303–308

visual reports, 326–330
voice in, 100, 101
of young children, samples of, 133
Writing center, 111, 464
Writing genres, 86, 87
Writing groups, 88–91
   comments of, 88, 89
   conferences with, 90–91
   revising in, 90
   sharing in, 89–91
   writing process for, 88
Writing notebooks, 355
Writing process, 84–104
   author's chair in, 95
   compliments in, 88, 89, 95
   correcting errors in, 91–92, 93
   defined, 71
   drafting in, 85, 86–87, 94, 103
   editing in, 85, 91–93, 94, 103
   for English learners, 94
   key features of, 85
   prewriting in, 84–86, 94, 103
   proofreading in, 91–92
   publishing in, 85, 93–95, 103
   reading process and, 71–72,
      102–104
   rereading rough draft in, 88
   revising in, 85, 87–88, 94, 99, 103

sharing in, 89–91, 95
teaching, 96–97, 485
what students need to learn
   about, 98
for writing groups, 88
Writing projects, 81. *See also* Projects
Writing rubric, 62, 64
Writing workshops, 35, 39, 479
   activities in, 47
   activity sheet for, 57
   assessment in, 486, 489
   classroom arrangement for,
      484–485
   conferences for, 486, 488
   establishing environment for, 481
   folders for, 481
   guidelines for, 487
   journals and, 194
   minilessons in, 47, 485
   poetry and, 387
   procedures in, 485
   proofreading in, 488
   reading process and, 80
   research workshop and, 340
   schedules for, 36, 46, 47, 485, 486,
      487–488
   setting up, 484–489
   sharing in, 486, 488–489

small-group conversations during,
   246
strengths and limitations of, 41
types of reading and, 77
vocabulary in, 165
writing process and, 96
Written language
   concepts about, 113–115
   critical literacy and, 17

Yellow Elephant: A Bright Bestiary
   (Larios), 375
*Yellow Star: The Legend of King
   Christian X of Denmark*
   (Deedy), 271
You Have to Write (Wong), 353
Young children
   fostering interest in literacy,
      113–126
   introducing to writing, 132–134
   minilessons for, 137, 139
   reading logs of, 186–187
   samples of writing of, 133

Zin! Zin! Zin! a Violin (Moss), 168
Zone of proximal development, 8, 167
Z Was Zapped, The (Van Allsburg), 361